The Economics of Development

THE IRWIN SERIES IN ECONOMICS

Consulting Editor

LLOYD G. REYNOLDS   Yale University

The
Economics of
Development

EVERETT E. HAGEN, Ph.D.

Professor of Economics, Emeritus
Massachusetts Institute of Technology

 1975

Revised Edition

RICHARD D. IRWIN, INC.   Homewood, Illinois   60430
Irwin-Dorsey International   London, England   WC2H 9NJ
Irwin-Dorsey Limited   Georgetown, Ontario   L7G 4B3

Revised Edition

First Printing, June 1975

ISBN 0-256-01735-2
Library of Congress Catalog Card No. 74–29749
Printed in the United States of America

Without the analysis of relationships among magnitudes, theories of economic development are at best based on casual empiricism. Two economists more than any others are responsible for organizing and conducting the quantitative analysis of development: Simon Kuznets and Hollis W. Chenery. Advance in our understanding of development, and therefore this book, owes much to them.

Preface

This is a revised edition of a book first published seven years ago. Since then, many more data have become available, analysis has advanced, and new analytical issues have arisen. The revision is therefore extensive.

Two completely new chapters have been added, one on the question whether exhaustion of the earth's stock of minerals will bring economic growth to an end, and the other on the relationships between economic growth and the distribution of income within growing countries. Two other chapters are essentially new: The chapter on population has been recast to focus attention on the relationship of food supply to continuing world growth, and the formerly very brief chapter on economic planning has been expanded to some four times its original length.

The discussion of the difficulties of innovation in agriculture and industry, presented to give concreteness to the economic analysis that follows, has been enlarged moderately and a brief discussion of the nature of so-called transfer of technology added. The discussion of growth theories has been reorganized. A new section in the second of the two chapters on growth theories presents the concept of leading sectors in a guise that is new and, I think, more logical than the conventional one. Growth in Saudi Arabia is discussed to illustrate this presentation. The discussion of entrepreneurship is considerably augmented.

In the first edition, the discussion of external finance and that of import substitution versus export expansion were separated in order that the former might be included in a group of chapters on the financing of development and the latter in a group on allocation. In this edition the alternative answer to this insoluble question of organization has been chosen. The chapters on external finance and that on outward- versus inward-looking policies have been placed together, so that the analysis of external finance and all aspects of allocation might be gathered within the framework of the policy issue of financial liberalization versus comprehensive intervention.

The result of these changes and additions is a considerably longer and, I hope, a richer book. The general approach of the first edition is retained.

As before, the association of various factors with the level or rate of change of gross domestic product or gross national product is analyzed. By intention, when income is concerned, GNP is discussed; when productivity is relevant, GDP. However, because growth rates for only GNP were available on World Bank computer printouts that were obtained, whereas ratios of various magnitude to GDP for five-year periods were presented in the printouts, logically inappropriate data are often related in charts. Where this is done, data for the oil countries, in which the difference between GNP and GDP is considerable, are omitted. For other countries, the illogic does not appreciably affect the statistical relationships.

Several readers of the first edition noted that it was inconvenient to refer from the graphs throughout the book to the table at the end of Chapter 1 to determine to what country a given number had been assigned. In the present edition the problem has been solved or at least ameliorated by two devices. On most graphs, countries whose data lie apart from the main line of scatter are named. Also, in addition to the assignment of numbers in an appendix to Chapter 1, for convenient reference a list of countries and numbers is given inside the back cover of the book.

Peter Kilby and an anonymous reviewer for the publishers both made suggestions for reorganization, changes in emphasis, and substantive additions that much improved the present edition. While I was working on this revision the International Bank for Reconstruction and Development had in preparation a new set of "World Tables," and I am indebted to Sang E. Lee of the Bank's Economic Analysis and Projections Department for making available to me computer printouts of data in advance of publication and of some data in a modified form that best suited my purposes.

My most immediate obligation is to my secretary, Gayle R. Hightower. In this period of financial stringency she also assists another faculty member, yet she has found time to be my statistical research assistant.

Almost all of the data used in the book were assembled and the relevant computations made by her. Her data sense even in a field strange to her and her intelligent questioning of occasional anomalous results prevented errors, some of which would otherwise probably have appeared in tables and graphs. I am indebted to her also for superintending the entire preparation of the final manuscript.

Cambridge and   Everett E. Hagen
Cataumet, Massachusetts
May 1975

Contents

List of Tables

List of Figures

I

The Growth of World Income

Though this book is concerned primarily with the lower income countries of the world, Chapter 1 discusses income and growth in the modern era in the low-income and high-income countries alike, and in all of the countries between. It does so because the growth of the lower income countries can be understood only in the context of growth in the world as a whole. Chapters 2 and 3 then consider whether and how exhaustion of the world's mineral reserves may retard future world growth, and whether inability to increase the world's food supply as rapidly as demand increases may distort it. The topics are of interest for their own sake—and they are receiving much popular attention. They are also relevant here, for future growth in the "less developed" countries will be severely constrained if growth in the world as a whole is severely limited by shortages of minerals or of food.

Yet the insertion of chapters analzying these topics interferes awkwardly with the flow of discussion that is of central concern in this book. Perhaps they are appropriately the topic of a different academic course. The conclusion is reached in Chapters 2 and 3 that there is zero probability of the abrupt exhaustion of the world's mineral resources and only a slight probability, given present and prospective human efforts, that food will be in shorter supply relative to demand in the future than in the past. If a user of the book is willing to accept that conclusion, or to leave the question in abeyance, he may move from Chapter 1 directly to Chapter 4. Or if he wishes, he may pause long enough to read the section of Chapter 3 titled "Population Growth and Income Growth in the LDCs" and then move to Chapter 4.

The Distribution of Income and Economic Growth among the Countries of the World in the Modern Period

1

In most countries of the world today there is occurring a continuing rise in average per capita income made possible by continuing increase in per capita productivity. The phenomenon has been given a name, *economic growth,* or, when account is taken also of the changes in economic (and social) structure that accompany it, *economic development.* That continuing increase in productivity—its possibility, causes, conditions, and effects—is the subject matter of this book.

Western economists tend to think of their own countries as having settled into permanent economic and social structures, and so view only the economics of growth and not that of development as relevant to them. The view is erroneous; with continuing economic growth, change in economic structure and economic institutions is continuing in high-income economies, as is change in social and political structure and institutions, whether as an effect or a cause of economic growth or as a common result of some third factor. But changes in many economic characteristics are occurring more rapidly in the lower income countries in the world, where growth is more recently under way, and the social concern about growth relates mainly to these countries, and so this book will deal mainly with lower income countries. It will nevertheless deal with most countries of the world, for in only 30 or 40 countries, the number depending on just where one chooses to draw the line, has economic growth been continuing for so long that their income has reached a level that is termed "high."[1]

---

[1] In a small number of very small countries at the other end of the range, economic structure is so primitive and economic growth so little in evidence that economists leave the study of these countries to anthropologists.

3

I shall be discussing both politically independent countries and non-self-governing areas. To avoid repeated use of the clumsy phrase "countries and dependencies," I shall refer to all of them as "countries." And, for convenience, when I refer to "economic growth" I shall often use merely the term "growth," since the context will make clear that I am not discussing any of the many other sorts of national or world growth or lack of growth.

POOR CONTINENTS, INTERMEDIATE CONTINENTS, RICH CONTINENTS

The reader will not be surprised to learn that the distribution of income is highly unequal. Table 1–1 presents the data for geographic regions and country groups.

TABLE 1–1
Per Capita GNP, 1971, Country Groups

Area	Average Per Capita GNP ($U.S.)
Asia (excluding Israel, Japan, and the Middle East)	$ 144
Africa (excluding Republic of South Africa)	170
Middle East (other than Israel)	376
Oceania (other than Australia and New Zealand)	463
Latin America	591
U.S.S.R. and Communist Europe	1,358
Japan, Israel, Republic of South Africa	1,890
Western Europe	2,296
Australia, New Zealand	2,797
Northern America	5,064

Source: *World Bank Atlas*, 1973.

They show Africa and Asia other than the Middle East with about the same level of income; that of the Middle East more than twice as high, largely because of its petroleum production; that of the small islands of Oceania still higher; that of Latin America about four times as high as Asia; and then the other areas of the world on a rising scale until the average for the United States and Canada combined is shown as 35 times that for Asia other than the Middle East.

The data are for gross national product (GNP), which is identical with gross national income, the income received by the country from production. Because a large share of Middle Eastern income from oil production flowed to foreign oil companies, the gross *domestic* product (GDP) of the Middle Eastern countries—the value of the output of those countries—was much higher than their gross *national* product.

The world's regional differences in income levels appear graphically on the world map of Figure 1–1. That figure may suggest a dichotomous

FIGURE 1-1
The Geographic Distribution of World Per Capita Income, 1971

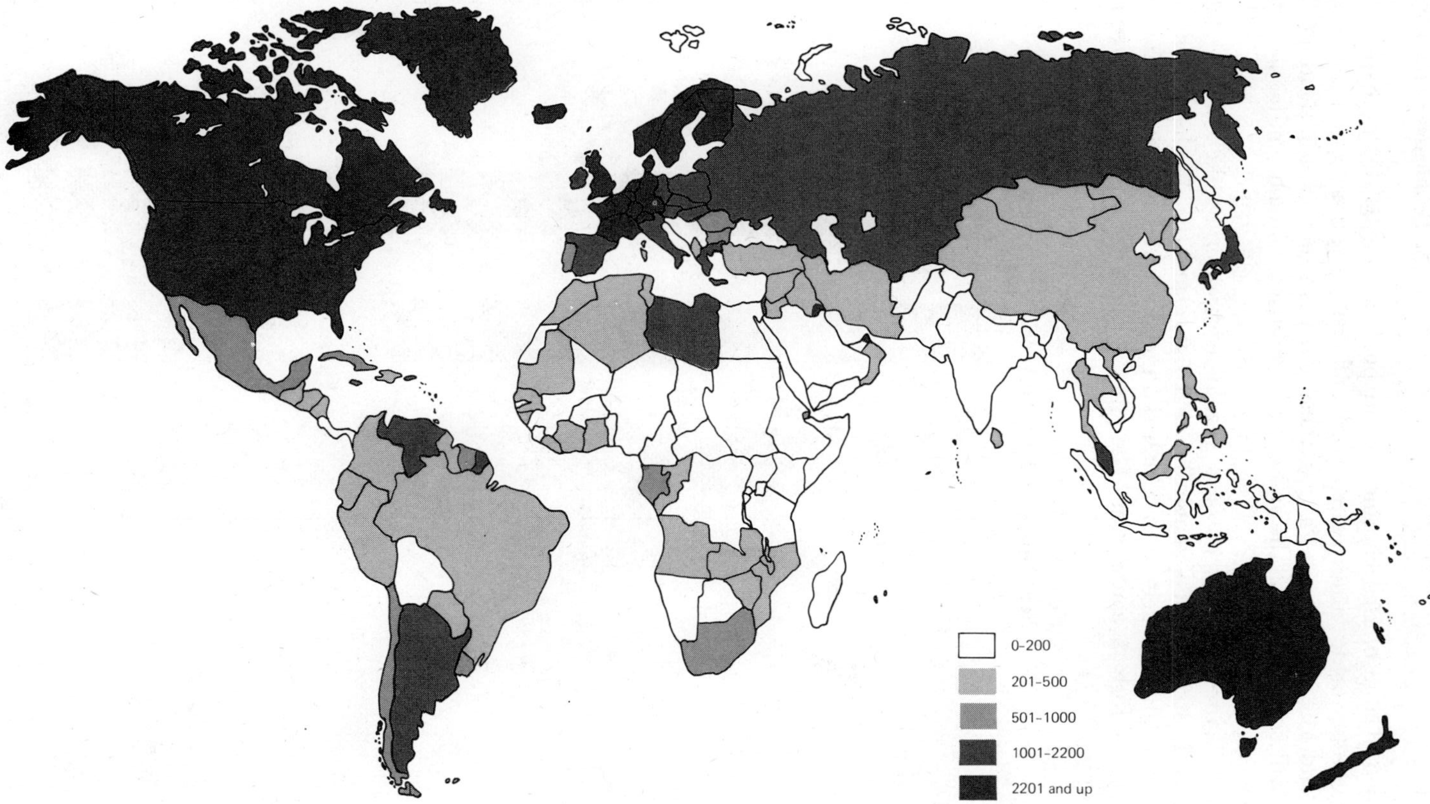

0-200
201-500
501-1000
1001-2200
2201 and up

world, one of rich continents and poor continents. Or perhaps a three-group world, with a poor Africa and Asia, a rather poor Latin America and Middle East, and a rich West. That suggestion is misleading, as we will see if we plot the individual countries of each continent along an income scale.

Figure 1–2 presents on a semilogarithmic scale the country data for 1971. Striking facts shown by that figure are the overlap among continents and the degree to which the income levels of the countries of the world form a continuum. Though the continuum is thin between $520

FIGURE 1–2
Per Capita GNP of the World's Countries, 1971

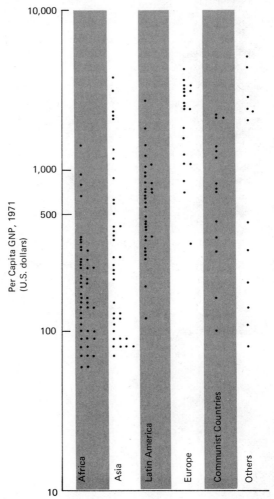

and $580, one cannot draw a line separating the "high-income" from the "low-income" countries except on an arbitrary basis. One may refer to the lowest income or highest income one tenth, one fifth, one half, or any other fraction of the countries of the world, but one cannot logically refer to the "low-income" and the "high-income" countries with the implication that there is a great gap between them. The conception of two groups of countries in the world, separated from each other in income level or level of economic development—"us" versus "them"—is a layman's stereotype not conducive to clear thinking about the process of growth.

Terms for Country Groups

A few words about terminology are pertinent here. Although the usage contradicts the facts, it is common to class countries of the world into two groups, high- and low-income, or (economically) more and less developed. An alternative classification sometimes used is of three classes, private-enterprise countries, Communist (or socialist) countries, and "the third world." Implicit in setting the "third world" apart is the same notion of dichotomy that underlies the high- and low-income stereotype.

The terms "developing" and "developed" countries are sometimes applied, especially in United Nations usage, to distinguish the supposed two groups. This usage would be somewhat absurd, even if two disparate groups existed, since a few of the countries included in the class "developing" are in fact not developing, whereas all of the countries excluded from that class and termed "developed"—the technically more advanced countries—are in fact continuing to develop. It may be suspected that the usage was adopted in the United Nations because it seemed indelicate to refer to lower income countries as "less developed." Actually, as applied to economic development or level of income, the term is an objective and nonpejorative one, which the lower income countries themselves do not seem to find offensive.

A separate term for a group of the lowest income countries has recently come into official use in the United Nations: the "least developed" countries. The United Nations organization known as UNCTAD (United Nations Conference on Trade and Development) was unable to agree on which nations are the "least developed" ones. During 1971 the United Nations Committee for Development Planning (a group of experts drawn from outside the United Nations organization) strove mightily to identify a group of countries to be termed the "least developed." A 1971 report of that committee presents as appropriate criteria (1) gross domestic product of $100 or less (in 1968), (2) a share of manufacturing in GDP of 10% or less, and (3) a literacy rate of 20% or less within the population 15 years of age and over (around 1960).

On the basis, applied flexibly to include countries eager to belong that met two of the criteria and were not far beyond the bounds of the third, the committee identified 25 countries of the world as the least developed. The countries thus included are 16 in Africa (Botswana, Burundi, Chad, Dahomey, Ethiopia, Guinea, Lesotho, Mali, Malawi, Niger, Rwanda, Somalia, Sudan, Uganda, United Republic of Tanzania, and Upper Volta), 8 in Asia and Oceania (Afghanistan, Bhutan, Laos, Maldives, Nepal, Sikkim, Western Samoa, and Yemen), and 1 in Latin America, Haiti.[2] These 25 countries had a combined population of 139 million in 1968.

Lastly, Mr. Robert S. McNamara, President of the World Bank, presented in 1973 the concept of "absolute poverty," which he stated characterizes nearly 800 million individuals, or 40% of the population of the "developing world."[3] Absolute poverty, he said, is "a condition of life so degraded by disease, illiteracy, malnutrition, and squalor as to deny its victims basic human necessities," "a condition of life so limited as to prevent realization of the potential of the genes with which one is born."[4]

Such classifications are useful for some purposes. The designation of "least developed countries" was a political one, responsive to the demands for special consideration of a group of members of the United Nations so large that their voting power is persuasive. The concept of "absolute poverty" was no doubt presented in an attempt to dramatize to callous men and women in high-income countries conditions in low-income countries. These purposes are legitimate. They do not, however, serve an analytical purpose; rather, placing groups of countries in separate boxes may confuse intellectual analysis. In the discussion of growth in this book, an attempt will be made to avoid the conception of dichotomies among the countries of the world with respect to growth. The conception presented will be of relative position on a continuum. However, writers will be quoted who refer to "the less developed" and "the more developed" countries, and quantitative analyses will be cited that group data by two such groupings. Hence, it will be impossible to avoid occasional use of two-class terminology, and I shall use it frequently in

---

[2] United Nations Committee for Development Planning, *Report on the Seventh Session* (*22 March–1 April 1971*), Economic and Social Council, Official Records: Fifty-First Session, supplement no. 7 (New York, 1971), document E/4990. The necessary data did not exist for the Maldives, Bhutan, Sikkim, and Western Samoa. It was assumed that the very lack of information was evidence of their low status on the scales.

[3] In an address to the Board of Governors of the World Bank Group, September 24, 1973 (Washington, D.C.: International Bank for Reconstruction and Development, 1973). See pp. 6–7.

[4] From estimates of income distribution by size in a number of lower income countries, made in the Development Research Center of the World Bank, it may be guessed that McNamara's estimate of the number of persons living in "absolute poverty" was actually that of the number of individuals with personal income (as that term is defined in national income accounts) below $50 per year.

the last half of the book, employing the terms "higher income" and "lower income" or (technically) "more developed" and "less developed" countries (MDCs and LDCs). The reader should think of the terms as referring to two ranges of a continuum. Whenever the implication is given of a dichotomy, of "we (homogeneous) advanced countries" and "those contrasting (homogeneous) backward countries," the reader should take the apocryphal Galileo as his model and murmur to himself, "It itsn't true."

THE WORLD DISTRIBUTION OF PER CAPITA INCOME BY INCOME LEVEL

If we group the country data underlying the array of Figure 1–2 into income classes, and make a few calculations, we arrive at Table 1–2. We

TABLE 1–2
World Aggregate and Per Capita GNP, 1971 Countries Grouped by Income Levels

Per Capita Income in Dollars	Population		Aggregate GNP		Per Capita GNP	
	Millions	% of Total	Billions	% of Total	Average ($)	% of World Average
More than 2,201 ...	468.9	12.4	$1,875.9	56.2	$4,000	451.5
(USA)	(207.0)	(5.5)	(1,068.4)	(32.0)	(5,161)	(582.5)
1,001–2,200	579.0	15.4	917.5	27.5	1,585	178.9
501–1,000	180.8	4.8	113.7	3.4	629	80.0
201–500	527.8	14.0	182.5	5.5	346	39.0
0–200	2,008.7	53.3	248.2	7.4	124	14.0
Total or Average ...	3,765.2	99.9	3,337.8	100.0	886	

Source: *World Bank Atlas,* 1973.

owe to the research divisions of the United Nations and the International Bank for Reconstruction and Development (the "World Bank") our ability to make such comparisons. Only in the last few years have the necessary income estimates been available. The comparisons they show are a little awesome.

What the Data Seem to Mean

If these data mean what they seem to mean, the peoples of successive groups of countries, as we pass down the income scale, live with incomes averaging 30%, 12%, and 7% of that in the United States, and at the bottom of the scale more than one half of the poeple of the world live in countries of which the highest per capita GNP in 1971 was less than one twenty-sixth that of the United States. The average income in that group was less than one fortieth that in the United States. The large majority of the people in that group of countries are the people of China and India, who together constitute 36% of the world's population. But the group also includes other countries with a total population of 670 million: more than 50 other countries or possessions in Asia and Africa, ranging in population from Indonesia and Pakistan downward to tiny communities, plus the one Latin American country of Haiti and some small islands.

It seems incredible that 70 or 80% of the people in this group of countries can stay alive. In fact, it *is* incredible. At this level of income they could not exist. But they not merely exist; they exist with a margin that permits them to increase in number. The second thing to observe about the data in Table 1–2, therefore, is that they are not true. The average income of the lowest income countries of the world is indeed a small fraction of that in the West, but not as small a fraction as that indicated in Table 1–2. It will require a rather long discussion to indicate the sources of error, but this is justified by the importance of the point.

The Sources of Difficulty

One of the difficulties is that measurements of per capita income are imprecise. There is a margin of error in the measurement of national product in any country. But beyond this there are biases that are correlated with economic development. They may not greatly distort the ranking of countries, but they certainly greatly distort cardinal comparisons of per capita product among countries at markedly different levels of development.

Much more basic, however, is the consideration that comparison of the incomes of countries at two markedly different income levels is in principle impossible. Consider, for example, comparison between India or China and the United States. The goods and services produced in either of those two low-income Asian countries differ so greatly in nature from those produced and consumed in the United States that to state that the American people produce a certain number of times as much goods and services per capita as do Chinese or Indians has only limited meaning. Nevertheless, as with various other impossible operations, we make the comparison as best we can because we need it. So, passing over the incomparability of the baskets of goods in low- and high-income countries, consider the other difficulties.

One source of bias is that the statistical coverage of economic activity becomes increasingly comprehensive as per capita income rises. Moreover, as an economy develops, an increasing share of production passes through the market. The housewife buys bread instead of baking it, etc. The national income statistician is well aware of the problem of estimating the value of production for own use, and always includes the major kinds (farm production and housing construction) in his estimates. But some other types of activity which are done by family members (sometimes almost as play) in an LDC, are purchased through the market at a later stage of development and are then included. Comparisons are therefore distorted in some degree.

A second source of possible statistical bias relates to intermediate products. Some products that conceptually are intermediate products (inputs in the production of other products) are counted as final products in the national income accounts of industrial economies, since to isolate them is extremely difficult and their inclusion does not greatly distort the evaluation of short-term trends within a single country. For example, as cities grow, increasing travel is required to go from the suburbs to and from work or to and from theaters, concert halls, and athletic stadia. Some share of this transportation is not part of the country's final product, but rather only a cost of attaining satisfactions of city living which are already adequately measured in the value of the output of the city's factories, offices, theaters, and so on. This is also true of smog eradication, prevention of water pollution, etc., and even of national defense insofar as the need for defense expenditures arises out of national frictions which themselves are a result of modern industrial life.[5] Hence gross national product is overstated.

However, these problems are not the major sources of the distortions in Table 1–2. Even if national product estimation were statistically perfect, it would be an ambiguous or inadequate measure of productivity or welfare. One basic difficulty is that if more than one good or service is being produced, then while the combination of goods in basket *A* may seem more satisfying than that in basket *B* to individual 1, that in basket may seem more satisfying to individual 2.

Comparison of real national income or product per capita between two countries (or between two periods in a given country) is comparison of the aggregate "quantity" of production in each, divided by the population in each. Since the physical quantities of different types of goods cannot be added, the aggregate quantity of production can mean only the *value* of aggregate production. For comparison between two situations, each product must be valued at the same price in both situations. But the relative prices of different goods are sure to differ in two countries. Except by coincidence, the two sets of goods will have a different relative value if priced at one country's set of prices than if priced at the other. (When two time periods are being compared, the problem is known to statisticians as that of choice between Laspeyre and Paasche weights.)

If the relative prices differ greatly, and if the relative quantities of goods produced differ greatly in the opposite direction (each country

---

[5] For a comprehensive brief discussion of the conceptual problems, see S. Kuznets (1947), pp. 10–34. For a more elaborate discussion, see Kuznets (1949), pp. 137–72. For technical appraisals of various conceptual problems and problems of measurement in United States national income accounting, many of which exist also in international comparisons, see also N.B.E.R. (1960), especially parts 1, 2, 3, and 6.

produces a relatively much larger quantity of the goods whose prices in that country are relatively low), then the indicated ratio of per capita product in one country to that in the other will differ greatly, depending on which prices are used. Table 1–3 illustrates the point. It is reasonable

TABLE 1–3
Hypothetical Comparison of National Products

	Country 1	Country 2
Production: Numbers of units		
Food	2	7
Clothing	5	3
Prices per unit		
Food	7	2
Clothing	3	6
Values, at Country 1 prices		
Food	14	49
Clothing	15	9
Total	29	58
Values, at Country 2 prices		
Food	4	14
Clothing	30	18
Total	34	32

to think of each country's relative prices as reflecting the tastes or preferences of the people of that country, given the availability of different goods. In the case illustrated in Table 1–3 it is possible to state that as measured by the tastes of Country 1, the production of Country 2 is more than twice as great, and that as measured by the tastes of Country 2, the production of Country 1 is slightly higher. No unqualified or absolute comparative statement can be made; the ambiguity must always remain.

Table 1–3 illustrates a practical problem, not merely a hypothetical one. The baskets of goods produced in different countries differ in many ways.

Some of the differences are closely related to income levels. As income increases, people change the relative amounts of different goods and services that they consume, and where the differences in income are great, these differences in consumption (and production) are great. Internationally, therefore, no valid comparison can be made except by specifying which country's preferences are being used as the yardstick.[6]

---

[6] Purists carry the matter further. The institutions of a country, for example those affecting the distribution of income, affect the types of goods that people would choose to have produced. Even if the relative production and prices of different types of goods were identical in two countries, no unambiguous comparison of welfare could be made if institutions affecting production choices differed.

The modern discussion of the measurement of economic welfare may be said to

Such a comparison requires a large amount of knowledge about production and prices in each country, knowledge that is unavailable for most countries. As a substitute, the method usually used to compare national products is to take the gross national product estimate for each country in its own currency, and to convert them all to a common currency by means of the exchange rate between currencies. This is the method used in Table 1–2. Each country's gross product estimate was converted to dollars by use of the exchange rate between that country's currency and the dollar (or, if a country has several rates, the average exchange rate which seems to best represent the average price of the country's currency in international transactions).

The exchange rate is determined by the prices in different countries of the goods and services traded in international trade. However, these are not representative of all goods and services produced. Indeed, use of exchange rates to compare the national products of two countries at different income levels systematically understates the national product of the lower income countries.

The reason is as follows. In low-income countries, goods and services whose production requires much labor and little capital are relatively cheap and relatively plentiful, whereas in high-income countries capital-intensive goods and services are relatively both cheap and plentiful.

The exports of a low-income country are not those products in whose production it is relatively most efficient. The reason is twofold. First, services cannot be exported, except for shipping and other services involved in international trade itself, and except for services to tourists which foreign tourists come to the country and buy. Moreover, many goods that are produced in low-income countries by highly labor-intensive methods cannot be exported; these are the locally used, unstandardized goods that constitute a large part of the nation's total production. The goods that are salable abroad by a low-income country are, with some significant exceptions, goods whose production is capital-intensive or land-intensive. Mainly, they are primary products. A low-income country is relatively less efficient in the production of these goods than in the production of the nonexportables.

On the other hand, the exports of a high-income country are also its capital-intensive goods.[7] These are the goods in which a high-income

---

begin with A. C. Pigou (1932). The most complete analysis of the problems of measurement is in P. A. Samuelson (1950). Samuelson's article contains a bibliography of essays concerning the topic from Pigou's discussion up to 1950. See also Pigou (1951), in which he states his understanding of the implications of Samuelson's article.

[7] Professor W. Leontief (1953) has shown that the imports of the United States are more capital-intensive than its exports, when land is treated as capital. That this is true, even though the United States has especially abundant supplies of land as well as other capital, illustrates the complexity of the set of influences at work. That the

country is relatively most efficient. To illustrate the result, suppose that the national product of Country Lowincome is 100 billion dekkars, and that of the United States is $750 billion; and that the exchange rate between the dollar and the dekkar is: U.S. $1 = 4 dekkars. If the exchange rate is used to estimate how much the national product of Lowincome is worth in dollars, the estimate will be $25 billion, or one thirtieth that of the United States. However, if all United States products were valued at their price in dekkars in Lowincome, their value might be 3,300 billion dekkars, indicating a national product of Lowincome one thirty–third that of the United States. And if the goods produced in Lowincome were valued at their prices in dollars in the United States, their value might be $75 billion, indicating production one-tenth that of the United States. The use of the exchange rate, in this example, distorts the comparison by one tenth, relative to direct valuation from country Lowincome's viewpoint, and by two thirds (or, using a different denominator, by 200%) in the opposite direction, relative to direct valuation from the U.S. viewpoint. Distortions are probably this great only for comparisons between the very lowest and very highest income countries, but considerable distortion exists whenever the difference in per capita income levels is considerable.

An Adjusted Comparison

The greater the difference in the income levels of two countries, the greater the difference in the ratios of labor costs to capital costs is likely to be, and hence the greater the understatement of the lower income country's relative income level. However, the degree of distortion is also affected by other factors, for example each country's wealth in natural resources. No formula showing the precise or even approximate amount of distortion in each intercountry comparison is possible. But some data are available to give a general impression of how great the distortions are. A comparison between five Western European countries and the United States showed that use of exchange rates undervalued their 1950 national products by from 37 to 63%, relative to comparisons based on United States prices. A similar comparison between eight Western European countries and the United States showed undervaluations of 1955 production by from 18 to 70%.[8]

United States is able to export products that are labor-intensive relative to those of its major trading partners (who are not the low-income countries) is presumably due to the fact that American labor is extremely productive, and not merely because of the large amounts of capital and land used in cooperation with labor. The general rule stated in the text applies with respect to the trade between the United States and the less developed countries.

[8] See M. Gilbert and I. B. Kravis (1954), and M. Gilbert and associates (1958).

By now, a number of other such estimates have been made[9] and several theoretical analyses of the problem have been presented.[10]

These considerations help to explain the data of Table 1–2. The calculation which shows that people live at average incomes one thirtieth or one fortieth that of the United States is a statistical mirage. By a crude adjustment of Table 1–2, Table 1–4 presents maximum estimates of the levels of income of the rest of the world relative to the United States.

TABLE 1–4
World Per Capita Gross National Product by Income Levels, 1971,
Adjusted Data

Per Capita Income (dollars)	Population		Aggregate GNP		Per Capita GNP	
	Actual (millions)	Percent of Total	Actual ($ billions)	Percent of Total	Average (dollars)	Percent of World Average
More than 2,201 ...	468.9	12.4	1,875.9	40.1	4,000	321.8
(USA)	(207.0)	(5.5)	(1,068.4)	(22.8)	(5,161)	(415.2)
1,001–2,200	579.0	15.4	1,376.2	29.4	2,377	191.2
501–1,000	180.8	4.8	227.4	4.9	1,258	101.2
201–500	527.8	14.0	456.2	9.7	864	69.5
0–200	2,008.7	53.3	744.6	15.9	371	29.8
Total or Average ...	3,765.2	99.9	4,680.3	100.0	1,243	

The adjustments were to multiply the data of Table 1–2 by the following ratios:

Products of Countries with
Per Capita Incomes
in Table 1–2 of: Multiplier

	Multiplier
$ 0–200	3.0
201–500	2.5
500–1,000	2.0
1,001–2,200	1.5
2,201+	1.0

---

[9] W. Beckerman (1966) lists all such comparisons that had been made at that date.

Hollister (1958), Tables 20 and 21, pp. 146–47 has made a comparison between Communist China and the United States for the years 1952 and 1955, though of course the data available to him were far cruder than those available for the European countries. His estimates of the value of U.S. products in yuan yield a ratio of U.S. to Chinese national product slightly *higher* than the ratio indicated by conversion *via* the exchange rate. His estimates of the value of China's production when priced at U.S. prices yield a value for 1952 2.21 times as high, and for 1955 2.37 times as high, as the value indicated by converting China's national product to dollars at the prevailing exchange rate.

[10] P. A. David (1972), B. Balassa (1973), and P. A. David (1973), summarize the argument and present bibliographies.

They are maximum in two senses. First, they aim to provide figures equivalent to the value each country's per capita product would have in the United States. This is the maximum way of valuing the products, but it is the "correct" way if the purpose is to indicate to Westerners the value in Western eyes of the per capita products in the low-income countries. It is maximum in another sense also. At least for many of the lowest income countries, the adjustments made in Table 1–4 may be a little too great, though for India it is probably not great enough. For some of the West European countries, also, the adjustments may be too small.

The intercountry per capita income ratios are now believable. The lowest income group of countries is shown as having incomes, on the average, about one fourteenth that in the United States. Anyone who will consider the average U.S. level of living, and will strip from it the clothing and shelter not needed in a warm country, eliminate highly processed and luxury foods, eliminate almost all travel, reading, commercial entertainment, vacation expenditure, etc.—and will consider too that the United States federal, state, and local units of government use about one fourth of America's production, whereas in the lowest income countries most of this share is available directly to the individual—will realize that income levels one-fourteenth those in the United States are sufficient to provide a way of living that is physiologically adequate for health. This of course does not mean that all persons in those countries in fact have enough food, clothing, and shelter for health—they do not—but it does help to explain why in countries that seem to be living at a level below subsistence, the population is actually increasing rapidly. Nevertheless, income in these countries is woefully low, relatively.

Hereafter, in referring to income levels in the less developed countries, I shall use data converted to U.S. dollars by use of exchange rates, because no other data are available. The reader should keep in mind that the data understate the true relative income levels of the less developed countries.

At this point the reader may consider a brief answer to the question: Why are the income levels of some countries so low relative to those of other countries? The proximate answer is clear. The dominant immediate cause is not colonial or imperialistic exploitation or suppression, or lack of good will, even though all of these have been present in some areas. The proximate answer is that a cumulative process of improvement in the productivity of techniques of production, going on in some countries of the world for several centuries, and at a slower rate for several preceding centuries, has raised their productivity and therefore their income to its present level. In the present lower income countries of the world, that process has been going on, at least at an appreciable rate, for only the last few generations. Low productivity is the dominant and defining characteristic of "underdevelopment."

Why productivity has not risen earlier is an historical question which will not be discussed here. It may only be noted—and will be noted at more length in succeeding chapters—that raising the level of productivity is a complex and difficult task, even if high levels of productivity are in existence elsewhere.

INCOME LEVELS AND RATES OF GROWTH

This section discusses recent rates of growth in all countries of the world for which estimates are available. First, however, a summary is given of the longer-run growth history of some of present high-income countries, for recent trends will be better understood in the perspective of that longer history.

A Century of Growth

Income in the present high-income countries of the world rose much more rapidly during the period between 1700 and the 20th century than did income elsewhere; that is why those countries have high incomes today. In 1700, the per capita income of the most elite countries of the world economically, namely Great Britain and the Netherlands, was probably not more than three or four times that of the average in countries containing the lowest income one half of the world's population. Today, the countries that have been growing longest have raised their income levels to the greater multiples shown in Table 1–4. They have not done so by a sudden burst of growth. Rather, their growth rates per century were rather moderate, compared with some other countries' rates since World War II—but their growth continued consistently.

Estimates for the 100-year period ending about 1970, presented in Table 1–5, show several facts: (1) Apparently in no country in which growth was under way in the mid-19th century has it ceased since then. (2) However, there are marked variations over time in the rate of growth in individual countries. They show up even if we compare only long time periods, such as the last 40 years of the 19th century and the first 71 years of the 20th. (3) Over this period, a growth rate averaging 2.5% per capita annually is a very fast one; only Japan and Sweden achieved it for the entire period. In these countries plus Russia-U.S.S.R., the rate has been markedly higher in the 20th century than in the last decades of the 19th. In the United States, which had a cyclical upswing at the end of the 19th century, it was markedly lower.

Sweden's remarkable performance during this period of more than a century has received less attention than it deserves. By it, Sweden has attained the highest per capita income in Europe and the second highest

TABLE 1–5
**Nineteenth and Twentieth-Century Growth Rates, Nine
Countries[11]**

	1860 or 1870 to 1900	1900 to 1971
Japan	3.0	4.1
United States	2.5	2.0
Sweden	2.4	2.7
Canada	2.2	2.0
Germany	2.0	2.1
France	1.5	1.4
Great Britain	1.4	1.3
Russia–U.S.S.R.	1.0	2.6
Italy	0.8	2.3

in the world, apart from the two high-income oil principalities. For all countries except Sweden, the 20th-century data of course reflect the disruptions of two world wars (though it is not conclusively evident that these reduced the average growth rate over the 65-year period).

Even though per capita income in other countries has also risen, these growth rates have given the average person in the high-income countries an increasing share of the world's income.

Data for 1938 made or compiled by Kuznets make possible a comparison of the distribution of the world's income in 1938 and in 1971.

In 1938, the United States had one fourth of the world's income. In 1971, with a smaller share of the world's population, the United States had more than 30% of the total. For the reasons indicated in this chapter, the data for both years overstate the true share of the United States, but the comparison between the one year and the other is valid. At the other end of the spectrum, while the population share of Asia and Africa combined rose from 61.4% to 66.1%, their percentage of the world's income fell.

The data do not give a true picture of the relative secular trends in the low- and high-income countries, for the great rise in the United States share of world income reflects mainly the fact that the depression of the 1930s affected the United States more seriously than any other country. At full employment in 1938, the United States would probably have had about as large a share of the world income as in 1965.[12] But even if the United States figures are subtracted from the world totals, the per capita share of Asians, Africans, and Latin Americans in the income of the rest of the world fell—not greatly, but appreciably.

The rise of the Soviet Union's share is especially impressive. Deriving

---

[11] Estimates from Kuznets (*Q.A.E.G.N.*, 1), Tables 1 and 2, for the period up to 1950 were combined with estimates by the International Bank for Reconstruction and Development for 1950–71.

[12] Between 1938 and 1941, U.S. GNP rose by more than one third.

TABLE 1–6

The Geographic Distribution of World Population and Income, 1938 and 1970

	1938			1970		
	Percent of World Population	*Percent of World Gross Product*	*Relative Income Per Capita (world = 100)*	*Percent of World Population*	*Percent of World Gross Product*	*Relative Income Per Capita (world = 100)*
U.S., Canada, Australia, New Zealand	7.0	29.5	419	6.8*	36.0	527
Of which: U.S.	6.0	25.4	429	5.6	31.9	564
Western Europe	9.9	27.6	275	6.0	20.0	333
U.S.S.R.	7.8	8.1	102	6.7	10.4	155
Southern and Eastern Europe†	8.2	10.8	129	6.7	9.7	145
Latin America	5.9	4.2	71	7.8	4.9	63
Asia	54.2	17.6	33	56.6	16.5	30
Africa	7.2	2.3	32	9.5	2.3	25

* Data for 1965 include minor islands adjacent to these areas.
† Includes countries east of West Germany and Austria, and the Balkan, Iberian, and Apennine peninsulas.
    Source: 1938: Kuznets (*Q.A.E.G.N.*, 1), Table 4, adjusted by revising the estimate of China's population in 1938 from 450 million. 1970: *UN Demographic Yearbook, 1972* and *UN Yearbook of National Accounts Statistics*, 1972, vol. 3. Estimates for some countries were made by the author by extrapolation or interpolation from data for other years.

an estimate for the Soviet Union in U.S. dollars has a larger margin of error than the same procedure for most other countries, because of the difference in the concepts of measurement of the national product and because of the absence of a meaningful foreign exchange rate. It is therefore possible that the GDP of the U.S.S.R. is overstated. This is more likely than understatement. But the error can hardly be more than 10%, and even with this maximum allowance for error the record is striking. The data show the U.S.S.R.'s share of non-U.S. world income rising by 40% while her population share fell.

Recent Growth, World Wide

These data, mainly for continental groups, are only very broadly indicative of changes in the distribution of world income among countries at various income levels.

Table 1–7 shows the average rate of growth from 1960 to 1971 of real GNP of the world as a whole and of countries classed into the income

TABLE 1–7
Average Annual Rates of Growth, 1960–71, GNP Weights, Country Goups
Classed by Per Capita GNP in 1971

| Per Capita GNP | Average Annual Rates of Growth in GNP (percent) | |
in Dollars, 1971	Per Capita	Aggregate
More than 2,200	3.4	4.4
1,001–2,200	6.3	7.4
501–1,000	4.4	6.5
201–500	3.4	6.0
0–200	2.1	4.2
World Average	(4.1)	5.4

Source: *World Bank Atlas*, 1973.

groups shown in Table 1–2. As compared with all previous figures, the global rates are amazing. Gross world product grew at a rate of 5.4% per year. This is a rate unprecedented in world history, a rate 3.4% faster than the rate of population growth. (Because of the weights used, the world rate of growth in per capita income shown is 4.1%, which implies a population growth rate of only 1.3%, whereas the actual was 2%. This anomalous result is explained in Appendix A to this chapter.)

But the rate of growth of per capita income in the lowest income group of countries was only 2.1%, and of the next lowest income group 3.4%, whereas that in the two next higher income groups was much faster. The very highest income group did not gain on any but the very lowest, but—taking these broad groups as units—below that very highest group the "income gap" was still widening.

By now, the reader may feel that he or she is drowning in data. But one more table will present data which must not be overlooked. The comparison by income groups of countries gives the impression that the wealthier countries, except for those at the very top, are steadily pulling away from the poorer. However, the data by groups conceals variations within the groups. Table 1–8, a matrix of income groups and growth rates for 1965–71, shows more fully what has been happening. A finer income division than in Table 1–7, and also six growth rate groups, are shown.

The data for some of the low-income countries are depressing. All of the 10 countries whose per capita income declined, except Cuba, had incomes below $400 per capita in 1965. Of the 39 countries with 1965 incomes of $100 or below, 17 had growth rates below 2%, and 10 below 1%. These latter are not only the least developed but the least developing of the world's countries.[13]

But the phenomenon equally significant for an understanding of

---

[13] Nine of the ten are among the United Nations' "least developed countries."

TABLE 1-8
GNP Per Capita, 1965, and Growth Rates, 1965–71, 152 Countries*

GNP Per Capita, 1965	−7% to 0	0–1%	1%–2%	2%–4%	4%–6%	6% →
6,400	Kuwait					
3,200		Iceland	United States	Australia Canada Europe, 5	Qatar West Germany France	
1,600			New Zealand	Brunei Netherlands Antilles	Asia, 1 Latin America, 1 Europe, 8	Czechoslovakia U.S.S.R.
800			Venezuela United Kingdom			
400	Africa, 2 Asia, 3 Latin America, 1	Lebanon Uruguay	Canal Zone	Africa, 1 Latin America, 4	Asia, 1 Latin America, 2 Europe, 3	Africa, 1 Asia, 2 Europe, 5
200	Swaziland Peru	Swaziland Peru	Africa, 1 Asia, 1 Latin America, 2	Latin America, 5	Africa, 2 Latin America, 3 Europe, 3	Bahrain
100	Senegal Cambodia	Egypt	Africa, 2 Asia, 2 Latin America, 2	Africa, 6 Asia, 5 Latin America, 2	Africa, 2 Asia, 3 Latin America, 3	Africa, 1 Asia, 4
0	Sudan Niger Africa, 4 Asia, 3 Latin America, 1		Africa, 6 Asia, 1	Africa, 9 Asia, 8	Africa, 4	Oman (25.1)

Growth Rates, 1965–71

* A number in a cell indicates that number of countries.

Notes: (1) "Asia" includes Oceania. (2) Each cell contains any country whose GNP or growth rate precisely equals the upper limit of the cell. (3) In nine cases, the 1965 income measure used was GDP. Sources: GNP, 1965–World Bank Atlas, 1967 ed. Growth rates, 1965–71–World Bank Atlas, 1973 ed.

economic growth in the world is the dispersion of growth rates at each income level. Not only the oil countries have risen in relative standing, though they have suddenly risen the most rapidly; 22 of the 39 lowest income countries had per capita growth rates above 2% per year, and five had rates higher than any country in the world with per capita incomes above $1,600 except Qatar, West Germany, and France. One third of the countries with incomes between $101 and $400, and almost two thirds of those between $401 and $800 likewise has rates of growth that exceeded all but three of the high-income countries.

The panorama of relative income levels, these figures show, is steadily changing. The sociologist Pareto wrote about the "circulation of the elites," the fact that, in any society, from one generation to another a number of families drop out of the group regarded as elite and others take their places. Among countries economically there is also a circulation of the elites. It has occurred over the long run, not merely by some accident during one six-year period. Great Britain, in the early 19th century the world's highest income country, in 1965 was the lowest income country in Western Europe, its per capita income much exceeded even by those of cold and mountainous Norway and arctic Finland. In 1920, Argentina was one of the world's high income countries, its per capita income equal to that of Austrialia.[14] That of Japan was less. And the shifts in the income rankings of these countries are only the most spectacular among those that occur decade by decade.

Until great noneconomic changes occur in the world's "least developed" countries, the ratio of their incomes to those of the world's high-income countries and to the countries just above the "least developed" will continue to fall. The range of the world per capita income will widen. Even if these "least developed" countries begin to grow, their relative incomes will continue to fall for a generation or more, for growth begins gradually, and the "least developed" countries will not quickly attain the growth rates of countries that have been growing for several decades or more.

---

[14] The estimates are rough ones. Observers of the time wrote of Argentina as one of the five countries of the world with the brightest economic promise.

The matter of weights explains the anomalous implication of Table 1–7 that the annual rate of growth in the world's population during the 11-year period was 5.4 minus 4.1, or 1.3 percent, whereas population data show a rate of about 2%. Countries with large GNPs had low population growth rates, hence the incorrect implicit result of a world population growth rate of 1.3%. The Table 1–9 comparison among income classes of growth rates in per capita income is the more nearly correct one, whereas the Table 1–7 estimate of the world's growth in aggregate GNP is the correct one.

Table 1–9 also arrives at an implicit incorrect rate of world population growth, 1.8%, because of the effect of using 1971 weights rather than current weights for each year. That table arrives at a much more incorrect figure for growth in gross world product. The correct figure is that of Table 1–7, 5.4%.

But except for these relationships, the concept is flatly erroneous that there is a fixed group of "low-income" or "less developed" countries of the world, whose incomes will remain low and will become steadily lower relative to those of a similar group of "developed countries." The group of "low-income" or "lower income" or "middle-income" countries is gradually but steadily changing. There will always be (relatively) low-income countries, but not the same ones. Those countries are low-income countries today whose growth rates, thus far, have been low. Apart from countries in which large valuable mineral deposits are discovered, or who by a cartel arrangement are able suddenly to obtain greatly increased prices for their minerals, even those low-income countries whose growth rates are relatively fast will rise in relative income only gradually, for "a stern chase is a long chase." Conversely, higher income countries with relatively slow growth rates will fall only gradually in relative income. As noted above, fairly rapid relative shifts, as of Argentina, England, and Japan, are exceptional, almost limiting cases. Yet the reader should think of a gradually changing kaleidoscope, not of a set of fixed income relationships.

APPENDIX A

RELATIVE GROWTH RATES, USING POPULATION WEIGHTS

It is worthwhile to reflect for a moment on what the aggregate GNP weights used in computing average growth rates in Table 1–7 mean. They mean that the percentage increase for a high-income country counts more in the average than the percentage increase for a lower income country with equal population. The point may be illustrated by considering two individuals. If the income of one rose from $1,000 to $1,100, an increase of 10%, and that of the other remained constant at $100, an average with income weights would not give the "sensible" result that on the average their incomes rose by 5%, but rather that it rose from $550 to $600, or by 9%.

We may compute an average rate of growth in income in another way: by first calculating the growth rate for each country and averaging the rates with the population of each country as weight. That computation gives the result shown in Table 1–9.

By coincidence, this computation shows the same rates of growth as with GNP weights for per capita and aggregate GNP in the highest income class. But it shows lower rates of growth in aggregate GNP for every lower income class, and in per capita GNP for three of the four lower classes. By any definition of the "income gap," it shows that gap widening more than do the calculations with GNP weights.

TABLE 1–9
Average Annual Rates of Growth, 1960–71, Population Weights, Country Groups Classed by Per Capita GNP in 1971

Per Capita in Dollars, 1971	Average Annual Rates of Growth GNP (percent)	
	Per Capita	Aggregate
More than 2,200	3.4	4.4
1,001–2,200	6.0	7.2
501–1,000	4.2	6.3
201–500	3.4	5.7
0–200	1.8	3.9
World Average	3.0	4.8

Source: *World Bank Atlas,* 1973.

Table 1–9, of course, does not achieve complete adjustment for the distortion of calculating income growth rates with GNP weights. Even in Table 1–9, the rate for each country is that in the country's aggregate GNP. If the rate of growth for each individual were known, and these rates were averaged counting each person as unity, the results would differ from those shown. For the lowest two income groups in Table 1–9, the rates of growth in both aggregate and per capita income would almost certainly be lower. For the top two income groups, they would probably be higher. The data of Chapter 7 concerning income distribution plus the data of Table 1–8 concerning rates of growth permit this deduction.

APPENDIX B

MACROECONOMIC DATA, 114 COUNTRIES

Table 1–10 presents data for population, income, and growth rates for all but some of the smallest countries of the world. For the countries to which numbers without affixed letters have been assigned, a variety of economic data is available. Data for these countries are used in many graphs throughout this book; the countries are identified on each graph by number only, except that countries that are exceptional cases on each graph are named. For each continent, a second alphabetized list of countries is shown, assigned numbers with letter suffixes. Fewer types of data are available for these countries; they are represented on only a few graphs.

The list of countries bearing numbers without letter suffixes, together with the numbers assigned them, is repeated inside the back cover, for ready reference. The numbers are the same as those assigned to countries in the first (1968) edition of this text.

TABLE 1–10
Population, Income, Per Capita Growth Rate, Various Countries

Country	Assigned Number	Population 1971 (millions— to nearest tenth)	GNP Per Capita 1971 (current U.S.$ to nearest $10)	Average Annual Growth Rate in GNP Per Capita 1960–71 (percent)
		Africa		
Algeria	1	14.4	360	3.5
Ghana	2	8.9	250	0.0
Guinea	3	4.1	90	0.1
Kenya	4	11.7	160	3.5
Liberia	5	1.6	210	2.5
Libya	6	2.0	1,450	17.6
Morocco	7	15.4	260	1.1
Nigeria	8	56.5	140	2.1
Rhodesia	9	5.5	320	1.1
Tanzania	10	13.2	110	3.1
Tunisia	11	5.2	320	2.8
Republic of South Africa	12	22.7	810	2.8
UAR	13	34.1	220	1.6
Cameroon	13a	5.8	200	4.0
Central African Republic	13b	1.6	150	0.4
Chad	13c	3.7	80	0.6
Congo	13d	1.1	270	0.9
Ethiopia	13e	25.2	80	2.7
Gabon	13f	0.5	700	5.2
Gambia	13g	0.4	140	3.6
Ivory Coast	13h	5.2	330	4.6
Malagasy Republic	13i	7.2	140	0.6
Malawi	13j	4.6	90	2.5
Mali	13k	5.1	70	1.4
Mauritius	13l	0.8	280	−0.4
Mozambique	13m	7.8	280	4.0
Reunion	13n	0.5	950	4.8
Senegal	13o	4.0	250	−0.4
Sierra Leone	13p	2.7	200	3.9
Somalia	13q	2.9	70	−0.9
Sudan	13r	16.1	120	—
Upper Volta	13s	5.5	70	0.9
Uganda	13t	10.1	130	2.1
Zambia	13u	4.2	380	2.5
		Asia		
Afghanistan	14	14.6	80	0.6
Burma	15	29.6	80	0.3
Ceylon	16	12.8	100	1.8
China (Taiwan)	17	14.9	430	7.1
India	18	551.1	110	1.3
Iran	19	29.8	450	6.5
Israel	20	3.0	2,190	4.7
Japan	21	104.7	2,130	9.6
Korea, South	22	31.8	260	7.4

TABLE 1–10 (*continued*)

Country	Assigned Number	Population 1971 (millions— to nearest tenth)	GNP Per Capita 1971 (current U.S.$ to nearest $10)	Average Annual Growth Rate in GNP Per Capita 1960–71 (percent)
Kuwait	23	0.8	3,860	−2.5
Lebanon	24	2.8	660	0.7
Malaysia	25	11.2	400	3.1
Pakistan	26	62.7	130	3.7
Philippines	27	37.9	240	2.5
Thailand	28	37.3	210	4.8
Turkey	29	36.2	340	3.7
Hong Kong	29a	4.0	900	5.8
Indonesia	29b	119.2	80	1.3
Iraq	29c	9.7	370	2.4
Jordan	29d	2.4	260	7.4
Singapore	29e	2.1	1,200	6.8
Syria	29f	6.5	290	3.1
Vietnam, South	29g	18.8	230	1.0

Latin America

Country	Assigned Number	Population	GNP Per Capita	Growth Rate
Argentina	30	23.6	1,230	2.6
Bolivia	31	5.1	190	2.5
Brazil	32	95.4	460	2.7
Chile	33	10.0	760	2.4
Colombia	34	22.3	370	1.7
Costa Rica	35	1.8	590	3.1
Cuba	36	8.6	510	−1.2
Dominican Republic ..	37	4.1	430	2.1
Ecuador	38	6.3	310	1.7
El Salvador	39	3.7	320	1.6
Guatemala	40	5.4	390	1.7
Honduras	41	2.6	300	1.7
Jamaica	42	1.9	720	3.3
Mexico	43	52.4	700	3.5
Paraguay	44	2.4	280	1.2
Peru	45	14.0	480	2.0
Puerto Rico	46	2.8	1,830	6.0
Uruguay	47	2.9	750	−0.2
Venezuela	48	10.6	1,060	2.3
Guyana	48a	0.7	390	1.9
Haiti	48b	4.3	120	−0.8
Nicaragua	48c	2.1	450	3.5
Panama	48d	1.5	820	4.4
Trinidad and Tobago ..	48e	10.6	1,060	2.3

Europe

Country	Assigned Number	Population	GNP Per Capita	Growth Rate
Albania	49	2.2	480	5.8
Austria	50	7.5	2,200	4.1
Belgium	51	9.7	2,960	4.2
Bulgaria	52	8.5	820	7.4
Czechoslovakia	53	14.5	2,120	3.8
Denmark	54	5.0	3,430	3.9

TABLE 1–10 (*concluded*)

Country	Assigned Number	Population 1971 (millions— to nearest tenth)	GNP Per Capita 1971 (current U.S.$ to nearest $10)	Average Annual Growth Rate in GNP Per Capita 1960–71 (percent)
Finland	55	4.7	2,550	4.0
France	56	51.2	3,360	4.6
Germany, West	57	61.3	3,210	3.7
Greece	58	9.0	1,250	6.7
Hungary	59	10.3	1,200	5.1
Ireland	60	3.0	1,510	3.6
Italy	61	54.1	1,860	4.4
Norway	62	3.9	3,130	4.1
Netherlands	63	13.2	2,620	3.9
Poland	64	32.7	1,350	5.2
Portugal	65	9.7	730	5.3
Romania	66	20.5	740	7.7
Spain	67	34.0	1,100	5.6
Sweden	68	8.1	4,240	3.6
Switzerland	69	6.3	3,640	2.7
United Kingdom	70	55.9	2,430	2.2
USSR	71	245.1	1,400	5.9
Yugoslavia	72	20.7	730	4.5
Cyprus	72a	0.6	1,100	5.7
Iceland	72b	0.2	2,480	3.1
Luxembourg	72c	0.3	3,130	2.6
Malta	72d	0.3	860	6.0
Oceania				
Australia	73	12.7	2,870	3.2
New Zealand	74	2.8	2,470	2.1
Papua/New Guinea	74a	2.5	320	4.7
North America				
Canada	75	21.6	4,140	3.8
United States	76	207.0	5,160	3.0

Source: *World Bank Atlas*, 1973.

BIOGRAPHICAL NOTE

The references in the text and footnotes to books and articles listed in the bibliography at the end of this volume will suggest sources for additional reading on specific topics.

During the past decade, many of the most important articles of the 1950s and early 1960s concerning economic development have been reprinted in one or more of these four volumes: Agarwala and Singh, eds., *The Economics of Underdevelopment;* Meier, Gerald M., *Leading Issues in Development Economics;* Morgan, Betz, and Choudry, eds.,

Readings in Economic Development; and, Okum and Richardson, eds., *Studies in Economic Development,* all published between 1958 and 1964. Meier presents the greatest number of selections, many of which have been cut—skillfully, but rather drastically. He has also added introductory notes to each section so that the volume can be used as a text. No comparably good collections have been published in recent years, partly because many recent writings are econometric analyses difficult to anthologize effectively.

The United Nations annual *World Economic Survey* presents the standard annual summary concerning the non-Communist and Communist economically more developed countries and the less developed countries, respectively. Each volume also deals with a selected special topic.

Statistical publications of the United Nations and its specialized agencies are comprehensive sources of data. Of most general coverage are three annual publications of the United Nations itself: the *Demographic Yearbook, Statistical Yearbook,* and *Yearbook of National Income Accounts.* The United Nations quarterly *Statistical Bulletin* presents current data. The standard source for statistical series relating to economic and financial matters, for members of the International Monetary Fund and for the world as a whole, is the Fund's monthly *International Financial Statistics.*

A convenient source of data on population, population growth rates, and rates of growth in per capita GNP is the *World Bank Atlas,* a slim pamphlet published occasionally by the International Bank for Reconstruction and Development. A wide variety of data relevant to economic growth, for the same countries, are presented in the Bank's *World Tables,* of which a new edition was in preparation late in 1974. Past editions, though not circulated widely, have been available to scholars.

A valuable, though now dated, source of historical and comparative data on many aspects of economic growth is the series of 10 supplements to issues of *Economic Development and Cultural Change* between October, 1956, and January, 1967, prepared by Simon Kuznets. Some of the data are presented, sometimes revised or augmented, and much textual discussion added in his *Modern Economic Growth: Rate, Structure, and Spread* (1966). A student of economic growth should examine library card files to see what additional volumes by Professor Kuznets may have appeared.

Limits to World Growth? The Question of Minerals Supply 2

It was taken for granted in the preceding chapter that growth in the lower income countries can continue indefinitely. It is time to question that assumption. If the world encounters limits to growth, the lower income countries will not escape their share of perhaps more than their share of the effects. If growth in the high-income countries is brought to an end by the noxious products of growth itself, perhaps growth can nevertheless continue in the less industrialized countries, but if the greedy demands of growth are constrained by the exhaustion of the supply of essential resources, growth must come to an end in the lower income countries as well. There will not be any complete exhaustion of resources, except in some rather crude model. However, some materials may become more and more costly to extract as they become scarcer—sufficiently costly in terms of the inputs required to bring growth in per capita income to an end and even cause it to fall. The effects, favorable on the lower income countries that provide large quantities of the materials, unfavorable on others, may be extreme. These matters need to be examined.

Economic growth, it has been said, cannot continue indefinitely in a finite world. Another way of putting the problem is that man, by his innovations leading to economic growth, and later by his intervention in the natural balance between births and deaths, has disturbed an ecological equilibrium. He must now suffer the consequences of the disequilibrium he has created.

Perhaps these simple statements set a useful framework for the analysis. The major relevant questions are the following: The accelerating

29

output of the world is consuming quantities of natural resources that are enormous relative to rates of a century or even a half-century ago, and enormous also relative to the proven world reserves of some of them. Must not world growth end, and fairly soon, by exhaustion of the materials from which to produce? Or, before this point is reached, will increasing pollution inexorably lower the level of human welfare? Will the world's population continue to grow indefinitely, creating indefinitely increasing demands for food that eventually cannot be met? Or, if changing human desires tend quite apart from the food supply to bring population increase to an end, will this happen soon enough?

Population increase, increase in the production of food, increased industrialization and with it increased mineral and energy use, and pollution interact. There are feedbacks. One affects another and thereby, perhaps, itself. All of these factors must therefore be considered together. They cannot, however, all be discussed simultaneously. This chapter discusses the questions of mineral (including petroleum) resources and pollution. The following chapter discusses population growth and food supply.

WORLD GROWTH IN THE MODERN PERIOD

Viewed in the broad sweep of human history and pre-history, improvements in technology and resulting rise in per capita income and consumption have probably been occurring (irregularly) since the Paleolithic (or Old Stone) Age and quite conceivably, if we had even the vaguest knowledge on which to base a statement, earlier. However, until the second millennium of the Christian era the rising trend was so slow, with forward movements and setbacks, that examination even at thousand-year intervals might not show progress during each interval. But by the end of the Middle Ages (or say the 15th century) economic growth and development in Europe had gathered sufficient speed to be noticeable per century. Gradually, led first by the Flemish and the Dutch and then by the British, there began the upsweep that led to the too narrowly named "Industrial Revolution" first in Western Europe and then in the areas of European contact. Unknown to the West, economic growth at an easily perceptible pace was also occurring in Japan from at least the 14th century on.

The mid-17th century is sometimes taken as marking the beginning of the modern era. This is a convenient date for economists to accept, since an estimate of world population is possible for the year 1650. England's per capita GNP, which, indirect evidence suggests, had been rising at an appreciable rate for two centuries or more before that time,[1] by 1650 had

---

[1] The indirect evidence is the economic changes that had been going on in England. Also, see E. Carus-Wilson (1941).

reached a level of perhaps $300 in 1970 United States prices, the level which the American colonies may have reached 140 years later, when they began their united nationhood. There is a wide margin of error in the estimates. Admittedly, to price 1650 production in 1970 prices, when many products of either year did not exist in the other, is a rather fanciful exercise, even more fanciful than directly comparing the physical volume of output of the lowest and highest income countries at the present time. However, both comparisons have a certain broad meaning.

Using England as a yardstick, and judging that average per capita income in the world as a whole was probably not less than one fourth and surely not more than one half that of England, we may estimate world per capita income in 1650 at between $75 and $150 in 1970 U.S. prices or, to select a single rough estimate, $100.

The world population in the year 1650 has been estimated as 550 million. Gross world product of that year, then, may be estimated at $55 billion in U.S. prices.

In 1970, the world's population had increased to about 6.5 times the 1650 figure. The gross product of the world, when each country's product is converted to dollars by the use of international exchange rates and the resulting figures are summed, was indicated in chapter 1 as some $3,050 billion—55 times as great as that in 1650. In chapter 1 I indicated reasons to adjust upward the per capita income estimates for the lowest income countries. It is reasonable to assume that the estimate for 1650 should be adjusted similarly. This adjustment would reduce the 1970/1650 ratio. However, with due allowance for such a correction, we may guess that the world's annual product had been multiplied by at least 20 times during the intervening 320 years. (Per capita income, then, had increased to 2-2/3 times its 1650 level, a rate of increase of about 0.3% per year over the 320 period.)

THE QUESTION OF FUTURE METALS AND ENERGY RESOURCE SUPPLY

The Acceleration of Resource Use

A world population of 550 million created little pressure on the land or its resources in 1650. The world's use of metallic minerals was insignificant in amount relative to the deposits later discovered. The use of coal for heating and as fuel in industrial processes was gradually increasing, especially in England, but at that rate of use even the deposits then known would have lasted an extremely long time. But with the rise in world production has come an awesome rise in the consumption of some mineral resources. As income rises, the income elasticities of demand for raw food and for clothing materials fall increasingly below unity, and that for manufactured goods taken as a group rise increasingly above unity. Hence, since 1650 the production of manufactured goods as a group has risen by more than 20 times. A much larger share of that production than in 1650 consumes metals, and much of it is energy-intensive, both because other power sources have replaced human power and because new materials and products involving energy-intensive production have been invented. And so, if we were to devise an index of the world use of all metals and energy, and had the data to extend the index back to 1650, it would show metals-plus-energy consumption in 1970 that was a much larger multiple of that in 1650 than 20, the estimated gross world product (GWP) multiple. As I have suggested, per capita gross product in the United States in 1790 was perhaps about $300 in 1970 prices. In 1970 it was 16 times as high. The rate of growth during the interval, much below 2% per year, is far below the recent world rate. To assess the magnitude of a possible world problem of the future, let us suppose that during the next 180 years GWP per capita increases only at the low average United States rate of the past 180 years. As is shown in the following chapter, demographers do not expect world population growth to level off until it has reached at least 8 billion, about 2-1/3 times the 1970 total of 3.56 billion. If a population of this size achieves a per capita income in the year 2150 that is 16 times that in 1970, GWP will then be some 37 times that of 1970 (or, in 1970 prices, more than $100,000 billion, compared with the $2,800 billion or so of 1970). Even with maximum allowance for a shift of demand from goods to services (whose production also requires the consumption of energy), it requires a most impressively expansive imagination to conceive of obtaining the materials and energy to feed that demand and especially to have fed the cumulative demand of the intervening period. If the mineral resources are not available, then GWP, in the aggregate and per capita, will have ceased to rise and will even have turned downward, perhaps sharply downward, unless men devise alternative sorts and methods of production, of great efficiency, not now conceived of.

The Short-Run Prospects

It is reasonably clear that if there is a problem it is a future, not a present, problem, and a long-run, not a short-run, problem. Apart from the 1973 rise in petroleum prices, the average cost of minerals (in the United States) has not risen (relative to other prices) during the past century.[2] The quadrupling of international petroleum prices in 1973 undoubtedly caused the minerals price index to rise precipitately, but that rise of course was not caused by a natural resource shortage. Moreover, perusal of the trade journals and of financial pages shows no sug-

---

[2] Evidence for the period 1870–1957 is presented in Barnett and Morse (1963), Resources for the Future, a research organization, has extended the relevant indexes (unpublished) to 1967. There was no marked increase, 1967–72.

gestion that minerals prices are about to rise. There is no indication that expert observers of the mining industry expect mineral costs to rise. Ergo, there is no present scarcity. To repeat, then, if there is a prospective shortage it is a long-run, not a short-run, problem.

Longer-Run Projections

The possible longer-run problem is made specific by projecting recent rates of increase in the consumption of individual minerals and associating the projections with estimates of world reserves.

The rates of increase in consumption of various minerals have differed, for several reasons. New products partially displace old ones using different metals. Shifts in the composition of demand occur as income rises. Improvements in manufacturing processes economize on the use of one or another material. Perhaps most important, some materials are substituted for others, most often newly developed materials for older ones. For such reasons, during the period 1950–70, U.S. consumption of aluminum and natural gas rose more rapidly than did GNP, that of lead, zinc, copper, manganese, iron, and coal (in descending order of rate of increase) rose more slowly than did GNP, and through a balance of influences U.S. consumption of petroleum and nickel rose at about the same rate as GNP. Since the invention of the electric generator, the consumption of electrical energy has risen at a much faster rate than has GDP, but the consumption of energy produced in older ways, more slowly.

World consumption of a few materials has decreased absolutely because of invention of a substitute possessing superior qualities. Silk and rubber are examples. There is no mineral of industrial importance of which this is true. The almost universal rule has been an increase, slow or fast, in the rate of consumption.

The potential problem is dramatized if we take as our point of view the seemingly obvious fact that the world's reserve of each mineral is a fixed quantity, and against that apparently hard fact portray the effect of an exponential increase in consumption. A rate of consumption that increases at 1% per year doubles in 70 years; at 2%, in 35 years; at 4%, in 18 years. Meadows and others, in *The Limits to Growth* (1972), illustrate the effect of exponential increase. Table 2–1 shows some of their data. At the 1970 rate of consumption of coal (about 217 million tons per year), and accepting the estimate of "known world reserves" presented in U.S. Bureau of Mines, *Mineral Facts and Problems, 1970,* those reserves would be exhausted in 2,300 years. However, the Bureau of Mines calculates an average exponential annual rate of increase in world coal consumption of 4.1% per year in recent decades. Projecting that rate of increase, world coal reserves would last only 111 years. Similarly, at the 1970 rate of consumption of iron, iron ore reserves would last 240 years,

TABLE 2–1
Calculated Exhaustion Periods for Mineral Reserves

1 Mineral	2 "Known" Global Reserve	3 Consumption in 1970	4 Exhaustion Period at 1970 Rate (years)	5 Calculated Rate of Growth in Use (% per year)	6 Exhaustion Period with Growth in Use (years)
Coal	$5. \times 10^{12}$ tons	$22. \times 10^{8}$ tons	2,300	4.1	111
Chromium	7.75×10^{8} tons	1.6×10^{6} tons	420	2.6	95
Iron	$1. \times 10^{11}$ tons	$4. \times 10^{8}$ tons	240	1.8	93
Nickel	$147. \times 10^{9}$ lbs.	$98. \times 10^{7}$ lbs.	150	3.4	53
Aluminum	1.7×10^{9} tons	1.17×10^{7} tons	100	6.4	31
Tungsten	2.9×10^{9} lbs.	$725. \times 10^{5}$ lbs.	40	2.5	28
Natural gas	1.14×10^{15} cu. ft.	$30. \times 10^{12}$ cu. ft.	38	4.7	22
Copper	$308. \times 10^{6}$ tons	$86. \times 10^{5}$ tons	36	4.6	21
Lead	$91. \times 10^{6}$ tons	$35. \times 10^{5}$ tons	26	2.0	21
Petroleum	$455. \times 10^{9}$ bbls.	$147. \times 10^{8}$ bbls.	31	3.9	20
Zinc	$123. \times 10^{6}$ tons	$535. \times 10^{4}$ tons	23	2.9	18
Tin	4.3×10^{6} long tons	2.5×10^{5} long tons	17	1.1	15

Source: Cols. 2, 4–6, U.S. Bureau of Mines, *Mineral Facts and Figures*, 1970, reprinted in Meadows et al., *The Limits to Growth* (1972), Table 1, p. 64; col. 3. calculated.

but at the calculated exponential rate of increase in consumption, 1.8% per year, only 93 years. These are among the longer-lasting reserves by these calculations. For copper the calculated exhaustion period with exponential increase is 21 years; for petroleum, 20 years; for tin, 15 years.

Mechanical projections of the past though these calculations are, they seem to lead by elementary but inexorable logic to the conclusion that the consumption of metals and energy must end at some time in the future, and that if the present rising trend in consumption continues, that end must come rather soon. Yet men who base their professional careers on knowledge of the minerals market do not expect this. If exhaustion of the world supplies of copper, lead, petroleum, zinc, and tin within the time periods shown in Table 2–1 were reasonably anticipated, there should be excitement in the minerals markets, hoarding of these metals, and intense bidding for ore deposits that offer any promise whatever. There is not. It is necessary to explain that seemingly irrational behavior.

Reserves and Resources

A first step in the explanation is to note that "known world reserves" are not quite what they seem. The term means something far different from "all the reserves in the world that men know about." The term and the alternative one, "proven world reserves," are technical ones which refer to mineral deposits that have been fairly well identified and that are of sufficiently high grade and sufficiently accessible so that they can be worked profitably at current metal prices and with present technology. If prices rise or techniques improve, "known world reserves" increase.

In addition to "proven reserves," geologists refer to "identified" and "hypothetical" "resources." Identified resources are known reserves plus other deposits reasonably well known as to location, extent, and grade which may be exploited profitably if the price rises or technology is improved. Hypothetical resources are undiscovered but geologically predictable deposits, deposits in areas that have not yet been explored. They may turn out to be "known reserves" or only "identified resources" when explored. For many minerals, companies do not explore new areas until known reserves are below anticipated use in, say, the next 20 years, hence almost by definition "known reserves" are below 20 years' use, and some of the data of Table 2–1 reflect not future shortages but merely present mining practices.

For some minerals, total "resources" are only moderately greater than "known reserves," but for others they are more than 100,000 times as great. This is true, for example, of lead (between 1.3 and 2 $\times$ 10^{12} tons) and zinc (between 5 and 6 $\times$ 10^{12} tons). Aluminum is now extracted from bauxite. It exists also in high-aluminum clays, dawsonite, alumite, and aluminum phosphate rock, and can be extracted from these, though only at costs above present aluminum prices. The world's aluminum reserves, including these other deposits, are almost unlimited.

Indeed, even "hypothetical resources" does not include the total world supply of any metal (even apart from such deposits as the solid iron-nickel core of the earth, whose extraction is beyond present human imagination), for estimates of even hypothetical resources omit deposits whose extraction would require techniques that are at present entirely unconventional. William Page has summarized responsible estimates of broader possibilities.

> Seawater has been estimated to contain 1,000 million years' supply of sodium chloride, magnesium and bromine; 100 million years' of sulphur, borax and potassium chloride; more than 1 million of molybdenum, uranium, tin and colbalt; more than 1,000 of nickel and copper. A cubic mile of seawater contains around 47 tons each of aluminum, iron and zinc; given around 330–350 million cubic miles of such water, we are talking around 16,000 million tons each. Such estimates tend to exclude special concentrations such as the Red Sea brines and sediments; these alone contain perhaps $2,000 million worth of zinc, copper, silver and gold, and perhaps ten times this level, at current market prices.
>
> It seems likely that manganese nodules, to be found on the seabed, contain a wealth of mineral; these may be 10^{12} tons in the Pacific alone, containing around 0.25 to 0.30% cobalt, 0.20 to 0.75% copper, 0.42 to 1% nickel, and 16 to 25% manganese. There may be vast quantities of iron, aluminum and zinc, to take only the industrially important minerals. Thus 1/50th of 1% of the ocean seabed could, in this sense, meet a year's demand on aggregate, at current consumption rates.
>
> The most pressing of the limits to growth in resource usage are not geological: Mother Nature has put on and in the planet ample for perhaps tens of thousands of years, but certainly sufficient for the world models' time period of up to the year 2100. The above figures may be horribly in error, but it is inconceivable that the principal qualitative point is entirely erroneous. What limits there may be come from man's economic and technological ability to exploit these resources.[3]

Several U.S. companies are now known to be at work on methods of collecting the manganese nodules. A legal difficulty seems at least as great as the technical one at present: the absence of any clear sovereignty over the ocean floor and the resulting uncertainty about whether exploitation of these deposits, even if commercially advantageous, would be allowed to continue.

It is also of some importance that the use of metals can be extended by increased recycling. The possible increase is the greatest for aluminum, copper, and zinc. A careful study of the matter concludes with an estimate that the potential recycling increase in the United States alone in

---

[3] *Models of Doom*, ed. H. S. D. Cole and others (1973), pp. 36–37.

aluminum would, over a period for 50 years, save 20% of the world's bauxite reserves as now estimated; in copper, about 15%; in zinc, about 40%. World-wide recycling would increase these figures.[4]

According to estimates presented and analyzed by William D. Nordhaus, unproven but recoverable petroleum deposits are greater than proven reserves. The recoverable oil in shale is three times that in total hypothetical petroleum resources. The supply of hydrocarbons in recoverable coal deposits is half again as great as that in all of these oil resources plus hypothetical natural gas deposits. And the energy available in the nuclei of U–238 and U–235 dwarfs that in all of these fossil fuels combined. Nordhaus's summary table is presented here as table 2–2.[5]

TABLE 2–2

Recoverable Energy Resources, by Type of Fuel and Regions of the World, 1970 (quadrillions (10^{15}) of Btu)

Fuel	United States	Western Europe	Persian Gulf and North Africa	Rest of the World	Total
Fossil					
Petroleum					
Proven reserves	213	70	2,543	756	3,582
Unproven but recoverable .	350	34	1,755	2,103	4,242
Coal	33,588	8,626	0	17,915	60,129
Shale oil	11,362	1,090	0	12,328	24,780
Natural gas	447	83	3,409	2,268	6,207
Total fossil	45,960	9,903	7,707	35,370	98,940
Nuclear					
U-235	—	—	—	—	1,504,100
U-238	—	—	—	—	206,970,000
Total nuclear	—	—	—	—	208,474,100
Total recoverable energy resources	—	—	—	—	208,573,040
Addendum: World energy consumption, 1965	—	—	—	—	154

[a] All fuels are calculated at their theoretical energy content. Nuclear fuels are not allocated by region. All quantities apply a conventional recovery rate to original resources in place.
Sources: Given in an appendix available upon request from Professor Nordhaus.

If his conclusions are correct, Nordhaus states,

> then the current "energy crisis" will blow over eventually. Real enough problems remain. Until supplies are expanded, the United States may

[4] Leonard L. Fischman and Hans H. Landsberg, in *Population, Resources, and the Environment,* ed. Ronald G. Ridker (1972), p. 98.

[5] "The Allocation of Energy Resources," *Brookings Papers on Economic Activity* 3 (1973): 542.

experience very serious shortages or very high prices. In any case rising prices are likely over the long haul, especially for transportation; adaptation to new, potentially difficult, technologies will present a problem; and several lean years on foreign exchange markets loom ahead. But we should not be haunted by the specter of the affluent society grinding to a halt for lack of energy resources (p. 570).

Even Nordhaus' estimates do not include the energy that may someday be harnessed by tapping geothermal sources or converting solar energy into electrical. That day will hardly be soon. Reykjavik now obtains more than half of its energy from a geothermal source, but in circumstances other than the remarkable ones of Reykjavik engineers do not think the promise of geothermal energy great at present. The cost of obtaining a large flow of electrical energy from solar energy by techniques now known has been estimated at between fifty to one hundred times the cost of producing electrical energy from other sources. Techniques not now envisioned except possibly by some "dreamer in a garret" will be needed to reduce that cost substantially. The possibility of these sources of energy, however, illustrates the fact that the limits are technological, not geologic.

From these estimates it would appear that the exhaustion of either metallic mineral or energy resources not only is not imminent but is not likely in the 20th or the 21st century, even with a continuing increase in the rate of consumption. However, the data perhaps suggest that before the world is far into the 21st century the inputs needed to extract each unit of most types of mineral resources (perhaps not energy resources) will increase unless techniques for their extraction are improved markedly. A steady increase in the number of units of input needed to obtain each unit of mineral output, and not exhaustion of resources in the sense that one empties a pail, is the problem that may face the world. If it occurs, how will it affect world growth?

FUTURE WORLD GROWTH

An End to Growth?

The answer is that if it occurs, the rate of world growth will slow down very gradually, and growth—per capita or in the aggregate—may come, very gradually, to an end. The bare outlines of an illustrative model are as follows:

Let the share of world productive activity initially devoted to resource extraction (say 2% after the estimates for the United States presented in Barnett and Morse, 1963) and let an initial rate of increase in labor productivity (in minerals extractions as well as elsewhere) through technical progress (say 2% per year) be assumed. Assume also that in natural resource extraction, the slope of diminishing returns to both labor and capital is increasingly steep, and that the invention of new natural resources and of new methods of extraction fail by a steadily increasing margin to offset this effect. Lastly, assume in accordance with the normal operations of the market that as mineral resources become more costly relative to other products and to labor the capital-labor ratio in production is progressively reduced.

If such a model were to be subjected to computer runs, the last two assumptions would have to be given precise quantitative form, and that form would determine the dating of various results. However, apart from this question of timing, one does not need to state the model mathematically or carry out computer runs to realize the nature of the results. For convenience I shall use symbols for some terms that will be used repeatedly during the next few paragraphs. Let:

R = output in resource extraction, in physical units,
M = all other world output, in physical units,
$Y = R + M$
r and m, respectively = per capita output in physical units in the two areas,
K = capital,
L = labor,
p_K = the unit price of capital,
p_L = the unit price of labor,
dr/dt = the time rate of increase in r,
dm/dt = the time rate of increase in m, and
dy/dt = the time of increase in total world output per capita.

As the marginal cost of resource extraction relative to other prices increases, it will be rewarding economically to use a decreasing quantity of minerals per unit of output of final products; yet because the price elasticity of demand for minerals is not infinite, their price will rise sufficiently that it will also be rewarding economically to shift an increasing share of the world's K and L into R. As the severity of diminishing returns in minerals extraction increases, such a shift *at an increasing rate* will be advantageous. Because of falling unit output of R per unit of input, combined with the increasing rate of transfer of inputs to the R sector, dy/dt will fall progressively.

Since the production of capital equipment is R-intensive, p_K/p_L will rise progressively. For any given set of known techniques, then, less K and more L will be used in production than would have been used at previous price relationships. This does not necessarily imply that during the early time period of the operation of the model the K/L ratio (in physical terms) will decline. It may merely increase at a slower rate than would otherwise have been the case. But as p_K/p_L continues to rise, a point will be reached after which the K/L ratio will decline absolutely. As p_K/p_L rises, inventive energy will no doubt increasingly turn to the devising of methods and products that economize on capital. No doubt the K/Y ratio will decline, and in part at the cost of the L/Y ratio. For this reason also, dy/dt will fall progressively.

The growth rate dy/dt will continue to be positive so long as the contribution of increase in productivity to Y is greater than the loss of Y through the shift of inputs from the M sector to the R sector. If, however, $\delta n/\delta K$ and $\delta r/\delta L$ fall progressively and without limit, as is assumed above, then inexorably dy/dt will fall, reach zero, and become negative. In words: if the pressure of diminishing returns in resource extraction increases too greatly, then (unless the pace of technical progress increases sufficiently) world output per person will reach a maximum and turn downward. This result will occur even if the world population remains constant.[6]

The rate of growth dy/dt will fall the more slowly, the greater the rate at which methods of economizing on natural resource inputs in industrial production, as distinguished from the substitution of labor for capital, are developed. With the sufficient invention of new cost-reducing natural resources or new cost-reducing energy sources, or a sufficient rise in the rate of increase in productivity anywhere else in the system, the growth rate will again turn positive.[7]

Limitless Growth?

This, then, is the way in which world growth will end, if it does. What are the requirements for indefinitely continuing growth in world output per capita?

Simply that technical progress shall be fast enough to offset the effects of diminishing returns in resource extraction.

The projections presented in Table 2–1 imply only a very limited degree of technical change in the use of metals and energy resources. The differential rates of growth in use of various metals in the recent past reflect not only changes in the composition of demand but also shifts in

---

[6] Whether it occurs faster with population and labor force increase than with none depends on the relative drain on resources of a given GDP with no population increase, or the larger aggregate but lower per capita GNP obtained through (labor force and) population increase.

[7] The model presented by Louella and Dennis Meadows and their colleagues has world output rising to a maximum and then collapsing catastrophically. The model behaves this way because of the assumed relationships among the variables, the most important with respect to this effect being that it is assumed that mineral resource use will continue to increase exponentially until world stocks are exhausted. That is, there are no prices, no relative costs, in the model. Such a model has limited empirical relevance.

the relative use of various materials in making given products. Those shifts in turn reflect technical change. However, projection of these rates into the future implies absence of technical change beyond this range.

If we project the longer-run past into the future, we will expect much greater technical change. Since 1850 petroleum, aluminum, nuclear-electric power, "artificial" fertilizer, and a whole array of plastics and synthetic materials have been invented. Aluminum was "invented" by discovering how to extract the metal from bauxite. Petroleum was "invented" by discovering how to extract useful products from it. Until well into the 19th century it was merely a smelly oil that sometimes fouled the surface of ponds.

If there had been no technical progress in the extraction and use of mineral resources during the past century, the deposits of minerals known a century ago would have been exhausted well before the present time and the dire predictions made by Malthus in 1800 would have come true. Starvation would have checked growth of the world's population, and the population that exists would be existing at a subsistence level unless control over births had held the total number below that which could barely exist. These results did not occur; exploration progressively uncovered additional natural resource deposits, technical progress reduced the cost of exploiting them, and technical progress also made possible progressively greater food yields per unit of land area.

Correspondingly, so long as an array of further inventions emerges progressively in the future, and especially if it includes an adequate rate of technical progress in the invention of new materials and the extraction of presently known ones, world growth and rise in world per capita income may continue, and even at the present rate of increase. (If, as seems probable, additional high-grade deposits of presently used minerals will not be found at the same exponential rate as in the past, then—to maintain the recent rate of world growth—technical progress will have to proceed at a faster rate than in the past.)

Technical progress in the exploitation of energy sources is perhaps of especial importance. For if sufficient energy is available, synthetic materials can be created to replace metals in many present uses, and technical progress may extend the range of replacement.[8] At the present time, the raw materials for all synthetics is hydrocarbons. If sufficient advance in energy creation occurs so that hydrocarbons are used only as a raw material and not as a fuel, they would constitute a raw material supply extremely large relative to prospective demand. The creation of synthetic products out of other raw materials, through synthetic advance, is of

---

[8] Technical progress in energy use may also be important. For example, since 1885 aluminum has been extracted from bauxite by the energy-intensive Bayer-Hall process. Reports in the trade are that a new process using about one sixth the electrical energy of the Bayer-Hall process is emerging.

course not excluded, though it is outside the scope of present technical conceptions.[9]

In *The Limits to Growth* (1972), Louella and Dennis Meadows and their co-authors assumed for purposes of modeling that all mineral resources are homogeneous and exist in a supply sufficient to permit the 1970 rate of use for 250 years. They assumed that use would in fact increase at an exponential rate that is a reasonable average of the recent rates for all important metals. On this basis, their model exhausts world mineral resources by dates usually between about the year 2030 and the year 2050, depending on other assumptions made, and world collapse occurs. However, the Science Policy Research Unit of the University of Sussex, taking the same model, altered it by assuming first a 1% per year rate of natural resource discovery (taken to include re-cycling) and of increase in the capability for pollution control, and then 2% per year rates. At the 1% rates, world collapse is postponed significantly; at the 2% rates, pollution ceases to rise when it reaches twice the 1970 level, and natural resource supplies grow rapidly throughout the period for which the model was run, namely to the year 2100.[10] (In this exercise, natural resource discovery may be taken to include technical progress which includes the exploitation of present identified low-grade reserves or invents new reserves.)

Men in 1800 were quite incapable of visualizing the inventions that have in fact occurred since that date. If comparable advances occur during the next 170 years, world growth may continue indefinitely, unimpeded. The story is told of the barber shop that kept a sign in the window reading "Free Shaves Tomorrow." It is possible that natural resource shortages, like those free shaves, will for an indefinite future period be prospective. If the world "comes to an end," it may do so because of social tensions before growth comes to an end because of natural resource shortages.

It is natural for a reflective economist to suppose that economic growth must some day end, for an economist knows that it is a most unusual model in which, if equilibrium is disturbed beyond its range of stability, the model does not move to another position of equilibrium later if not

---

[9] Not all technical progress will occur "automatically," that is, by the "spontaneous" mental activity of individuals or private organizations. In some fields it will require the organization of large-scale and long-continued endeavors by governments. One of its requirements in these fields is that men shall have enough foresight to be willing to pay the cost of the resources needed. If they do not have enough foresight, then they may suffer unpleasant and even permanent consequences.

[10] In its method, *The Limits of Growth* is based on Jay W. Forrester's *World Dynamics* (Cambridge, Mass.: Wright-Allen Press, Inc., 1971). In a rather devastating review in the *Economic Journal*, 83, no. 332 (Dec. 1973), William D. Nordhaus shows that Forrester's model is sensitive to his subjective assumptions, and no longer forecasts doom if assumptions regarding population, technical change, or substitution among inputs are changed in plausible (though of course uncertain) ways.

sooner. Man has grossly disturbed the ecological equilibrium, or quasi-equilibrium, of his relationships to the earth that existed for millenia. It is reasonable to suppose, to reify an abstraction, that someday "nature will have her own" again. Or, let us say that the process of entropy will not be forever defied. The writer shares this philosophic view. All that is said here is that the end of growth may be postponed "indefinitely," that is, so far as men can foresee the future.

POLLUTION

To this point in the discussion, I have ignored the problem of pollution, including in this term for convenience the accumulation of wastes and the degradation of the physical environment.

In the case of fuels, consuming means "using up," though there are residuals. In the case of metals it means "putting into use." Some small amount of the iron consumed in 1970 was used up through rusting. Virtually no copper or aluminum was used up; it was accumulating not only in the building, tools, and utensils of the industrial nations but also in their scrap heaps. Other wastes of urban living are accumulating in city dumps or as sludge in the oceans. Strip miners of coal and sometimes deep miners of coal leave the earth's surface degraded.

Accompanying these degradations of the environment is other pollution: pollution of the air and water and of some food supplies. Industrial corporations, individual entrepreneurs, city governments, drivers of cars, and other classes of polluters spew their chemical wastes into the air or dump them into rivers, lakes, and oceans. Farmers increase their yield by using insecticides whose harmful residues remain on food or accumulate in the tissues of animals who eat poisoned grass and of fish who swim in poisoned waters. Water seeping from cultivated lands into waterways so fills the water with residues of commercial fertilizers that neither plants nor fish can live, and the water becomes malodorous. From the various developments, humans are threatened with physiological impairment and shortened life.

Some degree of pollution is an accompaniment of life. Anyone who breathes pollutes the atmosphere; carbon dioxide is unhealthful for humans.

The person who denounces pollution is thinking of something which is excessive. Excessive pollution (including degradation of the environment) may be defined as activity which infringes on the liberty (including life) of some individuals without conveying an adequately compensating expansion of liberty (including more varied consumption or longer healthier life) on others. It is excessive pollution with which we are concerned.

Excessive pollution (including degradation of the environment) is not a necessary accompaniment of industrialization, urbanization, and population growth. The cause of excessive pollution may be stated simply but precisely in economic terms. It occurs because the persons or organizations that generate waste are allowed to dump it into the environment without paying the full cost of what they do. They are allowed to create external diseconomies without penalty because a framework of laissez faire, perhaps justified in simpler days, has been carried forward to more complex ones.

Excessive pollution may be ended by direct regulation or by taxing it. In some circumstances direct regulation is desirable; often taxation is more efficient. Effluent charges make pollution-intensive goods expensive, and so reduce their consumption. They make pollution-intensive methods of production costly, and so induce producers to abate the pollution either by countering it or by seeking other methods. They also generate revenue which the government can use to finance measures to reduce pollution.

In 1970, the United States spent perhaps $9.5 billion to abate pollution, or in 1967 dollars, $8.45 billion. The figure includes both governmental and private expenditures. The U.S. Council on Environmental Quality has estimated that to achieve and maintain the abatement in the emission of 14 major pollutants to the 1973 water and the 1975 air emission standards recommended by the U.S. Environmental Protection Agency would require annual expenditures rising by 1980 to $30.4 billion and by 2000 to $47.5 billion, both stated in 1967 prices.[11] These figures imply using an additional one tenth of one percent of GNP each year between 1970 and 2000 (say one twentieth of the annual increase for capita) to abate pollution. There may be no net cost whatever, for the increase in welfare not measured within GNP may be worth every dollar of the expenditure.

These are the abatement expenditures. Many of them will raise the cost of production in formerly polluting industries. This effect must also be considered. As GDP is conventionally measured, investment in pollution-avoiding equipment will not reduce GDP; less consumption but more investment will be recorded. However, as the production of goods by pollution-avoiding methods is begun, in many instances there will be a one-time decrease in real GDP (below what it would otherwise have been, not necessarily nor probably below what it was during the previous time period). The production of a ton of, say, copper will be more costly than before. It will use more productive resources, thereby reducing the production of other goods as that production is likely to be measured in GDP calculations. When the increased value of copper production has been deflated, GDP calculations will show no greater copper production and less of other production than would otherwise have been possible.

---

[11] See Ridker, *Population* (1972), pp. 45–50.

This result, however, is a reflection of the inadequacy of GNP measures; with the increase in the cost of copper production there was purchased greater health—or lesser un-health—than before. That this increase in welfare is not reflected in GDP calculations makes it none the less real.

The same effect will be avoided in the measurement of the deflated value of automobile production, if in calculating the Consumer Price Index a (more expensive) automobile incorporating antipollution devices is treated as "more automobile," not as a more costly version of the same automobile.

After this one-time decrease in (the rate of increase of) GDP, there is no apparent reason why the existence of antipollution devices and measures should reduce the continuing increase in productivity, as measured in GDP calculations, and in this respect those calculations will correctly reflect material welfare. Continuing urbanization and industrialization will bring increased crowding, the disappearance of trees and open shore lines, and the like, but these changes seem to distress only a minority of the population.[12]

As will be noted in the next chapter, increasing pollution of some bodies of water, pollution that at present we have no practical way of countering, may be the cost of increased food production.

The introduction of devices to abate other pollution, so far as it requires increased investment per unit of final product, increases the rate of consumption of the world's natural resource stocks. However, the effect is too small to modify appreciably the analysis presented in this chapter.

BIBLIOGRAPHIC NOTE

Forrester (1971) and L. and D. Meadows (1972) embody Forrester's view that the world faces doom. Of the many critical appraisals, Nordhaus (1973) and H. S. D. Cole et al. (1973) are the most comprehensive. Publications of the research organization Resources for the Future, Inc. (Washington, D.C.) present judicious analyses of the future demand for and supply of basic mineral resources.

---

[12] It seems probable thatt he rootlessness and anonymity of industrial life causes disruptions in home life which in turn breed anxieties, so that through these indirect and unrecognized effects industrialization decreases human happiness. Vance Packard's *A Nation of Strangers* (New York: David McKay Company, Inc., 1972) sketches some evidence of these results. These effects, however, must be separated from the question of whether the world's growth must come to an end because of exhaustion of natural resource stocks, other shortages of supply, or pollution.

Limits to World Growth? Population versus the Food Supply

3

Population growth was not mentioned in the preceding chapter except in passing, though the assumption of continued world population growth contributed to the projections in that chapter of continuing exponential increase in minerals consumption. In this chapter, attention is centered on population growth, for the question arises whether the world's population will increase to a number that cannot be fed or, more precisely, whether population increase will be checked not by the desire of people to have no further increase but by starvation and disease for a lack of an adequate food supply.

THE WORLD'S POPULATION HISTORY

The Rise in Total Population

Because of the accident that population censuses were held in both Roman and Chinese empires at about the beginning of the Christian era, a rough estimate of world population at that date is possible. It was between 200 and 300 million. In 1650 A.D., it was about 550 million. During the intervening 16½ centuries, the average rate of increase was little more than one twentieth of 1% per year.

At the end of this long period the rate was rising. The rise has continued. Between 1650 and 1750, using Carr-Saunders' world population estimates, the rate was 0.3% per year, and in four 50-year periods between 1750 and 1950 it was, successively, 0.4%, 0.5%, 0.6%, and 0.8%. By 1950, a spectacularly fast rise was occurring, caused largely by one aspect of technical aid to low-income countries from the United States

Public Health Service and the World Health Organization of the United Nations, namely, the introduction of public health and preventive medicine measures. These greatly reduced deaths from the "big killers"— tuberculosis, malaria, smallpox, and typhoid fever—and from infant diseases, and the rate of population growth rose sharply. The annual rate of world population growth in 1960 was about 1.8%, according to United Nations estimates. By 1970 it had risen to 2%, but was no longer rising. By estimates of the United States Agency for International Development, it was 1.9% in 1960, and remained at that level through 1973. This is the crude rate, the ratio of total births to the total population.

In 1970, the world's population, by continents, was as follows, in millions:

Asia	2,056
Europe and Asiatic U.S.S.R.	705
Africa	344
Latin America	283
Northern America and Oceania	247
World	3,635

At the growth rate of 2% per year, the population would double each 35 years. In the year 2000, the world's population would be 6,584 million; a century later, approximately 50,000 million. At a growth rate of 1.75% per year, population would reach about 5,600 million by the year 2000 and 35,000 million by the year 2100. These increases are hardly believable.

To understand the likely or even the possible course of future population growth, it is necessary to examine the sequence of change in death and birth rates known as the "demographic revolution" which has occurred in many countries.

The Demographic Revolution

The population growth rate increase since 1650 has not been simultaneous throughout the world. Rather, rapid population growth has been a rolling wave which spread from Western Europe and the areas of European colonization to the rest of the world. The rate increased first of all in England, then in the countries of Western Europe, and then in the areas peopled by European colonists—Canada, the United States, Australia, and New Zealand. Then it began to decline in all of these countries, in about the order in which it had begun to increase. Present indications, explained below, are that during the next 75 years population growth rates in those countries and in Japan, already low, will gradually decrease to zero. Yet population growth rates for the world as a whole reached successive record highs quinquennium after quinquennium up to

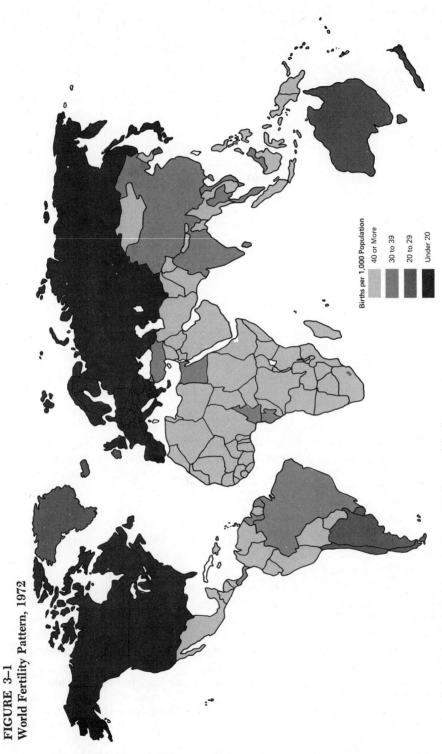

FIGURE 3-1
World Fertility Pattern, 1972

Births per 1,000 Population

40 or More

30 to 39

20 to 29

Under 20

Source: International Statistical Programs Center, U.S. Bureau of the Census.

at least 1960 and probably 1970 because the growth wave passed on to Latin America, Asia, and then Africa, and in many countries of those continents has reached heights it had never reached in the West. Figure 3–1 shows the birth rates of the world's countries in about 1972. The highest rates were in regions of relatively low population density in Africa, the Middle East, Latin America and Southeast Asia, plus densely populated Java. In China and India they were also impressively high. In six African countries plus Saudi Arabia, the estimated rate per 1,000 of population was 50 and in Afghanistan, 51.

To understand the "rolling wave" effect, it is necessary to understand the nature of the "demographic revolution." Consider first the Western countries.

Before the Industrial Revolution, both birth and death rates in Western countries were at or a little above 35 per thousand, or 3.5%, and birth rates were a little above death rates. Life expectancy at birth was below 30 years $(1,000/35 = 28)$. Death rates fell slowly, as income rose and medical knowledge advanced. Declines in birth rates began long after those in death rates. English records indicate that in that country death rates began to fall in the 1770s or 1780s, and birth rates not until the 1880s. On the Continent, the declines in both began somewhat later, and proceeded somewhat more rapidly, and the lag was somewhat shorter— say 50 to 75 years. In spite of the long lag, because the fall in death rates was so gradual the difference between birth and death rates never became extremely great, and the rate of natural increase (the population growth rate apart from the effects of immigration and emigration) nowhere rose much above 1% per year for long.[1]

Today, death rates are not far above 10 per 1,000, and life expectancy at birth in almost all of these societies is above 70 years (5 years or so higher for women than for men).[2] Birth rates are so little above death rates that if the birth and death rates at each age remain unchanged, the rate of population growth will taper to zero within the next 75 years.

The concepts of a "stabilized age distribution" and the "total fertility rate" are pertinent. For some time after death rates begin to decline in any country, population will be concentrated in the lower age groups, for declines in infant and child mortality are always conspicuous among the early improvements. Because babies and young children are no longer dying at the former rates, each family, on the average, will have more living children than previous families had. Crude death rates (rates per 1,000 of the entire population) will then be low, because infants, children, and adolescents have low death rates and there are many of them.

[1] The population growth rate in the United States, Canada, Australia, and New Zealand, where "empty lands" drew a large flow of immigrants, was much higher, and rates of natural increase were probably also higher in those lands for longer periods.

[2] A death rate of 10 per 1,000 implies an average life expectancy at birth of 100 years, and a death rate of 12.5 a life expectancy of 80 years, but only in a population with a stabilized age distribution.

But even if death rates at each age ("age-specific death rates") thereafter remain unchanged, crude death rates will raise somewhat again as this young population becomes older.

So also will crude birth rates, even though age-specific birth rates remain unchanged, because the individuals forming the "population bulge" will pass through the child-bearing years. Their children will create another smaller "population bulge" when they become parents a generation later.

But if age-specific birth and death rates remain unchanged, then eventually a "stablized age distribution" will be reached. A "stabilized age distribution" is one in which the number of persons moving up into each age group each year equals the number leaving that age group by death or aging. The percentage of the population that is of each age remains unchanged.

In a population with a stabilized age distribution, a life expectancy at birth of 70 years implies a death rate of 14.3 per 1,000 (1,000/70). In a number of Western societies, crude death rates fell temporarily not only below 14 but considerably below 10 per 1,000 at some time within the first several decades of the 20th century, even though life expectancy in the society was still well below 70 years. But by this time age-specific birth rates and even crude birth rates had also fallen to rather low levels, and even these unsustainably low death rates did not bring population growth rates of much above 1% per year.

Even though crude population growth rates in Western societies range from somewhat below to somewhat above 1% per year at present (in populations with somewhat young age distributions), they are headed toward zero. This is indicated by the present "total fertility rate." This is a rate determined by a survey covering one year, in which the number of children born to each woman in the population of age 15, age 16, and so on throughout the entire child-bearing period of 15–44 years, is observed. The "total fertility rate" is the number of children that each woman entering the child-bearing period will have if at each age she bears as many children as each woman of that age during the year of the survey bore that year, on the average. With present life expectancy in the West, if the total fertility rate is about 2.1 and age-specific birth and death rates remain unchanged, then when the population has reached a stable age distribution there will be no further population increase. In the countries of western Europe, the United States, Canada, Australia, New Zealand, and Japan, the total fertility rate is at about that level. (In the United States, in 1973 it was below that level—at 1.9.)[3]

As an indicator of future birth rates, it is complemented by information concerning the number of children that women just entering upon

---

[3] According to the National Center for Health Statistics, a division of the United States Department of Health, Education, and Welfare. *New York Times,* April 16, 1974.

child-bearing expect to have. In the United States and several countries of Western Europe, this information has been obtained, and has proved a remarkably accurate forecaster. In these countries, the present expectations of young mothers indicate no more future births than does the total fertility rate. Those expectations, that is, indicate that the rate of population growth is trending to zero.

In mid-1970, about 1.1 billion people lived in the group of countries listed above. (In mid-1975, somewhat less than 1.2 billion.) The population of these countries will increase for another 60 to 75 years. Yet unless population plans of later parents change, by the year 2050 the population of these countries will be approximately stable in size, at about 50% above the 1970 total, or 1.6–1.7 billion.

In Asian, African, and Latin American countries, however, the demographic revolution has begun in a way different from its beginning in the West, and no one knows now what the future course of birth rates will be or whether or not the demographic revolution will ever be completed.

In these countries, in the 19th century, both birth and death rates were above or near 45 per 1,000, almost 1% higher than the pre-Industrial Revolution rates of the West. (European rates before the Black Death of the 14th century are not known.) Because death rates were also high, over the 50-year period 1850–1900 the rate of population growth in Asia, Africa, and Latin America combined averaged only about 0.9% per year, but there existed the possibility of a rate of natural increase much faster than that which any Western country had experienced, if death rates should fall.

In recent decades, the possibility has become a fact. In a few countries, death rates began to be reduced before World War II under colonial rule. At the end of the 1930s they had fallen considerably in a few countries, notably Ceylon, Malaya, Singapore, and Taiwan. Then after World War II came the dramatic attack on major causes of death that has been noted above. Crude death rates fell from 35 per 1,000 or even more to 20, 15, and transitionally to even below 10 per 1,000. As a result, crude population growth rates reached levels never known in the West.

Between 1965 and 1970, persons concerned about world population growth began to breathe at least a little easier. In the Asian countries in which death rates had fallen markedly late in the 1930s, birth rates began to fall by about 1960, and in most of the countries in which death rates had been reduced rapidly soon after World War II, birth rates began to fall in the mid-1960s—20 years or less after the dramatic decline in death rates had begun. Figure 3–2 shows the relationship between crude birth rates in 1960 and those in 1970 in 53 countries with nearly complete registration of births.[4] But the fall was not uniform, and by 1972 it began

---

[4] I have this figure and Figure 3–1 through the courtesy of the U.S. Agency for International Development Office of Population.

FIGURE 3–2
Change in Crude Birth Rates Since 1960
(all larger countries with nearly complete birth registration)

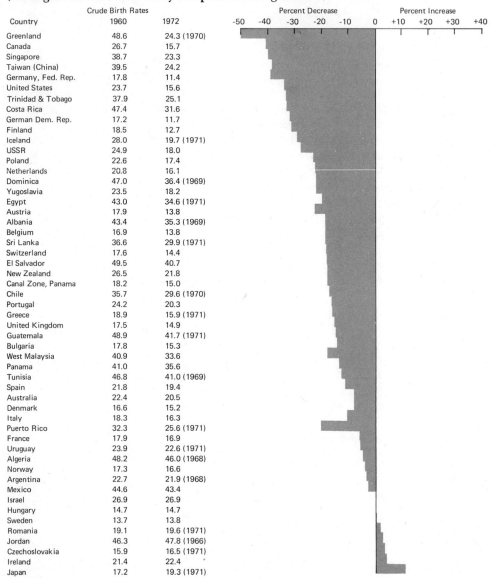

Country	Crude Birth Rates 1960	1972
Greenland	48.6	24.3 (1970)
Canada	26.7	15.7
Singapore	38.7	23.3
Taiwan (China)	39.5	24.2
Germany, Fed. Rep.	17.8	11.4
United States	23.7	15.6
Trinidad & Tobago	37.9	25.1
Costa Rica	47.4	31.6
German Dem. Rep.	17.2	11.7
Finland	18.5	12.7
Iceland	28.0	19.7 (1971)
USSR	24.9	18.0
Poland	22.6	17.4
Netherlands	20.8	16.1
Dominica	47.0	36.4 (1969)
Yugoslavia	23.5	18.2
Egypt	43.0	34.6 (1971)
Austria	17.9	13.8
Albania	43.4	35.3 (1969)
Belgium	16.9	13.8
Sri Lanka	36.6	29.9 (1971)
Switzerland	17.6	14.4
El Salvador	49.5	40.7
New Zealand	26.5	21.8
Canal Zone, Panama	18.2	15.0
Chile	35.7	29.6 (1970)
Portugal	24.2	20.3
Greece	18.9	15.9 (1971)
United Kingdom	17.5	14.9
Guatemala	48.9	41.7 (1971)
Bulgaria	17.8	15.3
West Malaysia	40.9	33.6
Panama	41.0	35.6
Tunisia	46.8	41.0 (1969)
Spain	21.8	19.4
Australia	22.4	20.5
Denmark	16.6	15.2
Italy	18.3	16.3
Puerto Rico	32.3	25.6 (1971)
France	17.9	16.9
Uruguay	23.9	22.6 (1971)
Algeria	48.2	46.0 (1968)
Norway	17.3	16.6
Argentina	22.7	21.9 (1968)
Mexico	44.6	43.4
Israel	26.9	26.9
Hungary	14.7	14.7
Sweden	13.7	13.8
Romania	19.1	19.6 (1971)
Jordan	46.3	47.8 (1966)
Czechoslovakia	15.9	16.5 (1971)
Ireland	21.4	22.4
Japan	17.2	19.3 (1971)

Source: Ravenhalt and Chao (1974). Data from U.S. Bureau of the Census.

to seem that in many countries in which birth rates had fallen the declines were tapering off at a level at which the population growth rate was above 2% per year.

In mid-1975, the world's population will be approximately 4 billion. Of that number of people, about 2.8 billion will be living in the countries in which death rates were rapidly reduced after World War II. The question most largely determining the future size of the world's population, or at least the size throughout the 21st century, is whether the population growth rate in the lower income countries will continue to decline after a pause, or will become stable at around 2%. As this is written, the trend even during the next few years—which may be a very significant indicator—is uncertain. As the age-stabilization process works itself out, the population growth rates in these countries will fall somewhat from their present level, and without further declines in age-specific birth rates the average population growth rate for the world as a whole will fall by say .1 or .2% from its present level. But it will fall further only if age-specific birth rates fall further.

The continuing decline in birth rates in Western societies occurred slowly during a long historical process of change in economic and social structure—rise in income, urbanization, industrialization, increase in education, etc. Perhaps birth rates will not fall further in the lower income countries until a comparable slow process has occurred. The result would be a very large increase in the world's population. Perhaps population increase will itself prevent some aspects of the historical change from occurring, and birth rates will never fall. The outcome is not known.

Figure 3–3 portrays the demographic revolution as it occurred in the West, and its alternative possible paths in the low-income agricultural

FIGURE 3–3
Variants of the Demographic Revolution

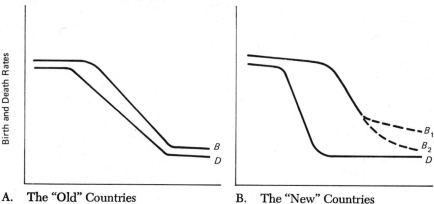

A.   The "Old" Countries   B.   The "New" Countries

countries in which death rates were suddenly reduced. The world's population future depends largely on which alternative path in Figure 3–3B is the more nearly correct portrayal of the future.

THE WORLD'S POPULATION FUTURE

Population Theories

There is empirical evidence of the statistical association of various objectively measureable conditions with birth rates.[5] Professor Irma Adelman (1963) presented a regression analysis among 37 countries ranging in income level from Morocco to the United States of the relationship between age-specific birth rates and four factors that may influence them. She found that birth rates tend to be positively associated with the level of per capita income and negatively associated with non-agricultural employment, the level of education increase, and the density of population per square kilometer. The relationships are such that if a rise in per capita income was caused by economic development (which brought a shift out of agriculture), and if a vigorous program of increase in education accompanied it, one would expect birth rates to fall. In a Rand Corporation study, in which individual families in Taiwan, rather than nations, were the unit of observation, T. Paul Schultz (1973) found a similar relationship among similar factors. Earlier (1967), Schultz had found similar evidence in Puerto Rico.

The findings raise difficult questions of causation. The Rand researchers and a number of other analysts tend to a purely economic explanation.[6] In peasant agriculture, the labor of growing children is useful, and investment in them yields higher returns than alternative uses of funds. As urbanization proceeds and children become less useful, birth rates fall. However, children are wanted as consumer goods, rather than merely as producer goods; hence there may be a positive partial correlation of birth rates with income level. But on the other hand, the cost of rearing children in the manner expected by one's social group tends to increase with income, relative to the prices of other goods; this substitu-

---

[5] The population forecasts of demographers have not been notably accurate, primarily because, there being no sure theory of the causes of population behavior, they have made forecasts mainly by projecting recent trends and have been forced to revise their projection when trends changed, as trends did shortly after the war and in the mid-1960s.

The Population Division of the United Nations prudently makes high, low, and intermediate population projections. Its medium projection to the year 2000, made in the 1960s, arrived at a world population of 6,130 million in that year. An average population growth rate of between 1.5 and 1.75% during the 25-year period 1975–2000 would yield that figure.

[6] A vigorous advocate of the thesis that economic factors are determining is G. S. Becker (1960).

tion effect may outweigh the income effect, and cause a negative partial correlation of birth rates with income level.

Actually, in various studies in various countries, both positive and negative simple and partial correlations are found.[7] By the assumption of different relative income and substitution coefficients in different countries, it is possible to explain all of the findings—since a decline in the relative cost of rearing children while income rises rarely if ever occurs. But of course the assumption of different coefficients in different countries is an implicit admission of the operation of factors not included in the formulation.

Recent demographic developments cause further trouble for the purely economic explanation. One of these is the decline in the 1960s and 1970s in the number of children that both young U.S. mothers and young European mothers plan to have. The decline is grossly inconsistent with any plausible economic coefficients applied to previous periods in these areas. Moreover, a similar difficulty is caused by the declines in birth rates in countries around the world shown in Figure 3–2, and in declines in smaller countries not shown in that figure. It is very difficult if not impossible to relate these changes solely to economic changes.

Even the statistical partial relationship to economic factors found in the analyses of the "economic school" is questioned by some observers, on the ground that many complex changes in the circumstances of life accompany the shift out of agriculture, the rise in income, and the rise in literacy and education. These may be surrogates for less easily observable and measurable but more fundamentally causal motivational changes with which the changes mentioned are usually but not always highly correlated.[8]

Some observers judge that a dominant motive determining the number of children wanted may be the importance placed in traditional rural life on perpetuation of the family through the male line (or, in a very few societies, through the female line. The argument is parallel). Since any given child born is approximately as likely to be a girl as a boy, this desire leads to families with a total number of children not far from twice the number of boys needed to insure that one will grow through adulthood

---

[7] See W. P. McGreevey (1974), pp. 3–8, for a summary of seemingly contradictory findings in different countries.

[8] To some students, the negative partial correlation between population density and birth rates (in Adelman's 37-country study) is fairly conclusive evidence of the importance of economic influences. Where conditions of life are harder, and where the size of farms is smaller, families have fewer children. That families have fewer children where conditions are harder seems abundantly evident to most students, including the present writer, and hardly needing statistical proof. Yet one must be wary of accepting even this correlation as clear evidence of the causal flow. High-population–density societies are old agricultural societies, probably differing from others culturally in various ways. The differences in population density may just possibly be surrogates for these cultural differences which are the "true" causal factors.

and parenthood. On the basis of this thesis, the recent decline in birth rates following by 20 years or so a decline in infant and child death rates is due to growing understanding that with the prior decline in infant and child mortality a lesser number of births is necessary to assure that a son will grow to parenthood, and the leveling off of the decline in birth rates which seems to have occurred is explained as due to the judgment that having two sons is needed for minimum assurance, sought even with fairly low infant and child mortality, that one will live through parenthood.

This thesis, like the economic one, is consistent with the observed data, for a shift from rural to urban life, increase in education, and rise in income all may imply a change in attitudes that would reduce the intensity of the desire for family perpetuation.

Even before the Pill, the spreading use of modern methods of contraception was used by some analysts to explain secular fluctuations not neatly explained by a more general theory. This special explanation is complicated by the recent fall in birth rates in the lower income countries, which demonstrates that effective methods of birth control are used (and hence must have been long available) in countries where the Pill or other modern methods are neither available nor can be afforded.

Psychoanalysts, to whose judgment in this field one must give serious attention, tell us that factors much less rational—that is, not the product of deliberate conscious calculation—affect birth rates. They suggest that the procreation of children (not merely patterns of sexual intercourse) is influenced by attitudes that operate within us without our conscious knowledge of them, which therefore exercise their influence through channels other than rational calculation. These attitudes have to do, among other things, with "manliness" and mastery on the part of the man, with fear of children and, on the other hand, relieving the emptiness of life on the part of the woman, and with many factors in the complex tensions between husband and wife. There is strong evidence of the operation of such influences in individual cases, but the social sciences do not yet have the knowledge or techniques to test them statistically. Perhaps the surge in birth rates that follows major wars—a surge throughout the population, not merely in families that have lost sons—is evidence. That such factors have changed during the postwar period in ways consistent with the recent declines in parental intentions is at least highly plausible.

Acceptance of the argument that unconscious, so-called "irrational" factors influence birth rates is also consistent with the known facts about the association of birth rates with rural versus urban life, level of education, and level of income, for it is plausible that changes in these would be associated in various ways with changes in motivations. (Strictly, one should say that there is *potential* consistency, for until we are able to measure the unconscious factors we cannot say whether or not the argument that they are important is consistent with other observed factors related to birth rates.)

I have commented briefly on what may be termed the economic, family perpetuation, and psychoanalytical theories of the determinants of birth rates (though the last is not a fully formulated theory but an assertion of the importance of one kind of influences). They are not mutually exclusive. The perpetuation-of-the-family theory is in a sense a sort of psychoanalytical theory. Probably virtually all observers who believe that these two sorts of influences are important would also agree that economic influences have an influence. All that they would reject is the somewhat dogmatic view that economic considerations are the sole factors at work (in this as in other human behavior), and that other factors are irrelevant.

On the thesis of economic causation, birth rates are not likely to decline further except as in the process of economic development the population moves from agriculture to other pursuits. On this thesis, the high birth rate itself, by increasing the agricultural population, will delay birth-rate decline. On the thesis of perpetuation of the family, further decline may occur somewhat sooner, some families settling for one son as confidence in the survival of children through parenthood increases still further. On this thesis, one would expect the provision of opportunities for education to have a somewhat greater effect than if one adheres to the economic thesis. Yet even on this thesis one would not expect birth rates to fall to a zero-growth–rate level until there had occurred a slow cultural change—of the sort presumably brought about more by other factors than by formal education—by which perpetuation of the family through a daughter was valued as highly as through a son, or by which the drive for perpetuation of the family weakened. This cultural change may occur in peasant agriculture as well as in cities, for the conditions of rural life everywhere are ceasing to be the traditional ones.

The only theoretical consideration that would suggest that there may possibly be a dramatically sudden slowing of the rate of world population growth is the possibility that the recently manifest firm tendency of young mothers in Western countries to have zero-growth–rate families is due to the disturbed world conditions of the modern era, and that these conditions will also exert a strong influence in the very near future in the lower income countries (where clearly there is a great deal of social tension).

A review of population theory suggests that only this possibility need qualify a firm statement that world population growth will not soon cease. Concerning the question: Will it ever cease, so long as the world can support a growing population at a constant or rising income? one must, in the writer's view, remain agnostic, since we know too little about the relative strength of various possible basic determinants to arrive at a firm conclusion.

A Minimum Estimate of Future World Population

A minimum estimate of the time when world population growth may cease and of the population the world will then have reached is possible. It is based on two assumptions and one fact. The first assumption is that in the countries with high population growth rates at present those rates will not fall *rapidly* to a level of only two children or slightly more per family—the zero-population–growth rate level in an age-stabilized population. The other is that that is the minimum level to which they will fall, even transitionally. The one fact is that even when (if ever) age-specific birth rates do fall to that level, population growth will continue for some further time during the period of transition from a young age distribution to a stable one.

On the basis of these assumptions and this fact, Tomas Frejka presents an estimate of minimum probable world population growth (as well as high alternative projections) in the *Scientific American* for March, 1973. After apparently careful quantitative projections, he concludes that population growth in the non-Western world, and thereby world population growth, will continue until at least the year 2150. By that date, by his minimum estimate, the countries with present high population growth rates will have a population of 6.5 billion, some 2.6 time their 1970 total of about 2.5 billion. As noted above, population size in countries in which fertility rates of about 2.1 are now in effect will have stabilized a century sooner at some 1.6 billion.[9]

Social changes not now foreseen may alter these forecasts, but at the present time it seems likely that in the 22nd century the world's population will total not less than 8 billion, double the 1975 total, if the world's production of food and other necessities permits. It may well total considerably more. (Forecasts are heard in popular discussions of the population problem that the world's population will double between 1974 and 2000. These forecasts are ill-founded.)

FOOD SUPPLY

The demand for food will increase faster than the population does if per capita income rises, for the demand per person will increase, but will increase more slowly than does per capita income. If population in the countries now containing about 70% of the world's people grows at a rate

---

[9] Western Europe, the United States, and Japan, which together have about 30% of the world's population, would then have about 20%.

of 2% per year, and per capita income grows at 3% per year, the demand for food in those countries may increase at more than 4% per year. In the higher income countries, with some 30% of the population, the increase in demand for food will be much less. For the world as a whole, it will nevertheless average some 3% per year. These figures apply to the next decade or two. If per capita income rises in the lower income countries, or if their population growth rate declines, the rate of increase in the demand for food will gradually fall.

How great are the prospects that the food supply will be increased at this rate?

It may be estimated (with a wide margin for error) that by 1970 the production of food (and of the raw materials for clothing) had increased to between 6 and 20 times the 1650 volume—perhaps to some 10 or 12 times.

This increase was not achieved by cultivation of a ten-fold land area, for most of the present cultivated areas of Europe, Asia, and Africa were probably in cultivation in 1650. The new lands were those of America, Australia, and New Zealand, plus lands of the older continents made usable by irrigation and the development of faster-ripening crops, and lands of inferior quality brought into use because of population pressure. Inspection of the globe and general knowledge of the regions probably under cultivation in 1650 and those in cultivation today suggest that the area of land cultivated today is hardly three times that cultivated in 1650—perhaps no more than double. If so, production per hectare has been increased at least three-fold and perhaps four-fold by improvement in seeds, added double- or triple-cropping through irrigation, increased use of commercial fertilizer, and changes in methods associated with these other changes. These advances in techniques have contributed increasingly to the increase in production, and increase in area has been of steadily decreasing importance, especially during the past century. Can technical advance continue to meet rising demand?

There is a sharp difference of opinion concerning this. To the writer, there seems no technical reason why agricultural production should not be increased at an equal rate with increasing demand due to increasing population and rising income, even up to the 8 billion or greater population of the 22nd century. This judgment takes into account the possibility of a shortage of food in 1975–77, discussed below.

The specific bases for the judgment are these: First, there exists a great reserve productive capacity in the present grain-exporting countries. When serious lack of rainfall in the Soviet Union and in South Asia in 1971 and 1972 resulted in a calamitously bad harvest in 1972 followed by a poor one in some areas in 1973, wheat prices in the United States more than tripled, from about $2 per bushel to over $6 at the peak early in 1974. World wheat prices rose by a larger percentage, since they had been lower before the shortage. The average world price of all major grains rose by the same order of magnitude. The supply response is of special interest here. The 1972 shortage emerged too late for Australian wheat producers to increase their plantings for the 1972–73 year, but in 1973–74 Australia harvested a wheat crop twice as large as that of 1973. The Canadian harvest increased by a lesser percentage. In 1973 the United States harvested a record crop of 1.71 million bushels, and in 1974 exceeded even that all-time record in spite of drought which injured the crop of spring wheat. Other grain crops, which mature later, were harder hit by the exceptionally wet spring, dry summer, and storms. Because of this unfavorable weather in the important American grain-growing regions and also in the Soviet Union in 1974, and because in 1974 and 1975 fertilizer shortages due to the 1973–74 curtailment of oil shipments reduced harvests in the low-income countries, until say 1976 or perhaps 1977 world stocks of foodgrains will probably remain low and prices high, and if the high-income countries are too selfish to share their grains, people in some areas of India, Bangladesh, sub-Sahara Africa, and elsewhere will suffer severely. This situation was duplicated often in the past when population and the demand for food were much less than at present. It is due to supply fluctuations whose mal-effects could readily be prevented by establishment of a world foodgrain storage scheme or by similar stockpiling in the major producing countries. The problem of supply fluctuation should not be confused with the question of world productive capacity. There is enough productive capacity.[10]

Second, productivity per hectare (and per agricultural worker) is continually increasing in the more developed grain producing countries. Agricultural output per hectare and per worker have both risen steadily during the past century in the countries of Western Europe and in the United States, Canada, and Japan.[11] The rise is continuing. Figure 3–4 presents data. There is no reason to expect any specific limit to that increase.

Third, the advances can be adapted to the low-income countries. On the average, agricultural output per male worker in Australia, Canada, New Zealand, and the United States is about 94% higher than in 11 less developed countries with which comparison was made. Ruttan has estimated the sources of the difference. A greater amount of land per worker accounted for only one tenth of it, whereas fertilizer and machinery

---

[10] The establishment of reserve stocks in ancient Egypt is recorded in the book of Exodus of the Christian and Jewish scriptures. Reserve stocks were established in Italy during one period in the history of the Roman Empire, as grain from the colonies flooded into Italy. Their purpose, however, was to dispose of an embarrassing surplus, not to provide protection against famine.

[11] This statement excludes Australia merely because the writer does not have data. No doubt the same increases have been occurring there.

FIGURE 3–4

Increases in Agricultural Productivity: New and Old "Developed" Countries, 1880–1965

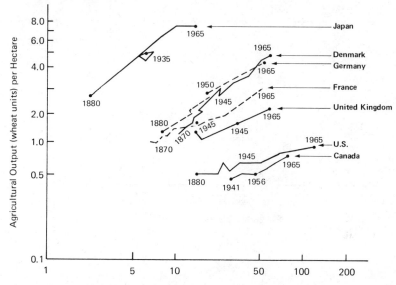

Agricultural Output (wheat units) per Male Worker

Historical growth paths of agriculture development in the United States, Japan and Germany, 1880–1965, and Denmark, France, and the United Kingdom, 1870–1965, and Canada, 1941–65.

Source: V. Ruttan (1973).

inputs and general and technical education were estimated to account for 61% of it (see Table 3–1). In 9 countries of Western Europe, agricultural output per male worker averaged 83.5% higher in recent years than in the 11 less developed countries. In this comparison, the amount of land per worker accounts for only 2% of the difference; technical inputs and general and technical education account for 64%.[12] That the differences are due not to resource endowments but to these other factors indicates possibilities for increase in output per hectare in the less developed countries.

Fourth, well-organized and adequately-financed research activity is accelerating the adaptation of improved seeds and methods to the less developed countries, and solving specific production and related problems of those countries. The research is conducted by seven international research institutions. It is financed by private U.S. foundations, the World Bank, the United Nations Development Program, the United States Agency for International Development, and other governments, and is guided by a common International Consultative Group. The re-

---

[12] V. Ruttan (1973).

TABLE 3–1
Accounting for Differences in Labor Productivity in Agriculture between Eleven Less Developed Countries (LDCs) and Four Recently Developed Countries (RDCs)

		Percent	*Index*
Difference in output per male worker		93.6	100
Difference explained:			
Total		90.0	96
Resource endowments		32.6	35
Land	9.7		10
Livestock	22.9		25
Technical inputs		24.5	26
Fertilizer	14.6		16
Machinery	9.9		10
Human capital		32.9	35
General education	19.5		21
Technical education	13.4		14

LDCs: Brazil, Ceylon, Colombia, India, Mexico, Peru, Philippines, Syria, Taiwan, Turkey, United Arab Republic.
RDCs: Australia, Canada, New Zealand, United States.
Source: Ruttan (1973).

search institutions (identified by their acronyms), their locations, and the matters on which they work are as follows. Where two or three are working on a common problem, their work is cooperative.

    IRRI: The Philippines—rice
    CIMMYT: Mexico—maize and wheat
    IITA: Nigeria—rice, maize, cowpeas, pigeon peas, sweet potatoes,
        yams, cassava, cropping systems for the low humid tropics
    CIAT: Colombia—cassava, beef cattle, swine, beans, rice, and maize
    CID: Peru—potatoes
    ICRISAT: India—millets, sorghum, chick peas, pigeon peas
    ILRAD: Kenya—East Coast fever, trypanosomiasis[13]

The first and second of these, the International Rice Research Institute and the International Wheat Research Institute (Centro Internacional de Mejoramiento de Maiz y Trigo), financed initially solely by the Rockefeller and Ford Foundations, developed from earlier improved seeds the "miracle rice" and "miracle wheat" that have been the basis of the "green revolution."

In 1974 the organizations that now sponsor this group of research institutions were discussing the establishment of a further unit for research in the special problems of agricultural production in arid lands. This unit may be in existence when this book is published. In cooperation with these international institutions, an Indian national research center is

---

[13] This listing is from R. W. Cummings (1974).

working effectively to adapt new rice and wheat strains to the differing conditions of different regions of India.

Those research centers are innovating *de novo* as well as adapting. The "green revolution" provides the conspicuous recent example. By 1973 the new varieties of rice were being planted on about 20% of the land in South and Southeast Asia on which rice is grown, and the new wheat varieties on about 30% of wheat lands. The areas on which the "miracle seeds" have been adopted are regarded as "very advanced" areas. Without further technical adaptation, their use on a considerable added portion of Asian rice and wheat lands is possible, and is proceeding gradually. At the same time, further adaptation which is already occurring is sharply reducing the amount of fertilizer needed to obtain high yields, and is increasing resistance to insects and plant diseases. And the development and steady improvement of these seeds is not an isolated phenomenon but only the most spectacular instance of a much more general continuing process.

The demand for food may press harder upon the world's growing productive capacity during the next generation than it has during the past generation for a temporary but fairly long-lasting reason. A variety of temperature and rainfall indicators from around the world indicate that the decade of the 1960s and the first years of the 1970s were a period more favorable to crop production than any of the several preceding decades. It is not probable that any lasting secular change has occurred; it is more probable that the world has simply been lucky for somewhat more than a decade (and then exceptionally unlucky for two years). Some meteorologists believe that the world has now passed the crest of a long weather cycle, and that conditions will not be as favorable as during the past dozen years for another 30 years or so. If so, the full exercise of the technical possibilities indicated in the discussion of the preceding several pages may be needed if, starting with the 1974–75 situation, supply is to increase faster than demand, thus reducing foodgrain prices relative to other prices. However, the price elasticity of the supply of foodgrains is high; it is reasonable to suppose that the continuation of relatively high prices will both bring out large current production and increase the secular rate of increase in production.

In summary, then, while there may be food shortages because of the lack of concern or administrative ineptitude of governments, the notion that there will be some grave biological difficulty in increasing foodgrain production as fast as the demand for food increases is without foundation.

One problem of future world food supply has not been mentioned. Implicitly, the discussion above has dealt with the production of calories. There is also a problem of possible protein deficiency, already a serious problem in some low-income countries. Research concerning ways to meet or prevent that deficiency is now going forward, but only on a scale that is probably inadequate. Foresight and the devotion of human energy to this problem as well as to that of calorie supply is necessary.

At this point it is possible to summarize the implications for economic development in the present lower income countries of the world which are present in the discussion in this chapter and the preceding one of the possible limits to world economic growth. They are as follows: There seems no reason to suppose that world growth will be limited by mineral or agricultural supply limitations during the foreseeable future so as to limit seriously the prospects for growth in the lower income countries of the world. (By "foreseeable future" is meant the coming half-century.) A stronger statement might be made, but this minimum statement is sufficient here. It follows that the analysis of economic development in the lower income countries can proceed without giving further attention to the question of aggregate world growth.

POPULATION GROWTH AND INCOME GROWTH IN THE LDCs

There is, however, a different question about the relationship of population growth to economic growth in the lower income countries that may be discussed here. This is the question whether population growth in those countries may not create an insurmountable barrier to progressive increase in their income levels.

Theories of a Low-Level Equilibrium Trap

The thesis about the effects of population growth which Malthus stated in 1800 is felt by many analysts to be applicable to the lower income countries today. In successive editions of his *Essay on the Principle of Population*,[14] Malthus restated his thesis with various changes, but the central themes remained the same. Briefly, he argued:

> that as the income of people rises above the subsistence level population will tend to increase because of a decline in death rates;
>
> that while the number of workers available to produce food will increase in the same proportion as the population, after some point they will not be able to increase the production of food in the same proportion, because of the limited quantity of land. In terms of later economic theory, diminishing returns to land will set in; and
>
> that therefore the supply of food per capita will decrease, income will be forced back to the subsistence level, and population increase will be

---

[14] Especially in the editions of 1803, 1826, and in the *Encyclopaedia Britannica* of 1824.

checked by famine, pestilence, and war, unless men and women check it by restraining their sexual desires.

Malthus recognized, in some of his successive editions, that the "subsistence level of living" might be a psychological minimum above the biological minimum. He recognized it grudgingly. To have admitted that any level of living once attained for a short time would become the psychological minimum would have destroyed his model.

In 1954, Leibenstein developed a model of economic development in which a low-income country will tend to be caught in the Malthusian trap, and will enter upon continuing rise in per capita income only if some powerful force (a great and rapid rise in the rate of investment, a great technical surge, etc.) raised the rate of growth of aggregate income above the maximum rate of population increase. A large ensuing rise in per capita income might then cause birth rates to fall.

Two years later, in 1966, Nelson developed a somewhat similar theory, giving the condition in which a low-income country might be held the name "low-level equilibrium trap."

An appendix to this chapter presents in a geometric model the essential elements of the models of Malthus, Leibenstein, and Nelson. Here it is of interest to note that up to the present the model seems of only limited relevance to reality.

Model and Reality

Up to the present time the model has been entirely irrelevant in the West. In no important respect has either population or the level of living behaved as Malthus predicted. We can see why this has been so by considering the experience of the West in somewhat greater detail than it has been summarized above.

There are 17 countries in the world in which a moderate or faster rate of aggregate output (1.5% per year or more) began before the end of the 19th century, and thus has gone on long enough so that it might be expected to have brought the Malthusian mechanism into play. Kuznets has analyzed population and national product data from about 1860 or later to about 1954 for 13 of them. The data are summarized in Table 3–2.

The following conclusions may be drawn from the data presented in Table 3–2:

1. Per capita income rose steadily in all of the 13 countries. (The percentages in column 3 are all consistently above those in column 4.)

2. Nevertheless, in none of the 13 did the rate of natural increase remotely approach the biologically possible maximum rate. Only in Canada, where vast empty lands cried out to be filled, did the rate of population growth, including that from immigration, touch 3% even for a

TABLE 3–2
Population and National Product, 13 Countries: Percentage Changes per Decade, Decades of Highest Percentage Population Change

Country (1)	Period* (2)	Percentage Change per Decade National Product (3)	Percentage Change per Decade Population (4)	Decade of Highest dP/dt Approximate Dates* (5)	Decade of Highest dP/dt Percentage Change (6)
Australia	1886/94–1945/54	26†	17†	1890–1900	21.5
Canada	{1870/79–1950/54	41.3	18.3		
	1870/79–1905/14	47.1	17.8	1899–1909	30.2
Denmark	{1870/78–1950/54	30.1	11.5		
	1870/78–1904/13	32.7	11.3	1913–1923	17.5
France	{1841/50–1949/53	15.3	1.3		
	1841/50–1901/10	18.6	1.9	1855–1865	4.7
Germany	{1860/69–1950/54	27.4	10.1		
	1860/69–1905/14	35.6	11.5	1894–1904	15.2
Ireland-Eire	{1800/69–1949/53	12.8	−3.5		
	1860/69–1904/13	11.6	−5.4	1938–1948	0.0
Italy	{1862/68–1950/54	18.0	6.9		
	1862/68–1904/13	15.7	7.0	1923–1933	8.0
Japan	{1878/87–1950/54	42.3	12.7		
	1878/87–1903/12	49.2	11.6	1937–1947	14.7
Sweden	{1861/68–1950/54	36.0	6.6		
	1861/68–1904/13	34.8	6.8	1938–1948	12.5
Switzerland	1890/99–1939/48	21†	7†	1894–1913	10.5‡
Russia-U.S.S.R. ..	{1870–1954	31.0	13.4		
	1870–1913	27.7	15.7	1870–1885	15.3§
United Kingdom ·	{1860/69–1949/53	21.5	8.0		
	1860/69–1905/14	25.0	11.1	1869–1879	12.4
United States	}1869/78–1950/54	41.2	17.4		
	{1869/78–1904/13	56.0	22.3	1873–1883	24.7

* Generally, Kuznets presents data for overlapping decades. His population data are shown as for intervals from one overlapping decade to another. The dates given in column 5 are the fifth years of the decades he cites.
† The decade rate from the first to the last period covered. Other percentages in these columns are trend-line rates.
‡ The decade rate for the 20-year period.
§ The decade rate for the 16-year period.
Source: Columns 2, 3, 4, Kuznets (*Q.A.E.G.N.*, 1), Table 2, except for Australia and Switzerland, which were computed from *ibid.*, Appendix Tables 18 and 5 respectively; columns 5, 6, ibid., Appendix Tables 1–5, 7, 9, 10, 13–15, 17, 18.

single decade during the 80-year period analyzed.[15] In no case except Canada and the United States did the rate of population growth exceed 17.5% per decade even for a single decade.

While data for the 19th century are not available for the other four countries with rapid rates of economic growth (Belgium, the Netherlands, Norway, and New Zealand), it is clear from general historical information about those countries that the course of events in them paralleled that in the other 13. Malthusian population trends have not appeared in any Western country whatever.

England provides some added evidence. A gradual rise in aggregate income occurred there in the 18th century. Estimates by Phyllis Deane (1955, 1957) indicate an average rate of growth in output for the century of about 15% per decade. She thinks that the growth was concentrated in the first half of the century. Population growth failed to keep pace with this moderate rate; it was about 6% per decade.[16]

Four years after Nelson presented his model, he published an article (1960) in which he tested its applicability to the case of Japan. His conclusion: the model is not applicable.

Why does the model fail? Basically, because two of its assumptions are not realistic. The first of these is that because of sexual appetites the birth rate will remain at a maximum even after death rates fall. Even long before recent methods of contraception were invented, this assumption proved false. The second nonempirical assumption is the implicit one that technical advance in the production of food, if it occurs, will be a one-time and more or less accidental event; that continuing technical progress will not occur. If birth rates had remained at maximum, then to bring rising per capita income the current of technical progress would have had to be so strong that it increased aggregate income at a rate higher than the maximum possible population growth rate. This turned out not to be necessary, because population growth rates remained more moderate.

Continuing technical progress is needed to offset or more than offset diminishing returns as the quantities of capital and labor continue to increase, but technical progress does continue. It has now continued so long in the West that the historical record reinforces the logical reasons for thinking of it as continuing indefinitely. It has also begun in many non-Western countries, and similarly there is reason to think of it as continuing indefinitely in those countries. There is no technical reason why it should not continue forever. It was stated in Chapter 2 that as natural

---

[15] In Australia, New Zealand, the United States, and Canada, during the early pre-industrial period of filling empty lands, population growth reached rates higher than those shown in Table 3–2.

[16] For other estimates of income and production in Great Britain during the 18th century, see Ashton (1955) and sources cited by him. Concerning Western Europe in the late 18th and 19th centuries, see H. Habakkuk (1963).

resources become scarce we have been inventing new ones. The significance of this is not that diminishing returns have disappeared; that there are no factors limited in amount—there are. We continually face the problem of augmenting them. But we have continually solved the problem. The future of diminishing returns has never arrived.

It might nevertheless be true that in the lower income countries of today, rapid population growth may be preventing rise in per capita income. However, the empirical evidence is that rapid population growth seems to be no hindrance.

Kuznets has shown that among 19 countries in which economic growth was occurring in the first half of the 20th century, and among a smaller group for which data are available back into the 19th century, there is a positive correlation between the rate of population growth and that of growth in income per capita.[17] He ranked the countries and calculated the rank correlation, then did the same for various subgroups that excluded countries whose inclusion might seem to bias the results. The correlation was positive not only in the case of the 19 countries but also in every subgrouping. The sample, especially when some countries have been excluded as indicated above, is small. Moreover, in only one of the eight groupings was the correlation significant even at the 5% level. But that the correlation was positive in every case in significant.

During the period covered by this study, population growth was a result of a cluster of factors associated with economic growth. The two had common causes. This may explain the positive correlations, but a similar result is reached in a study (Kuznets, 1967b) covering the period 1950–64, when population growth spurted quite independently of economic growth. Kuznets found a positive rank correlation between population growth and economic growth among 21 countries of Asia and Africa (excluding the more developed countries of Israel and South Africa), among 19 countries of Latin America, and among 40 countries treated as a single group. The correlations are not statistically significant, but that there is no negative correlation, much less a statistically signification one, *is* significant.[18]

Kuznets did find negative correlations among developed countries and among 63 developed and less developed countries as a single group, the latter significant at the 5% level. Both results were no doubt due to the rapid postwar economic growth and low rate of population growth of the developed countries. But the rapid economic growth is due to such special circumstances of the period—among which the lesser rate of population growth than the lower income countries is incidental—that one would hesitate to attach substantive significance to the result, even though there is statistical significance.

---

[17] Kuznets *Q.A.E.N.G* 1, Table 7, p. 29.

[18] Less comprehensive evidence of other research is consistent with these findings.

If we ask how this lack of relationship or even a positive relationship between the rate of population growth and the rate of growth in per capita income can be explained, the answer must be one of the following: (1) The result is mere coincidence. During this brief period in history, technical progress happens to be occurring with enough greater speed in countries with rapid population growth than in others to offset diminishing returns. This theory strains coincidence pretty severely. (2) The most rapid population growth is occurring in the lands with the lowest population density, where there is plenty of room. However, while this is true as among continents, it does not seem to be true as among the countries included in Kuznets' or the other statistical analyses. (3) Rapid population growth and rapid technical advance are joint results of some unknown third factor. (4) Rapid population growth is itself a cause of rapid technical advance.

The third and perhaps the fourth of these alternative explanations involves some causal link not now understood. However, there are some plausible reasons why rapid population growth may induce rapid economic growth that *are* understood.

Favorable: Less social overhead per capita is needed if the population density is greater. Population growth absolves entrepreneurs of errors in investment by providing an expanding market for the many products for which population size influences market size more than does the level of per capita income. Population growth creates "counter pressures"; it forces problems on the attention of entrepreneurs; it creates bottlenecks that make innovational decisions easier, in the way the Hirschman suggested. Lastly (actually a common factor underlying both population and output growth), vigor in procreation may be associated psychologically with innovational vigor.

Unfavorable: Rapid population growth reduces the capacity to save. It increases the burden of caring for children. Capital is diverted from innovation to mere expansion of capacity. It brings diminishing returns into play more sharply.[19]

As between such influences, it is conceivable that the balance of the effects is on the side of a neutral or positive relationship between the two types of growth.

Even though there is no general unfavorable result of population growth on the rate of growth in per capita product, in individual countries in which the death rate has fallen without much innovation in supply there can be a pseudo-Malthusian result. (Pseudo-Malthusian because rapid population growth was induced, not by rise in income, but by an exogenous force.) Starvation may always be close at hand. The sub-Sahara countries provide a conspicuous current example. Observers wonder, year by year, whether India's technical progress in agriculture is fast

---

[19] K. B. Griffin and J. L. Enos (1971) discuss the favorable and unfavorable factors.

enough. Boserup (1965) has argued that an increase in land shortage leads to fuller use of their own labor by cultivators, and not necessarily to a reduction in output per worker, but her illustrations suggest that this process is completed before population density in agriculture reaches that in India.

China of the early modern period presents a true Malthusian example. Between the mid-17th and mid-19th centuries, sweet potatoes, peanuts, and early-ripening rice were introduced into China. Their use made possible habitation of areas where the growing season had previously been too short or the soil not suited to the previous crops. Presumably as people moved to new lands, lessening population pressure on the old, the level of living of many persons, and average income in the country as a whole rose. But the rate of population increase probably also rose. When the new lands were filled with people, the level of per capita income apparently was no higher than before the introduction of the new crops had begun.[20]

The evidence cited above shows that the sub-Sahara countries and China of the 17th-19th centuries are not the general case.[21]

BIBLIOGRAPHIC NOTES

United Nations (1973) presents a comprehensive nonanalytical survey of current knowledge on all aspects of population. The volume replaces United Nations (1963), bearing an identical title. William P. McGreevey (1974) surveys critically but very briefly research on fertility determinants.

Theodore W. Schultz, ed. (1973 and 1974), present papers and discussion of two conferences on the economic theory of determinants of fertility. T. Paul Schultz (1967 and 1973) reports on research that applied the theory of economic determinants to Puerto Rico and Taiwan, respectively. G. S. Becker, in the 1960 N.B.E.R. volume *Demographic and Economic Change in Developed Countries*, first presents the theory of children as goods subject to the same influences that determine individuals' purchases of other goods.

Concerning a "low-level equilibrium trap," the books and articles mentioned in the text—H. Leibenstein (1954 and 1957) and R. R. Nelson (1956 and 1960)—cover the ground.

---

[20] Information concerning population and income in China before recent decades is so scanty that in part the account here is speculative. What is known is that new lands were occupied when the new crops had been introduced, that recent population estimates for China are much higher (between 100 million and 200 million higher) than the estimates previously accepted, and that the recent level of income is low enough so that it seems probable that it was not lower 300 years ago.

[21] Chapter 7 presents a discussion of the relationship between population density and economic growth.

II

The Positive Economics
of Growth

The term "positive" theory, contrasting with "normative" theory, is used in economics to refer to analysis that deals with causes and results without expressing value judgments. Chapters 4 through 12 discuss the growth process in this "positive," that is, "scientific," way.

Chapter 4 gives a sketch of the characteristics of the lowest countries, then presents an introductory overview of the growth process. Chapters 5 and 6 explain the difficulties of innovation in trade, agriculture, and industry, with some emphasis on technical, sociological, and "cultural," that is, psychological, difficulties. With this information, the reader can move to the purely economic theory which occupies almost all of Chapter 7 and later chapters with a surer appreciation of the importance of that theory.

Introduction to the Anatomy of Growth

4

The introductory overview of the process of growth presented in this chapter begins with a sketch of the characteristics of countries in which modern growth has not begun or has not proceeded far. They are in general countries in which the level of per capita income at 1974 prices is below or not far above $100 per capita. However, many of the qualities described apply to a number of countries with somewhat higher incomes as well. The sketch begins with economic characteristics, then moves to others.

CHARACTERISTICS OF THE LOWEST INCOME COUNTRIES

1. In the least developed countries, methods of production are predominantly traditional, "biblical." In agriculture, the wooden plow, the digging hoe, planting seeds by hand, threshing by walking oxen around and around over the heads of grain—these are symbolic of the methods in use. Burdens are commonly carried in pans or baskets on the head. The adjective "traditional" means literally only that things are done in the way they have "always" been done—for generations past. It implies also very low productivity. Nonagricultural production is very largely "cottage industry": family-sized enterprises using very little mechanical power. These too are traditional, or not greatly changed from traditional methods. In the larger towns and cities there may be a very few enterprises using methods introduced by foreigners—usually during colonial rule—or adapted by indigenous entrepreneurs from Western techniques. Even

73

these enterprises will be extremely small and the methods very simple by the standards of industrial countries. If the country has soil and climate suited to the larger-scale production of an agricultural or forest product for which there is demand in higher income countries, there may be larger enterprises to market the product. Only if the country has a valuable mineral deposit which a firm from an industrial country is extracting will there be a really large and capital-intensive enterprise.

2. It follows that the amount of capital used in production is very small. The amount of capital equipment per worker—in agriculture, in industry, and elsewhere—is a small fraction of that used in high-income countries. Little capital per worker is associated with little output per worker. The ratio of the value of capital to the value of output per year is pretty much the same as the ratio in high-income countries. To many economists, this paucity of supply of capital is the basic explanation of "underdevelopment."

3. Many other economists, especially among those who are practitioners rather than only theorists in the field of economic development, warn that the low volume of capital is a proximate cause which itself results from a more basis condition. In this view the more basic cause, which also explains the lack of capital accumulation, is the minimum presence, in both private enterprise and government, of the human attitudes and interests necessary for innovation and the administration of economic growth. In the term sometimes used by economists, there is low "absorptive capacity."

What is referred to is not lack of intelligence or training. Men may be sophisticated, and may be capable political administrators, military leaders, or intellectuals, but may be governed by motives that cause them to have no interest in running businesses effectively and cause them even not to observe what actions and arrangements are necessary for economic growth. That this is the one key factor in absence of growth is of course an oversimplification. But its great importance in countries in which little or no growth is taking place is clear. Judicious (and not prejudiced or supercilious) observers have said, for example, that the most prominent common characteristic of all or almost all of the 25 countries labeled "least developed" is this attitudinal one leading to relative lack of absorptive capacity.[1] Its presence or absence is of course a matter of degree. Where cultural change has occurred, perhaps over two generations or more through tensions in the relationships of modern life, different motivations may come to exist in increasing degree. Income will still be low for a long time because growth is a long process, but income is likely to be rising.

4. Except as foreign entrepreneurs are extracting a valuable natural

---

[1] They have said it orally, and not for attribution.

resource, some 60% or more of the aggregate output of the country will be in the primary sector: agriculture, forestry and fishing. Moreover, because value productivity is even lower in agriculture than elsewhere, an even higher percentage of the labor force—say 70% to 80%—will be engaged in these activities. Table 4–1 shows the average share of the

TABLE 4–1
Arithmetic Means of Shares of Major Sectors in National Product and Labor Force, by Groups of Countries Classified by Per Capita Economic Level, Early Postwar Years
A.   Shares in Labor Force, Including Unpaid Family Labor (percent)

Economic Level Classes	Rough Estimate Of Average Income (1974 U.S. $)	Number of Countries	Average Share of Sector		
			Primary	Secondary	Tertiary
I	2,400	8	15.0	40.2	44.8
II	1,400	7	31.1	31.1	37.9
III	900	6	29.4	28.3	42.4
IV	550	8	58.8	17.5	23.7
V	375	5	54.5	18.9	26.6
VI	275	7	64.8	15.0	20.2
VII	140	6	79.9	6.6	13.5

B.   Shares in National Product (percent)

Economic Level Classes	Number of Countries	Average Share of Sector		
		Primary	Secondary	Tertiary
I	7	13.2	38.1	48.7
II	6	17.2	41.5	41.2
III	6	19.2	29.2	51.6
IV	8	30.1	24.2	45.7
V	8	35.4	24.3	40.2
VI	10–11	42.5	17.8	39.3
VII	12–13	54.6	13.7	33.3

Source: Except for "Rough Estimate of Average Income," Kuznets, *Q.A.E.G.N.*, 2, p. 23 for shares in labor force and p. 10 for shares in product. Average income for each class estimated by present writer from Kuznets' index, same source, p. 7.

national product and labor force in each of the three economic sectors during early postwar years in each of seven groups of countries classed by income level. In this tabulation, the secondary sector includes manufacturing, mining, and construction. The tertiary sector includes all service activities, defined to include public utilities.[2] The estimates do not include Communist countries. The percentages given are simple averages

[2] Which in some tabulations are placed in the secondary sector.

of estimates for the countries included in each income class. Kuznets, who presents these data, gives only an index of the average per capita income level in each class; I have translated these into rough estimates of the average income level in U.S. dollars at 1974 prices.

An estimate of the sectoral distribution of the labor force in 1950 and 1960 in all "less developed" countries of the world as a group, and separately in three regions of the world, is given in Table 4–2. The countries covered presumably include Kuznets' classes IV–VII and part of his Class III. Neither tabulation presents data for the lowest income countries, Kuznets for lack of data and Table 4–2 because it averages entire regions. To estimate percentages for the lowest income countries, it would be necessary to project Kuznets' data beyond his Group VII: The labor force percentages in the primary sector, for example, are certainly higher in most of the 25 "least developed" countries than in even South and East Asia.

Tables 4–1 and 4–2, while giving an indication of the sectoral distribution of labor force and product in the low-income countries, also indicate changes as income rises that will be of interest repeatedly in the discussion later in this book.

The reason for the concentration of production in primary products is simply that at low incomes the first priorities of demand are for food, clothing, and shelter, and that since because of low productivity each agricultural family produces little more than enough for its own needs, a large agricultural labor force will produce a surplus only large enough to supply a small nonagricultural population. If too many men moved to

TABLE 4–2
The Structure of Employment, Lower Income Regions, 1950 and 1960

	Agriculture	Mining, Manufacturing, Utilities, and Construction	Commerce, Transport, and Other Sources
All less developed:			
1950	73.3	10.0	16.5
1960	70.7	11.5	17.6
Asia, South and East:[1]			
1950	75.3	8.8	15.7
1960	73.1	10.5	16.6
North Africa:[2]			
1950	72.9	9.7	17.2
1960	69.6	10.3	20.0
Latin America:			
1950	54.1	18.6	27.3
1960	50.1	20.0	30.0

[1] Excludes Middle East countries.
[2] Algeria, Morocco, Libya, Sudan, Tunisia and the UAR.
Source: Tables calculated by Bairoch and Limbor (1968).

nonagriculture, they could not eat. Conversely, a small fraction of the labor force in nonagricultural employment produces enough other products to meet the small demand for them. If too many men moved to nonagriculture, they would find no jobs.

Low productivity also dictates that the agricultural products shall be largely cereals and raw materials. Because the production of meat requires much larger inputs relative to the nutritive value of the output, the nutrition gained from meat is expensive. At low levels of income the demand for meat is small even apart from noneconomic forces such as religious taboos that may bar meat consumption.

5. In most very low-income countries, agriculture is predominantly peasant agriculture: cultivation by peasant proprietors, usually renters, rather than owners, on very small holdings. Even where land is plentiful, the typical holding will be no more than six to eight hectares (15 to 20 acres), since for most crops this is the greatest area that can be cultivated with one yoke of oxen or water buffalo or other beasts of burden, using primitive plows and drag harrows. Where population density is high, the size of holding may be as little as one to three hectares. Plots much larger than eight hectares are mainly tracts on which "dry cultivation" is practiced.

In other countries, large estates or ranches are common. They are of two types: large unproductive estates or ranches of individuals to whom operation of the establishment is more a way of life than an economic activity, and estates or plantations on which rubber, tea, cacao, or some other product adapted to large-scale production with wage labor is produced for the world market. Estate cultivation was initially produced by invaders from the West. The first type of large estate is most common in Latin America, the second in Asia, though in Argentina a commercial orientation is important on the large cattle ranches and wheat farms.

Table 4–3 in a somewhat complicated way shows the distribution of land holdings in ten selected countries, half of them with high income. Among the group, the concentration of land in large holdings in Uruguay and Guatemala is marked.

6. The marginal productivity of labor in agriculture in low-income countries is extremely low.

Employment in primary industries in the less developed countries is sometimes referred to as residual. The concept is that persons who can find employment elsewhere do so; those who cannot must be content to remain in the primary industries. This concept is closely related to that of "disguised unemployment" in agriculture. This in turn is sometimes stated in the stark form that the marginal productivity of labor in agriculture (and certain nonagricultural occupations) is zero. Other writers deny that any appreciable amount of labor in any country has zero marginal productivity. The empirical evidence is discussed in Chapter 9. How-

TABLE 4–3
Distribution of Farm Area and Farm Population by Size of Holdings,
Selected Countries, about 1950

1	2	3	4	5
		Percentage of Farm Land Area (numerator) and Farm Population (denominator) on Farms of:		
Country	*Per Capita GDP, 1960 (dollars)*	*Less Than 10 Hectares*	*50 Hectares or More*	*Relative Land per Person (col. 4 ÷ col. 3)*
Germany	1,338	24 / 69	37 / 3.4	31.3
Denmark	1,299	14 / 38	25 / 7.6	8.9
Norway	1,272	69 / 87	2.2 / 0.6	4.6
Belgium	1,237	46 / 77	9.4 / 1.5	10.5
Israel	830	17 / 48	69 / 43	4.5
Uruguay	485	0.7 / 21	95 / 48	59.4
Japan	456	91.5 / 99	8.5° / 0.7†	13.1
Guatemala	268	16 / 86	72 / 4.6	84.1
Libya	131	6.0 / 42	63 / 15	29.4
Hungary	—	78 / 91	1.0 / 0.1	11.7

Note: Percentages above 10 have been rounded to the nearest percent.
° Ten hectares and above.
† 1960.
Sources: Per capita GDP, 1960: Hagen and Hawrylyshyn (1969); distribution of farm population: United Nations (1963); distribution of farm land, ibid. and Food and Agriculture Organization (1955).

ever, almost no economist would dispute the statement that in many LDCs, since World War II if not before, the labor force in agriculture and in some service occupations has expanded to a size that has reduced its average productivity.

7. The ratio of exports to total production varies considerably. The exports are largely primary products. Johnston and Kilby (1975, p. 11)

note that countries in which mineral productions contributes more than 2% of GDP are typically exporters of minerals.

8. Because primary products fluctuate much more widely in price than do industrial prices, the foreign exchange earnings of the less developed countries, and hence their ability to pay for imports, fluctuate far more widely than do those of the more developed countries.

9. The ratio of population to material resources varies greatly. One of the fictions commonly believed about the low-income countries is that in all of them people jostle each other for space. The two huge low-income countries China and India, are densely populated; hence the bulk of the world's low-income population lives in densely populated areas. However, population density is low in many low-income countries in Southeast Asia, Latin America, and Africa. This is true whether the magnitude taken as the denominator of the population-resources ratio is area or some other measure of natural resources. As Table 4–4 shows, the amount of cultivable land per person is, as a minimum, more than 6 times as great in 21 countries of Asia and Latin America, including large countries, as in Pakistan, Taiwan, or Puerto Rico. It is nevertheless true that no low-income country today has the unused rich land available that was available in the United States, Canada, Australia, and New Zealand when their development began, and that few low-income countries today have as low man-land ratios as did the countries of Western Europe in 1700.

Population density is high in countries in which agriculture has long been practiced. The population density is evidence of their success in agriculture. It is also high in island plantation economies—the West Indies, Fiji, Mauritius, Ceylon—to which immigrant labor was brought and in which some endemic diseases were controlled.[3] Except for these plantation islands, wherever social organization was tribal and the economic base was hunting, herding, or fishing until modern times population density is low.

By and large, the natural resources of the least developed countries are little developed; the increasing utilization of natural resources is an aspect of economic growth.

10. The saving rate in the countries with per capita incomes under $400, taken as a group, is much below that of the higher income countries. Among countries with per capita incomes below $100 in 1965, the 1964 ratio of gross saving to GDP varied from just above 6% in Afghanistan and South Korea to more than 28% in Thailand. There was similar variability at income levels up to $300. Oil-rich Kuwait, though one would class it as among the least developed countries, had not only the highest per capita income in the world ($4,786 in 1965), if one treats the Arab Emirates as a single country, but also the highest saving ratio

---

[3] Hla Myint (1964), p. 32, makes these points.

TABLE 4–4
Persons per Hectare of Cultivable Land, Countries of Asia and Latin America,
Recent Years

3.0 and +	1.5–2.99	.50–1.49	0–.49
		Asia	
Pakistan	Ceylon	Afghanistan	Burma
Taiwan	China (mainland)	Philippines	Iraq
	India	Thailand	Iran
	Israel	Cambodia	Malaysia
	Japan	Laos	Saudi Arabia
	Lebanon	Vietnam	Syria
	Java		Turkey
	Nepal		U.S.S.R.
		Latin America	
Puerto Rico	El Salvador	Argentina	Brazil
	Jamaica	Bolivia	Chile
		Cuba	Colombia
		Dominican	Costa Rica
		Republic	Ecuador
		Guatemala	Honduras
			Mexico
			Paraguay
			Peru
			Uruguay
			Venezuela
			Guyana
			Surinam

Source: Iran, Saudi Arabia, Syria, U.S.S.R., Cambodia, Laos, Vietnam, Java, Nepal, Guyana and Surinam: estimated. Others: Food and Agriculture Organization (1964).

(43.8% of gross domestic product in 1964). Both fell during the 1965–72 period, as the population and spending increased.

11. Until the postwar period the lower income countries without exception were in the early phase of the demographic revolution. That is, birth rates were high, death rates were only a little lower, and the population growth rate was low. Death rates have now been brought down sharply, not by economic growth, but by public health and preventive medicine programs introduced throughout the low-income world by the United States Public Health Service and the World Health Organization.

12. In view of the economic structure of the less developed countries, it will not surprise the reader to be told that they tend to be nonurban societies. Where large cities do exist in nonindustrial countries, they are centers of government and administration or entrepots for foreign trade, and not the complex foci of economic life that they are in industrial high-income countries. Nor are smaller cities relatively as numerous; low-

income societies are, relatively, village societies, though towns and one or more cities of moderate or large size exist in almost every country.

13. They are not democratic societies. Traditional societies tend to be hierarchical and more or less authoritarian in political structure. Such structure persisted for centuries and in some societies for several millenia, up to modern times, and not necessarily because the masses were held in oppression by force. Hierarchical structure apparently seemed "right." Life was not all a matter of submission; hierarchy gave everyone at least some taste of power; even the lowliest peasant obtained his modicum of hierarchical authority as he became an older brother, a husband and father, and an elder in his village. Problems that could not be settled on the basis of traditional skill or traditional local knowledge were decided by cautious working out of village consensus, or passed further upward for decision on the basis of authority; individuals were thus relieved of the anxiety of responsibility. But, to whatever degree these considerations may have made hierarchical and authoritarian political structures satisfying during many periods in the past, the relationships that were satisfying have now been breaking down, and discontent is widespread. But where the discontent has found a popular solution, that solution has been not the establishment of democratic forms of government but the replacement of one dictator by another (Farouk by Naguib, then Nasser; Batista by Castro; etc.). The desire for authoritarian government persists. In other countries the discontent has been either relieved or suppressed by military dictatorships.

Voting participation has been low. In many lower income countries where it is now high, the votes cast seem to reflect loyalty to a leader rather than individual consideration of political issues. The process of voting is a modern innovation in these societies, imposed by colonial rulers who wished to introduce at least a façade of democratice practices. Previously, and of course also under colonial rule, this is not how leaders were chosen or policies decided. To large sections of the populations of many low-income societies, it still seems unnatural.

14. Written communication has not served the function in these societies that it does in more complex ones, and literacy is low. So also is the level of education, newspaper circulation, attendance at cinemas, and radio ownership and use. These facts would seem obvious without systematic empirical evidence; they are also well attested statistically.[4] The causes, of course, are lack of income as well as traditional tastes.

15. Lastly, in the less developed economies there is only a small and socially weak "middle class"; a relatively small number of professional men, salaried business managers and technicians, and self-employed businessmen above the cottage industry level. Typically, all of the "elites"—

---

[4] Taylor and Hudson (1972) present a comprehensive collection of relevant statistics.

from the central economically and politically powerful group through government, military, and religious officials and administrators, professional men, and lesser landlords down to village head men, with their families—constitute no more than, say, 2 to 4% of the population.

All of these characteristics, with the possible exception of the presence of large estates, change as economic growth proceeds. Indirectly, in due time economic growth is likely to cause a break-up of large, little-productive estates, but large, productive agricultural enterprises may survive the growth process or, if they are destroyed through political action at one stage of development, will reappear at a later one.

CHANGES CONCOMITANT WITH ECONOMIC GROWTH

Theories of how growth begins or why it does not begin will be summarized and evaluated in Chapter 7. In the remainder of this chapter, an ongoing process of increase in productivity and aggregate income is taken for granted, and changes in the economy and society that have been observed historically to accompany growth are discussed. Some are clearly results of growth. Some may be causes, or with growth may be joint effects of some third factor. The changes are progressive; change continues in high-income societies as in low ones. Up to the present time it gives no indication of approaching an end. It is reasonably certain that the nature of economic change in the higher income countries as productivity increases further in the future will be an extension of the changes that have occurred to the present. It is much less possible to predict that nature of future social and political change—for example, the impact of increasing economic and social complexity and mobility on democracy.

First an array of changes, both economic and noneconomic, are noted below; then more intensive attention is given to a type of change that will be of special interest to us, namely, change in relative output, productivity, and income in the three economic sectors.

Economic Changes

The major economic changes that accompany growth are the following:

1. Methods of production change in various ways, among which the following are conspicuous:

a. The ratio of capital inputs to labor inputs in production increases steadily, on the average, though not in every enterprise. In the process, capital goods become more and more complex.

b. The size of productive units, on the average, increases, measured by quantity of capital employed, labor employed, or output. The complexity of productive units increases also.

c. Division of labor among productive units as well as within them increases. To a greater and greater extent, enterprises become suppliers of material products or services to others. An increasingly complex productive network develops. More and more industrial products become standardized, their parts interchangeable. They also become increasingly complex, and their variety increases, as increasing income permits the average consumer to enjoy an increasing variety of consumption.

2. The markets available to producers become larger, in two ways:

a. The domestic market available to the average producer increases in size, both because per capita income rises and because steadily improving transportation and communication increase the geographical area which a given producer may serve. This is especially true of manufacturers and producers of perishable foodstuffs. Producers of agricultural staples may notice no change (though in fact their products may travel farther), and for many local services the market does not expand greatly.

b. The country's exports and imports increase. Thus many producers both buy and sell in an international market. Typically both imports and exports increase both absolutely and as a percentage of national product for a time. The increase in their ratio to national product then tapers off. Their later course varies greatly among countries, depending on the country's variety of natural resources and degree of specialization.

3. The structure of production, that is, the relative amounts of different types of goods produced, changes. The changes are not random; they follow a universal law. Inexorably, secondary industry increases in size relative to primary industry and then, as per capita income increases further, tertiary industry (services) increases in size relative to both.

4. The average value of output per worker becomes greater in secondary industry and then in tertiary industry than in primary industry. The differences persist. Once manufacturing has developed, only in the very exceptional case of a country that has a great comparative advantage in agriculture will the value of output per worker in agriculture ever thereafter be as high as in industry. Because of these differences in the value of output per worker, trends in the distribution of the labor force more or less parallel the trends in the distribution of production but there remains, apparently forever, a larger percentage of the labor force than of GDP in agriculture.

5. The composition of foreign trade changes. The imports of almost all low-income countries are largely industrial, though some import agricultural products and pay for them with mineral products. As income rises the share of consumer goods in imports falls and that of capital goods, raw materials, and fuels rises. (Consumer goods imports become a decreasing share of total consumption, and capital goods imports a decreasing share of domestic investment. The share of capital goods in imports rises because the ratio of investment to GDP rises.)

The exports of the lowest income countries initially are of primary products, together with perhaps a few handicraft products, since the country cannot compete internationally in the production of any others. The sale of primary or very slightly processed products will typically provide the major share of foreign exchange earnings during the first several generations of the development process, but the share of secondary products in exports will steadily rise. Resource-poor Japan provides an exception; handicraft and then manufactured products became dominant among her exports early in her modern development period. Manufactured products have rapidly become important among the exports of South Korea, Taiwan, and Singapore early in their development process.

6. The percentage of gross national income saved rises. This rise does not continue indefinitely. Rather, the saving rate rises to some higher level; then the rise tapers off.

It seems plausible that as a country's income level rises its people would save a larger share of their income because they can better afford to. However, this explanation of the increase in the saving rate is inadequate. Above a moderate level of income the absolute level of income in a society seems to have little to do with saving rates. This complex phenomenon is discussed in Chapter 13.

7. At least as measured by the income share of high-income receivers, the distribution of income after taxes in industrial countries is less unequal than in low-income agricultural countries. At some time during the period of development the desire of groups influential in the government to tax high-income groups or the ability to do so or both increases.

8. The country begins a demographic revolution. This process has been discussed in Chapter 3. Present rates of population increase are shown in Table 4–5.

Institutional and Noneconomic Correlates of Growth

It is worthwhile to repeat that the changes discussed in this section are not necessarily results of growth. It is easy to assume facilely that economic growth is the cause, all other change the result. In fact, causation probably runs in many directions among noneconomic and economic variables.

As the changes in the methods, productivity, and structure of production proceed, economic institutions also change progressively. Producers of food and clothing produce an increasing surplus above their own needs. An increasing share of production therefore comes to be for the market rather than for their own use. The use of money in the exchange of goods becomes increasingly convenient and necessary, and an ever-increasing share of entrepreneurs and workers engage in the production of goods of which they themselves use none, or an insignificant fraction.

TABLE 4–5

High and Low Rates of Population Increase, Asia, Africa, Latin America, 1965–71

Below 1.5 Percent		3.0 Percent or Above	
		Africa	
Angola	1.3	Libya	3.7
Gabon	1.0	Rhodesia	3.5
Portuguese Guinea	0.9	Togo	3.4
		Ivory Coast	3.3
		Rwanda	3.3
		Kenya	3.3
		South Africa	3.1
		Liberia	3.1
		Asia	
Cyprus	1.2	Kuwait	9.8
Japan	1.1	Qatar	9.6
		United Arab Emirates	9.5
		Brunei	3.6
		Jordan	3.4
		Syria	3.3
		Iraq	3.2
		Thailand	3.1
		Philippines	3.1
		Iran	3.0
		Latin America	
Jamaica	1.3	El Salvador	3.9
Uruguay	1.3	French Guiana	3.7
Puerto Rico	1.2	Mexico	3.5
Martinique	1.0	Ecuador	3.4
Trinidad and Tobago	0.9	Venezuela	3.4
		Guatemala	3.4
		Colombia	3.2
		Paraguay	3.1
		Peru	3.1
		Panama	3.1
		Nicaragua	3.0
		Honduras	3.0

Source: *World Bank Atlas*, 1973.

Commercial banking becomes of increasing importance, as do capital market institutions. Money, having replaced barter, is in turn largely replaced by bank debits and credits, and later an increasing share of financial payments are settled by bookkeeping clearing devices.

Cities become attractive loci of production for an increasing share of goods and become also increasingly attractive consumer centers. An increasing fraction of the total population comes to live in them, though as transportation facilities, vehicles, and communication improve, diffusion from the industrial centers occurs, until in the future industry may be rather evenly spread over large areas of some countries, with urban centers for commercial, governmental, and consumer purposes increasing the population density here and there.

Economic transactions become increasingly contractual, impersonal, and between strangers. Their chief sanction continues to be social expectation; but increasingly the sanction, if normal expectations break down, becomes legal enforcement rather than community relationships and power and status relationships.

Literacy, education beyond literacy, and "media participation" all increase. That is, increasingly people listen to radios, look at moving pictures, and later, as they become effectively literate, read newspapers and magazines.

In some senses, political participation also increases. To an increasing degree, individuals who previously had left it to their leaders to decide political questions come to have and express opinions about them, and thereby affect political decisions. However, the increase in political participation may taper off or even be reversed as a high degree of industrialization is reached. Participation in the formulation of national policies, as measured by the percentage of eligible voters who vote, is less in the United States than in various countries with lower per capita incomes, though this may be entirely unrelated to the U.S. level of income.

The earlier increase in political participation is an aspect of a change in political structure. In a study published in 1960, J. S. Coleman showed that if the countries of Asia and Africa were ranked by their level of economic development, and were then divided into three groups according to their political structure—authoritarian, semicompetitive, and competitive—there is correlation between the economic rankings and the political classification. The correlation also appeared among Latin American countries. "Competitive" here means that the interests and views of different groups within the society are taken into account in arriving at policy decisions, rather than decisions being handed down by authoritarian leaders.[5] Because of the establishment of military dictatorships in Brazil, Chile, and Uruguay since the Coleman study, the correlation in Latin America would be barely discernible today.

In other continents as well, the correlation between economic development and the democratization of government is far from perfect. In a

---

[5] See Almond and Coleman (1960). The analysis cited here is in the concluding chapter, written by Coleman. The index of economic development is not simply level of per capita income; rather, a weighted index derived by averaging together rankings in various measures of industrialization, urbanization, education, use of communications media, etc., was used. For a similar study, using the same method with somewhat later and additional data, see Hagen (1962).

number of countries, authoritarian government has persisted as income rose, or has reappeared where democracy had once been established.

Some of these changes are aspects of a change in the relationships of life known to political scientists and sociologists as "structural differentiation" or "role differentiation." In a traditional peasant society, many actions and decisions have simultaneously economic, social, political, and perhaps also religious aspects. The consumer unit, the family, is also the business enterprise. In some economies in which land is owned rather than rented, there is no institution of purchase or sale of land; the land one uses is part of the structure of the community, and one's family, having acquired the right to use it in some distant past time, retains that right as long as it continues to be a member of the community, but has no power to transfer it to anyone else. In any village, families maintain a relationship of cautious and careful reciprocity and power balance in which the exchanges of services and goods are parts of a web of social, political, and religious relationships. To fail in an economic exchange, or to abandon the web of economic reciprocity, would be to cause social, political, and perhaps religious offense. Social structure greatly affects economic relations. The person to whom one owes rent fairly typically also exercises political and social power, and may command one to sell one's produce to him, rather than merely bargaining for it. One must respect the wishes of elite persons—and it seems right that one should—and in economic as well as political or religious affairs. One may not conceive of the economic, social, political, and religious aspects of behavior separately; they fuse in most actions. Some of the comments above apply only to villages, but only less complex interrelationships exist in more urban communities. Only between bazaar traders and their customers are economic and other aspects of relationships likely to be fairly sharply distinct.

As economic development proceeds, these strands are gradually unraveled. With the development of the market, impersonal economic relationships, wider social and political contacts, increase in personal options, and general increase in the complexity of life, gradually the individual's various roles in life become increasingly separate from each other. Different types of relationship are no longer twined together into a single rope. One's various roles separate. For example, the sense that the only safe and proper business associates are one's relatives slowly weakens; gradually it becomes respectable for an elite person to work for salary, in a corporation, with nonrelatives. Economic theory alone becomes increasingly useful and sufficient in analyzing economic transactions.

It is tempting to suggest that expansion of the market and rise in income are the basic causes of this set of changes and the various noneconomic changes results. And certainly there is a great deal of truth in this statement. But causation may also run in the other direction, or in both directions, economic and noneconomic change each furthering the other. And some factors not mentioned in the paragraphs above may be the causes of both economic and noneconomic change. For example, one cannot reject out of hand the hypothesis that the association between technical progress and the emergence of more competitive (roughly, more democratic) government is due to the fact that in some eras of history some social forces cause an increase in self-reliance among erstwhile traditional people, and that this increased self-reliance is a cause of both the technical progress and the demand for an increased voice in political decisions.

A team of scholars who spent some years studying the process of industrialization around the world ventured the conclusion in 1960, and reaffirmed it in 1971, that

> industrial systems, regardless of the cultural background out of which they emerge and the path they originally follow, tend to become more alike over an extended period of time; that systems, whether under middle-class or communist or dynastic leadership, move towards "pluralistic industrialism" where the State, the enterprise or association, and the individual all share a substantial degree of power and influence over productive activities. The process of convergence moves sometimes faster and sometimes slower and is, on occasion, reversed, but it is a long-run development of fundamental significance. It points the general direction of change.[6]

One aspect of economic development not much stressed above is the increased instability of family life that it brings. Before economic change entered his society, the peasant villager tended to live from birth to death in his same village. As productivity rises and the patterns of consumption and production change progressively, an indefinitely continuing shift of the labor force is impelled. As business enterprises increase in size and in the geographic scope of their business, a series of moves becomes a normal part of an executive's career. Moreover, changes in modes of transportation and communication make changes in the location of one's home attractive: village life, town life, urban life, suburbanization, and exurbanization follow one another, and three of them often in the same lifetime. As income and economic complexity increase, these changes become more common. It has been estimated that one fifth of all U.S. families change their place of residence during each year. Probably few other countries yet face the same phenomenon in equal degree, but family instability is undoubtedly tending to increase in all developing countries.

This mobility constitutes the rootlessness of life so often commented

---

[6] Kerr, Dunlop, Harbison, and Myers (1971). See also the same authors (1964), final chapter. For a group of discussions of the same topic, see Faunce and Form (1969).

on in the United States. Many U.S. families, perhaps a large majority, make few permanent friends, take little part in the political or social life of their community, develop no sense of having a permanent home. Few U.S. children learn as children the relationships of life to which they must adapt as adults. Few parents raise their children in an environment which they understand from their own experience as children. We do not know what the effects of this rootlessness and this purposelessness (in a sense) of child nurture are. The effects, whatever they may be, on motivations, conscious and unconscious, on values, on hopes and diffuse fears and anxieties, are results of continuing technical progress additional to the social and political results sketched briefly above.

HOW THE THREE SECTORS FARE DURING GROWTH: CHANGES IN SHARES

Changes in relative production and productivity in the three sectors of the economy were mentioned above. They are discussed at some length here.

The Data

In the mid-1930s, A. G. B. Fisher formalized concepts that had been previously present in economic writings only in a vague form, by introducing the concepts of primary, secondary, and tertiary sectors of the economy. Fisher (1935) argued, without quantitative evidence, that as income rises demand shifts from the primary to the secondary and then to the tertiary industries.[7]

Colin Clark (1940, 1951, 1957), deriving a variety of economic estimates from refractory materials in imaginative ways (with, necessarily, wide margins of error), extended Fisher's analysis and in the process verified it. Using comparative international estimates as his basis, Clark demonstrated that the proportions of national output in the three sectors vary in general as Fisher has asserted and that the percentages of the labor force engaged in the three sectors varies correspondingly.

Hollis Chenery (1960) did a statistical study of the share of industry in the economic activity of 51 countries with a wide range of income levels, in 1950 or a nearby year. Their per capita incomes ranged from $50 (Burma) to $1,291 (Canada). The shift in the composition of production as one moves to higher levels of income among these countries probably corresponds roughly to the shift within each country as income rises over time.[8] The share of manufacturing in a country with a popula-

---

[7] See also Fisher (1939).

[8] Kuznets (1957, p. 17) concluded after studying both that "the direct evidence on long-term trends in the industrial structure of national product is remarkably consistent with that provided" by the intercountry data.

tion of 10 million, as calculated from Chenery's regression on income level and population size, rose from 12% of national income at an income level of $100 to 33% at an income level of $1,000. The share of primary production fell from 45% to 15%. The "growth elasticity of demand" for manufactured products was 1.44. That is, the percentage rate of increase in the consumption plus export of industrial products was about 1.44 times as fast as the percentage rate of increase in per capita income. Such a relationship cannot be projected indefinitely to higher incomes, for at some higher level it would indicate industrial production constituting more than total gross domestic product. But within the range of incomes studied by Chenery, the fit is moderately good, in spite of differences in country size, natural resources, trade patterns, and levels of technology at given levels of income.[9]

The data of Table 4–2 are impressive evidence that economic growth was proceeding steadily between 1950 and 1960, and impressive evidence also of its effects on the sectoral distribution of the labor force. Moreover, the intercontinental comparison in that table shows vividly the effects of the differences among the three regions in income levels.

From data for the high-income countries we can see how far the shifts in sectoral shares have proceeded. In those countries, the labor force share in the primary sector has declined to well under 10%. In many it is still declining. The percentage in the secondary sector rises steadily with income to a maximum somewhere between 30 and 50; then it too tends to decline. The maximum reached probably depends largely on the size of the country and on its net exports of manufactured goods, that is, on the

---

[9] Chenery's regression was log linear. Because postwar U.S. census data did not have the necessary breakdowns, Chenery included 1939 data for the United States, together with postwar data for all other countries except Italy. United States per capita income in 1939 was $1,065; the United States was out near the tail of the distribution. Since 1939 dollars had much greater purchasing power than postwar dollars, the regression coefficient is subject to some qualification. The use of postwar data for the United States, or the use of 1939 data revalued to postwar prices might have altered the coefficient appreciably. Though the United States 1939 data affected the regression, the United States lay off the regression lines. Chenery uses the regression to analyze changes only up to national income of $1,000 per capita in early postwar prices.

Yet as stated in the text the fit is moderately good. Chenery plotted industrial output 50% greater and 50% less in absolute amount than that indicated by a least-squares regression line relating per capita income and industrial value added in a country of given size. (The size selected was a population of 10 million.) An increase of 50% in industrial output corresponds to an increase in per capita income of about one third, according to Chenery's regression—the growth achieved in 20 years at a growth rate of 1.5% per year; and a decrease of 50% represents some 30 years less of growth at this annual rate. Only 5 of the 51 countries lay outside these lines. That is, the great majority of the countries were, so to speak, less than a generation ahead or behind the degree of industrialization their level of per capita income would suggest. The main cause of the deviation from the regression line were economies of scale in manufacturing (discussed in Chap. 12). The larger the population of a country, the higher the share of manufacturing in national output.

comparative advantage in manufacturing which it attains through economies of scale. The labor force share in the tertiary sector, above 50% in some of the highest income countries (and in Israel) has not reached its limit. All that can be said about ultimate limits is that that for the primary sector will be above zero percent and that for the tertiary sector below 100.

Figure 4–1 shows the historical trends in the United States. The share of the labor force engaged in the primary sector began to fall very early, in spite of the empty lands to be filled. Yet the figure shows vividly the long-continuing importance of agriculture. In spite of the booming industrialization of the United States, the absolute number of persons engaged in the primary sector rose until 1910. In any country in which economic growth is not rapid, the agricultural population may grow indefinitely. In countries without "empty lands," if growth is rapid the absolute decline in employment in the primary sector may begin sooner than it did in the United States, but it will hardly begin before two or three generations after the beginning of rapid economic growth.

In Chenery's analysis, the share of tertiary value added in national income other than transportation and communication rises very slowly between per capita income levels of $100 and $1,000, and the regression coefficient, though above unity, is not significantly different from unity at

FIGURE 4–1

Sectoral Distribution of Labor Force, United States (Historical)

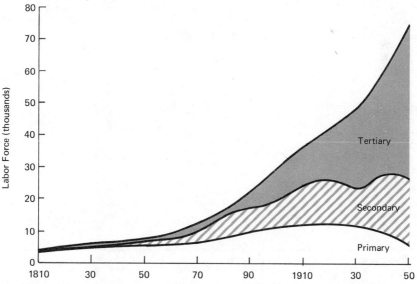

Source: Lebergott (1966), p. 118. Estimates for secondary sector for 1820 and 1830 interpolated.

a 95% confidence level. Rapid expansion in this sector at higher income levels was noted above. It would be surprising if there was a sudden change in trend. In fact, there almost certainly is not. The explanation seems to be as follows: The tertiary sector includes two distinct types of services: personal services mainly in the home, and professional, recreational, and other commercial services plus those of government. Let me term these Tertiary A and Tertiary B, respectively. As per capita income rises, the share of Tertiary B in national income probably expands from very low income levels onward. However, for reasons to be explained in the following section, the cost of services rises faster than the cost of other products, and the services of Tertiary A become too expensive to be afforded. The decline in employment and output in Tertiary A masks the rise in them in Tertiary B when the two are combined. But when Tertiary A has pretty much dried up, at incomes somewhat above $1,000 per capita in 1974 prices, the rapid rise in Tertiary B swells the sector as a whole.

As Table 4–6 shows, the relationship between the income level and the labor force share in the tertiary sector varies considerably among coun-

TABLE 4–6
Percentage of Labor Force in the Tertiary Sector, Related to Income Per Capita, Selected Countries

Country	GDP Per Capita 1960	Percent of Labor Force in Tertiary Sector, Recent Year
United States	2,817	53.1
Canada	2,063	46.6
Sweden	1,644	39.9
United Kingdom	1,353	47.5
Israel	830	57.4
Argentina	559	46.9
Chile	479	41.5
Japan	456	30.2
Mexico	346	26.1
Colombia	295	14.1
Portugal	285	26.9
El Salvador	232	22.4
Honduras	195	9.5
Ecuador	180	24.1
Egypt	151	29.4
Ceylon	138	36.8[*]
Philippines	137	19.9
Thailand	99	12.9
India	78	18.7

[*] Excludes electricity, gas, and water supply.
Source: GDP per capita, 1960: Table 1–8. Percent of labor force in agriculture: Kuznets (*Q.A.E.G.N.*, 2), pp. 75–80.

tries. Notably, the country's comparative advantage in trade and finance influences it. Lebanon, with a per capita GNP between $300 and $350, has some two thirds of her labor force in the tertiary sector, probably the highest ratio in the world.

The Causes

Why are there such great sectoral shifts? The cause most often discussed is shifts in demand as income rises, but this in fact is only one of three major causes.

The shift in relative demand is indeed an important cause. People's stomachs do not grow with their incomes, and at high incomes as at low they have only one body to clothe. As incomes rise they demand products that are more and more processed, and then more and more medical and professional care, recreation, travel, education and other governmental services. A second important cause is the substitution of domestic production for the import of manufactured goods. Up to some level of income this is a more important cause of the growth of industry than is the shift in demand. The third is a statistical illusion. Secondary and tertiary activities which at low incomes were incorporated within agriculture are separated from it as growth proceeds: "the making of clothing, utensils, furniture, weapons, jewelry, the processing of crops, the construction of houses, other buildings, and boats." "Fetching water, gathering fuel, educating, litigating, adjudicating, healing, regulating individual conduct, propitiating the Deity, waging war, and governing are increasingly turned over to public utilities and oil companies, and to teachers, lawyers, judges, doctors, policemen, priests, soldiers, and congressmen."[10]

Income Elasticities of Demand as Explanation

Engel was the first economist to suggest that there is a systematic change in the pattern of consumer expenditures as income rises.[11] His law describes the steady decrease in the share devoted to food. As income rises, people eat more, as the intercountry comparison of caloric intake in Figure 4–2 suggests. (The scatter is fairly wide; factors other than income affect caloric intake. Ireland, 60, is the extreme case. However, the large influence of income is clear.) But while absolute expendi-

---

[10] Kilby and Johnston (1972). The phrase within the first pair of quotation marks is by Kilby and Johnston. The second is quoted by them from Jones (1960). This point is also made by Bauer and Yamey (1951).

[11] The German statistician Ernst Engel, in a book published in 1857. He should not be confused with Karl Marx's collaborator, Friedrich Engels.

FIGURE 4–2
Caloric Intake Per Capita 1957–60, Related to GDP Per Capita, 1960

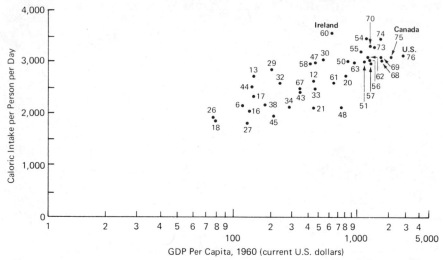

Source: GDP per capita, 1960, Hagen and Hawrylyshyn (1969); caloric intake, United Nations (1963).

ture increases, the share of income spent for food declines as income rises. In United States data, comparing families at different income levels, this effect is seen.[12] In the United States data, the percentage of income spent for housing (rent and utilities) remains about constant over a considerable span of income, then declines. Expenditures on clothing, transportation, education, and recreation increase more rapidly than income until high incomes are reached. Saving increases faster than income, and especially rapidly at high incomes.

These U.S. data suggest what happens to consumer demands, not to sectoral shares, as income rises. The latter vary quite differently. Farm receipts for foodstuffs rise more slowly than do consumer expenditures for the food products, for the percentage markup between farm and retail prices increases because of increased processing and other causes discussed later in this chapter. L. M. Goreux has estimated for various regions the income elasticity of demand for "farm foods," that is, the ratio

---

[12] In a much finer classification of goods, the absolute expenditure for many goods declines at some point as income rises, higher quality goods of similar types being substituted. Goods for which this decline occurs at low levels of income—relatively unattractive goods that must of necessity be used at very low incomes because they are cheap, but which are abandoned in part when income begins to rise—are termed "inferior goods." Potatoes and spaghetti are examples. In a broader use of the term, many goods become inferior goods at some level of income.

of the percentage rise in food payments to farmers to the percentage rise in consumer income. His figures are:[13]

Asia and the Far East, excluding Japan 0.9
Near East and Africa, excluding South Africa 0.7
Latin America, excluding Argentina and Uruguay 0.6
Japan 0.6
Mediterranean Europe 0.55
European Economic Community 0.5
Other Western Europe 0.2
North America 0.16

Hence as economic growth proceeds agricultural production as a whole declines in relative quantitative importance.

Shifts in Supply as Explanation

Yet in the expansion of manufacturing, shifts in consumer demand are less important than changes in the source of supply, at least until fairly high income levels are reached. The evidence is provided by Chenery's study.

Chenery multiplied the value added in each sector and subsector at an income level of $100 by 6, to arrive at the value each would have at an income level of $600 if the growth elasticity of demand for each was unity. There he calculated the value added for each at $600 from his regression equations, and analyzed from other data the sources of deviation from unit elasticity. For manufacturing, the increase in final demand directly and indirectly[14] accounted for 32% of the increased share of manufacturing. The replacement of imports by domestic production ("import substitution") accounted for 50%. The residual of 18% was not caused by increase in final demand. Chenery suspects that it was caused largely by the replacement of handicrafts and cottage industry by manufacturing (an illustration of the third cause mentioned above).

VALUE PRODUCTIVITY IN THE THREE SECTORS

As income rises, the demand for manufactured products continually rises relative to that for agricultural products. This simple fact is the explanation of much that is otherwise mysterious.

Industrial producers trying to recruit labor from agriculture in order to expand production to meet expanding demand cannot do so unless they are able to pay wages well above agricultural incomes. For, as is well

---

[13] A summary of Goreux's estimates is presented in FAO (1962), Table 12. The estimates are based on farm value during the period 1957–59. I have them from T. W. Schultz (1964), p. 13.

[14] That is, through increased production of intermediate goods.

known, labor is imperfectly mobile, and will not move from familiar circumstances to a new occupation and community unless a considerable increase in income is offered. The rising relative demand for industrial products therefore merely bids up their relative price, until this rise in price has increased the value productivity of labor, relative to that in agriculture, sufficiently so that a continuing flow of labor can be attracted to industry. The disparity will continue, so long as the demand for industrial products rises faster than that for agricultural products.[15] This aspect of the growth process, and not any inherent superiority of manufacturing industry, is the cause of the difference in value productivity.

This simplified and imprecise explanation of the process involved has omitted reference to some complicating factors. In certain very exceptional conditions the value productivity of labor may rise as fast in agriculture as in industry. The only historical case of importance in which this has happened is New Zealand, where immigrants colonized "empty lands" and the growing country's comparative advantage in agriculture was so great that the total rise (domestic and foreign) in demand for agricultural products was faster than that for industrial products. Conceivably, the value productivity of labor might rise no faster in industry than in agriculture if a flood of immigrant laborers into the manufacturing industry of a country swelled industrial output, but in fact this has not occurred. A flood of immigrants flowed into American industry from 1865 to 1914, and simultaneously the world eagerly bought the agricultural exports of the United States; yet the income elasticity of demand for industrial products outweighed these effects, and value productivity has remained higher in industry.

In some developing countries in which governments have stressed industrial development to the neglect of agriculture, the relative supply of agricultural products has increased less than the relative demand for them, and their price has risen relative to that of industrial products. India in the 1960s is an illustration. But in none of these cases has the process gone far enough to raise per capita income in agriculture to equality with that in industry—though in the absence of price controls this might have happened in a few countries if U.S. shipments of surplus agricultural commodities had not augmented the domestic supply.

The magnitude of the usual excess of the value productivity of labor in industry over that in agriculture is considerable. W. Arthur Lewis (1954, p. 150) has estimated that "there is usually a gap of 30% or more between

---

[15] Alternatively, productivity in industry may increase at a rate faster than that in agriculture—a rate fast enough to meet the faster increase in demand. This faster rate of increase in physical productivity also constitutes a faster rate of increase in value productivity. Value productivity in industry will continue to rise above that in agriculture until the disparity becomes sufficient to draw a continuing flow of labor from agriculture.

capitalist wages and subsistence earnings." This seems a minimum estimate of the differential which has been needed in the past to draw
workers from agriculture to industry. Rough estimates for a number of
low-income countries show per capita income in all nonagricultural
pursuits combined as between 2 and 2.5 times that in agriculture. For
example, to take two cases at contrasting income levels, in India the
average per-worker product in agriculture, forestry, and fishing in
1948–53 is estimated to have been only 42% of that in other industries,
even when unpaid family labor in agriculture is excluded. In the United
States, the corresponding ratio was 0.26 in 1870, 0.46 in 1910, and 0.56 in
1950. (Kuznets, *Q.A.E.G.N.*, 2, 2pp. Tables). These data overstate the
true difference in income between farm families and other families, for
farm families also obtain income from home and cottage industry and
petty trade. With allowance for these adjustments, a large differential
remains. Kuznets presents estimates of the sectoral distribution of income
over a long period in 14 countries (the lowest income country among
them being Hungary), and for recent years in 45 countries. The data
show a markedly higher income in manufacturing than in agriculture
except in Australia and New Zealand. The median of the ratios for the 14
countries in the 1890s was 1.42. In the 20th century the median ratio rose
to 1.89.[16] These estimates, of course, include profits and other nonwage
income. An estimate of weekly wages of agricultural workers and unskilled urban workers in nine countries in 1952 and 1953 shows a median
ratio of 1.43.[17]

The Rumanian economist Manoilesco (1931) argued that manufacturing is inherently more productive than agriculture. He was referring, of
course, to value productivity, not physical productivity. Comparison of
physical productivity is impossible, since different goods are produced.
Concerning physical productivity, only the rates of change can be compared. His argument is unclear, a fact that prolonged the attention given
to his book, for if the argument had been stated clearly it would have
been apparent that it was wrong. There is no such inherent difference.
The difference in value productivity is due simply to the effects analyzed
above of differences in income elasticities of demand.

Because per capita income in secondary and tertiary industries is much
higher than in primary ones, the intersectoral shift in the labor force itself
brings some of the rise in per capita income as development proceeds.
Kuznets (*Q.A.E.G.N.* Table 24) has calculated that intersectoral shifts
caused between 25% and 30% of the rise in per capita income in the U.K.,
the U.S., and Sweden during the first half of the 20th century (but only

---

[16] Incomes in manufacturing alone are probably typically 10% or 15% lower than in
all nonagriculture.

[17] Hagen (1958).

11% of that in Hungary). It may have caused 20 or 25% of the rise in per capita income income in Japan since World War II.

Elasticities, Cost Trends, and Income in the Tertiary Sector

The considerations discussed above explain phenomena puzzling to many laymen: why "farmers get an ever-decreasing share of the consumer's food dollar" and "the cost of services always keeps rising faster than other prices." The statements are exaggerations; they need qualification; but there is a good deal of truth in them.

The trends are easily explained. In personal services the rate of increase in productivity has been low because services remain relatively labor-intensive in spite of the invention of labor-saving devices. Incomes in services therefore lags as average per capita income rises, and workers shift to other occupations until the decreasing relative supply of services permits price rises which yield increases in real income paralleling (but always lagging behind) those elsewhere. This continuing process is the way in which, in any country, the sectors experiencing a slow rate of productivity increase share in the fruits of productivity increase elsewhere in the economy. This is why the price of haircuts, domestic service, etc., in any developing country, must rise secularly relative to prices in general, and why the mark-up between wholesale and retail prices steadily increases relative to the price or agricultural or manufactured products, so that the farmers in any country receive a steadily decreasing share of the consumer's dollar.[18]

On the other hand, both the rate of increase in productivity in transportation, recreation, and some communication services and the income elasticity of demand for them are high. Falling production costs and competition have therefore caused their prices to fall relative to other prices, even though rapidly increasing demand has caused the volume of these services to grow rapidly and income in some of these industries to rise rapidly. The income elasticity of demand for government services is so high that the share of the labor force engaged in producing them grows steadily even though they are labor-intensive and their relative cost therefore rises secularly.

THE GRADUALNESS OF GROWTH

One last aspect of growth may appropriately be mentioned here. This is its gradualness.

We used to think that rise in per capita income in each country begins

---

[18] And this is why an increase in wages and other incomes equal to the increase in productivity, in the industries where that increase is most rapid, is inflationary, even though prices of that industry remain constant.

rather abruptly.[19] However, as our historical information has improved, we have come to realize increasingly that in probably every developing country growth began quietly and gradually over a period of decades or even generations before it accelerated to a rapid pace easy to identify.

Three examples from the present high-income countries will illustrate. The English Industrial Revolution is sometimes dated as beginning in the 1780s, or at some time after the middle of the 18th century. Yet in fact technical progress in England had been gaining momentum for three centuries previously. In the 13th and 14th centuries, English wool exports consisted almost wholly of the sale of raw wool, mainly to the Flemish, who did the spinning and weaving. The Dutch were (especially a little later) the world's leading dyers and finishers. In the 15th century, England had advanced sufficiently in spinning and weaving techniques so that she began to spin and weave on a large scale and sell grey goods abroad in competition with the Flemish. By the 17th century, she had overtaken the Dutch in dyeing and finishing, and was selling finished goods abroad. By 1660, or soon after that date, she was producing two million tons of coal per year, perhaps five times the production of the rest of the world.[20] The most important proximate cause of her early use of coal was the growing exhaustion of her forests, but no doubt her coal consumption also resulted in part from her technological forwardness.

In the 17th century, having conquered coastal areas in India, she observed the cotton spinning skill of the Indians and the attractiveness of cotton fabrics for many purposes. Skillful and innovational English textile manufacturers took over and improved Indian methods. Several inventions very early in the 18th century (notably Kay's fly shuttle of 1704 and Newcomen's atmospheric steam engine) increased England's technical advantage in the textile industry and reduced her technical disadvantage in mining. The burst of inventions of 1750–1800 increased her cost advantage and brought a spurt of advance beginning in the early 1780s. Because she could undersell her continental competitors and surpass their quality, her production and exports increased at unprecedented rates, decade after decade, during most of the 19th century. Her rapidly expanding scale of production in turn drew British energies into devising increasingly effective methods of power-driven mechanized production.

But this was the cumulation of a four-century period of advance in techniques. She had been innovating more effectively than her neighbors since the 15th century. First she had overtaken and then surpassed them. The world market had been her reward. To date her economic growth from the 18th century and to assume that the availability of the world

---

[19] A widely read book that presented that concept is W. W. Rostow, *The Stages of Economic Growth* (1960).

[20] Singer, Holymard, Hall, et al. (1957).

market caused it is, to adopt a phrase used by Donald Culross Peattie, the "village idiot" theory of Britain's economic growth.[21]

Russia provides a second example. Russia's economic growth is sometimes assumed to begin with the Bolshevik Revolution of 1917; yet the best estimate is that per capita income in Russia rose at a rate of 0.75% annually between 1860 and the 1880s, and at a rate of 1% between the time and World War I.[22]

Japan provides a third example. It was not uncommon a few decades ago for American scholars to think of Japan's economic growth as having begun rather abruptly at some time within the last quarter of the 19th century. We now know that in some regions of Japan a sort of agricultural revolution took place slowly during the Ashikaga Period (1338–1568), and that even though factories had not yet appeared, productivity in handicrafts increased markedly during the Tokugawa Period (1600–1867). Japan's amazing growth in the late 19th and 20th centuries was only a flowering of an earlier process.[23]

So it is with the present lower income countries of the world. It is impossible to date the beginning of growth precisely, but study of the economic history of one of those countries after another has caused scholars to push back in time by several decades or several generations the period at which to place the beginning of growth.[24] The dates taken in many earlier studies as those when growth began may better be regarded as the dates for which fairly good economic statistics first became available.

---

[21] "The beginnings of spring, the true beginnings, are quite unlike [and much earlier than] the springtides of which poets and musicians sing. The artists become conscious of spring in late April, or May, when it is not too much to say that the village idiot would observe that birds are singing and nesting, that fields bear up their freight of flowering and ants return to their proverbial industry" Peattie (1935).

[22] R. W. Goldsmith (1961). Population growth and that of aggregate output were 1.5% higher. Goldsmith suggests that the figures for aggregate and per capita growth for each period have a margin of error of 0.25% in either direction. Concerning Russia see also P. Gregory (1972).

[23] See Reischauer and Fairbank (1958) and T. C. Smith (1955, 1959).

[24] See concerning: *Argentina:* Di Tella and Zymelman (1967); Diaz Alejandro (1967); Chaps. 1, 3, and 6; *Brazil:* N. H. Leff (1967); *Colombia:* Ospina Vasquez (1955); W. McGreevey (1965).

The Difficulty of Innovation: 5
Trade and Agriculture

I referred in the previous chapter to the view that the process of economic development in the lower income countries is an easy matter of their taking over and using the input-saving machines that have been invented in the West. That view is no longer held by competent students of economic development. It is a productive system, not merely individual pieces of equipment, that gives the West its productivity. Most industrial products of Western countries are made, not by single plants, but literally by hundreds of plants—in effect, by almost the entire productive complex. Few machines or industrial or agricultural plants will work as efficiently outside of the complex within which they fit as in it; most will only limp along at greatly reduced efficiency, and some will not work at all. The components and materials could not be produced efficiently in a single factory, for producing each efficiently depends on a scale of production reached only by selling to many buyers, and on components and supplies obtained from a network of firms. The agricultural and service industries of high-income countries also depend for their efficiency and the high incomes they yield on the inputs they obtain from many other firms in the country's productive system.

To adopt pieces of another country's productive system so that they will work well in isolation or within a rudimentary industrial complex and then to build upon them so that an efficient and dynamic integrated system evolves is a difficult process. To understand its complexity is to have the basis for understanding better the economies of economic growth. And so this and the following chapter are largely devoted to explaining the technical difficulties involved.

The complexity involved may be appreciated by first observing the obstacles to three types of technical advance: the transition from bazaar-type trading to fixed-price retailing, the improvement of techniques in agriculture, and the establishment of rather simple small factories in traditional economies; and then sketching the rather complex systemic nature of further industrialization. As a preface to the discussion, I shall describe the problem of introducing the use of the spade into tropical and semitropical low-income societies. The problem of the spade is symbolic of the nature of other problems.

IMPORTING THE SPADE

During two years of residence in Burma in the early part of the 1950s, which included brief visits to India, I observed that the invariable digging tool in the parts of those countries which I visited was the digging hoe. This is a hoe with a stout handle and a heavy blade perhaps 10 or 12 inches in width and 8 inches in depth. The process of digging consists of chopping into the soil with a vigorous stroke and then jerking the hoe backward so that the soil flies back past the worker. If the space in which to work is ample, if the soil is sandy or loose, if the hole to be dug is not too deep, and if it is not necessary that the sides be vertical or fairly precisely defined, the digging hoe is an efficient instrument. But if precise dimensions are required, if a deeper hole is required, or if the soil is hard or heavy, a spade seems to a Westerner far more efficient. The English, who have known about spades for a long time, were managers of much economic activity in lower Burma for a century and a quarter and in India for periods ranging up to three centuries. It occurred to me to wonder why they had not introduced that more productive Western instrument, the spade.

To discover one main obstacle is not difficult. Burma and India are hot, low-income societies in which manual laborers go barefooted or wear light sandals. The use in which the spade has its greatest advantage is that in which considerable pressure with the foot is necessary to press or jab it into the soil. It is precisely this use which is not feasible unless the worker wears heavy-soled shoes. The cost of shoes is prohibitive to a manual laborer of Burma or India. The cost to an employer would also be prohibitive unless—obviously a rare condition—his work included digging of the type for which a spade is advantageous continuously or at least frequently.

A simple technical adaptation seems sufficient to solve the problem. If a strap of steel, slightly convex, is fastened along the top edge of the blade of a spade, the bare foot can press on it without discomfort. However, the problem is solved only very imperfectly. If the soil is moist or of such material and consistency that it packs readily, some will be packed against this horizontal strap if the blade is pressed into the soil far enough to take a full load, and when an attempt is made to throw the spadeful of soil the blade will not "clear"; that is, part of the load will cling to the blade. If the metal strap is moved backward so that it does not project beyond the front of the blade, this difficulty is remedied but a new one appears. The spade becomes a clumsy instrument for digging at the edge of holes.

However, the problem is not insoluble. The solution has been known and used in some parts of Turkey, in Iran, and in at least several countries in north Africa for some generations and perhaps several centuries. Transversely through a heavy wooden handle of the spade or shovel, a few inches above the blade, a hole half an inch or more in diameter is bored. Through it a dowel about as long as the width of the blade of the spade is run. The bare foot can press down on the dowel without discomfort, there is no wall at the top edge of the blade against which soil packs, and the spade or shovel can be used with almost though not quite the same efficiency as in a shoe-wearing society.

The moral is probably obvious: a spade in use is not an isolated instrument. It is part of a complex. It cannot be transferred from the complex of a Western society to that of a tropical low-income society without adaptation to the new complex. The problem is a "system problem." I shall suggest that this general statement of the nature of the difficulty is pertinent to virtually all transfers of techniques from technically advanced countries.

FROM BAZAAR TO FIXED-PRICE RETAILING

A more complex problem is the shift from the bazaar system of retail trading to Western-style retailing, a shift which requires a rather complex favorable set of circumstances, even though it is obvious that bazaar trading is very wasteful of time and Western-type fixed-price trading is not. The point of departure for my discussion is the information presented by an American anthropologist, Clifford Geertz, in one section of his book *Peddlers and Princes* (1963b). His discussion is of a town in Java, but with some adaptations it has widespread applicability.

The most conspicuous feature of the bazaar system is the bazaar itself, in which many petty traders, in stalls or on portable stands or simply at convenient spaces on the ground, sell unbulky, easily portable, easily storable goods.

The price in each transaction is fixed in a process of prolonged haggling with each customer. This sliding price system seems inevitably to develop where goods are unstandardized and the value of the labor time spent in bargaining is low relative to the gain in the price of the goods which may be achieved. Bargaining occurs in high-income societies when these conditions pertain, as for example in exchanging a used automobile in part payment for a new one, or in arranging a large business loan from a bank.[1]

Within the volume of patronage of the bazaar as a whole, each dealer, situated between neighbors selling the same item, obtains his customers more or less by chance. The conspicuous competition is between seller and buyer, not between seller and seller. The gleam in each seller's eye is at the prospect of making a "killing" on an individual sale. There is little attempt to lure customers from other sellers, and to attract a steady clientele is of very minor importance among the goals of the individual trader.

The logic of the situation dictates this. To develop a reputation for selling at low prices would require foregoing most of the haggling which lends spice to the occupation, and by which an enlarged profit can occasionally be made; but this is not the main obstacle. Attracting customers would have to be by price or quality competition, and to develop a steady clientele it would be necessary to build a reputation for selling superior goods, or selling identical goods at low prices. But the goods are somewhat unstandardized ones, fabricated, often from unstandardized materials, by traditional craftsmen who do not follow precise patterns or cut to precise sizes and who cannot readily learn to do so. The bazaar trader cannot obtain standardized goods. In these circumstances, to establish a reputation for consistently maintaining a clear quality of price difference is impossible.

Behind the bazaar lies an elaborate manufacturing, processing, and trading mechanism, partly at the bazaar site itself, partly elsewhere. There are primary producers, traders in their products, processors (perhaps in two or more steps), assemblers of processed goods into larger lots, wholesalers and jobbers, and perhaps an added link between each. Typically there is extreme specialization of function and commodity among processors and of commodity among the petty retail dealers. (However, it is possible that both the multiplication of middlemen and the extreme degree of division of labor are results of recent economic stagnation and disruption leading to a great oversupply of labor, and are not intrinsic parts of the system.)

A system of credit extension binds together these various links in the productive and distributive chain. Every seller extends credit and every buyer seeks it. One aim of each dealer is to spread that scarce commodity, his capital, widely by doing business as much as possible with someone else's capital. A delicate process of extending just the right amount of credit occurs. If the purveyor of credit at any stage in the productive process extends too little credit, the recipient will seek out another who

---

[1] These reasons are mine. Geertz (1963b, p. 36) states that haggling occurs "where economic conditions are unstable, market information poor, and trading hyperindividuated." The hyperindividuation seems to me to be a result rather than a cause.

will extend more. If the purveyor of credit extends too much, the recipient may default.

Each trader short of the retail level (and any but the pettiest retailer also operates as a wholesaler or jobber at times) is typically engaged simultaneously in a number of deals. Often these are carried out through a variety of temporary combinations with other buyers or sellers. To diversify his risks and his chances of profit, and also perhaps simply because it is more exciting, he would rather have one fifth of each of five deals than all of any of them. Indeed, if he comes upon a deal of more than average profitability, he has some obligation to let other dealers share in it.

The conventional concept of interpersonal relationships in traditional society is that they are "functionally diffuse," that is, that they always take into account—in addition to economic factors—kinship, community, and other group relationships; relative political and social power; the need to continue to live in contact with the other party after the transaction is completed; and so on. This indeed is true among other groups but much less so of the trader. In the buyer-seller relationship of the bazaar, business is business. The bazaar dealer's activity is subject to ethical rules for which there are strong sanctions within his community, but these are not the rules or the sanctions of the other groups in the society. The stimulus of the bazaar dealer's way of life consists not only of his financial success but also of his multitude of contacts, the changing play of diversification of his risks and opportunities, and the challenge of the bargaining in each transaction.

What must such a bazaar trader do to make the transition to Western-type retail trading?

He must possess or acquire enough capital to cover the cost of a building, showcases, storage shelves, perhaps display windows, and other equipment, and a somewhat diversified stock of goods. This amount of capital may be large relative to his resources. This economic requirement in itself may be an important barrier.

Having this capital, he must give up the security of diversification of risks and instead risk in a single venture perhaps his life savings on which the security of his family depends. He must commit himself to overhead costs which are fairly large relative to his capital and his experience, and he must therefore enter upon bookkeeping-based price planning by which each sale will contribute a sufficient (but for competition's sake not an excessive) amount toward covering those overhead costs.

To make the venture succeed, he must also handle a new quality of goods. The reason is this: Since he has high capital costs compared to a bazaar trader, he must achieve lower labor costs if he is to compete successfully. He must therefore avoid the time-consuming haggling process which characterizes almost every bazaar sale. To this end his sale prices must be fixed. If he handles goods varying in quality and specifications, he cannot successfully maintain fixed prices. If quality and specifications varied, it would be advantageous for customers both to undertake a prolonged process of selection among items in his shop and to shuttle back and forth between his shop and the bazaar to benefit, so to speak, by arbitrage between the two markets.

Therefore, to reduce the time required for each sale he must obtain goods of reasonably uniform quality and specifications. He will not find the typical craftsman who produces for the bazaar prepared to provide them. Quite generally, inducing the new quality of craft work is not easy. Geertz reports that in Java tailors drew a fairly clear line between "old fashioned" craftsmen, who could not follow a pattern accurately and rapidly, and "modern" craftsmen, the small minority, who could. Even in that relatively modern country, Spain, in setting up a store in 1967 Sears Roebuck had much difficulty in getting suppliers of clothing to make standardized sizes of women's clothing. "If a woman likes my brand," a "manufacturer" told Sears, "she knows what size she is" (*Wall Street Journal*, March 27, 1967).

Moreover, the would-be store proprietor may not find the typical petty merchant-capitalist who organizes production of items for the bazaar ready to enter into a continuing agreement, even if he could arrange the necessary precision of production. The attractions of ever-renewed bargaining and the possible "quick killing" are too great. The storekeeper must therefore enjoy the coincidence of finding a supplier who, like himself, is seeking a new way of life, and is willing and able to produce to unprecedently exacting standards, and will enter into a continuing agreement to do so; or he must enter into production himself. Concerning imported industrial goods, obtaining uniformity is no problem, but most imported goods are relatively expensive goods, purchased only by a very limited clientele. The great majority of the items sold to consumers in a low-income society are domestically produced. Concerning these, the problem of obtaining uniformity is a complex one.

The storekeeper must also manage a staff of permanent employees. If he does his own manufacturing, the staff will be fairly large; if not, it will be small. In any event, he must become a supervisor. This type of continuing interpersonal relationship, quite alien to the somewhat abrasive dog-eat-dog tactics of the bazaar, is one in which the typical bazaar trader may feel uncomfortable.

Even if he does all of these things well, he will fail unless he meets one other condition. He must develop or find in his community a new type of clientele, one whose members will forego the pleasures of bargaining in the bazaar and be content to buy in a brief transaction at a fixed price. Moreover, because of their more exacting specifications, his goods will almost certainly be higher, not lower, priced per unit than those of the bazaar. This does not necessarily follow; he might conceivably save enough on labor costs both to cover his higher overhead costs per unit and to sell better goods at bazaar prices; but in practice the various cost elements usually work out so that higher prices are necessary.[2] Because of his higher prices and different trading style, his success depends on the coincidence of the existence in the community of a group of individuals who are socially restless, are endeavoring to strengthen their fledgling bourgeois status, and as a sign of their new status are seeking for better quality and a somewhat different style of goods than those found in the bazaar. If he attempts the transition in the absence of social ferment which produces a considerable number of such persons, he will probably fail.

In summary: To establish a fixed-price retail store, the trader must adopt a set of techniques and risks new to him. He must also sense correctly that a process of change is going on in the environment outside his enterprise, and take advantage of it. And he must, so to speak, alter himself. This phraseology is only figurative; he cannot change his own values and goals on command. However, he *is* deviant from his associates; if he were not, he would not have been motivated to make the transition. He must abandon his old skills, give up the constant challenge and stimulus and satisfactions of bazaar life, and remove himself to a lonely managerial function. Only an individual of considerable ability or luck will succeed. Many, of course, are succeeding. Innovation in trade as well as in agriculture and manufacturing is proceeding in almost all low-income countries.

TECHNICAL ADVANCE IN AGRICULTURE

Technical advance in agriculture, unlike that in local trading, depends in great measure on governmental action. In part, direct government measures to increase productivity are necessary; in part, the government must provide information, inducements, and assurances to cultivators. Altogether, the problem turns out to be at least as difficult as that of the transition from the bazaar to the fixed-price retail store.[3]

The Difficulties

Early capital-intensive investment can play its part. Irrigation projects may permit multiple cropping and increased yields on land already under

---

[2] Ultimately, the dominance in the market of uniform manufactured goods will work to his advantage, but initially he must deal in products made from the same materials available to producers for the bazaar.

[3] Among the various studies of the problems of technical advance in traditional agriculture, two of the more comprehensive are Schultz (1964) and Millikan and Hapgood (1967). The latter summarizes the findings of a six-week conference of highly-qualified experts.

the plow, or may convert land from waste to cultivation; drainage may do the latter; and roads or railroads may open up new regions. Irrigation has been important in India, China, the Middle East, and many other areas, and drainage in a few areas—for example, Israel. The Soviet Union has opened up large areas, in many of which, however, the growing season proved too short for effective cultivation. The effects of these measures, though important, are limited. New lands can be opened up only where "empty lands" exist; swamps drained only where they exist; and waters dammed only where the lay of the land permits. Moreover, these projects will not achieve their full benefits unless the glamorous large projects are accompanied by effective arrangements for field channels, the administration of local water distribution, limitation of the area served to that for which there is enough water, and assurance of water when it is needed. Premier Chou En-lai stated in 1959 that only one half of the area of Chinese land claimed to be under irrigation at that time could be adequately irrigated. Bardhan (1967), who notes this, also calculates on the basis of official Indian data that "only about 48% of the additional major and medium irrigation potential created since 1950–51 was utilized by 1955–56; the figure has gone up to 77% by 1964–65." The reason in India, as Bardhan notes, was not merely that administrators interested in the glamorous projects were less interested in the detail of making them work effectively, but also that favoritism discouraged maximum use. Administrative action to assure large landowners plenty of water made the supply to small peasants so uncertain that it did not pay them to make use of the facilities. The broader significance of this type of problem will be noted later in this section.

The peasant is usually a renter. He retains, say, one third or one half of his produce, the remainder going to his landlord.

He responds with alertness to economic inducements. The evidence is of two types. The first is historical: the surge of peasants in Southeast Asia and West Africa to new lands when the opening up of export trade created new markets for their products.

Second, various pieces of research done since World War II have given impressive evidence that within the limits of the products and production methods in which they are traditionally skilled, peasants are judicious in shifting among products, among methods of production, and in the ratio of capital to labor used in production in order to maximize their income.[4]

---

[4] Among the published writings in which such evidence is presented are: Schultz, 1964, chap. 3; Bateman, 1965; Bauer, 1954; Behrman, 1966; E. R. Dean, 1965; E. R. Dean, 1966; Falcon, 1964; W. O. Jones, 1960; Staley, 1961. The articles by Bateman and Behrman present the conclusions of doctoral dissertations at the Massachusetts Institute of Technology. To this evidence should be added that of two other unpublished doctoral dissertations at the Massachusetts Institute of Technology: M. Arak, 1967 and K. Frederick, 1965.

One fact sometimes cited as evidence of lack of economic motivation is the "backward bending supply curve" of labor found in some situations in Africa and Southeast Asia. Native workers came out of their villages to work in mines or on plantations, but after a few months of work returned to their villages. When wage rates were raised to encourage year around work, the result was that the native workers went back to their villages sooner. The conclusion drawn by some Europeans was that the workers could not conceive of wanting more than a certain amount of money. When they had accumulated this total, they quit working.

Anthropological research revealed more of the facts. Leaving their villages to work in the mines or plantations was extremely costly to the natives. They had to forego family life, and to default on community and religious obligations, both functional and ceremonial, of great importance to them. They needed small amounts of money to buy some staples—for example, salt. Apart from earning enough cash to make these minimum cash purchases, they left their villages only because rules imposed by the colonial rulers forced them to obtain a certain minimum of additional money income, for example to pay money taxes, on pain of imprisonment or other equally severe penalty. Once they had enough money income to meet these needs, the wage rate far less than compensated them for the psychic cost to them and their families of defaulting on their community obligations. Their behavior was economic and rational, and consistent with many other pieces of evidence that peasants respond judiciously and sometimes energetically to shifts in economic inducements.

However, as Hla Myint puts it (1964, p. 51), some peasants are ready to take advantage of *market opportunities* but not of *technological opportunities*. Shifting to new methods or crops is a much more difficult matter than shifting among known crops, and may involve large risks and anxieties.

First, in many types of change the peasant cannot act alone.[5] In the Philippines, the use of seeds brought to a certain community by a technical adviser promised a greater yield, but the plants would mature at a different time from the old variety. In this area, as crops approach maturity, rats and birds attack them for food. If the crops of the entire area mature together, the damage is spread widely, but if a single peasant or a few peasants adopted the new seed, the rats and birds would have converged on their fields and destroyed the crops.

Where it is proposed to breed improved cattle strains, this may be possible only if inferior cattle in the village are prevented from breeding with others and causing quick retrogression. In a village where cattle run freely, this can be prevented only by compulsion that will injure some peasants.

---

[5] Several of the examples cited in the text are from Whyte and Williams (1967).

In a number of countries, population increase and subdivision of holdings among children have progressively fragmented holdings. Examples are France, southern Italy, India, and China. It is difficult to arrange the land consolidation to the satisfaction of the peasants involved, for there are reasons why the plots were subdivided into scattered parcels. Those reasons often involve not merely family sentiment but earlier subdivision among heirs so that each received some of the land that was regarded as the richest, some that received the early spring sun, part of that with the best drainage, only part of that which floods in wet years, and so on. To arrange voluntary trades that will consolidate holdings requires a degree of mutual trust among villagers and a degree of faith in the results of the consolidations that would be rare in any country. It is rare among peasants. The common atmosphere among peasant villagers is one of mutual distrust or at least suspicion. The anthropological evidence concerning this is strong,[6] and a study of peasant history makes it easy to understand. Even where, on the surface, relationships within the village seem placid and even pastoral, residence in the village will reveal the cautious reciprocity and wariness of interpersonal relations, and psychological testing will reveal the distrust that underlies it. Since the peasant distrusts his fellows, the group action needed for some types of technical change may be impossible to arrange.

Second, the purely technical and economic problems are often very serious. In the first place, a change or set of changes financially advantageous in a technically advanced country, where yields are high, may not be so where yields are low. On occasion, according to Schultz, it gives no more than the same *percentage* increase in yield. If an improved rice strain developed in Japan increases the yield by 12%, the increase may be 600 or 700 pounds per acre. But in Burma, where the yield is only about one fourth as much, the 12% increase would be only, say, 170 pounds per acre. If the increased seed cost is equivalent to the proceeds of more than 170 but less than 600 pounds of rice, its use will be advantageous to an owner-cultivator in Japan but not in Burma.

Moreover, the improved strain or practice was probably developed in a country in which the cultivator owns his land and obtains the benefit of the entire increase in production. (Since the land reforms after the second World War, Japanese peasants have been landowners.) However, as noted above, in most countries the peasant is a renter, who pays as rent a fraction (say one third or one half) of his crop. Except in the unlikely event that his landlord will concern himself sufficiently with the processes of cultivation, and will trust his peasant's capabilities sufficiently to bear a share of the cost of the improved seed, the peasant must pay all of the increased cost but will retain only one half or two thirds of

---

[6] See, for example, Yang (1948), O. Lewis (1951), and Banfield (1958).

the increase in proceeds. In the example given above, adopting an improved Japanese strain of rice would pay a Burmese renter whose rent equaled one third of his crop only if its cost were less than the proceeds from 113 pounds of rice.

Even more important than these considerations in many cases is the fact that while an occasional method or new variety of plant introduced from the outside may be immediately useful, many—probably a large majority—will not be effective without adaptation. As is illustrated so strikingly in the United States by hybrid corn, many improved varieties of plants or animals often do not do well except in conditions of climate and soil rather closely parallel to those in which they were bred (Schultz, 1964, chap. 10). For example, a strain of a cereal that does well in one country may do poorly in another in which the days are longer or shorter during the growing season. Only when in the 1960s Rockefeller Foundation research scientists developed strains of rice and wheat that are photoinsensitive did this problem decline in importance.

Even though older wheat varieties were sensitive to differences in exposure to sunlight, wheat is much less "locality specific" than is maize (i.e., corn). Mexican wheat varieties are grown successfully from North Africa to India, but specific maize varieties have to be bred for various regions of a given country.[7] The Rockefeller wheat project in Mexico was much more successful than the maize project. One analyst attributes much of the difference in success to this difference between the two crops.[8]

Nevertheless, there was considerable difficulty in introducing the new wheat varieties in India. The reasons are illustrative. High population density in India has caused much farm land to be denuded of trees and shrubs, and has made land too scarce to use any of it to grow crops for fodder. Therefore, wheat with long stalks has been developed over the generations. The straw is used for fodder. In the irrigated areas of India, use of a much-increased amount of chemical fertilizer would seem advantageous. The wheat responded to increased fertilizer, but when fertilizer with a nitrogen content above 40 pounds per acre was applied, the heads became so heavy that the stalks often broke and the wheat failed to ripen. Only when a new short-stalk strain was introduced from Mexico in the mid-1960s did it become possible to use fertilizer with nitrogen content of up to 100 pounds per acre. Greatly increased yields have resulted. However, a moderate fodder shortage resulted. Moreover, the Mexican wheat is a red wheat. Indians prefer an amber wheat. To achieve full adoption of the Mexican wheat even where the fodder shortage is not a serious impediment will require finding a strain of amber wheat that can stand

---

[7] Evenson and Kislev (1974), p. 1312.

[8] D. T. Myren, in Wharton (1969).

heavy fertilization.[9] (The writer does not know, as this is written, whether this has been accomplished.)

In general, fertilizing, irrigation, planting, cultivation, and other practices which yield increased returns in one soil and climate may be disastrous or at least not advantageous in another. Or if they are disadvantageous they may be so only if a complex set of changes is adopted as one package. And it is impossible to know in advance just what the advantageous set will be.

In the words of the report of a conference of experts on agricultural change organized by the Massachusetts Institute of Technology Center for International Studies:

> The interdependencies among the factors are so strong that the effects of a package of factors are likely to be very different from the sum of the effects of each one applied by itself. . . . Additional fertilizer without water control may have little result, and the consequences of more water may be very modest if additional nutrients are not supplied. If both are supplied together, existing varieties that do as well as any others in the absence of water and fertilizer may not benefit as much from these new inputs as new varieties, specifically tailored to water and nutrient availability; yield on existing varieties may even be reduced by added water or fertilizer. Insects and diseases that are unimportant under existing practices may multiply dangerously under irrigated and fertilized conditions and require new measures of disease and insect control.[10]

Moreover, with the new seeds or practices, a new set of adjustments may be needed to annual variations in climatic conditions. With his traditional seed and methods of cultivation, the cultivator knows what adjustments to make in planting, manuring, cultivation—or all three—if the year is unusually wet, or dry, or late, or hot, or cold. If he adopts a new variety, or uses commercial fertilizer, he does not. And the expert from the country of origin of the new variety of the fertilizer does not know either, for there is no way to be certain in the new climate and soil except by extensive trial and error in those different conditions.

Hence a single change, and much more so a set of changes, increases the risk of loss even though in an average year the changes would be advantageous. Often the peasant cannot afford the risk. A potential increase of, say, 30% in average annual income is of no use to a peasant who is wiped out by making the wrong adjustment to climatic variation in the first year.

There are some items useful in peasant agriculture but not now used, mainly tools and equipment, which do not require such adaptation. Many

---

9 These facts are from Cummings (1967).

10 Millikan and Hapgood (1967), p. 16.

of them have been developed in recent decades in Japan, rather than in the West, because Japan needed equipment adapted to small-scale production, and devised it. However, the advantage even of many of these depends on the cost of the labor they displace, being much less where farm incomes (and thus labor costs) are low. And some of them lose even this lesser advantage until the use of machinery in the economy as a whole has developed to the stage at which local maintenance and repair are available.

This last point merits special mention. Westerners who see farm machinery in use all about them fail to realize that even if the saving in labor cost or the improvement in cultivation justifies its cost, its use is likely to be uneconomic until a sufficient volume of use emerges over a relatively short period to justify the establishment of local service facilities. To illustrate, the portable logging equipment used in Maine and New Hampshire has proved in recent years not to be usable economically in certain southern areas, because tree stands on which its use is appropriate were so scattered that too much time was lost in traveling to the nearest service establishment when a replacement part was needed. And New Hampshire observers are worried lest farming die out in some areas of northern New Hampshire because the farming land that remains fertile is sufficiently scattered so that the same problem exists.[11] In a low-income economy, the acquaintance with machinery is likely to be so slight and the tendency to introduction of any given type of machinery so slow that the necessity to cross this threshold constitutes an important barrier to its use.

Obviously, even if the peasant were vigorously innovational, because of the small size of his operations it would not pay him to spend his resources to seek out technical advances. The cost of finding improved varieties and practices, even if there were no cost of adaptation, would almost invariably be much greater than his small benefit. The cost of adaptation compounds the impossibility. The technical advances must be brought to him.

But—and this is the third type of difficulty—the peasant often has reason to distrust the persons who come to suggest changes to him. The technical adviser is likely to be an elite person or the agent of an elite person. In many countries almost every peasant has had a lifetime of experiences with landowners, rent collectors, moneylenders, and government agents which justifies his suspicion that anything proposed by an elite person is not likely to be to the peasant's benefit. If in Latin America the peasant is an "Indio" and the adviser is a mestizo, the negative reaction is automatic. If the expert is a foreigner, his advice is to be taken

---

[11] I have these items of information from R. A. Andrews of the University of New Hampshire.

with some reservation, since all foreigners are regarded as associated with the domestic elite groups.[12]

The peasant is likely to shy away from change for reasons that are deeper than these conscious ones. Facing the uncertainties that the prospect of change brings seems to cause the typical peasant to feel a degree of anxiety, and he may avoid the anxiety by deciding against change without realizing that his uneasiness has biased his decision. The common phrases "as cautious as a peasant," "peasant mentality," and so on, indicate how widely this characteristic of peasants has been observed. There is reason to believe that this attitude may be deeply bred into the behavior patterns of peasants in most or all traditional societies.[13] However, there is reason to suppose that the peasant will be more receptive to change, and more resourceful in making changes, in methods of production than in any other area of activity, for this is the area in which he is judicious and at least relatively resourceful. The peasant boy is not taught merely to follow traditional practices of cultivation by rote. On the contrary, he is taught how to meet annual differences in temperature, rainfall, and the like, and he is probably readier to use his own judgment in this area of behavior than in any other.

An extreme case illustrates the change that may take place in peasant behavior in a short period if the environment facing him changes drastically. In 1952 Cornell University rented the Peruvian hacienda of Vicos for a five-year period, and at the end of that period the government of Peru expropriated the hacienda and transferred title in it to the peasant occupants. From 1952 on, the American and Peruvian anthropologists managing the experiment acted consistently in ways that made it clear to the peasants of Vicos that they were respected, that the proceeds from production on Vicos would be used for their benefit, and that their desires concerning the terms of labor and the use of the hacienda's earnings would be met. Within a decade, as the peasants came to believe that this was actually true, from being passive and listless they became self-reliant and innovational. Productivity on the hacienda grew by leaps and bounds.[14] It would not be wise to draw broad conclusions about likely economic change from this experience, for two reasons. This was not an abrupt change from "traditionalism" to "modernism." Traditional atti-

---

[12] Too, if the adviser is indigenous, he may be poorly trained, indeed less expert than the peasant; and if he is foreign, he may be inexpert because he does not know the circumstances of production in the country.

[13] I have attempted to account for it, in *On the Theory of Social Change* (1962), Chaps. 4–8. The hypothesis advanced there is that this attitude arises from the early life environment of the peasant child. It is "bred into him" by his early environment, in ways explainable in terms of psychoanalytical theory.

[14] The most readily available summary of the facts of the Vicos "experiment" is presented in a group of articles which constitute the March, 1965 issue of *The American Behavioral Scientist*.

tudes had changed greatly in Peru before 1952—witness the fact that a Peruvian governmental Institute of Indigenous Indian Affairs existed and gave hearty and effective support to the Cornell anthropologists who proposed the project. Second, the change in the environment of Hacienda Vicos was more radical than could conceivably be duplicated elsewhere except on a small experimental scale.[15] Nevertheless, the change at Vicos is important evidence concerning possible responsiveness of at least some peasants to changes in inducements.[16] Unfortunately, with the withdrawal of the Cornell anthropologists from the project, there was retrogression, a fact that also has its morals.

However, the influences sketched above, singly and even more strongly in combination, indicate that if peasant cultivators are to carry technical progress forward they must be convinced by demonstration, not merely assertion, that the proposed changes will increase yields, that the government will administer effectively and dependably the measures (fertilizer supply, technical advice, etc.) necessary to make the new methods successful, and that they will actually receive the benefit.

The fourth type of difficulty in technical advance is that the government officials of many low-income countries have convictions and attitudes which prevent taking the steps that are necessary. A fairly extensive set of governmental measures is necessary. These measures are costly. And the groups who have traditionally dominated the legislative processes in low-income societies are precisely the landed groups who would suffer the cost of the research and demonstration, education, and land and tax reform. Where these groups are still powerful—which is everywhere where a social revolution has not occurred—they resist such programs strenuously.

These groups are not farmers; quite the contrary. They are distant from the process of cultivation. They regard the sweat and dirt of manual labor as pedestrian and demeaning, distasteful except to unrefined persons with inferior sensibilities and capabilities.[17] These landowners resist

---

[15] Violent social revolution might bring into power a government with intentions as favorable to the peasants of a country as the intentions at Vicos, but competency of management equal to that at Vicos would be impossible on a large scale.

[16] Danilo Dolci's success in getting Sicilian peasants to take concerted action to improve village conditions is another pertinent piece of evidence. My information is from a conversation with Mr. Dolci.

[17] Schultz notes (1964, p. 169) that it would not pay peasants to hunt out new methods, but expresses surprise that farmers who operate large enterprises in parts of South America have not found and adopted improved methods: "Why they have not done better on this score is a puzzle." The solution to the puzzle lies almost certainly in the elite attitudes toward manual labor in general and the grubby details of farming in particular referred to in the text. To be a farm owner is one matter, highly valued; to be interested in the plebian details is another. Effective innovation on large farms is almost invariably carried out first by *industrial* innovators who are expanding the range of their operations. Their relative advance in social position may later goad

the necessary measures not merely for pocketbook reasons, though those would be sufficient. They will not demean themselves by themselves performing the manual labor necessary for experimentation. Neither will they finance experimentation by the peasants. They have contempt for the cultivators and disbelief in peasant abilities. Feeling this contempt is probably essential to them; it justifies their own privileged position. One aspect of this contempt is a conviction that peasants are incapable either of benefiting from more than rudimentary education or of applying new methods successfully. These beliefs coincide conveniently with the short-run financial advantage of the landlords.

In the impressive understatement of the Center for International Studies conference (Millikan and Hapgood, 1967, p. 18), "Sustained growth in agricultural output requires technical, economic, attitudinal, and political transformations of the whole structure of rural society that cannot be brought about quickly."

In many countries new groups who believe in "modernization" have come to power. However, these groups may be as little willing to devote the country's resources or their own managerial abilities to the improvement of agriculture as are the landlords. The new leaders are likely to believe so fervently that industrialization is the key to modernization that they see little use in diverting resources or human energy from industry to agriculture. They too are likely to feel condescension or contempt toward the peasants, those living symbols of backwardness. They may favor large dam projects but not the unglamorous, painstaking process of research and demonstration or the reforms that are needed.

The Necessary Measures

A basic requirement for continuing increase in productivity in agriculture is continuing research, sponsored by either private foundations or by governmental bodies.[18] As noted in Chapter 3, this condition is being fulfilled, effectively, and will no doubt continue indefinitely. Consider, however, the type of governmental measures that are also necessary or facilitating.

1. The recent studies of cultivator response in a number of peasant

---

traditional landowners to action. It is reported that an exception exists in the Middle East, where the landlord class has itself initiated change, including entering into the modern processing of some agricultural crops.

[18] Griliches (1964), Peterson (1967) and Evenson (1971) have made estimates of the financial return within the United States to various pieces of agricultural research. Evenson and Kislev (1974) present an international estimate for wheat and maize. They show, incidentally, that research results (as measured by published papers) transfer much more effectively within a region, that is, to nearby countries, than over longer distances.

societies to changes in the relative prices of different products and changes in the relative costs of labor and other inputs justify the belief that an increase in agricultural prices will induce cultivators to increase their production if they believe that the increased price level will continue and that they will receive the benefit. But because the problems and risks in technical change are far greater than those in changes within known methods, the adoption of new methods will be minimal unless demonstrations of technical advances are brought to the cultivators and they are given convincing evidence that the advances are not unduly risky; that the inputs needed to carry out the changed methods will be available when needed; and that the benefits, or a rewarding share of them, will accrue to them, the cultivators, and not to the landlord or the tax collector.

If a low-income country were to carry out a large-scale program of improvement of roads from agricultural areas to the towns, the reduction in farm-to-market transport costs would be great, and the real income of cultivators would rise even though the cost of agricultural products to consumers simultaneously fell. In most cases, construction of storage facilities to prevent loss from rodents and insects and sharp declines in prices at harvest time would narrow the marketing margin still further. Some changes in other marketing facilities and institutions would also be pertinent.

2. If cultivators are to respond to "technological opportunities," it is necessary that they shall be informed of them and convinced of their feasibility. The results must be carried to cultivators by demonstration farms, technically expert village demonstration teams, and the like. But the experts must be expert. Evidence from China and India will illustrate the point. Concerning China, A. Eckstein (1966) has written: "Agricultural cadres often paid so little attention to the relationship between planting distance, depth of ploughing, soil moisture, crop strain, and soil fertility that applications of chemical fertilizer were at times not only wasted but even counterproductive." Bardhan, who cited Eckstein concerning China, notes the similar incompetence of many Indian "experts." "Farmers," he writes (1967, p. 22), "have often refused to adopt new inputs and technology . . . due to a better appreciation of their local unsuitability or technical complementarity than is to be found in the administrative officials pushing those programs (apart from the risk factors involved)."

3. In many countries, the governmental administration has been largely a mechanism for enforcing on the peasants the requisitions of landowners, moneylenders, and other economic elites, and for collecting taxes from whose expenditure the peasants perceive no benefit. Where this is true, there must be a broad change in the general tenor of administration if the cultivators are to be persuaded that the benefits of improved

methods will accrue to them. Accomplishing such a change is like moving a mountain.

4. The lesson that there has been a change may be demonstrated in community development schemes, and specifically in provision for self-help, grant-in-aid "rural public works" that are clearly responsive to the desires of the peasant cultivators. Community development schemes often are not, but rather are schemes to enrich local political bosses. The rural public works scheme in Comilla, then in East Pakistan, is discussed in Chapter 13. According to the reports available, the scheme was carried out in the spirit intended, and so as to benefit the peasants. But when United States surplus agricultural commodities ceased to be available in relatively large amounts to provide, through sale on the domestic market, the funds for the scheme, the public works program dwindled with them. Local enthusiasm was not sufficient to induce the appropriation of Pakistani governmental funds to continue the program.

5. Perhaps above all, the transfer of land ownership to cultivators, or as a minimum the institution of rental arrangements that will give cultivators dependable assurance that they will receive the income from increased sales proceeds, may be necessary to lend the necessary conviction. (Land reform is discussed in the section that follows.)

6. Literacy and elementary education presumably increase the ability of cultivators to receive information concerning improved methods and improved opportunities.

7. The capital market is not likely to function so smoothly that private benefit and social benefit seem identical in amount. If the other bases for success in technical advance in agriculture have been laid, the government will probably need also to intervene to increase the credit available to cultivators for production purposes.

Denmark, the United States, and Japan are the showcases of successful agricultural marketing and credit cooperatives. It is noteworthy that in all three countries much of the initiative for establishment of the cooperatives came from the farmers themselves. In a number of other countries, in which governments have attempted to confer (or impose) cooperative organizations on the cultivators from above, the results have not been outstanding. In some of these cases, the administration of the attempt has been half-hearted, inept, and corrupt. Even in India, where the quality of administration has been much higher, but where the government has also been the active party, the cooperatives are also primarily dispensers of government credit rather than self-help organizations.

The generalization is probably justifiable that unless self-help actually originates with the prospective recipients, and unless they are convinced that the program will be administered in their interest, the attempt to impose forms that have been effective elsewhere is not likely to be successful.

In Israel, the completely collective communities, the *kibbutzim*, and the communities organized for collective production, the *moshavim*, have been highly successful in solving new problems of production and in raising per capita agricultural income with great speed. But the motivation, the experience and problem-solving propensies of their members are so untypical that no deductions applicable anywhere else are justified.

8. Large-scale farms run like industrial organizations, and run on a large enough scale so that maintaining their own machine service centers is economic, may be established from scratch. But their establishment is possible only where large areas of land are available, and they are likely to be manageable only by farmers who are the heirs of generations of mechanical advance in agriculture, or by industrialists. The highly successful large mechanized farms of northwest Mexico are an example; they were established by Mexican industrialists.

Beginning in the 1930s, the government of the U.S.S.R. tried to increase agricultural production greatly by establishing large collective and state farms, each with its machine center. By and large the program was a failure, but its failure may have been due not to technical miscalculations but to the fact that this organizational structure was used to extract a large share of the output for urban use without compensation, leaving the collective members of state farm workers at minimal levels of living. Little incentive remained for effort or initiative.

Measures such as these eight seem to be necessary if in due course there are to emerge agricultural proprietors who not only seize upon technical improvements demonstrated to them but have acquired a sense that it may always be possible to improve today's production tomorrow, who look for and find methods that increase productivity in this crop this year, in that method year after next, in the other region five years from now, and therefore, on the average, in the country as a whole year after year after year. If such farmers are lucky enough to have, or politically resourceful enough to obtain, a government that will cooperate in the effort, productivity in agriculture may be expected to continue to increase each decade as productivity elsewhere in the economy increases.

LAND REFORM

One type of measure that affects the expectations of cultivators has attracted special attention. This is land reform.

Land reform may mean merely a transfer of ownership of parcels already under peasant cultivation from absentee landowner to peasant; a regrouping of scattered parcels into coherent units; or subdivision of large estates, haciendas, or ranches into small holdings and transfer of title to peasant cultivators. Usually, the transfer is by government compensation of the former owners on such basis as seems equitable and is feasible, and then sale to peasants on easy terms. The first type, involving no change in the management of production, can hardly have any but a highly favorable effect on productivity.

The second type is important in countries in which fragmentation of holdings has occurred. The difficulties in achieving exchanges that will consolidate holdings have been sketched above. Success may require that the government have or acquire lands of its own with which to enrich the exchanges, so that each peasant has a unified holding enough larger than before so that he is sure that it is superior even in spite of his fondness for those bits of especially choice land that he gave up.

The third type, division of large estates, is what is usually envisaged when land reform is referred to in non-Communist countries. The inequality of land holdings in the low-income countries is proverbial, and the proverbial picture is not greatly exaggerated. In the Middle East, as settled life replaced nomadic tribal life, tribal lands commonly became the personal lands of the tribal chieftain. In 1967 the *New York Times* reported the case of an Iranian father, sending his daughter to college in the United States, who gave her several villages to provide the income for her college education, as a fond U.S. father might have given her an automobile. In some areas of India, there are many large estates. In every country along the western half of South America, the conquistadores of the 16th century seized large estates for themselves, took the Indians under their protection to Christianize them and save their souls, and thereby (since the Church, which issued orders for humane treatment, was far away) had slaves to do their work. The land they took has remained in estate form—the *latifundia*—to the present time, while elsewhere in the same countries tiny farms—the *minifundia*—were formed as Indian villages disintegrated. The later creation of large holdings in the populated areas of Brazil followed somewhat the same pattern. In Argentina, in the 19th century, the government drove Indians off the land and distributed it in very large units to settlers who established the wheat farms of today (raising some cattle also). Today, in Latin America as a whole, holdings of more than 15,000 acres (25 square miles) constitute 1.5% of all farm holdings, but about one half of the agricultural land. This is true in spite of the fact that Mexico has no large feudal holdings; they were distributed after the revolution of 1910–20. In all of the rest of Latin America, except El Salvador, Costa Rica, and, after Castro, Cuba, these huge estates form the larger part of the farm area. They do not form as large a part of the cultivable land, for much of this estate land is suitable only for grazing.[19] In the Caribbean, Java, Ceylon, and parts of East Africa, agricultural holdings are also dominated by large estates.

A large part of the large holdings in many South American countries,

---

[19] The data from United Nations, 1951a, and apply to about 1950, but the situation has not changed much since that date.

especially those in the western half of the continent, are cattle ranches. While some of these are on infertile land, many are not. For example, until recent years extensive grazing has been practiced on land of market garden quality near Caracas, while fresh vegetables were imported to the city. Some grazing may still be done in the area. In Chile, Bolivia, Peru, and Guatemala, the practice prevails of giving peasants who are virtually serfs the right to cultivate small plots of land, in return for which they are obliged to work a certain number of days per week (often, three) on the lands of the estate owner. It prevailed also in Chile at least until the late 1960s. In the Middle East, large holdings are commonly rented to peasants for peasant-scale cultivation. In other areas of the world, the large estates are typically plantations, run as large-scale units. They may produce sugar in the West Indies and Java, rubber in Malaysia, wheat in Argentina, sisal, sugar, tea, coffee, or tobacco in Africa, and various other commodities in all of these places. The plantations in eastern, central, and southern Africa are owned by European settlers; most of those elsewhere are indigenously owned. In Africa south of the Sahara, much land is still held in communal tenure. On much of this, "shifting cultivation" is still practiced. The cultivators burn and slash, cultivate for two or three years, then abandon the plot to let nature partially restore the fertility of the soil while they move elsewhere. Many of the European-owned estates, for example in Kenya, were formed by occupying these lands while they were thus unoccupied. This was often done by purchase of the rights from the indigenous tribal groups, who sometimes did and sometimes did not understand that they were giving up the land permanently.

In a few cases the small holdings nourish high-yielding specialized crops. A frequently and appropriately cited example is the highland peasant coffee plots of Colombia, where, as the television advertisement says with little exaggeration, Juan picks the ripe beans every day; and where he earns a fair living. But where the small holdings are grain lands, on which income from the crop is eked out with that from the sale of eggs from a few hens, the peasant may live little above subsistence, and little better than the serf on the hacienda.

Land reform is said to release peasant incentive and energy, to promote education and community development in general, and to have other socially desirable side effects. The United Nations is more or less officially in favor of land reform, and the Alliance for Progress made land reform one of its yardsticks of whether a country is socially progressive and would therefore use economic assistance to social advantage. But the problems and the economic advantage or disadvantage of land reform differ with these different types of large-scale ownership and operation.

Where plantation agriculture is practiced, a shift to peasant ownership would typically cause a sharp and permanent decline in production, because large-scale operation is the more efficient form. Before undertaking this change, a country needs to consider whether the satisfaction the peasant may feel in ownership is worth the cost to the rest of the economy of the loss in output, and whether the peasant will feel satisfaction when he sees that production has fallen. Moreover, the shift will require capital that the owner formerly provided. The fall in sugar production in Castro's Cuba was due partly to the loss of the capital and the management formerly provided by the owners of the sugar plantations. In the sugar zone along the northeastern coast of Brazil, an obsolete industry holds on on large plantations organized around sugar "centrals." There is near-starvation now. Land reform would mean absolute starvation unless the government took over the centrals and modernized them—or subsidized them while it found other crops that would thrive in the area, provided the technical advice for a transition, and accomplished the transition gradually. There are some exceptions to this rule that production would fall; with respect to some tree crops in some conditions of cultivation, small-holder cultivation is efficient.

Where the landowners are merely feudal landlords and peasant agriculture is now practiced by tenants, production would presumably rise if the peasants obtained title to the land and full claim to the proceeds—provided that the seeds and equipment now furnished by the owners were provided by someone else. Marketings might fall, and might rise above their former level only if production rose progressively and markedly. For where a landlord had extracted a large part of the crop as rental, and marketed it, peasant tenants who became owners would probably consume a larger share of their own grain, divert some land from grain farming to the raising of a few chickens and pigs, and live better and sell less. This happened in eastern Europe, and would have happened in the Soviet Union if the government had not used force to collect the grain from the peasants. The percentage of food-grain production in China that was marketed fell from above 35% during the first half of the 1950s to below 31% in 1956 and 1957 (Ishikawa, 1965, Table 8.) This was undoubtedly one reason for the formation of communes in 1958.

But where the owner is a feudal lord who maintains his own estate and obtains listless labor from ill-fed serfs who eke out a bare subsistence on their own plots, transfer of ownership to the peasants would probably increase production enough to increase marketings also—provided again that the necessary capital were made available.

Lastly, on many haciendas of Latin America, the land is not in cultivation at all. It is held because landowning is a way of life. Much is idle; or because cattle ranching is more esteemed than agriculture, cattle roam fertile acres. With capable administration of land redistribution, to peasants who would convert the land to cultivation, production would rise quickly and markedly.

The problems in effecting the latter two types of land reform are political as well as economic. The present owners are economically powerful, and they are able to call upon the conservative sentiments of traditional societies. The low-cost way of accomplishing transfer of ownership is to compensate the present owners with long-term low-interest bonds (which in effect is partial confiscation), but the political resistance is intense. Fiscal measures to penalize unproductive use of land are a less drastic means of change, but these run into severe administrative problems, especially in the mountainous areas of western South America in which there exist no good cadastral surveys and where there is extreme difficulty in making them.[20]

Warriner's Summary

Land reform is as land reform does. It increased production in Egypt and Japan, reduced it in Iraq, Bolivia, and Chile.[21] In a 1969 book, Doreen Warriner presents the most authoritative survey of the execution and degree of success of land reform in 13 countries (Denmark, Italy, Yugoslavia, Bolivia, Brazil, Chile, Cuba, Mexico, Venezuela, Egypt, Iraq, Iran, and India). She comments on the relationship between the provisions and administration of land reform and its effect on production, which

> . . . may or may not be favorable depending on the conjunction of factors which influence incentive. . . .
> When the rate of compensation payable is high, as in India, or when estates are purchased at market values, as in Chile, Peru and Venezuela, and where the ex-tenants must pay high purchase installments, then the effects on investment in agriculture can be unfavorable. . . .
> On the basis of this range of experience, it appears that the more revolutionary the method of redistribution, the greater is the likelihood of reducing production; the more compromising the method, however, the greater is the likelihood of incurring high costs of expropriation. Yet this is too neat an antithesis, since in fact several reforms have increased production without incurring high costs, notably Egypt and Japan, while in Mexico the reform indirectly stimulated investment in agriculture by private landowners. But of the countries observed, only Iran seems to have succeeded, up to a point, in avoiding both dangers. . . . In Iraq, Bolivia and Venezuela, the laws were framed to provide for an integrated

---

[20] Thomas Carroll (1961) surveys "The Land Reform Issue in Latin America." Hirschman (1963) presents a history and critique of land use and land reform attempts in Colombia which illustrates vividly the difficulties involved. Barraclough and Domike (1966) present a comprehensive analysis of agrarian structure and related matters in seven Latin American countries.

[21] Philip M. Raup, "Land Reform and Agricultural Output," Chap. 8 of Southworth and Johnston (1967).

organization to support the farmers, and Cuba had a rational policy aim of diversification. Yet in practice the political impetus which drove through expropriation—communism in Iraq and Cuba, left-wing syndicates in Bolivia and Venezuela—could not work on these lines; success does not follow the prescriptions. The revolution brings sudden and violent change, but agriculture demands continuity; the kind of people who make revolutions are not, as a rule, the kind who can organize for increased production. . . .

If there is one lesson of universal validity that emerges from all this experience, it is the need for putting more practical intelligence to work. If there is one good state land settlement in Brazil among many bad, that is because one man, an engineer, devoted himself to it; if there are good Japanese farmers in Brazil, that is because farming efficiency has been bred into them and their organization. If there are well-managed state and cooperative sugar factories in Maharashtra, that is because faith in cooperation could be translated into action by Professor Gadgil and others; and if there is a good joint farming cooperative, a saint-politician will be found behind it. If the Iranian reform in its first stage got carried out quickly and effectively, that was because a powerful and original mind conceived a bold strategy. If in Venezuela there is one really well-to-do intensively cultivated settlement, that is because it found a labor leader with drive to organize it.[22]

Land Reform in Chile

The most recent land reform action in Latin America is that in Chile. (The only other notable one was that in Mexico in the 1920s). The Chilean operation is a classic example both of the motives other than equity and increase in productivity that may affect land reform movements and of how not to proceed if productivity is an important consideration.

Beginning in 1966, under a moderate reform administration, large estates of rich farm land that was not being cultivated intensively—in some instances hardly at all—were taken by the government and redistributed to peasant tenants and workers. Compensation was in 20-year bonds bearing interest at 5%, with an inflation adjustment in the bond value equal to three fourths of the rise in the cost of living index. Peasants who became owners decided through their own organization what share of the land they wished to divide up into individual plots and what share should remain undivided to gain the advantages of large scale cultivation. The proceeds from the latter were divided among the workers according to labor inputs, with labor graded and weighted

---

[22] Excerpts from Raup's essay, Warriner's book, and other useful comments on land reform are presented in *Development Digest* (U.S. Agency for International Development), April 1970.

according to the skill involved, much as in the most recent arrangement in China. However, the redistribution was hampered by both legislative resistance and administrative inexperience, and proceeded slowly.

Then, after the Socialist government of Allende had gained office in 1970, redistribution was accelerated. All farms above 250 acres in size were to be expropriated, including ones already intensively cultivated; in fact small and medium-sized farms were also expropriated, the selection of farms being haphazard; and peasants were encouraged to occupy lands and the police were ordered not to interfere. The motives presumably were an ideological sense of equity, a desire for revenge on political opponents, and a desire also to gain rapidly a strong base of political support among the peasants. But technical advice was neglected, and production fell. It fell also on farms not (in the owners' views, not yet) expropriated.

After the military overthrew the Allende government in 1973, the police and army aided former landowners to reverse the situation, though one may assume that it is not entirely reversible and will never return to the pre-1966 condition.

Land Reform in China

Under a Communist government, land reform may of course mean something far different from any of these "capitalist" types. In China, immediately after the Communist government gained power in 1949 it confiscated the lands of the landlords and richer peasants and distributed the land to poorer peasants and landless farm workers. Then between 1952 and 1957 individual peasant farming was replaced by production by "mutual aid teams," then by agricultural producers' cooperatives in which the income from production was divided on the basis partly of land owned and partly of labor contributed, then by cooperatives (or "collectives") in which income distribution was wholly on the basis of labor contributed. The land had for practical purposes become collectively owned, except for private garden plots whose produce could be sold or bartered in rural free markets. In 1958 there was very rapid amalgamation of collectives into huge communes having an average membership of 4,000 to 5,000 households or say five times that many individuals. The private garden plots and rural free markets were abolished.

The purpose of the successive collectivization and amalgamation was not primarily to permit machine use. Neither was the motivation merely ideological. Rather, peasant farms in China had become so small and so fragmented that their operation as individual units was very uneconomic. J. L. Buck's authoritative work (1937) reported that in 22 provinces surveyed in 1929–33, the average farm contained only 4.23 acres, and was divided into 5.6 fragments. Average farm size subsequently decreased further.

A commune was not merely a large collective farm. It was a political and administrative unit of government, and owner of rural nonagricultural enterprises. As agricultural producing units, the communes as set up in 1958 failed, probably partly because of ideologically-guided inefficient management but perhaps mainly because the relationship between an individual's work and his income was so slight that incentives declined. After an agricultural crisis in 1960, there was a gradual return to areas operated by production teams of 60 to 80 households. Private garden plots and rural free markets were restored. Further, a system of scaling the value of different types of labor, developed earlier, was introduced generally. Under it, skilled, technical, or managerial labor was given a greater return than ordinary labor.

Agricultural production rose fairly rapidly again. In 1967 the Chinese government began to re-institute communes. In 1973, according to a Chinese official, there were 76,000 communes. However, labor scaling was continued, and the announced intention to abolish again the private garden plots and rural free markets may not have been carried out fully. In spite of the later political disturbances in China, agricultural production has continued to rise—from 108 million tons in 1949 to 250 million tons in 1971 (reduced by drought to 246 in 1972), according to a Chinese report.[23] One reason, as a visiting team of highly qualified U.S. agricultural experts discovered in 1974, is that the Chinese had developed a short-stemmed rice capable of bearing heavy heads and yielding high yields with large applications of water and fertilizer before "miracle rice" was developed in the International Rice Research Institute.[24]

BIBLIOGRAPHICAL NOTE

C. Geertz (1963b) gives an insightful and delightful account of the difficulties of the transition from bazaar to fixed-price retail store in an Indonesian village.

Hayami and Ruttan (1971), Mellor (1974), and B. Johnston and P. Kilby (1975) present surveys and analyses of the role of agriculture in economic development. The first gives impressive econometric analysis. Mellor's book is a revision of a 1966 volume. The excellent volume by Johnston and Kilby gives especial attention to structural transformation and to the interaction between advance in agriculture and that in industry. Eicher and Witt, eds. (1964) and Southworth and Johnston, eds. (1967) gather together useful essays. Specifically concerning problems of in-

---

[23] I have the number of communes and the data on production from Aziz (1973).
[24] *New York Times,* October 7, 1974.

creasing productivity in agriculture, see T. W. Schultz (1964), and Millikan and Hapgood (1967), the latter of which reports on a 1964 conference of specialists on the problem.

Concerning land reform, see D. Warriner (1962) and (1969), and the essay by Philip Raup in Southworth and Johnston. K. R. Walker, *Planning in Chinese Agriculture* (1965), is good but now dated.

6

The Evolution of Industry: Relationships with Agriculture and Infrastructure

THE DIFFICULTY OF INNOVATION IN MANUFACTURING

The student of industrialization almost always takes as his starting point a situation in which the "dawn of proletarianization" has already occurred. He is interested, not in the transition from production in the individual household to production in petty industrial shops, but in the transition from these "cottage industries" to manufacturing, and in the later development of manufacturing. In this chapter too it will be assumed that cottage industry has already developed. The difficulties to be discussed are those of moving from the cottage-industry stage to the factory stage.[1] We picture a country with no factories, and ask: What difficulties will be faced in establishing them?

Prospective industrial enterprisers can usually enter any of a variety of industries serving their domestic market without fear of foreign competition. For some products, transportation costs provide a natural protection. This is true, for example, of brick and tile. For others, the products of industrial countries, designed for a high-income market, are not suitable for the low-income country's market. Or, more precisely, the foreign product has some advantages but is often sufficiently ill-adapted in other ways so that to most buyers the domestic product is more attractive at the relative prices of the two. Sandals and some agricultural implements are examples of such products. For a variety of products, the manufacturers of, say, Hong Kong, Singapore, and Japan are more of a threat than those of the West, because they make products better

---

[1] Illustrations of the difficulties of the earlier transition are found in the preceding chapter.

128

adapted to a low-income country's market. For such products, and for many manufactured in the West, tariff protection or other protection against imports may be needed for some time if indigenous factory production is to succeed. But tariff protection is commonly available to any enterpriser of a low-income country who offers a plausible proposal to produce a wanted industrial product.

Typically, however, the earliest industry is established by displacing, not imports, but the products of indigenous cottage industry. It would seem to many Western observers that there should be little difficulty in these cases. They assume that factory production is more efficient than traditional methods. In the production of certain products, this is true. But it is not true in general when the factory must operate within a nonmodern productive complex. A single factory, small or large, introduced into a nonindustrial society often will be less productive than traditional methods. For many products, modern production and modern productivity can emerge only by a developmental process, because of the difficulties discussed in this chapter.

For convenience, those difficulties may be classed under the three heads of cultural, technical, and economic barriers, though each difficulty has all three aspects in some degree.

Cultural Difficulties

Worker Attitudes. The prospective factory manager in a nonindustrial country faces certain difficulties in interpersonal relations not experienced except in minor degree in industrial countries, and ones of which the Western analyst considering the industrialization process is often unaware.

One of these is a certain type of difficulty in obtaining careful work by factory operatives. The difficulty is not merely lack of familiarity with the characteristics of machines. Workers in any society learn with great speed when motivated to do so, as for example in driving and caring for a truck or tractor of which they are proud. The difficulty which is unique, at least in degree, is a lack of interest in working efficiently, even willingness to do bad work, due to a sense of isolation and alienation that seems to be felt by most workers coming from a traditional social environment into the impersonal social system of a factory.

The problem differs depending on the economic and social structure of the country at the time when industrial establishments begin to be introduced. Three cases may be distinguished. The first is that of a well-functioning traditional peasant society. This case is typified by the Asia of a century or so ago. The second case is that of hacienda agriculture, common throughout Latin America. In the third case, traditional peasant agriculture has already been disrupted by the forces of history.

In a traditional peasant society that is functioning well, cultivation of small farm plots is by the proprietor (who may be an owner or, more usually, a renter) and members of his family or extended family. There are few landless laborers and few urban menial wage workers. Urban workers are self-employed craftsmen, craftsmen-merchants, or retainers. In such a society there are few candidates for industrial jobs. A craftsman or cultivator who becomes a factory worker suffers a considerable measure of loss of his sense of independence and productiveness, and of his social status in his village—for in the social scale of a traditional community, a factory worker is only a menial. He also loses his bond to a patron, who in the old round of village life had provided ritual leadership in times of emotional stress, some economic security in time of petty crisis, and guidance concerning affairs outside of the narrow range within which the inferior had competence—for example, public affairs. He also loses his religious base. The homage or propitiation he had traditionally offered to the unseen powers was given in part in ceremonies related to his traditional occupations. When he moves to a job in a factory, in some degree he may be abandoning his gods, and may expect to be abandoned by them.

These facts may be summed up by stating that a cultivator or crafts-man in a well-functioning traditional society feels rewards in his work and in the social relations that accompany it. The economic return it yields him is only one aspect of his satisfaction—indeed, emotionally it may be rather incidental. When he moves to a factory, however, the work itself is likely to offer him very little satisfaction. All he gets out of his job is the wages, and these may be paltry repayment for the losses he has suffered.[2] Even though he moved willingly and even eagerly, he may find later that he has abandoned valued facets of his life that he did not realize he was abandoning. He will be a poorer industrial worker because of his sense of loss.

Where hacienda agriculture exists, there are no similar attachments to a traditional situation. On a typical hacienda, the peasant has the right to cultivation of his very small plot of infertile land, but he is virtually a serf, not a tenant-cultivator. To such peasants, a move to a factory may be liberation, not a step downward. However, since they are serfs and not free to move, and since the estate owners are probably in a position to block establishment of factories that might induce peasants to flee the hacienda, the potentially favorable attitudes of workers may not come to fruition.

The well-functioning peasant society described above is rare today. In

---

[2] "The traditional rewards for work that flow from the character of the social rela-tions enjoyed at work give way to rewards that may be considered extrinsic to the work itself, in that they are rewards *for* the performance, rather than *in* performance. . . . In short, work tends to become dominantly instrumental rather than consummatory in its gratifications" M. M. Tumin (1960), pp. 281–82.

most societies, the traditional structure of peasant agriculture has broken down under the stresses of disorder or "modernization." A shift to factory work may not involve any emotional loss to these workers. The loss has already occurred.

It does not follow that the wage worker who has become a factory hand will be a contented and efficient or conscientious worker. If, as an agricultural worker cut off from attachment to the land, or an urban menial, he felt rejected by his society and perhaps by his gods, he may feel the same sense of alienation in the factory. The shift may simply give him a target on which to focus his restlessness and bitterness. Thus, though the recruitment of factory workers will be easier, obtaining their emotional commitment to industrial life may not. The class tensions which run so high in some Latin American countries—perhaps especially Argentina, Brazil, Chile—may be a result of such feelings of rejection and abandonment.

From this discussion of the likelihood of adverse worker attitudes, it would be easy to gain an exaggerated impression of the economic impact of labor problems in early industrialization. Workers who need income may work, unhappily and resentfully, but still well enough to hold their jobs, even if they are "alienated."

These difficulties are relative, not absolute ones. Where the traditional social structure has been breaking up for several generations and industrialization has been proceeding slowly for the same length of time, landless workers in agriculture or menials in towns may be so divorced from the traditional system of attachments and rewards that they do not feel the emotional losses described above even when they first move to factories. This seems to be true, for example, in Puerto Rico.[3]

A group of studies of migration from rural areas to towns and cities in Latin America and Africa are reported on briefly in Chapter 9. Uniformly, the migrants were from among the better educated (a few years of schooling) and, economically, the more secure young adults in their rural communities, not the landless and desperate. The deduction is drawn by some observers that by the time of these studies, the late 1960s, they no longer felt a deep attachment to the land. They had become, it is concluded, merely "economic men." In a now well-known 1969 article, also discussed in Chapter 9, John R. Harris and Michael Todaro suggest that young men migrate from rural areas to towns and cities because even if they are employed in the cities for a considerable part of the year their annual income is higher than on the farm.

However, it is well to be cautious in drawing conclusions from these facts. What seems to happen is that the rural family selects the appropriate one of its members to seek work in the city, and supports him while

---

[3] See P. Gregory in Moore and Feldman (1960).

he is conducting his search. If he succeeds, he then remits part of his income to augment the rural family income. And even if he is the best-educated young member of the family and sent for that reason, he and the family as a whole may be alienated and somewhat desperate. He may be driven off the farm by economic distress just as surely as if he were landless, and may feel social disaffection which makes him a reluctant and unmotivated industrial recruit. Or, on the other hand, he may be fairly cheerfully making his way in life. Without further psychological investigation, we cannot know what the implications of the family decision are.

Even where the initial emotional loss is great, in time workers do make the best of factory work and the associated round of life. Nevertheless, these problems increase the difficulty of successful establishment of a factory.

Foremanship.   In conditions of worker alienation, to operate a factory with a reasonable degree of efficiency would require unusually capable foremanship. The foreman is the immediate supervisor of the operatives. By virtue of his supervisory position he might replace the old patron. Unfortunately, however, being a foreman presents great difficulties to an individual in a nonindustrial society. Almost universally, observers of early industrialization mention the low quality of foremanship.

In function, a foreman is a supervisor, responsible for directing the workers to perform the tasks assigned to them. But he is also a helper. He should also know more about the petty technical problems and sources of difficulty in each worker's job than does the worker, and through that knowledge help each worker maintain the flow of output. On occasion he should be a spare workman, pitching in to help break bottlenecks.

However, since the foreman has the authority to direct a group of subordinates, in a traditional society he is on the verge of becoming one of the lesser elites. One of the evidences of eliteness is the exercise of authority. Moreover, the sign of eliteness in a traditional society is that the individual does not demean himself by concerning himself with the details of manual labor. The nonelite individual who has become a foreman is likely to have in exaggerated form the sense that an elite gives orders and is above concern with menial tasks. Hence he is not likely to perform efficiently the menial tasks associated with his job.

To put the matter in another way, effective foremanship requires a combination of attitudes of eliteness and alert concern with grubby tasks. These attitudes are antithetical in a traditional society, and an individual attempting to combine them is likely to be so conflicted within himself that he is not able to function with high efficiency.

This explanation is, of course, only hypothetical. However, the problem of foremanship is so ubiquitous in early industry that some forces as deep-seated as these must cause it.

Other Interpersonal Relationships. One element of the moral code of traditional culture is an overriding obligation to take care of one's family, relatives, and the members of one's group. It is overriding in the sense that it may take precedence over the requirement of honesty to others, as a person from an industrial society interprets honesty. Because the obligation is so strong, in forming his management staff an enterpriser cannot appoint the most competent available persons from his entire society, for they may cheat him to provide the better for their relatives and friends. Conversely, he must honor his obligations to a relative even though that relative is not extremely competent.[4]

This dependence on one's relatives also has a positive aspect. One can rely on them for a degree of support and loyalty that may be less easy to obtain in an industrial society.

The traditional need to select one's associates from only the members of one's immediate group is commonly mentioned in the Western literature. It is less well known that a related difficulty exists in dealing with customers or suppliers. The traditional mores are illustrated in Professor Levy's statement of the ethics of interpersonal dealings in traditional China. His statement is widely applicable elsewhere, and the past tense in which he couches it might appropriately be altered to the present tense with reference to nonindustrial countries. "One was adequately protected in private dealings," he states, "if one had established either directly or through a carefully chosen go-between a personal bond with those with whom one dealt. Strangers, however, were fair game in a radically *caveat emptor* fashion that would horrify the most rapt laissez-faire idealists of the modern West."[5] Even in the industrial city of Medellin, Colombia, a leading businessman, discussing business practices in the region, said to the writer in 1958: "In our contractual relationships we do not depend on enforcement in the courts. Court processes are too cumbersome to be effective. If we have not gained confidence in a man through personal contacts or recommendations, we do not deal with him."

Technical Difficulties

Technical Aspects of Management. Even as the factory manager faces these cultural problems, he will face a set of technical problems that are bewildering if he has not had industrial experience. He must select his equipment. In large degree he will have to depend either on the apparent reputation of a manufacturer or on technical advisers whom he engages

---

[4] His decisions are probably not conscious ones. He "instinctively" distrusts strangers and is unwilling to entrust policy decisions, the hiring of staff members, the firm's financial secrets, or the handling of money, to persons not members of his primary group.

[5] M. J. Levy, Jr., in Abramovitz et al., p. 463.

more or less on faith. Having arranged for the erection of a plant and installation of equipment, he must create a management structure whose requirements he does not fully understand, and must arrange for the training and supervision of a raw work force in processes with which neither he nor the work force is acquainted. He must face the technical problems of the maintenance and repair of the strange and fairly complex machinery and its occasional adjustment. Moreover, he will have to purchase raw materials with awareness both of the range of capability of the factory's machinery and the relative financial advantage of different qualities, which alter as their relative prices change.

These problems are learning problems. But the learning required is not simple, and the prospect may deter any but the boldest entrepreneur from making a large technical move at one step. Few men are likely to have gained relevant experience in a foreign-owned factory, for until industrialization is under way, foreign-owned industrial establishments are likely to be extractive ones. This is why run-of-the-mill operators of small shops may never make the transition. Even for energetic, judicious, and self-confident native enterprisers the transition may be from cottage industry to workshop to a modest degree of mechanization to a true factory, and may require a lifetime, or the combined lifetimes of father and son.

Absence of an Industrial Complex. The basic technical problem, not soluble by a learning process, results from the fact that the factory is not situated within an industrial complex.

The earliest factories will probably be ones that do not need to depend on other plants for an assured flow of inputs. If they did, they probably could not exist. For example, apart from raw cotton a cotton textile factory needs few current inputs except lubricants and some simple chemicals. But even such a self-contained factory may face difficulties of power supply which force it to provide its own power; of machine repair and replacement; of transportation and communication; and of expert technical advice when complications arise. I referred at the beginning of the preceding chapter to the fact that almost every factory in an industrial country owes its efficiency in part to the fact that it obtains components, materials, and services from many other plants, whose efficiency in turn depends on the fact that they specialize and that they produce specialized products in a volume made possible because they sell to many customers. An early factory in a nonindustrial country must somehow devise substitutes for the presence of many specialized suppliers from whom it can obtain bolts, gaskets, valves, wire, specialized cloth or dyes or rubber products, and a dozen or several dozen other components produced if necessary to high quality and fine specifications; casting, forging, and machining services for maintenance and repair; and technical advice if needed. This is one of the two greatest difficulties in the industrialization process. (The other is the economic problem of factor prices, discussed below.) So smoothly does the industrial system of a technically advanced country run that it is not easy for residents of such a country, even residents reasonably well informed about industrial processes, to realize the problems of establishing a single factory in, so to speak, a wilderness, and running it so that its cost of production is less than that of traditional processes even though the relative costs of labor and capital are in effect "stacked against it."

Economic Difficulties

These cultural and technical difficulties are compounded by economic ones.

Capital; Foreign Exchange. Difficulties due to shortage of capital and of foreign exchange must form an important part of the subject matter of any book on the economics of development. In this book they are discussed at length in Chapters 7 and 17. The reader is merely reminded here that he does not have a balanced view of the barriers to economic development until these too have been taken into account.

The small size of the market in a low-income country with poor transportation is also often mentioned in the economic literature as a deterrent to industrialization. The argument is discussed in Chapters 7 and 10. The conclusion is reached that it is greatly overstated. The size of the market is more likely to be an obstacle at a later stage in development.

Relative Factor Prices. A basic and universal difficulty is that mechanized methods may be disadvantageous in a nonindustrial society simply because labor costs are low. This difficulty is referred to by economists as that of relative factor prices. The "factors" referred to are labor and capital.

Some modern industrial processes performed by machinery could not be done by labor-intensive methods (methods using much labor relative to the amount of machinery) no matter how much labor was employed. The necessary precision could not be attained or the chemical process carried on except by mechanized methods. With respect to these processes, the fact that labor is cheap is irrelevant.

However, a second reason for a high degree of mechanization in industrial countries is to save labor even in processes that can readily be done by hand. As the cost of labor per man-hour in industrial countries has risen with rising productivity, it has become cheaper to do many things with much machinery and few workers even though they can be done with technical adequacy by a larger number of workers using simpler equipment. For two centuries inventive effort has been channeled into devising increasingly labor-saving and capital-using machines and methods.

The labor-saving aspects of these machines are inappropriate in a low-income economy. The machines cost even more than in an industrial country, for they must be imported from the industrial country. The rate of interest on the capital invested is also likely to be higher. But labor may cost only, say, one tenth as much per man-hour. Hence a machine which is economic in an industrial country because it saves the labor of, say, 5 workers and involves an annual cost (for amortization interest, and maintenance) less than that of their services, would be an expensive luxury in a nonindustrial country where 20 workers could be hired at an annual cost much lower than that of the machine. As an example of this situation, U.S. engineers who were asked to recommend a mechanized process for loading rice onto ships in Burma found that even by giving a mechanized bulk-loading process the benefit of every doubt in their calculations they could not arrive at a cost as low as that of "coolies" transporting the rice from warehouse to barge and barge to ship in 212-pound sacks.

Professor Hoffmann found that this consideration was important in the German weaving industry even in the 19th century. Mechanization in German weaving, he states, proceeded slowly until after 1865 because "so long as the wages were low, the mechanical loom had no cost advantage over the hand loom."[6]

In such cases, the real cost of a capital-intensive method to the country, not merely its financial cost to an entrepreneur, is higher than that of labor-intensive methods.

If machines ideally designed for low-income countries were available, in the early stages of development the only machine methods adopted would be certain ones that are technically impossible without the machines, plus ones by which with a fairly small amount of capital a very high aggregate labor cost was saved. As wages rose with economic development it would become economic to use increasing increments of capital to save labor.

In fact, this is what happens in the course of development, but the choices facing enterprisers in nonindustrial countries who are purchasing Western machinery are not as simple as those suggested above. Many machines devised in the West incorporate both labor-saving features that are wasteful in low-income countries and technical features for which there are no feasible labor-intensive alternatives. The one must be bought with the other. The mechanization of auxiliary operations such as in-plant transportation can be avoided, but in the fabricating processes themselves, the enterpriser must either use a machine that incorporates expensive labor-saving features or use a nonmachine method (producing a somewhat different product). The greater the labor-saving element

---

[6] W. G. Hoffmann in Rostow (1964), p. 109.

inseparably incorporated in a machine, the greater the likelihood that a private entrepreneur who tries to introduce the capital-intensive method in a low-labor-cost economy will fail.

In summary, then, the cultural problems of moving directly to modern factory production in a nonindustrial society are the reaction of workers to the partial destruction of their world involved in their shift to factory work, the psychological contradictions of foremanship, and the narrowness of the group whose members are members of one's community and hence are trustworthy in economic transactions. The purely technical problems are the complex problems of machine management and the absence of an industrial and related institutional complex. The economic problems are lack of capital and of foreign exchange, in some instances the smallness of the market, and the very high cost of capital relative to labor. A further aspect of the problem is that of entrepreneurship itself. Persons with traditional attitudes will not be entrepreneurial in technical and economic affairs. Lack of effective entrepreneurship in these fields is one basic reason why the problems sketched in this and the preceding chapter are overcome only very slowly.

As in the cases of change in trade and in agriculture, the problem is a "system problem." Resourceful men overcome the resistances, and change proceeds, as the data on economic growth presented in Chapter 1 testify.

A SCHEMA OF TECHNICAL STAGES IN INDUSTRIALIZATION

In a certain sense, as countries industrialize they all follow the same path.

There is some uniformity among nonindustrial countries with respect to the types of goods and services they produce: They start the process of industrialization from a common base. All produce a cereal that is the mainstay of the diet. If the country's climate is adapted to growing wheat, then the people have learned to like wheat; if rice, then rice. Most produce cotton, a few wool, and a very few some other fiber, as the basic material for clothing, and spin and weave it. Virtually all produce shoes or sandals, some type of sugar, some type of fermented alcoholic beverage, and some leather and wool products. The simple services produced are also uniform, and there are various other similarities.

There is also variation, caused mainly by differences in climate and in natural resources; and as industrialization proceeds there are differences in the relative demand for various industrial products. These are caused mainly by differences in physical circumstances and in national policy—for example, defense policy. These differences in preindustrial production and in industrial demand have caused differences in the goods produced and therefore some differences in methods. But there are common elements in methods, even though different goods are produced, and certain characteristics of the process of industrialization appear with surprising uniformity in all or almost all countries.

An industrial complex evolves in a definable series of steps. The sequence is determinate enough to be called a set of stages, for the characteristics of each stage, taken as a group, differ from those of the others, and the events of each stage lead to those of the next.[7] The dividing lines between stages are not sharp; the process is as gradual as organic growth; perhaps an apt comparison is with the human growth stages of infancy, childhood, adolescence, and adulthood. However, no one would wish to claim as unequivocal an existence for the stages of industrial development as for those of human growth, for intrusions from the outside may alter the former in ways for which there is no close parallel in the biological case.

At first view, the constraints on the sequence seem essentially engineering ones, but since the basic question is the cost at which products can be produced they are also fundamentally economic ones. The engineering underlies the economics.

A typical sequence in the development of an industrial complex is first described below. Variations from it are then commented on. I have put the description in the present tense, with an occasional historical excursus.

1. Advance in Self-Contained Processes

At some point in time, enterprisers who feel secure in managing small wage-labor shops are ready to attempt further steps in change. One causal or permissive factor is usually observation or indirect knowledge of a more advanced process abroad; technical re-discovery *de novo* is extremely rare. Advance is by no means automatic or routine. Colombian history provides an example. There is an impressive record of successive attempts and failures, along with successes, in the region of Colombia around Bogota (the Sabana) between 1830 and 1890. This was the region that had the greatest contact with Europe. In the region of Antioquia, much more isolated, the first stages of advance came later, but were much more rapid and assured when they did come.[8] Failures also plagued Japanese entrepreneurs in the 1870s and 1880s, even though from their observations of European power they were convinced of the superior efficiency of machine methods. Probably if the detailed history of any industrial country during the early phase of industrialization were

---

[7] See Kuznets' statement of the logical requirements of a schema of stages, in Rostow (1964).

[8] See the detailed account of industrial development in the two regions in Ospina Vasquez (1955).

known, many early failures would be found. They are testimony to the presence of the difficulties surveyed above.

Early successes are improvements in the production of goods already familiar and widely used in rougher forms—for example, sugar, soap, matches, rice or wheat flour, leather, footwear, sawn lumber, bricks, and textiles and textile products. Plants producing coarse or rough paper for packaging may be established. So also may a quasi-modern cement plant. The brewing of beer is usually introduced early, and beer takes over the urban market from the traditional crudely fermented, moderately alcoholic drink. In many instances the brewer begins to make glass bottles when he begins to brew beer; bottle-making is not a complex process. Small semimodern brick kilns, making brick of uniform dimensions, sturdier and more free from warping than the traditional product, succeed. Slightly mechanized methods of making earthenware, improving its quality and increasing its uniformity, are introduced. In many countries, production of a new agricultural crop becomes important at or before this stage; for example, coffee in Colombia in the 1880s after its limited production for a generation or two previously. If so, the production of tools for its cultivation often occupies the energies of some of the early innovators, and its processing those of others.

In many of these processes, the introduction of mechanical power coincides with that of machinery for more uniform processing. In the 19th century, the source of power was often a water wheel whose motion was transmitted to machinery by means of pulleys, belts, and gears. Later, the water wheel may have driven an electric generator. Or, depending on the time in history when the plant was established, the motive source may have been a steam, gasoline, or diesel engine. In any event, usually the plant provided its own power; dependable power was not available from an outside source. And even today a new factory in a nonindustrial country is likely to have its own auxiliary motor because the public electricity supply is likely to fail.

In most Latin American countries, as earlier in Great Britain, the first brewer was a German immigrant. Some of the other early industrial innovations are also by immigrants. They are likely to be immigrants from countries only a generation or two ahead in the industrialization process who see greater opportunity or greater freedom in the still less-experienced country. The national market for advanced industrial products is not yet large enough to be attractive to corporations from industrial countries.

Two common qualities define these enterprises:

1. Almost all of the advances are in the production of goods with whose qualities producers are familiar because similar products were previously produced by traditional methods. Often, imports may already have partially displaced the traditional goods. Domestic production then

replaces some imports, but only because the domestic producers are given protection against imports by high tariffs, quotas, or in some cases merely high transportation costs.

2. The processes introduced are largely "straight-line, self-contained" processes. They do not require the feeding in of a considerable range of supplies and components from other industrial plants. With relatively little qualification, they take a raw material and by a straight sequence of processes turn it into a finished product. The only industrial products needed as inputs are auxiliary materials of which a large enough supply for a long time can easily be stored, such as lubricating oil. As noted above, even power is self-supplied. Thus there is no need either to obtain dependable flows of supplies from other parts of an industrial complex or to solve a considerable range of new technical and managerial problems simultaneously. So conspicuous is this quality that I have termed the stage that of "advance in self-contained processes."

Another conspicuous characteristic is that the new methods involve only a moderate increase in the use of capital per worker. Nevertheless, certain minimum plant sizes are necessary. The first cotton-spinning factories in Japan during the period from 1867 to 1883 had 2,000 or fewer spindles each. Each factory remained alive only through government subsidies. The first financially successful spinning mill was that of Shibusawa, in Osaka, which opened in 1883. It had 10,500 spindles. However, its success was not due merely to its size. It also was better located than its predecessors, and employed the best of the few technicians then available in Japan.

Many of the new methods of production use types of work teams, relationships of workers to machines, types of work leadership, management organization, institutions of worker payment, and the like, drawn out of the practices of the traditional society. However, as the introduction of new methods proceeds, more and more frequently is it necessary to organize workers into teams of uncongenial sorts or to assign them to isolated tasks, doing work whose rhythm is largely dictated by machines. The development of foremanship and increasing delegation of authority is required. As the entrepreneurs master these changed methods, no doubt workers too are adapting to them more or less fully, more or less resentfully; execution of the function of foremanship is gradually becoming increasingly effective; and both workers and managers are learning more and more securely elementary control of specifications and quality.

For some of the new products the market is uncertain, for the products are of a distinctly new quality, and their sale must depend on a shift from traditional consumer demand. The converse of a fact stated in chapter 5 in the discussion of the transition from the bazaar is now pertinent: success in selling these new products depends on the simultaneous appearance of new enterprisers in trade who make the shift from bazaar to retail store and handle them, and the emergence of socially restless consumers moving up to the "middle classes" who buy them.

2. Increase in Interrelationships

Two developments now occur. They are readily distinguishable from each other, and I have struggled to order them in time so that they might be termed separate stages, but they occur so concurrently with each other that it is better to regard them as aspects of a single stage.

From one of the two arises the term with which I have labeled this stage. Even in the first stage there had been a few instances of production by some industrial enterprises for others: paper for packaging or wrapping many articles, bricks for construction, coal for steam engines. Now "linkages" appear in greater volume,[9] for the growing volume of production now causes several industrial enterprises in combination to become markets for one or another component, material, or auxiliary item large enough so it pays some local entrepreneur to enter upon its production. Examples are cement blocks, cardboard cartons, simple cast parts, wire, bottles, sulphuric acid, caustic soda, and other simple chemicals.

Rolling mills that would look like toys to any steel producer are constructed, in some cases to roll nothing but light reinforcing rods. Tools and very simple machines for the new industries begin to be made within the country. If a dominating type of farming provides a large market for certain types of farm machinery, simple agricultural machines also begin to be produced domestically.

Unlike most of the production processes of the first stage, the production of these component materials and products replaces imports.

"Forward" linkages also appear. That is, either the plants producing some of the new industrial products, or other plants, begin to process those products further. For example, sugar refineries begin to produce alcohol and syrup also. To some cotton gins there is added a press to extract much of the cottonseed oil and a chemical process to extract more. Cement plants begin producing cement tile and tubes and perhaps also asphalt sheets and limestone tile.

One sort of improvement in specialized supplier operations is perhaps especially important as a basis for later advances. This is improvement in casting, forging, and machining. Capability develops to do more elaborate and more precise work than before, and to work in other metals than merely iron. The importance of this local service for repair, maintenance, and other metal-working is great.

---

[9] The term is Hirschman's (1958).

The second aspect of this second stage is that methods of production become continually more capital-intensive and more removed from traditional ones. For example, textile plants become much larger and more complex, and truly modern cement plants appear. They are not simply larger; they use more capital per worker. The development is a continuation of the preceding development, and if this were the only change one would hardly be warranted in referring to it as a separate stage, yet the increasing capital-intensivity and complexity is conspicuous enough to be noted. Several factors make this development possible. Management has gained experience. With an increasing scale of production, further mechanization is economic. The rising cost of labor as its productivity increases makes the further substitution of capital for labor economic. The plowing back of profits provides the increasingly experienced managers with the necessary capital. Sometimes they are able to borrow capital at this stage. Growth in the size of the market is stressed in much of the literature as a cause of the emergence of larger enterprises, but the growth in managerial experience and capability may be more important. When entrepreneurs are ready to tackle management of more complex enterprises, it often turns out that the market has lain waiting for them since the days of purely traditional methods.

3. The Expansion of Light Engineering

By this point in its technical development, the economy is becoming capable of working metal in increasingly diversified ways. Some fairly simple advances in light engineering in the earlier stages of progress have been mentioned above. In due time, light engineering begins to expand more rapidly than industry in general. An increasing variety of metal containers, components, and simple tools and machines begins to be produced within the country. The production within the country of almost all component parts of bicycles is symbolic evidence that this stage is well advanced, and is of more than symbolic importance, for bicycles are an important early form of local transportation.

The expansion of light engineering includes the production or the partial production within the country of many products previously imported.

Some simple light engineering products which do not involve too-exacting specifications, and which include few components too complex to be produced domestically, are produced within the country except for the import of those components. Twentieth-century examples are commercial air conditioning systems (domestic production of conduits and mountings, with importation of the motor, refrigeration unit, and fan) and refrigerators (domestic production of the casing, importation of the insulating material, compressor, and motor).

4. Control of Quality and Tolerances

Now there occurs a long stage or stages of progressive improvement in control of quality and of size tolerances in metal-working industries. This makes possible more complex products and more efficient techniques and permits the establishment of new industrial plants. The strands of industrial interrelationships increase greatly in number and complexity.

As this stage proceeds, the government may decide to enforce by foreign exchange and import controls the domestic production of some components for complex products. The process is uneconomic; it is costly to ship a product from an industrial country minus some component and then install the component in the country of sale, and costly also to ship many components and assemble the product in the country of final sale.

However, when the state of technical advance in the country permits, local assembly is often forced by governmental policies. This has been true since the second World War in all of the larger Latin American countries, from which all of the examples of expansion of light engineering are drawn. When capital goods imports, capital flight, a worsening of the terms of trade, or more commonly the last two in combination, had caused scarcity of foreign exchange, the government refused import licenses to the suppliers of certain finished commodities unless they agreed to assemble and then increasingly to manufacture their products within the country. Once domestic assembly was occurring, the way was open to domestic production of as many components as technical capabilities permitted, and these capabilities and this production expanded. Almost any country as it develops technically will presently be assembling some simple machines, and at least the larger countries will find assembling a main channel of entry into the fabrication of transport vehicles, industrial engines, electrical machinery, and various other fairly complex metal products.

Advance in techniques in other types of manufacturing also proceeded. As it did, the complexity of interrelations of supply continued to increase. The manufacture of components and assembly of products in itself involved new interrelations. Development of the metal-working industry added a new dimension to the relationships, and among the industries producing light metal products, nondurable consumer goods, construction materials, and the construction industry itself, interrelations of growing complexity contributed to the increase of productivity. In the countries that have so far reached this stage, strands of supply relationships among concerns began to take on the appearance of a net.

During these stages of technical change, certain institutional and financial changes that cannot be attributed with certainty to any one stage occur.

As ventures are entered upon which are both new and larger than traditional ones, the diversification and limitation of individual risk becomes of increasing importance. The adoption of corporate institutions, or some adaptation of traditional institutions which accomplishes the same purpose, appears within industry.[10] Though the concept that a business enterprise is a family entity dies hard, it is gradually replaced in many sectors of industry and some of trade by some professionalization of management.[11] Depersonalization of relationships among business firms proceeds more or less *pari passu.*

The adaptation of other traditional contractual and financial practices to the new business complexities also proceeds. Commercial banking appears fairly early. A few of the most successful companies sell stock through a network of contracts, but a general capital market will be a late development.

5. The Stage of Industrial Complexity

The stages of advance in self-contained processes, establishment of initial interrelationships, and expansion of light engineering involved a minimum of several generations and perhaps a much longer period from the time when the first innovation steps became conspicuous in the erstwhile traditional economy. For lack of the information necessary to make further differentiations, even roughly, all later technical progress may be lumped together as a fifth stage, the stage of increasing industrial complexity. The following description of this stage is drawn from the experience of the technically advanced countries.

It will be marked by the expansion and increase in complexity of the metallurgical and chemical industries, the development of the heavier metal-working processes, ultimately with fine tolerances, and perhaps the development also of an advanced electronics industry. The state ultimately reached will depend largely on the size of the economy.

The transition from light engineering to heavy engineering and advanced industrial metallurgy, chemistry, and electronics has not been studied. To casual observation the technical jump involved seems very large. How it is accomplished is puzzling. A guess may be ventured that

---

10 In Antioquia, where mining was of importance two centuries or more before the beginnings of industrialization in the 19th century, a form of limited-liability organization was devised and applied to mining ventures before industrialization began. See Hagen (1962), p. 373.

11 The present head of a Colombian industrial enterprise that is one of the largest in Latin America in its field, and large even by United States standards, told the author in conversation that when he returned to Colombia in the 1930s after obtaining a technical education in the United States, and took a corporate job rather than establishing his own family business, he was looked upon with some condescension as a man willing to be a mere hired hand.

the explanation is twofold: progress into the advanced techniques may be by a series of not very large steps that go unnoticed, only the fairly spectacular final result attracting attention; and on the other hand, by this stage in industrialization entrepreneurs are ready to take rather large jumps.

The relative growth of these industries is not the only distinctive characteristic of the fifth stage. Another is continued increase in specialization and in supply interrelationships. The net becomes a web. Ultimately the web becomes so elaborate that in a sense there are no independent productive establishments; there is only a productive complex, though perhaps one with thicker and more numerous strands of interrelationship within some subcomplexes than among them.

In a country that advances far into this stage there may develop a productive system which, perhaps with the import of the components embodying the world's latest technical advances, will be able to produce any known product within some area of specialization. Japan has recently reached this point of wide technical versatility. Its technical prowess in specific fields illustrates that a latecomer may reach and push back some world technical frontiers.

The countries labeled the world's 25 "least developed" by the United Nations Committee for Development Planning, and perhaps a handful more are at the beginning of stage 1; various countries of Latin America are somewhere between the end of stage 2 and the beginning of stage 4; southern Italy is hardly in stage 3; Sao Paulo is beyond stage 4 and well into stage 5; various regions of India are at each of the stages from 1 through late 4; as in any large country, different regions of Brazil and India are at different stages in the development of an industrial complex. Somewhere in stage 4, foreign firms begin to be able to manufacture effectively in the country, and they become increasingly important as the country progresses into stage 5.

During the progressive elaboration of an industrial complex, there occurs introduction of more advanced methods in individual processes. While this is mentioned only in passing in the schema of stages above, it is an important part of the process of industrialization. For example, each of the types of plants mentioned as appearing in stage 1 may continue to exist, becoming more and more complex (and usually more capital-intensive) during the industrialization process, and may be found flourishing in stages 4 or 5.

This technical advance in individual processes occurs because of increased specialization, the increasing size of the market with rising income and thus an increase in possible scale of production, the increased knowledge and skill of the producers and progressive ability to handle increasingly complex methods adapted from abroad, and because of new creative ideas that are not merely induced by specialization or the investment in knowledge. The progressive development of an industrial complex plus this process inextricably interwoven with it constitute the process of industrialization.

The discussion so far has given the impression of a rather diffused and balanced process of technical advance, similar in every country. But while there are important comparabilities, there is also a good deal of product specialization. Innovational energies in a society are channeled into one field of production or another by the opportunities created by a natural resource advantage (England, New Zealand, the Netherlands, Denmark), lack of natural resources (Japan, Switzerland), a major invention or group of inventions (also England), concentrated government demand (the Soviet Union), or other factors. As a result, technical advance and the development of industry are concentrated—though never wholly so—in that field and those to which it has important linkages. The country then imports components, complementary materials, and finished industrial products in which it does not specialize. The United States has the most diversified industry in the world. Yet economically the case of the United States is not greatly different from that of Western Europe. Shipments of components and materials that in the United States are regional, are international in Western Europe because there are political boundaries.

This specialization does not limit the applicability of the schema of stages, since that schema relates to techniques and interrelationships, not to types of products.

COMMENTS ON THE INDUSTRIALIZATION PROCESS

The Pace of Advance

Broadly speaking, advance to each stage of the schema is a necessary condition for advance to the next.

However, no country will repeat precisely the technical steps of others, for two reasons. One is that the steps require innovation within each country, and because men and resources differ, the entrepreneurs of different countries will innovate in ways differing in large or small degrees. The other is that the technical steps available to any generation differ from those available to preceding ones. The development of the steam engine, the internal combustion engine—first gasoline, now diesel—and the electric generator and motor each offered new opportunities. The development of radio communication obviates passage through earlier communication stages. And so on.

Yet the need for the evolutionary construction of a productive complex makes the concept of "leaping from the 17th century to the 20th" futile. But the pace in different countries will be different. What happens is not the bypassing of a developmental process, but rather of taking larger steps along it—donning two-league boots if not seven-league boots. The greater the technical ingenuity and entrepreneurial resourcefulness, the larger the technical steps that can be taken and the difficulties of component parts and materials and complementary production that can be met.

The pertinent historical case is that of Japan, where industrialization surged forward beginning in the 1880s. The clans who overthrew the feudal Tokugawa regime and the Meiji restoration of 1868 sent scores of Japanese nobles already well educated in Japan to Europe for technical training, and brought a few technical advisers to Japan. Simultaneously, the government established a number of industrial enterprises, absorbed their losses, and then if they began to operate successfully sold them for pittances to private investors. It provided an assured market for others. Amusingly, the process was not the result of a far-sighted and broadly-based plan of stimulating the enterprises that would most advance Japanese industry. Rather, the government simply fostered in one of these two ways enterprises to produce goods that the government itself used in large quantities—paper, coal, and so on. Moreover, it did not sell its plants to entrepreneurs judged the most promising; rather, it rewarded the nobles (or in some cases merchants) who had supported the overthrow of the Tokugawa government. However, these were also the men most deeply motivated toward industrial progress.

Simultaneously, eager entrepreneurs (many with financial assurances from the government) erected plants to produce for the private market. In doing so they made technical leaps greater than those that have been made in any other country. In 1867 the first cotton-spinning mill in Japan began to operate, and within a five-year period in the 1870s the following first factories in various industries began to operate: silk reeling, 1872; soap, 1873; glass, 1873; Western-type paper, 1874; cement, 1875; matches, 1875; beer, 1876. Brick-making plants and wool-spinning mills opened apparently during the same period. The list is not complete. These are the dates of initial, not necessarily successful, operations. A scholar writes of the Japanese factories of the 1880s: "What came out of the machine [in a paper mill] did not look like paper, and no one knew what was wrong." And: "all three [pioneer cotton] mills encountered breakdowns, cracked gears, and broken pistons, and they were often operated with broken parts impossible to repair."[12] Another student of early Japanese industrial development states of one of the early spinning mills: "During the first seven years and very possibly the first thirty-five years of the firm's operation, English technicians were never far away."[13] The accounts seem contradictory, but possibly both are correct.

---

[12] Kee Il Choi (1967). The list of early factories is also from Choi.
[13] G. Saxenhouse (1974), p. 152.

The entrepreneurs persisted. Some failed, but many succeeded, and Japan entered upon modern industry more rapidly than any country had done before her and almost certainly more rapidly than any country will in the future.

Japan's burst of industrialization was spectacular. But one should be cautious in generalizing from the case. Since the 6th century Japan has shown a unique ability to adapt from abroad what was useful for her national life. Moreover, she did not enter upon industrialization in the 1870s in a state of technical innocence. There had been two centuries of innovation in Japan before the Meiji Restoration, in handicraft production on an increasing scale (though not with power-driven machinery) and in business methods. Marked and progressive increase in productivity in agriculture had occurred even much earlier.[14] Japanese nobles of the clans that took power had been studying the Dutch language and Dutch industrial methods before 1800, and studied them fairly intensively from 1800 on.[15] Their interest during the entire 19th century in acquiring the technology necessary "to protect themselves from the barbarians" (that is, Europeans) was intense. A small cadre of individuals had become well versed in Western industrial techniques and had been experimenting with some of them since soon after 1800—a fact not known in the West until historical research since the second World War uncovered the facts.[16] Before mid-century the Japanese had established metallurgical laboratories. Between 1850 and 1853 technicians of the Saga han (clan) built several successful reverberatory furnaces, using a Dutch book as a guide, and in 1853, the year of Commodore Perry's first arrival, they cast a satisfactory iron gun. "Even though this gun is not the equal of those made in the West," wrote the Japanese translator of the book used in building the furnaces, "the difference is not very great." To this background was added what must be termed Japanese genius.

All or virtually all of the low countries in which rapid technical progress has not yet begun or has barely begun are far more traditional in some relevant institutional and cultural respects than England was in 1750, other countries of Western Europe in 1800, or Japan at the time of Meiji Restoration in 1868. There is no reason to expect in any of the low countries the burst of supreme industrial talent and energy which alone would make it possible to parallel Japan's achievement.

Investment in low-income countries by foreign companies might conceivably provide the technical base for larger-than-average jumps, but

---

14 Reischauer and Fairbank (1958), p. 557; T. C. Smith (1959), Chap. 7.

15 Until the 17th century Holland had been in the technical forefront among European nations, and through Holland's merchant voyages around Asia and up to the East Indies Japan had become acquainted with Dutch prowess.

16 For a summary of some relevant facts, see Smith (1955), Chap. 1. The statement about the iron gun is from Smith, p. 4.

that it *will* do so is unlikely. The types of plants which might provide such aid are ones producing for the domestic market. Foreign firms do not establish many such plants in low-income countries, for several reasons. The host government is often not hospitable. The productive processes used by the foreign firm in its own country are usually not well adapted to transplantation to a simpler industrial environment. Executives in industrial countries are usually too fully engaged with the problems and opportunities of investment in their own country to be interested in a small venture in areas that are foreign in several senses. Acceleration by foreign firms of the later stages of industrialization is much more likely and much more frequent.

Inevitable Progress?

If each step in the sequence of industrialization sketched above paves the way for the next, this raises the question of whether the sequence is self-sustaining. Started on the road, are the entrepreneurs of a country fairly certain to learn from each step the way to progress to the next? The answer must be a qualified one: no, in the early stages of industrialization; perhaps yes and perhaps no, in the later stages.

At least in the early stages, the process of industrialization may itself generate resistances that will check it. In his classic study of the recruitment and commitment of labor to industry, Moore (1951, p. 304) concludes:

> Agricultural improvements, that is, the introduction of processing, are not necessarily "on the road" toward industrialization where they establish a new equilibrium based on relatively unskilled labor. . . . In any case of moderate, adaptive innovation, the reaction of workers to the new situation may be sufficiently hostile to prejudice rather than promote further changes of the same variety.

Moore (ibid.) suggests also that

> . . . decentralized industry may fit the previous social structure so completely that the small increase in production has no further implications either for capital accumulation or for attitudinal changes that would lead to continuing transformation.

And Nash (1958), in his study of the town of Cantel in the Guatemalan highlands, portrays an adaptation by the Indians (to a textile factory that employs almost a fourth of the town's workers) so satisfying that no motivation for further change seems to exist and no further change is likely.

However, there are no clear cases of stoppage once economic growth has continued long enough so that per capita output is several hundred dollars per year. In Argentina and Chile, class tensions are high. After smoldering for a long time they have burst into the open in cost-push inflationary pressures far too intense to be contained by monetary means. Large-scale capital flight has also resulted. Yet in each country economic growth, though slowed, seems to be continuing; that is, per capita income is apparently continuing to rise, though the vitality of the growth may not be entirely certain for another decade.

In the intermediate and later stages of growth, the demand for imports generated by the process may be greater than can be met. Development may be retarded (see Chapter 17). But there is no evidence that it may be stopped.

Hence it is possible that through the learning steps which it provides and the funds for further investment which it generates, after a certain point the process of industrialization is self-sustaining.[17] However, another explanation of continued growth is also plausible. Growth begins only if a fairly high degree of innovative energy and values that channel it into industrial management and technical innovation exist among members of a society. Once social conditions have generated this innovative energy and these values, they may be self-perpetuating for six or a dozen generations through the home environment they create. As long as they exist, they may carry industrial innovation along as a current carries a boat.

This thesis, which rests on psychoanalytical considerations, seems plausible to the writer, but there is no point in spelling it out here. Even if it is correct, it would be agreed that so long as a son does not feel oppressed or disregarded by his father, the example of a father contented in his entrepreneurial role tends to attract a son to a similar role. In this sense, innovation may be self-perpetuating. On the other hand, it is thought that the rootlessness of industrial life tends gradually to create a home environment which lessens innovative qualities and turns values elsewhere. Hence the question whether and for how long economic growth is self-sustaining is at best a very complex one and at worst a mere semantic quibble. No further attention will be given to it in this book.

Variations from the Schema

The schema sketched describes a more or less typical sequence of industrialization—the "natural history" of industrialization, or the order in which an industrial system is likely to be evolved by indigenous entre-

---

[17] This is consistent with the earlier version of Rostow's thesis of self-sustained growth (Rostow, 1956 and 1960). In Rostow (1964), he has dropped the prefix "self-" from his terminology. It is not clear whether he adheres to the thesis of self-sustenance.

preneurs who have knowledge of techniques used elsewhere. There are variations on this order. They may be discussed under the headings of *enclave activities, managerial immigration, footloose industries,* and *pressure production.* In part they imply a somewhat different sequence of industrialization and in part they are simply excrescences which do not greatly affect the industrialization process.

Enclave Activities. Some extractive industries or industries partially processing extractive products are profitable in a nonindustrial environment because of the high value of the primary materials they extract, even though their costs may be increased greatly by the absence of an industrial complex.

To obtain petroleum or minerals for the world industrial market, industrial corporations drill oil wells in the Middle East; extract tin, tungsten, and lead in Burma, and copper in Zambia and the Congo; establish a huge hydroelectric, mining, and aluminum refining complex in Ghana; and so on. Such activities are commonly termed "enclave activities." They are called this because they are usually almost wholly detached from the domestic economy. They are cysts: in the economy, but not of it. This is not necessarily by the choice of the corporation involved; it has no alternative. It must import its equipment, industrial supplies, management, and technical staff. Even if it processes materials to the finished stage, it does no (or an insignificant amount of) marketing in the host country; there is no market there. Of necessity, it builds its own railroad and port facilities. It makes minimal adaptation in its management and personnel structure, because its management is Western and its requirements for indigenous labor are not complex. The hypermodern methods it employs are much the most economical method of extracting the ore or petroleum, because the labor-saving devices also incorporate highly efficient chemical or physical techniques.

The operations may be valuable to the low-income country. They may provide income to indigenous workers and foreign exchange earnings to the economy as a whole. They may teach to some of their workers mechanics' skills that are useful elsewhere.

A corporation conducting an enclave activity is usually eager to train technical personnel from within the indigenous country, not so much to save money as to increase its acceptance in the society. If it does so, it may help the country to prepare more rapidly than otherwise for an advanced technical stage. Moreover, if the company officials put their minds to it, they may train indigenous individuals to produce some of the supplies they need, and may aid in the establishment of indigenous firms supplying them.

However, on the whole the transfer of techniques from these extractive behemoths has been extremely limited. To entrepreneurs and workers of the traditional economy, the capital-intensive activity of a modern mine, ore-concentration plant, oil refinery, or other such plant is a sort of fantasy, not related in a meaningful way to the traditional technical activities. Except for a few repair and maintenance activities, the processes are much too far removed from ones present in the society for transfer to take place. Hence the early establishment of these activities does not materially alter the sequence of industrialization, which in spite of the presence of the enclave activity must proceed step by step as sketched above.

What is true of such plants is almost equally true of some capital-intensive very "advanced" plants erected by the governments of some nonindustrial countries as symbols of modernity. Many such plants exist as "monuments" but do nothing to foster either a process of technical innovation or the emergence of an industrial complex.

Managerial Immigration.   However, the degree to which each industrial enterprise must have a supporting industrial network varies among enterprises. The looser the dependence of a given type of plant upon inputs from a complex around it, the more readily and profitably it may be established at an early stage of industrialization. If raw materials, markets, and the economic environment are favorable for the establishment of such plants, the necessary capital and management may be imported. In their contacts with the productive activities around them, such plants may vary between the extremes of moderate acceleration of the industrialization process to enclave status. If they are in the range of the spectrum near the former extreme, they may accelerate industrial development.

Footloose Industries.   Certain types of industries, which may or may not become enclave activities, are attracted to where dextrous workers—perhaps not entirely without a mechanical background, and willing to perform a routine precise operation day in and day out in order to increase their income—are available at wages that are low relative to those of the parent company's home country. These processes involved have two characteristics. First, they are largely self-contained; their efficiency does not depend on the presence of an industrial complex. Second, they produce products—almost always components of larger products—of high unit value and low weight, so that transportation costs to the country where the processing will be done and back for final assembly are not important within the component's total cost. The archetype product of this sort is a small component of an electronic instrument, requiring hand wiring or assembly. The operation may require precision to a fine industrial tolerance. This can be provided, for the plant may be equipped with delicate apparatus. The ideal location for footloose industries until recently was Taiwan, Hong Kong, or South Korea, but wages in these places are becoming too high, and firms with footloose processes to place are moving elsewhere.

The establishment of such plants is too recent to permit firm judgment concerning their contribution to the process of industrialization around them. There is no obvious reason that it should be great.

Pressure Production. There is a principle that "anything that can be produced at all can be produced anywhere if cost is not a consideration"—that is, if resources are available to import all the necessary talent, expertise, skills, ar.d materials, and to establish all the required supplying activities regardless of the diseconomies involved. Armaments are the product in whose production this principle is often applied, at least in moderate degree. They may be made domestically even though they could be obtained much more cheaply by using the productive resources involved to produce and trade goods in which the country has a comparative advantage. Government demand provides the market. A high degree of protection against imports may create an essentially similar situation for other products. By definition the arrangement reduces the country's level of living at the time. The basic diseconomy is in the production of materials, components, or even complete products for which neither the market nor the industrial complex for efficient production exists. However, if the productive process is one in which the country later will grow up to efficiency—that is, will have the needed productive complex and the necessary market either at home or abroad—then, weighing future time against present time by appropriate weights, the action may raise the country's average level of living over time. The country may acquire comparative advantage, which is not a static thing. And if the productive resources used could not in fact be readily shiftable to other production, the present loss may not be great.

Later Comers

The Late-Comer Theses. Many writers, noting the rapid development of some countries that began development late (Russia, Japan), have argued that, in general, late comers ought to be able to grow more rapidly than their predecessors. The simplest form of this thesis is merely that a late comer can advance more rapidly than the pioneers because the pioneers have already developed advanced methods.[18] There is logic to the hypothesis. One advantage is that if an advanced technique has been developed elsewhere, its possibility is known, and some of the exploration that would otherwise be necessary can be dispensed with. United States nuclear scientists have stated that this fact, and not necessarily knowledge through espionage of the precise methods, was a very important factor in the rapid Russian development of atomic and nuclear fission.

---

[18] Most of the writing on the late-comer thesis was done a dozen years and more ago. Ames and Rosenberg (1963) discuss the logic, and present a bibliography.

The other side of this coin is that copying the technique may not be the most advantageous thing to do; the possibility of imitation of technical features of a process may thwart the development of a still more advantageous process. But on balance there is almost certainly great technical advantage in having a ready-made advanced technique as one of the alternatives. Adaptation will usually be necessary, but part of the problem is solved.

It is sometimes added that the late comer can move directly to advanced techniques, passing over intermediate ground. For example, Campbell (1960, p. 165) suggests that the Russians could industrialize rapidly because "their task was not complicated by the presence of existing plants and an already familiar technology, and they could build a modern industry from the ground up." The thesis of a simple mechanical substitution of the 20th century for the 17th is untenable. Campbell's statement may more appropriately be interpreted as an expression of the "fossilization" thesis, also advanced by other writers. Habakkuk (1962, p. 220), comparing British and U.S. technology in the 19th century, concludes that "such lags as there were in the adoption of new methods in British industry can be adequately explained by economic circumstances, by the complexity of her industrial structure and the slow growth of her output, and *ultimately by her early and long-sustained start as an industrial power.*" (The italics are mine.) Svennilson (1954) in explaining European economic sluggishness during the interwar years, argues that resistances to adoption of new technologies are much greater in industrial societies than in nonindustrial ones that offer "virgin soil" to industrialization. Such arguments are best justified as cases of the general principle suggested by the anthropologist Kroeber (1944), that when a pattern of activity has worked very well in a society, the members of the society may cling to it even when changing conditions have made it dysfunctional.

On the basis of the "fossilization" plus the "leapfrogging" thesis, a stronger form of the late-comer proposition has been suggested, namely that late comers can be expected to overtake and surpass countries that began development earlier, before the late comers in their turn become fossilized. On the basis of qualitative arguments alone, it is impossible to evaluate the likelihood of this. The country whose trend at present suggests the greatest probability that it will overtake and surpass the leaders is Japan, but before Japan could do so at present relative rates of growth, many eventualities could intervene. Certainly the relative pace of development of less or more developed countries as groups at present does not give comfort to the thesis that they will presently overtake and surpass the world's leaders, but as was noted at the end of chapter 1, a number of them are overtaking and surpassing some countries that have been ahead of them.

The Stimulus of Backwardness. Gerschenkron advances an alternative or additional thesis of the effects of backwardness on the pattern of growth. Drawing his generalizations from a study of industrialization in Europe, he suggests that the more backward a country's economy was on the eve of its industrialization, the more pronounced were certain other characteristics of its industrialization, namely (1) the discontinuity of the start, (2) the stress on bigness of plant and enterprise, (3) the stress on producer goods as against consumer goods, (4) the pressure on the levels of consumption in order to finance investment, (5) the magnitude and the coerciveness of the role of special institutions designed to increase the supply of capital for industry and to centralize entrepreneurial guidance, and (6) the inability of agriculture to offer a growing market for industrial goods.[19] While he claims validity for this thesis only in Europe, he sometimes applies it more widely.

The thesis suffers from the ambiguity of his concept of backwardness. Economic backwardness, he states (1952, pp. 43–44), "defies exact measurement," but he suggests that in ranking a country one should consider its level of per capita output, the relatively favorable or unfavorable nature of climatic conditions and natural resources, and the presence of such conditions as a high percentage of illiteracy and a religious attitude that urban ways of life are displeasing to the Lord. He suggests that in practice, since the relevant measures on the whole tend to point in the same direction, European countries can be ranked unambiguously.

The thesis has limited applicability. Spain, Portugal, and India, among other countries, present examples inconsistent with it. These countries are industrializing and were surely backward according to his criteria on the eve of their industrialization, yet their industrialization processes have hardly any of the characteristics he suggests. Scrutiny of other countries does not suggest that if agreement could be reached on their degrees of economic backwardness there would be high correlation between backwardness and the characteristics of industrialization indicated.

However, a not unrelated hypothesis may have wider empirical relevance. Suppose that technical advance is under way in a nonindustrial country, but is held back by *political institutions* such as serfdom and the extensive controls exercised by the tsars in Russia, or the feudal rule and even more comprehensive economic controls exercised by the Tokugawa in Japan. In these cases one may think of economic and technical capability as having advanced far ahead of actual economic structure and performance because of political barriers that prevent the latent economic

---

[19] Professor Gerschenkron has presented aspects of his hypothesis in various places. It is clearly defined in the following two articles in combination: Gerschenkron (1952) and (1964). His relevant essays are also gathered together in Gerschenkron (1962). The summary of his thesis in text above is taken from Gerschenkron (1952, p. 353) and (1964, p. 142).

change from becoming actual. Then, if the forces for change burst through the old political bonds and destroy them, a spurt of change and most or all of the qualities of industrialization suggested by Gerschenkron might occur.

The "Transfer" of Industrial Technology

Few products or processes are invented *de novo* in low-income countries. With certain exceptions, industrial advance at every stage depends greatly on the acquisition of knowledge from a more industrialized country. This statement is not inconsistent with the emphasis in this and preceding chapters on the need for adaptation and domestic innovation.

We do not yet know much about the process by which technical knowledge passes from one country to another; we have assumed that the process is simple and have paid little attention to it. "It is a striking historiographical fact," writes one scholar, "that the serious study of the diffusion of new techniques is an activity no more than fifteen years old."[20] "The diffusion of technology in the modern world," another states, "has been largely limited to techniques not unfamiliar to St. Paul or Mohammed: the movement of persons and the transmittal of written documents."[21] It is difficult to think of other possible means.

In the insightful chapter 2 of his book *Technological Change and Economic Development*, W. Paul Strassman reminds readers of the complexity of the process of "transferring" technology:

> Technological information can range from advice for improving performance of a given installation to recommending a daring invention using newly discovered principles of nature. The bulk of activity today in technological transfer is diffusion of routine advice about standard processes. Information flows to newly industrializing nations so that managers can arrange the layout of machinery, adopt preventive maintenance schedules, forecast and plan production properly, control inventories and quality, reduce scrap, use proper depreciation methods, improve hiring and training practices, and balance work incentives. A harder transfer occurs when new equipment is not to be installed or used according to standard foreign or local practice. If the equipment is to be redesigned, even more knowledge is needed; and information flows must increase, especially if redesign first calls for scientific exploration. An interesting order of flows is the diffusion of knowledge about information channels themselves.
>
> Information about manufacturing processes is immensely complex and heterogeneous, and it is sent only sporadically to widely separated places in poor countries. If enormous libraries were shipped abroad, the knowl-

---

[20] N. Rosenberg (1972), p. 3.

[21] W. Parker, in N. Rosenberg, ed. (1971).

edge would get there physically but with no effect on productivity. The books would need readers who require training, and therefore schools; the schools need teachers—and, in any case, not all is clear from books, for not enough combinations of circumstances can ever be covered. Books must be complemented by experience, and experience in operating modern industry is precisely what underdeveloped countries lack and seek. . . . Experience is embedded as "judgement" in the human tissues of those who have long participated in a species of events.

The modes of transfer are many: Migration; travel abroad by low-income country individuals; popular magazines; technical journals; trade journals; catalogues; machinery salesmen; the follow-up service of machinery sellers; staff engineers; consulting engineers; management consultants. Formal education: vocational, technical, scientific; training programs; technical assistance flowing from voluntary associations, governments, and international organizations; research; development, and engineering processes; research institutes and laboratories, in the contributing countries and in the recipient countries. Direct private investment from abroad; licensing agreements; the observation of production processes in the plant in the industrial country.

And even as a summary listing, the list given is surely not complete. There is a paradox in the demand for and flow of information which the market cannot solve. For no one can know how much to bid for information unless he already has the information. Learning pays, but how much? As Strassman puts it, the entrepreneur cannot "simply keep spending until marginal gains vanish, for discoveries never pass in review prearranged according to merit like the nobility at a coronation."

None of these methods of the transmission of technical knowledge is likely to be fully effective. Any of them is of very limited usefulness without personal contact. No written material conveys full information, especially since adaptation is virtually always necessary and the written material is unlikely to provide the needed information about adaptation. But human contacts too are fallible. Information often passes as if through a series of relays (again, Strassman's phrase), at each of which it is filtered and something may be lost, since the agent at the relay does not know fully what it is important to transmit.

Formal education in less developed countries is likely to be by instructors with a longing for the modern, disdain for practice, and inadequate knowledge of it; and in industrial countries, by instructors also primarily interested in the modern and the "advanced" and without knowledge of the problems relevant to less industrialized countries. In any event, instructors in schools are not likely to understand fully processes that are not yet in use in the country. Technical assistance is likely to be limited by advisers' lack of knowledge of the framework within which the process must operate and sometimes by their conviction that things can best be done just as they were done in their home country.

The institutional framework of little-industrial countries—as real a fact as the industrial framework—is not conducive to effective work by detached research institutes or laboratories. These in the less industrialized countries are likely to be sterile almost until the time when they are no longer needed. As a United States National Academy of Sciences committee has observed (1974) in a statement that illustrates the stage nature of modes of advice as well as of industrialization:

> Industry must go through certain evolutionary phases before it is ready to make commercial use of R&D efforts. As in the United States, so in the LDCs, the development of basic engineering capabilities—the ability to manage quality-control systems, introduce materials specifications and standards, maintain tool shops, and establish other production-support activities—normally must precede more ambitious developmental and applied research on product design, new materials, equipment design, and other changes in production or processing techniques.

Casual empiricism suggests that travel—travel abroad by an entrepreneur of a nonindustrialized country, or (no longer frequent) migration into that country by a man who intends to establish a business and thereafter live there—is a typically important ingredient at the very first stage of industrialization; and licensing agreements and formal research are of major usefulness only at a very advanced stage. But other channels or flows surely complement these even at these stages. Which ones, and to what degree? What are the "natural" and "normal" and most effective means or combinations of means at stages between? No one, apparently, knows much about this. At least no one has written systematically about this.

Technical Advance in Infrastructure and Agriculture

Concurrent with advances in industry, and interwoven with them and with each other, are technical advances in agriculture and in the construction and operation of infrastructure facilities. Advances in both fields both facilitate advance in industry and depend upon it. If any of the three fields lags too much, progress in the others is severely hampered.

Successive advances in manufacturing industry make the construction of successively more complex infrastructure facilities economic, and each judicious advance in infrastructure also supports further industrial advance. The market alone will not call forth this interwoven advance in an optimum pattern, even if there were no special problem of mobilizing the "lumps of capital" necessary to construct infrastructure. For to a greater degree than projects in other sectors, many infrastructure projects yield benefits for which a private enterpriser cannot collect payment, or which to obtain the maximum economic advantage ought to be provided to the public without charge. These benefits are discussed in Chapter 15 under the headings "External Economies" and "Public Goods." Because of them, many infrastructure projects will be constructed at the time and operated in the way optimum for economic growth only if they are provided by the government. And of course governmental action will not automatically bring them about at the right time. Foresighted government planning is required.

In a closed economy, there must be a fairly close relationship between technical advance in agriculture and that in industry, in order that the growing industrial class will have food, and growing industry a sufficient market. Even here, however, some flexibility is provided by the adjustment link, the terms of trade between the two sectors. In an open economy, imports provide an added adjustment factor. Agriculture also provides savings to finance industrialization.

In some historical cases, notably England and Japan, some types of technical advance in agriculture began early. This has also been true in some present low-income countries. In these recent cases, the early technical advance in agriculture has been by individuals not from the landlord class who, finding lands not under peasant cultivation that are suitable for new uses, have begun the cultivation of, say, cocoa or coffee or sugar cane.

Even in these cases, when industrial advance began (in the processing of agricultural products), it gained momentum of its own, and advance within traditional agriculture remained slight until industrial development was well under way. The reasons are social, not technical. Traditional landlords or estate owners are not innovative. Where cultivation is by tenant peasants or is on more or less feudal estates, the set of institutional and technical circumstances which render technical progress in agriculture so difficult are not likely to be breached until (1) innovation in industry has somewhat disrupted old socioeconomic relationships, and (2) simultaneously some successful industrial innovators look for new fields in which to exercise their talents.

Some of the members of the emerging business class may then become political leaders and carry forward the alterations in sociopolitical institutions which are already under way. Others may carry forward technical progress in agriculture outside of *traditional* agriculture. Such men, rather than traditional landlords, are responsible for the opening up of new lands and the rapid increase in agricultural output in recent decades in Mexico, Colombia, and some other Latin American countries. Later, with the steady erosion of peasant agriculture institutions by industrialization, urbanization, and the modern equivalent of the enclosure movement, peasant agriculture will follow along.

To some extent, technical progress in agriculture depends on technical progress in industry. Notably, mechanization in agriculture depends in great degree on the ability of the economy to service and repair the equipment conveniently. To a much smaller degree, technical advance in industry depends on that in agriculture, for when the stage arrives at which laborers in agriculture have been acquainted with machinery from childhood, agriculture will send more capable workers to industry than it did earlier. They will also probably have less unfavorable attitudes.

Concluding Comments

The facts presented in this chapter reinforce the general conclusion that economic development is a complex and difficult matter. Consideration of the step-by-step process by which complex productive systems evolve should remind the economic analyst that in applying economic criteria for choice among development projects, he must take into account the technical readiness of any given country for each project, which of course affects its economic readiness.[22]

Acquaintance with the range of difficulties in technical progress may also prevent erroneous assessment of the effects that can be achieved by some given type of economic action. Some U.S. economic aid programs in the late 1940s and early 1950s were based on the assumption that if only advanced techniques (modern "know-how") were presented to the technically less developed societies, economic development would proceed rapidly. This turned out to be true in some cases, and egregiously in error in others. It was then assumed by some individuals concerned with the programs and by many academic analysts that the missing ingredient was economic resources; technical advice plus economic aid would do the trick. Again, in some countries the assumption was proved wrong. The most current thesis which selects one factor as the key to success or failure is that "investment in human resources"—that is, appropriate education—is the additional ingredient needed to accelerate growth rates. This is surely as erroneous as the two earlier theses; there is reason to be suspicious of any formula that stresses any one factor as the missing key. Technical information, resources for investment, and education are all important, but singly or in combination they will accomplish greater effects in some countries than in others, depending on saving propensities, the innovational talent and energy, the grip of traditional institutions, the productive complex that has already evolved, and other factors in each country.

But for an economic theorist, the most important conclusion to be

---

[22] In varying degree this consideration is ignored, to their detriment, in the analyses in Chenery (1953), Chenery and Kretschmer (1956), Eckstein (1957), Galenson and Leibenstein (1955), and Kahn (1951), among others.

drawn from the fact of interwoven complexities in technical progress is neither of these. Rather, the theorist is impressed by the fact that it is not necessary to create any new and unique theories of economic barriers to explain why low-income countries, seeing the West's affluence, do not more rapidly adopt Western methods of production. It is not necessary to assume that low-income countries are too impoverished to save; that their markets are too small to absorb the output of factories using improved methods; that any increase in income will quickly be wiped out by an increase in population which it induces; or any other easy generalization. All of these hypotheses merit exploration, but even if none of them holds up under investigation the failure of low-income countries to reach Western levels of productivity quickly need not seem puzzling. The interrelationships among the economic, technical, social, and attitudinal problems will make economic growth difficult even if a good deal of creative energy is being exerted to bring it about.

With the belief that some dramatic difficulty must exist dispelled, we are in a better position to consider whether the empirical evidence supports or brings into question the various theories of economic barriers.

BIBLIOGRAPHICAL NOTE

Concerning problems of labor recruitment and commitment, the classic early study is Wilbert Moore, *Industrialization and Labor* (1951). W. Moore and A. Feldman, eds., *Labor Commitment and Social Change in Developing Areas* (1960) is a standard later work. The 1969 article by Harris and Todaro mentioned in the text is a counterbalance to the "alienation" thesis, yet may be consistent with it. Kerr, Dunlop, Harbison, and Myers, *Industrialism and Industrial Man* (1964) is a culminating work in a large research project that studied the role of labor and management in economic growth. This paperback edition is somewhat revised from the original 1960 edition. A valuable bibliography is presented. See also by the same authors, "Postscript to 'Industrialism and Industrial Man,'" *International Labor Review,* 103 (June, 1971).

7

Theories of Development:
How Growth Begins

There is an unsettled issue in the analysis of how economic growth begins. It is whether increases in the productivity of supply—increases in the number of units of output per unit of inputs—commonly begin without any previous economic change, or whether on the other hand an increase in aggregate demand—which normally would have to be an increase in foreign demand—necessarily or at least typically begins the process. Available data provide no answer on which all analysts agree. The exports of most and perhaps virtually all, developing countries increased during the early decades of development. (For data, see for example Kuznets, *Q.A.E.G.N.*, 2.) The question is whether the export increase was a response to foreign demand and caused the acceleration of growth or whether foreign demand merely, in Adam Smith's phrase, provided a "vent for surplus" which the increasing productive economy produced.

Theories of demand-led growth and growth originating in improvement in supply are contrasted and evaluated in this chapter. It may be well by way of introduction to dispose of the notion that the low income of low-income countries constitutes an almost absolute barrier to growth. Early post-World War II theorists, seized by an unquantified image of low-income peoples bound in a morass of poverty, believed this, and were pessimistic about growth ever starting. (It was already in progress, but they did not yet have enough data to realize this.) Some brilliant but rather bizarre theories about how it might possibly be started resulted. The entire conception is unrealistic. Because it still hangs on in some

162

writings, it is worthwhile to get it out of the way. This "introduction" will occupy more than one third of the chapter. A more fruitful discussion of the issues of demand-led versus supply-initiated growth can then be presented.

THEORIES OF VICIOUS CIRCLES

One of the best known statements of the theory of vicious circles shackling low-income countries is that by Ragnar Nurkse (1953). Hans W. Singer had made a brief but fairly complete statement of the doctrine earlier (1949), but Nurkse's fuller statement attracted more attention.

The theory is that two mutually reinforcing vicious circles perpetuate low income. Either alone would be sufficient to do so. One consists of the relationships among lack of capital, income, and saving. Because income is low, there is little capacity to save. The low income is a reflection of low productivity, which in its turn is due largely to the lack of capital. The lack of capital is a result of the small capacity to save, and so the circle is complete.

The other vicious circle relates market size, income, and investment. "The inducement to invest," Nurkse wrote, "may be low because of the small buying power of the people, which is due to their small real income, which again is due to low productivity. The low level of productivity, however, is a result of the small amount of capital used in production, which in its turn may be caused at least partly by the small inducement to invest." The circle is complete; there is little inducement to invest because, income being low, the market is small; so long as there is little investment, income will remain low and the market small.

If there were inducement to invest, there would be no savings to finance investment, and if there were savings, there would be no inducement to invest them. There is no way in which the circles can be converted into upward spirals.

When the thesis of two vicious circles is heard by persons who have a mental image of low-income countries as immobilized in a morass of poverty, it seems so self-evidently true that no investigation seems needed to confirm it. The thesis is internally consistent. The flaw in it as an explanation of the real world is that neither low income, low productivity, and low saving, nor low income, small market size, and low investment in the low-income countries in fact form the vicious circle that is adduced. The unreality of the thesis is sufficiently evidenced by the fact that even while it was being presented, growth was proceeding in many if not most of the countries supposedly hopelessly immobilized in poverty. This is shown both by the partial data for increase in GDP from 1950 on presented in Chapter 1 and by the sectoral shift between 1950 and 1960 in the labor force, indicated in Table 4–2. Data that reached farther back would show growth occurring earlier also. However, instead of dismissing the theory with this general comment, it will be useful to examine some aspects of it further.

Critique: Market Size

Nurkse cited as examples of the smallness of the market the impossibility of profitable shoe production in a hypothetical economy with income so low that few persons wear shoes, and a supposed volume of use of steel too low to absorb an economic level of output of a modern steel mill. He might have cited other and more obviously correct examples: electric light bulbs, aluminum, automobiles, television sets. But all this is irrelevant. A growth process does not require that a low-income country has a sufficient market to justify the production of every industrial product, but only a market large enough to justify improved methods in the production of goods already in use in the country.

Demand for a considerable range of such goods, ample in amount to take off the market the output of a more productive plant, was present in virtually every low-income country, even the smallest ones, before the process of modern growth began, and was present not merely in the country as a whole but in separate regions or cities. Examples of such products are soap, matches, sandals, rice or wheat flour, sugar and various sugar products, textiles, and clothing and other textile products, bricks, cement, and some other construction materials. A large enough market for many or all of these products usually existed even if only primitive transportation facilities were available to distribute the products.

In an earlier book, I have noted examples of this in two valleys of Colombia that were then isolated (Antioquia and "the Valley"), the larger of which could not have had a gross product of much more than $100 million (in 1965 prices) at the time:

> The first modern sugar refinery was established in one valley of Colombia and the first modern textile mill in another between 1900 and 1910, when the population of the entire country was not more than six million and the level of per capita income [converted to dollars by the exchange rate] probably less than $100; and each valley was so isolated from the rest of the country by barriers to transportation that the market for each enterprise initially was confined primarily to its own valley—at a maximum estimate one fifth of the total national market in one case and much less in the other. Both flourished, as did a stream of other improvements (Hagen, 1962, p. 43).

This was true even though initially the only "roads" except for local ones extending a few miles from the larger towns were mule paths. Goods had to be carried in or out of the valleys on mule or human back.

Growth has begun in such markets with the introduction of methods that reduce the unit cost of production or, what is the same thing, produce a more attractive new or improved product with the number of inputs formerly used to produce an older one. The latter has apparently been the first step much more often than the former. Production of more uniform cloth, whiter flour, more fully refined sugar, and nonwarping bricks are examples. Even a fairly small improvement in productivity in the improvement of such traditional products, permitting a small reduction in price or sale of an improved product at the same price as the traditional one or a price not too far above it might capture a sizable and already existing market, and in the way sketched later in this chapter may initiate a growth process.

The new production may also be for the foreign market, which of course would take an increased supply of staples that from the viewpoint of a producing country was virtually unlimited. That initiating process will be discussed later in this chapter. The point being made here is that the domestic market in low-income countries was also adequately large and was the target for many early innovating entrepreneurs.

C. P. Kindleberger (1965, chap. 9) presents an attractive variant of the size-of-market argument. He notes that in a traditional society much production is for a local market only. A very large percentage of the goods consumed in a village may be produced within 10 or 15 miles of the village. If there is a single producer of some handicraft item, reducing his cost of production and price will increase his sales very little. There is more than one producer of most commodities or handicraft products even in a single village, but the concept of production as a family affair, not an enterprise to be expanded by reducing costs and taking sales away from other families, may dull any incentive to ponder ways of improving methods. However, if improvement in transportation and changes in marketing institutions expand the market so that it includes a region or the country as a whole, the situation is radically altered. If the producer can reduce his price or improve his product, he can take sales from 100 or 1,000 other producers with whom he has no personal ties. Hence the incentive to improve his methods may be increased. The enlarged market creates a qualitatively, not merely a quantitatively, changed situation.

The argument has a degree of cogency. Perhaps if transportation from villages were better, there would be more innovation in them. When the Tokugawa forced the heads of Japanese clans to spend alternate years (more or less) in Tokyo, and held their families in Tokyo at all times, the travel and family maintenance created a need for money, and under the pressure of this need, the availability of a large market, and contact with urban attitudes over a period of nine generations, loyal retainers did steadily though very slowly increase their productivity in handicrafts and agriculture. But to elevate the transportation change to a general theory of growth (Kindleberger does not) overstates its importance greatly.

At some stage in the growth process, limited market size may retard growth. This is perhaps the fact that was somewhat confused in the minds of early postwar theorists. The case of the small Central American countries provides an illustration. The market in each of these countries was ample in size for the first steps in industry. In each, factories appeared in consumer goods industries long before the move early in the 1960s to unite the markets of these countries through establishment of a Central American Common Market (CACM). But the small individual markets did presently hamper production of the goods with ambitious producers who had gained experience wished to turn to, and the establishment of a common market for many goods accelerated industrialization. By about 1970, however, most industries able to produce efficiently for a market of the size of the Common Market had been established, and the acceleration ended. The larger market had become too small. (Dissension among the member countries also plagued the CACM.)

Consideration of such facts has led some analysts to the conclusion that if a larger market were available in a nongrowing, low-income economy, a wider range of manufacturing enterprises would be economic, and that because of this wider range of opportunities some innovation would occur sooner. This may be true, but it may be suspected that the instances are very few. The main difference between a smaller and larger national market is that larger establishments would be economic in the latter. But these larger establishments tend to be also more complex establishments, using not merely larger machines but more complex combinations of machines and processes. It is probably that as growth begins they are barred not by the size of the market but by the lack of managerial and technical experience of the entrepreneurs. A few decades later, with growing experience in simpler industry, the managers will be ready to handle them. Hla Myint has coined a relevant phrase. The economies that are relevant, he writes (1954, p. 155) are not economies of scale but "economies of experience." Market size and economies of scale are discussed further in Chapter 12. Here it may merely be noted that the size of the domestic market has not been a barrier to the initiation of growth.

Critique: Inability to Save

The vicious circles thesis of inability of low-income countries to save ignores both the self-financing of dedicated entrepreneurs and the implications of the extreme inequality of income distribution in low-income countries. When direct evidence is sought, it too brings this aspect of the vicious circles thesis into question.

Of course not all early entrepreneurs have all of the resources that they might effectively use, but it seems clearly not the common case that desirous entrepreneurship is present but saving is lacking. The 25 "least developed countries" illustrate the lack of entrepreneurship. The problem of aid to these countries is first to study the countries to see what projects might be effective, then to plan the projects, then to provide the funds, then to provide the management of the projects.[1] In countries in which the growth process is well under way, either lack of domestic savings or lack of foreign exchange may limit the rate of growth, but neither is a highly visible problem in countries in which growth has hardly begun. The evidence is both direct and indirect.

There seems to be no society in history which was too poor to wage war, even a large-scale war relative to the size of the society, when emotions were aroused. Any considerable war requires a share of the nation's manpower and other productive resources which would be sufficient for a significant rate of capital formation. And while the disruption of war has often caused hardship and death, historical records suggest that the diversion to war of a considerable fraction of the resources of the population at large, in even the lowest income societies, has often occurred without causing starvation or death—though of course, sometimes either the disruption of war or the preemption of resources has caused both.

The lowest income societies have often been able to build magnificent monuments. As Cairncross (1964, p. 251) has written: "Anyone who looks at the pyramids, cathedrals, and pagodas that civilizations have bequeathed, can hardly regard the construction of railways, dams, and power stations as imposing an unprecedented burden on a poor community."

No one would expect the lowest income groups in low-income countries to contribute savings for investment. But they do not do so in any society. Apparently, the families forming the two or three lowest income deciles of any population dissave. At least, this is true in the highest income society of the world, the United States. Saving is roughly zero in the next decile or two and a low fraction of income in the decile or two next above. It is only because of the relatively high rate of saving by families and single individuals in the highest several deciles of the income distribution in any society (saving both out of their personal incomes and by the companies of which they are the major owners) that there is a considerable net flow of saving in the economy as a whole. In 1950, the 10% of United States income receivers receiving the highest incomes after taxes, who received 29% of aggregate income, saved 20% of their income.

---

[1] One study of the sub-Sahara countries within the group of 25 "least developed" countries was carried on by the United Nations and another for the United States Agency for International Development, in 1973 and 1974. The statement in the text is based on the writer's knowledge of these studies plus less direct knowledge of the other "least developed countries."

The bottom 90%, on the average, saved only 3%.[2] By parallel, to understand the saving potential of any economy, it is necessary to consider the highest income groups, and the highest income groups obtain a larger share of the country's income in low-income countries than in high-income ones.

For some countries it is possible to make estimates of the share of total national income received by, say, the 10% of income receivers (families and single individuals) with the highest incomes. Such estmates for nonindustrial countries are subject to considerable margins of error. Kuznets has selected estimates that he regarded as tolerably acceptable. Figure 7–1 presents them for seven low-income and seven high-income countries. In Chapter 9, Table 9–1, estimates for the income received by the upper 20% of income receivers are shown. The evidence is striking. Even when incomes before payment of personal taxes are compared, the highest income groups in low-income countries receive a much larger

FIGURE 7–1

Income Shares before Taxes of Upper 10 Percent of Income Units (Families or Tax Returns), Selected Countries, Late 1940s and Early 1950s

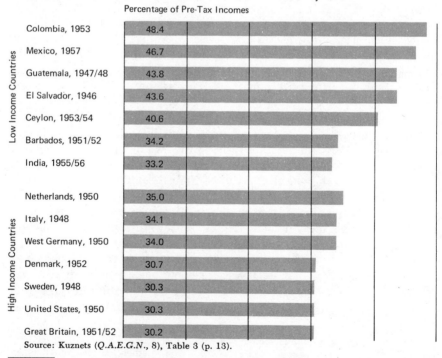

Percentage of Pre-Tax Incomes

Low Income Countries

- Colombia, 1953 — 48.4
- Mexico, 1957 — 46.7
- Guatemala, 1947/48 — 43.8
- El Salvador, 1946 — 43.6
- Ceylon, 1953/54 — 40.6
- Barbados, 1951/52 — 34.2
- India, 1955/56 — 33.2

High Income Countries

- Netherlands, 1950 — 35.0
- Italy, 1948 — 34.1
- West Germany, 1950 — 34.0
- Denmark, 1952 — 30.7
- Sweden, 1948 — 30.3
- United States, 1950 — 30.3
- Great Britain, 1951/52 — 30.2

Source: Kuznets (*Q.A.E.G.N.*, 8), Table 3 (p. 13).

[2] Kuznets (*Q.A.E.G.N.*, 5), p. 22, n. 8. Derived from the United States Bureau of Labor Statistics *1950 Survey of Consumer Finances.* For summaries of other statistical evidence, see Duesenberry (1949) and Brady (1951).

share of the country's income than is true in the more developed countries. The disparity with respect to income after taxes must be much greater, since the percentage of high incomes legally due as taxes has probably typically been less in the low-income countries, at least until after World War II, and in any event actual collection of taxes legally due from high-income families is far less effective in the low-income countries.

W. Arthur Lewis (1955, p. 236) draws a moral: "Least of all can those nations plead poverty as an excuse for not saving in which 40% or so of the national income is squandered by the top 10% of income receivers, living luxuriously on rents." William Nicholls, U.S. agricultural economist who is better informed than any other U.S. scholar concerning Brazilian agriculture, has stated (in Saunders, 1971, p. 218) that out of high incomes obtained from agriculture in the United States, portions "found their way into saving and private domestic capital formation . . . while in most of Brazil they were dissipated in private and public 'conspicuous consumption.'"

We do not know, in fact, that high-income landed families in low-income countries do not save. We only believe, on the basis of imprecise evidence, that they seldom invest savings in productive activities. Historically, some of the landed rich have on occasion been innovative. The "agricultural revolution" that preceded the Industrial Revolution in England was carried out by them. The German Junker class modernized German agriculture. In Iran, large landowners have established food-processing plants to process products of their land—and thereby have raised the level of income in the country. Such instances are apparently rare, but it seems fairly clear from available data that if there is little saving and productive investment in a low-income country, this is because men are not motivated to make it, not because they cannot.

The Demonstration Effect

Some theorists who assume that there is no saving at all by high-income families in low-income countries, or very little saving, believe that the explanation is that high-income individuals in the less developed countries are acquainted with the consumption levels of the West and are driven to attain them and are therefore psychologically unable to save. In a U.S. community, Duesenberry (1949) suggests, low-income families save nothing or spend beyond their income because they cannot bear to be too distant in their consumption standards from persons with whom they associate. He calls this effect the "demonstration effect." Just so, it is argued, high-income groups in low-income countries do not save because with increased international communication their standard of comparison is a Western one.

Certainly high-income families in low-income countries often have patterns of consumption that are partially "Western." Nevertheless, it is not certain that the demonstration effect keeps them from saving. It may merely alter their consumption from traditional to Western forms. High-income families of lower income U.S. communities have contacts with wealthier U.S. communities that must be closer than the contacts of high-income families in low-income countries with the West. Yet a study by Dorothy Brady (1951) showed that these American families save about the same percentages of their incomes as do families in their relative income bracket in high-income communities. This fact suggests that the comparison which most potently influences the U.S. families' allocation of their incomes between consumption and saving is that with the other families of their own communities. By parallel, one may hypothesize that if the high-income families of low-income societies were entrepreneurial in their motivations, their contact with the West would not prevent them from saving in substantial amounts. It has been suggested that the saving and investment of the West provide a model that might be expected to provide a demonstration for them, if demonstration effects were important.

It may be that two other factors of much greater importance in deterring investment by the members of the landed class and the high-income members of the professional classes are their already comfortable social situation and their distaste for associating themselves with the grubby process of manufacturing, the crass businesses of finance and trade, or the menial matter of problems of agricultural production.

THE SUPPOSED NEED FOR A "BIG PUSH"

One corollary of the too-low-income, too-low-demand thesis is the doctrine that through some mechanism there must be a marked increase in aggregate demand if growth is to be stimulated. Facts refuting the notion have been presented above. Yet the thesis of the need for a "big push" (perhaps better called a "big pull") has aspects that merit examination.

Thesis Stated

The best known exponent of the need for and efficacy of such a "big push" to initiate growth is P. N. Rodan. In a 1943 article, as a part of an English wartime study of how to bring about the development of Eastern and Southeastern Europe after the war, he had proposed the establishment of a large trust to plan and finance investment in the entire area simultaneously. He had argued the need for increased demand and had added the idea that the capital gains, as existing properties rose in value as development proceeded, would insure success. After the war Rodan expanded his thesis so that it became a general argument about how economic development in low-income countries might be started.[3]

Rodan emphasizes two considerations not given much stress by Nurkse or Singer. Low-income countries, he argues, are often on dead center because no potential investor anticipates investment by other men, and therefore none of them anticipates a market large enough to justify an investment, even though if all of them invested and if the pecuniary external economies were taken into account, every investment project might be advantageous. The difficulty does not exist in advanced countries both because the general expectation there is one of growth that will yield pecuniary external economies and because the market does a much better job of signaling to each producer the prospective effects of the plans of others.

To this concept of lack of a demand stimulus, Rodan adds a special difficulty on the supply side. Lack of infrastructure makes other investment uneconomic, and because of low saving capability the lump of capital needed to build the infrastructure is not available. Infrastructure, or social overhead capital, is the type of capital goods that serve not merely one industry but many, and once installed have low variable costs relative to total unit costs. Transportation, power, and communications facilities, and some other sorts of urban utilities are the chief types. Efficient projects of these types, it is suggested require large units. Low-income countries cannot accumulate the large lumps of capital needed.

The remedy, Rodan argues, is a comprehensive investment program, by which many investment projects, undertaken simultaneously, will create the demand for each that will make it profitable, and by which infrastructure facilities will be made available at the same time as industries to use them. The program must of course be carried on either by an overall planning body or under assurances from that body that convey conviction to all investors that the entire program of investment will be carried forward.

To the charge that the concept of such a program, in a society that is not sufficiently imaginative and innovational to find even one advantageous investment project and mobilize resources to carry it out, is a mere fantasy, Rodan replies that of course capital would have to be provided from outside; that the increased demand for labor implied in the investment program could be met in the disguised employment that is rampant in agriculture in such countries; and that the vision of such a bold and promising program might stir imaginations and evoke enough energies to make such a "big push" a success even though the society had

---

[3] He has presented his argument in various places (e.g., 1961a) but most comprehensively in Rosenstein-Rodan (1961b). Nurkse (1958) presents a similar but less elaborate argument. Rodan presented the argument orally to students and others for a number of years before putting it into print.

not been motivated to carry out a lesser program. He does not consider the question of whether the society would have the managerial and innovational attitudes and capability (as distinguished from enthusiasm and energy) and the necessary initial productive complex to carry out such a program.[4]

Is a Lump of Capital Needed?

No systematic empirical evidence has been adduced to support the lump-of-capital argument. Like the size-of-market argument, this argument is stated as axiomatic, or as so surely justified by casual common-sense observation that no further proof is necessary: "Everyone knows that large plants are the most efficient, and that they require cheap power and good transportation and communication facilities, and that poor countries do not have the savings to finance these." But when one shakes off one's preconceptions, for a combination of empirical and theoretical reasons, the argument seems less persuasive.

The choice is not often between very large facilities or no facilities. Almost any type of infrastructure facility can be built in various sizes. Roads may be dirt, graveled, blacktopped, or paved, light-duty or heavy-duty, and may be built in any width the traffic calls for. Electric generators vary in size from small diesel units to the largest hydro or nuclear plants. Local telephone systems and even microwave transmission towers are relatively inexpensive. A city can afford the urban utilities it "needs," since these are proportional to its size and functions. Railroads are perhaps the least divisible type of infrasturcture, but until a heavy volume of bulk traffic calls for the service of a railroad, road or water transport is a fairly good and finely divisible substitute. And while unit. cost varies with the facility, the view that there is a dichotomy in costs—that unit cost is "high" in small or lower-grade facilities and "low" in large higher-"quality" ones—is overstated. There are indeed large cost variations, inverse to the size of the infrastructure plant if it can be used at capacity. But in a nonindustrial low-income country, a large infrastructure plant could not soon be used to capacity. The services of a large infrastructure facility built as early as the argument implies would be exorbitantly costly per unit, since for a long time only a small fraction of the capacity would be used.

The "lump-of-capital" argument implicitly assumes that power-communications-transport-labor coefficients in production are fixed, in the secular course of development. Without certain power or transport or communication facilities, advance is throttled. But of course it is not.

---

[4] Currie (1966) presents a vivid and forceful argument which incorporates many parts of the "big push" thesis, and applies them to the development problems of Colombia.

Economic history suggests a principle of continuity and flexibility in growth. There are many alternative paths of advance; many ways of improving techniques other than by moving from cottage industry to industrial plants of the size found in the United States; many ways of reducing costs other than by introducing large infrastructure facilities.

Reduced to more reasonable dimensions, the role of infrastructure facilities in development is coordinate with that of many other pieces of capital equipment and changes in management practices and in institutions. Increasingly large infrastructure facilities have their place in the course of development, but they deserve no special niche as absolute or near-absolute prerequisites to growth.[5]

It remains true that there may be a market bias against construction of "lumpy" social overhead capital facilities at the optimum time in the course of economic growth because of the difficulty of accumulating the necessary sums of capital. Hence there is a strong case for governmental or international financing of them. However, that in the absence of government or international action they may be built too late is a far weaker statement than that their absence is a crucial or especially important barrier to growth. On the other hand, because they are obvious and glamorous objects of international aid to economic growth, there is reason to judge that many of them are now being built too soon, that is, at a time when alternative expenditure of equal size would advance development further.

Counterpoint: Hirshman: Induced Decision-Making

Hirschman (1958, chaps. 3 and 4) attacks the "big push" proposal as unnecessary, impossible, and undesirable. "It combines a defeatist attitude toward the capabilities of underdeveloped economies," he states, "with completely unrealistic expectations about their creative abilities. . . . The conception of the traditional economy as a closed circle dismisses the abundant historical evidence about the piecemeal penetration by industry that competes successfully with local handicraft and by new products which are first imported and then manufactured locally." These need no expansion of demand to find a market. Moreover, it ignores the fact that some new products are sufficiently attractive to make people work harder or longer to earn more income in order to buy them. Thus their availability creates its own market.

---

[5] I have noted the development of textile and sugar production in Colombia in the complete absence of the infrastructure facilities presumed to be prerequisite. Conversely, development under the British of all types of infrastructure, in addition to the spur of greatly increased and thereafter steadily increasing export demand did not generate continuing development in Burma. Many other examples of the ineffectiveness or non-necessity of modern infrastructure could probably be cited.

Moreover, Hirschman notes, in the Rodan thesis a people that is "entirely uninterested in change and satisfied with its lot is . . . expected to marshal sufficient entrepreneurial and managerial ability to set up at the same time a whole flock of industries." This would require "huge amounts of precisely those abilities . . . likely to be in very limited supply in underdeveloped countries. . . . If a country were ready to apply the doctrine of balanced growth, then it would not be underdeveloped in the first place."[6]

Lastly, the program is undesirable. The scarcest factor in the LDCs is the ability to make decisions. This capacity is weak in government as well as in the private sphere; a policy based on the fact of sluggishness of decision-making in private activity which assumes that the government is all-wise and vigorous is unrealistic. A crucially important and effective factor in stimulating growth is the creation of circumstances that make the advantage of a course of action so obvious that even weak decision-makers will act. The approved policy for economy is to make the non-obvious initial decisions that create bottlenecks or at least imbalances (scarcities) and thus make the advantages of further steps obvious to timid decision-makers. The creation of surplus capacity in infrastructure will improve the opportunities for "directly productive activities" (Hirschman's phrase) and may thus facilitate their establishment—though it will do so at great cost. On the other hand, establishing directly productive enterprises that create a bottleneck in infrastructure will thereby make the desirability of improved infrastructure obvious and thus induce a decision within government for its construction. This order of procedure—beginning with directly productive activities—is at least as conducive to growth as the opposite one. In general, growth proceeds by advances that create bottlenecks. Responding to them creates others, at other points, and thus development proceeds, transmitted from one sector to others through linkages, in a continuous moving picture of unbalance.

Critique

If Rodan's thesis is interpreted as meaning that there must be a "big push" to get growth started, the thesis is of course flawed, for growth has very often begun quietly, gradually, without even a little push. Moreover, the concept of starting everything at once in a society that lacks the ability and energy to start even a few things is a peculiar one. Hirschman's criticism is well taken. But no one who has noted the surge of growth in South Korea, as United States government funds poured in in procurement during the Korean and Vietnam wars and as economic aid between them, and that in Taiwan, similarly stimulated by a great flow of

---

[6] The quotations are from Hirschman (1958), p. 53.

U.S. government funds, would deny that a great bulge of demand is highly favorable to growth. There are other reasons for the rapid growth of South Korea and Taiwan; few persons would claim that the same inflow of purchasing power would bring the same results in any country; but that a large increase in aggregate demand is a highly stimulating factor in favorable circumstances can hardly be questioned.

On the other hand, Hirschman's position that the optimum way to stimulate economic growth is to "bring about the circumstances" in which further desirable steps are obvious is subject to somewhat the same sort of attack that he directs toward the "big push" doctrine. To paraphrase Hirschman's statement about the "big push," if a country were able to make the decisions necessary to create those circumstances, then it would hardly be a country of ineffective decision-makers in the first place. Hirschman seems to need a deus ex machina to take the initial important steps. It must be concluded that Hirschman's thesis is more effective as a criticism of the "big push" or balanced growth thesis than as a positive prescription for growth policy. Formally, there is a way out of the dilemma: it may be assumed that a country has a few bold and judicious leaders, who by expanding some activities will create bottle-necks that will indicate profitable investment possibilities to their most timid fellow entrepreneurs, but a theory based on this assumption is pretty fragile.

The Neo-Marxists: Baran

Paul Baran (1957) presented a neo-Marxist view of why growth does not occur.

Karl Marx had no explicit theory of economic growth, but merely a theory of how the curtailment of demand resulting from the appropriation of surplus value by capitalists would cause the collapse of the capitalist system. Implicitly, he assumed that continuing technical progress is a natural phenomenon which needs no explanation. However, Baran applied the Marxist view of the world explicitly to the problem of development. Gathering together the several theories of peculiar barriers, though giving them a Marxist twist, and combining them with standard Marxist views of class oppression, he presented a coherent and integrated neo-Marxist theory of the barriers to economic development. The ingredients are two:

1. A special version of all of the hypotheses of peculiar barriers. The market is too small—because of the profits retained by the ruling coalition of owning classes. Income ample for saving for investment is received by these classes, but they do not invest. The conception of constructing infrastructure "transcends by far the financial and mental horizon" of these groups. In general, the situation is marked by monopolistic market arrangements, lack of external economies, and a divergence

between social and private advantage, in which private advantage is pursued.

2. A political theory. An alliance between feudal landlords, industrial royalists, and the rising bourgeois capitalist middle classes imposes a government that can take no forward-looking step.

In addition, Baran sketches the disruption of the feudal coherence of the backward societies by the invasion of capitalism. That invasion ended paternalistic relationships, ended also the partial or total self-sufficiency which gave stability to economic life, and instead subjected the areas to the vagaries of the world market. Since the developing bourgeois middle classes failed to lead the popular movement for social amelioration, the ousting of feudal overlords, and democracy, that movement failed. This thesis, however, is presented as an explanation of social disruption, and only indirectly as an explanation of the lack of growth.

No technical or entrepreneurial problems exist. If the ruling alliance had the will, economic development (and social progress) could proceed without difficulty.[7]

Beneath the polemics, this thesis has a good deal in common with some of the argument presented and to be presented in this chapter. It was implied in the three preceding chapters that the market opportunity is not seized because innovation is difficult and it will be argued later in this chapter that if the difficulties are not surmounted this is because insufficient innovative entrepreneurship exists. It was suggested earlier in this chapter that the landed elites of low-income societies do not save and invest productively because their attitudes toward life constrain them. Baran agrees concerning the overt behavior but he will have none of this coddling concerning its causes. The reason men who might act do not, he states, is that they are evil men. But this of course is characterization, not analysis.

If one regards the propensity of men not to save as evil, one must still ask, if one wishes to gain more than a superficial understanding, why men are evil. And as for their ability to innovate in the circumstances facing them if they choose, this is a factual question, concerning which the facts seem to contradict the Baran assumption. His thesis will be unsatisfying except to persons who believe that the devil theory of history is adequate analysis.

INCREASE IN DEMAND AS INITIATING FORCE

The discussion above indicates that adequate inducement to invest and adequate ability to save have existed in the static conditions of low-income countries. The question remains, nevertheless, whether an in-

---

[7] A. G. Frank (1967) presents a similar view of economic development in Latin America.

crease in foreign demand may not in fact have typically been the initiating force in growth.

One source of confusion concerning the relationship between demand and growth may be got out of the way in beginning the discussion of this thesis. In some writings on the question of demand-led innovation, there is confusion between an increase in GDP due to a Keynesian effect and an increase due to increase in productivity. Of course an increase in exports, however caused, raises real GDP, if there was slack in the economy. The issue here is the quite different one of whether an increase in demand, or steadily increasing demand, causes more productivity-increasing innovation than would otherwise have occurred.

In one respect, a high level of exports may certainly facilitate growth. A high level of exports provides high earnings of foreign exchange. If a shortage of foreign exchange for the purchase of capital equipment would otherwise exist, booming exports will relieve it. There is no controversy about this fact; it is not related to the issue being discussed here.[8]

A priori, the inducement effect of expanding demand is indeterminate. It may cause producers to say to themselves, "How can we take better advantage of this booming market?" or on the other hand may cause them to feel "We are doing fine" and to continue their methods unchanged or even to slacken their efforts. Until psychology is able to tell us what differing qualities of men cause some to react in one way and some in the other to the same stimulus, the economist's discussion of the question must be an empirical rather than theoretical one.

The Staple Theory

Out of the 1901–11 boom in Canadian wheat exports and the concomitant boom in Canadian economic growth has arisen the "staple theory" of growth, first stated in fairly complete form by Melville Watkins (1963). The theory, Richard Caves writes (in Bhagwati, 1971, p. 404),

> describes a sequence of events whereby the rapid expansion of some commodity exports, requiring a substantial input of natural resources but relatively little local processing, induces higher rates of growth of aggregate and per capita income through a higher rate of capital formation, inflows of capital and labor to the region, and expansions of output and productivity in other sectors via various linkages, externalities, induced innovations, and the like. The resource-based product is called a staple, and the term is used equivalently to name the model.

---

[8] As they increase foreign exchange earnings, exports simultaneously reduce a country's resources available for domestic use and, if domestic resources are the bottleneck, may retard growth. See the discussion of the "two gaps," in Chapter 17.

I noted in the opening paragraph of this chapter that accelerated economic growth and an increase in exports are associated. Caves claims a relationship in some cases in which an increase in exports is causal. "In countries most clearly matching the export-led growth model," he writes (p. 429) "the rate of export expansion appears to be connected to the movements of at least some of the following variables: rate of capital formation, money supply, rate of domestic saving or capital inflow, unemployment or net immigration, and the growth of the import-competing manufacturing sector." The only cases he cites, however, are Canada and Australia. If there is a considerable degree of innovational energy in a country, there is a priori reason to suppose that the availability of a buoyant foreign (or domestic) market will increase innovation in order to supply the increasing demand. Whether expanding demand will create such energy is a more complex question.

Market expansion may have played an important causal role in the earliest stages of economic development in Colombia in the third quarter of the 19th century. Papanek (1967) cites market expansion in Pakistan after separation from India as perhaps the most important cause of the rapid technical progress that has occurred in Pakistan subsequently. Rapid technical progress probably began only when the market began to expand rapidly. Certainly, rapid industrialization began only then. But of course other forces that may be an adequate explanation were at work, notably the well-known release of creativity caused by uprooting and migration to a new situation in which it is not possible to move in old ruts.

Economic progress in Britain in the late 18th and first half of the 19th century and in Sweden and Denmark in the 19th century seems to show innovations to increase productivity in order to take advantage of new export opportunities—certainly expansion of the market nourished innovation in England even if it did not initiate it.[9] Douglas North (1961) makes the expansion of exports a prominent theme in his discussion of economic growth in the United States from 1790 to the Civil War.[10] It seems plausible to argue that reciprocal causation between expansion and innovation existed. Nurkse (1961) mentions seven countries in advancing the thesis that exports were the "engine of growth" in the 19th century. The seven are Argentina, Australia, Canada, New Zealand, South Africa, the United States, and Uruguay.[11]

In many other instances exports have failed to induce growth. Indonesia's economic retrogression after independence, the retardation of

---

[9] See A. J. Youngson (1959), C. P. Kindleberger (1961), and W. W. Parker (1961)—all cited by Caves.

[10] He also states the thesis in North (1964).

[11] The 1961 volume presents earlier essays.

Argentina's economic growth since about 1920, Bolivia's economic inertness, and the failure of a 70-year tide in world demand for Burma's rice to set a growth process in motion can be cited. Increased demand for the industrial products of a developing country, it is agreed, has often been innovation-induced, rather than the other way round. Vigorous innovation in England much preceded the spectacular rise in her exports in the 18th century. The fact that "Britannia ruled the waves" in that century has sometimes been mentioned as the cause of her conquest of the world market for textiles. This is erroneous. By the 18th century, men-of-war were not driving competitor merchant ships off the seas. Any country that could get the orders could hire shipping to deliver them. England captured the market because she could deliver the best and the cheapest textiles.[12]

Exports have had little relationship to the Russian economy either during the period of her early vigorous growth, 1860–1914, or subsequently.[13] The rapid rise in Japan's exports after about 1890 was the planned result of a feverish search for industrial and handicraft products that could be produced cheaply enough to earn foreign exchange, rather than a response to world demand for primary products in which Japan's natural resources gave her a comparative advantage; with the exception of silk, such primary products were nonexistent. The rapid economic growth of Sweden and Denmark in the last two decades of the 19th century and the first of the 20th are probably also cases of rapid export expansion resulting from innovation, rather than causing it.

Irving Kravis (1970) has presented the most systematic critique of the thesis that exports to the industrial countries ("the center") were the "engine of growth" in newly-developing countries ("the periphery") in the 19th century. If exports were the engine, he argues, we should expect to find at least some of the following features in the economic history of the periphery countries: (1) a large and/or growing share of exports in domestic production; (2) an association between the timing of changes in exports and in GNP with the latter following the former; (3) a concentration of exports in sectors marked by relatively rapid growth and/or rapid growth of industries linked to the export industries; (4) the attraction of foreign capital to export industries or to industries supported by them.

He surveyed the data available in a number of secondary sources concerning the seven countries discussed by Nurkse, whose growth during the 19th century or the last half of it was marked. He found none of

---

[12] During the same century she made great progress in steel refining. The cause often given for that advance is that she was *losing* the steel market to continental competitors who had lower labor costs and better ores.

[13] Relatively small imports of needed materials or equipment were important at times.

the four characteristics present. He found, moreover, that some countries with rapidly increasing exports grew rapidly, while others did not. Moreover, Kravis notes a GATT study of the exports of 58 less developed countries during the period 1951–61 to 1964–65. The study showed that the difference between superior, middle, and inferior export performance by these countries depended very little on differences in world demand for their products and much upon the degree to which a country gained a larger share of the total market and the degree to which it diversified its exports. (The latter was a less important distinguisher than the former.) In short, a country's own innovative efforts were the major determinant of its increase in exports. Kravis concludes (p. 858):

> The idea that there was a powerful expansionary impact from the center's demand for food and raw materials, which was the main factor generating growth, can be true, if at all, for but a few countries. . . . nor was export expansion by periphery countries the differentiating factor determining the extent and quality of their growth.

Trade, he suggests, was the handmaiden, not the engine, of growth.[14]

Caves (p. 437) makes the necessary qualification to the "staple theory." After listing ten possible linkages between exports and growth, he states that this list "indicates the range of consequences that export-led growth may have, depending on the product in question *and the traits of the economy in which it is produced.*" There can be little disagreement that in a society characterized by qualities conducive to growth, market expansion may be a stimulating factor. All that can be objected to is statements that make it the general or necessary cause of growth.

There is one last consideration that makes the thesis of increasing demand as the trigger of growth attractive to many economists. Given the fragility of the vicious circle or need-for-a-big-push theses, if increase in demand is not the explanation of the beginning of growth, then there seems to be no economic explanation, and economists are given to finding economic explanations of economic phenomena. To the extent that increase in demand or some other change in external economic circumstances is only a partial explanation, then differences among countries in innovational behavior must be due to differences among men, and the beginning of growth in a country whose economy has been static must be due to changes within men. The assumption of such causal forces, which lie completely outside the purview of economics, seems to make many economists uneasy, but it may be valid nevertheless. These personality theories of the beginning of growth or the rate of growth are discussed briefly in Chapter 11, "Entrepreneurship."

---

[14] For criticism of Kravis' criteria and analysis, see Crafts (1973), and for Kravis' reply, see Kravis (1973).

IMPROVEMENTS IN SUPPLY AS INITIATING GROWTH

If an expansion of demand is not a necessary condition for the beginning of growth, and if the low income and size of the market of low-
income countries are not important barriers to growth, then growth may
begin simply through the introduction of improved methods of production by innovative entrepreneurs. An improvement in methods of production here refers to a change in method by which the same output is
produced with fewer inputs or, what amounts to the same thing, a
product with improved quality is produced with no more inputs than
before.

The improvement will typically though not necessarily be one using
more capital and less labor, with the increase in capital cost being less
than the decrease in labor cost.

Such an innovation in supply does not necessarily lead to growth in the
aggregate or per capita income of the economy. It may instead lead
merely to increased concentration of income, and to increased unemployment. Consider carefully the following possible sequence of events.

The innovator is able to produce the good with fewer inputs per unit
of output then before. He will therefore be able to sell the good at a price
that will widen his profit margin—at the same price as before, in which
case he obtains the entire benefit of the reduction in cost per unit, or, if
he wishes to expand his sales, at a somewhat reduced price, but one
which still widens his margin of profit. In either case, fewer inputs will be
employed per unit of the purchasers' expenditures than before. Aggregate
consumer expenditures will be "buying less inputs" than before. Hence
some inputs, almost certainly labor inputs, will be "laid off"—"disemployed," to use the convenient English term. They will be disemployed in
the establishment of the innovating entrepreneur if he sells the product at
the same price as before and therefore sells the same number of units as
before, or in other establishments if he attracts purchasers by reducing
his price. The reader can easily work out the logic of the fact that the
result will be net disemployment in the economy as a whole; that any
increase in employment in the innovator's establishment will be less than
the decrease in employment elsewhere.

Indeed, if the innovator does not spend his increased income, there
will be a downward multiplier effect, because of the reduced spending of
the workers who have been laid off. Only if the innovator spends as much
of his increased income as the disemployed workers had been spending
of theirs when they were employed will that be avoided. His spending
will not cause re-employment of the disemployed workers, but will only
replace their former spending and keep unemployment from spreading.
If he does spend as much of his added income as the disemployed

workers had been spending of theirs, the level of aggregate GNP will be maintained. If he spends less, aggregate GNP will fall.

A cost-reducing (or quality-improving) innovation, in short, does not in itself expand GNP. It expands productive capacity, but simultaneously creates such "technological unemployment" that aggregate income does not rise, and may fall.

It should be noted that the word "unemployment" is used here to include the disguised unemployment that exists as workers laid off from industrial jobs disappear into the families of their rural relatives and the underemployment that exists as individuals unable to find other income-earning activity resort to petty services with extremely low productivity or hold jobs as retainers of wealthy patrons. That is, it includes economic unemployment, partial or total, whether or not discernible in statistics.

How then can innovation in supply initiate growth?

The analysis above must be qualified by considering one aspect of the innovation. The innovation commonly involves an increase in the amount of capital equipment used. Assume that this capital equipment is sufficiently costly that it is purchased not out of the innovator's current income but rather out of previously accumulated savings, his or someone else's. If so, its construction will cause an increase in employment. The increase will be only temporary; once the equipment has been constructed, employemnt will fall, and the loss of man-hours of work, over the lifetime of the equipment, will be greater than the man-hours spent in constructing the equipment by a margin sufficient to more than cover interest costs. Otherwise, there would have been no net saving in production cost.

Suppose, as is commonly the case, that there was some unused productive capacity in the economy. Suppose that it was sufficient to accommodate the construction of the capital equipment. Then a temporary slight bulge in employment and a subsequent decrease in employment to a continuing level lower than the pre-innovation one will be the only effects of the innovation on employment.

The increase in productive capacity caused by the innovation may however become an actual increase in output and income in the following manner. Suppose that not one but a number of innovations occur, simultaneously or close enough together in time so that the bulges in employment and income caused by their demands for capital equipment overlap. Suppose indeed that there is a continuing stream of innovation, which involves a continuing flow of capital formation financed not out of the current receipts of innovators but out of accumulated past savings or by credit creation. That continuing flow of capital formation, plus the multiplier effect which it creates, may cause a rise in employment more than equal to the direct technological disemployment. If the flow of innovation and capital formation is an increasing one, so also may be the creation of income and employment.

Moreover, the demand for the construction of capital equipment plus the consumer spending of the increased income received may press upon productive capacity of the relevant section of the economy, and may thus cause producers other than the innovators to engage in capital formation to increase their productive capacity—an accelerator effect. This non-labor-saving capital formation and the multiplier effect which flows from it will create re-employment and increase GDP. This secondary capital formation plus its multiplier effect is probably always more important quantitatively in turning a potential expansion of income and employment into a real one than is the capital formation-cum-multiplier directly associated with the innovation. Through this total process of technological disemployment plus re-employment, a secular expansion of aggregate and per capita income—economic growth—occurs.

The joint presence of disemployment and re-employment is reflected in the fact that in the "less developed countries," between 1955 and 1970 manufacturing production rose by about 7% per year and manufacturing employment by about 4% per year.[15] That output grew faster than employment indicates that technological disemployment occurred; that net employment increased indicates that the employment-inducing effect was greater than the disemployment effect. Ergo, growth.

This is the classic process of economic growth, as seen by most economists. However, there is no principle of economics that indicates that in any given country all of the disemployed will be re-employed during the same time period or even at any time, or that the expansion of output will absorb into employment all of an expanding labor force. Secular unemployment and growth may continue side by side.

There are two other possible methods of re-employment or increase in employment. One is shift of the disemployed workers to agriculture, from which, presumably, they came. If idle land is available, or if the slope of marginal productivity of labor on land already in use declines only gently, this sort of re-employment may proceed fairly smoothly and aggregate GDP will rise. If the increased agricultural production replaces imports, the terms of trade need not turn against agriculture. Or the added agricultural production may simply increase a surplus for export. No increase in world demand is required unless the country produces so large a share of the world output of its export product that its increase in exports materially affects the world price. However, if the slope of the marginal productivity of labor in agriculture descends steeply and there are no idle lands to which to escape, then the return of workers to agriculture will have these favorable results only in small degree and will be merely a disguised increase in the number of the employed.

The third possible path to re-employment is that the disemployed workers may offer to work for lower money wages than before. The

---

[15] United Nations, *Growth of World Industry*, 1972 ed., p. 542.

reduction in wages may cause employers to increase the proportion of labor to capital used in production. Moreover, the falling price level, by increasing the value of money balances held by families, may cause them to increase their spending, thus expanding aggregate demand.[16] This shift in methods of production to more labor-intensive ones would presumably involve a change in the types of goods produced as well. Many economists believe that the entrepreneurial flexibility needed for such shifts rarely exists in less developed countries, even if wages are flexible, and that the much more common sequel to disemployment is the absorption of the surplus labor into agriculture and petty services without appreciable increase in output. Moreover, they argue, the flexibility of industrial wages assumed in this thesis does not exist. Nevertheless, the possibility of a productive adjustment of methods of production and products produced to a change in relative factor prices must be recognized. It will be discussed in Chapters 17 and 19, which deal with the allocation of productive resources.

In this sketch of growth through innovation without prior increase in demand realistic? Three noted development economists have thought so. Economic growth occurs, they have said, when innovating entrepreneurs get at work. No other condition is necessary.

Adam Smith.   Adam Smith thought this. Smith was the first "development economist." At a time when few other men appreciated the possibility of ever-rising levels of living, Adam Smith sketched central aspects of the process of growth. In his great 1776 work, he stressed the role of innovation in that process. Innovation, he said, occurs because of the division of labor, and the division of labor in turn occurs because of the natural propensity of men to "truck, barter, and exchange." The division of labor leads to an increase in the dexterity of workers, an elimination of the wastes of time involved when a man does more than one task, and (above all, we would say today) to the invention of better machines and equipment, both because the division of work into simpler and simpler components makes it easier to devise machinery to do each component and because specialization may include concentration of the efforts of some men or the development of machinery.

The division of labor, Smith stated, is limited by the extent of the market, which by determining the total volume of each product that can be sold determines how finely it pays to specialize. But he believed that economic development is cumulative, for he noted that the size of the market is not of a fixed magnitude. Once division of labor increases productivity, the resulting increase in national income (and population) both enlarges the market and permits an increased flow of saving. The two effects together permit further division of labor and invention of

---

[16] The "Pigou effect."

machinery; a further expansion of income and enlargement of the market and of the savings flow results; and so on and on.

We know now that much technical progress occurs quite apart from the division of labor; nevertheless we must recognize the force of Smith's analysis. He recognized that his hypothesis requires an answer to the question of why technical progress occurs more in some countries than in others—in his day, more in England then elsewhere. His answer was not that the English had a special genius or that an increase in demand stimulated the English but rather that the political institutions of England, which gave men great freedom, were highly conducive to innovation.

Schumpeter. In the 20th century, Joseph A. Schumpeter argued, as Smith had, that innovation occurs when innovative men exist. The (business) entrepreneur acts, Schumpeter said (1934, pp. 93–94):[17]

> . . . to found a private kingdom, usually, though not necessarily, also a dynasty. The modern world really does not know any such positions, but what may be attained by industrial or commercial success is still the nearest approach to medieval lordship possible to modern man. *Its fascination is specially strong, for people who have no other chance of achieving social distinction.* . . .
>
> *Then there is the will to conquer: the impulse to fight, to prove oneself superior to others, to succeed for the sake, not of the fruits of success, but of success itself.* . . . The financial result is a secondary consideration, or, at all events, valued as an index of success and as a symptom of victory, the displaying of which very often is more important as a motive of large expenditure, than the wish for the consumers' goods themselves. . . .
>
> Finally, *there is the joy of creating, of getting things done, or simply of exercising one's energy and ingenuity.* This is akin to a ubiquitous motive, but nowhere does it stand out as an independent factor of behavior with anything like the clearness with which it obtrudes itself in our case. Our type seeks out difficulties, changes in order to change, delights in ventures.

The italics are mine.

Lewis. More recently, W. Arthur Lewis implicitly presents a similar conception, though since his central interest in the relevant article (1954) is the saving rate, he terms the central figures in his model capitalists rather than innovators or entrepreneurs. "A country's saving rate is low," Lewis writes, "not because the country is poor but because its capitalist class is small." As those of its businessmen who have capitalist temperaments invest, profit, save, and invest, the saving rate and the investment rate rise and growth proceeds.[18]

---

[17] The English translation was published in 1934. The book was originally written in German in 1912.

[18] Lewis's model is discussed in Chapter 8 of this book.

Lewis's reference to saving introduces the final question concerning this simple supply theory of the beginning of growth: Without some previous change which increased the capacity to save in low-income economies, how could the early innovations have been financed? The question of saving is discussed at some length in Chapter 13. Here it is sufficient to state that one important source, and probably a sufficient source, is the one indicated in Lewis's statement: the expanding savings of entrepreneurs from initially small but rapid expanding enterprises.

NATURAL RESOURCES, CLIMATE, AND GROWTH

Certain views of natural resource paucity[19] and climate as barriers to growth, not related to either the demand-led or supply-initiated theories, may be considered here to round out the discussion of theories related to the beginning of growth. Two views of natural resource paucity as a barrier are fairly prevalent, especially among laymen, but one is illogical and the other is of limited empirical significance.

Resource Paucity as a Barrier

The association of natural resource abundance with high income is seen in the present affluence of the oil-producing countries, and in the United States, Canada, Australia, and New Zealand, though of course in these latter cases many other factors are also causes, and monopoly pricing plays its part in the post-1973 extreme affluence of the oil countries. At the low end of the income spectrum, before post-World War II disorder disrupted the Burmese economy, because of her more plentiful mineral production and agricultural land per capita Burma had a slightly higher per capita income than India, with technology inferior to India's. On the other hand, Java, Jamaica, the United Arab Republic, and to a lesser degree India and China suffer from extremely high population density relative to their natural resources, or those that have so far been discovered and exploited. But among the world's highest income countries are Japan and Switzerland, two countries which rank very high indeed in paucity of natural resources.

It may be granted that a country's natural resource endowment affects its income level. The fallacious view referred to above refers not to income level but to change in income level. It is that some countries will find it especially difficult to grow at all and—in the extreme version—cannot hope to grow, because their populations are so large relative to their natural resources. Consideration of the economic histories of Japan and

---

[19] The term commonly used is "resource scarcity." "Paucity" is the precisely accurate term.

Switzerland should convince anyone that as a minimum the view needs qualification. Here, we may note the fallacy involved.

Assume that two countries with identical incomes per capita, say $100, are being considered. In one, population density is high; in the other, low. We may then ask, with lesser natural resources per capita, how did the first country achieve the same income level as the other? The answer is that it must have either more capital per head, or better techniques per unit of capital, or both. Each starts today with the techniques and natural resources that it has today. Now, with each starting from that condition, suppose that innovation, combined with capital formation, occurs in both. Other productive inputs (labor, natural resources) being given, with added capital embodying improved methods, income will rise—in both. The logic is as simple as that.

It has been noted that "countries lacking resources will turn to manufacturing at an earlier stage in their development in order to make up for their lack of primary products for export and domestic use."[20] The statement identifies income level with stage of development, in this context a misleading identification. It is illuminating to turn the statement on its end. Countries with few natural resources will achieve a given level of income only by achieving a higher level of technology (that is, only at a later stage in their technical development) than countries more blessed with resources. This technology will usually include a greater degree of industrialization.

However, a resource-poor low-income country is handicapped. The economic principle of variable proportions tells us that a country with ample natural resources per capita will thereby get a higher yield from the same proportionate increase in capital per capita, in the absence of technical progress. There is not conceptual reason why technical progress should not raise the level of income in countries with high population density relative to natural resources as rapidly as in those with lower population density. But in the world as we know it this probably will not happen. The reason is that the basket of known techniques to draw upon and adapt does not include many designed for labor-intensive production.

This advantage of low-income countries applies with full force only to activities in which natural resources are an important input and in which the country is limited to use of its own natural resources. It applies especially, therefore, to agriculture, forestry, fishing, and mining. It does not apply to tertiary services, and except as transportation costs in the import of raw materials reduce the net income generated, it does not apply to manufacturing industry.

However, low-income countries, typically, have not achieved technical

---

[20] H. B. Chenery (1960), p. 647.

flexibility great enough to permit them to take great advantage of imported materials. The more advanced a country's technology, the less its dependence on its own resources. Again, Japan and Switzerland provide the examples. The Netherlands may be added. Earlier than either of the other two, Holland made the world her oyster by developing a great merchant fleet. England followed suit, but combined this with pioneer technical progress in manufacturing. As world trade increased in volume and in freedom, Japan took advantage of it without a great fleet. Switzerland's imports are more local; she exports goods and financial services to the world. Sweden has the reputation of producing fine automobiles, which in fact are produced all over Europe. Singapore provides the most recent example of very rapid rise in income without natural resources. The manufacturing and distribution enterprises that have been induced to come to Singapore depend no more on her natural resources than on those of Upper Volta.

Postwar data, perhaps surprisingly, seem to indicate that population density is no deterrent whatever to economic growth, even in low-income countries. The data indicate this, at least, if the area of cultivable land can be taken as a good measure of the total natural resource stock. While this measure fails to reflect other valuable natural resources, there seems no reason why it should give a biased estimate—no reason, that is, why cultivable area as a measure should over- or understate total resources in densely populated countries relative to others.

Figure 7–2 presents the data. As the figure indicates, from 1960 to 1970 the rate of economic growth in the densely populated countries of the world was fully as high as in the less densely populated ones.

This evidence is inconclusive, since (like some other figures in this book) it presents only a simple correlation where a multiple regression is appropriate for full analysis. The relationship shown is a little surprising. There are several possible explanations. One is the fact noted: that only in primary industry does the man-land ratio necessarily affect the contribution to GNP of added investment. A second one is that, at a given level of per capita income, investment benefits more from economies of scale in a more densely populated country. (The following chapter discusses this matter.) While this may be true in manufacturing, it seems surprising that it would offset the effect on returns to investment of lesser resource abundance in primary industry. However, where investment is going on disproportionately in secondary industry, it may. Other possible explanations are that capital formation, technical progress, or the discovery and exploitation of natural resources is occurring at a more rapid proportional rate in the more densely populated countries. However, it is difficult to see why this should be true.

If we define "natural resources" broadly—to include all aspects of

FIGURE 7–2
Economic Growth Rates, 1960–65, Related to Population Density, 1960

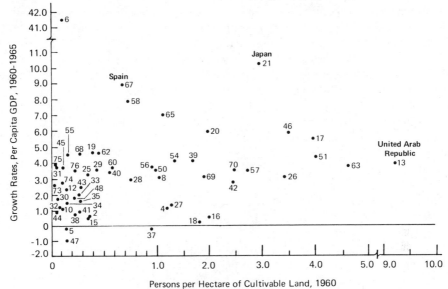

Persons per Hectare of Cultivable Land, 1960

Source: Growth rates, 1960–65: Hagen (1968), Table 1–8; Persons per hectare of cultivable land, 1960: U.N. Food and Agriculture Organization, *Production Yearbook, 1964.*

nature—we may include here discussion of the effect of climate upon growth.

Climate and Progress: Huntington

A well-known geographer, Ellsworth Huntington, argued in a series of books that lack of development in the present "backward" areas of the world is due in large part to the effect of their climate on man.[21] Human energy and achievement in all fields are greater, his thesis runs, where the climate is moderate and above all variable. Occasional thunderstorms, which increase the quantity of ozone in the air, are especially favorable. (Amused critics noted that his description of a climate ideal for human achievement coincides remarkably with that of New Haven, Connecticut, where he lived and worked.) Peoples who live in hot, humid, nonvarying climates are doomed to a perpetual lesser rate of advance in economic prowess and civilization. Huntington buttressed his arguments with much episodic argument and also more systematic data, some purporting to show ingeniously that at the time when rapid advance in material

---

[21] He summarized his arguments, and moderated some of his earlier theses about the dominating importance of heredity, in Huntington (1945).

civilization in some subtropical areas of the world stopped, the stoppage occurred because the climate had changed.

Huntington's evidence is not convincing to geographers in general, and his thesis has gone out of favor.[22] However, a second thesis which he advanced (1945, chap. 21) has lasted longer. This is that the subtropics were most conducive to the first stages of advance in civilization, but that when means of coping with colder climates had been developed, the temperate zones became more favorable. The thesis is Toynbeean. The subtropics, where grasses grew lushly and animals could easily be raised in domesticity, encouraged man to settle down, to grow cereals, and to begin to accumulate artifacts. Moreover, the clays of the subtropical rivers were ideal for making lasting written records, and encouraged the development of written communication. But the climate provided little stimulus, and so man grew lax. However, when he had made sufficient technical advance to protect and nourish himself in colder climates, those climates stimulated him, and the continued advance of civilization occurred in the temperate zones.

A thesis stated in such broad terms lacks rigor. It is consistent with the general facts of human history, but this may also be true of alternative theses. If accepted, the thesis possesses little predictive power concerning the longer run future of the tropical and subtropical areas, for today any of various conditions in the world or in their own countries may provide stimulus to the peoples of the warm climates, and through technical advances man's ability to cope with the supposed adverse conditions of those climates is steadily increasing.

Climate and Progress: Lee

Dr. Douglas H. K. Lee, professor of physiological climatology at John Hopkins University, doubts the deleterious effect of tropical climate on human performance, but suggests his own reasons for thinking that the climate of the tropics creates great barriers to increase in productivity in agriculture.[23] They are that tropical areas tend to monoculture, and "pure stands invite disease" and pests; that weeds grow more luxuriantly in the tropics; and that the use of fertilizers is more difficult.

Professor Lee's thesis runs into two difficulties: that artificial fertilizers are now being used with great success in tropical areas with no difficulty except that of adapting their use to local conditions; and that in coarse cereals, in which there does not seem to be any greater tendency to monoculture in the tropics than elsewhere, the ratio of yields per acre in

---

[22] For vigorously presented criticisms of Huntington's thesis about the effects of climate on human energy and performance, see Bates (1952) and Simey (1946).

[23] H. K. Lee (1957).

the tropics to those in the temperate zones seems as low as in the case of rice, cotton, and other monoculture crops. This latter comment is casual empiricism; the writer has not done a systematic study.

Yet the fact remains that almost all of the poor countries of the world lie in the tropics. The major ones lying elsewhere are Afghanistan, Pakistan, and China. And the only tropical countries with even moderately high incomes are the oil countries. Afghanistan's poverty can be blamed on its desert. Because of the other two exceptions it is possible to argue that the cause is isolation, not climate. The Europeans who might have brought the virus of growth penetrated neither the tropics nor China. Yet the factor of climate looms so large that it would be foolish to ignore it.

In discussing it I shall be guilty of dichotomizing falsely, for convenient summary discussion. When I refer to the tropics, I shall not mean *all* the tropics, and some "tropical" conditions exist in nontropical areas. Latitude is a matter of degree. Altitude, coastline, mountains blocking rainfall or capturing it, and other factors all cause variations. But in crude summary generalizations we may refer to tropics versus nontropics.

It is not necessary to resort to belief in the stimulating effects of ozone to believe that the tropical climate has been a deterrent to economic growth. Consider simpler facts.[24] Tropical soils apparently need to be protected from the sun if the organic matter and micro-organisms necessary for fertility are to be preserved; hence when the lush tropical cover is removed, the soils deteriorate unless alluvial overflow replenishes it annually, and rains leach out the main plant food. Hence the laterites of a large part of the humid tropics.[25] Winter, which kills many weeds, pests, and disease-bearing organisms, does not occur in the tropics, a fact that may be a greater ill than the lushness with which desirable plants as well as undesirable competitors grow is a benefit. Locusts are peculiarly a tropical pest. Trypanosomiasis, a disease carried by the tsetse fly, prevents the raising of cattle and draft animals over most of tropical Africa. Humans are subject to malaria (largely eliminated from the subtropics, but not from the tropics), bilharzia or "snail fever," a parasitic disease from which 150 to 200 million persons in Africa, the Middle East, and Central America plus an unknown number in China suffer, and from a variety of other parasites carried in the blood not known in the temperate zones except as carried there by visitors to the tropics. Bacillary and amoebic dysentery are common. The idea that only visitors "not used to the water" suffer from them is a fiction. The cumulative debilitating effect of these various plagues must be extremely great.

---

[24] I have these from A. M. Kamarck (1972), whom I cite rather than the sources which he cites. I am indebted to Peter Kilby for calling my attention to Kamarck's manuscript.

[25] Hence also the virtue of "shifting cultivation," which allows protective cover to grow back after two or three years of crop growing.

These plant, animal, and human difficulties may fully explain the economic backwardness of tropical countries. Not all tropical countries are affected in the same way, or equally affected, depending mainly on their altitude and rainfall pattern. Economic theory has paid little attention to these factors in growth, probably largely because they are not subject to economic analysis (though their results are). Another reason may be that until recently little could be done about most of them; it is still true that there are many of them on which attack is still ineffective. But many of the problems can now be ameliorated. Economic growth can occur in the tropics, and indeed real income is rising in many tropical countries. But the reader may keep these tropical climate-related conditions in mind as a probable major cause of the present low incomes of tropical countries.

SOCIOLOGICAL FACTORS

Somewhere in the discussion of theories of growth, theories of the effects of social and political factors should be mentioned, and though they are not uniquely theories about the beginning of growth they may be mentioned here.

By the statistical technique of factor analysis, Irma Adelman and Cynthia Morris (1965) have measured the association between 22 social factors and the level of GNP per capita in 74 less developed countries. The social factors, they found, "account for," that is, are associated with, 66% of the variation in per capita GNP. (See also the fuller exposition in Adelman and Morris, 1967.)

The procedure was as follows. On each of the 22 qualities, they ranked each country into one of 9 or of 12 groups, which were then given numerical values ranging between 1 and 100. Some of the characteristics ranked are highly objective, for example, extent of literacy. Others are rather subjective, for example, intensity of nationalism and degree of national unity. For each characteristic, the authors assigned each country a rank on the basis of certain studies by political scientists, then submitted the judgmental rankings to the criticism of some 30 regional experts of the United States Agency for International Development, and modified the rankings where the separate suggestions of two or more experts for correction were consistent.

Some of the subjective rankings may have been influenced (unconsciously) by the respondents' knowledge of whether the country being ranked was experiencing growth, and at what pace it was growing. This is an unavoidable weakness in the method.

In factor analysis, the variables whose association with an "observed variable" (in this case, GNP per capita) is being tested are grouped into "factors." The items grouped as a common factor must have a substantive association. That is, they must measure qualities that are in some sense aspects of "the same thing." But the groupings must also have another common quality: the variables grouped as one factor must show an approximately equal degree of statistical association with the observed variable, when the influence of the other factors has been allowed for. If they do not meet this test, the grouping into factors is inappropriate, and must be redone.

In this study, Adelman and Morris grouped the 22 variables into four factors. The first represents the degree of differentiation of social roles and degree of development of integrating (mainly communication) devices to integrate the differentiating groups. (For example, of the seven variables included, one measures the degree of breakdown of extended kinship, village, and tribal complexes into nuclear families; another is the use of mass communication media.) The second factor is the degree of Westernization of the political system. The third is the type and nature of leadership; and the fourth the degree of social and political stability. The "factor loadings" (analogous to partial regression coefficients) indicate that the first factor "explains" 42% of the variation in GNP per capita, the second 18%, the third 5%, and the fourth between 1 and 2%. Performing the factor analysis by continents indicated that as development progresses, the influence of the first factor tends to decline and the second to increase.

The study, like any statistical association, does not show causation. That must be deduced by the analyst from the nature of the factors studied. In this case, the authors conclude that the degree of relationship shown "lends support to the views, long held by development economists, that, in the last analysis, the purely economic performance of a community is strongly conditioned by the social and political setting in which economic activity takes place." The associations shown may also be due to the converse fact that the social and political structure and functioning of a country are affected by its level of income and rate of growth.

BIBLIOGRAPHICAL NOTE

The standard expositions of the theories of vicious circles are: R. Nurkse (1953), H. W. Singer (1953), and P. N. Rosenstein-Rodan (1943). Albert Hirschman's attack on the conception is in his *Strategy of Economic Development* (1958). W. A. Lewis' classic article, "Economic Development with Unlimited Supplies of Labour," in *The Manchester School* (1954) is reprinted in A–S, M–B–C, and O–R. See also his further discussion (1958) and (1972).

Theories of Development: How Growth Proceeds

8

Some important topics in growth theory, including theories about balance, leading sectors, dualism, and growth points, deal with the growth process rather than with how growth begins.

BALANCE OR LACK OF BALANCE DURING THE GROWTH PROCESS

The Theses

Some economists, and not necessarily those who adhered to the vicious circles or "big push" hypotheses, have argued that there must be balance during the growth process if it is to continue. In its weakest form the principle asserted is merely that as growth occurs there must be some expansion in all sectors of production except in the production of "inferior goods" and except as imports satisfy demand. In its strongest form the thesis states that as growth occurs the output of the several sectors of the economy must be increased in proportions rigidly determined by the changing composition of rising demand and by input coefficients in production.

Under certain rigorous conditions, this strong form must hold. In a closed economic system, if there were fixed input coefficients in production, and if the price elasticity of consumer demand were zero, then an absolutely inflexible balance would have to be maintained. The allocation of increasing consumer demand among final goods would be completely

194

determined by the income elasticity of demand for various products, the allocation among capital goods by investment choices and requirements, and the output of each industry feeding other industries by the input coefficients of each industry. In such an economy, incidentally, only by coincidence would the demand for each type of input equal the available supply; except by coincidence, only one type of input, the bottleneck input, would be fully employed.

The opposing theory is that in its essence the growth process is one of unbalance. An innovator makes an advance in one field, and to meet the resulting demand expands production in it. This creates increased demand and shortages of components or materials and a rise in their price. This opportunity induces expansion in those fields. Perhaps infrastructure now becomes congested. The government or a private entrepreneur is induced to provide it. And so on.

Schumpeter, who proclaimed that innovation occurs in bursts or waves, lesser men following the great innovator who first makes an advance, would have found the conception of rigid balance in growth incredible. He (1939, vol. 1, p. 102) describes the growth process as follows:

> Progress—in the industrial as well as in any other sector of social or cultural life—not only proceeds by jerks and rushes but also by one-sided rushes. . . . We must cease to think of it as by nature smooth and harmonious. . . . On the contrary, we must recognize that evolution is lopsided, discontinuous, disharmonious by nature. . . . The history of capitalism is studded with violent bursts and catastrophies which do not accord well with the alternative hypothesis we herewith discard. . . . Evolution is . . . more like a series of explosions than a gentle, though incessant, transformation.

Hirschman, who attacked the "big push" theory, attacked the theory of required balance during growth as vigorously, and expounded the thesis of lack of balance as the engine on growth. The balanced growth theory, he writes (1958, p. 62):

> . . . is essentially an exercise in retrospective comparative statics. If we look at an economy that has experienced growth at two different points in time, we will of course find that a great many parts of it have pushed ahead: industry and agriculture, capital goods and consumer goods industries, cars on the road and highway mileage—each at its own average annual rate of increase. But surely the individual components of the economy will not actually have grown at these rates throughout the period under review. Just as on the demand side the market can absorb "unbalanced" advances in output because of cost-reducing innovations, new products, and import substitution, so we can have isolated forward thrusts on the supply side as inputs are redistributed among users through price

changes, and at the cost of some temporary shortages and disequilibria
in the balance of payments or elsewhere.

Criticisms

The statements by Schumpeter and Hirschman are surely reasonably
accurate descriptions of the growth process. The balance thesis in its
strong form is untenable, for three reasons (all of which are stated in
Hirschman's analysis). First, price elasticity in consumer demand for
various goods will accommodate a differential between the relative rates
of increase in consumer demand for various goods and the relative rates
of increase in supply. Second, even in the fairly short run, and even more
so over periods of a few years, some input coefficients are not rigidly
fixed. Hence some input scarcities can be accommodated. Entrepreneurs
can and do adapt to differential relative pricing and differential relative
availability of inputs. Third, with some qualification, goods whose production it does not seem economical to expand can be imported and
goods whose production is expanded at a rate faster than that which
domestic demand expands can be exported.

However, there are limits to the flexibility permitted by each of these
factors. Income elasticities of demand do determine the relative movement of the demand schedules for various goods, but a sharp rise in the
price of a good because of its scarcity does not eliminate the effects of the
scarcity, though it may be the best remedy available if the scarcity has
occurred. Some input coefficients are virtually fixed, and many others can
be varied only moderately. Some goods are not exportable or importable
at all, and many may be imported or exported only at inordinate expense.
Thus for a considerable share of the goods and services used in a country,
growth is best served if production rises in at least roughly the same
proportion as demand. When it is observed that without adequate infrastructure growth will be severely hampered; that the agricultural sector
must be producing an adequate surplus if industrialization is to proceed,
and must augment the urban market for industrial goods if industry is to
thrive; or that there must be an excess of exports over the value of
consumer goods imports, the desirability of balance in production is
being recognized. (Putting the agriculture-industry relationship in the
way in which it is stated above is singularly agricocentric; it could as well
be stated that the industrial sector must produce a sufficient surplus and
must provide a sufficient market for agricultural products; but the
Physiocratic viewpoint is the one commonly taken.) But these points are
not in dispute, nor are they inconsistent with the thesis of the desirability
(and inevitability) of unbalanced growth.

Keeping growth of production in balance with anticipated growth in
demand is of course not relevant to the cases of export-oriented or import-
replacing innovation.

Scitovsky: Concentration and Dynamism

To the other arguments, Scitovsky (1959) adds one concerning the advantages of unbalanced or concentrated investment for its own sake. It begins with consideration of the importance of economies of scale. Rapid expansion of one industry at a time, Scitovsky argues, is required to expand an enterprise or industry rapidly to the size at which unit cost is the lowest, that is, to take advantage of economies of scale. If each of five enterprises is expanded by 20,000 units of production capacity each year, in order that they may "take in each other's washing," the techniques added each year and thus the final plant may be less than optimum. If, instead, the productive capacity of one was expanded by 100,000 units in the first year, in advance of demand, a second by an equal amount in the second year, and so on, at the end of five years the country might have five enterprises each more efficient than in the alternative case. The level of income thereafter would be higher. Meanwhile, production in the plants expanded early would temporarily be at high cost, because they were operating below capacity, and unless imports could meet the growing demand there would be relative shortages of the products of the other plants. Where the loss involved is too great, it would pay to have balanced growth and to introduce the most efficient large-scale methods at a later date by scrapping equipment not yet fully depreciated and replacing it with an efficient large unit; but otherwise concentration of investment may bring superior results.

Scitovsky goes on to an argument much beyond mere economies of scale. He argues that a rapidly growing industry attracts man's energies, and that with a rapid rate of expansion there are both more opportunity for and more receptivity to new methods. He notes that an association between the rates of aggregate growth of industries and their rates of increase in productivity is well established by statistical studies in various industrial countries.

One's decision concerning the degree of balance or unbalance that is desirable in growth will depend on one's appraisal of empirical factors, rather than on abstract economic logic.

EXTERNALITIES; GROWTH POINTS

External Economies

The concept of technological external economies has been present in economic literature for a long time. The productive activity carried on by one firm may reduce the inputs needed by another firm per unit of its production, in such a way that the firm conferring the benefit cannot collect compensation for it; or the productive activity may increase the inputs required per unit of production in another firm, in such a way that the firm causing the added cost cannot be required to pay compensation. Or, the benefit or injury may be bestowed or received by a consumer. Such effects are termed technological external economies and diseconomies (sometimes, collectively, externalities).

A bucolic example of an external economy is the benefit that flows from establishment of an apple orchard near an apiary. Since the bees now have to fly a shorter distance to get their nectar, they will produce more honey. An industrial example is that of a new mine opened near an older one, from which the new mine operator must pump water. His doing so reduces the flow into the older mine and hence reduces the pumping costs of the owner of that mine. In these days when much attention is being given to pollution, the reader hardly needs examples of external diseconomies.

Whether the bestower of a benefit (or an injury) can collect payment (or be forced to pay) is often an institutional rather than a technical matter. If the law is changed so that payment can be enforced, the economy is no longer "external."

Technical external economies must be distinguished from pecuniary external economies, advantages to a firm resulting from the activity of another firm which, unlike technological external economies, do accrue through market operations, and which accrue even though the first firm's inputs per unit of output are not affected. The establishment or expansion of one enterprise, by increasing the demand for the products of a supplier, may increase the latter's profits. Or, a supplying firm, perhaps by a technical advance or because production on a larger scale has reduced its unit costs, may reduce the price of its product, and thereby the cost of production of a firm to which that product is an input. This firm's profits may thereby be increased. In the broadest sense of the term, the concept includes also an increase in profits resulting from an increase in demand caused by the expansion of income in the economy as a whole.[1]

Growth Points

Because of technological external economies arising from proximity to appropriate other firms, growth in industry and in some types of service

---

[1] The concept of pecuniary external economies was first expounded by Scitovsky (1957). Until then, technological external economies were referred to without the use of the first adjective. In an economy in which growth is not occurring (more precisely, a static economy in equilibrium) there can be no other type of external economy but technological. Only in a growing or technologically changing economy can pecuniary external economies appear.

External economies of either type must be distinguished from economies of scale, the economies in production that a firm may gain because its own level of production is larger. Economies of scale are discussed in Chapter 12. A pecuniary external economy consisting of an increase in demand may of course be larger than otherwise because economies of scale are gained.

tends to be concentrated geographically. It centers around "growth points" or "growth centers," or, to use the stronger French term, *poles de croissance*. It is argued that the geographic spot at which growth begins in an economy will form a focus of growth, and that the attractiveness of this center for further growth will at least for a time increase regional disparity in income and in innovational energy.

One of the external economies involved is the availability to each firm of semiskilled, skilled, white collar, or technical workers who have been trained by other firms. Any firm training workers loses some of them. If other firms are clustered nearby, those losses are offset by the recruitment of workers who have been trained in other firms.

Much more important is another technological external economy resulting from clustering. This is the advantage resulting from the mere closeness of sources of supply, maintenance and repair services, and technical consultancy. Any firm in a low-income country that has to stockpile machinery components or to send 1,000 miles to obtain technical advice understands keenly the advantages of clustering.

The importance to a firm of having these and other needed facilities nearby is illustrated by the difficulties encountered by the government of Italy in its attempts after the second World War to attract firms to the region in and near the "heel" of Italy's "boot." When the construction of infrastructure plus the rather generous financial incentives offered by the Italian government during the 1950s had induced a much smaller movement of industry to the area than had been hoped, the European Economic Commission commissioned a research study to determine the conditions needed to encourage an industrial enterprise or a group of interlocking enterprises to move.

That study, as reported in the London *Economist* (Nov. 7, 1964) concluded that

> . . . most firms, despite the incentives, could not afford to sacrifice the "external economies" (i.e., benefits that come from the industrial environment rather than from the particular firm's own efforts) that they would enjoy if they invested in the north.

It was found

> . . . that external economies depended on something much more specific than being surrounded by a lot of other industries. For many firms it was vital to have several highly specialized auxiliary firms close at hand, providing them with components, carrying out a single operation in the productive process, or looking after servicing or retooling. . . . It appeared that for many industries the vital consideration was closeness to their auxiliaries rather than closeness to markets or basic supplies. For their part, some auxiliaries might need to have several large firms to serve before they could operate on an economical scale. . . . It appears that the common classification of industries into supply-orientated (sic), market-

oriented, and footloose . . . is inadequate, unless supply-orientation is taken to cover the much more specific requirement of closeness to auxiliary industries.

The industrial development of the Italian south has progressed modestly in recent years, but would not have had even this moderate success if it had not been for the industrial projects established in the region by the large government-owned business enterprise, the Institute for Industrial Reconstruction, whose decisions were heavily influenced by considerations other than market ones (see S. Holland, ed., 1972).

And so industrial enterprises as well as some types of service enterprises tend to cluster, up to the point where congestion, the main external diseconomy of clustering, other than pollution, outweighs the advantages of closeness.

The tendency is not all-encompassing. For types of production in which economies of scale are small or end at a small size, location near rural markets or near sources of supply may be economic. Keith Griffen (1973) reports that textiles production, food processing, and the production of construction materials appear in all parts of Taiwan, and that in the northern and central areas over 60% of rural income is from nonfarm sources. In China, also, there is much dispersion of some industry to rural areas.[2] In China this was done predominantly by decree, to lessen urban congestion, and in Taiwan there are apparently considerable direct and indirect subsidies to rural industry, so that it is not clear in either case whether the result is uneconomic or whether on the other hand it is the social optimum when diseconomies which urban producers impose on the community but for which they are not required to pay in other economies are taken into account. In Japan some small-scale rural industry still persists. Mainly, these small enterprises make components or materials for large-scale industry. Their continued existence is due largely to the lower incomes which none-too-mobile producers will accept, and, as the income differential between rural and urban Japan shrinks, the number of rural industrial enterprises is also rapidly shrinking. The income differential is also important in Taiwan and presumably in China, so that in these countries also the existence of all of the present types of rural industry is hardly an equilibrium situation.

Whatever may be optimum in some instances, the net advantage for much the larger share of manufacturing lies in clustering. As economic development proceeds, industrial concentration increases. At a late stage, some local decentralization occurs and, also, "megalopolises" emerge, in which for, say, 300 miles there is no countryside but only industrial urbanism of varying intensity. "Spread" has occurred from growth points until they merge.

---

[2] See C. Howe (1971) and J. Sigurdson (1974).

Perroux, the author of the term *poles de croissance* (1955), saw nothing ominous in this tendency.[3] On the contrary, he recommended locational concentration to take advantage of the natural forces (mainly technological external economies). Myrdal (1957b) saw a danger in this tendency. He complemented or extended the concept of growth points with his thesis of "spread" and "backwash" effects. Growth, he said, tends to spread from the growth point, but a contrary effect may more than counteract this one. The growing center is attractive to firms by reason of the external economies that it presents, but not only to firms. It is also attractive to individuals as consumers. As a result, it will attract the most talented and alert individuals and leave outer areas denuded of capital and talent. This "backwash" may not merely retard the development of other regions but actually lower their economic level below what it would have been if the growth center had never emerged. Myrdal advocated policy measures to prevent this adverse effect. The importance of the effect and the necessity for the policy measures are matters of controversy.

There is a phenomenon in agricultural growth that may be termed a variety of growth point effect. Tang (1958) and Nicholls (1961) portray the growth point and spread effects in rural development in the southern Piedmont during the past century. The greater efficiency of agriculture near industrial centers is striking. More recently (in Saunders, 1971) Nicholls has documented the close correlation between industrial growth and agricultural modernization in the Brazilian state of São Paulo.

SECTOR ANALYSIS: DUALISTIC MODELS

It was noted in Chapter 4 that as income rises in an economy the structure of production continually changes for several reasons. As this process goes on, there are transfers of labor, of products, of income, and perhaps of saving among the sectors of the economy, and also triangular trade among the primary and secondary sectors and abroad. An important aspect of the theory of the growth process is the analysis of those transfers and exchanges.

In even the simplest analysis of growth, the economy is disaggregated into the consumer goods and capital goods sectors or, on the income side, into consumption and saving. This may be termed vertical disaggregation. Sectoral analysis disaggregates it horizontally. The disaggregation may consider, say, five sectors: the primary, secondary, and tertiary private sectors, government, and the "rest of the world," but in a more simplified and manageable analysis the theorist is content with two

---

[3] The concept is also developed by Hirschman (1958), Chap. 10. Hicks (1959), especially pp. 163–66, discusses the causes of interregional inequality during the process of growth.

sectors. These are thought of as the modern and traditional sectors, which are conceived of as the "leading sector" or innovational sector and the rest of the economy, or the capital-intensive and labor-intensive sectors, or, suggestively, merely manufacturing and agriculture. Or, in an open economy, the sectors considered may be agriculture, manufacturing, and the rest of the world.

The first two-sector or dualistic analysis was on social rather than economic grounds. The Dutch economist Boeke concluded that Indonesians do not respond to economic incentives, and deduced that the cause was an immutable Oriental personality, to be contrasted with economically rational Western personality. Boeke presented the thesis in a book published in two volumes (in 1942 and 1946).[4] His view had lost credit with other social scientists even before it was conspicuously contradicted by the rapid economic advance of a string of areas from Japan to Singapore; it need not be discussed further here. Hou (1965, chap. 7) portrays a dualism that is both economic and social in China during the century ending in the 1930s, and many writers (for example, Broadbridge, 1966) have contrasted two economic sectors in Japan. Dualism here refers to a marked difference in methods in two sectors: traditional versus modern, labor-intensive versus capital-intensive, little productive versus highly productive. Dualism as it is now emphasized in development theory has nothing directly to do with these socioeconomic observations of countries where the contrast is assumed to be especially sharp, but rather is merely analysis which treats of separate "horizontal" sectors. It provides useful insights into the growth process.

Causes and effects of expansion of industry relative to agriculture as income rises were discussed in Chapter 4. Technical progress in trade, industry, agriculture, and infrastructure was discussed in Chapters 5 and 6, and it was noted that technical progress and capital formation in each depends in part on technical progress and capital formation in all. These are sectoral analyses, though that in Chapters 5 and 6 was more largely sectoral engineering than sectoral economics. Sectoral economic analysis will be important in many of the remaining chapters of this book. Here it will be sufficient to present an overview of some of the sorts of transfers and exchanges the dualistic analysis will deal with.

The Structure of Consumption

Some early discussions made heavy going of the process by which industrial production emerges as productivity and income rise. They conjured up the need to assume zero marginal productivity in agriculture, so that some workers could shift to industry without reducing agricultural production. The need is a myth.

---

[4] Now available in a later edition, 1953.

It has been frequently stated that there must be an agricultural surplus if industry is to develop. The statement has been made with an air of greater profundity than it merits. The content is merely that so long as all of an economy's workers engaged in agriculture are producing no more than enough to feed and clothe themselves, no industry will emerge. The economy cannot afford it. This was noted in Chapter 4. Above the subsistence level of income, agriculture depends on industry for a market and for a supply of goods as truly as industry depends on agriculture. The relationship is symmetrical. Agriculture has no special importance.

Resources for Industrial Investment

A shift of workers from agriculture to industry does not result in any flow of saving; it merely alters the composition of production to match the changing composition of consumer demand. But if the industrial production requires capital equipment, someone must refrain from consumption in order that productive resources can be diverted from the production of consumer goods to the production of that equipment. The problem of saving must be dealt with.

One model, by John Fei and Gustav Ranis (1964), assumes that the saving, like inputs for industrial production, must come from agriculture, and somewhat ponderously sketches a model in which the migration of inputs and the transfer of savings occur together. W. Arthur Lewis' 1964 model, discussed briefly in the preceding chapter, assumes that capitalist entrepreneurs provide the saving by plowing back profits from their expanding ventures. Lewis' model is discussed in Chapter 9 and the Fei-Ranis model in Chapter 13.

LEADING SECTORS AS FOUNTS

The "Leading Sector" Concept

Both Hirschman and Scitovsky, in their essays cited in this chapter, state that a rapidly growing industry may become a "leading sector," creating demand for supplies from other industries that will stimulate innovation in those industries. More generally, a leading sector is any sector of industry that expands first or is expanding most rapidly at any given time and is thus "leading the way" into growth or to further growth. Hirschman had coined the term "linkages" to refer to the relationship between a leading sector and other industries, and had used the concept in presenting his thesis of unbalanced growth. The conceptions of a leading sector and linkages are prominent in Rostow's 1964 elaboration (or revision) of part of his thesis about stages of growth.

The argument is a little tricky. First, in some writing it seems to be argued that any linkage increases the amount of increase in demand; instead of getting an increase in one industry, the economy gets it in two or more. Where the linkage is to a capital goods industry, to construct productive capacity, there is of course an accelerator effect and an added increase in demand (though not necessarily in innovation), but where the linked industry merely supplied components, the argument is incorrect. The increase in the demand for the final product is the total increase in demand; whether the product is produced wholly in one industry or in two or more is immaterial. The concept of linkages (merely an offshoot of input-output analysis) is a useful tool in analyzing the structure of production (that is, the composition of output) in an economy, but apart from this it does not deserve much place in the analysis of growth.

A qualification to this statement seems to be necessary insofar as the linkages are "forward" ones, providing new materials to customer industries, rather than "backward" ones, providing demand to supplying industries. The provision of a new product that becomes a new material in a customer industry may make possible an increase in productivity in that industry.

Productivity Increase through Input Shifts

Yet it may be suspected that the users of the concept of leading sectors have correctly sensed the importance in increases in productivity of sectors leading technical advance, but have misidentified the nature of the contribution. By way of a bridge to what I believe to be the correct analysis, consider another and logically quite unrelated process, that of gain in average productivity apart from increase in productivity in any sector.

If inputs shift from a sector in which the average productivity of inputs is low to one in which it is high, the value of output in the economy will rise, and a time series for GDP will show an increase in productivity in the economy, even though techniques and productivity remain unchanged in each sector.

This effect causes a significant share of the increase in output per worker in some countries at some times shown by GDP statistics. Denison (1967) has made estimates of the sources of growth of national income per person employed in the United States and Western Europe during the period 1950–62. He estimates that of the average annual increased output per unit of input in the United States during this 12-year period, 0.25% was due to improved allocation of resources, compared with 0.75% due to advances of knowledge and 0.30% due to economies of scale. In Germany, he estimates that 0.76% was due to improved allocation of resources, compared with 0.75% due to advances of knowledge and 0.62% to economies of scale.[5] It has been estimated that of Japan's very rapid rate of increase in output per unit of input during the postwar period, as much as 2% per year may have been due to the shift of labor and accompanying capital from agriculture and petty industry and services to larger scale industry.

This result would not be achieved if technical advance were not occurring in the sector to which inputs "migrate," for the migration would not occur if the income differential between sectors was not widening. And so the sector whose advance is drawing inputs from other sectors may appropriately be termed a leading sector, though not in the sense in which that term has been used in the literature.

Leading Sector as Fount

There is still another way in which one sector may "lead," and this process may be the one which analysts groping for an explanation of their sense of the importance of surging sectors may have confused with transmission of technical advance through input-output relationships. In quite a different way a sector in which productivity is increasing more rapidly than elsewhere in the economy may pump its increasing income throughout the economy.

The process is best illustrated in the extreme case in which rapid rise in productivity, creating an "unlimited" supply of foreign exchange, is occurring in one sector of the economy and no rise at all is occurring in other sectors. I shall first picture such a limiting case and then draw conclusions that apply in less extreme circumstances.

The limiting case may be termed an "oil economy." I shall define an "oil economy" by stating a set of hypothetical empirical conditions from which by only moderate simplifications we may derive a model. The statement is made with no specific country in mind. The reader may, if he wishes, think of Saudi Arabia, Kuwait, Abu Dhabi, or Dubai as illustrating the model.[6]

Workers constituting between 0.1% and 1% of the labor force extract and refine petroleum. The annual gross product is $400,000 per man. One tenth of the value of petroleum production goes abroad as profit and return to capital to the foreign oil companies that hold the petroleum concession. One or 2% of the remainder consists of costs (other than profit and return to capital), and the balance—about 90% of the gross

---

[5] His estimates are discussed in Chapter 10.

[6] This model is drawn with little modification from E. E. Hagen, in J. N. Bhagwati and R. S. Eckaus, eds. (1972). The original was written before the 1973 rise in the price of oil. The hypothetical income shares have been adjusted to current price relationships.

value of petroleum output—becomes (foreign exchange) revenues to the government. Other governmental revenues and other foreign exchange earnings are small. The country levies no customs duties. No immigration is permitted.

The country as a whole has a population of between 50,000 and 10 million. It is a desert country. The nonpetroleum productive sectors are agriculture and a fabricating and service sector which I shall refer to as "sector three." Sector three is divided into government and private sub-sectors. Between 60 and 80% of the labor force is engaged in agriculture. There is little cereal or textile production; agriculture consists almost wholly of nomadic goat and camel herding. The goats and camels provide food and materials for clothing and shelter. Goats are also sold for meat and the proceeds used to buy commodities from sector three; few other agricultural products are marketed.

The government subsector purchases the construction of economic infrastructure, educational and medical facilities, other public buildings, and most urban housing; produces education, medical care, and general governmental administration; and trains workers for these activities. The government makes no transfer payments. There is little private capital formation in sector three.

The Model. We simplify the hypothetical empirical conditions in certain respects. Assume a petroleum sector small in manpower but large in value-added, as in the hypothetical empirical case. There is no value production in agriculture (the agricultural population subsisting on zero income), no private capital formation in sector three, no government revenue and no foreign exchange earnings except from oil. There is full employment throughout the economy, at low-value productivity except in the petroleum sector.[7] Population and the labor force are constant in size. As the model progresses physical productivity per worker in each non-petroleum sector remains constant, but petroleum output can be increased without increase in employment. There exists a monetary authority in which the treasury deposits the foreign exchange revenues accruing to it. The monetary authority disburses them to pay for foreign purchases by the government, and issues local currency which it sells to the treasury in exchange for foreign exchange. With this local currency the government finances its domestic expenditures. The monetary authority then has the foreign exchange available to sell to private importers or for private transfers abroad. There is no other currency issue or credit creation. (We ignore the fact that the petroleum concessionaire sells foreign exchange to the monetary authority to obtain local currency with which to pay its local salaries and other domestic expenses. We could, if we

---

[7] Dudley Seers, "The Mechanism of an Open Economy," *Social and Economic Studies,* vol. 13 (1964), pp. 233–42, presents a model in which petroleum revenues determine the level of employment.

wished, make assumptions concerning expenditures out of this income identical to those we make concerning the expenditure of government revenue, and lump the two together in operating the model.)

There is no other government revenue. There is no food or textile production in agriculture; all food and textiles consumed in the nonagricultural sectors are imported. The marginal consumer propensity to import is 0.4, and the marginal consumer propensity to save is 0.1. There is no saving but consumer saving; government expenditures equal its revenues. World prices of petroleum are constant, as are the prices of imports.

Let us designate output in the petroleum sector, less that share which flows abroad as return on capital plus profit, as "national" value-added in that sector, and use the following symbols:

Subscript T refers to the non-petroleum sector.
P = output in the petroleum sector.
P_d = national value-added in that sector.
G = government expenditures, and G_d domestic government expenditures.
Y = aggregate money income and Y^* aggregate real income, in the economy as a whole without subscripts and within sectors with appropriate subscripts.
y = per capita money income and y^* per capita real income.
C = consumer expenditures, C_d consumer expenditures within the country, and C_M consumer imports.
S = saving.
K = the Keynesian multiplier.

We assume that an increase in petroleum production is accomplished with no additional domestic cost, so that the entire increase in national value added in the petroleum sector accrues to government. (We could, if we wished, assume increases in wage and salary rates in the petroleum sector, and incorporate them in the model without complicating it by the procedure referred to in the preceding parentheses.)

We begin the operation of the model by assuming an increase in petroleum production to a new higher level and thereby in the level of government expenditures both within the country and abroad. An increase in Y_T results. The Keynesian multiplier applies:

(1) $$\Delta Y_T = K\Delta G_d.$$

The leakages are saving and importing, and with the propensities to import and to save given above,

(1a) $$\Delta Y_T = 2\Delta G_d.$$

There is no foreign exchange constraint, regardless of the share spent domestically. For by familiar Keynesian analysis, money income will rise only to the level at which the leakages equal the exogenous flow of expenditure, in this case increases in G_d financed by the sale of foreign exchange by the treasury to the monetary authority, which in turn equal the foreign exchange revenues accruing to the treasury. If all of the increase in saving is invested abroad, the incremental quantities of foreign exchange supplied and demanded will be equal. If part of saving is held domestically (hoarded), the monetary authority will accumulate foreign exchange.

Let us assume for the moment that there is no migration from agriculture to sector three, so that the entire increase in income in sector three consists of an increase in *per capita* money income. In a closed economy at full employment, the entire increase in money income would be inflationary; the aggregate increase in money income would be equaled by an increase in money costs. However, in an "oil economy," real income will increase by a large fraction of the increase in money income, for a large fraction of the increase in expenditure out of the increased incomes in sector T (all of which are consumer expenditures) is for imports, the price of which is not affected by the increase in money incomes. These costs do not increase. The increase in exports that pays for them was costless. Therefore, even if *per capita* money incomes increase without increase in productivity, only a part of the increase in incomes causes an increase in costs.

$$(2) \qquad\qquad \Delta Y_T^* = (\Delta C_M / \Delta C)\, \Delta Y_T.$$

Since there is no population increase, equation (2) also holds for *per capita* income. Expenditures of the income of the high-productivity sector has pumped an increase in real income out throughout the economy.

This result, however, may be regarded as occurring in the third phase of increase in income in sector T rather than in the first. To introduce the first phase, assume that before the increase in government domestic expenditures the differential in real income *per capita* between agriculture and sector three was the maximum under which there would be no migration, and that over a considerable range the elasticity of intersector migration with respect to the real income differential is infinite.

The increase in G_d would then instantaneously induce a flow of migration such that neither *per capita* money incomes nor the price level in sector three would rise, the entire increase in Y_3 flowing to an increased labor force in sector three. The money and real increases in aggregate income in the sector and in the economy as a whole would then be identical.

If the elasticity of intersector migration with respect to the real income differential is infinite but with a time lag, and an increased differential induced only a low rate of intersector migration per time period, then the labor force, *per capita* money income, and *per capita* real income in sector three would all rise temporarily, money income more than real income, but the continuing inflow of labor would gradually reduce *per capita* money incomes (hence costs) and *per capita* real incomes to their initial level.

Without population increase, the agricultural labor pool would gradually dry up. Assume that after a certain flow of migration, further increments of migration would occur only at successively greater real income differentials. Term this transitional period "phase two." After some total amount of migration, migration would cease, thus ushering in phase three. During phase two, the relationship between the rise in *per capita* money income and that in *per capita* real income in sector three is that shown in equation (2) for aggregate income, but the Keynesian effect is divided between increasing *per capita* money (and thereby real) income, and expanding the size of the sector three labor force. When that expansion ceases, assuming that ΔG_d is sufficient to carry the economy to this point, the process will enter phase three, in which the entire impact of income expansion is on *per capita* incomes. During phase two as well as phase three, some degree of inflation accompanies any increase in aggregate (and *per capita*) real income.

The Three Laws. Whether the proportionate rate of rise in per capita real income in the nonpetroleum sector is greater than that in national value-added in the petroleum sector depends on the share of domestic to total incremental government expenditures, the magnitude of the multiplier, and the relative size of the two sectors. If there is no population change and no migration between the petroleum and nonpetroleum sectors, $\Delta Y_T/Y_T$ and $\Delta y_T/y_T$ are equal, and we can treat them interchangeably.

$$(3) \qquad \Delta Y_T = K\Delta G_d > \Delta P_d \text{ if } \frac{1}{K} < \Delta G_d/\Delta G$$

But $\qquad 1/K = (\Delta C_M + \Delta S)/\Delta Y_T.$
Therefore

$$(3a) \qquad \Delta Y_T > \Delta P_d \text{ if } (\Delta C_M + \Delta S)/\Delta Y_T < \Delta G_d/\Delta G.$$

That is, if ΔY_T is to be greater than ΔP_d ($= \Delta G$), the multiplier effect must more than offset the fact that part of their increment in government revenue is spent abroad.

$\Delta Y_T > \Delta P_d$ if, for example, $\Delta C_M/\Delta Y_T = 0.4$, $S/\Delta Y_T = 0.1$, and

$$\Delta G_d/\Delta G > 0.5.$$

These inequalities refer to absolute increases in money income in the nonpetroleum and petroleum sectors. The relative magnitude of $\Delta Y_T/Y_T$ and $\Delta P_d/P_d$ depends, in addition to the ratios above, on Y_T/P_d. If the two sectors are equal, then equation (3a) states the conditions for $\Delta Y_T/Y_T > \Delta P_d/P_d$. Any decrease in the ratio Y_T/P_d of course increases the ratio of $(\Delta Y_T/Y_T)/(\Delta P_d/P_d)$, *ceteris paribus*.

The sector in which money income (or national value-added) is increasing at the faster proportionate rate is of course growing in size relative to the other, thus reducing the inequality in the proportionate rates of growth. Hence we arrive at the law: *In a country with an important petroleum sector and no technical progress in the nonpetroleum sector, the relative rates of growth of aggregate money income in the latter sector and of national value-added in the petroleum sector will tend toward equality. If the relative population (labor force) of the two sectors remains constant, the statement also applies to* per capita *money income and national value-added.*

The absolute difference between $\Delta Y_T^*/Y_T^*$ and $\Delta Y_T/Y_T$ is of course smaller, the less the degree to which the multiplier effect bids up the price level in sector three and the greater the degree to which, conversely, it expands the work force by means of migration from agriculture. Hence a second law of petroleum economies: *The relative rates of growth in aggregate real income in the nonpetroleum sector and of national value-added in the petroleum sector will tend the more strongly to approach equality the greater the elasticity of migration from agriculture to non-agriculture with respect to the income differential between them.*

The trends in sectoral and aggregate gross product in Saudi Arabia, shown in Table 8–1, during the 1960s illustrate both laws, though the migration into sector three was largely from abroad rather than from agriculture.

When a continuing rise in the demand for labor in sector three has exhausted the labor pool in agriculture, output in the nonpetroleum sector will cease to rise, but real income will continue to rise as money incomes rise. This rise will be accompanied by inflation. Hence law three: *In the absence of technical progress and labor shifts, real* per capita *income in the nonpetroleum sector of the economy can rise only during a process of inflation.* (This statement of course disregards transfer income.) Hence if real *per capita* income is continuing to rise secularly in the nonpetroleum sector of a petroleum economy without inflation and without intrasector migration, this is evidence that technical progress is occurring in that sector. This statement assumes that no unemployment exists.

All Economies as Oil Economies. This model of an "oil economy" portrays no more faithfully than do other models the details of the actual situations from which it is derived. In the desert petroleum-producing

TABLE 8-1

Estimates of the Gross National Product of Saudi Arabia by Industrial Origin, at Factor Cost, 1382|83–1388|89*

Sector	Millions of Saudi Riyals of Year 1386/87		Average Annual Growth Rates (percent)
	1382/83	1388/89	
Agriculture, forestry, fishing	879.2	923.9	0.8
Mining and quarrying:			
Crude petroleum and natural gas	3,843.1	6,972.1	10.4
Other mining and quarrying	17.5	39.3	14.4
Manufacturing:			
Petroleum refining	553.2	961.4	9.6
Other manufacturing	157.0	299.0	11.3
Construction	380.6	753.8	12.1
Electricity, gas, water and sanitary			
services	87.1	208.3	15.6
Transport, storage and communications ..	537.3	1,172.1	13.9
Wholesale and retail trade	559.0	1,151.7	12.8
Banking, insurance and real estate	47.3	95.7	12.5
Ownership of dwellings	413.4	577.9	5.7
Public administration and defence	778.9	1,099.4	5.9
Services:			
Education	213.3	391.9	10.7
Medical and health	91.9	129.0	5.8
Other services	191.5	307.6	8.2
Gross Domestic Product	8,750.3	15,083.1	9.5
Factor income payments abroad	2,154.8	3,331.3	7.5
Gross National Product	6,595.5	11,751.8	10.1

* A.D. 1963–1969.
Source: Saudi Arabian Monetary Agency, Annual Report, 1389–90 AH (1970).

countries, there is population increase, production in agriculture, private capital formation in the nonpetroleum sector, government revenue other than that from petroleum, technical progress (though typically at a very slow rate), etc. These divergences from reality do not lessen the usefulness of the model. It applies to countries other than the petroleum-producing desert countries. To suggest this wider applicability, let us summarize the essential qualities of an "oil economy."

In the first generalization, the economy and its setting consist of five parts: the Fount, the Farm, the Market, the Bank, and the Source of Supply. The Fount has extremely high productivity in the production of a commodity for the world market, and the Farm low productivity.

The agencies that capture the foreign exchange earned by the Fount exchange it for local currency at the Bank, and spend that in the Market. The process bids up money incomes of the persons in the Market and draws individuals into the Market from the Farm. All exchange their incomes for foreign currency at the Bank and import goods from the

Source of Supply, otherwise known as the Rest of the World. So long as the expenditures by the Fount rise, real income in the Market will rise without change in technology.

This is the oil economy. In the oil economies of the period since the Second World War, the Fount has been either petroleum production or the United States Government. In South Vietnam, expenditures from the Fount offset physical destruction in part, and in South Korea and Taiwan they initiated the process of growth carried on by the resourceful people of those countries.

The model is still too limited. In the second generalization, we need neither Farm, Bank, nor, very much, the Rest of the World. We need only the Fount and the Market. The Fount may also be the Source of Supply. If the prices of goods provided by the Source of Supply to the Market fall while money incomes are being bid up in the Market, then the entire country may experience economic growth and rising real income without inflation. The other sectors of the economy, which constitute the Market, are carried along by the rising productivity of the Fount, and prosper in the pleasant delusion that they too are increasingly productive.

In this version, the textile and steel industries were the Fount in 18th- and 19th-century England, wheat or cotton farms in 19th-century United States, Canada, and Australia, sheep or cattle ranches in New Zealand and Argentina, dairies in Denmark, hydroelectric power in Norway, metallurgical factories in Japan. The oil economy, after all, is only the limiting case of the diffusion of the fruits of technical progress among the various sectors of an economy.

More prosaically, the analysis suggests that in many countries a sector in which a prolonged surge of productivity took place provided both income to other sectors whose output per man was advancing less rapidly, and increasingly inexpensive goods on which to spend that income, or the exports with which to finance an increasing flow of imports. In this sense certain sectors led their countries' rise in income, and did so neither by the transmission of technical advance through supply connections nor merely by drawing inputs from less productive sectors, but rather by providing low-cost output and simultaneously pumping out the income with which to buy it. This, it is suggested, is the true version of "leading sectors." In this sense, manufacturing industries were leading sectors during some stage of growth in all but a few countries of the world. Insofar as technical progress (portrayed in a different model) spread to the other sectors of the economy, the rise in income was the faster and more prolonged.

If this model is empirically useful, long-term price series should show prices in the leading sector thus defined falling relative to prices in other sectors. The price data necessary to test the thesis are not readily available (and the same price behavior might be consistent with other models as well).

STAGES OF GROWTH SCHEMAS

Note should be taken in this chapter of several schemas of stages of growth, schemas that are more descriptive than analytical, but nevertheless useful.

The Historical School

During the 19th century, the German "historical school" (really, two or three schools of writers, in successive generations) evolved schemas of the stages of economic development. Friedrich List wrote of the pastoral, peasant, agricultural-manufacturing, and agricultural-manufacturing-commercial stages. Bruno Hildebrand referred to the stages of exchange: natural (that is, barter), money, and credit. Gustav Schmoller thought the evolution from village or manorial to town to territorial to national economies was significant. Karl Bücher and Werner Sombart introduced classifications with greater sociological content. Bücher contrasted closed household, town, and national socioeconomic systems, and Sombart described fairly richly concepts of precapitalist and early, high, and late capitalist systems.

Stages: Rostow's Schema

Rostow's later stage schema is a distant relative rather than a lineal descendant of these.[8] In Rostow's schema, once the static stage of traditional life has been disturbed, the society passes through the later stages of establishment of the preconditions for growth, takeoff, drive to maturity, and high mass consumption. During the period of establishment of the preconditions, "the insights of modern science [begin] to be translated into new production functions" (Rostow, 1960, p. 6); the idea spreads that economic progress is possible, an effective centralized national state is built, education broadens, new types of entrepreneurs come forward, commerce widens, economic institutions change, etc.

The period of takeoff is "the interval when the old blocks and resistances to steady growth are finally overcome" (Rostow, 1960, p. 7). The changes sketched above proceed. During a period of "a decade or two" or "two or three decades" investment rises rapidly, the basic economic, political, and social structure of the society are transformed, and thereafter a steady rate of growth can be sustained.

During the drive to maturity, a period of about 60 years after the beginning of takeoff, the nation acquires mastery of the most advanced

---

[8] The first presentation of the schema is in Rostow (1956). The most comprehensive presentations are in his 1960 volume and in his essay in Rostow (1964).

existing technology, and can produce anything it chooses, at least in its chosen area of specialization. Thereafter, in the age of high mass consumption, the economy's leading sectors shift toward durable consumer goods, and a large share of the population acquires a high level of living.

Rostow has been sharply and correctly criticized for two aspects of his presentation:

1. The limited content or tautological nature of most of his distinctions between his stages. As one reads his essays quickly, the stages seem to be given distinctly different characteristics, but as one searches more carefully for distinguishing marks, most of them vanish. Thus "basic economic, social and political transformation" turns out to be indistinguishable from earlier or later economic, social, and political transformation. The "drive to maturity" turns out to have the same characteristics as the earlier process of growth. High mass consumption turns out to exist at any time, relative to earlier times. The use of consumer durables, now that they have been invented, occurs earlier in real life than does the "drive to maturity" that is supposed to bring it about. And so on. Except for the one specifically stated criterion of the change in the rate of investment during the period of takeoff, no one scrutinizing a society with Rostow's book in hand would know what to look for to distinguish the stages.

2. The invalidity of this one quantifiable criterion. The supposed upward surge in the rate of investment (and presumably also the rate of growth) during a crucial period of takeoff turns out to exist only in a few countries. The facts elsewhere contradict the schema.

Rostow may have based his concept of such a period on the history of the country with whose growth he is most familiar, England. A surge of industrialization did occur there, beginning early in the 1780s. Similar surges occurred in the Soviet Union and in Japan. But in these countries they occurred because political revolution burst the bonds that had previously been hampering growth. These are special cases. As data for other countries have been accumulated, it has become clear that in economic development there is usually no such phenomenon as a takeoff. Gross and net capital formation rose fairly steadily in most Western European countries from about 1850—the date when data begin—until the first World War. To divide the rise into periods would be entirely artificial.[9]

Hence the schema of stages must be rejected. But Rostow's essays present rich and perceptive suggestions of the changes that must occur if a country that was traditional is to become technically progressive.

At the end of Chapter 7, the possible influences of climate on the

---

[9] See Kuznets (*Q.A.E.G.N.*, 7), app. tables.

beginning of growth were discussed. That discussion is also pertinent to the rates of continuing growth.

BIBLIOGRAPHICAL NOTE

The following books, among others, give useful summaries of development and growth theories, but without clear distinction between the two: I. Adelman (1962), B. Hoselitz (1960), G. M. Meier and R. E. Baldwin (1957). H. J. Bruton (1965), presents a lucid discussion of what may be termed the "conventional wisdom" of theories of the development of the low-income countries, but without any empirical materials. As indicated in the text, A. O. Hirschman (1958), dissents from most of the conventional wisdom, and specifically from the concepts of the vicious circles as barriers and the "big push" or balanced growth as a feasible strategy. P.A. Baran (1957), gives a Marxist view. I. Adelman and E. Thorbecke, eds. (1966) presents a number of growth models.

A somewhat ponderous presentation of dualistic theory in relation to saving and capital formation is Fei and Ranis (1964). Jorgenson's two articles (1961) and (1969) are indispensable for the theorist interested in dualism. Paauw and Fei (1973) relate theory to Southeast Asian experience in an illuminating way.

The Rostow schema of stages is presented in his *Stages of Economic Growth* (1960), and his concept of the role of leading sectors in his essay in L. H. Dupriez, ed. (1955). Both are criticized and defended in W. W. Rostow, ed. (1964).

Theories of noneconomic determinants of economic development are provided by the books by Huntington and Lee, mentioned in the text, plus the following: B. Hoselitz (1960); the essays by Landes and Sawyer in E. M. Earle, ed. (1951); A. Gerschenkron's essay in *Explorations in Entrepreneurial History* (1953); and the ensuing exchanges between Landes, Sawyer, and Gerschenkron in the May, 1954 issue of that journal. The analysis by I. Adelman and C. T. Morris of the association between sociological factors and economic growth, in the article discussed in the text, is presented in expanded form in a book by the same authors (1967). Concerning theories of entrepreneurship, see Chapter 11.

9

Economic Growth, Unemployment, and Income Distribution

To complete an introductory overview of the growth process, we must survey what is known about the effect of growth upon the distribution of income. To introduce this discussion, it will be useful to define two conceptual tools, because of their frequent use, even though having introduced them we shall pretty much discard them.

THE LORENZ CURVE AND THE GINI RATIO

Inequality of income distribution is often portrayed on a "Lorenz curve," as in Figure 9–1. If the distribution of income were entirely equal, it would be represented graphically by the 45° line. Along that line, each 1% of the population receives 1% of national income. In fact, however, the curve of income distribution in any country (say curve A) sags below the 45° line. The lowest income 10% of the population receive less than 10% of the income, the next 10% almost certainly also receive less than 10%, and so on up to some point at which, graphically, the curve A has a slope of just 45°, after which point higher income deciles each receive more than 10%.

The Italian mathematician Gini proposed an algebraic measure of the degree of inequality: the ratio of the area between the line of equality and the income distribution curve to the entire area below the line of equality. In the case of perfect equality, the Gini ratio is zero. If one person, represented at the extreme right of the box, received all of the income, the Lorenz curve would follow the perimeter of the box, and the

FIGURE 9–1
Two Lorenz Curves Yielding the Same Gini Ratio

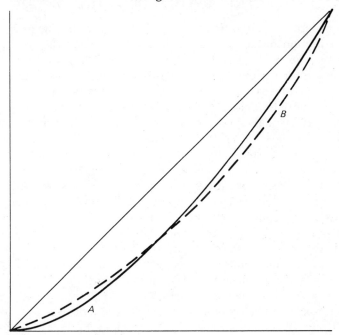

ratio would be unity. If one Lorenz curve lies entirely below another, the Gini ratio will necessarily be higher for the lower curve. However, two curves may cross. The Gini ratio may be identical for the two, or may show greater inequality for one, while other measures show greater inequality for the other.

Thus the measurement of income inequality may be ambiguous. In Figure 9–1, the income share of the lowest income 40% of the population is less on curve A than on curve B, but the share of, say, the lowest income 70% is less on curve B and there is greater income concentration at the top. It is impossible to state indisputably on which curve inequality is greater. The question is not merely academic. If, for example, 5% of the labor force, which was unemployed, gains unemployment during a cyclical upswing, an increase in profits may benefit the top income groups at the same time and a crossing of curves such as from A to B may occur.

Because of such ambiguities, in the quantitative discussion in this chapter reference will usually be made to change in the income share of given segments of the array of income receivers, rather than to the Gini ratio or to inequality in general terms.

INCOME DISTRIBUTION BEFORE GROWTH

From general considerations one would expect the inequality of income distribution to have varied considerably among the world's lower income countries before the economic growth of the 20th century began.

One reason for variation in income distribution relates to land ownership. In a nonindustrial economy in which cultivation of the soil is by small-farm proprietors each owning his land, the distribution of income will be relatively equal. No one should suppose that the Lorenz curve will approach congruence with the 45° line. There will still be a capital city, if not a trading or industrial city, and there will be towns serving regional needs. There will be high-income governmental and professional leaders, whose high incomes contribute considerably to income inequality. If there is a class of "big traders," they too will have high incomes, perhaps the highest in the country. Urban incomes will average not less than two or three times rural ones. And even among farmer-owned family-size farms, there will be differences in size, efficiency, and income. Yet, relatively, income inequality as well as the income level will be low.

There are few such societies today. Irma Adelman and Cynthia Morris (1973), in a study of income distribution and growth in 43 countries, single out six countries whose economies are more or less like this: Burma, Chad, Dahomey, Ecuador, Niger, and Surinam.[1] Using as a yardstick of income inequality the share in income of the lowest income 60% of the population, after grouping the countries by common characteristics the authors note that among the 4 groups into which the 43 countries divided, the one with the least inequality was this group of 6. In each of the six, farming is predominantly on small subsistence farms and there is only a limited industrial sector, in which almost all factories are small. It may be assumed that only a few individuals in these countries have very high incomes. There has been little development and little concentration of land ownership to yield high incomes, and so there is relatively equal income distribution.[2] The average share in total national

---

[1] The three African countries included are in the United Nations list of the 25 "least developed." The other three are not.

[2] Adelman and Morris note another characteristic of this sub-group of six countries: manufactured goods comprise less than 10% of total exports in each, and the four commodities that rank highest among exports in each country comprise more than 75% of exports. In Surinam the dominant export is bauxite; in each of the other countries it is one, two or three tropical agricultural products. The significance of the concentration of exports for income distribution may be discounted. Within another subgroup of 24 countries, whose average income inequality equaled that in the entire group, the more exports are diversified, the higher is the income share of the lowest income 60%. The cause of export concentration in the subgroup of six no doubt is that the climate or natural resources of each happens to favor a single commodity or a very few commodities.

income of the lowest income 60% in the entire group of 43 countries was 26%; the share in the subgroup of 6 was 34%. (The highest percentage in any of the 43 countries was 38% in Israel.)

Contrasting with these countries are the more numerous ones in which before modern growth began there existed a class of individuals holding large tracts of land which they operated as estates or rented to peasant tenants. Where this was true, the large landowners historically were descendants of aliens, as on the large estates of Latin America. In India, which was not an integrated nation until the last half of the 19th century, large landlords are in many cases the descendants of conquerors from other regions of the country. There also were and are large landowners in some countries of the Middle East where the population seems to have been relatively homogeneous ethnically and religiously. Tribal land may gradually have become the personal possession of descendants of tribal chieftains. Income was surely more unequally distributed in these economies than in those in which this concentration of wealth did not exist.

Historically, the less egalitarian social and economic structure often emerged from a more egalitarian earlier state, but landlordism and large estates have persisted over such long periods of time (three centuries in parts of Latin America, longer in India, several millennia in Egypt) that their presence should be regarded as a traditional state rather than as a first step in a growth process.

Another relevant classification of traditional economies is into those with and those without surplus labor. Here and hereafter I shall use that term—"surplus labor"—to refer to a portion of an agricultural labor force not necessarily with zero marginal productivity but with productivity which though positive is low relative to average labor productivity, or to labor in petty services whose productivity is low relative to that of equally capable labor in other occupations. Surely where a large pool of surplus labor thus defined is present, the distribution of income is highly unequal by any measure. The inequality differs in nature from that caused by landlordism or estate-ism. The latter tends to cause concentration of income at the top, whereas the presence of surplus labor tends to cause income to be especially low for, say, the bottom 40% of income receivers.

Societies with both landlordism or estate ownership and surplus labor would be expected to have the highest degree of income inequality. The two conditions may tend to go together. Not enough quantitative evidence is available to test this thesis. The distribution of income is also affected by the nature and richness of natural resources, the social and political structure inherited not only from colonial days but from the distant past, discrimination among ethnic or cultural groups, and many other factors, as well as by the degree of concentration of wealth ownership and the presence or absence of surplus labor.

At this point I shall digress to consider whether surplus labor defined as above really exists in more than negligible amounts.

The Concept of Surplus Labor

W. Arthur Lewis makes the existence of surplus labor of even lower productivity than that defined above the basis for a well-known theory of how development proceeds. He asserts as an empirical fact that in many less developed countries there exist large reservoirs of labor whose marginal productivity is "negligible, zero, or even negative" (1954, p. 141). This labor is found, he says, in agriculture, petty trades and services, domestic service in the houses of wealthy men who keep retainers because their position calls for doing so, and in other areas. That such labor exists, he states, is "obviously the relevant assumption for the economies of Egypt, of India, or of Jamaica," though not for some parts of Africa or Latin America.[3] Rosenstein-Rodan (1943) asserted the same fact earlier, in his analysis of problems of postwar development in Eastern and Southeastern Europe. Their judgment is shared by some other students of economic development, but they present no evidence.

Employment in primary industries in the LDCs is sometimes referred to as "residual." The concept is that persons who can find employment elsewhere do so; those who cannot must be content to remain in the primary industries. This concept is closely related to that of "disguised unemployment" in agriculture. This, in turn, is sometimes stated in the stark form that the marginal productivity of labor in agriculture and certain nonagricultural occupations is zero.

The concept of zero marginal productivity of labor needs definition. Strictly, it means that if a small amount of labor were withdrawn from production, the same volume of aggregate production could be obtained with the remaining labor with no change whatever in methods. However, a less rigorous definition is appropriate. This is that if a small amount of labor were withdrawn, the same output could be obtained with the remaining labor with only simple changes in management and the addition of only a small amount of simple capital equipment. As applied to peasant agriculture, the implication is that a peasant family has it within its administrative and financial capability to make the adaptations necessary to maintain the level of aggregate production.

Employers who behave as "economic men" would not hire workers unless their marginal productivity equaled the wages paid them. But a peasant family may continue to support an added family member even though his presence merely spreads among five men work that could be done by four, and a wealthy patron may support unneeded retainers

---

[3] The most widely accessible presentation of Lewis' view, and of the effects of an unlimited supply of labor on economic development, as he sees them, are found in his 1955 book, but his 1954 and 1958 articles present his views in more detail.

because of noneconomic considerations. And even though the marginal productivity of labor in agriculture is zero, "surplus" family members may remain on the peasant farm unless a wage markedly higher than their share of the family's income is offered in town.

Several empirical studies bring the existence of labor with zero marginal productivity into question. In a statistical study of prices and wages in Egyptian agriculture after World War II, B. Hansen (1966) demonstrated convincingly that the seasonal relationships between price and wage movements and the ways in which the two varied among different areas were consistent with the absence of surplus labor at peak seasons and very difficult or impossible to reconcile with the presence of surplus labor. In a nationwide study of Indian farm management, Paglin (1965) found that in each of five regions which he analyzed separately, output per acre declined as the size of the holding increased. This suggests that the application of additional labor per acre on the smaller plots increased production, hence that there was little or no surplus labor on plots of any size. Moreover, from 11% to 57% of the labor used, even on plots of 2.5 acres and less, was hired. The percentage increased with size of plot. The most plausible explanation is absence of surplus labor, though certain other theories of work and of employment practices could also be consistent with the data.

T. W. Schultz (1964, Chap. 4) analyzed effects in India of the severe influenza epidemic of 1918–19. He estimated that deaths from the epidemic caused an 8.3% fall in the agricultural labor force. The acreage planted in 10 provinces studied fell from 1916–17 to 1919–20, when weather was comparable, by 3.8%. From statistical relationships which suggest a marginal productivity of labor of 0.4, Schultz concludes that this fall in acreage was about the percentage decline which would be expected from a labor shortage of about 8.3%, and hence that there was no previous redundancy of labor whatever.

The demonstration is not conclusive, however. Apparently there was somewhat less rainfall in 1919–20 in some of the provinces, which might account for some small part of the acreage reduction. Calculations including data for three additional provinces yield an estimate of a higher marginal productivity of labor. This estimate suggests that a reduction in the labor supply of the amount estimated should have caused a greater fall in acreage (or, more precisely, in output) if there was no redundancy initially. And, perhaps most important, the deaths from the epidemic probably were not evenly distributed. If, for example, one half of families suffered a loss of two labor force members out of six, and the other one half suffered no loss, then the fall in acreage would be expected even if the previous labor supply on all holdings was moderately redundant.[4]

---

[4] See Sen (1967a, 1967b) and Schultz (1967b).

There is no direct empirical evidence showing the existence of surplus labor.[5] However, certain general considerations suggest the likelihood that the marginal productivity of labor will approach zero in a technically static economy, and historical developments provide fairly convincing evidence of the existence in some societies of some, and possibly a large amount of, agricultural labor with low marginal productivity.

The general considerations are as follows. In peasant societies, the family rather than the individual is the economic as well as the social unit. That as a boy approached manhood he should strike out on his own if there was little need for him at home has not been a part of the prevailing ethic. Indeed, until recent times there was no place for him to go.

Historically, the population density in all peasant societies apparently has increased slowly. The most densely settled ones are merely those in which peasant agriculture has existed the longest. In the old settled agricultural societies, notably China and India, the size of small holdings has been reduced progressively generation after generation by subdivision among heirs, until it is far below that which could be cultivated with one yoke of oxen.

Considering these facts, it seems most plausible to assume that family size has been determined by the average, not marginal, income of family members. That assumption necessarily leads to the conclusion that the marginal productivity of labor in a peasant family is below subsistence.[6]

Another historical development suggests the presence of surplus labor. This is the acreage devoted to production of agricultural staples in West Africa and Southeast Asia when European conquest, the advent of traders, and for Southeast Asia the opening of the Suez Canal opened world markets to cultivators in those areas. In the 25 years following the opening of the Suez Canal in 1869, Burma's rice exports rose to seven times the 1869 level, and Burma became the "rice basket of Asia." Between 1913 and 1953, Nigeria's oil and oilseed exports increased to seven times the initial level, even though her cocoa exports were also expanding rapidly, and during the same 40 years Ghana's cocoa exports increased to 13 times the initial level. Between 1918 and 1950 the area under cotton in Uganda increased about 11-fold and the area under subsistence crops about 7-fold.[7] These multiples are not large merely

---

[5] The literature is reviewed in Kao, Anschel, and Eicher (1964).

[6] An intermediate thesis, that family size was checked at the size at which the marginal productivity of the last member was equal to his subsistence, leaving the family average above subsistence, is more implausible than the first alternative. It is difficult to see on what principle this criterion would have been adopted.

[7] The data for Burma are from Furnivall (1948, app. 1). Hla Myint cites the other data, which he draws from various sources. He draws the conclusion presented here,

because the initial bases were tiny. Ghana became a major world cocoa exporter, and Burma the world's greatest rice exporter. Moreover, the increases were not attained by rapid technical advance, except possibly in Uganda. Rather, peasants simply flooded onto unused lands when the new market opened up. (Introduction of estate agriculture by European immigrants was important in Uganda.) The amount of land under cultivation and the volume of production increased at rates far in excess of any possible rate of population increase. It is true that peasants with marginal productivity no lower than average might have abandoned old lands in favor of new ones yielding higher income, but in that case one would expect historical accounts of depopulated areas, and there seem to be none.

If this analysis is correct, we have the rather curious situation of extremely low marginal productivity of labor even though land was not scarce. Moreover, the cases do not demonstrate low marginal productivity of labor and land combined for lack of capital. There is no evidence that capital equipment was regarded as in short supply. Rather, the situation seems to have been one of sharply declining marginal utility of the only crops they knew how to produce. Added quantities of the staple would have been of little value, since (I hypothesize) other cultivators also had all they wished to use for consumption plus all they could trade for staples or handicraft articles that they themselves did not produce. In addition, the cultivators must have had little contact with the outside world, and no conception of the possibility of producing new types of goods to widen their range of consumption. The situation was not one of low marginal utility of aggregate income. No doubt the peasants would have been glad to add to their capability of sponsoring and participating in village feasts and festivals and religious giving.[8] However, they had no way of converting their production capabilities, by either trade or production, into the types of goods and services that would have increased their real income. In short, the marginal productivity of their labor was very low indeed.[9] When trade offered an output for additional produce,

---

that the marginal productivity of labor must initially have been zero. See Hla Myint (1964, pp. 38–39 and 43).

[8] This was certainly true in Southeast Asia. I assume that similar desired types of added consumption existed in West Africa.

[9] This is not a bizarre or unique situation. Consider the case of a teacher in a secondary school in the United States who would like to augment his income by working for two months during the summer, but who is not equipped for, or lacks the initiative to find, seasonal work that is available. The marginal productivity of his labor is zero or negligible. If a program of summer teaching is established, he is promptly available for additional production. Something similar was true of the peasants of Southeast Asia and West Africa, with the difference that they were available the year around rather than only seasonally.

That in cases like those in Africa and Burma cited here, the rural workers had

thereby providing income to buy increased handicrafts or newly imported goods, or to pay for increased participation in village activities, the fact that large amounts of labor could be drawn from existing peasant plots without appreciable (perhaps without any) reduction of output there promptly became apparent.

There are few areas in the world today that could be opened up by peasant labor alone. The situation sketched is purely an historical one. But the existence of these rather spectacular cases of internal migration, suggesting the presence of large amounts of labor with low marginal productivity, should make us wary of dismissing too readily the assumption that it existed elsewhere.

If a family chose to have so many members that the marginal productivity of their labor measured in a modern economic sense was low, the addition of the "last" member must have served a satisfying function, and it is somewhat anomalous to apply the abstract concept of low marginal productivity to the situation. However, two facts of recent history and one theoretical consideration related to modern economic change argue strongly that surplus labor as I have defined it now exists in large quantities, whatever may have been true historically.

One of the facts is the postwar rapid population increase, which has resulted in rapid increases in the labor forces of most low-income countries beginning at about 1965. The major part of the population increase was in rural areas. That the economies of these countries were flexible and adaptive enough to absorb the labor force increase without a marked fall in its marginal productivity in agriculture is unbelievable. Relevant data are presented later in this chapter.

Related is the migration from farms to towns and cities that has occurred in virtually every low-income country since World War II. It is not reported that the movement from the countryside has reduced agricultural production. That fact strongly suggests that the family members who migrated were "surplus."

The theoretical consideration is that the process of growth, in its early stages, almost certainly created unemployment—of the sort that in industrial countries we term "technological unemployment." The great likelihood of this is argued later in this chapter.

For these reasons, the presence today of considerable numbers of "surplus" workers seems certain. I shall continue the discussion in this chapter as though it were an established fact.

---

previously been producing handicraft products and local services, rather than nothing, is suggested in an unpublished manuscript by S. Hymer and S. Resnick (1967). As they point out, it follows that rising agricultural income, making possible the purchase of industrial products, may increase rather than decrease the supply of agricultural products to the nonagricultural center. They suggest the "inferior goods" concept mentioned in the text below.

INCOME DISTRIBUTION DURING GROWTH

For the reasons mentioned above, one would expect rather wide differences in the degree of inequality of income distribution before growth begins. We are interested in knowing what changes occur as growth proceeds. A number of case studies show that an early effect of growth is to increase the inequality of income distribution. The income of workers remains constant, or perhaps decreases, while that of entrepreneurs and the professional classes rises. But for how long does that trend continue? What changes occur at later stages in growth?

Some of the causes of high or on the contrary low inequality before growth began will persist. For example, the degree of concentration of land ownership may continue to affect the distribution of income throughout the growth process unless land reform alters the concentration of ownership. The society's rules of inheritance will have important effects: primogeniture versus division of property among all sons or all sons and daughters. Population density relative to natural resources will have a continuing effect.

On the other hand, a number of factors may alter the distribution of income as growth proceeds: among others, the rate of growth of industrial output, that of agricultural output, the rate of population growth, the education provided by the society for its members, trade and migration between the two sectors, the inward- or outward-looking character of the nation's trade policies, and whether the country remains capitalistic or turns to socialism. An integrated theory of the effect of economic growth on income distribution does not yet exist, but it is possible to give at least some minimum quantification of the effects of some of these influences. Before that is presented, let us look at the resultant of all of these influences combined: the overall change in income distribution as growth proceeds.

Not enough historical series exist to give direct evidence. Estimates of income distribution in 66 countries at various income levels provide the best and only surrogate that exists.

The estimates were made in the Development Research Center of the International Bank for Reconstruction and Development. The data from which they were drawn, like all estimates of income distribution, are necessarily uncertain, and there are large conceptual differences in what was measured in different countries. Moreover, to convert estimates to a uniform basis, as has been done by the World Bank research workers, it was necessary to depend upon free-hand Lorenz curves drawn to whatever data was available, and then to read the share of the lowest income 40% and the highest income 20% from them—a precarious procedure. One must regard the measures of inequality presented as only very rough estimates.[10] But the differences in income distribution shown are so great that clearly they reflect real differences. To a person interested in this subject, the changes as income rises are rather spectacular.

The selection of countries was neither systematic for the purpose at hand nor random. These are simply all of the countries of the world for which estimates could be made. There is no apparent reason to suppose that bias exists on this account except that the lowest income, least developed countries are under-represented.

The relationship to per capita income of the income share of the lowest income 40% of the population of each country ranges widely. However, a systematic relationship appears if the countries are grouped by income level. I have classed the countries into six income groups by drawing dividing lines at $100, $200, $300, $500, and $1,000 of per capita income. The group with income of $100 or less is reasonably representative of countries in which a sustained growth process has not begun, even though India and Pakistan, in which such a process seemingly has begun, are included.

Table 9–1, which presents the tabulation, shows for each income level the income share of the lowest income 40%, that of the highest income 20%, and the ratio between the two. The income share of the highest income percent rises as one moves from the lowest income group of countries to the $100–$200 group and the $200–$300 group, remains higher, even though falling, in the next two income groups, and only in the group of countries with incomes above $1,000 is it lower than in the countries in which growth has not begun. The income share of the lowest income 40% follows a course the inverse of this, reaching its lowest point

TABLE 9–1
Income Levels and Income Shares*

1	2	3	4	5
		Income Share (in percent) Of		
Income Level	*Number of Countries*	*Highest Income 20%*	*Lowest Income 40%*	*(3/4)*
$100 or less	8	46.1	16.4	2.8
$101–$200	5	57.9	13.4	4.3
$201–$300	13	67.9	11.1	6.1
$301–$500	8	57.6	11.6	5.0
$501–$1,000	15(12)	50.6(54.0)	15.3(13.5)	3.3(4.0)
Above $1,000 ...	17(15)	44.9(46.6)	16.1(14.8)	2.8(3.1)

* Data in parentheses exclude socialist countries. Col. 5 is computed from Table 9–2, not from the rounded figures of Table 9–1.
  Source: Table 9–2.

[10] See Chenery, Ahluwalia, Bell, Duloy, and Jolly (1974). The estimates are presented in Chap. 2, Montek Ahluwalia. Ahluwalia states: "The data are weak, but they are also the only data we have."

in the \$200–\$300 group of countries, and becoming approximately as high as at incomes below \$1,000 only in the group above \$1,000.

Statistic analyses by Adelman and Morris and by Chenery and his associates confirm the relationships indicated in Table 9–1, with some differences in the precise income levels at which trends reverse.[11]

It is regrettable that data for the distribution of income after the payment of income taxes were not available, for these data concerning pre-tax income give a distorted impression of income distribution in high-income countries relative to that in low-income countries. The highest income 20% of income receivers in high-income countries (except perhaps Italy) pay heavy income taxes. To a much greater degree, in low-income countries they do not. Data for the distribution of after-tax income would show the income share of the highest income 20% in high-income capitalist countries reduced by say one fourth or perhaps one third from the estimates shown in Table 9–1, while the shares of the low and middle income groups increased. (Indirect taxes also affect income distribution, but in the low-income countries as much as in high-income ones.) A similar adjustment, but a smaller one, would be appropriate for the income class between \$500 and \$1,000. The reversal in income shares would then be shown at lower per capita incomes, and the ratios in higher income countries would be more favorable relative to those in low-income countries.

The same adjustment would remove much of the difference between the indicated income inequality in socialist and capitalist countries, since the income distribution shown in Table 9–2 for socialist countries corresponds to the after-tax, not pre-tax, income distribution of capitalist countries. Yet a considerable difference would remain. It is probable that on a fully comparable basis[12] income inequality is less in socialist countries, for while the inequality of labor income seems as great in Communist countries as in others, the elimination of most private property income lessens inequality.[13]

Yet even if the indicated adjustments are made, the data show that the inequality of income distribution is greater at income levels from \$200 to \$500 than at incomes below \$100, is at least as great in the income group \$500–\$1,000, and that the distribution of incomes is markedly less unequal only in the group of countries with per capita incomes above

---

[11] In the analysis by Chenery and others, the share of the lowest income 40% turns upward at a per capita income of about \$800. I have read this per capita income level from Chenery, Ahluwalia, Bell, Duloy, and Jolly (1974), Fig. 1–2.

[12] An impossible criterion, since full conceptual equality is impossible because of the differences in economic structure.

[13] The share of the lowest income 40%, the highest income 20%, and the ratio between the two, for the three socialist countries in the \$500–\$1,000 income class and the two in the above \$1,000 class are, respectively: 22.9%/36.9%/1.6 and 25.8%/32.2%/1.25.

$1,000. This is a sobering fact, if the lower income countries may be expected to repeat the history of the higher income ones, for at a rate of increase of 2% per year it would take more than a century and one half for countries with per capita incomes of $75 to reach an income level of $1,000.

In presenting the pre-tax data, Ahluwalia divided the 66 countries into three groups on the basis of the degree of income inequality (measured by the income share going to the lowest income 40%), and classified the countries in each group by income level. Table 9–2 presents a similar matrix, but with five income levels rather than three.[14] The comparison among income classes in the high- and moderate-inequality country groups is somewhat similar to that for income groups undifferentiated by degree of inequality, but within the low-inequality group even pre-tax income inequality, as measured by either the share of the lowest income 40% or the high-low ratio, is less in every higher income group than in the group with per capita incomes below $100, and the income share of the highest income 20% is not higher in any higher income group than in the group below $100 (except for statistically insignificant increases of small fractions of 1%). The after-tax comparison, would of course be much more favorable to the second highest and especially the highest income group of countries.

What shall one make of these comparisons? Is there a type of country that is "high inequality" and another that is "low inequality" by nature, and will continue to be so at whatever level of income? Can one accept the cross-national comparisons as indicating the probable future secular trend within individual countries?

The answer to the first question may be a qualified Yes. A person acquainted with the economic institutions and social structure of some of the countries in the lower income groups of the high-inequality column of countries will recognize in them a structure that will tend to perpetuate high income inequality at whatever level of income, in the absence of social revolution.[15] One would see similar characteristics (tending toward high inequality) in only a few of the countries in the other two inequality groups. On the other hand, however, three of the high-income capitalist countries in the low-inequality column—Australia, Canada, and the United States—historically had large "empty" areas and no fixed social structure. These qualities probably tended toward low income

---

[14] To avoid cells with very small numbers of cases except at the $300–$500 income level, I have combined the two income classes with incomes of $200 or less shown in Table 9–1.

[15] With some diffidence, this statement may be made of the Philippines, Rhodesia, Senegal, Honduras, El Salvador, Malaysia, Brazil, Gabon, Costa Rica, Mexico, South Africa, and Panama, and perhaps with more knowledge of some of the remaining countries. History may of course falsify the implied forecast.

inequality. These two qualities in combination are not present in any lower income countries of today.

It follows that if no new forces intervene, income inequality in these present high-inequality low-income countries may never moderate to its level in the present high-income countries. But at least five new forces will be at work. First, many of the lower income countries have just undergone severe strain associated with the attainment of independence. That transition in their histories surely interferes with the simple projection of the future from the past, even though one may not know in what direction the change may be. Second, throughout the world today there are social expectations that were not present even 40 years ago; surely these will exert pressure upon the distribution of income. Third, as will be shown in Chapter 12, expenditures for education are greater today than previously in the early stages of growth. There is both presumptive logic and some empirical evidence, discussed later in this chapter, that increased education is associated with lessened income inequality. Fourth, the social pressure mentioned above may in a number of cases lead to social-political revolution, with results on income distribution that will depend on the nature of the revolution. Last, the future rate of growth in per capita income of a number of the present low-income countries may be faster than was typical in any but the very recent past. Sweden, with an average rate of growth over a prolonged period of not much more than 2% per year, thereby rose steadily in income rank to become one of the world's very highest income countries today. A rate equal to Sweden's average historical rate characterizes many of the lower income countries today (see Chapter 1, Table 1–8). It will be shown shortly below that relatively rapid growth is conducive to decrease in income inequality.

Yet the data have *some* implication for secular trends. To believe that the differences in income inequality between the lowest income countries and the countries in the next several higher tiers of income are mere accident—that the latter countries always had greater inequality than the present lowest income countries—would require remarkable faith in coincidence. It is more plausible that in the past at least the process of economic growth increased income inequality, then later decreased it. The countries with incomes above the lowest level reached their higher levels by a process of growth that, except for its lesser average speed, is not dissimilar in its economic aspects to the growth process now occurring. Hence one translation from the cross-national data to a secular forecast seems warranted. There is no justification in these data for the optimistic view that the early process of growth will in itself ameliorate the relative economic condition of the lowest income groups in low-income countries. The opposite presumption exists. These data reinforce the view arrived at by direct empirical observation that in many, though

TABLE 9–2
Degree of Inequality, Income Levels, and Income Shares

	High Inequality Share of Lowest 40% less than 12%			Moderate Inequality Share of Lowest 40% between 12% and 17%			Low Inequality Share of Lowest 40%, 17%*	
$0–$200	Lowest 40%	Top 20%		Lowest 40%	Top 20%		Lowest 40%	Top 20%
Kenya	10.0	68	Burma	16.5	44.8	Chad	18.0	43.0
Sierra Leone	9.6	68	Dahomey	15.5	50.0	Sri Lanka	17.0	46.0
Iraq	6.8	68	Tanzania	13.0	61.0	Niger	18.0	42.0
			India	16.0	52.0	Pakistan	17.5	45.0
			Madagascar	13.5	61.0	Uganda	17.1	47.1
						Thailand	17.0	45.5
Average	8.8	68		14.9	53.9		17.4	44.8
$200–$300								
Philippines	11.6	53.8	Zambia	14.5	57.0	Korea	18.0	45.0
Ivory Coast	10.8	57.1				Taiwan	20.4	40.1
Senegal	10.0	64.0						
Rhodesia	8.2	69.0						
Tunisia	11.4	33.6						
Honduras	6.5	65.0						
Ecuador	6.5	73.5						
Turkey	9.3	60.8						
El Salvador	11.2	52.4						
Average	9.5	61.1		14.5	57.0		19.2	42.5
$300–$500								
Malaysia	11.6	56.0	Dominican Republic	12.2	57.5	Surinam	21.7	42.6
Colombia	9.0	61.0	Iran	12.5	54.5	Greece	21.0	49.5
Brazil	10.0	61.5						
Peru	6.5	60.0						
Gabon	8.8	67.5						
Average	9.2	61.2		12.4	56.0		21.3	46.0

$500–$1,000

Country			Country			Country		
Jamaica	8.2	61.6	Guyana	14.0	45.7	Yugoslavia	18.5	41.5
Costa Rica	11.5	58.5	Lebanon	13.0	61.0	Bulgaria	26.8	33.2
Mexico	10.5	64.0	Uruguay	16.5	48.0	Spain	17.6	45.7
South Africa	6.2	58.0	Chile	13.0	56.8	Poland	23.4	36.0
Panama	9.4	59.4				Japan	20.7	40.0
Average	9.2	60.3	Average	14.1	52.9	Average	21.4 (19.1)	39.3 (42.8)

$1,000 and up

Country			Country			Country		
Venezuela	7.9	65.0	Argentina	16.5	47.4	United Kingdom	18.8	39.0
Finland	11.1	49.3	Puerto Rico	13.7	50.6	Hungary	24.0	33.5
France	9.5	53.7	Netherlands	13.6	48.5	Czechoslovakia	27.6	31.0
			Norway	16.6	40.5	Australia	20.0	38.8
			Germany, W.	15.4	52.9	Canada	20.0	40.2
			Denmark	13.6	47.6	United States	19.7	38.8
			New Zealand	15.5	42.0			
			Sweden	14.0	44.0			
Average	9.5	56.0	Average	14.4	46.7	Average	21.7 (19.6)	36.9 (39.2)

* Data in parentheses exclude socialist countries.
Source: Copyright World Bank, 1974.

probably not all, countries the first effect of growth on the distribution of income is to increase its inequality.

The data suggest that in the past the worsening trend in the distribution of income may have continued not for a decade or two but for one, two, three, perhaps even six generations. As indicated above, even if this translation from cross-national to secular deductions is correct for the past—it may not be—it would be hazardous to extend it to the future. But the implications present in the data indicate that it will be worthwhile to pay careful attention to the mechanisms that may be at work affecting income distribution.

THE CAUSES OF CHANGE IN INCOME INEQUALITY

The Rate of Growth, Unemployment, and Income Distribution

The growth effect of early innovation was discussed in Chapter 7. Disemployment and re-employment are of importance here, for they perhaps affect the income share of the lowest income 40% of a country's population more than any other force that impinges on it. As noted in Chapter 7, the direct effect of an innovation in production is disemployment of workers. Indirectly, however, through capital formation and the multiplier, an act of innovation may create employment. If the temporary increase in demand is sufficient to cause a secondary accelerator and multiplier effect, the employment and income creation is increased.

If innovation occurs slowly, each temporary burst of income- and employment-creation will be small, will not press on the productive capacity of the economy so as to create an accelerator effect, will not offset disemployment, and there will be increase in unemployment and no increase in aggregate income. A stagnant level of per capita income, then, may not reflect a technically static economy. It may mask a slow process of innovation and an accompanying gradual increase in unemployment and steadily worsening distribution of income. A rise in aggregate (and unless population growth prevents, per capita) GNP occurs when innovations occur in close enough succession so that the accompanying capital formation is a continuing stream which, with its multiplier effect and the secondary accelerator and multiplier effect, causes a secular expansion of income and employment. This force for re-employment of the technologically disemployed has been too much neglected in the theory of growth, yet as asserted in Chapter 7 it is almost certainly more important quantitatively in the expansion of income than is the capital formation directly associated with innovation.

Growth in GNP feeds on itself. The more rapidly GNP is growing, the greater the accelerator effect and the faster the rate of growth, up to the limit permitted by the presence of idle labor or the pace of innovation.

But, as the analysis of the accelerator shows, this relationship also has its negative side if growth is slow.[16]

It may be expected, then, that a rate of growth of aggregate GDP and GNP ranging from zero upward will be associated statistically with a rate of change in employment moving from negative to zero to positive—from net disemployment through zero to net re-employment. Where there is no labor force increase, a moderate pace of innovation, generating a moderate degree of multiplier-accelerator-multiplier effect, will be sufficient to prevent disemployment, and to create a continuing rise in aggregate and per capita GDP and GNP without a worsening of the distribution of income. The faster the population is growing, the higher the rate of growth in aggregate GDP that will be needed to prevent disemployment or, beyond that, to cause net re-employment.

And, of course, increase or decrease in unemployment affects the distribution of income in indirect as well as direct ways. Innovation with disemployment will obviously widen the income disparity between, say, the top decile and the disemployed decile or so of the labor force. Indirectly, that disemployment may reduce the income share of the bottom 40% or so of the labor force, for when a disemployed worker returns to his agricultural family he reduces the per capita income of the family, and the existence of surplus workers also depresses industrial wages or keeps them from rising as much as they otherwise would.

Re-employment has opposite effects. Every withdrawal of a worker from agriculture to industry raises not only his income but also that of the remaining agricultural family members who share the family's food or the income from it. A worker in industry may eat more than he did when he was a low-productivity and low-income member of a rural family. More certainly, the remaining members of a farm family will eat better now that their income per capita has increased. The amount of produce marketed will not increase by the full amount the migrant member of the family was eating while still within the family. This is well attested to by empirical evidence. On both counts, the terms of trade will turn in favor of agriculture, even if the shift of a worker from agriculture to industry did not appreciably reduce agricultural production. Change in the terms of trade in favor of agriculture tends to lessen income inequality. As re-employment continues and the marginal productivity of farm workers rises, each shift will cause a greater reduction in agricultural production (or lessen its increase), and the change in the terms of trade will be greater. At the same time, increasing real wages will have to be paid in industry to obtain workers.

Here, then, we have one thesis of change in income distribution as growth proceeds. The faster the rate of growth in aggregate GNP, rela-

---

[16] Familiar Harrod-Domar considerations are involved.

tive to the rate of population growth, the less rapid should be the unfavorable change or, across the zero line, the more rapid should be the favorable change, in income distribution.

To test that hypothesis, associated data for the rate of economic growth and the change in income distribution in individual countries over time is needed. Chenery and associates had such estimates for 18 countries for recent periods. Their Figure 1–1 is presented here as Figure 9–2. I have drawn a vertical line at a rate of growth in GNP of 6%. Of the 7 countries growing at a slower rate, the income distribution as measured by the share of the lowest income 40% was worsening in 6. Of the 11 countries growing at a faster rate, income distribution was improving in

FIGURE 9–2
Growth and the Lowest 40 Percent

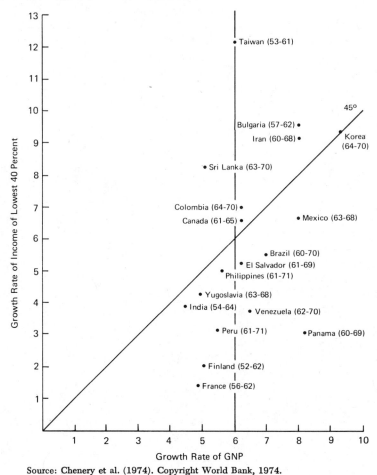

Source: Chenery et al. (1974). Copyright World Bank, 1974.

5. A computation that substitutes increase in per capita income for that in aggregate income yields a comparable relationship. Apart from possible errors in the estimates, the data indicate that other factors were exerting important effects on the distribution of income, but they also indicate a relationship between rate of growth in GNP and change in income distribution that can hardly be more coincidence.[17]

The Level of Income and the Degree of Inequality

This thesis about the relationship between rate of growth and change in income distribution leads directly to an important thesis about the relationship between income levels and income distribution. It is shown in Chapter 1, Table 1–7, that at the present time the rate of growth is slow in the lowest income countries as a group, and is increasingly rapid as income rises until the income group above $1,600 is reached. Data going back to 1950 indicate that the average rates of growth in low-income countries were slower two and three decades ago than in the 1960s. A reasonable assumption is that up to income levels above $500, rates of growth have been too slow to offset the disemployment effect of innovation. This simple thesis alone could explain the worsening income distribution shown in Tables 9–1 and 9–2 as one moves from the lowest income levels up to the $500–$1,000 group. It is not suggested that this was the only influence at work, but that it must have been an important one.

In some degree this effect must continue in the future. For economic growth begins gradually and slowly. There is no instant conversion of crowds of traditional producers into innovators. Investment and innovational capability, and with them the rate of growth, increase gradually, not suddenly. Hence the creation of surplus labor, or increase in the pool of surplus labor if one already existed, seems highly likely in the early phases of growth, and with it increase in the inequality of income distribution. England between 1770 and 1820 or 1830 provides the earliest example. The contemporary examples are many. If the pace continues slow, surplus labor may continue to exist indefinitely. India provides perhaps the most conspicuous example of its mass continuance. It seems paradoxical, therefore, that India is a low-equality country, according to Table 9–2. The explanation presumably is that poverty in India extends well into the upper income 20% of the population. The very wealthy class constitutes only perhaps 1% or 2% of the population.

Two other forces, not mentioned above, may be expected to tend to improve income distribution at some intermediate level of per capita

---

[17] Adelman (1974) presents a similar analysis. Because some estimates of income distribution were revised and added estimates made after she wrote, her data differ somewhat from those underlying Figure 9–2.

income. If factory workers move gradually to higher skills, learned either on the shop floor or in school, their wage incomes will rise. Further, if innovational entrepreneurs increase in number or widen their activities, they will come increasingly into competition with each other and their profit margins will shrink. Both factors may help to explain the reversal of the income inequality trend at incomes between $500 and $1,000.

W. A. Lewis: Unlimited Supplies of Labor

W. Arthur Lewis' well-known 1954 article entitled "Economic Development with Unlimited Supplies of Labor" has been mentioned in previous chapters. The model presented in the article deals mainly with how the increase in the rate of saving and investment necessary for growth in a low-income economy may come about, but the model is pertinent here because changes in the inequality of income distribution necessarily occur concomitantly.

As noted earlier, Lewis introduced his model by asserting as an empirical fact that in many less developed countries there exist large reservoirs of labor whose marginal productivity is "negligible, zero, or even negative." These workers, Lewis posits, are living at a subsistence level, and are available in "unlimited" numbers for employment in the "capitalist sector" of the economy, at a wage equal to the subsistence level of living plus a margin sufficient to overcome the friction of moving. I shall term this wage the "subsistence-plus" wage. In Lewis' model, the real wage in industry remains constant at this level until the pool of surplus labor is drained dry.

Another assumption of the model is the existence of a group of capitalists who by their nature are savers and investors.

Central aspects of the model are presented in Figure 9–3. In this figure, the quantity of labor employed in the capitalist sector is measured on the horizontal axis, and output and real income on the vertical axis; OS is the subsistence level of income, OW the subsistence-plus wage of the capitalist sector, N_1Q_1 the marginal productivity curve of labor employed with a given amount of capital, N_2Q_2 the curve with a larger amount of capital, and so on. Along each curve the employer will add labor until the point Q at which its marginal productivity no longer exceeds the wage. The areas N_1Q_1W, N_2Q_2W, etc., represent his "profits," using that term to refer to return on capital as well as profits above that amount.

Having initially invested the capital represented by the N_1Q_1 curve, employing WQ_1 of labor, the capitalist will plow back his profits to reach the N_2Q_2 curve in the process employing added labor and increasing his profit flow. And on to N_3Q_3, N_4Q_4, and so on. The many "little islands" of which the capitalist sector consists will grow, the share of profits in the

FIGURE 9–3
Capitalistic Investment with Unlimited Supplies of Labor

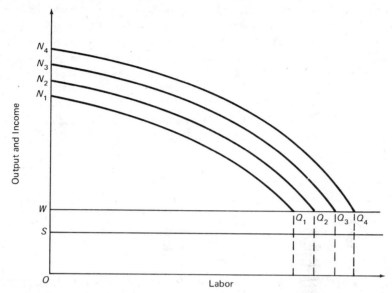

national income will grow, and—because capitalists by nature are high savers—the ratio of saving to national income will grow. And, though this is not the point with which Lewis was concerned, the income share of the top few percent of income-receivers will also grow.

At the same time, re-employment will proceed. Lewis does not term it "re-employment," for his model, being one of capital formation and not innovation, has no disemployment.[18] Lewis notes in his article that the capitalist sector may create its own supply of labor by destroying (through its competition) enterprises in the non-capitalist sector, but this observation is not reflected in the model.

Lewis recognizes conditions in which the rise in the economy's saving rate will cease. It will cease, he says, when the "little islands" which comprise the capitalist sector touch each other, competition among capitalists begins, and the rise in the ratio of profits to national income ceases. Another and related development occurs. The supply of surplus labor begins to dry up. Competition within the capitalist sector for labor then begins to pull up wages, not only of workers newly recruited into the sector but of all workers.

The model provides valuable insight into the source of saving for

---

[18] He deals with technical innovation at somewhat greater length in his 1958 sequel article.

capital formation in the early phases of growth. Its simplifications depart too far from reality for the most useful analysis of changes in the distribution of income. Because there is no disemployment in the model, the early increase in the inequality of income distribution is not indicated. Because the shift in terms of trade as surplus labor is drawn from agriculture is not reflected in the model, that aspect of changing income distribution is ignored.[19] Lastly, since there is no disemployment in the model, all capital formation, no matter how slow, decreases unemployment, and the significance of the rate of economic growth is not recognized. Nevertheless, the sharp presentation of one aspect of a relevant process contributes to understanding of the process of change in income distribution as well as of the process of growth.

Population Growth and Inequality

It will hardly surprise the reader to read that an inverse relationship is to be expected between the rate of population growth and the rate of change in the income share of, say, the lowest-income 40% of the population.

Most population increase in the lower income countries takes place in rural areas. Unless a large flow of rural-urban migration takes place, rapid population growth causes a rapid increase in the rural population.

When rapid population growth begins in any country, temporarily the percentage of the rural population below working age swells; then the agricultural labor force swells. Because of diminishing returns, agricultural output does not increase in the same proportion, except in countries in which idle land is plentiful. In other countries, rapid growth in the agricultural labor force will not prevent the population increase from depressing per capita incomes in this low-income sector of the economy unless rural-urban migration is rapid enough to absorb the labor force

---

[19] Lewis assumed that until the pool of surplus labor in agriculture (and services) is exhausted, labor can be drawn into industry at a fixed real wage equal to the subsistence level of income plus a margin sufficient to induce migration into industry. Dale Jorgenson (1967) has shown that in such a model, in which real wages in industry remain fixed in spite of expanding industrial production and regardless of the rate of increase in aggregate or per capita income in industry and in agriculture, the terms of trade cannot be determined within the model but must be set exogenously, as by a monopolist who pays little attention to maximizing his income.

If productivity rises in agriculture, and if the rural population is increasing, it is possible that the combined effect of the increase in population, the income elasticity of the demand for agricultural and industrial products respectively, and the elasticity of demand for agricultural products with respect to the relative price of agricultural and industrial products, may in combination happen to hold real income per capita in agriculture constant. In that case real wages in agriculture might remain constant. This is a knife-edge effect not considered in Lewis' model.

increase and prevent this effect. Hence, rapid population growth tends to increase income inequality.

The World Bank cross-national comparison shows results consistent with this expectation. The income share of the lowest 40% of the population was found significantly correlated negatively with the rate of population growth over the preceding decade. Moreover, additionally there was a barely significant negative relationship between the share of agriculture in GDP and the income share of the lowest income 40% of the population. The two factors are not entirely independent.

Rural-Urban Migration: The Harris-Todaro Thesis

Throughout the lower income world, since World War II there has been much migration from rural areas to towns and cities. There is hardly a city in a lower income country that does not have around it an arc of shanty towns with rows of "houses" built of packing box boards and tin sheets salvaged from cans, and beside them clusters of very modest but more presentable residences. An appreciable fraction of the residents are unemployed. (The order of magnitude is 1/10, 1/5, possibly 1/4, not one half.) Flight to the city has suggested to many commentators that the most miserable of landless laborers flee agriculture in desperation, hoping to be cared for by someone, somehow, in the city.

This turns out not to be the case. A number of careful studies have shown that the rural migrants to the city are young, many of them new entrants to the labor force, that on the average they are better educated than the average person in the rural community which they left—a statement that does not imply more than a few years of education—and that in their rural community they were economically better off on the average than the average person of their age. Ridker (1971) reported this concerning South Asian areas; Wayne Nafziger (1969) reported this concerning Nigeria; and a dozen young social scientists who had recently completed studies in Latin America or Africa, who met at a conference at the Massachusetts Institute of Technology in 1972 agreed that this was true in every case in which their studies had collected relevant facts.[20]

After a study of rural-urban migration in East Africa, Michael Todaro (1969) set out an explanatory hypothesis, and John R. Harris and Todaro (1969) applied it to East Africa. Rural individuals, the authors suggest, migrate to cities even when knowing that the prospect of unemployment faces them, if they calculate that their annual income even in spite of unemployment during part of the year will exceed the agricultural income which is their alternative. Though Harris and Todaro do not ex-

---

[20] These careful research workers noted that their data might not include all rural-urban migrants. Some may have given up and returned to their rural area after being unemployed for some time.

plore the point, the calculation may consider expected urban lifetime income, not merely the immediate likely income rate.

The migrants, then, are not the most desperate rural individuals, but rather probably the most mobile because they were the most self-reliant and resourceful. Perhaps they are the ones whose families can best afford to support them in temporary urban unemployment. Presumably the families do support them and in their turn, if they find work, they remit income to their parents.

On this hypothesis, rural migration will continue at a rate that will not permit urban unemployment to disappear until the differential between rural and urban incomes shrinks to a certain minimum. If the rate of increase in employment in urban areas rises, the rate of in-migration will also rise, and unemployment will be maintained at the former level.

The urban unemployment, then, is not necessarily an indication of stagnation or of a condition regarded by the individuals experiencing it as extreme poverty. Rather, it may be a tolerable aspect of an upward ladder, a stage in a process of sectoral shift. Yet one should not be too sanguine in interpreting it. If rapid population increase places great pressure on rural incomes, then even though the calculation of the migrants is of increased annual income in spite of urban unemployment, they may be fleeing extreme poverty. The entire family by whose decisions the individual migrates may be desperate.

Increased Employment in Nonagriculture: An Illustrative Qualification

The speculative use of recent data will indicate the general magnitude of the likelihood that the expansion of the "capitalist sector" or, more broadly, the expansion of output discussed in a previous section, will absorb the increase in the labor force that is occurring during the decade of the 1970s.

Table 9–3 presents an estimate of the rate of growth in the labor force in lower income regions during the decade. The estimate was made in 1966. It nevertheless has little margin of error, for it does not depend on population growth estimates. Virtually every person who will have entered the labor force in any country by 1980 was already born in 1966. The table shows rates of labor force growth during the decade averaging 2.3% per year in the "less developed" world and ranging from 1.2% per year in Central Africa to 3.4% in Central America. The average rate is probably approximately the highest the world will know, since during the last half of the 1960s birth rates declined in many lower income countries. Assuming that labor force absorption must occur mainly in industry or in services associated with the expansion of industry, what are the prospects that in any given country the expansion of employment will prevent an increase in the pool of surplus labor?

TABLE 9–3
Estimates of Growth of the Labor Force in Less Developed Regions:
1950–65 and 1970–80

	Average Percentage Rates of Growth per Year	
	1950–65	1970–80
Developed countries	1.1	1.0
Less developed countries	1.7	2.3
Regions		
Other East Asia	1.8	3.1
Middle South Asia*	1.4	2.0
South East Asia†	1.9	2.5
South West Asia‡	1.9	2.8
West Africa	2.2	2.3
East Africa	1.3	1.8
Central Africa	1.0	1.2
North Africa	1.1	2.6
Tropical South America	2.7	3.0
Central America	2.8	3.4
Temperate South America	1.5	1.5
Caribbean	1.8	2.3

* Includes Ceylon, India, Iran and Pakistan.
† Includes Burma, Cambodia, Indonesia, Malaysia, the Philippines, and Thailand.
‡ Middle East countries.
Note: Excludes Sino-Soviet countries.
Source: Turnham and Jaeger (1971), p. 31. Derived from data given in Ypsilantis (1966).

A crude calculation, using quantitative relationships roughly estimated from a variety of recent data, is possible. The calculation is as follows. Industry (manufacturing, mining, and construction) expanded at a rate exceeding 7% per year during the 1960s in the range of countries with per capita incomes from below $100 to above $500. This is the average rate for the entire group. I shall assume that it is the rate at each income level. It is reasonable to assume that its rate of growth during the decade 1975–85 will be slightly faster, or say 8% per year. It is reasonable to estimate that the share of industrial employment in total employment in the lowest income countries is four fifths that of industry's share of output and that this ratio declines as industry expands; that when industry expands industrial employment will expand at three fifths of the rate of expansion of output; that for each worker in industry 1.25 workers are employed in commerce, transportation, public utilities, and other service occupations serving industry or distributing its products, and that for each added in industry 1.25 workers will be added in these industry-associated service industries. (The industry-related services referred to do not constitute the entire tertiary sector.) The expansion of employment in industry, it should be noted, is net "re-employment." Two fifths of the expansion in output will require no increase in employment; three fifths will occur through increased employment. This ratio would certainly not apply at rates of expansion near zero, or at rates of expansion double the average rate of 8%, but it is reasonable to use this relationship for rates of say 2% on either side of the average, which is the range that is relevant.[21] It should be noted that the increase in employment in the industry-associated services are not caused by the expansion of industry. Industry does not have magic initiating power. Rather, increase in employment in industry and in industry-related services are concomitant resultants of the same expansion of demand.

From these assumptions, Table 9–4 can be derived. The term "industry-associated" in the table includes industry itself. The present share of industry in the national product varies from 10% or less in the lowest income countries to about 30% in countries with incomes of say $500 to $700 per capita. Calculations are therefore shown for industry shares of 10%, 20%, and 30%.

TABLE 9–4
Expansion of Employment: Hypothetical Calculation, Assuming 8 Percent Rate of Growth of Industry per Year

1 Share of Industry in National Product in Percent	2 Share of Industrial Employment in Labor Force (percent)	3 Share of Industry-Associated Employment in Labor Force (percent)	4 Growth of Industry-Associated Employment as Percentage of Total Labor Force (Col. 3 × .048)
10	8	18	.86
20	14	31.5	1.51
30	20	45	2.16

A conclusion from the calculation then is that in the lowest income countries, except perhaps in Central Africa with its low labor force growth rate, the pool of surplus labor will almost certainly increase, and that in the highest of the three income groups of countries being considered the expansion of nonagricultural employment associated with the

---

[21] The relationship between industrial output and employment shares is estimated from Kuznets, *Q.A.E.G.N.*, 2, from Turnham and Jaeger (1971), and from scattered other data; the relationship between the rates of growth of output and employment in industry from *The Growth of World Industry*, 1967 and 1972 editions, the ratio of industry-associated employment to manufacturing employment from Kuznets and other labor force data and from Turnham and Jaeger, p. 109, table 5–2. The data are inconsistent. Some of Kuznets' data show a higher percentage of the labor force than of output in industry, a most unlikely statistic. The ratio of the employment growth rate in industry to the output growth rate in industry was above 3/5 for the period 1955–65, but below 3/5 for 1955–70. The ratio for manufacturing only in Taiwan, 1953–69, shown in Bruton (1974), p. 11, was only .5 (6.3/13.0). It is highly probable that at this high rate of growth in manufacturing output, the ratio would be lower at lower rates of output growth. As stated in the text, the coefficients used in my calculations are subject to such error that the margin of error in the results is great.

growth of industry will just absorb the increase in the labor force at intermediate rates of population growth and will draw down any existing pool of surplus labor at lower population growth rates, but will not absorb a labor force increase (in the economy as a whole) of much above 2%. In countries with per capita incomes (and industry shares in gross product) intermediate between these two groups, the results on the surplus labor pool will also be intermediate.

The assumptions underlying these calculations are subject to such wide margins of error that the calculations should be regarded as no more than an exercise in method. For example, the increase in nonindustry employment associated with increase in industrial employment may be much overstated. The data as presented, however, give a sense of the forces at work. With diligent research they could be refined.

Even on the assumption that the calculations in table 9–4 are correct, it should not be concluded that where not absorbed by industrial growth, labor force increase will necessarily add to the pool of surplus labor. Labor absorption is also going on in some agriculture, as the section that follows indicates.

Innovation in Agriculture

Innovation in agriculture and the expansion of agricultural production, like this pair of processes in industry, may have either net employment-creating or net disemployment effects, even while they raise aggregate income within agriculture if they do not have too adverse effects on the terms of trade between agriculture and industry. Because agriculture is the low-income sector of almost every low-income country, shifts in income distribution within agriculture may have effects on income distribution on the country as a whole quite different from comparable shifts in income distribution within industry.

Innovation in agriculture may increase the inequality of income distribution within the sector, at least for a considerable time and perhaps indefinitely, since the larger farmers, with more capital and better channels of information, who may also be the more able and innovational farmers, are likely to be the early beneficiaries and if the new methods require complex techniques and access to limited resources such as irrigation water, may be the only beneficiaries unless strong policy measures are adopted and implemented by the government. This effect was feared with respect to the "green revolution." In an early survey of the effects of the "green revolution," Donald Freebairn writes in summary:

> Rapid technical progress in agriculture has the capacity to increase significantly agricultural production; recent successes in Mexico, India, Pakistan, and the Philippines serve as indicators of the results that can be

expected. At the same time, the technologies, with their implicit imple-
menting policies, seem to work toward heavy concentrations of potential
benefits. Without being able to specify numerically the degree of concentration, the larger sized landowners . . . combine their connection with
the information networks producing improved technology with control
over the requisite resource base, including access to the production inputs
and the means of financing them. In addition, because of their social and
political status, they can influence policies that enhance their own positions relative to those in weaker positions.[22]

If introduction of the new technologies is accompanied by increased
mechanization, disemployment of peasants or farm workers is likely to
occur, and the increase in income inequality within agriculture will be
augmented.

However, these considerations are not conclusive concerning the
change in income distribution in the rural sector. The technology of the
"green revolution" requires more labor per acre-year (with given machinery) than do the older techniques, and by shortening the growing
season permits two crops per year in some areas where only one crop per
year was grown previously. The need for labor is increased accordingly.
The introduction of tractors, by speeding the preparation of the ground
for planting, may increase the possibility of multiple cropping and thus
may increase, not decrease, the demand for labor. The introduction of
tube wells has had this effect, both by permitting the growing of a second
crop during the dry season and by permitting a shift to higher value
crops whose cultivation is more labor-intensive.

A survey conducted in Pakistan, India, Thailand, Malaysia, and the
Philippines in 1971 and 1972 by 30 social scientists, on behalf of the
International Rice Research Institute, showed that the green revolution
had had these labor-absorbing, not labor-displacing, effects. Over half of
the 2,400 farms surveyed on which the new technology had been adopted
used more hired labor from within the village, 30% hired extra labor from
outside the village, and 40% used more family labor. "The villages where
labor-saving technology had been most widely adopted since the introduction of modern varieties also reported the larger number of farmers
with increased employment of family and hired labor," stated a summary
of the study.[23]

This report went on to state that the size of farms and the form of
tenure had "not changed dramatically." The implication perhaps is that
there had been some adverse change.

With increasing agricultural income, off-farm rural employment is
generated in appreciable amounts. Gibb (1972) found that in an area of

---

[22] Poleman and Freebairn (1973), p. 109.
[23] *New York Times*, Sept. 23, 1974.

the Philippines in which agricultural income rose by 25%, nonagricultural employment increased by an equal percentage in a poor rural town, by about 45% in a wealthy rural town, and by about 65% in a "local [that is, agriculture-based] urban center." Hence the net effect on labor incomes and on the distribution of income in rural areas may very well be favorable. The a priori assumption that technical progress in agriculture will worsen the distribution of farm income is not justified.

If agriculture employs, say, 80% of the labor force, an increase in the income share of the wealthiest farmers will increase the inequality of income distribution. Where growth has proceeded sufficiently so that the labor force share of agriculture is considerably smaller, an increase in the incomes of the wealthier farmers may decrease inequality in the country as a whole, by some measures of inequality, for even those farmers may be in the low-income 50% or 60% of the population. This is especially likely to be true if the larger farmers are peasant farmers rather than landlords or great estate owners.

Education and Inequality

Adelman and Morris, in the statistical study of 43 countries referred to earlier in this chapter, analyze factors affecting the degree of income inequality as growth proceeds. Necessarily, differences among countries at different levels are taken as surrogates for changes during growth. The main method of analysis is hierarchical. The authors determine the ranking or position of each country with respect to a number of characteristics thought to affect inequality of income distribution. Then they divide the sample into two groups with markedly differing average inequality and range of inequality, on the basis of that characteristic that seems (by a statistical process) most reasonably to divide them. They then split each of the two by a similar process, then split one of the resulting four into two. Thus they have two groups, four groups, and six groups, at different stages of their explanation, each consisting of countries with a degree of inequality differing significantly from that of the countries in the parallel group. They then assign causation to qualities distinguishing the groups which seem logically to be causal. The measure of income inequality was in one analysis the income share of the lowest income 60% of the population; in a second analysis, the income share of the highest income 5%.

Alternatively, a multiple regression was used. The dependent variables were the income shares and per capita income of the lowest income 40%, lowest income 60%, highest income 20%, and highest income 5%. The independent variables were GNP per capita, and in various combinations rate of improvement of human resources (educational development), extent of the direct economic role of the government, and rate of growth of per capita GDP. While the authors believe that the hierarchical analysis is more illuminating and less sensitive to errors in individual measurements, they note that the two analyses are consistent.

In both analyses, they find the income share of the lowest income 40% positively correlated with educational development in the country.

The World Bank analysis indicates the same relationship. In this analysis three multiple regressions were run, using as the dependent variable the income share of the top 20%, the middle 40%, and the lowest income 40% respectively. The independent variables were the rate of growth in GDP during the five years preceding the year for which income distribution was estimated, primary and secondary school enrollment rates, the share of agriculture in GDP, and—using dummy variables— whether a country was in the high income group and whether a country was socialist.[24] The regression showed a significant positive relationship between school enrollment rates and the income shares of the lowest income and middle 40% of the population. Primary school enrollment was more significant for the lowest income 40%, secondary school enrollment for the middle income group.

The conclusion drawn by both Adelman and Morris and the World Bank research group is that education decreases inequality. Persuasive logic supports the deduction from the statistical association. That an individual may increase his income by gaining education relative to someone else is irrelevant; if everyone gained more education and moved upward, no one would have moved upward relatively and the distribution of income would not be changed unless somehow the change in the labor force caused a reduction in the share of income going to capital. But with general education the demand for higher level jobs may be expected to increase, that for lower level jobs to decrease, and the income margin between them to lessen.

However, the reader should be warned not to move uncautiously to further conclusions. If the result is due to education, is it a result of the supply of or the demand for education? One of the authors (Adelman, 1974) cites five countries as examples of the importance of education: Israel, Japan, South Korea, Singapore, and Taiwan. All five, however, are inhabited by peoples in whose cultures love of learning has long been conspicuous. In other cultures, in which a school certificate seems to be regarded commonly as a symbol with which one can obtain a clerical job, would growth be furthered by an added supply of education? The answer apparently is, Yes, since a statistically significant relationship was found in the entire World Bank sample.

But another question also presents itself. Respect for education has associated with it respect for people. Possibly this attitude, rather than the education which results from it, is at the root of attitudes and policies

---

[24] See n. 4.

that reduce income inequality. Education and lesser income inequality may be joint results of this common cause, rather than education being the causal factor. Or, more probably, both sorts of causation may be at work. If broader education were offered to people not characterized by the same cultural attitudes, would income inequality be reduced, or reduced by as great a degree as expected? It is not certain.

Other Factors

In their analyses, Adelman and Morris find the degree of income inequality associated not merely with level of per capita income and emphasis on education but also with the extent of the direct economic role of the government and with the presence or absence of export-oriented policies (and associated labor-intensive methods of production). The direct role of government was measured largely by government expenditure on infrastructure, health, and education. The effect of export-oriented policies will be discussed in Chapter 18, "Outward- or Inward-looking Orientation."

Out of these analyses, at least the outlines of a theory of income distribution during growth and in the presence of population growth emerges.

GOVERNMENTAL MEASURES TO REDUCE INCOME INEQUALITY

Let us turn from positive to normative theory and consider what a government may do to lessen income inequality. Various measures are possible.

1. Emphasis on education has been mentioned. The education must be appropriate. Elementary "practical" education for the many rather than higher education for the few is in point. Education is discussed further in Chapter 12, though the emphasis there is on its contribution to growth rather than to lessened inequality of income distribution.

2. Measures to alter relative factor prices are often urged by development advisors. The goal suggested is to end governmental interference with the market: to end interest-rate subsidies, import subsidies, prohibitive tariffs, tariff exemptions for capital goods, artificial support of exchange rates, special exchange rates, and the like that in one way or another subsidize capital or protect its use, and to end labor-union restrictions, minimum wage laws, requirements of expensive social security measures, and other measures that raise the cost of industrial labor. Such measures, which would let foreign exchange rates settle at their own level without import or foreign exchange restrictions, may at the appropriate stage in development accelerate the development of industrial

enterprises that can compete in the world market and thus accelerate long-run economic growth. It is argued that they will have a favorable effect on the inequality of income distribution by inducing more labor-intensive methods of production and by inducing a shift in the basket of goods produced, toward goods whose production is more labor-intensive. The contrary argument is that the elasticity of substitution between labor and capital in manufacturing is so low that the result would be slightly more employment at much lower wages.[25] These arguments are discussed in Chapter 18, in the context of discussion of such "liberalization" on growth rates.

3. Direct employment of low-income individuals at adequate wages, as in rural public works. This use of the "hidden rural savings" which surplus labor constitutes is discussed in Chapter 13, "Domestic Saving."

4. Redistribution of the ownership of capital and thereby of the income from capital. The conspicuous ways of accomplishing this are through land reform, the socialization of large enterprises, for example in infrastructure, and inheritance taxes. The first, which has been discussed in Chapter 5 on trade and agriculture, will not have the favorable effect intended unless steps are taken to maintain productivity of small farmers after the land reform. The second will not have the effect intended, and may have an unfavorable effect on both the rate of growth and the distribution of income, if the enterprises are not run efficiently after being nationalized. The third is difficult to administer effectively in the absence of the complex records that evolve only as the country industrializes.

5. The institution of a government which carries out a full socialization of the means of production is of course the extreme case of increase in the economic role of the government. It will be noted that the socialist countries for which data is included in Table 9–2 (Bulgaria, Poland, Yugoslavia, Czechoslovakia, Hungary) have Gini ratios among the lowest. To suggest socialism as a measure for reduction in income inequality, however, would be vapid and superficial, not only because of the many other impacts of socialism on life to be considered but also because the adoption of socialism is not a policy to be considered by an advisory committee and then accepted as one might decide on higher taxes or a tariff reduction, but rather the resultant of social, political, and cultural conditions within which economic analysis is a rather minor element.

6. Income redistribution through taxation and government expenditure, for health care, education, housing, and direct payments to selected groups or classes. The caveat noted above about the possibility of redistributive taxation applies here as well.

7. Alteration of relative prices; for example, to reduce the price of

---

[25] See Chenery and Raducel, in Chenery (1971).

mass-used consumer goods. If this is done by administrative decree, it may reduce their availability instead.

The several measures requiring government expenditures will compete with each other and with other governmental measures for funds.

Many measures included within the five rubrics above may be politically impossible because groups whom they would affect adversely have too great an influence in the government, or because the appeal of "modernity" in industry, meaning capital-intensive projects, is too great; or may be impossible administratively because the necessary administrative institutions, talent, and energy, and data on which administration must be based, do not exist. Some of these conditions change as growth proceeds; this, as well as the direct economic effects of growth discussed throughout this chapter, may be a reason that after a certain point in growth inequality tends to diminish. Because of the political, attitudinal, and administrative difficulties, many observers are pessimistic about the likelihood of hastening the process. There is no need to discuss the political difficulties further here. Some of the other measures listed are discussed briefly or at some length at appropriate places in later chapters.

BIBLIOGRAPHICAL NOTE

Chenery, Ahluwalia, Bell, Duloy, and Jolly (1974), and Adelman and Morris (1973), used in the text, will be the standard references on the relationship between growth and income distribution. Lewis (1964), (1968), and (1972) are valuable theoretical analyses. No single book pulls together studies of the question of surplus labor. Todaro (1969) and Harris and Todaro (1969) break new ground concerning rural-urban migration. An especially insightful and judicious discussion of the role of labor in economic development is H. J. Bruton in E. O. Edwards (1974).

Capital Formation and Technical Progress

10

No other factor has brought such explosively rapid increase in the income of the people of a country as the discovery and exploitation of a sufficiently valuable natural resource deposit, such as the petroleum deposits of two handfuls of countries. This statement would be true even in the absence of the cartel-enforced increase in petroleum prices. But for the great majority of the countries of the world, there have been no comparable increases in known natural resources. In these other countries, much the most important factors in rise in per capita income are capital formation and technical progress.

Economists are agreed that capital formation or technical progress or the two in combination are the dominant causal forces in economic growth, but there is difference of opinion concerning their relative importance. The difference is asymmetrical; some economists believe that investment in physical or in human capital is virtually the entire explanation of rise in output, but no economists believe that it is unimportant. The evidence concerning the two causal factors is surveyed in this chapter. One's conclusion with respect to that issue may affect one's judgment not only about prospects for the lower income countries but also about the effects upon their growth of various policies of the higher income countries.

ANALYTICAL TOOLS; DEFINITIONS

The Production Function

The factors that determine the productive capacity of an economy may be summarized in a "production function," that is, a statement of the relationship between the volume of output and the volume of various

250

inputs in production. In the most general statement, as below, the production function does not indicate the nature of the quantitative relationship between the inputs and output—the decrease in output that will result if one input is decreased, or the increase in some other input or inputs that will be necessary to maintain the same volume of output. Rather, it indicates only that there is a relationship. In these very general terms, we may state:

$$Y = F(R, K, N, E, t) \tag{1}$$

That is, output is dependent on the flow of inputs of natural resources, capital, labor, entrepreneurship (or management), and some other factor that may vary with time. The symbol N may represent not a number of persons but a number of labor units in which a trained man is more than one unit. If we wish to recognize psychological, cultural, and social differences among societies or in different time periods as causal factors, we may add another symbol, C, thereby splitting off an element that would otherwise be included within t. In stating such a mathematical formulation, one is implicitly assuming that each of the inputs represented is homogeneous, so that its quantity can be measured unambiguously. In reality, of course, there are many types of each of these inputs, so that we should write: $Y = F(R_1, R_2, R_3, \ldots K_1, K_2, K_3, \ldots \text{etc.})$. But though the assumption of homogeneity is unrealistic, it is useful for exposition. Conceptually also, we could if we wished introduce another variable representing the scale of production to indicate that this is a separable factor that affects the relationship between inputs and output.

The reader may state that all that the production function does, in this general form, is to note that the volume of output depends on a number of things, and that this is no great discovery. This is true, but the production function also states that output does not depend on anything else, at least in a degree that is important enough to be taken into consideration in analysis. The absence of any variable in a function implies that the coefficient of that variable is zero. That is an important limitation, and permits us to restrict analysis to a set of considerations that the mind can comprehend efficiently.

Moreover, the production function indicates a number of variables which research workers should try to quantify. As will become apparent in this and subsequent chapters, attempts have been fairly successful, and a great deal of understanding of the process of economic growth has been gained through quantification of some or all of the variables of equation (1) and analysis of the statistical relationships between them and growth.

For purposes of exposition of the production function, the variables of equation (1) are often reduced to two, by regarding land as a form of capital, ignoring entrepreneurship and social-cultural factors (which are difficult to quantify in any event), and taking the function as of a given moment in time, thus eliminating t. The function may then be portrayed geometrically. It is assumed here that the reader is acquainted with that formulation, and with its properties.

The production function, represented geometrically, is an elegant device on which to illustrate the implications of returns to scale and of decreasing returns. It is an awkward representation on which to portray technical change, for with any technical advance the entire function must be redrawn, since technical advance yields increased output per unit of capital or labor or both. The function as drawn, that is, rules out technical change. Nevertheless we sometimes use it in discussing technical progress because we have no better geometric tool.[1]

Definitions

Technical progress, or advance in the state of technical knowledge, consists of the invention of new methods or new products, that is, the creation of new mental constructs, and the introduction of these constructs into the processes of production in a society. The term "innovation" is commonly used to refer to this second step.

The distinction between invention and innovation is conceptually not a sharp one, for if a new method has been devised in someone's brain but not yet put into use, there are always unforeseen problems yet to be solved. The invention will not work precisely as it exists in the mental construct; the process of invention is not yet complete. However, the loose distinction between devising the mental conception and putting it into effect is a convenient one, and I shall follow the usual usage.

Innovation may merely benefit one person at the expense of others. We are concerned here only with innovation that increases productivity in the economy as a whole.

Capital formation is the use of productive resources for the construction of added capital equipment. Capital formation may consist of the construction of added units of a type of equipment already in use to supply an enlarged labor force with tools ("capital widening"). Little innovation is involved. One can also think of capital deepening without much innovation: the introduction of pieces of equipment already conceived of but not previously in use because not enough capital was available. Yet if the equipment has not before been actually constructed, some innovation is involved.

Some innovation consists of reorganization of productive processes without any change whatever in the capital equipment used. Innovation often occurs without *net* capital formation, through replacing a worn-out

---

[1] Concerning the production function, see the "Bibliographical Note" to this chapter.

capital instrument with a more efficient one that constitutes no more capital than the old one. But almost all innovation in production requires gross capital formation, and much of it involves net capital formation. The innovation is, so to speak, embodied in the capital. Innovations are incorporated in a large share of capital formation recorded by accountants as merely replacement. When a machine wears out, it is replaced not by an identical one but by an improved one (one that contributes more to output than did the same number of units of the former capital). If capital is being provided for an expanded labor force, this capital too will embody improvements rather than merely copy the old.[2]

It is easy to weigh the relative importance of capital formation and technical progress from a certain viewpoint. Increase in the amount of capital used per worker is not conceptually necessary even for indefinitely continuing economic growth. However, without continuing technical progress, indefinitely continuing growth cannot be conceived of, because of the diminishing marginal productivity of capital. But this is a philosophical, not an empirical, distinction. Without exception, in countries in which technical progress is occurring, net capital formation is also proceeding. It is therefore an empirical question whether the one or the other makes the contribution to increase in productivity. The issue is not merely one of statistical attribution, for there are two questions: What share of increase in productivity can be assigned to each? and, Is either in the main the moving force which induces the other? If the share attributable to capital formation is large and if capital formation is the prime mover, then income in the low-income countries can be raised at almost any desired rate by providing enough capital. If some other less manipulatable factor is important, then the problem is less malleable. The first question is discussed below, then the second.

CAPITAL FORMATION OR TECHNICAL PROGRESS: STATISTICAL ATTRIBUTION

Figure 10–1 illustrates the fact that a large share of increase in output is not accounted for by increase in capital inputs.

Kuznets (*Q.A.E.G.N.*, 6, pp. 19–21) analyzed data for 10 economically

---

[2] The difficulty of conceiving of the meaning and measurement of a constant (or changed) quantity of capital when its physical specifications change has been urged especially by Mrs. Joan Robinson (for example, in J. Robinson, 1954) and discussed at length in the economic literature. The meaning of the text is sufficiently clear without discussing that problem here.

Nicholas Kaldor (1957) has argued that a distinction between capital formation and innovation is "arbitrary and artificial," since even as innovation shifts the production function, by introducing more capital-intensive methods it causes movement along an isoquant toward the capital-intensive end. (See also Kaldor and Mirlees, 1962). His argument is unwarranted. Conceptually and statistically, it is possible to distinguish between the two types of change.

FIGURE 10–1
Gross Domestic Investment and Aggregate Growth Rates, Less Developed Countries, 1960–70

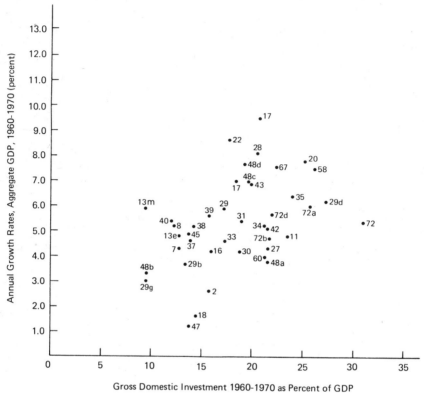

Gross Domestic Investment 1960-1970 as Percent of GDP

See endpapers of book for number key for countries.
Source: Economic Analyses and Projections Department, World Bank.

advanced countries from the mid-19th century to the late 1950s. In each study, he found that when he ranked the countries by the percentage of national product they spent for capital formation and by the rate of growth in their output, there was no significant correlation between the two rankings. From the mid-19th century to World War I, each 1% per year increase in productivity in Italy required net investment of 5.3% of net domestic product. In the United Kingdom, the ratio was 3.3, in Germany 4.8, in Sweden 2.6, in Japan (data beginning with 1885) 1.6. Some influence that made the yield of capital formation greater in some countries than in others must have been at work. Some of the differences are due to differences in the type of industry suited to the country, and the quality and quantity of natural resources, but others, for example the low ratios for Sweden and Japan, cannot plausibly be accounted for except by superior innovational talent and energy.

Johnson and Chiu (1965) analyzed the relationship between rate of investment and rate of growth in *NNP* per capita for 44 countries for the period 1950 to 1962. A scatter diagram of the data shows no discernible relationship, and one of the data for the 12 European countries included shows only a faint and dubious relationship. Clearly, some factor other than capital formation seems to increase productivity.

Quantitative Studies of the U.S. Economy

Increase in output per worker or per man-hour is due either to increase in the quantity of inputs, primarily capital, cooperating with labor, or to increase in output per unit of total inputs. In principle it is easy to distinguish between the two.[3] The first attempts at statistical attribution, in the 1950s and 1960s, dealt with output in the United States. They treated all increase in output per man-hour not attributable to increased capital inputs as attributable to a single other variable termed "technical progress." The findings are presented in Table 10–1.

Both of Abramovitz's estimates and the higher estimate of the share attributable to technical progress in the Solow and Massell studies used as a final step the "remainder" method.

The rate of increase in output per man or man-hour attributable to capital inputs was first estimated. The remaining increase in output per man or man-hour was then assigned to "technical progress." This method has an error analogous to analyzing the causes of increase in size of a rectangle which has increased in both dimensions by first measuring the

---

[3] Where there are only two types of input, capital and labor, the necessary measurement is as follows. Let Q be an index of output, L an index of labor input, and K an index of capital input. Let α be the share of output attributable to labor and β that attributable to capital in the base period, so that $\alpha + \beta = 1$. Then the rate of change in "total productivity," the productivity of all inputs in combination, is, for discrete changes:

$$\frac{\Delta P}{P} = \frac{\Delta Q}{Q} - \alpha \frac{\Delta L}{L} - \beta \frac{\Delta K}{K}$$

and the rate of change in the productivity of labor inputs per hour is:

$$\frac{\Delta P}{P} = \frac{\Delta q}{q} - w_K \frac{\Delta k}{k},$$

where q is output per man hour, k is capital per man hour, and w_K is the share of output attributable to capital in the base period. This is Solow's measure of technical change. Kennedy and Thirlwall (1971) present this formulation of Solow's measure in a survey article on technical progress. Unfortunately, in the survey, by presenting the claims of Jorgenson and Becker without evaluating the bases on which those writers attempt to assign all increases in output to increases in inputs, they give those studies undeserved weight. Otherwise the fairly exhaustive study is illuminating.

TABLE 10-1
Attribution of Productivity Increase, United States

Author and Scope of Study	Share Attributed to Technical Progress
Abramovitz: *NNP* per capita, 1869-78 to 1944-53	.80-.95
Solow, with correction by Hogan of an arithmetic error, and definition of lower limit by Levine: Private nonagricultural output per man-hour, 1909-49	.81-.90
Massell: Manufacturing output per man-hour, apparently 1919-55	.67-.90
Massell: Same, by different method	.87

Sources and notes: See the "Appendix" to this chapter.

ratio by which the length has increased, attributing a proportionate share of the increase in area to it, and assigning all of the remainder of the increase in area to increase in width. The nature of the resulting error, assigning to width a result that is due to increase in both length and width, is shown in Figure 10-2. Because of it, these estimates understate the share of increase in output that is attributable to capital, and overstate the share of "technical progress."

The lower of the Solow estimates (actually by Levine, using Solow's data) and the lower of the Massell estimates define the magnitude of error due to this cause, for in these estimates the contribution not attributable to increase in capital inputs was calculated first and the contribution of capital inputs treated as the remainder. The "true" estimate of productivity increase per unit of input is therefore between the lower and higher estimates (assuming no other sources of error).

These limiting estimates show a very striking result. Of all of the increase in output per man or man-hour, as a maximum less than one third is attributed to capital formation, and the data suggest that the best estimate is less than one fifth. The rest is due to increase in factor productivity.

The estimates are subject to a qualification of some importance. They imply that the effects of technical progress are disembodied, that is, do not depend on the rate of capital formation. Actually, many technical advances can be put into use quickly only because the economy is expanding, capital deepening is also going on, and so a goodly amount of new capital equipment is being produced in which to incorporate the new methods. The indicated contribution of increase in productivity should not be assumed to pertain, even with the same rate of technical progress and of other relevant changes (discussed below), if the rate of capital formation varied greatly from that of the historical record. The converse is also true; capital formation would not continue to make the indicated contribution if technical advance faltered, and would presum-

FIGURE 10–2
The Attribution Problem

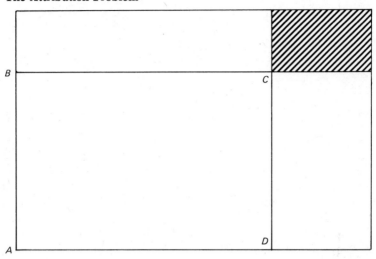

When the length and width of the original rectangle ABCD are increased, is the shaded segment of the increase in area due to increase in length or in width?

ably make a greater one if the pace of technical advance increased markedly.[4]

Studies of Norway, Finland, and Great Britain have confirmed the importance of increase in factor productivity.[5] The highest attribution to capital formation is in a study of Israel by Michael Bruno (1962). He estimates that capital formation was responsible for between 50% and 60% of increase in output per capita in Israel during the period 1953–64. A. L. Gaathon (1961) had reached a similar result for the period 1950–59.

Abramovitz, Solow, and the other early estimators realized that not all recorded increase in the productivity of inputs is due to technical progress, though they may have underestimated the importance of other factors. Among other factors are economies of scale, improved training of workers, shifts of workers or of capital from one sector to another (mainly, from agriculture to elsewhere), organizational improvements, and effects of a shortened work week on efficiency. Researchers whose

---

[4] Probably much more than half of all technical progress is embodied, that is, depends on new capital to carry it, though Denison, in the estimates discussed in the next section of the text, assumed that equal parts of technical progress were embodied and disembodied.

[5] See the sources cited in Kennedy and Thirlwall, p. 18.

interest was directed to empirical research by the studies of the 1960s soon realized that the contributions of these other factors are so large that to term the entire group "technical progress" was grossly misleading. The term "the Residual" (preferably spelled with a capital "R") came to be applied. A more neutral term would be simply "other," since the factors are not a residual, but the term is nevertheless well established in the literature.

COMPONENTS OF THE RESIDUAL: DENISON'S ESTIMATES

Edward F. Denison (1967), making use of such clues to the importance of various factors as are suggested by bits of research, and necessarily making generous use also of his own good judgment, has presented estimates of the specific sources of growth in aggregate output and in output per person employed between 1950 and 1962 in nine Western countries."[6] His estimates are useful not only for the magnitudes they suggest but also because of their indication of the complexity of the factors that make up the Residual. Table 10–2 summarizes estimates of the sources of increase in output per man-hour for the United States and for western European countries taken as a group.

It was noted above that Denison's figures are in large part based on judicious judgment rather than on some sort of econometric exercise. Only the estimates of land capital inputs are results of fairly precise statistical procedures. Denison *assumes* that about two thirds of the decrease in hours was compensated for by a resulting increase in output per man-hour. He derives his estimate of the contribution of increased education on the *assumption* that of the income differentials that appear when men of the same age are classed by educational levels, three fifths are the result of the education. He lays down the quite arbitrary judgment of the increase that growth in the size of the national market added to the increase in output that would otherwise have been caused by all other forces. And so on. His figures quantify his judgments, rather than resulting from some sort of statistical exercise. The estimates should be given only the credence which careful evaluation of the partially (or wholly) subjective reasoning underlying them suggests to the reader of Denison's thoughtful study. But with due qualification on this account, the estimates indicate two things clearly: the approximate share of increase in output per worker attributable to factors other than inputs, and the general order of magnitude of the factors included. Even though increase in education, with a generous estimate of its effects, is included in factor inputs, 63% of the increase in output per man-hour in the

---

[6] In a previous book (1962) he presented estimates for the United States for the periods 1909 to 1929 and 1929 to 1957, and in a later book (1974) extends these estimates to 1969 and elaborates them.

TABLE 10–2
Sources of Growth of National Income per Person Employed, 1950–62
(contributions to growth rate in percentage points, and index)

	United States		Northwest Europe	
Sources of Growth	Percent	Index	Percent	Index
National income per person employed	2.15	100	3.80	100
Total Factor Input	.79	37	.73	19
Capital	.60	28	.65	17
Land	−.03	− 1	−.04	− 1
Labor				
Hours of work	−.17	− 12	−.14	− 3
Age-sex composition	−.10	− 12	.03	1
Education	.49	23	.23	6
Output per unit of input	1.36	63	3.07	80
Advances of knowledge	.75	35	.76	20
Changes in the lag in the application of knowledge, in general efficiency, and errors and omissions ..	—		.56	15
Improved allocation of resources	.29	13	.68	18
Economies of scale	.36	17	.93	24
Irregularities in pressure of demand	−.04	− 2	−.01	− 0
Other			.15	4

Source: Denison (1967), Tables 21–1 and 21–3.

United States and 80% in Europe are attributed to other factors. But among those other factors, in the United States variables other than technical progress yield almost as large as contribution in the estimates as technical progress; and in the special conditions of postwar Europe, three times as large a contribution. These other variables are not added ones thrown in from the outside; rather, apart from the postwar reconstruction process, they are resultants of the growth process itself.

Hence they are neither independent of each other nor additive. They are, generally speaking, effects of the increases in per capita income and the changes in techniques resulting from capital formation and technical progress. These two remain the important originating factors in rise in output and income per capita.

Is There Residual Technical Advance?

These estimates, or their implication that there is an element in rising output that is unexplainable by economic calculus, have been challenged. Some economists, while agreeing that there are increases in productivity due to such factors as economies of scale and increase in worker efficiency associated with shorter hours, deny that there is any unexplained technical advance. They assert, that is, that technical advance is the product of investment—investment not in physical capital but in education and research. Professor Theodore Schultz, a prominent member of this school, writes (1964, pp. 136–39):

> Advance in knowledge and useful new factors based on such knowledge are all too frequently put aside as if they were not produced means of production but instead simply happened to occur over time. This view is as a rule implicit in the notion of technological change. . . . What is concealed under technological change . . . are particular (new) factors of production that are adopted and employed because it is profitable for firms to do so. . . . These new factors are produced means of production. . . .

Professor Schultz and his associates have cited as illustrations a number of cases of the high rate of return on the expenditures for various pieces of research into improved agricultural methods. These are examples of produced technical advance.

The view, in other words, is that there is no increase in total factor productivity. Output increases no faster than do inputs, properly measured.

An extreme example of this view is found in a 1967 article by Dale W. Jorgenson and Zvi Griliches. They try to show that estimates for the United States presented in a 1962 book by Denison grossly understate increases in labor and capital inputs, and that if these were appropriately measured there was very little greater increase in outputs than in inputs. However, careful criticism by Denison (1969) of their adjustments (the most important of which he termed, with convincing demonstration, "magnificent in its implausibility") brought somewhat reluctant acknowledgement of errors by the two authors. After this exchange, it appears that the concept of a significant degree of productivity increase not attributable to increase in inputs is well established for the United States, unless it is believed that innovation is simply a return to investment in research.[7]

Learning by Using

It is a more subtle point that the effects of innovation and capital formation are inextricably interwoven. Numerous examples have been cited in the literature of continuing increase in labor productivity without capital formation.[8] These are sometimes taken as indicating the independence of advance in productivity from capital formation. It may however

[7] Becker (1964) does so. His argument is tenuous, in part for the reasons indicated in Chapter 12. The Jorgenson-Griliches and Denison articles are reproduced and a rejoinder by Jorgenson-Griliches added in a 1972 Brookings Institution publication listed in the bibliography under Jorgenson.

[8] Arrow (1962) cites three. Kennedy and Thirlwall (1971), pp. 38–39, add several.

indicate something more complex. This is suggested by a bit of analysis to which little attention has been paid in the economic literature.

In a 1972 article, Emile Benoit presents a brief summary of an elaborate study of the effects of growth of defense expenditures in developing countries. The main finding that interested him is that the burden of defense expenditures seemed positively, not negatively, correlated with rates of growth in nondefense GNP. Benoit analyzed data for 44 lower income countries for the period 1960–65 and for a lesser number of countries for the period 1950–65—in each case, all of the countries for which he could get data.

Robert Dorfman (1972) commented on that article. In a multiple regression for the period 1960–65, Benoit had found a significant positive correlation of the defense burden (defense expenditures not contributed from abroad) with nondefense growth. Dorfman performed additional regressions. He found that in an analysis for the five year period, differences in the rates of domestic investment and the inflow of external resources together accounted for only 22% of the differences among countries in growth rates ($R^2 = .22$), while with defense expenditures added, R^2 rose to 0.41. But if the period 1950–65 was used, domestic investment and inflow of resources accounted for 63% of differences in growth rates, and defense expenditures added nothing to the explanation. "The hypothesis comes to mind," Dorfman wrote (p. 11), "that investment and foreign resources are indeed the effective variables that determine the growth of the civilian economy,[9] within this simple model, *but that their influence . . . is subject to considerable lags*" (my italics).

The deduction one may draw is that working with new capital equipment effectively requires a learning period much longer than has usually been assumed. If long lags are introduced, statistical studies may attribute to capital formation a considerably higher share of increase in output than has been attributed in studies not assuming such lags.

Or should the delayed increases in productivity be regarded as adjustments not to new capital equipment but to the new methods incorporated in that equipment, that is, to innovation? The question is a rhetorical one. The question is unanswerable. What the findings of the analysis seem to indicate is rather that the processes of capital formation and innovation are so related that insistence on attribution of increase in output per man-hour to one or the other obscures understanding of the process of growth.[10]

---

[9] The growth rate data excluded defense GDP.

[10] Kenneth Arrow's 1962 article, whose title is "The Economic Implications of Learning by Doing," presents an elegant exposition of the implications of the assumption that each act of capital formation is more productive than the one before it because the advances made in learning by doing are embodied in successive acts of investment.

Unproduced Innovation: The Significance of the Controversy

In a sense the statement that all technical advance is produced is trite. Of course technical advance typically results from effort. The issue is whether it is produced mechanically by investment in education and in research, as automobiles or suits of clothes are produced, so that if for example the Japanese rate of investment (gross investment between 30% and 40% of GNP) were somehow imposed on another nation that had as good an educational system as Japan, Japan's rate of economic growth would be duplicated. (It would be necessary, presumably, to believe that the differences in economic performance of, say, the Singaporeans, and Taiwanese, and the Koreans on the one hand and the Burmese and the Malays on the other hand are explainable without reference to differences in the peoples themselves.) Or whether, on the other hand, there are differences in innovational performance among nations and between different eras in time that are not explainable by a calculus of investment. From this viewpoint, the hypothesis that innovation is explainable as a product of investment seems unqualifiedly untenable. Since the human differences involved are largely those of entrepreneurship, broadly defined, they are discussed in the following chapter.

Capital Formation or Innovation: Which Leads?

If one thinks carefully about the capital-formation–innovation problem, one realizes that the estimates discussed above do not fully answer the question whether innovation has an influence entirely separate from that of capital formation. Perhaps innovation occurs only when it is induced by capital formation. Or perhaps the degree of technical progress, explained by noneconomic influences, largely determines the rate of capital formation. Can one country accomplish more with given additions to capital than another because it is more innovational? In contrasts among countries and among industries, there is some pertinent evidence.

Two students of the Japanese economy studied the relationship between investment and growth in Japan from 1890 to 1931. With few exceptions, when the growth rate rose, the amount of investment needed to yield a given increase in capacity declined.[11]

Using a regression method earlier devised by W. E. G. Salter (1960), and data by Salter, Leif Johansen (1961) analyzed the increase in productivity in 28 groups of British industries from 1924 to 1950. As between industry groups, he found that the share of the increase in productivity attributable to technical progress (i.e., not accounted for by capital

---

[11] Ohkawa and Rosovsky (1962), p. 24, cited by Leibenstein (1966), p. 20.

formation alone) was the greater, the faster the increase. K. A. Kennedy (1971) found the same to be true in Eire during the post-World War II period.[12] It is a reasonable deduction that in all three cases the rate of technical progress was the autonomous factor and the rate of capital formation the induced factor.[13]

Some nonstatistical evidence concerning the United States supports this conclusion. During the past several years the author has had systematic discussions with groups of executives of large U.S. corporations, a total of more than 100 executives. These executives have been unanimous in stating that up until the monetary stringency of 1965–66, the level of capital formation of their corporations was determined by their needs for expansion and the number of new products and processes they had evolved that seemed worth investing in. They had had available from the company's "cash flow," or had readily obtained, all of the capital they found it worthwhile to invest. When asked what they would have done if given, say, 25% more capital to invest, they answered almost unanimously that they would not have been able to make added productive investments; the capital would have been wasted. Except for executives from telephone or railroad companies, they felt that even a 1% reduction in interest rates (which is a rather large reduction) would not have altered their plans appreciably. In short, in the terms that have been used here, they felt that the rate of capital formation in their industries was wholly determined by the flow of innovation; the flow of innovation induced a flow of capital formation appropriate to introduce it.[14]

If one divides the rate of investment (the ratio of gross domestic investment to gross domestic product) by the rate of growth, one obtains the "incremental capital-output ratio" or ICOR. This ratio, discussed further in Chapter 13, is, strictly, the increase in a country's capital stock, over a period of years, divided by the increase in the country's productive capacity, expressed as output per year, during the same period. (Or,

---

[12] He found very low correlation during 1926–38, but attributed this to the unusual nature of the period. While any such explanation is suspect, his is very plausible.

[13] Johansen's conclusion may be put in another way: a small increase or decrease in capital formation is associated with a greater change in the rate of increase in productivity. However, the implication that capital formation is the controlling factor is almost certainly false, for there is no reason to believe that the availability of capital to the 28 industry groups varied in the way that would be implied. It is much more plausible that differences in the demand for capital, because of differences in technical progress among the industry groups, accounted for the differences in capital formation. Inspection of the industry groups gives no reason to assume that economies of scale account for the differing increases in productivity.

[14] In general, these men also felt that there is a limit to the results that can be produced by research. Research is important, and the volume that is useful varies in different industries, but the flow of results depends in part on the "state of the arts," and increasing research expenditures by, say, 50% will by no means bring 50% more technical advances per year.

productive capacity should be lagged slightly, to allow for the time needed to complete investment projects and put them into operation.) If the ICOR is calculated for an industry rather than an entire country, it is the ratio of the increase in the industry's capital stock to the increase in its per-year value added capacity. Since productive capacity is difficult to measure, statisticians usually measure actual output instead. If, say, $3 billion of investment in a country during a given 5- or 10-year period is associated with an increase in annual output (GDP) of $1 billion, the ICOR is 3. If the ICOR is to measure what it purports to measure, the country or industry must be operating at capacity at the beginning and end of the time period being considered, or an estimate must be made to correct for the divergence from capacity.

Figure 10-3 shows the relationship between ICORs and rates of growth in aggregate GDP in 43 countries during the decade of the 1960s. The relationship is clearly a negative one. The faster countries grow, the lower their ICORs or, the lower a country's ICOR, the faster it grows.

How shall one account for this? The most plausible explanation, it would seem, is this: the more capable innovators the people of a country

FIGURE 10-3
ICORs Related to Growth Rates, Less Developed Countries, 1960-70

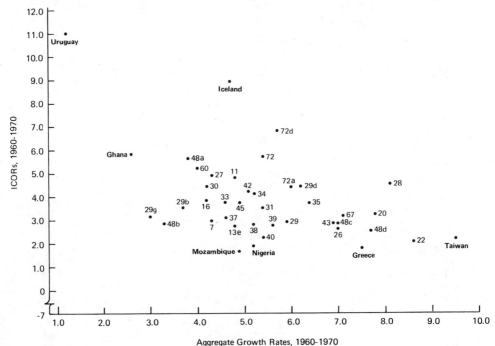

Aggregate Growth Rates, 1960-1970

Source: Economic Analyses and Projections Department, World Bank.

are, the more efficiently they will design and use new capital, and both because of this greater effectiveness (lower ICOR) and as a direct result of their greater capability in innovation, the faster will be their rate of growth.

THE LESS DEVELOPED COUNTRIES

Of course what is true in countries whose advance is at the forefront of technical knowledge is not necessarily true of technically less developed countries. Central emphasis is still placed on difficulties in capital formation by many economists studying economic development in the low-income countries. Perhaps one reason it has been assumed that difficulties in innovation may safely be neglected is that to a person who is not an engineer or innovating entrepreneur the process of innovation seems to go forward "automatically" in the West; it is something to which one need pay no attention. Another possible reason for minimizing the problem of innovation in the LDCs is the assumption that since the techniques requisite for high productivity and high levels of income have already been invented in the West, they need not be invented again, and thus no innovation is required to introduce them to the low-income countries.

Yet this seemingly obviously sensible view, like many "obviously sensible views" about technical matters, is distorted and incomplete. This will probably be clear to a reader who reflects on the difficulties in innovation in low-income countries that were discussed in Chapters 5 and 6. Innovational ability is needed for technical advance in these countries as it is for technical advance in higher income countries. Superiority in innovational capability and energy seems of great importance in Japan's amazing economic performance since the second world war. This factor seems important in the economic prowess of the Chinese in Thailand and Malaysia, who did not bring capital with them but accumulated it by their entrepreneurial efforts. In the very rapid rise in income in densely populated Hong Kong, external capital has played a larger part, but sheer entrepreneurial talent and energy also seem very important. Other less spectacular examples might be cited. It is probably that in other countries, also, differences in the effectiveness of innovation have played an important role, and one quite separate from the role played by the availability of capital.

Economic theory can go no farther than to recognize the operation of a noneconomic factor. Its explanation lies in the fields of personality theory and sociology. Since this is a text in the economics of development, and in any event relatively little explanatory theory has been developed in those other fields, little attention is paid in this book to the presumably relevant sociological and personality factors. However, the nature of explanations offered in those fields is surveyed briefly in the following chapter.

SOURCES AND NOTES TO TABLE 10-1

APPENDIX

M. Abramovitz, in "Resource and Output Trends in the United States since 1870," *American Economic Review* 46 (May, 1956), 5–23, reprinted as National Bureau of Economic Research Occasional Paper 52 (New York: 1956), divided an index of NNP in 1929 prices by an index of capital and labor inputs in 1929 prices. The lower estimate used the same NNP series, but inputs with 1869–78 weights. A shift of the NNP series to 1869–78 weights would have raised the estimate. The method used implies neutral technical progress, and involves the "remainders" method. That is, the contribution of capital is computed first, and all remaining increase in productivity attributed to technical progress. In the Thirty-Fourth Annual Report of the National Bureau of Economic Research (New York, 1954), entitled "Economic Progress and Economic Change," Solomon Fabricant presents an estimate that of the increase in output per capita in the United States from 1871 to 1951, 90% is attributable to technical progress and only 10% to capital deepening. This estimate is presumably based on a preliminary version of the data used by Abramovitz. It is subject to the criticisms of Abramovitz's estimate stated above.

R. M. Solow, "Technical Change and the Aggregate Production Function," *Review of Economics and Statistics,* 39 (August, 1957), 312–20. W. P. Hogan, "Note," ibid., 49 (1958), 407–11, and R. M. Solow, "Reply," ibid., 411–13. H. S. Levine, "A Small Problem in the Analysis of Growth," *Review of Economics and Statistics,* 42 (1960), 225–29. Solow assumes that the return per unit of labor and of capital is equal to the marginal product of each. By this method he avoids using weighted units of aggregate inputs and also avoids the assumption of a linear production function, but his results indicate that a linear function gives a good fit. He uses the "remainders" method, thus overstating the share of technical progress. Levine redid the computation, using capital formation as the residual.

B. F. Massell, "Another Small Problem in the Analysis of Growth," *Review of Economics and Statistics,* 44 (August, 1962), 330–35. The estimates first cited in Table 10–1 treat first capital formation, then technical progress, as the residual. The alternative estimate, 0.87, avoids the remainders problem by using a method which assumes that rates of increase in output and technical progress are exponential through time. This assumption does not strain the facts greatly for the period 1919–55, but would do so if extended for another decade.

BIBLIOGRAPHICAL NOTE

Except for mere reportorial discussion and lack of analysis of the essays by Jorgenson and others claiming nonexistence of a residual, Kennedy and Thirlwall (1971) presents a comprehensive analysis of the literature. The studies mentioned in the "Appendix" just above are basic early ones. Denison's three books and his exchange with Jorgenson are important. See also OECD., *The Residual Factor in Economic Growth* (1964). J. Jewkes and others (1958) and C. F. Carter and B. R. Williams (1958) probe the origins of innovation. R. S. Eckaus (1962) discusses the problem of choosing and finding appropriate technologies in LDCs.

Concerning the production function, for lucid discussions illustrated with geometric diagrams see A. W. Stonier and D. C. Hague, *A Textbook of Economic Theory* (1957) or C. E. Ferguson, *Macroeconomic Theory* (1975). R. G. D. Allen, *Mathematical Analysis for Economists* (1953), chaps. 11 and 12, has an excellent discussion in algebraic terms of the use of the production function in economic analysis. For advanced discussion of the topic, see the symposium in the 1962 issue (vol. 29) of the *Review of Economic Studies*. T. Scitovsky, "Two Concepts of External Economies" (1957), introduces the concept of pecuniary external economies.

Entrepreneurship 11

Much economic theory ignores entrepreneurship. This is because little economic theory deals with innovation. The model used—a very useful one—is one in which the "state of the arts" is constant. The national product then depends only on the absolute and relative quantities of land, labor, and capital available. However, when such a model is used for the study of economic development, one central aspect of the process is excluded by definition. Entrepreneurship is the human input into innovation. Since effective entrepreneurial behavior must be treated as being present in different degrees in different countries and at different times, a study of this behavior is a necessary part of the study of innovation.

The economist is interested primarily in the input entrepreneurs provide, rather than in their psychological characteristics or their origins. Yet it is worthwhile to delve a short distance into the social and psychological questions of what kind of men these are and why or when and where they appear. The information that can be given in a brief sketch will, it is hoped, provide a useful setting for the reader's further study of the economics of the emergence of innovation.

THE NATURE OF THE FUNCTION AND THE MEN

The entrepreneur faces the problems and takes the risks. When Yusif Sayigh (1962, Chap. 4) listed entrepreneurial functions and asked 207 heads of Lebanese business firms which four of these (or others) they regarded as their most important contributions to their firms, the two most often ranked high in their replies were conceiving the idea and designing the organization, that is, converting the idea into a functioning organization. These are the entrepreneurial functions par excellence. Where management is innovational, it is also entrepreneurial. The distinction between management and entrepreneurship becomes blurred.[1]

Changes in the Entrepreneurial Function

Entrepreneurship is not a homogeneous function, nor is it carried out in the same way in different circumstances.

As economic development proceeds, enterprises involve more equipment, larger numbers of workers, larger numbers of highly trained persons, more complex and more technical operating problems, and more complex relationships to suppliers, customers, and government. An increasing number of decisions must be delegated by the general manager to subordinate executives. Moreover, the network of decision making becomes more complex. Both the simple line organization that sufficed in small firms and the only slightly less simple line-and-staff organization that functioned well in slightly larger and more complex firms become inadequate.

A. H. Cole (1946) described the stages of rule-of-thumb, informed, and sophisticated management. Alternatively, he termed them empirical, rational, and cognitive management. It has been said that the most important quality of the executives of large business corporations today is not knowledge of the productive processes but the ability to select capable and innovational subordinates. There is some truth in this, but the point is easily exaggerated. The top manager must make complex substantive decisions, even though he may rely on subordinates for the technical capability to carry them out. Today, the most sophisticated management of large U.S. corporations increasingly involves the use of high-speed and large-capacity computers for purposes of management control. "Modern" managers can master the use of computers to yield bases for decisions involving complex situations and large masses of information. "Old-fashioned" ones cannot. A line is being drawn, not unlike the line between modern and old-fashioned craftsmen described by Geertz.

---

[1] Peter Kilby (1971) lists 13 aspects of the entrepreneurial task. Four deal with technical innovation in production, three with purchasing and marketing, and three with personnel, financial, and production management. The others are perceiving opportunities, obtaining resources, and dealing with the public bureaucracy. Students of economic development whom he cites identify technology and production management as the areas where indigenous entrepreneurial performance is least satisfactory in lower income countries. Kilby and the scholars he cites drew their conclusions from enterprises already in operation—when in the minds of the Lebanese entrepreneurs the most important functions of entrepreneurship had already been completed.

The standard texts on business organization discuss the sole proprietorship, the partnership, the corporation, and many intermediate forms of organization. The shift from one form to another is correlated to some degree with the increasing size of organization and complexity of management that accompany economic development.[2]

The Nature of the Entrepreneur

Joseph Schumpeter's statement of the motives of the entrepreneurial man was quoted in Chapter 7. He said, it will be remembered, that the entrepreneur acts "to found a private kingdom. . . . Then there is the will to conquer: the impulse to fight, to prove oneself superior to others, to succeed for the sake, not of the fruits of success, but of success itself. . . . Finally, there is the joy of creating, of getting things done, or simply of exercising one's energy and ingenuity." It is possible to sketch more fully the qualities which in combination the business entrepreneur has in greater degree than other men. The sketch is drawn from studies of innovational businessmen, in literature and in field research, and from personality theory.[3] It is entirely consistent with Schumpeter's characterization of motives.

In common with all effective entrepreneurs, the business entrepreneur trusts himself. That is, he feels that the world is amenable to his management; that if he tackles a problem with energy and thought, the result will be good. Facing a problem may raise tensions within him, but not tensions that deter him; he is drawn to problems. He finds satisfaction in facing them because each problem tests him, and he expects the result of the test to be satisfying.

In these respects, he is like all innovators. In others, he contrasts with the intellectual innovator, the conceiver of new more satisfying explanations of things (in physical or other sciences). He has no sense (the traditional man has and the intellectual may have) that working with

---

[2] In India, as the British introduced fairly large and fairly complex business organizations into a society in which the attitudes of industrial Britain did not yet exist, they created the device of the "managing agency." British or other investors not resident in India could have the direction of a venture there undertaken by a managing agency of Britons who were resident there. The somewhat peculiar phenomenon emerged of a company operating in India (or Burma) with all the usual organization of an industrial company except that it was run by a quite separate company. The same managing agency often directed enterprises in several different industries. Before the British left India, managing agencies of competent Indian industrialists had emerged. These are still prominent in India, though apparently the formation of new managing-agency contracts is now uncommon. This type of organization does not seem to have developed elsewhere. Its introduction into India met a problem of the time but perhaps at the cost of retarding the evolutionary process of economic growth.

[3] See, for example, Warner and Abegglen (1955), Abegglen and Warner (1955), Phelps Brown (1953), Fromm (1947), McClelland (1953 and 1961), Hagen (1962).

material things—with engines and materials, clean or dirty—is grubby and demeaning. Directly or vicariously, he works with his hands most of his life. Unlike the intellectual, he finds only incomplete satisfaction in working with ideas. The resolution of an intellectual inconsistency does not excite him as it does an intellectual. He derives his satisfaction from tangible, not merely mental, results.

He is flexible and pragmatic. If one method of operation of one structure of relationships does not solve his problem, he is ready to try another. He does not mind friction with others, or does not mind it so much that it inhibits him. But he is not overtly aggressive, since he needs to work with people. He likes the sense that he can operate with them in such a way that they will help him to achieve his goals. (This varies to pleasure in dominating people, an attitude that is effective in only certain specific types of entrepreneurship.)

His central satisfaction is in solving problems—material problems, and problems of relationships with other persons. This problem-solving, whether or not he recognizes the fact, is an end in itself, not merely a means to an end. He wants recognition of his success. His "reference group"—the group whose approval gives him satisfaction—is not, like that of the intellectual, some set of thinkers living, dead, or not yet born, but people around him. He wants position that gives him recognition within his organization and his business world. The position he gains is satisfying evidence that he has been a good problem-handler. He wants money, too, as evidence of his success. If his desire for position and money exist too greatly for their own sake, rather than as evidence of achievement, he is likely to become the manipulative innovator of whom Eric Fromm writes (1947). He will then be not innovative but only cunning.

There is a hazard in this portrayal of the nature of the innovational entrepreneur. It gives an impression of all or nothing. Either the entrepreneur is innovational or he is not. That is wrong. Innovation may vary from arranging a window display more attractively or making cleaning a shop floor more efficient by shortening the handle of a broom through beginning the production of artificial "bones" from the inner layer of animal hides for sale to U.S. department stores, to constructing the first crude internal combustion engine or introducing a textile factory successfully in a country without dependable power, supplies of textile fibers, or precision machine shop or foundry facilities. An entrepreneur may innovate a little, or a moderate amount, or a great deal, with regard to minor or major matters. The conception should always be of variation in degree.

The most elaborate studies of the possible relationship between personality and innovational activity have been made by D. C. McClelland. McClelland began this work by giving groups of U.S. college students "projective" tests of "achievement motivation" (also termed need for achievement, or, for brevity, *n ach*), a quality of personality which causes an individual to feel satisfaction in performance evaluated against a standard of excellence. He found significant correlation between the students' scores on these tests and their behavior in experimental situations, and also between their *n ach* scores and statements by their mothers of the tasks they expected their children to do independently at various ages. Achievement motivation refers not to desire to attain great position or fame, but to pleasure (or perhaps a reduction in one's state of anxiety) in solving problems. These results are reported in a 1953 book.

Later, McClelland attempted to obtain statistical evidence of a relationship between the degree of achievement motivation present in various societies and the economic achievement of the societies. In a later work (1961), he reports on attempts to measure the degree of achievement motivation present in various countries at various periods in history and to correlate it with economic advance in those countries. Measurement of changes in achievement motivation from one period to another in a given country was done by scoring comparable writings at different periods for evidence of this quality. The studies include, among others, ones of ancient Greece, Spain in the late Middle Ages, and England from Tudor times to the Industrial Revolution. Since the time lag that has to be assumed between change in the degree of achievement motivation and the resulting change in the pace or presence of economic advance varies greatly from one to another of these studies, the results are less than fully convincing.

In a study of achievement motivation and economic progress in the 20th century, he took as his universe all nontropical countries for which the necessary data could be obtained, except for the tiniest ones. As his measure of economic growth he used electricity production, a variable with respect to which far more precise international comparison is possible than with respect to gross product or national income. (The two periods he studied were 1929–50 and 1952–58. Total energy consumption, converted to common units, was available for many countries for the earlier period, though perhaps not at the time for the other, in United Nations publications. It is a more representative measure.) To measure achievement motivation, he had school readers scored for this quality. He then related nations' scores on achievement motivation in about 1925 with their increase in electricity production from 1929 to 1950, and scores on achievement motivation in 1950 with increase in electricity production from 1952 to 1958, and found statistically significant correlation.

This study, however, is marred by statistical weaknesses that markedly lessen the impressiveness of the conclusions. He assumed that another factor, initial level of electricity use, also affected the rate of increase in each country, but instead of doing a multiple regression with this initial level and the need achievement scores as the independent variables, he did a simple regression between initial use and rate of increase, and then a second simple regression between need achievements and the deviations. Since the two independent variables may themselves be related causally, the method may lead to invalid results. Worse, he also adjusted data for two countries with conditions that he regarded as exceptional, and, without explanation, used aggregate data for one period and per capita data for the other, and a logarithmic relationship for one period and an arithmetic one for the other. Statisticians would find unconvincing two parallel studies in which, quite unnecessarily, such differences in method were used in the regressions.

Independently of the empirical studies, one may assume that there is likely to be a significant relationship between the degree of achievement motivation present in a society and the country's rate of economic growth. If one accepts the thesis that personality is one important determinant of human behavior, this conclusion almost necessarily follows. But McClelland's attempt at statistical verification is not satisfying.

WHENCE AND WHY MEN BECOME ECONOMIC INNOVATORS

It would be wrong to conclude that men are born as innovators, or become so in infancy and childhood, and will be innovators "come hell or high water." No doubt because of lessons they draw from their early life experiences, some men will face any given situation with more self-reliance and resourcefulness than will others, and in this sense will be more innovational. But entrepreneurial behavior, like all other behavior, is a product jointly of personality and external circumstances, and the discussion in this section will consider both. Because it is not possible to consider why men become innovators without considering their positions in society, *why* and *whence* are considered jointly.

THE GROUPS WHO INNOVATE

Social Origins

Early innovating entrepreneurs do not emerge at random from all groups in a society. Rather, they come disproportionately from some one social group that is distinguishable from other groups in the society by some set of social characteristics that preceded its innovativeness.

In 17- and 18th-century France, economic innovation was clearly correlated with Huguenot religious belief. The Huguenots were middle- and upper-class townspeople, but barred by their religion and perhaps also by their bourgeois attributes from membership in or close association with the king's court.

In Russia, when in 1667, for diplomatic reasons, church ritual was revised to accord with Greek practice, the revision included the use of three fingers rather than two in making the sign of the cross. This implied equality of Christ with God the Father and God the Holy Ghost, in a trinity, an implication that was sacrilegious to millions of Russians. These "Old Believers" seceded from the church, were condemned as schismatics, and from then until the Bolshevik Revolution of 1917 were persecuted now and again with varying degrees of severity. The Old Believers were prominent in the accelerating economic growth that occurred in Russia during the last half of the 19th century. In 19th-century India, the community known as the Parsis—the name derives from their origin in Persia ten centuries earlier—was prominent far out of proportion to its numbers in industrial innovation in western India (see Ashok Desai, 1968).

In none of these cases has a statistical study been made that would quantify the relative participation of the group in innovation, but it seems clear from less precise evidence that each played a disproportionate part within its society. In other cases, the participation of a select group has been quantified.

A study by the present writer found that in the English Industrial Revolution the Protestant Dissenters provided some ten times as many innovating entrepreneurs between 1760 and 1830, in proportion to their numbers, as did the Anglicans.[4]

In a Japanese village, Clifford Geertz (1963b, p. 49) found that apart from some Chinese-owned enterprises, the firms in which the transition to manufacturing was occurring were owned and operated predominantly by Reform Muslims. In Lebanon, the shares of various religious groups in the population and among the innovating entrepreneurs (Sayigh, 1962, p. 69) were as shown in Table 11–1. In proportion to their number, Christians provide 4.5 times as many innovators as do Moslems, and Jews 13 times as many.

TABLE 11–1
Religious Affiliation of Lebanese Entrepreneurs

Group	Percent of Population	Percent of Innovating Entrepreneurs
Christian	50.0	80.2
Jewish	0.4	1.9
Moslem	44.0	16.4
Druse	5.6	1.5

[4] Hagen (1962), pp. 294–309. There is an arithmetic error in the text. The Nonconformists (Dissenters), who numbered some 7% of the population, contributed 43%, not 41%, of the English and Welsh entrepreneurs in the sample studied, and thus about 10, not 9, times as many as the rest of the population in proportion to their numbers.

In West Pakistan, in 1959, two "communities" (quasi-castes) constituting less than 0.2% of the population controlled more than 44% of the private Pakistani-owned industrial capital surveyed by Papanek (1967, p. 42).

George B. Sansom, a standard historian of Japan, states that "the organization of Japan at and following the Restoration of 1868 was in great measure the work of samurai of the lower grades." A survey of 196 corporate executives and individual business entrepreneurs of the period between 1868 and the early 20th century shows that a very large percentage came from the "outer" clans—those whom the Tokugawa had held in a socially inferior position for two and one half centuries—and investigation of a smaller sample shows that among those whose father's social rank could be determined, lower rank samurai of the outer clans and "wealthy peasants" (descendants of men of erstwhile rural samurai rank) were common. (During the Tokugawa era some "ordinary" peasants became relatively wealthy. The reference to a special class of "wealthy peasants" is not to these, but to the "rustic samurai" of the previous period, who became classed as peasants by the Tokugawa, and who were local community leaders.) For lack of data, no stronger statement can be made, but here too the suggestion of the incomplete data is that the economic innovators came in large proportions from two of the lesser elite whose members had felt repressed socially (who had been supervisors, if not performers, of labor with the hands).

The major settled areas of Colombia are divided into three regions, Cundinamarca, also known as the Sabana (the area around Bogota), Antioquia, and the Valley of the (Upper) Cauca. They are separated by rugged mountain ranges over which until after World War II there was only poor transportation except by air. Historically, the Bogota area has had much the most and closest contact with Europe. The Bogotanos, who historically formed the political and social elite, did—and still do—look down upon the Antioqueños as rustic and somewhat crude, yet the Antioqueños, like the business people of the other regions, claimed to be of Spanish stock little tainted by mixture with Indian blood. Hence they too were "elite." A gradual acceleration of economic growth occurred in Colombia at the turn of the 20th century until shortly after World War II. The writer surveyed the history of all nonfinancial private business concerns in the three regions shown in a 1956 census of industry as employing more than 100 workers. One hundred ten of the 141 enterprises for which information was obtained were founded by "Old Colombians" (a term that excludes both foreign firms and those founded by recent immigrants or not so recent immigrants regarded as still "foreign"). Of the 110, 75 or 68%, were founded by Antioqueños, who in 1905 constituted about 40% of the population. In proportion to population, more than three times as many Antioqueños became entrepreneurs as Old Colombians of other stock.[5]

As against this handful of cases—including important cases—there are no studies known to the writer showing a more or less random distribution of early innovating entrepreneurs among the population.

If one asks why these groups had turned to crafts or crafts-cum-trading work, gradually became established in it, and then burst out at a later period in industrial innovation, various ad hoc partial explanations can be offered for various groups, but the one common quality that suggests a general explanation is this: all were groups of neither plebians nor social leaders but rather of lesser elites and, as I shall indicate a few paragraphs below, lesser elites who were not fully accepted socially by the leaders of their societies and who had reason to feel unjustly or unreasonably derogated.

Economic Background: Occupational Origins

In all but the most primitive societies there are many small craftsman-traders (who sell their own products) and a smaller number of larger trader-financiers. It is to be expected that entrepreneurs in developing commerce would come largely from these groups, probably mainly from the latter. Few relevant studies have been done. In his survey of business enterprisers in present-day Lebanon, Sayigh (1962, pp. 75–76) found that among the fathers of those engaged in finance, a field in which Lebanon has specialized, 44% had been traders, 25% had been professional men, and 6% had been "financiers." The traders may of course have been trader-financiers. Among the fathers of those engaged in providing services, 29% had been traders, 16% industrialists, 12% professional men, and 43% had been engaged in various other occupations.

Many industrial entrepreneurs too emerged from trading families. A study of the 47 British innovators in manufacturing mentioned in Ashton's *The Industrial Revolution* (1948) for whom information concerning their fathers' occupation was available showed that 17 of the fathers had themselves been manufacturing proprietors, 10 artisans or laborers in industry, 12 cultivators, 4 professional men, and only 4 in trade.[6] However, Ashton's study deals mainly with heavy industry and the textile

---

[5] Hagen (1962), 364–65. One hundred sixty-one firms were included in the total sample. Seven of these were elsewhere than in the three main regions. No information was obtained about 13. Of the 141, 9 were subsidiaries of foreign companies, and 29 had been founded by persons regarded as of foreign origin. Since there is a tendency in Colombia to term a person an Antioqueño if *either* of his parents is Antioqueño, the figures given in the text somewhat overstate Antioqueño participation, but the correction on this account would not be great.

[6] Hagen (1962), p. 302. Information could not be obtained concerning the occupations of the fathers of 25 other innovators in manufacturing.

industry, thus omitting consumers goods industries such as brewing, concerning which we have no data. Just over one third of the fathers of the industrialists surveyed in Sayigh's study in Lebanon were themselves industrialists; 31% had been in trade and 35% in various other occupations. Alexander (1960) determined the preceding occupation of 63 industrialists of the Aegean region of Turkey. After weighting his stratified sample so that it more accurately represents the total group of industrialists, he found that less than one tenth (8%) had inherited their industrial position from their fathers; 43% had themselves been in trade before moving to industry, 19% had been farmers, 17% craftsmen or skilled workers, and 12% had other occupational backgrounds. The movement of some members of Iranian landowning families directly into manufacturing industries has been mentioned. From this scattered evidence it is clear that trade is an important source, but that no simple generalizations concerning other occupational origins of industrial entrepreneurs are warranted.[7] And concerning trade as a source, the statistics are ambiguous. It has been asserted that "a commercial revolution must precede the industrial revolution." The sketch in Chapter 5 of innovation in trade in Indonesia shows the close relationship between change in trade and change in manufacturing. But a "trading family" from which an industrial innovator emerges may be either a family that for several generations has consisted of "great traders" or one whose head two or three generations earlier was a craftsman-trader, a son and perhaps grandson expanding the scope of activity, and a member of the next generation innovating as an industrialist. The route in England was often the latter over a period of two or three generations. By steady expansion of activity in an energetic family, the son or grandson of an artisan or small craftsman-trader had become a large merchant in London or one of the other cities who obtained his goods by "putting out," that is, supplying materials and capital to craftsmen who made the products he sold, and he or his son established a true factory. It seems likely that a more or less similar route would be revealed in many instances in other countries in which the family origin is listed simply as "trade."

Common Qualities

We now have seven cases: England, France, Russia, India, Japan, Colombia, and Pakistan. (I omit Java, since the innovation there was petty and was in trade rather than in production in the layman's sense of

---

[7] Harris (1967, Chap. 8) shows that in Nigeria, of a sample of 262 industrial entrepreneurs, the fathers of 25.1% had been subsistence farmers and 19.4% cash-crop farmers, 21.7% traders, 17% self-employed artisans or contractors, and 3.8% employed artisans. The remaining 13% were of scattered occupational background. However, Nigeria was never a peasant society, and no deduction concerning likely or possible trends in such societies should be drawn from these data.

that word.) If one asks what common qualities distinguish the seven groups who led their countries into innovation in a great diversity of circumstances from their fellows in the society, or from others who might have been expected to be innovators, certain answers quickly suggest themselves. There were distinguishing characteristics.

First, they were native. This is worth mentioning because there is a thesis that innovators will be "outsiders," aliens in the society. This was not true in these societies. As will be noted a few paragraphs farther on, these groups were outsiders in a sense, somewhat estranged from the leaders of their societies, but in race, residence, and culture they were flesh of the flesh, bone of the bone of their societies.

Second, they were not the economic or social leaders in their societies who had the most wealth available for investment and, in most cases, the greatest opportunities to be acquainted with technical advances in other countries. This opportunity is not relevant to the cases of the Huguenots of France or the Protestant Dissenters of England, who were very early innovators and had little to learn from abroad, and who moreover had as close contacts as anyone in their societies with new methods that may have developed in the Low Countries. (English traders learned of the spinning and weaving of cotton in India; English entrepreneurs then seized upon the knowledge.) In the case of Pakistan, the facts are not clear. The Parsis in India may have been in better position than others to learn of foreign developments because of their contacts with the British East India Company—though one must ask why they more than others chose to make those contacts. In Russia the industrialists to whom the tsar had granted monopolies, in Japan the Tokugawa, in Colombia the Bogotanos (and in Java the wealthier elites)—all these had much more contact with foreign countries than did the groups who became the innovators. And in all seven countries except perhaps for India, top economic and social groups were better placed to provide or obtain capital for investment if they had wished.

Third, with slight qualification the innovating groups were ones whose members were used to working with their hands or to supervising such workers. They did not object to "getting their hands dirty." That is, they did not have the disdain of traditional elites for manual labor. This was directly and obviously true in France, Russia, Colombia, England, and probably India. It may seem untrue of Japan, insofar as the innovators were samulai, but in fact they were lesser samurai (of the outer class), whose duty it had been to supervise the estates of their lords. In Pakistan, this familiarity with hand labor may be less true, but at least the innovators in industry—many or most of them in jute production—were working with materials with which they were familiar and with whose processing they had been concerned even if they themselves had not been processors.

To some observers, this is sufficient explanation; the innovators were persons doing things that were extensions of what they were accustomed to do. But though this may be a necessary condition, it is not a sufficient one. For there were many other members of the same societies with this same background who did not become early innovators or far fewer of whom became early innovators: non-Huguenots in France and non-Dissenters in England; Tokugawa samurai in Japan; producers on the Sabana and in the Valley in Colombia, Pakistani not of these two tiny business communities, probably non-Old Believers in Russia, and so on. And in other countries groups with about the same experience in production did not. Other forces must also have been at work.

Fourth, then, every one of the seven groups we are considering had for generations been derogated in its own society—looked down upon unjustly and unreasonably, in their own eyes—by the social leaders of the society. The innovating groups were, in a sense, "outsiders," but they were native outsiders. They were all protestant dissenters, though not all Protestant Dissenters. This is the most striking common quality apart from their work experience. In England, Protestantism had arisen from a stream of protest at abuses and immorality in the church that was trickling and then flowing more strongly from the 14th century—and earlier—on. Langland's *Piers Plowman*, Wycliffe's attacks on the "Caesarian clergy," John Ball and the other itinerant "poor priests"—all these were of the 14th century. In the late 15th and early 16th centuries, Colet, More, and Erasmus wrote. Out of these beginnings Protestantism gradually arose. And throughout its existence its adherents were ridiculed, "harried," and persecuted by the elites of the society whom they, the Protestants, thought ungodly.

Throughout a somewhat similar history, in France the Huguenots were persecuted and ultimately destroyed by force of arms. In Russia, from the 17th century on the persons who clung to what they believed the true faith, the only faith that would bring them salvation, had been belittled and often harshly persecuted. In Japan, the traditional rights of the outer clans had been denied them from the time of the ascendancy of the Tokugawa soon after 1600; they were subjected to regulations and constraints that were undignified and humiliating. In Colombia, the Bogotanos expressed their contempt for their crude and crass fellow countrymen, the Antioqueños, who were in fact of the same Spanish stock that was the Bogotanos' claim to eliteness.

In India, the Parsis, who fled from persecution in Persia at the end of the 7th century, were uprooted again in the 14th by Muslim invaders of northwest India and are found in the 15th in a different area, where they were uneasy intruders who made their living increasingly in "tax farming, shipbuilding, shipping, and trading" (Desai, 1968), and who, though they became well-to-do, undoubtedly felt the condescension and contempt with which the landed elite looked upon their cultural differences and the grubby, demeaning fields in which they worked. The Pakistan innovators were survivors of an uneasy history in Hindu communities in India, in which they had felt the derogation of the larger community.

It is surely not coincidence that groups whose members historically have worked with their hands are groups that are looked upon with some disdain by traditional leaders. Members of the group are derogated because they work at distasteful work. But it is also true that members of the group work at occupations distasteful to traditional elites because, since they are looked down upon, they are not admitted to the channels of social advance in traditional fields. The causation is mutual; research to determine which came first, for example in England after the Norman Conquest, would be hopelessly intricate. But it is clear in history that the two often go together.

That innovation is associated with a sense of social derogation explains an aspect of innovation in England early in the Industrial Revolution that might otherwise be puzzling. A number of large and titled landed pro-prietors were early innovators, though not in industry. They innovated in agriculture, and at least one, later, in mining. On examination of these cases it turns out that these individuals, though members of the titled country elite, were not a part of the inner titled group associated with the king's court, and were looked down on by the court elite. They too suffered from a sense of derogation.

Lastly, in five of the countries the cultural differences between the groups that produced innovators and their fellows in their societies included religious differences. The innovators were Huguenots in France, Dissenters in England, Old Believers in Russia, Parsis in India, Muslims in Pakistan whose history was in Hindu India. There appears to be nothing unique and common in the substance of these religions, but only in the relationship of their adherents to the dominant religion: dissent. And in two cases, there was no overt religious difference. The outer clans in Japan were apparently as Buddhist as the Tokugawa. In Colombia, the Antioqueño innovators were as piously Catholic as other Colombians, though it seemed to the writer and a fellow research worker that there was a subtle difference in attitude, symbolized by the plaques or pictures of Christ on the cross on the walls of their offices. Without exception, each Colombian executive in 1958 had such a representation hanging on the wall behind his desk. Many of those in Bogota were subdued in style. The color tones were muted. In Medellin, central city of Antioquia, in more cases the flesh was stark white, the blood that flowed from Christ's wounds bright red. The pronouncement of the religion was, so to speak, more garish. Perhaps it was simply less self-conscious, and without "art."[8]

---

[8] An unpublished study indicates a statistically significant correlation between the percentage of non-Catholic population in Latin American countries in 1960 and the

EXPLANATIONS

Three Theories

Out of these facts, perhaps a theory can be built.

Weber. A well known sociopsychological thesis concerning innovation by the Protestant Dissenters derives from their religious "ethic." In 1904–5 Max Weber wrote his *The Protestant Ethic and the Spirit of Capitalism* (English translation, 1930). He argued that the Protestant Dissenters who brought about the Industrial Revolution in England were motivated not merely by a desire for profits but by an ethic, inculcated in them by their religion, which caused them to work continually, compulsively, and systematically to increase production. This systematic (Weber says "bureaucratic") and ascetic endeavor, and not the pursuit of profit, is the true "spirit of capitalism."

The pursuit of gain is as old as man himself, but this new spirit appeared with Calvinist religious doctrine. The pertinent belief, the Calvinist doctrine of predestination, was that whether each individual will be saved was determined by God before the individual was born, and that a man whom God has elected to salvation is also ordained to live a good life while on earth. Calvinism also taught, Weber asserts, that man's duty to God is to glorify Him by making His earth fruitful. Because of these two beliefs, Weber argues, the individual was driven compulsively to augment production to relieve his perpetual anxiety that he might not be among the elect, that is, to reassure himself by bringing forth "good fruit" that he was "a good tree."

Some Dissenters adopted a softer variant of Calvinism. They accepted the idea that no man is worthy of salvation, and that some are saved purely through God's mercy. However, they believed that the choice is made by God during a man's lifetime. No man can live perfectly and thus earn salvation, but by a good life a man can "put himself in the way of grace," that is, increase the probability that God's grace will fall on him. Weber argued that a man who believed this would also strive unceasingly. Weber advanced arguments, of varying degrees of persuasiveness, to explain why other groups of Calvinists did not react as the Protestant Dissenters of England did.

---

level of per capita income. The study was first suggested and done by Eduardo Garcia, with data for the late 1950s. It was later done more elaborately by the writer. The elaboration consisted of doing a multiple regression between population, number of non-Catholics, and aggregate GNP, to avoid the remote possibility of spurious correlation because for each country the same denominator, population, appears both in per capita GNP and percent of non-Catholics. One should not take this study alone as strong evidence of the importance of either the religion or dissent. Protestantism is associated with urbanism. Urbanism may conceivably be the cause of both Protestantism and growth.

His argument is incomplete in the sense that he offers no explanation of why one group of men and not another should have happened to accept the Calvinist tenets. This is certainly as great a mystery as why these tenets should have had the effect that he posits. But the thesis he does propose is in itself of great interest.

But Weber's empirical evidence will not withstand intense scrutiny. Kurt Samuelsson (1961) has attacked almost every piece of evidence advanced by Weber: data that Calvinists in Germany sent their sons in greater numbers than did Catholics to technical schools, his thesis that the duty of working ascetically and making the earth fruitful is uniquely a Calvinist tenet, and his claim that such a doctrine is systematically advanced in Dissenter preachings. In tone, Samuelsson's essay is an ex parte attack rather than a dispassionate treatise, but with one exception his criticisms are accurate.

For example, one main part of Weber's argument is a summary of the writings of Richard Baxter, a leading writer of advice for laymen of the dissenting sects, especially from Baxter's *Christian Directory*, where he claims the Protestant ethic is vividly set forth. The writer has read the *Christian Directory* carefully. Weber's quotations are correct, but the brief passages he selects do not present a systematic summary of the book. Baxter gave advice concerning almost any topic, to Christians in almost any situation in life. His advice is discursive. The Devil could cite the *Christian Directory* for his purpose as readily as he could the Bible. No one not already acquainted with the "Protestant ethic" would be likely to derive it from the *Christian Directory*.

Yet the statistical association between Dissent and economic innovation in England is far too strong to be dismissed as coincidence.[9] There is a connection, even though Weber's explanation of its nature is not acceptable.

McClelland. McClelland concluded in his 1953 book that achievement motivation, which causes economic innovation, is inculcated in early childhood, and specifically is the greater, the greater the insistence of parents on early independence by children. He recognized in a 1961 book that the matter is more complex. Insistence on independent achievement before the child is capable of it results in anticipation of failure by the child, and he will avoid facing it. Low achievement motivation is bred into him. There are many other complexities.[10] Nevertheless, the evidence is strong that the child learns, quite unconsciously, early in life,

---

[9] Samuelsson denies that the Protestant Dissenters contributed disproportionately to innovation during the Industrial Revolution. He bases the denial on the grossly inaccurate undocumented estimate that Dissenters constituted half of the population of England. As noted above, a better estimate is 7% (see Hagen, 1962, pp. 304–9).

[10] See, e.g., the article "Socialization" (by Irving L. Child), in the *Handbook of Social Psychology*, vol. 2.

the patterns of behavior that are safest and most rewarding, and that this learning greatly influences his adult behavior. Thus McClelland's general point is much more solidly based than his specific formulation of it. His only attempt, however, to explain why the sort of childhood environment that would inculcate higher than average achievement motivation appears more frequently in some societies or some social groups than others was his suggestion that the Protestant Ethic caused innovation, not because the dogma drove men to unceasing toil to prove their worth, but because the soberness and sternness of the Protestant attitude toward life led to early independence training for children. The speculation is permissible.

Withdrawal of Status Respect. A broad cultural argument concerning the origins of innovative entrepreneurship in traditional societies, consistent with the facts about innovating groups summarized above, has been advanced by the present writer (1962). The argument asserts that the personality typical in traditional societies, the hierarchical and authoritarian social systems of those societies, and traditional economic conditions interlock to create a system in quasi-stable equilibrium. In the rather authoritarian home environment of infancy and childhood, initiative by the child brings not reward but rebuke or restraint. The child learns to avoid anxiety by not using his initiative. Rather, he waits for directions.

This environment thus inculcates a personality in which attacking problems, except in certain very narrow spheres, arouses anxiety. Moreover, since there is little self-reliance, depending on a hierarchy of social authority is satisfying, as is being able to direct the individuals below one in the hierarchy not by virtue of having shown one's competence but by virtue of one's authority. Hence there is little innovation in techniques or in social structure. Personality, social structure, and economic limitations are mutually supporting and perpetuating. The society is in a quasi-steady state, a noninnovational one.

The problem is then posed how change may come about from within the society. It is suggested that an important factor is some historical accident (usually, accession of a new group to power, but also certain other types of events) that causes a change in the behavior of the top elites, so that middle level or lower elite groups feel that their performance in the society is being curbed, their status no longer fully respected. The cases of Russia, England, Japan, and Colombia are examined, and it is argued that such an historical change occurred in each. It is argued that the resulting social tensions have two results, among others: (1) Rejection by members of the derogated groups, over a period of several generations, of some values of the top elites who now are behaving improperly. Since the derogating groups are traditional, the effect is partial rejection of traditional values. (2) Over a sequence of generations, there is less consistent control of children in the homes of the derogated groups, largely because of withdrawal of fathers into their own problems and anxieties. As a result, children are freer to use their initiative, and in certain circumstances which are sketched in presenting the theory, some of the children of succeeding generations become much more innovative. In time, then, individuals of above-average self-reliance and innovative ability, chafing at the unreasonable condescension of the top elites toward them, casting about for ways of proving their worth (to themselves as much as to the derogating top elites), and willing to get ahead in occupations which the traditional elites spurn, gain success economically by technical innovation.[11]

The main claims of the broad thesis to consideration are: (*a*) It offers an explanation of the prolonged persistence of traditional hierarchical and authoritarian political structure throughout the world's history—a better explanation than the dubious one that small groups of top elites could preserve a hierarchical social structure merely by force for centuries or several millennia. (*b*) There is a modest amount of empirical evidence of home environments and child training in traditional societies that is consistent with the model, and ample social-psychological evidence of the importance of early childhood environment for adult behavior. (*c*) The thesis is consistent with the facts about innovating groups summarized in this chapter.

However, the whole schema is drawn with such a broad brush that at best it is suggestive. Except for quantitative evidence of the role of

---

[11] It is important to realize what is not being said here. It is not being said that any derogated group will turn to economic innovation. It is being said that any derogated group will gradually turn away from the values of its derogators. If the derogators are traditional, and economic prowess is a promising channel of escape from their derogation, then the derogated may turn to economic activity of sorts which the traditionalists look on with distaste. But if the derogators are themselves businessmen, the derogated group may turn away from business. It is believed by some analysts that this latter effect constitutes a bar of importance to economic growth in some ex-colonial societies. Native groups were severely derogated by their colonial conquerors. The conquerors were economic as well as political masters, and the native individuals (unconsciously) associated satisfaction in economic life with contempt for them, their race and culture and values. By accepting the economic values of their masters, they would also be accepting a conception of themselves as worthless. So in psychological self-defense they rejected the modern values of their conquerors and clung compulsively to the only values that seemed to give them worth, traditional (and anti-innovational) values and attitudes. So the thesis runs. It may be a partial explanation of ineffective economic performance in India, Burma, Indonesia, and a number of African states. In any event, the precise nature of the principle stated in the text must be noted.

It is a converse of this principle that a minority group so completely and ruthlessly suppressed by an alien majority that no avenue of escape whatever seems open may simply relapse into inertia. Given sturdy enough personality, however, some of its members may turn to inner achievement, which can be blocked by no external force. This face may be an element in the achievements in philosophy and mathematics of European Jews at the beginning of the modern era.

derogated groups of lower elites as innovators, the evidence offered is historical rather than statistical.[12]

Aliens versus Natives: Great Traders

Why have alien groups nowhere led a society into continuing technical progress? Why have the great traders nowhere done so, except perhaps in the case of Pakistan? The two circumstances are related.

Aliens entering a new society have usually been traders, partly because it is easier to set oneself up in trade in a new country than to fit into the complex of social relationships involved in industry or agriculture, perhaps also because trading and finance were more congenial to the attitudes of persons who pulled up their roots in their home culture and set out to make a life for themselves within an established alien culture. Perhaps they did not enter industry because of those attitudes. But in any event a sufficient reason may be that they feared to. Aliens are often fair game. Aliens who are becoming well-to-do are uniformly regarded as exploiters. Capital embodied in fixed equipment can readily be levied on or destroyed by a dominent majority that turns against the aliens.

If a native group, too deeply rooted in the culture to be regarded as alien—too like the other members of the society in history, dress, manners, traditions, even if deviant in some respects—if such a group forges ahead economically in fields that were traditionally distasteful, a problem is created for the rest of the society. The derogators have now become inferior in an important respect—economically. A familiar principle of sociology comes into play, the principle that it is relative status, not absolute position, that moves men. The erstwhile superior majority presumably now chafes; some members of it will see the newer sort of activity as not so demeaning after all; and the society as a whole may follow its minority into economic growth. To follow in a new field is not so difficult as to enter upon it, and the less innovative majority may readily join the process.

An illustrative instance of the importance of relative status is cited by Epstein (1962). When one of two companion Indian villages received irrigation in the 1930s, whereas the other, on somewhat higher ground, did not, because the water would not flow up to it, little change occurred in the fortunate village during the next two decades except multiple

---

[12] In this model, social and technical innovation must come from disturbances in the social structure which through their effects on home environment lead to change in personality. Some writers have assumed that I was thereby arguing that innovation cannot occur in any society without change in personality. This is not my view. The evidence of innovation in some circumstances because of the destruction of old ruts, and without prior change in personality, is fairly strong. Only in the model sketched, which I think is an important one but which I do not regard as encompassing all of the relevant causal factors of life, must the contrary be true.

cropping and much increase in income. But the residents of the "dry" village acted as though the relative reduction in status goaded them to innovational fury. Economic, social, and political change had burst out in that village by the mid-1950s.

Innovational activity because of insecurity of a previously satisfying status may explain the movement of Iranian landed groups directly into industrial activity (mainly, the processing of agricultural products), a move that elsewhere has been rare.[13] Agricultural innovation by the German Junkers after the middle of the 19th century may have a similar explanation.

But if a group that can readily be regarded as purely alien forges ahead, there is an easier route to restore the relative status that is regarded as just. Unalloyed envy may express itself. The native majority is not likely to emulate the alien group that is becoming superior; it is likely to crush it.

Great traders were usually members of an alien group, and insofar as they were what has just been said applies to them. Chinese in Southeast Asia, Marwaris here and there throughout India, Marwaris and other Indians in Southeast Asia and East Africa, individuals from the Middle East in many Latin American and African countries, Jews in many countries throughout history provide examples. But many studies by anthropologists testify that even where they were native (as in China and Japan), the great traders were a group apart. Chapter 5 described the differences between the motives and attitudes of bazaar traders and of other producers, and the difficulties bazaar traders would have in changing to a role in which they were in constant supervision of subordinates. The discussion in that chapter described also their function outside of the web of social obligations that surround other economic transactions in a village. That description, enlarged, applies to great traders. The great traders seem to have a different image of the world. They are regarded as crass and unproductive by their fellows; they distrust those fellows; and they are not likely to move into the noncommercial world.

The bar of course is not absolute. Individuals from every social group have been innovators in any field. Papanek notes that the two tiny Pakistani business "communities" that had become owners of 44% of the country's industrial capital by 1959 were trading communities. In the disturbed conditions of the new nation pure traders may have acted more boldly than elsewhere. In any event, considerations such as those

---

[13] The Iranian change is discussed briefly by Meyer (1959, Chap. 3). He suggests that it occurred because the threat of land and tax reform made insecure the traditional landed haven, and because the oil consortium agreement of 1954 and the Iranian seven-year plan gave promise of expanding markets for Iranian industry. The general pressure of the outside world on the Middle East, with its resulting psychological unease, may also be mentioned.

sketched just above probably explain why great traders, even though they have the capital and the information necessary for innovation in other fields, have nowhere unless in Pakistan led a society into even short-lived economic growth.

Groups, Not Individuals

Economic growth requires innovation by many individuals, not isolated single men, for no more complex reason than that if an isolated individual becomes an economic innovator, this in itself will not be enough to lead to growth. However, one added comment is in point about the fact that the many individuals appear within a single distinctive social group. A single individual who defies the conventions of the society, who does things that are looked upon as gauche, ungentlemanly, will be squashed by the social disapprobation. The social pressure will deter most such deviants. For a successful social movement, the individual needs the protection of approval of a group important to him. Hence turning away from old ways of behavior to economic innovation in "grubby" fields occurs within groups such as the Protestant Dissenters, the Old Believers, the Antioquenos, and so on.

This comment needs qualification. Individuals outside of these groups were also early innovators. The groups provided disproportionate numbers of innovators, not all of them. But it is likely not only that each innovator carried within his head his own "reference group" (a suggestion that conflicts with that just stated) but also that the existence of the social group active in the new field provided psychic support to other individuals.

Social Mobility and Social Blockage

It has often been stated that the availability of upward social mobility is conducive to economic prowess. The generalization is incomplete. Social blockage as well as the openness of social channels is required to create incentive. If traditional ways of gaining increased social status are not open because the derogated group is not accepted into them, or is not accepted socially even if it enters them, and if in addition an economic channel is open and there is no institutional bar to gaining wealth and thereby at least one sort of status, then the blockage plus opportunity are conducive to economic prowess.

There was a good deal of upward mobility through traditional channels in England in the later medieval and early modern period. Yeomen became larger landowners; larger landowners became titled; service of the court might bring recognition; and so on. The names of land registers show considerable "circulation of the elite." But the Protestant Dissenters were at such odds with the top elites that such channels would have brought little reward to them. In one of two ways—nonacceptance into traditional channels, or refusal of the recognition accorded others in those channels—social blockage of traditional channels must be present if the availability of other less highly regarded channels is to be attractive.

Education and Entrepreneurship

Formal education is likely to do little to make an individual more self-reliant or less anxious when he faces new problems—in technical terms, to increase his "need achievement." The inculcation of mental concepts relating to logical thought or decision making apparently has relatively little such effect. Differences among individuals in this quality have been fairly deeply rooted in them by the process of socialization before formal schooling begins. The individual's tendencies are reinforced and elaborated or, on the other hand, confused, contradicted, and blunted by the models of behavior set by instructors and other seniors during the individual's school years, by his friendly and admiring or distrustful and hostile relationships with these mentors—mainly by whether he gains a sense that they value him—by his sense of success or the lack of it in relationships of various types with his school fellows, and by various other such influences. These experiences during the school years are almost certainly less important than those of the preschool years in determining which way "the tree will incline," but they are important. But there is little support in modern psychology for the notion that entrepreneurial attitudes can be taught by formal instruction.

But education gives the entrepreneur more knowledge, better tools, acquaints him with a wider range of alternatives. In these ways an increase in education of pertinent types increases a man's capability to conceive of and establish new productive ventures or widens the range of ventures which he is well fitted to conceive of and establish.

Since increase in the quality of labor through education is discussed in the chapter that follows, no more need be said here.

Old Ruts or New Actions

Lastly, it has often been noted that men often innovate with great effectiveness when their old ways of behaving are no longer possible—when, as the older anthropologists say, the "crust of custom" is broken. If one cannot tread along in an old rut, or if doing so no longer yields the former satisfying results, then if one has a certain degree of self-reliance, one will consider how to act most effectively.

This thesis implies that without any change whatever in their degree of innovativeness or in economic circumstances, where derogation develops groups will innovate. On the other hand, perhaps it is a mild version of another form of the same thesis that continuous expansion of the market, or even a one-time discontinuous increase, may but will not necessarily spur innovation.

A. J. Meyer (1959, Chap. 3) attributes the rise in entrepreneurial activity in the Middle East during the three decades following 1930 in part to the depression in Europe, the expulsion of individuals from various countries, and the Arab-Israeli war. In Colombia, a major shift of capital and entrepreneurship from commerce to industry occurred in Antioquia between 1905 and 1915, when the opening of roads and the Panama Canal greatly reduced the profit opportunities in commerce.[14]

That migrants to America moved to an area in which the social structure and economic facilities of their homelands were entirely lacking may account in part for their innovative vigor in American colonial and United States history. (The bountiful natural resources waiting for them must also be given their due.) The Hindu refugees from Pakistan and the Muslim refugees from India have both been exceptionally effective business innovators, even though each group settled among ethnic fellows, so that the minority thesis mentioned above does not apply.[15] The innovational vigor of immigrants, other than lower economic class immigrants, to a society already well structured has been noted in various other places as well. It has been argued that the physical destruction by bombing in Germany and Japan, and the demonstrated nonviability of a previous way of life in Germany, France, Italy, and Japan, may be important causes of the rapid rate of technical progress in those countries since World War II. The achievement of the three European countries may be contrasted with the relatively poor rate of rise in productivity in Britain during the same period. The British social system scored well during the war, so that old ruts seemed satisfying after the war. Though the circumstances are sufficiently complex so that any dogmatic opinion is unwarranted, this thesis about one important strand in the causation is plausible.

THE INSTITUTIONAL FRAMEWORK

For Whom Do They Innovate?

The conception commonly expressed in Western writings of a generation or more ago, that an individual will function efficiently in economic endeavors only if he is working in a private enterprise to further his

---

[14] On the broad plain of the Sabana, the erstwhile traders turned to a landed life; in the Valle (around Cali), for reasons that are not immediately obvious, they sank into relative obscurity: Hagen (1962), pp. 374–76.

[15] Since Papanek (1967, Chap. 2) notes that certain groups of Muslims already in West Pakistan have also been effective innovators, one should not stress the effect of migration exclusively.

individual interests, has been proved false by history. Depending on his view of the world and the circumstances of his life, the entrepreneur may act effectively on behalf of himself, his family, his community, his country, some other social group, or the business organization to which he is attached.

The family-centered firm is ubiquitous in nonindustrial societies. The phrase refers not merely to a firm run for the financial benefit of the family—that could be said of most small U.S. firms—but one managed (usually) by the senior family member, that depends on relatives for its capital (though of course it may also borrow from banks when well established), and that draws its managerial members only from among relatives.

The patrimonial management[16] of the family firm has often been attacked as inimical to innovation. The most important criticisms made are that obligations to one's relatives force one to dissipate one's capital in loans or gifts to them, and to employ incompetents as managers. Associated, it is suggested, are refusal to delegate authority, hence neglect of foremanship, and stress on safety and security that causes excessive caution in evaluating even small risks. Landes (1949, 1954) has sketched the degree to which the desire to preserve the family patrimony has made the managers of French family firms cautious to the point of being noninnovational. Many writers have noted similar phenomena in low-income countries.

Yet the criticism is, as a minimum, too sweeping, for wherever economic innovation gets under way widely in a country, family firms, which are also family-oriented, have been innovational. For until economic development has proceeded some distance, there is no other form of private indigenous economic organization. Wayne Nafziger (1969) concluded from a study of Nigerian entrepreneurs that the support of the extended family helped a would-be entrepreneur to obtain apprenticeship training and to establish a firm, but that the demands of the family upon him hindered his use of the capital he accumulated to expand the firm.

Of course, some of the attitudes mentioned above, and others related to them, may prevent innovations. They are aspects of a country's culture. Aversion to yielding authority to subordinates, inability to arrange effective foremanship, anxiety in the face of risk, and overly high valuation of the security of not changing practices are characteristics of traditional and authoritarian cultures, characteristics that would exist even if family firms were somehow outlawed. Among the attitudes common in such societies are the priority of the moral duty to care for one's kin, which makes conflicting commitments to non-kin subsidiary, and, correlatively,

---

[16] Harbison and Myers (1959, Chap. 4) classify the sources of management authority into patrimonial, political, and professional.

the fact that persons outside of one's kin or "pseudo kin" group are likely to take advantage of one if they can do so to the benefit of their own group. Where such values prevail, patrimonial management in the family firm is not an obstacle to the innovational conduct of business but a necessary condition for it. I have written earlier (1957):

> Where one can neither trust a stranger or an acquaintance as a business associate, nor persuade him to lend one money, then the extended family may be a necessary source of capital and a necessary bond between business associates. Its abolition would not modernize the society; in the circumstances it would merely paralyze large-scale relationship.

Khalaf and Shwayri (1966), noting the importance of the family-oriented firm in Lebanon, argue this side of the case persuasively. In a culture such as that of Lebanon, they state, property and kinship create a sense of responsibility and of loyalty, necessary for the efficient conduct of business, that would not otherwise exist.

The United States is usually cited as the country that extols the virtues of private enterprise. And though various other countries could also be cited, economic development by private enterprises has succeeded so well in the United States that the strength of support for private enterprise is not surprising.

In U.S. corporations there is a high degree of loyalty to the organization as such. In *The Organization Man* (1956), William H. Whyte, Jr. has painted a picture of corporations demanding submissive conformity of their officials. This is a caricature. In recruiting and promoting executives, U.S. corporations stress nothing more than the ability to make competent judgments. In a person with a high degree of such ability, they will put up with a considerable degree of idiosyncrasy. They require that an individual who is to be one of a group of executives be a person who is able to work with others. This is not conformity. However, they do in effect demand conformity in one important respect: U.S. business life attracts and puts a premium on men to whom the interests of the company become their interests, so that, among other results, in the allocation of their time between their business careers and their families, their families sometimes come out second best. However, this loyalty is to the concept of a career in a corporation, rather than an indissoluble tie to a given corporation. It does not prevent the individual from accepting a position in another firm, and operating with full zeal there, if the transfer promises him more income or, perhaps more important, a wider scope of managerial activity.

In the United States, as well as in other countries that stress private enterprise, individuals have nevertheless seen an opportunity for public service, or to exercise their abilities, in public corporations, and have managed them with distinction. Examples are Lilienthal in the Tennessee

Valley Authority, Mattei in Italy's ENI (Ente Nazionale Idrocarburi), and Bermudez of Pemex (Petroleo Mexicano).

In the Soviet Union, individuals who are government employees have innovated so effectively as to give that country one of the world's higher rates of economic development during a period that included two destructive wars.

Like the U.S. convictions of the effectiveness of private enterprise, governmental operation of virtually all economically productive activity in the Soviet Union is probably the result of historical experience, but of one contrasting to that in the United States. In tsarist Russia, there was extremely little public enterprise. Agriculture was feudal or (even after the freeing of the serfs in 1861) quasi-feudal, and industrial enterprises were owned by nobles, often with monopolistic franchises from the tsar. The Communist government radically reversed this situation. Perhaps the following explanation is plausible. Russian nobles were self-centered, callous, and contemptuous in their treatment of the classes beneath them. The lower and middle classes and intellectuals of Russia so bitterly hated and distrusted the nobles, who would naturally be the owners and managers if there were private enterprise in Russia, that they could not conceive of business operation by private firms as being in the public interest. I do not mean to imply a conscious decision by this chain of reasoning, but rather a deep-seated emotional attitude. As a consequence, the operation of economic activity by the state "automatically" and "inevitably" seemed to them the necessarily best form of economic organization, and aroused their emotional support sufficiently so that they have innovated with effectiveness and satisfaction in government enterprises. This explanation is only a broad historical speculation, but it offers an explanation of an historical development that otherwise lacks historical explanation.

In some of the least developed countries, the hostility toward large private ventures has been combined with such traditional attitudes of the managers toward industrial activity and such managerial incompetence that public operation has been disastrously wasteful. In some ex-colonies the compulsion to appear modern caused by the humiliations of the colonial system has led to grossly wasteful "showcase" expenditures. These of course are not results of public enterprise, but results of something much deeper which is also the cause of public enterprise. At the other extreme, in the Soviet Union hatred of the old elites was combined with a high positive valuation on serving the government and with high technical and mangerial competence, and the result has been a rapid rate of economic growth. It seems highly likely that in the Soviet Union economic growth during the past 50 years would have been slower under a mixed enterprise system, just as it seems certain that in the United States it would have been slower under a socialist system. Hence no general judgment concerning the superiority of private or socialist enterprise or the optimum mix of the two is possible. The decision must depend on the national temper, a factor which is not notably easy to evaluate.

Japan during the Tokugawa era (1600–1868) provides an example of loyalty to a different entity. During the Tokugawa era there was a great deal of economic innovation. Many an entrepreneur, effective in conceiving and promoting technical progress in agriculture or crafts, appeared, to whom service to his feudal lord or the preservation and enhancement of the enterprise he had created or inherited took precedence over his own interests or those of his natural family. The formal rule of inheritance was that the family property passed to the first-born son. However, if that son was incompetent, for the sake of the enterprise a father often created a new first-born son by adopting a capable young man, who then inherited the property (and the family responsibilities).

The case of the American Indians illustrates the persistence of traditional community values of a different type. Before European occupation of the North American continent, American Indians had been entrepreneurial enough, in both warfare and some economic activities. Shifts from hunting to agriculture, and the adaptation of the horse to their purposes by the Sioux, are cases in point. Indian leadership (in most tribes) had been on behalf of the tribe or of small kinship bands within the tribe rather than of individual families. Conquest and subjugation by the European immigrants crushed Indian entrepreneurial activity for several generations, but in the mid-20th century, here and there, resourceful tribal leaders are becoming active. They are barred by the forces of history from achievement in war, but in politics and economics they are innovating effectively. And, in some degree adhering to their former values and rejecting those of their conquerors, they are innovating on behalf of tribal enterprises, rather than for their individual economic advancement.[17]

France illustrates still a different pattern. Napoleon, who saw a need to educate entrepreneurs to counteract French "bureaucratic" tendencies, founded the *École Polytechnique*. Subsequently, the other *grandes Écoles* sprang up. Their graduates, some of France's ablest men, technically trained, have ever since moved easily from private business to government and back again, as the occasion demanded, and acted ably in either. When in government they have taken for granted that they could make business decisions more capably than the private business executives directly concerned, and have often done so, and through the elaborate

---

[17] Some American Indians have left their reservations to enter into other U.S. communities. A few of these have established small enterprises—often service shops of some type—in communities near their tribal homes, but most have taken industrial jobs in large cities. Most Indians of all of these groups are of mixed blood, and hence also have a mixed cultural heritage, as do many who remain on the reservations.

French system of regulatory commissions and governmental and quasi-governmental investment banks have coerced or persuaded private executives to adopt the policies they prescribed. In Shonfield's words, "These are men who take pride in assuming personal responsibility; their habit is to assume the initiative, and to think up formal justifications for their actions afterwards."[18]

It has sometimes been said that if entrepreneurship is "in a man's bones," he will be an entrepreneur under any auspices. There is something to the point, but the examples cited above suggest that it is easily overdone. That U.S. entrepreneurs would have innovated with as much zeal and effectiveness as bureaucrats, or Soviet entrepreneurs as executives of private corporations, or the leaders of American Indian bands or Japanese during the Tokugawa era for their personal economic advancement, seems extremely doubtful.

Institutional Supports

It need be mentioned only briefly that innovational entrepreneurship is fostered by appropriate governmental supports. The most fundamental of these is simply competent governance. Government that provides the legal institutions and judicial, administrative, and infrastructure services conducive to efficient production also facilitates innovation in production. Legal institutions, bolstering cultural practices, that free business of the need for personal acquaintance and personal trust are important. So long as the need for that practice persists, some types of innovation will be hampered. The development of effective capital markets, also important, is discussed in Chapter 13. This too depends on gradual changes in attitudes at least as much as on laws and organizations.

In many less developed countries, especially in Asia, governments themselves have established many industrial and mining enterprises. (Public utilities are typically governmentally owned in most countries. The United States is one of the exceptions to the general rule.) In part this has been done for motives similar to those that were suggested above as the motives for the emergence of government ownership of any enterprises in the Soviet Union. The colonial histories of these countries created an emotional antipathy to large private enterprises, especially if foreign-owned, and to many persons in those countries only a governmentally owned enterprise seems sure to be in the public interest. A reason that on the surface seems more logical has sometimes been re-

---

[18] Shonfield's *Modern Capitalism* (1965) presents a thoughtful analysis of differences among Western nations in the institutions and operation of capitalism. For a brief description of French so-called "indicative" planning after World War II, with reference to the role of these administrators in it, see Hagen and White (1966), Chaps. 9 and 10.

ferred to as the "vacuum" reason. No private entrepreneurs capable of establishing such enterprises are available, and if the government does not establish the enterprise it will not exist. Unfortunately, in many enterprises set up by governments partly for this reason, the management necessary for the economic operation of the enterprise has not existed after the government set up the shell, just as it did not exist previously. Government acquisition of a firm does not improve its management unless there are good managers within the government. The enterprises— some of them badly advised in the first place, some of them economically advantageous if they could have been well managed—have been burdens on the economy rather than aids to development.

The Industrial Corporation in Japan

The nature of Japanese industrial management at the present time provides an example of the extremely effective adaptation of factory management to traditional attitudes concerning interpersonal relationships. Since the rate of increase in productivity in Japan from the 1880s to the 1960s has been the highest in the world, the system has clearly been extremely successful.

The simplest exposition of the relevant aspects of Japanese factory organization is that by James C. Abegglen (1958 and 1973). He describes relationships between employees and their corporations which are widely prevalent in larger Japanese companies. His account perhaps overstates their generality.[19] Yet they are still very common.

Major features of the pattern are as follows. Companies hire young men and women for worker class jobs ("those who work") as they leave school, and for managerial positions ("those who direct") as they leave college, after fairly intensive investigation of the individual's background and reliability and in the case of managerial positions of his general ability. The company will not seek workers from among individuals already employed in industrial jobs elsewhere, for (after a probationary period, in the case of the worker class) there is a lifetime commitment between an individual and his company. He will not move to accept a better job, and the company is committed to retaining him until retirement except in instances of the most extreme provocation, such as several unexplained absences for periods of weeks. During such absences, until the man is discharged, his family receives his wages, for he continues to be an employee. Economic slack, causing a downturn in sales, is not sufficient justification for discharging or laying off workers. Similarly, an executive, once he has become attached to a given corporation after his

---

[19] This is indicated in Jean Stoetzel (1955). In large part, the observations in the text are based on conversations of the writer with a considerable number of Japanese executives in 1956, 1960, and 1974.

graduation from college, owes and honors loyalty to that corporation throughout his business career, and the corporation has a converse obligation to him. He would no more think of moving to any position whatever in another corporation than he would of stealing from the company's till.[20]

The obligation not to lay off employees does not work hardship on employers as often as might appear, for a company may succeed in a voluntary appeal to some of its employees to return to their family village for a time, to aid the company, or to retire early in return for a bonus in addition to regular retirement pay; and the turnover among women employees is sufficient so that their number may be reduced in moderate degree rather rapidly by not making good attrition. However, the obligation to retain workers has typically been recognized even when it imposed a heavy financial cost on the company.[21] The decision of a mining corporation in the 1950s to discharge some workers, after the offer of bonuses for early retirement had not brought a sufficient reduction in the work force, caused a long and bitter strike.

Within both the worker ranks and the management staff, the members of one "class" (one year's recruits) are almost never promoted over those of another. Yet within this limitation, superiors seek out ability among the men under them, and promote the most able, with as close scrutiny and search for the best men as anywhere in the world. Advancement of workers in pay is on the basis of seniority and size of family, with a very small variation based on function and deficiency. In managerial positions, overt assignment of responsibility for a function and thereby of credit for successful performance or blame for failure is avoided. Though executives must in fact know who among them are capable and effective, formal assignment of responsibility or credit is avoided through the use of management committees on whose ambiguous shoulders responsibility falls. Indeed, extreme care is taken to avoid any formal or public imputation that one executive or one worker has not performed as well as another.[22]

---

[20] See Abegglen (1958). In the 1960s, in Japan's persisting extremely tight labor market, this loyalty broke in some degree. As early as 1963, Ezra Vogel presented evidence that the loyalty of workers to employers is much less than absolute; the evidence has been increasing since that time.

[21] The security thus afforded the workers is somewhat reduced by the high bankruptcy rate among Japanese companies in recent years, associated with the displacement of the less progressive by the more progressive. However, the firms going bankrupt have typically been small firms employing relatively few workers.

[22] A group of 11 Japanese small industrialists visited the Massachusetts Institute of Technology a few years ago, after having visited a few large U.S. industrial plants. At these plants, several incentive payment systems had been explained to them as examples of advanced management systems which resulted in markedly different wage payments to different workers because of their differential productivity. I asked the Japanese visitors whether these systems were not irrelevant to Japan. The conversation

To a person acquainted with Japanese history, the origins of this form of personnel relationships in Japanese factories is clear. It is a direct transference to the factory of the former reciprocal obligations between an individual and his lord. The personality traits that made the former bond so compellingly necessary still exist.

The success of the system is probably explained by one positive and one negative element of those persisting attitudes. The positive factor is the great need to perform one's obligations to one's superior loyally in return for his fulfilling his obligations toward one. This has been as effective an inducement to Japanese workers and executives to labor diligently and competently as other incentives have been to Western workers. The negative factor is the extreme shame felt in the Japanese culture at being exposed as having failed at formal fulfillment of the responsibility of one's position. Apparently a Japanese executive who cannot avoid the perception that his peers or superiors are saying to him, in effect, "You have failed to perform the duties of your station" would feel such shame that he could not continue to function, even though his previous contributions to the company's success had been great. Apparently also, workers who gained such a perception through the fact that fellow workers of equal seniority had been promoted above them in rank or salary would be affected in a similar way. To avoid this, invidious distinctions are avoided. That everyone may know the true facts of relative ability is not important, if they are not formally signaled. Yet Japanese industrial success is surely also due in large degree to a factor quite separate from these, namely, the high degree of innovational ability of Japanese. These arrangements of structure are ones in which Japanese are freest and most motivated to exercise those abilities.

Industrialization might have been impossible in Japan if these imperatives of Japanese personality had been ignored, for the impersonal and contractual relationships between Western employers and employees and the Western discrimination among employees were indecent and immoral to the Japanese, and work probably could not have been carried forward under them. An organizational innovation of great creativity was necessary to permit industrialization to proceed.[23] Because that innovation

---

was through an interpreter, and when an American participant asked a question, the answer was usually first by the Japanese team leader, then by his deputy, the other team members waiting deferentially until these two had spoken. However, as the interpreter finished my question, the 11 men spontaneously nodded emphatically and said simultaneously: "Hai" (that is, "yes"). When I asked whether they had the right to discharge workers in case of a decline in production, one after another surprised me by asserting firmly that they did. Then one added, as an afterthought, and the others agreed, "Of course we would not. It would not be right."

[23] Since this deep mutual sense of comprehensive obligation exists (or has existed), there is a corresponding intense sense of treachery or abandonment if either side seems

was made, industrialization proceeded with impressive rapidity and efficiency. But, with the growth in scale of Japanese factories, it has been impossible to preserve the full paternalistic employer-employee relationship. The relationship between supervisor and worker is not a full substitute for the old unforced personal relationship. A corporation is not a samurai or a lord. This is no doubt one of the reasons for the bitter industrial strife which has appeared in postwar Japan. This is also no doubt one, but only one, of the reasons why relationships within Japanese corporations are changing—probably to the detriment of Japan's future rate of technical progress.

"Technical Activism" in China

The government of China is not neglectful of the need for innovative entrepreneurship, and has a well-defined program of encouragement of "technical activism." Facilities and resources are made available to persons recognized as innovative in agriculture or industry. During the three years 1965–68, about 100,000 persons were given the rank of technician and some 10,000 the rank of engineer. The rewards are both this recognition and, in a national competition, money payments. The individual identified as innovational is given education, is made a member of an appropriate professional society, and is sent the technical information which is distributed systematically.

In the early 1950s, industrial management was one-man management. By the 1960s this had been changed to committee ("3 in 1") management by a "Revolutionary Committee." Late in the decade, one member of the committee was a professional manager, one was elected by the workers, and the third represented the Party. The result could be managerial confusion; it could also be innovational suggestions by individuals not constrained by the acceptance of conventional methods. There is some evidence suggesting a movement in the early 1970s toward more professional management.

In larger establishments, there may be a research and development staff, to which such individuals are assigned. In peasant agriculture and decentralized industry, technical activism by individuals is the alternative to this more formally organized effort.[24]

---

not to fulfill its obligation. This is probably an important factor in the radicalism of one segment of the Japanese labor movement and in the bitterness and intransigence seen in some Japanese labor disputes mentioned in the text.

C. Kerr, J. Dunlop, F. Harbison, and C. Myers (1964) suggest that the compulsions of the industrial system are causing industrial relations in the various countries of the world to draw slowly toward (not necessarily to) a common point. Nothing in the Japanese case contradicts this possibility, for the Japanese system is changing.

[24] This information is from R. P. Suttmeier (1974).

BIBLIOGRAPHICAL NOTE

Weber (1930), Samuelsson's criticism of Weber (1961), and McClelland (1953) and (1961), all cited in the text, are important studies of origins of innovative action. See also Hagen (1962). Two books of wide scope concerning management in the course of industrialization are Kerr, Dunlop, Harbison, and Myers (1964) and Harbison and Myers (1959). The 1971 article by the four authors is a useful sequel. Concerning Japanese management and industrial organization, see Abegglen (1958) and (1972)—an up-dating of the 1958 book—and the criticisms of his thesis implicit and explicit in Stoetzel (1955) and Vogel (1963). Suttmeier (1974) presents a valuable insightful analysis of China's organization for innovation.

Other Factors in the
Production Function

12

Increase in per capita output due to increase in natural resources and in the quality of labor, and to economies of scale, are discussed in this chapter.

NATURAL RESOURCES

It was noted in Chapter 7 that paucity of natural resources does not bar economic growth. Whatever the relative amounts of labor, capital, and natural resources being used in a country, capital formation plus technical progress can raise per capita income. What is primarily in point in this section of this chapter is the impact on lower income countries of *increase* in their stock of natural resources, whether or not that stock is relatively limited. There will be no mystery to the effect: the countries themselves, foreign exploiters, or usually both in varying degree, benefit.

For economic purposes, a country's stock of natural resources is not that for which an omniscient and prescient person would see future use for, but that which the country and the world know about and can use. In 1800, apart from the spices, perfumes, and rare woods of the Orient, the natural resources of the world's lower-income countries were largely unknown. In effect, the resources did not exist. Since that time, they have been created, in effect, by exploration, by improvements in transportation and communication that brought them closer to users, and by technical advance which made them usable, or more usable. Apart from this, the value of known natural resources rose as demand increased with rising world income. Only the first of these results, the economic creation of natural resources, is considered at this point.

The list of illustrations could be long. The teak forests of Burma and Thailand were of only petty local value until they were discovered by foreigners. The rice lands of those countries increased enormously in value and in their contribution to income when the Suez Canal was opened. The discovery of copper deposits in Peru, Chile, and Rhodesia much increased the income of those countries, as the discovery of iron ore deposits enriched certain other countries.

The value of certain tropical lands soared as techniques increased the number and improved the quality of finished products that could be made from natural rubber, and as the rubber tree productivity of those lands was discovered. Then the natural resources were destroyed again in large part when synthetic rubber was discovered and improved. The discovery of a method of extracting aluminum from bauxite made deposits valuable that previously had little value. The invention of nuclear fusion did the same for uranium deposits.

Michael Roemer (1970) has described the results of natural resource discovery in Peru and in waters that Peru controls. In 1950, no iron ore was being mined in Peru. Fishing and copper mining together contributed 1.4% of the gross national product. Then foreign firms began to extract the iron ore and increased the extraction of copper. And after 1955 nylon fishing nets replaced the weaker, heavier, and less durable cotton nets, and the development of sonar "fish-finders" revealed the tremendous schools of anchovies that were being missed. The catch multiplied from 59,000 tons to 8.5 million tons in 11 years. In 1966, the extraction of anchovies and tuna from the sea and of iron and copper from the land yielded output more than sixteen times that 1950 output—more than 9% of a total GNP about 2.3 times as great.

Among the results were large government royalties from copper, the creation of four new industries (making boats, fish nets, processing equipment, and jute sacks) serving the fishing industry, employment of not far from 3% of the nonagricultural labor force in fishing, the fish meal industry, and those supplier industries, and foreign exchange earnings from the fishing and fish meal industry alone that constituted one fourth of the country's total.[1]

The most spectacular example, of course, is the petroleum discovery and extraction that elevated Saudi Arabia, Iran, and Libya from poverty to affluence, and made the poor sheikdoms of Abu Dhabi and Qatar the highest income countries in the world. And this even before the establishment of a monopoly price for petroleum made these countries even far richer.

---

[1] I am indebted to Peter Kilby for this summary of Roemer's information.

There is little more to be said. Added examples would hardly make the point more forcefully. Dozens of the world's countries have benefited, though in lesser degree, from the discovery of new natural resources or the creation of new resources through technical change. In summary, the results are added employment, income, and foreign exchange. The foreign exchange effects are discussed further in Chapter 17.

IMPROVEMENT IN LABOR FORCE QUALITY

Increase in the size of the labor force, other inputs being unchanged, will tend to lower average per capita income. If the resulting larger agregate income and larger number of consumers in combination make economies of scale possible, that effect may offset the diminishing returns-to-labor effect, though only in a most unusual production function would it offset diminishing returns fully. We are concerned in this chapter, not with these effects, but with increase in the number of units of labor input without increase in the number of workers, that is, with improvement in the quality of the labor force.

Consider first the effects of socialization. There are intercountry differences in the productive capacity of workers. Some of them are due to differences in their physical condition, others to their socialization, and still others to their formal education.[2] In the broadest sense, the term *socialization* includes all of the environmental experiences that influence an individual's qualities. I shall use it to include all such influences except formal education and training.

Socialization

Some of the economists who stress the importance of "investment in human resources" seem to assume that all differences in worker capability other than those due to inherited qualities and physical condition are attributable to deliberate education and training, and can be created by deliberate policy. This is naïve psychology. Differences among individuals in motivation and capability at adulthood are caused in large part by other aspects of the environment to which the individual is exposed

---

[2] Most social scientists doubt that there are significant intercountry differences in intelligence, or, more precisely, in the innate determinants of intelligence. There is no definitive verdict concerning this question, since intelligence tests are "culture-bound." The most that responsible social scientists will say is that they have no evidence of any ethnic or other national differences in the hereditary determinants of intelligence. I refer to the hereditary determinants rather than to intelligence itself, since the evidence is mounting that intelligence at adolescence or adulthood is greatly influenced by early environment—by its psychological impact and probably also by the presence or absence of brain damage caused by inadequacies of diet. Concerning the latter, see McDermott (1966).

during infancy, childhood, and adolescence. To put a complicated matter overly simply, they are determined in an important degree by the generalizations the individual draws, from the first year of life onward, concerning the nature of the social world about him and the safest and emotionally most rewarding way to behave in it. And much of the effect on the individual is entirely unintended by his parents or anyone else.

To cite an extreme example, the typical individual brought up in a slum, with no father present in the home much of the time, and in a community environment that suggests to him that neither his immediate group nor the society outside it has respect for him or concern for his welfare, will be a poorer grade worker than the individual brought up by dependable parents whose behavior and attitudes toward him convey to him a sense of his worth, and in a community that accepts him. The two individuals are likely to have different degrees and qualities of formal education, but it would be absurd to say that these are the causes of the differences in work attitudes and behavior. The principle that applies in this extreme example applies also to the effects of any other differences in environment. There may be differences among societies in typical individual motivations and capability due to these factors, for childhood environment and patterns of childhood training differ among societies.

This point is stressed here to suggest that the reader avoid too-facile attribution of differences in productive, especially innovational, capability to differences in formal education and training. Little more that is relevant to economic growth can be said about these topics. In Chapter 5 it is noted that members of peasant societies, like those of other societies, are responsive to economic incentives. The prevalence in nonindustrial societies of attitudes that cause difficulties in the transition to industrial work is mentioned. In Chapter 11 a hypothesis of the greater prevalence of noninnovational personality in traditional than in other societies, due to differences in socialization, is summarized.

The Effects of Education

Deliberate education and training are also of great importance, for of course appropriate knowledge greatly increases productive ability.

Education may be acquired in educational institutions, via training courses on the job, or by way of "learning by doing." The latter two methods train workers for specific productive jobs; educational institutions provide more general training. Education of all three types, but especially in educational institutions, is partly consumption, partly preparation for future production. Expenditure to produce physical equipment for future production is termed investment. In ordinary usage, expenditure to prepare human beings similarly is not. There are at least two reasons. Capital is usually thought of as a market commodity and, except where slavery is still practiced, human beings cannot be bought and sold. Also, distinguishing the investment aspects of education from the consumption aspects is difficult; the two are joint products.

It is of some importance to distinguish the significance of different levels of educational expenditures. A constant level of educational input per student is analogous to gross capital formation with zero net capital formation. That is, it is precisely analogous to replacement of depreciated capital. New workers are being trained to replace retiring ones. An increase in expenditures for education in order to provide the same quality and quantity of education per person to an expanding population is precisely analogous to capital widening. If, on the average, individuals are given more training than before by means of increased educational expenditures per person, then, insofar as the increase is to prepare them to produce, rather than to give them satisfaction as consumers, the increase in educational expenditure is analogous to capital deepening. Insofar as new knowledge to be taught or new methods of teaching have been devised, this is analogous to technical progress. The advanced technique may be introduced with or without net investment (increase in educational expenditure per student). And increased expenditure per student may mean a greater "investment" per student, or may mean only that with a rise in average income in the society, teachers are being paid better. Hence an analysis of educational expenditures per student gives only a general and uncertain indicator of the contribution of education to the training of workers. Yet it is often the only indication available.

Edding (1966) presents data for selected industrial countries showing that the percentage of national income or gross national product spent on education in educational institutions has been rising steadily during the 20th century, except when war intervened. The rise does not seem to be merely a result of a high income elasticity of demand for education. Edding also presents data showing the ratio of educational expenditures to national income for high- and low-income countries in about 1950 (see Figure 12–1). While there is a high degree of correlation between per capita income and educational expenditures, the percentages at low incomes are as high as those in the advanced countries were early in the 20th century, at much higher incomes. It seems that the course of history has shifted national tastes in favor of much increased expenditures for education. It is indicated in Chapter 14 that a similar shift has occurred with respect to total current government expenditures.

A number of estimates have been made which are first approximations to estimates of the return to investment in education. The method, in general, is to estimate the lifetime incomes of persons with different levels of education and the costs of obtaining the different levels of education (including the earnings foregone while in school), and then to calculate the rate of return per year throughout life that is implied by the figures,

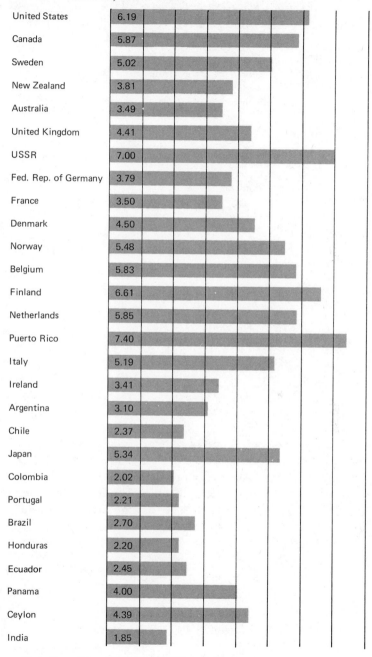

FIGURE 12–1

Educational Expenditures as Percent of National Income, Selected Countries, about 1950

United States	6.19
Canada	5.87
Sweden	5.02
New Zealand	3.81
Australia	3.49
United Kingdom	4.41
USSR	7.00
Fed. Rep. of Germany	3.79
France	3.50
Denmark	4.50
Norway	5.48
Belgium	5.83
Finland	6.61
Netherlands	5.85
Puerto Rico	7.40
Italy	5.19
Ireland	3.41
Argentina	3.10
Chile	2.37
Japan	5.34
Colombia	2.02
Portugal	2.21
Brazil	2.70
Honduras	2.20
Ecuador	2.45
Panama	4.00
Ceylon	4.39
India	1.85

Note: Countries are listed in descending order of per capita GDP in 1960.
Source: Edding (1966), Table 2, p. 40, and Table 3, p. 41.

on the assumption that the increase in income can be attributed to the increase in education. Table 12–1 presents such estimates for the United States and India.[3]

TABLE 12–1
"Rates of Return" to Education, India and the
United States (Percent)

	Rates
India, certain urban areas, early 1960s	
Secondary school education	10–12
College and postgraduate education	16–17
United States, native white urban males, 1939	
Secondary school education	16
College education	14.5

Note: Each figure is derived by estimating the difference in life-time income of persons who did not have the education indicated, then calculating the annual rate of return to the cost of the education which that difference in lifetime income would constitute. Becker presents estimates for college education ranging from 13% to 15.5%. He regards 14.5% as the most probable or representative estimate.

Source: India: Harberger (1965). United States: Becker (1964), Chap. 4 and p. 128.

These are not in fact estimates of the rate of return to education, for the differences in lifetime income are also due to differences in ability and motivation, and general knowledge indicates that these are connected with education. On the average, persons of greater mental ability certainly seek out and have access to more education, and their greater ability, rather than merely the education, gives them higher income. Similarly, the basket of personality elements that collectively constitute motivation is almost certainly positively correlated with education (persons more highly motivated toward working effectively will seek a greater degree of education), and undoubtedly affects lifetime income. Studies which do not separate out the effects of these factors therefore certainly overstate the causal influence of an individual's education on his income, and probably overstate it greatly. It is quite clear that there is only a limited causal relationship between education as such and lifetime income. An empirical study of Algeria which brings out the covariation with other factors is presented in John Simmons (1974). The quantitative significance of the estimates shown, therefore, is that the true increase in an average individual's earning capacity due solely to his formal education, calculated as a rate of return on the total

[3] Schultz (1963) presents an extensive bibliography of discussions of the return to investment in human resources.

cost of the education, is less, and probably much less, than the percentage shown.[4]

The conclusion to be drawn is not that the advantages of increased education to a less developed country (or a more developed country) are necessarily less than is commonly assumed, but merely that they cannot be calculated in this simple way. First, the "joint product" aspect must be considered. The increased income of educated individuals reflected in the

---

[4] Becker (1964) considers both problems. From the studies that he cites, one might conclude that perhaps 7% to 10% of the additional income earned by college graduates, and a much larger share of that earned by high school graduates, is due to greater ability. If so, the calculated rate of return to college education would be reduced by 20% to 30%, or to about 9% to 12%. But Becker's adjustments for ability and motivation are grossly inadequate. For lack of data, he is unable to differentiate among students who ranked in the bottom 60% of their high school class, or among students who ranked in the lowest 45% of a sampler in intelligence tests. Also, one of his analyses is based on the assumption that students' ranks in college would be the same as their ranks in high school, but disregards the fact that many of the lowest ranking would not gain entrance to college. Further, Becker grossly assumes that brothers have similar degrees of motivation (since they have similar parental and social background), and by citing income differences between brothers with different degrees of education, he believes that he has eliminated the motivational factor. However, as psychologists interested in the analysis of personality testify, among the most pronounced differences in motivations are often those between brothers. Differences in parental care of a second or later son (because of their experiences with earlier siblings) and rivalry between brothers which leads the younger one to try to differentiate himself from the older are among the causal factors. If one of two brothers goes to college and another does not, this is almost prima facie evidence of differences in ability or motivation. Even where economic limitations make it impossible for more than one sibling to be sent to college, relative motivation may enter into the choice of the one to be sent. Hence differences in income associated with differences in education level among brothers are very probably caused in considerable part by differences in motivation. The fact that these differences are of roughly the same magnitude as the differences Becker found in other groups he studied suggests strongly that motivational differences may account for part of the income differences he attributes to education elsewhere in his study.

Concerning motivation, Becker suggests that the estimated effects of education on income shown in a study by Morgan, David, and others (1962) that attempts to "partial out" the effects of "achievement motivation" do not differ greatly from other estimates. However, their measure of achievement motivation is an indirect one which, as their own several comments indicate, will hardly bear this weight.

From these considerations, and consideration of the magnitude of the "rates of return" shown in Table 12–1, one may suspect that for most of the individuals receiving high school and college education in the United States, the increase in subsequent income to the individual does not justify the cost. (There is no reason to assume that the United States is unique in this respect.) But of course the increase in his material income and his enjoyment of life because he and all other high school and college graduates received those degrees of education may nevertheless be far greater than the total cost. The increase in the productivity of a worker because the workers around him are educated may be considerable, and the increase due to the fact that some of them are is certainly great. Similar considerations apply to consumption.

A further consideration has been noted by R. S. Eckaus in an unpublished manuscript. Incomes rise secularly because of rising productivity. A person who began work, say, 4 years after another because he extended his schooling, would earn higher income per year in each of his careers than did the other, 4 years earlier. Most studies incorrectly attribute all of the difference to education.

figures is due not merely to education but also to their ability and motivation. But it is not due simply to the sum of the three. In part, at least, it is due to a relationship more analogous to the product of the three; and the product of three numbers, any one of which is zero, is also zero. It is quite possible that as the degree of a person's intelligence and his motivations favorable to productivity increase, increased education is increasingly important to permit him to achieve his potential (except in certain exceptional roles).

Furthermore, education undoubtedly yields important "external economies" in production. That is, the education of one person makes the work of other persons more efficient. In part, this benefit is captured in estimates such as those presented. Since the data are averages for entire groups of persons receiving a given level of education, they include the benefit to each person resulting from the education of others at the same level. But the data do not reflect the increase in the productivity and income of a college graduate because of the elementary and secondary school education of the men and women he will work with, or the increase in their productivity because a broadly or technically educated man is present to manage the process. (Consider the effect on productivity in general if there were *no* technically trained men.)

When to these effects of education are added the consumer elements and citizenship effects, the case for devoting a large amount of resources to education is amply strong. But development planning may be distorted if it is based on attractively quantified calculations which overstate and oversimplify the direct effects.

McClelland's Analysis

McClelland (1966) has tried to measure the effects of education on economic growth by making comparisons among countries. He relates the economic level of 28 countries in 1929 (measured by their electricity production per capita), their secondary school enrollment ratios to population in 1930, and their economic growth rate, 1929–50. For lack of the directly appropriate data, he uses the ratio of secondary school enrollment in 1930 to population as a measure of the level of education possessed by members of the labor force in each country during the period 1929–50. He assumes the first two variables to be causal and the rate of economic growth the resultant. In a second test he relates electricity production per capita in 21 countries in 1950, the "educated adult stock" in each (estimated years of secondary education among adults 30 to 40 years of age per 1,000 inhabitants) in 1950, and the rate of economic growth, 1952–58. Results of the former analysis are shown in Table 12–2. The results of both analyses appear to constitute strong evidence of the influence of education on the rate of economic growth.

TABLE 12–2

Countries Classified by Economic Level (1929), Secondary School
Enrollment Ratios (1930), and by Rate of Economic Growth, 1929–50

Economic Level: Electricity Produced, 1929	Secondary School Enrollment per 1,000 Inhabitants, 1930	Economic Growth Rate, 1929–50*
Kwh/cap > 800		
U.S. (962)	44.3	+1.86
Canada (1855)	31.8§	+1.73
Sweden (811)	18.8‖, ¶	+3.17
Norway (2850)	18.7	−0.03
Kwh/cap 150 to 500		
England (269)	50.2†, ‡	+1.65
Denmark (158)	40.5§	+0.14
Netherlands (290)	32.2	−0.10
Australia (359)	26.2‖	+1.13
New Zealand (484)	21.4	+1.86
Japan (247)	15.7	−0.44
Finland (324)	14.0	+0.74
Austria (380)	13.8‖	−0.12
France (378)	10.3‡	−0.55
Chile (211)	10.0	−0.43
Italy (260)	6.8	−0.62
Kwh/cap 150		
Ireland (33)	12.4¶	+0.33
Hungary (100)	6.5	−0.26
Poland (100)	5.1†	+0.03
Argentina (119)	4.9	−0.61
Spain (107)	4.4	−0.63
Portugal (36)	4.3	−0.52

* Deviations in standard score units of gains in electricity produced per capita over gains predicted from regression of 1929 production level on 1929–50 gains (see McClelland, 1961, Chap. 3).
† Estimate based on interpolation or extrapolation from existing annual figures.
‡ Estimate for private schools added, based on ratio of public to private enrollments at other time periods.
§ Figure only approximate because of complications in the school system in the province of Quebec.
‖ Estimate for technical school enrollments added, based on ratio of general to technical enrollments at other time periods.
¶ Underestimates due to unavailability of enrollments in first and second years of secondary education given in some primary schools.
Source: McClelland (1966), p. 267. Data for electricity produced in individual countries added from McClelland (1961), p. 91.

However, the study suffers from the statistical deficiences of the underlying study, discussed above, and also from an additional one. In presenting this second step of his analysis, McClelland groups the countries by electricity production per capita in 1929 (in the second study, 1950), in order to show the effect of education on growth at each level of electricity production. The method, however, is subject to the difficulty that the correlation shown between education and growth depends on the division lines selected in grouping countries, and there are no "right" or "wrong" groupings, except that the bands grouped should be as narrow as is consistent with having a minimum number of cases in each band. If McClelland had excluded the two countries with electricity production per capita far below 100 kilowatt hours (Ireland and Portugal), and had grouped together the six countries between 100 and 225, and in a separate group the five between 245 and 325, he would have shown no or very slight evidence of correlation in these groups, and might have concluded that education has an influence on the rate of growth only at higher income levels. This ambiguity bedevils this method of presentation.

Even if a multiple regression indicated a significant relationship between educated adult stock or prior secondary school enrollment and economic growth, this relationship would not prove the causal influence of education. The relationship would also appear if populations varied in their innovational capacities (because, for example, of differences in socialization), and if the more innovational peoples were both more favorably motivated toward education and more successful in economic growth. That is, it is difficult to determine by statistical analysis in which direction the causal influence runs.

Other studies do not provide stronger evidence. It must be concluded that although assigning a causal influence to education seems justified on a priori grounds (more precisely, on the basis of casual empiricism), up to the present we do not have strong statistical evidence to support the assumption.

Even though one accepts the judgment that education can contribute greatly to productivity, one must be cautious in assuming that the level and types of education provided in technically advanced countries will increase productivity in less advanced countries. To take the extreme example, skill in the use of high-speed computers would be useful to extremely few individuals working in, say, Ceylon, and to none in Ruanda-Urundi. The point is relevant to lower levels of education as well. The mix of education that is applicable depends on the technical stage at which a country stands.

Learning on the Job

Productivity is of course increased by not only formal but also informal education. Much training in manual skills is on-the-job training, and even at the level of management training some U.S. corporations say, "We do not care much whether a prospective employee is a graduate of a liberal arts, management, or technical course. If his college career and personal qualities make him seem a good prospect, we will give him a training course after we hire him." Some apprenticeship programs do not involve even formal on-the-job training: rather, the training is pure watching and learning by doing. Sheer continuing industrial experience also brings improvements not only in skills but also, in many instances, in work attitudes, regularity of attendance, etc. This factor is no doubt important at the level of top management also.

PLANNING AN EDUCATIONAL PROGRAM

Any less developed country, in planning a development program, must decide how great its expenditures for education should be. The problem is not merely a choice between educational expenditures and other developmental expenditures; the estimate of the productivity of educational as well as of other developmental expenditures should be a determinant of the total amount of resources to be allocated to development. Two overly simple and contradictory methods of estimating the more advantageous level of educational expenditures have been proposed.

The Fixed-Input Coefficients Approach

There are two ways in which the task of estimating the optimum level and nature of expenditures for education can be approached. One is to estimate the rate of development of the country; on the basis of this estimate, to estimate its needs for persons with various levels and types of training, at various future times (say 1 year, 5 years, 10 years, 20 years in the future); then to plan the educational program that will meet those needs; and lastly to plan the training of teachers so that they will be available in time to do the teaching in time to produce the needed trained men. Requirements impossible to fulfill by the target dates by use of the supply of indigenous teachers that can be trained in time may exist. The problem can be met in part by importing teachers for a period. Even so, the time needed for some types of training is so long that the necessary education cannot be conferred in time. This is one reason why the importation of experts may be required.

There are so many possibilities of wide margins of error in this process of estimate, and these possible margins widen so rapidly as the time period being considered increases that very broad ranges of error indeed may exist. However, the likelihood of deficiencies if nothing is done (which means, if the previous level of present trends in education is allowed to continue) is so great that a forecasting procedure is preferable.

This method of forecasting assumes fixed coefficients of inputs of trained labor in production. That is, it assumes that certain numbers of men with certain training will be needed, absolutely, for a given basket of production. The question of the cost of obtaining them does not enter the calculation. More precisely, it is assumed that the cost will not be so great that development will be furthered by using resources for some other purpose rather than meeting the estimated demand fully.[5]

The Infinite–Price–Elasticity–of–Demand Approach

An alternative approach is as follows: (1) to assume that each level of general education prepares individuals for a range of types of jobs that will be needed, and that will yield the income now earned by persons with that level of education (that is, it is assumed that there is no need to determine educational requirements for various jobs; the present market evaluation of school graduates at each level is sufficient indication of the value to the economy of added individuals with that education); (2) to determine those incomes; (3) to calculate the cost per student of each level of education, including the earnings foregone by the students; (4) by comparison of costs and future incomes, to calculate the education per student that will yield the highest return. Preparing to give the optimum pattern of education may require withdrawing teachers from one level of teaching to train them for a higher level, drawing ex-teachers back into teaching, or importing teachers.

Unless by coincidence returns are equal, computations will, of course, show that the net return to education up to some level is greater than that to lesser or greater levels. From the nature of the assumptions made, it would follow that in the future all children should be educated up to that level and none beyond it (except to train teachers to provide the education up to that level). The conclusion is subject to one qualification only: that education up to one level may yield the highest return only up to a volume of children for whom indigenously trained teachers can be provided. If teachers must be imported, the added cost of providing the education might make a lesser level of education, one that can be provided by indigenous and less costly teachers, more advantageous.

This method of estimate assumes that an indefinitely large number of workers with each level of education will be found as productive and offered as high incomes as are the present graduates at that level; and that the relative advantage of training up to this level, and this level only, will not be altered as the supply of persons with lesser and greater education shrinks in the future. This is the extreme opposite of the assumption that a given number of workers of each type, no more and no

---

[5] R. S. Eckaus (1964) presents a discussion of computing educational requirements by this method. To illustrate, he presents a tabulation, drawn from the United States population censuses of 1949 and 1950, of the distribution of workers among occupations in the United States, and combines this with a tabulation prepared by the United States Department of Labor of the training requirements for each tabulation. The two classifications are not consistent; he had to reconcile them.

less, is required. The opposite assumption is justified by assuming that each category of labor is highly substitutable for each other category and perhaps for capital also. The assumption may be justified over a moderate period of time if the number of educated workers is not increasing very rapidly.

This model avoids the hazardous estimation of future demand for various types of workers. But it does so only at the cost of simplifying assumptions that make it reasonable only for moderate increases in the numbers of individuals to be educated rather than for larger increases, and only for fairly short-term rather than longer-term planning.[6]

More Complex Models

The truth, of course, is somewhere between the two approaches. If the supply of persons with one type and level of training is too short, someone with another level or type of training will find his way into the job (and production methods or the choice of projects may be altered in the process). On the other hand, if there is an oversupply of some types of workers relative to demand, they will not automatically shift to other types of work without cost. Their productivity will be less than otherwise. And if there is an undersupply, their productivity will be greater than otherwise.

Professor Adelman (1966) has presented a "linear programming" model which, recognizing these facts, combines some of the qualities of the two approaches. She applied the model to Argentina. She divided the Argentinian economy into nine "sectors" of work, and from empirical data derived an assumption of which of six levels of education is needed in each sector. She also estimated (or guessed at) the marginal productivity of workers with each level of education in each sector. Previously, she had done a projection of Argentinian production, and had proposed a development program for a 20-year future period (in units of 5 years each). Taking this projection, and her estimates of educational needs and productivity, she was able by mathematical manipulations and use of a high-speed calculator to do a projection which made a mutual adjustment

---

[6] Bowles (1967) presents this method, and applies it to Northern Nigeria. His model yields the conclusion that educational expenditures should be concentrated on primary education, since the net yield per student is higher than that of providing advanced education (because of the zero opportunity-cost of the student's years in school, and the very small opportunity-cost of providing teachers, relative to the cost of providing university graduates to teach in high schools); and that a temporary reduction in primary school enrollment, to give teachers further training, would be advantageous. Bowles' model would provide the indicated level of education for every child. The model assumes that all children are equally educable. No problem of aptitude or motivation for education is allowed for. This assumption, however, could easily be modified to allow for differences in receptivity to education. A rough quantitative basis for the necessary estimate would not be difficult to find.

between the amount of education of each level and the amount of production in each sector. That is, the computations caused both shifts in the education of each level to be provided, because of production needs, and shifts in the pattern of production, because of the availability of workers with the various levels of education.

In principle, this sort of computation is superior to either of the two pure approaches. However, each of those begins with some fairly concrete facts: training needs in each type of job, and earnings of persons with various levels of education, respectively. In the Adelman model, so many additional hazardous estimates and assumptions must be made (for example, an estimate of the marginal contribution to production of workers with each level of education in each sector, and the assumption that their relative contribution in each sector would not be altered by shifts of labor between different uses), that the model must be regarded as a fascinating analytical exercise rather than as having great empirical reference.[7]

A Tentative Conclusion

Educational planning requires forecasting manpower needs one and even two decades in the future. The actual future needs will be determined by the types of production, and the methods advantageous in each, that emerge during that future period. These will be affected not only by the country's innovational successes and rate of investment during that period, but also by changes in world demand and by technical progress. The uncertainties are such that only broad judgments about educational programs are likely to have great significance: the emphasis to be given to primary education, secondary education, technical education, etc. In view of these facts, it is possible (and to the writer seems probable) that educational planning that is marginal in a broad sense will be superior for a long time to come, and may even be conceptually superior indefinitely, to laying out a blueprint for the educational structure as a whole running to a point, say, two decades in the future. That is, planning the broad changes that are feasible and advantageous for the next five years, and then considering five years from now what is feasible and advantageous for the next five years, and so on, may be superior in principle to a longer-range blueprint. Models which suggest probable or possible needs, say, 20 years from now may provide perspectives that will and should influence the near future planning, but it would be a mistake to use them for more specific purposes. This may be true in principle because of the uncertain nature of the future, and not merely because we

---

[7] Tinbergen and Bos (1964) present another model designed as a basis for educational planning.

have not yet accumulated enough information or developed sophisticated enough methods to feed into the models.

It is sometimes suggested that by overemphasizing humanistic education, and thereby turning out graduates for whom there are no jobs in the society, an LDC may create a corps of frustrated and alienated individuals who may be a source of social instability. The argument assumes both that individuals make relatively little choice of type of education, but rather become humanists, social scientists, or engineers, depending on what their colleges happen to be teaching, and also that their emotional attitudes and reactions are altered basically by their college career.

The argument may put the cart before the horse. Investigation of a small sample of individuals by the writer suggests that it does. Inquiry concerning five such frustrated intellectuals in Burma indicated that they had been emotionally unstable and socially rebellious while or before they were in secondary school, and suggested strongly that they had chosen to become humanistic intellectuals because they were insecure and anxious to become elite, and regarded such grubby subjects as engineering with distaste. One would not wish to generalize from such a small sample, but it does suggest careful scrutiny of the generalization that the provision of education is the cause of the social alienation of the educated unemployed, or even of their unemployment.

Two experienced students of development especially concerned with the role of education (Edwards and Todaro, 1974)[8] have argued that development of the educational system that is excessive for purposes of economic development is fostered by pressure outside the educational system. The result is both the creation of a class of educated unemployed, and the use of resources to provide secondary and higher education that would more productively be used elsewhere. They suggest that reduction of public subsidies to higher education would minimize the distortion, but recognize that education reduces social and political biases in hiring and promotion against "caste, race, creed, tribe," and that these biases as well as that against those with less formal education must be reduced if excessive expenditures for education are to be reduced. They are not optimistic about the prospects for correction of the distortion.

ECONOMIES OF SCALE

From Adam Smith onward, economists have been intrigued by the theory of economies of scale. It is appropriate that economists dealing with economic growth should be equally concerned with it, for one of the

---

[8] Edgar O. Edwards of the Ford Foundation and Michael P. Todaro of the Rockefeller Foundation.

most conspicuous developments as technology progresses and income rises is progressive increase in the average size of plants in almost all industries.

The Sources of Economies of Scale

As the size of a plant increases, up to some size the number of units of input required per unit of output will decrease. This effect is an "economy of scale." Usually, there is then a range of size within which cost per unit of output (i.e., number of units of inputs required) is roughly constant. At still larger sizes of plant, unit cost rises again (diseconomies of scale).

These statements also apply to the size of a firm, if the firm is a management unit rather than merely a holding company.

Unit cost may also decrease, reach a minimum, and then increase as an industry grows in size, even though individual plants are already at optimum size and the number of plants rather than their size increases. Presumably it does so in any industry over some range of size.

Economies of scale are due to indivisibilities of men or material objects. Economies of scale of a plant may be due to the fact that a large or complex machine may do more than twice as much work as any that can be devised with one half the depreciation and interest cost. A large press may stamp out more than twice as many auto body parts as one costing half as much—which indeed may not be powerful enough to stamp out any at all. If the volume of output of a plant is large enough so that a worker can work continuously at one process rather than shifting from one to another of four processes, the time he would spend moving from one to another is saved, his skill is probably greater, and investment in machines or tools that are idle most of the time is saved. And if the market becomes large enough so that he can work full time at one process or subdivision of a process, this fact may stimulate the design of an improved machine for that one process or subprocess. A better way of putting this is that if the volume is large, the inventor has a wider option, for he can devise either a machine of small capacity (and use several of them) or one large machine, whereas for a smaller volume of production he has only the former option. Hence larger scale increases the probability of an advance in technique. If one man has the ability to manage a plant employing 300 men, part of his ability is wasted and unit costs are increased if there are only 100 men for him to manage. By a sort of law of large numbers, the volume of inventories that must be maintained rises less than the volume of production and sales, for one need not expect that all buyers will reorder at once or all flows of supply fail at once. This too is due to indivisibilities, in a more subtle sense—indivisibility of the size of orders, because of considerations of transportation and clerical work. If transactions were continuous flows, economy of inventory scale would not exist.

The diseconomies of size of plant arise largely from the increase in complexity of administration as the size grows; and from increases in the transportation cost of inputs, as they must be brought from farther away; and of finished products, as they must be shipped to more distant customers. The lowest unit-cost size of plant may be one at which many components are made in volume below lowest unit cost, because increasing plant size to that at which the components were produced most cheaply would raise administrative costs per unit too much. In this event, if the industry grows to include several plants of minimum-cost size, jointly they may use enough of some components so that a separate firm specializing in the production of those components may reduce their unit costs. This sort of specialization is the reason that there are economies of scale in an industry beyond the size at which all plants are of minimum-cost size. The components involved often are specialized services. Diseconomies of scale of an industry arise mainly from increases in the unit costs of inputs whose production requires natural resources sufficiently limited in amount so that diminishing returns set in.

Where there are barriers to the flow of goods, capital, labor, or management among countries, there are also economies of scale for an economy as a whole. It is difficult to see why there should be diseconomies of scale of an economic system, if by a larger economy we mean one with proportionately more material resources as well as more people.

Economies of scale are especially conspicuous in manufacturing, mining, power, transportation, and communication industries. Minimum-cost size of plant varies greatly among different industries within these industry groups. But up to some size of plant, economies of scale exist in any type of production. Even in primitive production, an enterprise so small that it does not require the full time work of one worker is in general uneconomically small, and unit cost will fall as the scale increases up to the capacity of one worker (or one family). Where draft power is animal power, peasant farms smaller than the size that can be cultivated with one yoke of oxen or water buffalo are uneconomically small. For "wet cultivation," a size of 15 to 20 acres, the maximum one yoke–one family size, seems to be the minimum-cost size. For "dry farming" the minimum-cost size may be much larger. In the plains states of the United States, there was a time when 40 acres was the minimum-cost size for grain farms. Three generations ago, 160 acres may have been the minimum size in many localities. Today, with the development of power machinery and large-scale plowing, cultivating, harvesting, and threshing equipment, minimum cost apparently is achieved only at several thousand acres in wheat farming. But beyond some size of farm, unit costs rise because the economies of the indivisible large machines so far invented have been achieved and costs of management rise.

Firms that require large-sized plants for minimum cost will of course survive only where the market for their products is large enough to permit adequate scale; though if they have protection against competition and the demand curve for their products is not too steeply sloped, a size below their minimum-cost size may be large enough.

Market Size, Industrial Experience, and Minimum-Cost Production

Average plant size increases over time, and no doubt would even in a fairly large economy of constant size, because advance in techniques reveals new methods by whose use unit cost will be reduced more if the plant is enlarged than if it is not and whose use may require a larger plant if any cost reduction is to be achieved. (Of course new techniques permitting smaller size are also developed, but these are far fewer.) Average plant size increases in growing low-income economies. Perhaps the reason is that with rising income the market expands, but perhaps market size is not the limiting factor in these economies. Entrepreneurs may not yet be ready to manage plants of a size that the market would justify. Hla Myint's comment that "economies of experience" must be present before "economies of scale" can be attained has been mentioned. His point is well taken.

Even if the thesis of limits to managerial capability reflects reality more accurately than does the thesis that small scale prevents the beginning of development, it remains true that scale is an important consideration in assessing the future of low-income countries. For considerations of scale suggest (even though not very precisely) industries that will not be economic four or five decades in the future if producers must depend on the market of that country alone, and this consideration may affect the policies of far-sighted leaders concerning regional integration, the establishment of regional industries, trade policy in general and other matters.

The size of the economy may restrict growth in a quite different way. The larger an economy, the smaller the percentage increase in its output and income needed to justify one added plant of given size in any industry. Hence the risk of expansion is less. An example of this difficulty is provided by nuclear power plants. The minimum feasible size of nuclear power plants is large. Production cost when the plant is used much below capacity is exorbitant. A small economy whose natural resources are such that nuclear power would be cheaper than any alternative source may nevertheless never be able to afford a nuclear power plant, because absolute growth in the demand for power may be so slow that, no matter when a nuclear power plant was constructed, it would be used at such a low fraction of capacity for so long that it would be uneconomic unless it displaced existing sources of power supply.

One effect of small size of the economy on the development of new industries has not been mentioned. In a country in which there is room for only one or two enterprises in a given industry, the opportunity exists for marketing to be monopolistic, and for the price to be held above the cost of production. This fact creates policy problems that are absent or less acute in countries large enough so that there is competition among many enterprises, though monopoly may appear there because of other circumstances.

Scale and Size of Market: The 1957 I.E.A. Conference

The relationship of size of the economy to economic efficiency of industries was explored at the 1957 conference of the International Economics Association.[9] The conferees, in considering the types of manufacturing that flourish in industrial countries of various sizes, found it convenient to classify countries into size groups. Somewhat curiously, the criterion used was population, not gross national product or some combination of per capita and gross national product. The country groups used were those below 10 million in population, those of 10 to 15 million, those of the size of France and the United Kingdom (around 50 million), and the United States. The following conclusions were reached concerning economies of scale.

1. In most manufacturing industries, most technical economies gained by increasing the size of plant or firm are very largely exhausted by firms of moderate size. Beyond this size there is a plateau of roughly constant unit costs. Even small countries can support most industries.

2. However, for certain industries—those producing automobiles, aircraft, locomotives, and heavy machinery, both mechanical and electrical—the minimum cost size is larger. The minimum-sized economy required to sustain these industries is ordinarily one of between 10 and 15 million population. There are exceptions, among them Australia (because of its higher per capita income, though the conference proceedings do not discuss this reason for its being an exception). Sweden, whose automobile industry emerged to prominence after the date of the conference, is a similar exception.

3. In economies with larger markets, there is a greater degree of specialization. The typical firm produces a narrower range of products than a corresponding firm in a smaller country. Differences in this respect are noticeable not merely between countries of 10 to 15 million population and, say, France or the United Kingdom, but also between the latter countries and the United States.

4. In larger markets, production of services as well as of goods is specialized. There is greater dependence on specialist firms. Like special-

---

[9] E. A. G. Robinson (1960).

ization in general, differences in this respect are noticeable between
countries of 10 to 15 million population, France and the U.K., and the
United States.

5. In larger economies, less growth (in percentage terms) is needed
to provide a market for an added efficient unit of production. Hence the
risk of investment in expansion is less.

The omissions from this list of generalizations are as remarkable as the
inclusions. The conferees were distinguished economists. Yet, so static
has the economic analysis of scale been that it did not occur to them to
mention four other rather obvious and important facts relating economic
development to market size. They are:

6. The size of plant that is minimum cost in a country depends on the
level of the country's managerial capability.

7. Whether a plant of minimum cost size will find an adequate market
in a country with a given population depends on the country's per capita
income.

8. Technical advance in a country increases the size of the country's
market.

9. As the world's technical margin moves outward, some new products
possible at the margin require larger industries, hence larger economies
to support them, than the largest previously required.

The first three of these four generalizations have an a priori analytical
basis. The last is more nearly a purely empirical observation, but seems
justified by the world's history since the Industrial Revolution.

Both population and per capita income are determinants of market size
in the aggregate and for any given product. At a given level of per capita
income, a country with a large population will support some manufacturing industries that a smaller country will not. Both Chenery (1960) and
Maizels (1963) have computed multiple regressions of the effect of per
capita income and population on manufacturing production in the 1950s.
Chenery used data for periods between 1950 and 1955 for 34 to 50
countries at all levels of income, except that (apparently because postwar
U.S. census data did not provide the necessary classifications) he used
1939 data for the United States. Maizels used 1955 data for 39 countries,
excluding the industrial countries of Europe, United States, and Japan,
and excluding also low-income countries in which manufacturing is of
slight importance—mainly some countries of sub-Sahara Africa and a few
smaller countries of Latin America.

Dividing all manufacturing into 15 groups, Chenery found a significant partial regression of manufacturing production on population for 9
of the 15, and for manufacturing as a whole. That is, he found that an
increase in manufacturing production per capita is associated with an
increase in population, at a given level of per capita income. This means
that in a country with larger population, manufacturing production is a

larger share of total production. This presumably is true because economies of scale make manufacturing more economic relative to other production. The tendency for production per capita to increase with population, in Chenery's calculation, applied to about 40% of manufacturing output in economies with a per capita income level of $300 and 57% at a level of $600. The elasticity of manufacturing output as a whole with respect to population size (holding per capita income constant) was only 0.20, but even this effect was important enough so that "an increase in population from 2 to 50 million [would cause] manufacturing output per capita to nearly double and the sectors having *significant* economies of scale to more than triple" (Chenery, 1960, p. 645; italics mine).

Maizels, however, dividing manufacturing into six more aggregated groups, found a significant (positive) correlation with population for only one group, basic metals, and found a weakly negative correlation for food, beverages, and tobacco.

Chenery's data are preferable in that they are more disaggregated, but this difference hardly explains the full difference in the statistical results. It is possible that because Chenery's calculation includes a few nonindustrial countries and the Western industrial countries, it distorts the relationship among the "semiindustrial" countries. A linear relationship may not be appropriate for the three groups in combination. The true influence of size of economy of scale may lie somewhere between the Chenery and Maizels calculations.

In any event, large population is not enough. For example, an indefinitely large number of persons with annual incomes of $60 each will not create a market large enough to support an automobile industry. Expansion of the demand for many industrial products accelerates as per capita income rises above a certain level. The income level at which this occurs varies with the products.

Neither did it occur to the conferees to consider the implications of the fact that the size of the market needed for minimum-cost production by an industry is not a constant, but depends on the state of techniques in the industry. The volume of production needed for minimum cost production of jet aeroplanes is much greater than was that for DC–3s, and that for supersonic planes is much greater than that for jets. The volume of production needed for minimum-cost production of tin cans increased greatly when certain automatic production processes were devised; that for automobiles increased when an improvement in alloys made possible the stamping out of parts in huge presses; and so on.

Equally important for the study of development, the generalizations concerning necessary and sufficient scale apply only to countries that possess the technical capability to operate the techniques which any given scale implies. Conversely, a country with a high level of technical capacity may produce a good successfully, and export it, even though its own market alone is not large enough to support the industry. Burma, with its population of more than 25 million, possesses neither the market nor the productive capacity for any of the manufacturing industries which, the conference concluded, can thrive in a country of this size. But automobile production is well established in high-income and high-technology Sweden, even though the population of Sweden is less than half as great. No doubt when their technologies and incomes have risen above present world levels, many countries smaller than 10 million in population will support some of these industries.

If the I.E.A. conference had been held in the 1960s, the conferees might have considered the cases of products for which still larger production volumes are required for minimum cost: high-speed computer systems, supersonic aeroplanes, and interplanetary space vehicles. The enterprisers of most European countries do not regard themselves as large enough to attempt the production of high-speed computers. France and Great Britain think it necessary to combine to attain the size of productive complex necessary for the production of supersonic airplanes. And only the Soviet Union and the United States deem themselves large enough, at the mid-20th-century point of technical progress, and—even with the government being the organizing unit—to undertake the production of interplanetary space vehicles. And as techniques and men's vision advance, it may be hypothesized that neither of these countries alone will have sufficient resources or market for some technically feasible and perhaps attractive ventures, even with the government summoning up the necessary resources; and still later some technically feasible and attractive venture may be beyond the economic scope of the entire world at that time. Some ventures in the exploration of space may be illustrative of each of these cases.

BIBLIOGRAPHICAL NOTE

In the 1960s there appeared a group of publications on the improvement of human capabilities through education, none by personality theorists and some disregardful of the evidence of personality theory concerning factors that limit or enhance the receptivity of individuals to education (and thereby disturb the purely economic view). See for example T. W. Schultz (1963 and 1967a) and H. Correa (1963). Harbison and Myers (1964) stress the role of education in growth. C. A. Anderson and Bowman (1965) present a useful collection of essays on the subject of education and economic development. See also B. A. Weisbrod (1964). E. A. G. Robinson and J. E. Vaizey, eds. (1966) present the proceedings of a conference held by the International Economic Association. The essays by Eckaus (1964), Bowles (1967), and Adelman (1966) are discussed in the text and identified in footnotes.

III

The Allocation of Resources for Optimum Growth

The remaining seven chapters of this book deal with the allocation of resources between consumption and investment and with their allocation within both areas to best serve present and future welfare. I have not written "to maximize growth," for the problem is more complicated than that. Maximizing growth may not maximize even future welfare, much less welfare in the present and future considered together. The complexities of allocation have been implicit in some of the discussion above. In Part III they are gradually brought into the open.

Any measure for the financing of investment from either domestic or foreign sources (Chapters 13–14 and 17) affects the allocation of investible resources (Chapters 16, 18, and 19) to some degree, and any measure affecting the allocation of investment alters the flow of income into investment in some way.

Domestic Saving: General Considerations

13

FINANCIAL LIBERALISM VERSUS SELECTIVE INTERVENTION

There are two contrasting sets of policies for the management of resources for development. Each ranges across both financing and allocation. One may be referred to as "financial liberalism," the other as "comprehensive intervention."[1] Neither set is quite, like history, a seamless web, for it is logically possible to separate some policies that would be regarded as belonging to one set from the rest of the set. Yet the two groups of policies arise from such opposed views of the nature of the economic world that each group forms a psychologically if not quite necessarily logically coherent whole. There are no countries that have adopted the complete course of action that the financial liberalists prescribe; even the few countries that they point to—usually, South Korea and Taiwan—intervene to a considerable extent. One can, however, name a large group of lower income countries that intervene rather comprehensively, and only a few that stand in the middle ground between these and the few where in the main liberalist policies prevail, so that thinking of

---

[1] Edward S. Shaw (1973) refers to the first as "financial deepening," by virtue of the fact that a prominent aspect is the accumulation of financial assets at a faster pace than accumulation of nonfinancial wealth. Ronald I. McKinnon (1973) terms it (or the movement toward it) "financial liberalization." Both refer to the opposite set of policies as "financial repression." While both men are professors at Stanford University, the view they express should not be thought of as representing a "Stanford school" of thought; many economists elsewhere express similar views. McKinnon acknowledges his debt to Shaw.

the two sets of policies as polar opposites is not an extreme distortion. To describe the two sets of policies will provide a convenient frame of reference for the two final parts of this book, and it will be convenient and also conducive to clarity to describe each in its pure form.

Policies of selective intervention arise from the view that the allocation of resources induced by the market is in general or at least very often inimical to the public welfare, and from a view of manufacturing and especially capital-intensive manufacturing as especially desirable because it is "modern." The purposes of intervention, then, are to foster growth in general and especially the growth of manufacturing industry. This involves the replacement of traditional by modern methods of production but especially "import substitution," the replacement of importing goods by their domestic production. Avowedly, the purpose is also to obtain an equitable distribution of income, but this consideration turns out to be of secondary importance, easily sacrificed in the supposed interest of growth.

The goal is pursued by intervention of various kinds. By fiscal devices: discriminatory tax levies, selective tax exemptions, subsidies. By administrative regulations to make ventures of certain types more attractive by limiting them to selected firms by means of franchises, permits, licenses without which entry is forbidden. By credit and interest mechanisms: ceilings on permitted interest rates, government loans to favored industries at low interest rates, credit quotas. By legal regulation of the profits of foreign firms, and of minimum wages in large-scale manufacturing. By protection of existing domestic manufacturing enterprises or ones about to be born against foreign competition by means of tariffs, import quotas or prohibitions, provision of foreign exchange at selectively low rates to selected industries or for the purchases of some or all types of capital goods, especially capital goods for manufacturing (rather than for small-scale production or for agriculture). The result is that foreign exchange will be scarcer than otherwise for other importers, and is unavailable or available only at higher cost for imports of all other capital goods or consumer goods.

This situation is accentuated by the fact that officials who favor these policies also usually favor and establish official exchange rates that overvalue the currency. This, so far as foreign exchange is available, makes all imports cheaper; one unit of domestic currency buys a larger amount of foreign goods than otherwise. But the same policy penalizes exports and discourages them or makes them impossible, since sales in foreign currencies at the world price will yield an artificially low amount of domestic currency. Hence the total supply of foreign exchange is reduced, whereas the imports of favored importers are increased because of the reduction in cost. Thus the supply of foreign exchange for general imports is even lower, and the cost where there is no regulation is bid even higher than if the domestic currency were not overvalued. Administrative control of all imports is then likely to be thought necessary, and the result is the complete unavailability rather than merely very high price of imports regarded as least essential, including—if the foreign-exchange crunch becomes severe—the intermediate products needed by some producers.

Because competition by domestic producers with foreign ones is made more difficult by this foreign exchange rate policy, subsidies to exporters or to industrial exporters may be established. A complete set of import and export subsidies would amount to devaluation of the currency. Selective subsidies (or equivalent), necessarily burdening nonfavored sectors, are in the nature of the policy.

The costs of some manufacturers who have been favored may continue indefinitely to be high relative to the costs of foreign producers because of their own sloth within protection or because the country does not have the raw materials, the size of market, or the industrial complex that would permit efficiency. If so, they may require and may receive permanent protection and may even so be able to produce only for the domestic market—at prices that would exceed import prices if imports were permitted.

A few countries eager to develop manufacturing who follow policies of selective intervention open their doors wide to foreign manufacturing firms, and may even grant tax favors. However, the view of the world that underlies selective intervention is likely to include a judgment—or feeling—that foreign corporations will thwart the public interest and must be closely circumscribed. In many lower income countries, foreign corporations are therefore admitted only with restrictions that cause many multinational corporations not to enter.

The advocates of financial liberalism state that forced saving through governmental budget deficits that cause inflation is a necessary result of the policy of selective intervention. It is certainly not a necessary result, but it is true that the financial restrictions mentioned above are likely to reduce the volume of private credit expansion, and thus permit or make necessary a budget deficit to achieve the financial expansion that could and might otherwise occur privately. Deficit financing sufficient to cause inflation may but need not be associated.

Comprehensive selective intervention probably induces the earlier development of some manufacturing than would occur otherwise. It is likely to bring about a high-wage industrial sector. It almost certainly causes duality; that is, lower income in agriculture, petty services, and perhaps small industry relative to income in other urban sectors than would otherwise exist. The advocates of financial liberalism assert that the large excess capacity found throughout manufacturing industry in many lower income countries is due to policies that make capital artifically cheap and grant valuable import privileges to manufacturing firms. These and other effects are discussed in this and the following chapters. The relative effects on growth of selective intervention and financial liberalism are discussed in Chapter 18.

The essential features of financial liberalism can be stated briefly: freedom of interest rates from regulation and absence of discriminatory taxes, subsidies, or regulations of any kind as among industries or among individual enterprises, including foreign-owned enterprises. This includes absence of any tariffs or other restrictions, controls, or subsidies on imports, exports, or foreign exchange movements. Necessarily, it also includes allowing the foreign exchange rate to settle at the level at which the demand for and supply of foreign exchange are in balance. It includes also absence of minimum wages.

Higher interest rates will result, interest rates rising to the order of magnitude of 15% or 20% higher than the inflation rate, judging from the experience of South Korea and Taiwan during relevant periods.[2] These are rates that reflect the demand for and scarcity of capital, rates at which all available capital is wanted. Individuals or firms are also likely to feel that savings are more secure. The results of these two conditions, advocates of financial liberalism argue, will be a lower level of consumption and a higher level of saving available for capital formation. (Small variations in "real" interest rates, say between 4% and 8%, do not seem to affect saving appreciably, but it is plausible that a rise in real interest to 12%, 15%, or 20% does so.) There will also, it is argued, be less or no export of capital from the country, and greater private credit expansion which will take up slack in the economy if any exists, hence less and perhaps no need for governmental deficit financing of investment.

If these liberal policies are adopted while manufacturing industry is still in its infancy, its early development will probably be slower. Advocates argue, however, that the emergence of manufacturing enterprises able to compete in foreign markets will be faster, and that manufacturing industry as a whole and national production as a whole will grow more rapidly. They also argue that with capital costs not artificially low and labor costs not artificially high, methods of production in manufacturing and elsewhere will be more labor-intensive, partly because the change in relative factor costs will induce production of a different mix of products. Thus, it is concluded, under financial liberalism the distribution of income will be less unequal.

These contentions will be discussed in this and the following chapters.

Under a policy of financial liberalism, there may be temporary protection or subsidy to infant industry, though because "temporary" protection or subsidy is politically difficult to remove, the more extreme advocates of financial liberalism oppose even this. Some financial liberalists, for ex-

---

[2] See McKinnon (1973), pp. 109 and 115.

ample McKinnon (1974), argue that land reform that reduces agricultural output is likely to be a part of selective intervention policies, but there seems no strong reason why it should be more associated with this than with the opposite policy.

With this frame set forth, let us consider the obtaining of resources for investment.

THE NEED TO SAVE

Given the existence of a large enough number of entrepreneurs wishing to invest and capable of investing effectively, except for a capital inflow the limit to a country's rate of capital formation and its rate of growth is its restriction of consumption and diversion of productive resources from the production of consumption goods. The resources thus freed can be used for the production of capital goods or of goods for export to finance the import of needed capital goods that cannot be made within the country. In money terms, the limit is the flow of savings that can be generated to finance investment and to permit exports the proceeds from which can finance capital goods imports. Not all exports are available for this purpose. Some merely imply specialization in satisfying consumption demands and will be used to finance the import of consumer goods imports; only proceeds in excess of those used for this purpose can finance capital goods imports. An inflow of capital from abroad can finance capital goods imports or consumer goods imports, thus lessening the need for domestic saving.

Productivity-increasing innovation without capital formation is conceptually possible in individual instances, by managerial improvement, by technical inventions, or in other ways, but there is no recorded case in which it has been sufficient to obviate the need for a marked rise in capital formation to bring about development in any nongrowing economic system as a whole. The question may then be asked, How high a rate of saving and investment is needed to bring about a given rate of growth in GDP and GNP?

Net saving equal to 4% or 5% of GDP normally yields no economic growth, for this is about the ratio needed for mere capital widening for an annual increment of 1% or 1.5% in the labor force. At higher rates of population growth, the percentage of GDP that must be invested merely to "keep up with the labor force" is correspondingly higher. True, investment out of depreciation allowances will constitute an added 3% or 4% of GDP, even in a technically static low-income economy, and if that investment begins to embody technical advances, it can contribute to growth even though the bookkeeping of firms shows it as merely replacing depreciated equipment. But it cannot contribute enough, and if there is to be development, the ratio of saving to national product must rise significantly.

Estimating Capital Requirements

There is no a priori principle by which to estimate the rate of capital formation required to achieve a given rate of growth. All that can be done to estimate the capital formation needed in country A is to examine the ratio of capital formation to growth in productive capacity[3] (the ICOR, defined in Chapter 10) in a country or countries thought to be similar to country A, or the past ICOR in country A. There was a time, soon after World War II, when for want of a better figure economic analysts discussing the prospective development of a low-income country took 3 as a first approximation estimate of the gross ICOR. This figure had a very limited empirical base: the experience of the United States since about 1870, and scattered rough estimates for a few "less developed" countries. It was better than no estimate, and indeed is not too far from the average of ICORs for recent years in developing countries. However, the variation in ICORs among countries at similar levels of income is so great that an average ratio has a wide margin of error. Rather than 3 or 4, the ICOR may be 2, or perhaps 5 or 6 or 7. Recent estimates show the following ICORs for the period 1960–70: Uruguay, 11.0; Iceland, 8.9; Thailand, 4.5; Taiwan, 2.2; Nigeria, 1.9; Mozambique, 1.6.

Those ICORs and the others shown in Figure 11–3 are conceptually very crude measures. In some of these countries new natural resource deposits were discovered; in others, not. In some the labor force was increasing much more rapidly than in others. No doubt innovation was proceeding at various rates in various countries. The sectoral composition of increase in output varied; capital requirements per unit of added output are much higher in housing and infrastructure than the average ICOR in agriculture, manufacturing, or services. Norway's ICOR is high because of the importance of shipping and hydroelectric production in its economic activity. A country's population size, by affecting the size of its industrial sector at any given level of income, affects its ICOR. Its geographical size and population density both probably affect its ICOR by affecting its need for infrastructure per unit of GDP. The ratio of capital formation and of growth in GDP to the level of GDP are much higher in some countries than in others. All of these factors and others affect capital requirements per unit of added productive capacity. Until more research has been done on the factors causing variations in ICORs, the best estimate of a country's ICOR for the next decade is probably its ICOR for the past decade, with quasi-objective allowance for marked

---

[3] Or the ratio between the percentage of each to GDP.

change in circumstances. A short appendix to this chapter discusses the concept of the ICOR and its measurement further.

The Optimum Rate of Saving

A country's prospective ICOR will have little relationship to the percentage of their national income that the people of the country collectively save. The question arises whether a planner should choose a growth rate for his country and then ask how the saving needed to finance it can be generated, or should accept some given saving rate as optimum and then plan the growth rate that that flow of saving will finance.

The neoclassical economists once thought they knew how to define the optimum rate of saving, and they were willing to accept whatever rate of growth resulted from it. The market rate of interest on riskless loans, they said, reflects the society's evaluation of the relative desirability of present and future goods, and the optimum rate of saving is the saving rate stimulated by that rate of interest. This market decision, as the neoclassical economists visualized it, is influenced by the increase in future income anticipated by the savers as a result of their saving. If the rate of interest is 4%, then 1.04 units of goods one year from now, $(1.04)^2$ units two years from now, or $(1.04)^n$ units n years from now are regarded as equal in desirability to 1 unit now, and any larger amounts of goods at the future dates are regarded as more satisfying. Then, if investment will yield more than a 4% rate of return (after allowance for risk), the future goods it will yield are more desired than present goods, members of the society will save and invest to obtain the preferred future goods, and that rate of saving which just finances all investment projects which meet this criterion is the optimum rate. Indeed, the interest rate settled at 4% because this is the rate at which the flow of saving by persons willing to save if they could earn a 4% rate of return just equaled the flow of investment which would earn this rate or more. The choices made by individuals between present consumption and future consumption are one blade of the scissors by which the market rate of interest is determined. The other blade is the bidding by would-be investors for funds. If a society saves very little, this is because its members have a very high rate of time preference, so that even if interest rates are high the net flow of saving is small—equal to the small flow of investment that can earn this high rate of return.

There is a large element of truth in this neoclassical view. If almost no individuals in a society save over their lifetimes this is certainly because they do not find the investment opportunities open to them attractive enough to induce them to save. But economists are no longer so sure that these choices have much relationship to the rate of interest, or that this behavior, aggregated for the society, yields a result that is optimum in the judgment of the present and future members of the society taken as a group.

First, economists are less certain that future goods are of less value to individuals, taking their choices both now and in the future into account, than are present goods. The two supposed reasons for this preference are the diminishing utility of successive increments of income and "pure time preference." It is an observed psychological fact, it is argued, that successive increments of income give diminishing satisfaction. Hence an increment of future consumption will have to be greater than the decrement of present consumption required to yield it, to be equally desired. But Duesenberry observed that the choice a family makes of the shares of its income to be consumed and saved respectively depends on its position in the income distribution, not on its absolute income. Saving by each family seems to depend more on keeping one's consumption up with the Joneses than on calculations concerning the future, and the percent of income saved by the community does not rise even though the society's per capita income rises. This fact casts doubt on the applicability of the diminishing utility of income thesis, and indeed throws into confusion the entire attempt to compare the present and future utility of increments of income.

As for "pure time preference," no doubt an individual may prefer an increment of consumption now to one at a future date, but at the future date he will probably prefer it then to having had it earlier. So in assaying the community's optimum distribution of income over time, there seems no reason to weight any one moment in time more heavily than another.

There are other reasons for doubting the validity of the market rate of interest as a measure of time preference. First, Keynesian theory suggests that the rate of interest is determined in part by choices by individuals and firms concerning the amount of funds they want to hold liquid even at the sacrifice of interest, and hence is hardly a measure merely of time preference. Second, full employment may be maintained in an economy either by an easy money policy combined with a high level of government receipts relative to expenditures, or by a tight money policy combined with a lower level of government receipts relative to expenditures. Interest rates will be lower in the former case than in the latter, and investment will be greater. Which more truly reflects the society's preference as between present and future?

Moreover, other factors that have little to do with interest rates influence saving decisions. An individual may prefer to save more, to increase the society's income in the future, if his government imposes saving on all other individuals through fiscal policy, than if he alone were saving. But the votes which decide governmental action in the matter will be on a one vote per person basis, not according to income. Hence they are two long steps removed from the money market.

Many people in low-income countries today want higher levels of income for their countries partly because they want their countries to be given more recognition by the technically advanced countries. Time preference has little to do with the matter.

In the light of these considerations, and others that might be raised, the concept of an unambiguously defined optimum rate of saving and investment seems to many economists to be a will-o'-the-wisp.[4] In fact, people save and invest a fraction of their incomes for purposes and perhaps because of unconscious motives that have little to do with rational growth rates. In a democracy, saving by the government will be determined by complex sets of considerations, many of which have little to do with economic growth. The collective decision may be influenced by the presentation to the public of a great national purpose, but only in the largely fictitious case of a dictatorship that can disregard the public will on such issues can a planner think of greatly altering the national saving rate by his decision.

THE SOURCES OF SAVING FOR EARLY INNOVATION

Broadly speaking, there are four possible domestic sources of funds for capital formation within a nonindustrial, low-income economy, and only four. Savings may be obtained through their thrift or by coercion from (1) agriculture (cultivators or landlords), (2) trader-financiers, or (3) consumers, or the savings rate may rise through the increasing plowing back of profits by innovators. The broad bases are the first and third. If a large flow of saving is to be obtained quickly in a traditional economy, part of the value of agricultural production must be siphoned off for investment; this may be done by reducing the income of the peasants, the landlords, or the consumers, many of whom will of course be the peasants. In a private enterprise economy, this siphoning off will presumably be done by interposing a tax between the cost of production and the retail price of mass-consumed goods; in a socialist economy, it may be done by interposing a markup on the price of the goods as they pass through the hands of the state. Japan financed rapid industrialization by siphoning off the large stream of income that had previously gone to the feudal lords. The Soviet Union did so by forced levies on the peasants and by imposing a large markup, only part of which was a substitute for the "rent" previously taken by feudal landlords. In the few fortunate countries rich in petroleum or other natural resources, a fifth source of revenue exists: the revenues from exploitation of these resources. In addition to these domestic sources, funds may be attracted from abroad.

The financing of early growth is virtually always by private initiative and from private sources. Virtually no government is ready to take the

---

[4] Sen (1961) discusses most of the considerations stated above, and also others.

actions needed to divert energies from traditionally satisfying activities to the management of development, and to divert resources from traditional uses to investment, until a corps of private individuals in the country have entered upon growth, and provide the demand and the support for effective government action.

Landlord Entrepreneurship

In at least three historical cases, landowners have been contributors in important amounts to investment and progress in agriculture. In England, nobles and members of the landed gentry carried out the enclosures and later, in the 18th century, both conceived of new projects connected with the land and invested large amounts of money in them: new methods of cultivation, toll roads, and canals. They were the entrepreneurs as well as the investors. As noted in Chapter 11, these were not members of the most elite group of lords and landowners. Rather, they were the "country gentry," somewhat looked down upon by their court cousins. In Germany, the Junkers carried out changes in agricultural methods that required both their personal involvement and, in some cases, sizable investments. And in Japan, which in this respect as in so many others is a special case, landlords and peasants have cooperated, with initiative from both, in technical progress. There are records of increases in agricultural yields during the Ashikaga period, 1336–1582.[5] It is not clear whether landlord-peasant cooperation, with dual initiative, was the vehicle at this early period, but it clearly was from the early Tokugawa period until the end of landlordism after World War II.

In many other countries some early agricultural innovation has been carried out and financed by an occasional deviant feudal landlord. In some parts of Latin America and Africa, early agricultural as well as industrial innovation seems to have been by self-financing, restless entrepreneurs who had been neither traditional landowners nor traditional peasants but rather were "economic men" in societies that had never jelled fully into a traditional state. In other traditional societies, there has been little early agricultural innovation. Technical progress in agriculture has lagged after that elsewhere. There is no recorded case in which early peasant initiative or finance has been of great quantitative importance.

The Expansion of Peasant Production

The expansion of agricultural production by peasants by the occupation of idle lands when a world market was opened up to them is sometimes discussed as if it had been the beginning of technical innovation in agriculture. In fact, it was not. The peasants merely flooded onto

---

[5] Reischauer and Fairbank (1958), p. 557.

new lands and produced crops by the same old methods. But this development required investment to clear the new lands and plant the crops, and a "wages fund" to sustain the peasants while they carried out the investment.

The exploitation of mineral resources and the establishment of plantation agriculture, in the early period of Western colonial control or domination of a less developed country, was financed by the Western enterprisers who promoted the ventures—first from their own external funds, later partly or wholly from the profits of the ventures. But when Western traders opened world markets to the peasant cultivators of the less developed countries, the financing of expanded agricultural production was usually by trader-lenders of the country itself or of other less developed countries and by intention but not in the end by the peasant cultivators themselves.

The main peasant-produced agricultural exports are rice, from Southeast Asia, and cocoa and palm oil, from West Africa. Cocoa and palm oil are plantation products in Brazil, Indonesia, and Malaya, but in West Africa cacao and palm trees are grown by peasant proprietors, who between or alongside them grow food for their own use. In Southeast Asia rice itself is of course the main peasant food. Idle land was available in both areas, needing only to be cleared and planted. The trader-financiers provided the "wages fund" on which peasants lived for a year, and the peasants cleared the land and planted the crop. Since the increase in the value of the land was then more than the amount of the year's subsistence, the peasants should be regarded as contributing the saving, in kind, by their labor in building up this wealth. Often, the peasants soon lost their land. The "subsistence fund" which the money-lender had advanced was recouped with interest. By this process large areas were opened up, production greatly expanded, and the level of income of peasants undoubtedly raised.

There is little opportunity for repetition of the process. There are few remaining areas in the world that could be opened up by the work of groups of peasant families alone. Perhaps there are some in Africa.

Trade and Commerce

Early innovation in trade and commerce has usually been financed by the traders themselves, who came into the business from other countries with resources previously accumulated, or plowed back profits from local trading.

Early Industrial Investment

The members of the landed class in probably every less developed country have sufficient capital and sufficient income to finance even relatively large industrial ventures, but their contribution has been small. In no country has the landed group contributed a considerable fraction of early investment in industry. However, parallel to the several instances of landlord innovation in agriculture, there is at least one case of landowner entry directly into industry. In the Middle East some large landowners have since 1950 established manufacturing plants to process the products of their lands.

Some growth theorists when considering the possible sources of industrial financing seem to have in mind implicitly the static economic model of value and distribution theory, used so powerfully and fruitfully in much economic analysis but not intended to apply to the growth process. In this model, because it is static, there can be no source of saving to finance innovation except one that already exists before innovation begins. On this basis, a surplus in agriculture, the one large sector of the economy before industrial innovation began, must finance early industrial investment. Theorists have developed two-sector models to illustrate how the agricultural surplus was accumulated, and how transferred. They are concerned with such problems as how there could be a surplus labor force in agriculture available to be recruited for capital formation in industry, how its food supply in industry was provided, once it had transferred, and how savings could emerge to finance the use of this labor in capital formation rather than in the production of consumer goods.

One of the most elaborate of these models is that of John Fei and Gustav Ranis.[6]

The Fei-Ranis Model

The model is explicitly one of a dualistic economy, in which the marginal productivity of a considerable share of agricultural labor is zero. Workers can therefore leave the agricultural sector without reduction in agricultural production. Consumption per capita of remaining cultivators in the model remains constant. The food previously consumed by the workers who transfer to industry is therefore available to be sold to the industrial sector, where the new industrial workers buy it out of their wages. All of these workers can be employed in producing capital goods, for there is no increase in the aggregate demand for consumer goods, since (in the model) all of the income received by agriculture from the sale of this food is saved. The savers become owners of industrial capital. The model is thus consistent; there is a flow of workers into industry and

---

[6] Fei and Ranis (1964); but an earlier paper (1961) presents the core of their analysis.

a flow of saving to permit their use in capital formation rather than the production of consumer goods.

The assumptions underlying the model have some peculiar implications, however. Why were workers with zero marginal productivity given employment in agriculture? Hardly by landlords, except for the tiny number of family retainers. The realistic explanation is that they are members of peasant families, who will not turn away members to starve. However, there is ample evidence that peasants whose income rises increase their consumption. Thus if redundant peasant family members shifted to industry, in this way increasing the per capita income of the families which they left, those families would provide none or only a share (probably a small share) of the saving needed to support the migrant workers in capital formation.

The authors recognize the problem. The simple model which I have summarized above abstracts, they say,

> from the important problems of who *owns* the emerging agricultural surplus and who *owns* the newly created industrial capital goods. . . . On the one hand, the ownership of the released agricultural surplus may be in question, i.e., may vest in the cultivator, the landlord, or the government; and on the other hand, the ownership of the newly created industrial goods may be vested in government, the industrialists, or even possibly in the workers. In all such realistic cases when the released worker does not "carry" his own released consumer bundle with him, institutional arrangements must be devised to effect the necessary transfer.[7]

The "institutional arrangements," they imply, are someone else's business. Yet without consideration of those arrangements the model is of limited empirical significance. The authors refer to Japan repeatedly, and may have drawn their model from observation of Japan, yet there is no historical evidence that in Japan there were "surplus" agricultural workers. Rather, the government took over in taxes a large share of the income that had previously flowed to the feudal lords, which they had been spending on consumption. Similarly, the government of the Soviet Union reduced consumption to finance capital formation. Where this is done, there is no need to assume the prior existence of surplus labor; coercive reduction in consumption will free resources for capital formation even though they had previously been highly productive. The model is much more elaborate than is necessary to explain such cases.

If surplus workers do transfer from agriculture to capital formation, there of course is no need for saving in agriculture to permit this. Saving anywhere in the economy will serve the purpose. Actually, saving in

---

[7] Fei and Ranis (1964), p. 26. The italics are theirs.

traditional agriculture has contributed relatively little to the financing of development. The Fei-Ranis model is discussed here because it attracted considerable attention when first presented. It did so partly because of the static view then held (discussed above, in the preceding subsection) of the sources of saving, and it contributed to understanding of relationships between income and resource flows, but it discusses what is largely a "non-event," and is of limited empirical relevance.

Plowing Back Profits

Where else, then, may the saving that financed early industrial innovation have come from in "real life"? Historical evidence is not sufficient to make firm statements, but the following seems probable. Not in a large flow from merchant-financiers as a group, because of the mentality sketched in Chapter 11 in discussing industrial entrepreneurship. Nor from small craftsmen as a group. Cottage industry proprietors collectively probably do not save much. Moreover, they seemingly typically have a peasant or petty shopkeeper mentality that does not include sufficient breadth of vision or inclination to risk-taking that would lead them to put their savings into larger ventures, their own or someone else's. Landes (1949, 1954) and Sawyer (1954a, 1954b) have argued that the petty bourgeois, family-centered, antirisk-taking mentality of French shopkeepers hobbled French economic development in the 19th century. Gerschenkron (1953) has replied that the expense of coal supply for power was the cause of perpetuation of the family firm.[8] The fact that a similar phenomenon is found in many other countries suggests that the Landes-Sawyer thesis hits upon the more important cause.

But some craftsmen-traders whose small businesses had prospered through their capability became industrial innovators, and some merchants whose larger businesses had prospered through their capability became industrial innovators. As noted in Chapter 11, these latter probably were not members of a traditional merchant-financier class but rather men who earlier had been small craftsmen-traders selling their own products, or, more likely, the sons or grandsons of such men, who had moved on to larger things.

Once they were small industrial innovators, they had financed themselves from the plowing back of their profits into their businesses. A small producer devised an improvement which increased quality or reduced costs. A profit margin appeared. He lived frugally, expanded his business from his earnings, and presently, in say 10 or 20 years, through the plowing back of his profits he became a major industrialist.

A reader of historical biographies is impressed by the frequency of this

---

[8] See the further discussion by this author, 1954.

route to industrial innovation. Samuel Smiles' biographies of English industrialists, an occasional account in Ospina Vasquez's book *Industria y Proteccion en Colombia, 1810–1930* (1955), and brief references in writings concerning Japanese industrialization, are all impressive.[9]

W. Arthur Lewis' model of "development with unlimited supplies of labor," summarized in Chapter 8, portrays precisely this process of plowback. This, Lewis suggests, is the major way in which the rise in capital formation from "4 or 5 percent" to "about 12 or 15 percent" of national income occurs. To the present writer this model seems to portray much the most important process by which early industrial development is financed. In Lewis' model, there is "surplus labor," with low though not necessarily zero marginal productivity. The present writer has indicated in Chapter 8 the judgment that such labor probably exists in considerable amounts in many economies because of the present rapid increase in the total labor force, if not previously. However, as noted in Chapter 8, the existence of surplus labor is not a necessary condition for the freeing of resources for capital formation in Lewis' model (though the model would be materially altered in some respects if this assumption were removed).

LABOR-INTENSIVE CAPITAL PROJECTS

It has been suggested by various writers that the "hidden rural savings" (Nurkse's term) embodied in the under-used labor of low-productivity agricultural workers can be captured directly, by drawing those workers into labor-intensive rural capital projects. If those workers have zero productivity, the social cost—loss of other output—is zero, it is said; if they have positive but low productivity, the cost is low. Dams, irrigation or drainage channels, wells, roads, village water reservoirs, rude village schools, river bank improvements to contain rivers in flood time— all these and other rural public works call out to be constructed. Government action to mobilize such labor in the construction of such projects has been urged.

The difficulties that lie in the way are greater than appears on the surface.[10] In the first place, workers cannot build capital projects with their bare hands. There must be some cooperating capital equipment. This includes not only the capital equipment directly used in the project but also, if the project is a large one, construction of a community in which the workers can live. Its provision will require either a net addition

---

[9] Smiles' accounts are well varnished. He adulated the subjects of his biographies. But this probably does not greatly distort his evidence concerning the point in question here. Ospina Vasquez's book is the standard work concerning early economic development in Colombia. The present writer was also impressed by a number of accounts that he heard orally from the sons or grandsons of Colombian innovators. Concerning Japan, see for example Hirschmeier and Yamamura in Kilby (1971).

[10] Nurkse (1953, Chap. 2) gives a succinct statement of the difficulties.

to saving elsewhere in the economic system or diversion of a flow of saving from some other capital formation. But let us assume that the cost of capital equipment amounts to 20% of the cost that would be incurred in building the project in the normal way. If, then, a labor-intensive method is substituted (involving a different engineering design), and otherwise idle labor would provide the remainder of the productive effort, then the project would still seem to be, to the extent of 80% of its value, socially costless except for the sacrifice of otherwise idle time.

The net gain is the greater, the greater the degree to which (other things being equal) the project is labor-intensive. If a dam can be built with the use of large tractors, cranes, and rollers, and alternatively with the labor of thousands of additional workers using hand scoops, hand-operated simple hoists, and manually-operated tamping devices, which together constitute less capital than would otherwise be needed, and if the workers would otherwise be unproductive, then there is a net increase in the capital formation of which the economy is capable.

Apart from the "leakage" (Nurkse's term) involved in the cost of capital equipment used in the labor-intensive method, another item has sometimes been referred to as a cost to the economy in such labor-intensive projects. This is the increase in goods that must be provided for consumption. Increased consumption goods will be required for two reasons: because the erstwhile underemployed workers will eat more, now that they are working vigorously, and because the cultivator families from which they were drawn, having higher income per remaining member, will consume more.

While a cost is involved, it is not a net cost to the economy. That is, the added cost is matched by an added benefit. The additional consumption goods must be provided, but their cost is precisely equaled by the increased consumption of the workers and peasant families concerned. If the purpose of economic development is to increase the material welfare of members of the society, the increase in consumption directly accomplishes the desired result. A transfer is involved. The added goods consumed must be produced or imported. Some other investment project or some other consumer must then have less. But of course a transfer is not a net cost to the society. There is an aspect of the increased consumption that may not be costless, even in this sense. The consumer goods must be transported to the site of the capital project.

The greatest cost involved may be neither the cost of capital equipment nor the (sometimes negligible) change in transportation costs, but rather the provision of management. There are few models of labor-intensive projects. A partly original engineering design may be required. Innovational engineers and capable administrators in general are among the scarcest resources of less developed countries. The mobilization of the necessary engineering management may therefore be the most difficult aspect of the labor-intensive project; if that management is diverted from other work important in economic development, the cost may be high.

As a result of these considerations, the labor-intensive projects that promise the greatest benefit are those near the homes of the workers who will be employed (to minimize food transport and, if near enough, the provision of new housing), and simple enough in nature so that elaborate new engineering design is unnecessary.

One of the best-known successful programs for the use of underemployed labor to construct labor-intensive public works is a program executed during 1962 and following years in the province of Bangladesh, then East Pakistan, of which Comilla is a central city. Under the direction of the head of a government Academy for Village Development established at Comilla, a man of considerable administrative capability and devoted to village improvement, a pilot program of local public works was executed in a seasonally dull period, January–April, 1962. Its success led to provincewide programs during the following four years, under the general direction of an able provincial official. Roads were resurfaced and new roads built, canals that had filled in reexcavated, culverts and bridges constructed, sand erosion control dams built, and dikes and embankments for flood and irrigation control built. Altogether a considerable number of million man-months of paid work have been executed by villagers. Floods that would otherwise have ruined or damaged spring crops were prevented, and marketing costs considerably reduced. The costs were initially borne by the central government, and those after 1963 out of the proceeds from the import of surplus U.S. agricultural commodities obtained through a $621 million loan from the United States government.[11] After 1965, the size of the program had to be reduced because of a reduction in the amount of U.S. surplus commodities that could be made available, and the program apparently had dwindled to nonexistence some time before the Bangladesh war for independence disrupted the society. It had been opposed and where possible obstructed by landlords because of the lessened dependence of peasants and increased cost of agricultural wage labor that occurred even though the work was performed mainly in the off-season. That increase perhaps testifies that the labor employed had not been entirely unproductive previously.

The United Nations Food and Agriculture Organization, which is an enthusiastic proponent of the use of agricultural surpluses for this purpose, estimated in a 1955 publication that almost half of the total cost of labor-intensive capital projects will consist of the increased consumption

[11] This information is summarized from R. Gilbert (1964). Gilbert presents figures which indicate that the reduction in transportation cost resulting from some of the rural roads built increased the peasants' gross revenue from their produce by about 6 percent.

of agricultural products of the types then available as surpluses, and that this share of the cost can therefore be financed by obtaining surplus products. The existence of surplus agricultural products in high-income countries, especially in the United States, was a more conspicuous fact of life then than 20 years later.

LATER STAGES OF DEVELOPMENT

Marginal Saving Rates

As development proceeds, the flow of savings by corporations increases in size. An increasing flow of individual savings is invested in savings institutions or in securities in the capital market and is thus made available to investors. Government captures an increasing share of the national income in taxes, and an increasing share of government expenditures is devoted to public capital formation. A flow of saving sufficient to finance growth at some positive rate can be taken for granted. The discussion above has dealt mainly with the "natural history" of the saving process in early growth. One question concerning the natural history of savings in later stages of growth remains. Can the percentage of private income saved, plus the willingness of citizens to bear increasing taxes and of the government to hold down its current expenditures, be expected to rise sufficiently with rising income to finance an expanding development program?

Many persons hoping for the rapid development of the less developed countries place high hope in the marginal saving ratio. If a country begins to develop so that its per capita income begins to rise, then surely private individuals and the government can be expected to save a relatively large fraction of the additional income. If they do, the average saving ratio will rise steadily, and the country will become increasingly capable of financing its own domestic investment, though not necessarily the foreign exchange cost of that investment. For example, if a country with per capita national income of $100 saves 8% of it, and if it saves one fifth of increments of income, then when income has risen to $150 per capita the average saving ratio will have risen to 12%. The high marginal saving rate may occur because of a tendency of individuals to save high fractions of increments to income, or because the government feels able to levy high taxes on rising incomes. However, the hope that average private saving rates will rise cumulatively as income rises must rest on the assumption that people will continue to save high fractions of added increments of income, even after they have become used to them. The Duesenberry (1949) study of saving makes this seem very unlikely. And heavy government taxation of rising incomes runs into the difficulty that it is very difficult to administer a tax levied specifically on increases in income, and a merely graduated income tax hits persons whose incomes have not risen as well as those whose incomes have. It may therefore be resisted vigorously even after incomes are rising on the average, though perhaps not as vigorously as when they were not rising at all.

If profits are rising as a share of national income (as is to be expected), then the saving ratio should be rising because of the high saving propensity of profit receivers, but it may not rise enough to finance an ambitious development program.

As the rate of saving and investment increase in a country and economic growth begins, per capita income also rises, so that there is a positive statistical relationship between the income level and the saving rate. But beyond this early period, the saving rate seems not to rise as income continues to rise, and the positive statistical relationship disappears. Mikesell and Zinser (1973) have summarized studies of savings-income functions in developing countries. More data are available for Latin America than for other lower income areas. Hollis Chenery and Peter Eckstein (1970), using a simple linear savings function, calculated coefficients for each of 16 Latin American countries for the period 1950–64, or about that. Mikesell and Zinser made comparable estimates for periods running usually from 1953 to 1968. A remarkable aspect of the two sets of estimates is the great differences for individual countries, even though there was large overlap in the periods covered. However, in both studies the median and average ratios of saving to national product were between 10% and 15% and in neither study was the marginal ratio consistently above the average ratio. Between 1951 and 1964, per capita income in the 16 Latin American countries rose markedly, on the average—probably by 20% or more. Chenery and Eckstein note that during that period the average saving rate rose only from 16.3% to 16.9%. This very small rise is well within the probable error of the estimates.[12]

However, in a cross-national per capita study, Luis Landau found a significant positive relationship between level of income and level of saving in Latin American countries. He studied 20 countries for each of four periods, 1950–52, 1956, 1958–60, and 1961. He found that countries with higher levels of per capita income tended to save higher percentages of gross national income, though the differences decreased over the 1950–61 period. S. K. Singh (1971) reached the same conclusion in a cross-national study of 70 countries for the 1960–65 period.

These time series and cross-national studies are made consistent if we assume that causation does not run from the level of income to the saving rate but rather in the opposite direction. The higher income countries are

---

[12] Mikesell and Zinser calculated a linear function relating the log of saving to the log of income for the 16 countries for the same periods as their calculation of a linear function relating the absolute figures, thereby obtaining estimates of the elasticity of saving with respect to income. For only 6 of 18 countries was the elasticity above unity.

higher income countries because over a period of years, from the time when their incomes were lower, they had been higher savers and investors (and presumably also more effective innovators).[13]

If this is the correct explanation, then the hope for more rapid growth does not lie in the greater opportunity offered steadily by gradually increasing income, but must lie in some other change that may occur within societies. The hope for a high marginal saving ratio depends on the temper of the country in question. It cannot be depended on to appear universally. It was noted above that Singh reached a contrary conclusion, but even Singh found that a rise in GNP from $100 to $1,000 per capita was associated with only an 8 percentage point increase in the saving rate, half of it due to increase in depreciation allowance rates.[14] Given those figures, at a rate of increase of per capita income of 2% per year it would take 50 years to increase the saving rate by 3%.

Among the other causal factors affecting saving rates are the rate of growth in per capita income and the ratio of exports to GNP. Figure 13–1 presents data concerning the relationship of the rate of growth of per capita income to the saving rate. The scatter is very wide, but there is a diffuse positive relationship. If income is rising rapidly, the data suggest, families fail to adjust their consumption upward rapidly enough to achieve a "normal" relationship to their income, that is, the relationship that would pertain if their income were constant. Duesenberry (1949) observed this phenomena in the U.S. economy; it appears elsewhere as well. It is a partial explanation not only of extreme phenomena such as the very high Japanese saving rate but also of moderate differences in saving rates associated with moderate differences in growth rates. Thus, high growth feeds on itself. (Note that a converse explanation of the relationship—high saving rate financing high investment rate and thereby causing or permitting a high growth rate—is also possible.)

A similar loose positive relationship between saving rates and export rates is shown in Chapter 17, Figure 17–2. This relationship is less easily explained. In part it is due to high government saving rates; exports are easy to tax, and government revenues tend to be higher in relation to GNP in countries with large exports. Perhaps also, exporters are high savers. Or, high export rates yielding high foreign exchange earnings in many instances remove one constraint on investment, and may make possible a utilization of productive resources more fully than elsewhere, and thus, with greater prosperity, more saving. Neither of these theses is

---

[13] Landau concludes that the income level is causal, because the relationship holds true in short-run time series as well as in cross-national analysis. His evidence conflicts with the more broadly based statistical analyses summarized in the text.

[14] Singh used a complex saving function: $(S/Y_g) = a_o + a_1 [Ln (Y_g/Pop)]^{-2} + a_3 [Ln (Y_g/Pop)]^{-4}$.

FIGURE 13–1
Savings as Percent of GDP Related to Per Capita Rate of Growth, 1960–71
(less developed countries)

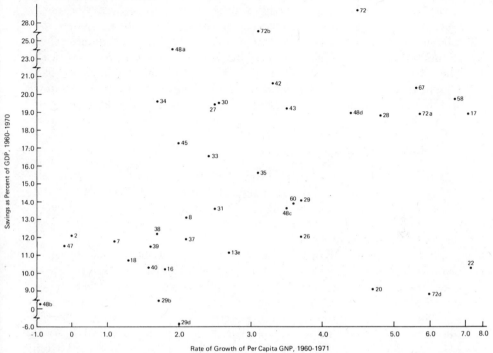

Source: Per capita rates of growth, Table 1–10; Savings, Economic Analyses and Projections Department, World Bank.

well tested empirically; these influences have not been adequately separated out from other influences.

Interest Rates and Saving Rates

Shaw and McKinnon claim that the high interest rates that prevailed in South Korea and Taiwan during the 1960s stimulated very large flows of saving and accumulations of financial assets. The rates of interest on one-year deposits exceeded the rate of change in the wholesale price index by 18.6% at the peak in Taiwan, and by 22.1% in South Korea. The ratio of M_2, the sum of demand deposits, currency, and time and savings deposits, to GNP rose to 47% in Taiwan and to 35% in South Korea by 1970. These ratios compare with ratios ranging from 18% to 30% in Chile, Colombia, Venezuela, Brazil, India, Pakistan, Argentina, Turkey, Ceylon, and the Philippines in 1968 or 1969, 56% to 59% in the United Kingdom,

France, and Belgium in 1969 or 1970, and 70% in the United States in 1970.[15]

Yet that the high accumulations in South Korea and Taiwan resulted primarily or largely from their high interest rates is uncertain. McKinnon himself unwittingly illustrates the reason for doubt when he quotes the following conversation (p. 123): Economist: "Why do the Japanese save so much?" Man on a Tokyo street: "Because our income grows so fast." The rates of growth of income in South Korea and Taiwan may have had a great deal to do with the rapid increase in time and savings accounts and thereby in M_2 in those countries.

Institutional Supports

The discussion thus far in this chapter has ignored the channels through which savings flow from saver to investor, if these are not the same person. Such channels, when they function well in industrial economies, not only improve the allocation of resources; they probably also increase the aggregate flow of saving.

Financial intermediaries, institutions that are not themselves the saver or the investor, but merely accumulate and transfer the funds, are slow to take root in nonprogressive economies. They become important when technical progress and "modern" economic institutions have become built into the society, but they are not effective in the early stages. Of the initial funds of 486 industrial enterprises in Nigeria surveyed in 1965 (Harris, 1967, chap. 7), only 6% or possibly 8% were obtained from financial intermediaries (banks, 6%; moneylenders, 2%). More than two thirds (68%) were own savings, loans or gifts from one's family, or loans or gifts from friends; 7% were loans from suppliers. The remaining 17% were loans from Nigerian investors, from the government, loans from or investment by foreigners resident in Nigeria, and one case of government investment.[16]

Direct lending by the owner of money to the user is as old as human specialization. Traders, whose principle of business is to operate to as large an extent as possible with someone else's capital, early develop the practices of obtaining or extending commercial credit, borrowing or lending on the security of goods, and transmitting funds via commercial banks or their equivalent. Moneylenders lend to peasants on the security of a forthcoming crop, or, where land is alienable, on the security of land.

---

[15] McKinnon, pp. 109 and 115 for South Korea and Taiwan, 95 for the 10 semi-industrialized countries, and 94 for the 4 industrial countries. The semiindustrial countries are listed in the ascending order of the percentages.

[16] The survey included all sources from which one fourth or more of the capital had been obtained.

Pawnshops flourish in probably every low-income country.[17] Cooperative marketing associations or producers' cooperatives are less viable. Fostered "artificially" by the government, they often wither and die.

But the practice of refraining from consumption to exchange income in return for a certificate of debt, in order to obtain interest in anticipation of undefined future need, is slow to develop. Interestingly enough, the first contingency for which the members of low-income societies become ready to save money regularly is death. An early sign of economic development is the appearance of large office buildings in the cities of a country, built with the funds of the insurance societies that have developed. The core of their business is often business insurance of various types, but they will also have sold a large volume of small life insurance policies—so-called "industrial life insurance"—whose petty premiums the agent appears at the door weekly to collect. Savings banks and savings and loan associations are institutions that first come into their own in urban communities, and then only after development is under way. At a later stage, they become very important, especially in the financing of home ownership.

Larger capital market intermediaries—investment banks and securities markets—are still later to appear. Before they can function effectively, a number of concepts alien to traditional societies must become accepted and imbedded in institutions. These include the concepts of: that impersonal legal person, the corporation; the dependability of impersonal contractual obligations, because of the attitudes of the business community (more than through action in the courts); the security of paper claims; the anticipation of future production as wealth. Capital markets, that is, consist not only of a complex of financial organizations: commercial banks, investment banks (in Europe called merchant banks), insurance companies, savings and loan institutions, securities exchanges and their auxiliaries, and others, but also of a web of legal institutions and practices.

Capital markets cannot be created by fiat, or by erecting on paper a set of institutions that would be desirable if only people used them. The refusal to loan to others than family members in a traditional economy is due not to blind tradition but to a justified belief that only family members will respect one's interests. By the criteria used by U Tun Wai, a staff member of the International Monetary Fund (Tun Wai, 1957, p. 194), in the mid-1950s capital market transactions in Latin America were "significant" in scope only in Chile, Colombia, Cuba, and Peru; and in Asia, only in Japan. However, then as later, securities markets play some role in the accumulation of capital by large corporations in India. Shares

---

[17] For a discussion of the establishment of state pawnshops in the colonial Dutch East Indies, see Furnivall (1948).

of stock were marketed as early as the 1880s in Japan, when industrialization was in its infancy, but even after the second World War there was no public market for government bonds. The government sells its bonds through a process of allocation of quotas to the commercial banks, which the banks by convention are obliged to accept.

Sixteen years later, surveying capital markets again, U Tun Wai and Hugh Patrick (1973, p. 268) wrote:

> With only a few exceptions (for example, in Brazil, India, Malaysia, and Singapore), markets are thin, with little or no trading and with relatively few and insignificant amounts of new public issues by private corporations. With a somewhat larger amount of issue, the market for government debt may appear to be more developed, but its sales are mainly to captive buyers. Information is poor and manipulation is substantial, especially for private issues.

"The explanation as to why capital markets are relatively unimportant in LDCs," they add, "lies in a combination of historical circumstances, current level of economic and financial development, and government policy." As changes in attitudes permit, the skillful development of financial institutions can facilitate investment and also perhaps increase saving, but in advance of changes in attitudes, the creation of formal institutions seems of little effect.

Borrowers are always willing to borrow from financial intermediaries: it is the inability of these institutions to accumulate funds, not any lack of market for their services, that prevents their early development. Therefore, government-chartered institutions that obtain loanable funds by credit creation may emerge early and may accelerate development. Examples are the "wildcat banks" and other commercial banks of the United States between the 1820s and the Civil War, and the commercial banks chartered by the government of Japan in the 1870s. Although in the United States case, many ill-judged and wasteful loans were made, nevertheless the development of the area between the Alleghenies and the Mississippi was probably considerably accelerated by the operations of these banks.[18]

In France, beginning with the Credit Mobilier in 1852, and then in Germany and in the smaller countries to the east and south of these, private joint-stock banks sprang up which often were the entrepreneurs as well as the financers of new ventures. In the aggregate they played a quantitatively important role in the development of large-scale industry in their countries. These private investment banks have continued to be important in Germany. In France, they abandoned their entrepreneurial role in considerable degree as time passed, but public and quasi-public

---

[18] Patrick (1966) argues the "supply-leading" rather than merely "demand-following" possibilities of financial intermediaries.

banks have continued to exercise a permissive if not an active entrepreneurial role. Without their endorsement, the flotation of new large issues of securities has been difficult or impossible. In the successive French development plans of the period after World War II, the administrators referred to in the previous section have enforced their guidance of French investment plans by arranging that the government banks require approval of the officials of the *Commissariat au Plan* before endorsing bank loans or bond issues.

The existence in the United States of a very active market for equity as well as debt securities has relieved U.S. corporations of the necessity for such connections with the banking community or the government. In some countries, for example Japan, sponsorship by a given large bank is a necessary aspect of the life of a large corporation. It receives all of its capital, throughout its life, from that bank. The U.S. capital market is the freest in the world, the only one in which foreign securities may be floated without any government restriction except to insure the validity of the issuance and the accuracy of the information provided concerning them.[19]

The skillful elaboration of a set of legal and financial institutions comprising a capital market in Brazil in the mid-1960s was one factor in Brazil's rapid economic growth since 1968.[20] Their importance in this respect should not be exaggerated; Brazil, whose growth in aggregate GNP was at a rate of 9% per year after 1968, had also grown at a rate of 8.3% per year from 1957 to 1961. The 9% rate after 1968 followed three years of recessions caused by severe anti-inflationary measures; the average growth rate from 1964 to 1974 is lower. Yet the post-1968 growth is remarkable.

The institutions established provided attractive yields to savers during inflation; created a long-term debt market that functioned; and created also a reasonably effective market for new equity issues. None of these were created *de novo;* financial arrangements between lenders and borrowers had previously been used to offset inflation, and there had been transactions in debt and equity issues in banking institutions and in no less than nine securities exchanges. However, the economic officers of the new military government established more effective devices, the most widely known one being the issuance of government bonds "indexed" with respect to both inflation and foreign exchange rate devaluation. The bond holder received both interest payments and a principal repayment

---

[19] Yet at the height of the U.S. balance of payments crisis in the late 1960s, a 15 percent tax was levied on the purchase of foreign securities not already owned within the United States, and the transfer of funds abroad by American corporations was regulated by the government.

[20] See Ness (1974).

at maturity adjusted upward by whichever of the two indexes had risen the more.

In the less developed countries, there has been a great vogue of formation of government development banks or development corporation. These, however, have commonly served more as merely financing than entrepreneurial agencies.[21]

APPENDIX

THE ICOR: FURTHER COMMENT

The concept of the ICOR (developed since World War II) contrasts with an older one used in static economic analysis, the marginal (physical) productivity of capital. The marginal productivity of capital, or MPC, is the ratio of the increase in output to an increase in capital causing it when no other input changes in quantity and there is no advance in technical knowledge. That is, MPC is the partial derivative of output with respect to capital. The concept is not one of change over time, as capital is added, but rather a comparison of the output that could be obtained with or without the added capital, but with other inputs adapted to work most efficiently with the specified added amount of capital, at any given time. The capital is thought of as maintained perpetually, the increase in output being the perpetual flow created in addition to that needed to replace depreciation of the capital. Or, if the capital is thought of as being used up and not replaced, the MPC is the rate of return net of depreciation that the capital will earn during its lifetime, that is, the rate at which the value of the incremental flow of output must be discounted to yield a present value equal to the cost of the capital. This is the general formula of which the perpetual flow formula is a special case.

In the ICOR, the ratio is inverted; the capital requirement forms the numerator, the change in output the denominator. Because introduction of new techniques and increases in inputs other than capital both reduce the amount of investment needed to increase productive capacity, the ICOR is much smaller than the inverse of the MPC. The MPC may be 8/100, the ICOR 100/20, 100/30, or even 100/50.

Conceptually, the ICOR must be taken net, in both the numerator and denominator. Investment that merely replaces capital that is worn out does not increase capacity. However, the figures are often taken gross, for several reasons. The calculation is a rough one in any case, and as an indicator of future gross capital needs the ICOR based on capital formation and national product figures gross of depreciation is probably as

---

[21] Perera (1968) presents the most recent survey of development banks around the world.

accurate a tool as one in which the calculation was made net of depreciation and then the need for capital formation to replace depreciation was reintroduced in estimating capital needs.

Conceptually, allowance can be made for the effect of the various factors influencing the ICOR that were mentioned. A group of English economists making an estimate in 1965 of the capital needs of various British industries to 1975 made allowance for one important variable, the rate of expansion of the industry, which—as mentioned in Chapter 10—is inversely correlated with the ICOR. They estimated the ICOR for each industry by a regression of the ICOR on the average (rather than incremental) ratio of capital to annual output and the rate of growth of the various industry groups.[22]

The ICOR estimates now available, together with data now available for some of the other variables mentioned above, would permit a useful multiple regression. The guess may be hazarded (and may be wrong) that the regression would leave a large share of the variation in ICORs unaccounted for.

Because investment does not give rise to an increase in productive capacity until the investment has been completed, it is appropriate in calculating an ICOR to measure the increase in capacity during a period beginning and ending a little later than that during which the investment goes on. A six-month lag might be appropriate, but since many data are available only for annual periods, a lag of one year is sometimes taken. If the time period considered is fairly long—say, 10 years—whether or not a lag is assumed will not affect the ratio greatly.

A fairly long period must be taken for another reason. The denominator of the ratio, conceptually, is the increase in productive capacity. However, few estimates of productive capacity are available. Rather, we have data for actual GDP. We must use these, and choose periods beginning and ending at a time when we think that the ratio of actual production to productive capacity was about the same. The possible margin of error is great if the period for which the ICOR is calculated is only a year or two, but lessens if a longer period is taken.

General considerations do not give any clear indication whether ICORs should be expected to be positively or negatively related to income level, other things being equal. The cost of producers' durable goods per unit of output may be expected to be higher in low-income (less-industrialized) countries, because more of the producers' durables must be imported. On the other hand, the cost of construction of simple structures may be lower. The capital cost of early increases in agricultural output may be less, though this is controversial.[23]

---

[22] W. Beckerman and associates (1965). They use a linear relationship. A logarithmic linear one might be more logical. See Walters (1966), pp. 818–22.

[23] For a fuller summary, see W. A. Lewis (1955), pp. 202–7.

BIBLIOGRAPHICAL NOTE

While the thesis of the virtues of "financial liberalization" has been developing for two decades, the comprehensive statements are in Shaw (1973) and McKinnon (1973). McKinnon presents more empirical material. Concerning saving rates, the theoretical basis in Duesenberry (1949) is highly relevant. Fei and Ranis (1964) and Paauw and Fei (1973) have been mentioned in the bibliographical note to Chapter 7.

Monetary, Tax, and Fiscal Policy: Inflation

14

Interest rate policy, specifically the presence or absence of ceilings on legal interest rates, may significantly affect the areas into which institutions possessing investable funds will place them. To a person who believes in the efficiency of the market, it seems evident that the allocation of investable resources made by private financial institutions and investors attempting to maximize interest returns will further growth more than will administrative determination of the channels into which savings shall flow. This is not to be taken as condemnation of all selective intervention with regard to interest rates. For example, governmentally induced low interest rates on low-cost housing construction may be administratively a more effective means of securing housing for low-income families than measures that would be economically more efficient if feasible. But so far as growth in aggregate income is concerned, the market is likely to be more effective.[1]

Monetary Policy's Limited Role

Apart from the effects of removing legal limitations on interest rates, monetary policy as conventionally defined can do much less in lower

---

[1] Even in the absence of capital market institutions, whose formal establishment will not cause them to function before their time has come. McKinnon expresses faith in the rapid development of capital markets, if not interfered with by government. He states (1973, p. 2) that his analysis focuses on "semi-industrial" countries. His faith is better based concerning such countries than concerning ones at earlier stages of growth.

income countries than in the more developed ones to influence the flow of resources into investment. In the more developed countries, credit creation by the commercial banks is the major source of funds for short-term business uses, and it is also an important source of intermediate-term loans. Central bank policies, by affecting the volume of reserves of commercial banks, may make short- and intermediate-term credit easy or difficult to obtain. Moreover, the supply of bank credit also influences long-term interest rates, and the rate of interest on long-term loans influences the volume of investment, especially in capital-intensive projects.

Most of these lower-income countries also have central banks or monetary agencies, but those banks lend less to the commercial banks than in the more developed countries, and influence their supply of credit and their interest rates much less. This is true partly because much commercial banking is by branches of foreign banks, who depend on their head offices for their loan funds, and partly because monetary institutions necessary to make central banking an effective instrument of control have not developed. For example, "open market operations" by the central bank are not possible, because large impersonal markets for securities do not exist. Moreover, since the capital market is little developed, the tightness or looseness of commercial bank credit has less effect on interest rates. In some less developed countries monetary policy is little more than an aspect of fiscal policy. Commercial banks do not buy government bonds except under pressure, and almost the sole source of financing of a government deficit is the central bank.

Fiscal Policy

It was noted in the first section of the preceding chapter that a tight (conservative) fiscal policy may increase total investment by freeing resources for private investment. The argument needs qualification. A government sufficiently disciplined to carry out such a policy is probably also sufficiently disciplined to use a relatively large amount of its tax revenues or borrowing for public investment. The question considered here is: In what other ways may fiscal policy contribute to the allocation of resources to development?

By tax policies, the government can influence the "climate" for private investment. Whether differences in tax policy within a nonconfiscatory range have a great deal of influence is a matter of difference of opinion. Apart from tax policy, the main fiscal measure to be considered is the mobilization of investable funds by the government itself and their use for either government investment or loans to private investors. The mobilization may be through a surplus of revenues over nondevelopment expenditures; if there is slack in the economy, by deficit financing of capital expenditures, or by forced saving through inflation-causing deficit capital expenditures if there is no slack in the economy. To understand the prospects for noninflationary development expenditures or loans by the government, it is necessary to survey the entire fiscal system in the low-income countries.

It is a generally accepted fact that government services are a type of tertiary product for which there is a high income elasticity of demand, so that as per capita income rises the ratio of government expenditures to GNP rises. Yet Figure 14–1, showing the relationship between general government consumption expenditures in 1964 as a percentage of GDP and GDP per capita in 1965 for a large number of countries, indicates no statistical relationship. ("General government expenditures" exclude expenditures of government enterprises.) If defense expenditures were eliminated, the expected relationship would probably be seen, but only very loosely, with a wide spread of countries at any given income level, and with only a small average difference between lower and higher income countries.

Yet there is no inconsistency here with the conception that government consumption expenditures rise as income rises. They do. But there has

FIGURE 14–1

General Government Consumption as Percent of GDP, 1970, Related to GDP Per Capita, 1970

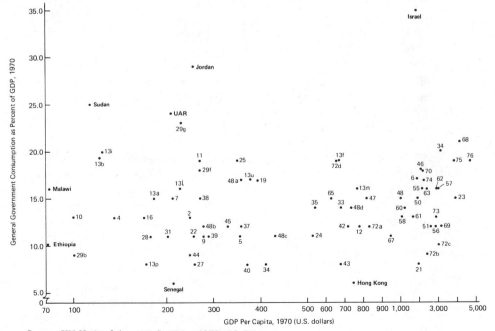

Source: *UN National Accounts Statistics,* 1972, vol. 3.

been a change during the past generation or so in the concept of the obligations of government. The government consumption expenditures of lower income countries are no doubt higher than were those of present high-income countries when their per capita incomes were as low as those of the lower income countries today, and if the incomes of those latter countries rise to present high-income levels, their general government consumption expenditures per capita will presumably be a higher percentage of GNP than are those of the high-income countries today.

This secular change was suggested by Martin and Lewis (1956) in an analysis of 1953–54 government expenditures in six high-income countries and ten less developed ones of which eight were British dependencies. The two authors, separating "basic" government expenditures from those for defense, public debt, and agricultural subsidies, found that there was not much difference between the rich and poor countries in the percentage of national income spent for "basic" purposes. They concluded that in the high- and low-income countries alike, government expenditures had increased over time because of a changed conception of the role of the state. The facts in these countries may have been affected by the fact that the pattern of government expenditures was set by British colonial administrations. But a similar secular trend was observed in Chapter 12, in a larger sample of countries, with respect to expenditures for education. The demand for "modern" governmental services and expenditures—notably but not only for education, health and medical care, and social security transfers—has been strong. Where governments in developing countries have been short of funds for investment, this is because they have not been able or willing to hold down current expenditures as well as because they have not been able to increase tax revenues.

The demands of modernization have reached some low-income countries more than others. This is one cause of the wide spread of expenditure percentages in those countries. Another is the difference in their revenue sources. H. H. Hinrichs (1966) demonstrated that government revenues in low-income countries are highly correlated with their level of foreign trade. In fact, a formula stating that the percentage of government revenues to national product equals 5 plus one half of the percentage of imports to national product is a good estimator. The reason is simple. Imports and some types of exports are attractive targets for taxation, and are easy to tax. And one must conclude from other data that, having obtained the tax revenue, the governments spend it. A sort of Parkinson's law seems to hold.

Hinrichs shows another surprising fact (using data by Kuznets for 1950–58). At the lowest levels of income, budgets are balanced. In the industrial countries, they tend to be balanced again. But at intermediate levels, an "expenditure gap" appears. At this level governments meet the pressure for current services and for development expenditures by spending beyond their revenues. A Parkinson's law does not hold after all. The surplus of expenditures is not necessarily in domestic (and perhaps inflationary) expenditures. The deficit may be in foreign exchange, and financed by economic aid. The data do not permit a clear determination on the point.

Tax Structure and Tax Policy

In the lowest income countries, the traditional sources of governmental revenue are traditional types of direct taxes. In Asia, land taxes were most important; in Africa, head taxes; and in some countries, taxes on livestock.

An expert from an industrial country, advising the government of a low-income country concerning the taxes it should add to strengthen its revenue base for development purposes, may have a natural tendency to recommend "modern" forms of direct taxes. However, in less developed countries, choices of equity must be made among the taxes that it is economically, politically, and administratively feasible to levy and collect, and the situation differs from that in more developed countries on all three counts.

An income tax can be administered effectively only if the economy is predominantly a money economy, business institutions have become sufficiently complex so that fairly complex financial records are kept, the level of administrative honesty and efficiency is high, and political attitudes are such that collection of taxes levied on economically powerful and socially eminent individuals is possible. In many of the lowest income countries, the first two and the last of these characteristics are absent and the third is present only partially if at all. The highest income groups are too powerful politically to permit even moderate rates of taxation to be levied against them. For example, a proposal for a personal income tax rising to 4% in Guatemala in 1966–67 was blocked by a group of economically powerful high-income individuals who charged that such a tax is communistic. Equally important, taxes levied on high-income individuals are unlikely to be collected. In all but a few of the countries usually classed as "less developed" it would be unthinkable for a government employee (of the lower middle class) to challenge a socially and economically eminent individual as a tax evader and issue an instruction to him to produce records or respond to an investigation.

Where this is true, as among the individuals subject to income tax the tax actually collected is likely to be regressive, for it can be collected from low- and middle-income salary earners. Moreover, at the rates at which it can be levied on this limited group it will not yield much revenue; revenue must be sought elsewhere.

Taxes requiring complex records are irrelevant, whatever their abstract merits of equity or incentive may be. For example, the tax on spending (as contrasted with income) recommended to two or three less developed countries by a distinguished economic adviser[2] to encourage saving, would be futile in most less developed countries, for where records of income are grossly deficient evidence from which to deduce a family's total spending is nonexistent.

Taxes on land are only roughly equitable. Yet in less developed countries they have much to recommend them. They obtain revenue. If land ownership is concentrated, their incidence is on a high-income group. If landlords were collecting approximately the maximum feasible rent before the tax, they cannot pass any great share of the tax back to renters. And, if the tax is set on land valuations that are reassessed only, say, every five or ten years, the land tax, insofar as it affects incentives to technical progress in agriculture, is conducive to progress, for the landlord knows that any increase in the yield of his land will be free of tax until the next assessment. Where dominating political influence has passed from the landed group and their peasant "clients," a tax levied on the potential value of land in its most productive use (measured in some approximate way) may be feasible, and may bring into cultivation large estates of rich land held for cattle grazing because the owners find this a congenial way of life.

When an expanded tax base is sought, indirect taxes and export taxes (which in low-income countries are with considerable justification considered direct taxes) will probably have to be the main source of revenue. The canons of tax theory suggest that such taxes should be collected at the final point of sale to prevent "pyramiding." However, in less developed countries the tax may be more equitable if it is collected at the point of manufacture or import, for with tax administration considerably less than perfectly efficient, the prospect of actual collection at the point of manufacture or import is better than when the commodity has entered the channels of trade. Selective excises or customs duties, on items consumed mainly by the well-to-do, may have a higher degree of progressivity than any other tax, even though their incidence is uneven among persons of the same income level. The relative importance of customs varies greatly; they are a major source of revenue in many small, low-income countries.

Export taxes, hardly known in industrial countries, will be the greatest source of revenue in some countries. Export taxes are often chosen either on the theory that they burden the foreign buyer of the commodities taxed, or on the theory that the exporter is a rich company that can afford to pay. The first ground is almost always ill-based. Unless a country is a major world supplier of a commodity (or unites with other suppliers in a

---

[2] Professor Nicholas Kaldor.

cartel), its tax will not affect the world price appreciably and therefore will be absorbed by the exporter or passed back to producers. Even if the country is a major supplier, the export tax will reduce sales and the country's proceeds from the exports if the demand is price-elastic.

If the exporting firm is also the producer, the burden of an export tax is likely to fall on the firm, except in the fairly rare case that the tax so affects the firm's economic calculations that it both induces and permits the firm to drive a harder wage bargain than it would otherwise. A few countries have established government marketing boards. The purpose is to obtain revenue, to maximize proceeds by establishing an export monopoly, or to counter cyclical fluctuations. Unless the country produces so large a share of the world supply of a commodity that it can affect the world price, the profit of a marketing board, like an export tax, is simply a tax on a selected group of domestic producers, justified on equity grounds only if these producers are in an especially favorable economic position.

Any foreign firm is likely to be regarded as a fair target, if a formula can be devised that will burden it more than domestic companies, and a foreign company that is exploiting a country's natural resources for export is the fairest of all. The extreme case is the international petroleum companies, which because of the noncompetitive structure of world petroleum prices earn unusual profit margins. Until the 1940s, as a maximum these companies paid royalties and profits taxes equal to, say, one fifth or one sixth of their gross earnings. The Creole Petroleum Company agreement with Venezuela—for approximately a 50–50 division—broke the pattern. During postwar years the petroleum companies were progressively forced to yield larger shares, until before the end of the 1960s the governments were collecting two thirds or somewhat more of gross earnings in royalties, fees, and taxes. Then, in the early 1970s, the governments of the oil countries began moving to become part owners of the oil companies' producing subsidiaries. They negotiated a price for part ownership based on oil companies' investment costs, not market value, and paid for it out of oil revenues. Lastly, in 1973, the Middle East countries, which had been pressing oil prices upward, approximately quadrupled them while adopting measures to limit oil companies' profit margins on crude petroleum, and to increase the government's share of the revenues. Other producing countries followed. In general, the absolute level of company profits was not reduced by this last change, though some oil countries are trying to accomplish this.

Before the end of the 1970s, governments will no doubt be full owners, formally or in fact, with the oil companies sharing in profits as a return for their management of the enterprises. The discovery of new oil fields, the entry of new firms seeking drilling rights, and the fact that capital was already sunk and could not be withdrawn put the oil companies in a none too strong position, regardless of the provisions and specified duration of their original agreements. They will continue to profit from the spread between oil prices at the wellhead and prices to the buyers of fuel products, though the oil countries are taking that spread into account in their calculations of an appropriate division of oil revenues between themselves and the oil companies.

Sometimes the geese that were laying golden eggs have been killed or wounded by tax policies. Progressively heavier taxes levied on copper or copper companies by an impoverished Chilean government during 1949–54 reached a level in the latter year at which it was not worthwhile for the companies to expand their operations. In 1966 a new administration required the companies to take it into partnership, and aided the companies to expand their (and its) operations and profits. The leftist government that gained office in 1971 nationalized the copper mines. Output and revenues fell sharply, partly because of lack of labor discipline but perhaps more largely because Chilean as well as foreign technical experts and managers resigned their jobs and left the country. The military regime that took power in 1973 invited the copper companies back. Presumably government revenues from copper will rise again.

Apart from these special cases, as a country leaves its traditional state and enters upon economic development, it must turn to indirect taxes. On grounds of equity within the limits of political and administrative feasibility, this is what it should do. In most of the low-income countries of the world today, indirect taxes produce more revenue than direct ones, even if export taxes are counted as direct taxes. The taxes will include a heavy dose of import and export taxes, if imports and exports have become increasingly large relative to the national product as development got under way. There is evidence that they do rise until industrialization has proceeded some distance. The smaller the country, the greater the probability that this will be true.[3] Only later, as still more revenue is sought and as economic complexity produces more financial records, will the newer forms of direct taxes, corporation and graduated personal income taxes, become increasingly important. The ratio of direct to indirect taxes, even including export taxes in the former, will fall below unity as soon as the country alters the traditional tax system, and then will gradually rise again as the country becomes more and more industrial.[4]

Table 14–1 compares the shares of direct and indirect taxes in total

---

[3] Eckstein and Deutsch (1961) advance the thesis that the ratio of foreign trade to national product rises and then falls. While the thesis is disputed, the facts seem to be in their favor. Concerning the relation of population size to foreign trade share, see Chapter 17 below, especially Figure 17–1 and the accompanying text.

[4] Hinrichs (1966) presents a fascinating chart in which he shows this trend in the direct-indirect tax ratio during the course of "development time," and relates the tax structure of various countries at various dates to it.

TABLE 14-1
Direct and Indirect Taxation, LDCs and MDCs
(percentages of total tax revenue)

	Direct		Indirect
	Total	Of Which Export Taxes Are	
Europe: 10 high-income countries, 1950–59	59		41
Africa: 8 countries, 1961–62*	43	13	57
Asia: 8 countries, 1958†	35	11	65

   * Ghana, Kenya, Nigeria, Rhodesia, Sierra Leone, Tanganyika, Uganda, Zanzibar.
   † Afghanistan, Burma, Ceylon, Malaya, India, Pakistan, Philippines, Thailand.
   Sources: Europe: Kuznets, *Q.A.E.G.N.*, 7, pp. 68–69; Ceylon and India: U.N., ECAFE, *Economic Survey of Asia and the Far East, 1960* (Bangkok, 1961), Chap. 6. Nigeria and Zanzibar: Due (1963), Chap. 2.

taxation in low- and high-income countries shortly after World War II.

Drastic declines in tax collections after the transition from colonial rule to independence occurred throughout most of sub-Sahara Africa, and in Burma, Indonesia, and apparently to a lesser degree in Ceylon. These declines illustrate the administrative problems. Of course the problem in most of these areas was much broader than merely tax administration.

Noninflationary Deficits

The governments of many developing countries resort to deficit financing because they see no feasible alternative, because they think the economy needs an expansionary stimulus, or because they are irresponsible. They sometimes resort to it on a scale that leads to inflation. Before considering the desirability or undesirability of inflation tolerated for this purpose, we should consider the limits of noninflationary deficit finance.

Deficit finance is noninflationary if it is merely the spending abroad, to purchase capital or other goods for import, of funds which the government has previously accumulated abroad or can borrow abroad. Domestic deficit spending may also be noninflationary.

Unemployment of labor and underemployment of management and capital equipment may exist in the less developed countries. In a low-income country in which investment is sluggish, there may be overt unemployment, even though it is hidden by the tendency of unemployed urban workers to return to their rural homes. If so, deficit financing may appropriately be pursued simply to increase aggregate demand. Very few economists would criticize it in these circumstances. A policy of spending to the point of incipient or slow inflation, to draw the country's productive resources into full use, also has much to recommend it. If the expenditures are developmental ones, so much the better for development. However, a mere increase in aggregate demand is not a remedy for low productivity, and often not a remedy for underemployment. The underemployed may not be geographically, industrially, or occupationally mobile, and management and capital may not be available to offer them more productive employment even if the demand for products is increased.

It is conceptually possible to spend to the point of creating inflationary pressure, but to curb the pressure by direct price and wage controls in most sectors of the economy, in order to induce a rapid shift of resources to those sectors in which prices and wages are permitted to rise. This is the device used with such success in the United States during World War II. It has been termed the "disequilibrium system."[5] However, it requires an extensive administrative machinery, a high degree of administrative efficiency, and a high degree of public approval. These are not likely to be present in programs of economic administration in the less developed countries, and this possibility is therefore of more academic than practical interest.

Lastly, it should be noted that more deficit financing than otherwise is possible, without causing inflation, if individuals or firms are accumulating increasing amounts of cash. Some saving is always in the form of cash accumulations, when GNP is expanding, for at higher incomes individuals choose to hold more cash, and more cash is also needed by business firms if they are handling a larger volume of business. As their incomes rise, individuals tend to hold not only more cash but cash equal to a higher fraction of their incomes. The ratio of the money supply to GDP tends to increase fairly rapidly during the period of "monetization" of the economy, the period when farmers shift from subsistence farming to production for the market. McKinnon (1973) suggests that where a capital market is not functioning well and investors finance their own capital expenditures, this increases the amount of money held idle as investment increases, for the investors must hold money until they have accumulated enough to pay for a piece of equipment. He may underestimate the availability of credit from suppliers. He makes no attempt to quantify the presumed effect.

However, these tendencies are offset wholly or in part by improvements in transportation and communication, which permit business to be handled with smaller cash balances, and by technical advances such as improved bank clearing systems. The tendencies on the two sides seem to be about equal, for Figure 14–2, which shows a wide scatter, shows only a slight tendency for the ratio of money to GDP to rise with income. The data of Figure 14–2 are for 1970. A similar figure, in the first edition of this book, with data for 1965, also showed a wide scatter but showed some tendency for the ratio of money to GDP to rise with a rise in the

---

[5] Galbraith's phrase (1947).

FIGURE 14–2
Money/GDP Ratio, 1970, Related to GDP Per Capita, 1970

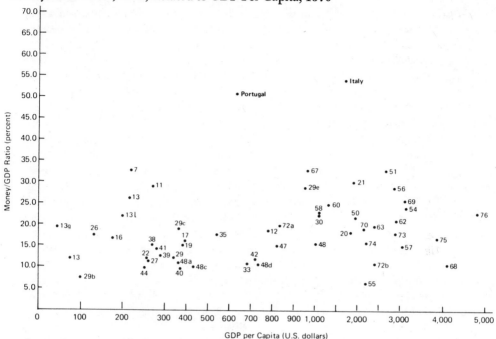

Source: GDP per capita, U.N. *Yearbook of National Accounts Statistics, 1972*, vol. 3. Money/GDP ratio, *International Financial Statistics*, vol. 25, October–December 1972.

level of income. Whichever may more truly represent the underlying trend, the tendency is slight.

Figure 14–2 does suggest an increase in money held at least equal to the increase in GDP. Even this increase gives a quantitatively significant opportunity and even necessity for increase in credit expansion. Individuals and firms are increasing their stocks of idle money. Credit must be expanded, and the funds used, in equal amount, to prevent a deflationary effect. Either government deficit financing (for either investment or current expenditures) or an increase in private debt must occur. If GDP is expanding at a rate of 5% per year, the money supply must be expanded at about that rate, or in a typical country by about 1% of GDP. This expansion, if used for investment, yields a significant increase in the rate of investment.

Inflation and Economic Growth

Does inflation accelerate economic growth? Retard it? Does economic growth necessarily cause inflation ultimately? These questions, discussed in this chapter, divide theorists and economic growth practitioners alike.

Inflation may be due to the upward pull of excessive aggregate demand or the upward push of costs. Consider demand-pull inflation first.

The governments of less developed countries may engage in deficit financing to the point of inflation, even rather rapid inflation, not to increase aggregate demand for its own sake, but to divert resources to investment by creating new money and hiring them with it. There is no question that the immediate purpose can be attained. A government agency can undoubtedly hire men, equipment, and management to construct a road, a hydroelectric plant, or a steel mill, by offering them enough compensation to attract them from other work. That the men and materials will be hired away solely from other investment projects, and not at all from the production of consumer goods, is very unlikely. Hence the immediate result is to increase the volume of investment in the country. The policy questions are whether, if a significant degree of inflation results, the aggregate level of productive investment will be greater in the somewhat longer run, and, if it is, whether the other effects of the inflation constitute a cost too great to justify the benefit. Inflationary spending cannot achieve more than a minor increase in aggregate investment, for the added money incomes created increase the demand for consumer goods also, and government investment gains only if it "keeps ahead of the multiplier." The policy question concerns a marginal, but of course possibly an important, difference.

Growth-Stimulating Effects

One basic argument in favor of the policy is that the developmental projects are executed. Resources are diverted. It may have been impossible to levy or collect the necessary taxes, but inflation requires no administrative skill.

Second, it is argued that mild inflation diverts income to the mercantile and industrial classes, who are the saving and investing classes. This redistribution of income in itself increases the share of the nation's product that will be used for developmental purposes. The argument is sound, provided that entrepreneurial spirit exists among these classes, that the inflation continues to be mild, and that effective countermeasures to prevent the redistribution of income to higher income groups are not adopted by other groups. A country must be both wise and lucky to meet these requirements.

It is argued that inflation need be neither extreme nor prolonged. The investment projects being carried on in the country may include some that will permit the expansion of the production in a short time: the import of fertilizer, the digging of tube wells, the construction of factories that will quickly begin production of goods much in demand. If the inflation-causing margin of expenditures is small enough, and the magnitude of such projects large enough so that, as they raise income, the increase in saving will soon be as large as the inflation-causing expenditure margin, then inflation will cease.

Limiting government investment to a carefully calculated level of this sort is "fine tuning" not likely to be followed in practice if the urge to spend in order to develop exists. Moreover, the increase in saving will end inflation only if the saving is not invested in added investment. The groups whose income and saving is increased by the new projects may conceive of new projects in which to invest their savings. The supposed self-limiting nature of the inflation will then be illusory. Of course, if the continuing inflation buys this continuing increase in the rate of investment, to many persons concerned this will seem a cheap price to pay.

It is suggested that the country may be more certain of a quick end to the inflation if the government either operates the projects, so that increased profits flow to the government, or siphons off a share of the increased profits in taxes. If the government can operate the projects efficiently—an important qualification—it will receive the profits, but the question remains whether the government itself can or will wish to resist the temptation to re-spend the increased income. Whether the tax system can act in an anti-inflationary manner depends on its nature. Where the corporate profits tax and the graduated personal income tax are absent, or not collected, inflation is likely to increase government costs more rapidly than revenues increase. A growing government deficit then feeds the inflation, and becomes chronic.

Evils. One major argument against the inflationary finance of development projects is the danger that the inflation will be chronic or perhaps even accelerating. One element of this argument has just been stated. Another is the assertion that once inflation has begun a cost-push process is likely to keep it going.

Inflation occurs because some group in the country—in our example, the government—is using newly created money to bid scarce goods away from someone else. The level of living of some group or groups in the country which finds that its income will buy less goods than before must fall. The classes most likely to find their living level reduced, because they have not shared the benefit of rising prices, are wage and salary earners: professional men, government employees, and industrial employees, if they are not organized. But many industrial employees are organized into labor unions, and whether organized or not, in a democratic country they and the government employees are likely to make effective demands for protection against inflation. This protection takes the form of frequent increases in government salaries and the imposition of frequently increased minimum wage standards for private industry. Demands of cultivators for price supports or income supplements, if the high level of demand has not already inflated the prices of their products, and of importers and exporters for devaluation, will follow. Each concession to one group will raise prices further and bring renewed demands from the other groups. Thus a cost-push force may be added to the demand-pull effect, and the mild, short-lived, self-limiting inflation may turn out to be more rapid, continuing inflation.

Second, inflation, by raising domestic prices relative to foreign prices, tends both to divert to the domestic market some output formerly exported and to encourage imports. Thus it worsens the balance of payments. This imbalance may be corrected by devaluation or increased protectionism. Either increases the cost of goods formerly imported, and contributes to the cost-push element in inflation. Devaluation, by increasing the amount of domestic currency received from exports, also adds to the demand-pull element.

Moreover, the threat of devaluation both repels foreign capital and causes a flight of domestic capital to foreign havens. If the holders are confident that one devaluation will be the only one, they will bring their money home after devaluation has occurred, but if they fear successive devaluations they are likely to leave it abroad.

Continuing inflation diverts investment from projects expected to produce income into channels expected to give protection against the inflation by yielding a capital gain. One of these is inventory accumulation, in anticipation of profits on price rises. Moreover, the groups whom inflation benefits are likely to include not only high savers but also luxurious spenders. For this reason there will be increased demand for the services of luxurious urban apartment houses, resort hotels, night clubs, and the like. This demand increases the likelihood of capital gains from their construction, and on both counts resources tend to flow into such projects. Inflation seems always to accelerate the development of cities. Hence land itself in urban areas is purchased for a price rise, and the circulation of money from landowner to landowner may keep it diverted from productive investment. Insofar as the individuals investing in these luxury construction ventures or land speculation are persons who are attracted by "a quick buck" and would not enter upon industrial or agricultural ventures in any case, little has been lost, so that this excrescence is less damaging than it appears, but these opportunities created by inflation attract more sober entrepreneurs also, and there is always some loss.

Empirical Evidence. These disadvantages appear in their extreme form only if inflation is fairly rapid. A person who recognizes them fully may still believe that deficit financing of developmental expenditures, kept within moderate bounds, will foster growth. That within a fairly wide range of each, any rate of inflation is consistent with any rate of growth, is indicated in the period from 1950 to 1965 by the association of price stability with no growth or slow growth in Burma, Ceylon, and India; of price stability with rapid growth in Pakistan, Thailand, and Japan; of rapid inflation with a zero or low rate of growth in Indonesia and Argentina; and of rapid inflation with moderate or rapid growth in Brazil and Turkey. Somewhat more systematic evidence is provided by more comprehensive data for Asian and African countries and for Latin American countries. Figures 14–3 and 14–4 present this data.[6] The Latin American data are presented separately from those for Asia and Africa because the differences in inflation rates are so great that the effects may be different. In no Asian or African country except South Korea did the cost of living rise by more than 70% between 1960 and 1970. In only 11 of the 18 Latin American countries shown did it rise by less than this, and in 4 it rose by between 600% and 3780%. Both scatters are wide. In neither Africa-Asia nor Latin America is there much indication of a relationship

FIGURE 14–3
Inflation and Growth Rates, African and Asian Countries

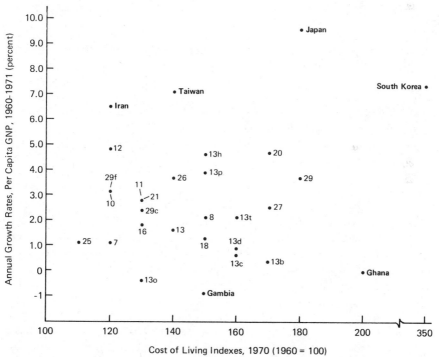

Source: Per Capita Growth Rates, Table 1–10; Cost of Living Indexes, calculated from data in *International Financial Statistics*, various issues.

[6] Indexes of wholesale prices would be more appropriate than the cost of living indexes used in Figure 14–3 and 14–4 but the former are available for the period only for a much smaller number of countries.

FIGURE 14–4
Inflation and Growth Rates, Latin American Countries

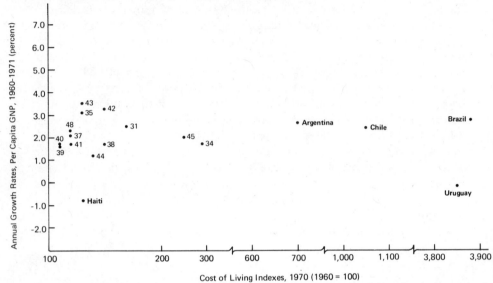

Source: Per Capita Growth Rates, Table 1–10; Cost of Living Indexes, calculated from data in *International Financial Statistics*, various issues.

between the rate of inflation and growth. Data relating inflation, 1950–64, to growth rates, 1960–64, presented in the first edition of this book, showed a possible negative lagged relationship in Latin America and a distinct positive lagged relationship in Asia-Africa. I concluded at that time that a moderate rate of inflation, reflecting demand sufficient to take up slack in the economy, accelerated growth, while hyperinflation, as in some Latin American countries, deterred it. The data for the entire decade of the 1960s contradict this conclusion (except that it is possible to conclude that there is a very loose positive relationship in Asia-Africa).

In a study of 43 countries, Henry Wallich (1970) presents a more rigorous analysis. He did a multiple regression with aggregate GNP growth rates for 1956–60 and 1961–65 as the dependent variables, and income per capita, the rate of population growth, and in some runs the ratio of investment to GNP as independent variables.[7] In other runs investment was omitted, since the close relationship between investment and growth makes the inclusion of both statistically suspect. He initially intended to test the hypothesis that the rate of current inflation is positively related to growth rates, because of the demand which inflation reflects, but that past inflation is negatively related, because of the

---

[7] The population data used were average annual growth rates, 1946–55. Other data were averages for each of the five-year periods 1956–60 and 1961–65.

retarding effects of the distortions resulting from past inflation. He found it impossible to separate out present and past inflation, because of collinearity between them, but found, contrary to his expectation, that "over a five year period the [assumed] negative longer run effects outweigh the possible positive short run effects. When investment is excluded, an increase in the rate of inflation by 1 per cent lowers the rate of growth by 0.04 percentage points. When investment enters, the effect is reduced to 0.03 per cent." This is a small effect. An inflation rate of 30% per year, not uncommon in several Latin American countries, would imply a reduction in the rate of growth of aggregate GNP by about 1%. But to apply the coefficient to these extreme cases is of doubtful validity.

The differences between inflation rates in Asia-Africa and those in Latin America are so great that assuming a linear relationship among a single group of 43 countries may be unwarranted. On the other hand, Wallich's multiple regression is a better instrument than the simple regression implied in Figures 14–3 and 14–4. On the basis of these data, it is impossible to make a strong statement about the effects of inflation on growth, except that whatever that effect is, it is not large.

Curbing Demand-Pull Inflation

The means of curbing inflation that is due merely to excessive money demand is simple: eliminate the excessive rate of creation of money income. If that advice and the discussion of it in this section seems unreal to some readers, this may be because there are fewer and fewer countries in which the pull of demand seems to be the only cause of inflation. But in this section let us consider the case as an important theoretical case. All inflation is "demand-pull" in the sense that it can be stopped by sufficiently stringent monetary policy if the country is willing to endure the concomitant results.

The curbing of income creation has been the formal recommendation of the International Monetary Fund concerning inflation anywhere. Apparently without exception, its agreements to support the currency of a country have required stringent fiscal-monetary policy. The position that virtue requires monetary restraint sufficient to prevent inflation is a necessary one for the Fund. It is difficult to see how an agency whose purpose for existence is the treatment of monetary problems could formally adopt any other viewpoint. That the IMF at times recognizes the unvirtuous necessity of relaxing monetary restraint is indicated by the fact that in a number of instances, among them that of Argentina (discussed later in this chapter), it has not withdrawn its support of the currency when a country has perforce broken the restrictive agreement.

One danger of the abrupt application of monetary policy so stringent that it is inconsistent with the continuation of rising prices is that a quick reduction of the excessive rate of expansion of the money supply is likely to cause a temporary depression. The reason is that during inflation, projects are likely to be in existence that are profitable only during inflation. These are likely to be checked quickly by monetary stringency, and inventory accumulation even reversed, but there may be a considerable lag before other projects replace them.

These considerations argue for a gradual approach to stringency. However, if the undue creation of money income is tapered off only gradually, individuals are not likely to believe that the government will really end inflation. In this event, the expectation of continuing inflation will itself prolong the inflation.

It is sometimes recommended that abrupt action should be taken and a temporary depression be risked, but that to cushion it a program of public works should be associated with the anti-inflationary fiscal-monetary policy, to offer employment to workers disemployed. The most appropriate works program would be one using labor-intensive methods of construction. Such a program would of course require additional government expenditure, and inflation would be less starved than otherwise. Nevertheless, the interests of equity would be served if while inflation-caused profits (and probably all profits) were being squeezed, this employment was offered to workers laid off because of the profits squeeze. The equity would be only a rough one, for during the anti-inflationary squeeze many low-income profit receivers are likely to be hurt almost as much as the workers disemployed. But measures for even rough equity may be better than no measures.

McKinnon (1973, pp. 84–88) argues that if a ceiling on interest rates is carefully removed when counterinflationary measures are applied, deflation of the money supply can be prevented (the ratio of money stock to the price level remaining constant) and recession prevented or lessened. The argument has no empirical basis.

A danger of the application, abruptly or gradually, of monetary policy stringent enough to check rising prices is that the inflation may be cost-push as well as demand-pull. In this case the impact on employment rather than prices will be all the greater. Depression will precede price stability, not merely because of a lag in the substitution of sound projects for inflation-caused ones, but because of the competition of workers, farmers, and industrialists for income shares as the rise in money incomes is checked. Workers may refuse to accept reductions in money incomes, or may demand rises in money incomes in order to "catch up" with prices, and employers unwilling to take the necessary reductions in profit margins, or lacking the working capital to pay the wages demanded, may reduce their output. If the difficulty is only the temporary one of needed adjustments because some incomes rose before others in inflation, that is, only transitionally cost-push, then there need be only a temporary period of adjustment. When the various economic groups see that inflation really is checked, they will presumably relax demands based on expectations of continuing inflation, and will concede further income increases to groups whose money incomes had lagged, and stable income relationships will return. But if the difficulty is a more basic disagreement between workers and employers concerning an equitable distribution of the national income, then price stability may imply not temporary but continuing depression. This is a problem of cost-push inflation, now to be discussed.

LATIN AMERICAN INFLATION

By Contrast, Cost-Push Inflation

Some Latin-American theorists believe that the rapid inflation that is prevalent in some Latin American countries is due neither to demand-pull nor cost-push forces nor the two in combination, but rather to a set of forces not recognized in conventional theory. As an introduction to discussion of their thesis, the theory of ordinary cost-push inflation is sketched.

Cost-Push Inflation

Under perfect competition, each employer will offer work so long as the wage needed to attract additional workers is not higher than the marginal value productivity of additional workers, and each idle worker will offer himself for work so long as the real wage offered is high enough to attract him. If some workers are idle, their attempt to obtain jobs will bring real wages down. Employers will then offer added employment. Wages will settle at the level at which every person is at work whose minimum offer price is not higher than his marginal productivity. Competition among employers in selling their products will keep prices down to the marginal cost of producing each unit of output.

Suppose now that both employers and workers have organized to reduce competition. Suppose that through collusion employers raise prices. With money wages constant, these price rises constitute a reduction in real wages. Labor unions then strike or threaten to strike in order to obtain compensating increases in wages. Employers find it advantageous to yield, but, having done so, they restore their increased profit margins by raising prices further. The process is repeated. Such an inflationary spiral might, of course, begin with a demand by labor unions rather than an increase in prices by employers. The succeeding steps would be as above. This is the ordinary conception of cost-push inflation. Or cost-pushes may take over the inflationary process after the pull of excessive demand has begun it and has changed income relationships in a way that seems inequitable to some participants in the economic process but reasonable to others newly benefited. Or wage cost-pushes may occur in the absence of unions because of the intense feelings of unorganized workers.

If the government takes steps to see that the money supply is not increased, yet this cost-push pressure causes further increase in prices, then when prices are raised there may not be enough money in the economic system to handle all payments. Some employers may be bankrupted, or as a minimum may have to reduce their volume of production. Unemployment will appear. As the volume of production shrinks and unemployment increases, unions will be in a weaker position to demand further wage increases, and employers in a position where further price rises become less and less advantageous. At some level of unemployment and reduced production, there will be an equilibrium of strength between the two parties at which, if the fiscal-monetary authorities hold the line on money expansion, the inflation will come to a halt. This may be at a very small degree of unemployment or at a very high one, depending on the intensity with which the two sides push their demand.

A moderate increase in productivity may make it possible for employers to obtain the increased profits they had originally sought, even while raising wages, without increasing prices, and would make it possible for workers to obtain the higher real wages they had originally sought without forcing a reduction in profits, even though prices are not increased. Hence if the goal of workers is a certain absolute level of real income, and the goal of employers an absolute amount of profits, inflation might come to an end with full employment in spite of the cost-push factors. But if workers demand that their wages shall continue to increase as fast as productivity does, and employers have as their goal profits increasing as fast as aggregate sales do, and if these demands are inconsistent, then the cost-push inflationary pressures may continue forever.

In this latter situation, workers and employers are bargaining for shares of the national income. If the sum of the share that unions feel will maximize worker income or be equitable, plus the share that employers judge will maximize their income or be equitable, is more than 100%, then whenever one of the two parties succeeds temporarily in getting the share it thinks right the other will act to increase its share. As long as the fiscal-monetary authorities grant the necessary increases in money income, inflation will continue.

Industrial collective bargaining is typically not for absolute amounts, but for shares of income. There is no absolute criterion for the share of the national income that it is equitable for labor to obtain. That is, there is no absolute criterion on which labor unions base their wage claims. Neither is there any absolute criterion for the share of profits when there is collusion among employers. However, in Western industrial societies, at least until almost 1970, workers and employers regarded each other as not unreasonable men, and each others' offers as not wildly unreasonable. The unions knew that "too high" money wage demands in one sector would be matched by "too high" demands elsewhere, so that price rises would be general and would offset part of money wage increases. Therefore, each union pressed for enough to strain the willingness of employers to give, in order to be sure that its workers fared fairly well relative to others, but not for so much as to be "out of the ball park." The result was a close enough approach to agreement between unions and employers on the division of the expanding pie so that the average annual wholesale price increase was small.

In the United States, from the 1957–59 average to 1965, the rise averaged less than 0.4% per year, and from 1957–59 to mid-1967, less than 0.7% per year. In the postwar period of very high demand in Western Europe, demand-pull and cost-push pressures together brought some annual price increases of more than 5%, but these were unprecedented. Then at the end of the 1960s, inflation accelerated in both the United States and Western Europe, even before the sharp rise in food prices in 1973 and that in oil prices at the end of that year added factors quite outside the range of usual cost-push elements. By mid-1974, with those unusual cost factors contributing, the cost of living was rising by 7% per year in West Germany, almost 12% in the United States, more than 13% in France, 16% in Britain, and 23% in Japan. The question arises whether the West is not experiencing in lesser degree the causes of inflation about to be described with reference to Latin America. The Latin American phenomenon may be interesting for reasons other than merely its relationship to economic growth.

The Monetarist-Structuralist Controversy

Many of the economists who argue that inflation must be tolerated in the process of economic development do not argue for its deliberate creation. They argue that there are forces in the course of development, quite different from the pull of excessive aggregate demand, that tend to produce inflation, whatever the intentions of the government, and that measures necessary to check the expansion of the money supply will be so damaging to the development process that they should not be used. These economists urge anti-inflationary measures as vigorously as do "conventional" economists, but they argue that the appropriate measures are ones of a type quite different from the conventional ones of merely fiscal and monetary restraint. The appropriate measures take a longer time to execute, and during this time inflation should be tolerated, in order that development shall not be seriously retarded. This school of thought has been conspicuous in Latin America.

The problem of rapid inflation has been most conspicuous in Latin

America. Figure 14–5 shows the spectacular rise in prices from 1950 to 1964 in three of the four largest Latin American countries, Argentina, Brazil, and Chile, and by way of contrast, the slow price rise in the fourth, Mexico. The extremely rapid price rise brought on the controversy about causes. The "conventional" view, that the cause of inflation in Latin American countries, as elsewhere, is the creation of too high a level of money income and demand, is known as the monetarist view. The contrasting doctrine concerning causes and cure that is about to be summarized is known as the structuralist view. The structuralist view is sometimes attributed primarily to economists associated with the United Nations Economic Commission for Latin America, but many other econ-

FIGURE 14–5
Price Rises, 1950–64, Four Latin American Countries

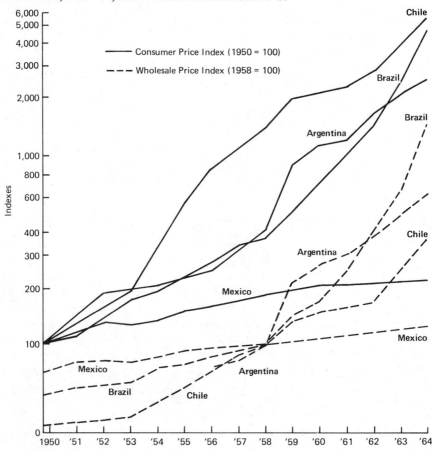

Source: Growth rates, 1950–65: Hagen (1968), Table 1–8. Price indices: *International Financial Statistics,* various issues.

omists who have studied economic development in Latin America also hold it.

It would be a mistake to assume that one group of economists believes that the causes of inflation in Latin America are wholly monetary, whereas another group believes that monetary expansion is not a causal factor at all. The views actually held by individuals are much more complex. However, the intellectual content of the controversy will be made clearest if the structuralist theory is sharply contrasted with the monetarist. The structuralist view of the inflationary process differs considerably from the cost-push thesis. The structuralist argument has received enough attention that it is evaluated here at some length. It is an internally consistent theory; yet it is very doubtful that the causes adduced are in fact the major causes of Latin American inflation.

The Structuralist Argument: Exposition

The structuralists say (*a*) that increases in the prices of one or another type of goods are initiated by increases in demand due to developments to which insufficient attention is given in conventional inflation theory; (*b*) that because of certain "basic" factors in the situation suppliers do not respond to increased demand by increasing the supply of goods; and (*c*) that the price rises spread and become general inflation because of certain "propagation" factors. I shall describe the initiating, basic, and propagation factors in turn.[8]

Initiating Factors. The views concerning the initiating factors may be subdivided into the "simple" and "sophisticated" views. (These are my terms, not ones generally used in the literature.) The "simple" initiating factors are simply failure of supply in some sector of the economy to increase as much as demand increases. Some supposed causes are as follows:

Suppose that growth of population and of cities occur. As a result, the demand for agricultural products grows. If the growth of food production is sluggish, food prices will rise. Or, suppose that some workers are drawn from food production to production of capital goods. An increase in saving may have financed the investment, so that aggregate demand does not increase. Nevertheless, food production will fall, and the shortage of food will cause price increases.

Or suppose that import demand rises with population growth, without an equal increase in exports. The resulting shortage of foreign exchange will force devaluation or increased protection, and in either case an

---

[8] Grunwald (1961, pp. 108–23) presents a concise summary of the structuralist thesis. My sketch of the initiating and "basic" factors is drawn primarily from Economic Commission for Latin America, 1962, and to a lesser extent from Grunwald. Both are reprinted in part in Meier (1964).

increase in the price of imported consumer goods and of imported raw materials and components whose price enters into the cost of domestic products.

The wide fluctuations in export earnings of most less developed countries are well known. A decline in these earnings will have the same effect as an increase in the demand for imports.

The structuralists agree that demand-pull or cost-push forces—for example, an excessive rise in demand caused by undue budget deficits, or cost-raising wage rises—may also be initiating factors.

What I have termed the sophisticated view of the initiating factors relates to interaction between fluctuations in foreign exchange earnings and government policies. When foreign exchange earnings are high, income and both investment and consumer spending in the country are high. When foreign exchange earnings and income fall because of a fall in the volume of exports or a worsening of the terms of trade, the government is likely to expand credit or resort to deficit financing to finance a continued high level of investment and income and prevent recession. But for lack of foreign exchange, imports must fall. The shortage of imports would cause rises in their price in any event. The credit expansion makes the impact on prices greater by preventing the slackness in the domestic economy that would otherwise reduce the demand for imports and also wholly or partly offset the effect on the price level of the shortage of imports. The demand-pull effect of the credit creation and the cost-push effect of rising import prices both initiate price rises.[9]

Basic Factors.   Next, there are "basic factors" which prevent production from increasing adequately in response to selective increases in prices. The exposition of these basic factors is largely an elaboration of the obvious characteristics of LDCs: factors of production are not mobile; entrepreneurship, domestic saving, and foreign exchange are scarce. However, the structuralists assert that other factors are also important. The management of industrial production is monopolistic. Producers prefer to keep production low and raise prices when demand increases. Even if new industry does spring up, its costs and prices will be high, because of inexperience, small scale of operations, and monopolistic tendencies. It is asserted that government action could take the place of the inadequate market forces in inducing new production and the shift of labor necessary to accomplish it, providing saving, and curbing nonessential investment, but government policy is often too shortsighted to accomplish these changes. This part of the argument rather idealizes the capabilities of government and also the beneficial results of such policy actions.

The inequality of income typical of less developed countries is usually

---

[9] For this "sophisticated" version see, e.g., Prebisch (1961), pp. 3–9.

given importance among the basic conditions in the structuralist argument. It is thought to contribute to the problem, in that imports and domestic production cater to the luxury spending of the high-income groups. The argument seems to be that capable entrepreneurs do exist, and if they were not busy serving this market they would use their energies expanding production for the mass market and thus checking inflation.

A tax structure that causes government revenues to fail to keep pace with inflation is mentioned as another "basic" factor.

Propagating Factors. Under the heading of "propagating factors," the structuralists stress first the interaction between domestic price rises and the balance of payments, already mentioned. Price rises decrease exports and increase the demand for imports, and thereby cause a shortage of foreign exchange and necessitate devaluation or restrictions on imports. The resulting increase in import prices feeds the inflation. The rest of the "propagating factors" are simply familiar cost-push elements. In the absence of these, an initial price rise in any sector of the economy would merely bring about a series of other diminishing rises, tapering to a stop. For the initial price increase was only in certain prices; the percentage wage increase needed to offset that initial rise would be less than the initial percentage increase in the selected prices; the further rise in prices due to devaluation or an increase in protectionism would be still smaller, since only imported goods are affected; and so on, in a diminishing series. But if every economic group is able to achieve a temporary restoration of its former real income, in an economy in which total real income has fallen or some one group has obtained an increased share of the pie, then inflation will continue indefinitely.

One proviso must be added. Inflation can continue indefinitely only if the money supply continues to expand in passive response to the continuing increase in the demand for money. But the structuralists recognize this. They do not contend that inflation is independent of the money supply, but only that expansion of the money supply is not the active and initiating factor.

The Structuralist Argument: Criticism

The structuralist argument is often presented as a unique theory of inflation. So it is, in total. But when it is broken down into its three parts, the fact emerges that each of the three is largely familiar. The equally important fact emerges that with significant qualification concerning the "basic" factors each of the three is sound, on the appropriate assumptions.

None of the factors presented as initiating inflation would do so in a perfectly competitive economy. For except for factors that are simple demand-pull inflation, each "initiating factor" that causes an excess of demand for some products simultaneously causes a deficiency of demand for others. In a perfectly competitive economy, each price rise somewhere in the economy would be matched by a price decline somewhere else, and the price level would remain stable.

Consider, for example, the growth of urban demand as an initiating factor. The increase in urban income which causes the increase in demand must have been brought about by an increase in the production of industrial goods and urban services. If part of the income is used for the purchase of agricultural products, the inflationary excess of demand for agricultural products is matched by a deflationary deficiency of demand for industrial and tertiary products. Careful analysis will indicate that there is a similar matching in the case of every other initiating factor.

However, we do not live in perfectly competitive economies. We live in economies in which wages and prices tend to ratchet upward. The prices of agricultural products rise when demand for them increases, but the prices of industrial products for which demand simultaneously decreases do not necessarily decline. Moreover, the demand-pull elements in some of the structuralist initiating factors—for example, the "sophisticated" argument about the effect of income maintenance in the face of falling export earnings—are certainly sound. When the inability of less developed economies to change the structure of production or to introduce new techniques, quickly, or the unwillingness of national leaders to do so is added, and the cost-push and other propagating factors are added, an internally consistent and persuasive theory of inflation, independent of demand-pull initiating forces, emerges.

However, one link in the argument is weak—that concerning the "basic factors" and their controllability. There is often monopoly in industrial production in the lower income countries because the market is small enough so that potential competitors hesitate to enter into competition with an established producer. Other opportunities are more tempting. But even where this situation exists, monopolists as well as competitive producers do expand their production when demand increases, and the contribution of the difference in their behaviors to inflation is easily exaggerated.

Moreover, the idea that if the distribution of income were less unequal there would be more production for the mass market, and that this production would prevent or materially lessen inflation, is a peculiar one. First, the difference in the distribution of demand that is attainable by change in income distribution is limited. Secondly, the conception that producers for the low-income market are not affected by inflation has little basis. The two arguments seem to derive less from logical analysis than from a feeling that monopoly and income equality are bad and must be the causes of this as well as other evil results.

However, even if the "basic factors" element of the structuralist argument is omitted, a consistent argument remains. But even though this is granted, one may doubt that this set of conditions in fact accounts for the rapid inflations in some Latin American countries. The phenomenon to be explained is rapid inflation in certain Latin American countries only— in Argentina, Brazil, Chile, Bolivia, Colombia, Ecuador, and Uruguay, but not in Mexico or any of the Central American countries; and in those Latin American countries but in no other developing country in the world in equal degree except Indonesia and South Korea. The structuralist argument has no elements that would not seem to apply fully as force- fully to all other developing countries in the world. Why, then, is hyper- inflation unique to certain areas in Latin America?

"Aggression Inflation"

There are apparently some inflationary forces unique or almost unique to Latin America. They are probably merely an exaggerated form of cost- push factors, but the difference in degree is so great that it suggests separate classification. In a society in which the employers and workers distrust each other in an extreme degree, there may be a very large degree of disagreement concerning the division of the pie. If the distrust is sufficient, *any* offer of the other party may seem grossly unreasonable because this is the only kind of offer one would expect the ill-intentioned other party to make. More than this, collective bargaining may be an aggressive procedure in which the satisfactions consist partly of the pleasure found in attacking the other party. In such an atmosphere, with fiscal-monetary policy attuned to maintaining some approximation of full employment, price increases of 15% or 25% or 50% per year might occur because initially the social tensions cause disagreement to the extent of 10% or 15% concerning the division of the "social dividend," and there- after the expectation of large price increases causes labor to increase its wage demands and employers to increase their price increases. And of course others in the society will also use their political influence to obtain escalations of money incomes which will contribute to the inflationary spiral.

Inflation in Argentina and Chile

Such aggression seems to be an important element in the rapid infla- tions of some Latin American countries. Argentina and Chile may be taken as illustrations. Few cases show more clearly than Argentina a monetary policy of a purely passive nature. Events were in the saddle, and the monetary authorities had no choice but to accommodate their policies to the situation.

Argentina. In May and June 1962, the writer interviewed individually some 15 or 18 leading Argentinian businessmen and a smaller number of non-Peronist labor leaders concerning the social tensions present in Argentina. The mutual fear, suspicion, and hatred expressed was extreme. It is a fair brief characterization to state that the employers regarded the workers collectively as an alien evil horde. When asked how the workers might again be integrated into the society, each businessman responded in almost the same words, as if reading from the same copybook, "They must be educated to change their ideas. They must be taught to work harder."

The labor leaders expressed equal distrust and perhaps an equal degree of hatred of the country's business and other leaders. Some of the political leaders, they agreed, were financially honest, but they had no faith that any of the leaders of the 39 parties then formally organized in Argentina had any concern for the welfare of anyone but the small special interest or ideological group that he headed. These were the attitudes of the more moderate leaders. Unfortunately, I did not have time to gain access to the Peronist leaders. Their bitterness, it is reasonable to assume, was greater. The social distrust is evident in the murderous guerilla warfare that has broken out in Argentina in the 1970s.

It should be added that in Argentina, and to a greater or lesser extent in several other Latin American countries, the distrust of the country's leaders was objectively justified during the period surveyed here by the actions, or inaction, of the government. Corruption was rife. Absence of urban utilities, even sanitary facilities, in the expanding low-income sections of cities was not a matter of concern. No responsible official seemed troubled by the decay of railroad service. One got the impression that it seemed demeaning to some (perhaps many) social leaders to appear concerned about the welfare of the lower income population. Perhaps it raised questions about one's loyalty to one's own class. These attitudes may be a result of the group tensions.

In 1946, General Juan D. Peron had been elected president. Mutual fear, suspicion, and hatred between industrial workers and employers had been expressed verbally in Argentina for a generation previous, but until the rise of Peron the workers had been almost impotent. Peron made this class hatred the basis of his political appeal.

Between 1946 and 1950 he moved skillfully to concentrate power in his hands, and by 1950 had dictatorial powers. He then forced employers to increase markedly the wages paid and "fringe benefits" granted to workers, especially but not only industrial workers, and tried to hold industrial and agricultural prices down, though with only a moderate degree of success, by direct controls. Between 1935 and 1946, the estimated share of wages in the gross domestic income was 42% or less. (It may have been somewhat higher before the depression of the 1930s.)

Under Peron, during 1945–49 it averaged 47%, and during the period of his maximum program, 1950–55, 53%.[10]

In September, 1955, Peron was ousted by the armed forces. During the following two years, price controls were progressively removed. Employers pushed their prices upward; unions responded with wage demands; and the accelerated cost-push spiral shown in Figure 14–5 began.

Events during 1960–63 will illustrate the role of monetary policy in this development. By this time, the government had called upon the International Monetary Fund to support the peso, and the IMF had agreed to do so in each of several successive annual agreements. In an attempt to check the inflation, increasingly stringent monetary restrictions were agreed on and adopted. They did not check the inflation. Monetary expansion continued during the 1960s, through borrowing of money abroad and depositing it in Argentinian banks. When the foreign lenders asked repayment, beginning late in 1961, business continued somewhat as usual for a time through the device of "paying" bills with promissory notes. Then progressively increasing unemployment and bankruptcies appeared, and in mid-1962 the monetary restrictions were removed to prevent political revolt. The price rise had hardly paused.

Chile. Briefer reference to Chile will indicate that a similar element may be important there. Schott (1959) notes that continuing though gradual inflation had been proceeding since at least 1875. A cost of living index used since 1928 showed annual increases averaging about 6% during 1931–35, 8% during 1936–40, 16% during 1941–45, 20% during 1946–50, and 22% during 1951 and 1952, and then followed the even more spectacular rates of rise shown in Figure 14–4. Schott wrote:

> The monetary authorities, finally, had virtually no choice but to permit a rising rate of expansion of bank credit and the money supply, both to finance growing Government deficits and to meet the increasing demand for money to finance transactions at higher cost levels.
>
> More basic factors in Chile's socioeconomic structure contributed to the long-term nature and the intensity of the inflation. The most important of these was what Chileans themselves often call the "struggle" or even "civil war" between the country's major economic interest groups. In essence, each of these groups utilized the particular instruments of economic policy that it could best manipulate in an attempt to secure for itself a larger share of the real national income. Salary earners . . . secure legislation. . . . Wage earners made use of strikes, legislation aiming at larger social benefits, and Government subsidies. . . . Businessmen found protection in . . . monopolistic positions. . . . Farmers obtained guarantees. . . . Exporters and importers utilized preferential exchange rates and quotas.[11]

---

[10] Hayn (1962).

[11] Schott (1959), in Meier (1964), p. 221. See also Hirschman's (1963) essay on inflation in Chile.

Aggression Inflation: Conclusion

As a tentative hypothesis of the causes of the rapid inflation unique to some Latin American countries, I suggest the intense distrust and hostility among social groups present in these countries, combined with perceptions of the political situation by the lower socioeconomic groups that make them dare to press their demands.

But why should these class tensions be uniquely great in some Latin American countries? One dominating fact of Latin American history provides a possible answer. This is that "colonialism was domesticated," that is the European conquerors became "indigenous" and perpetuated their rule in ethnically dual societies. A large fraction of the population was treated for generations virtually as slaves, then as slave-like inferiors. Even though distinctions are no longer so sharp, it is reasonable to believe that high tensions have persisted. They were complicated by late 19th- and early 20th-century waves of immigration, especially in Argentina and Chile, of people who were of European stock sharply different from that of the Spanish and Portuguese elites, and who in their turn, drove to get ahead.

The hypothesis is presented as a tentative one that needs interdisciplinary testing. Its relevance here is that it fills a void left by the seeming inadequacy of the demand-pull, cost-push, and structuralist theses. If in some degree the inflations now in process in Western countries are due to the emergence of similar even though lesser class distrust and hostility, this must be ascribed in the West to the disruption of social cohesion and the degree of disintegration of family life that accompany the ever-continuing destruction of communities and community life caused by technical progress and specifically industrialization. If this factor is present (it may not be), its presence bodes ill for both the containment of inflation and the preservation of social stability. But these observations are a digression from the immediate concerns of this volume.

Supply-Cost Inflation and Growth

Ordinary cost-push, structural, and aggression inflation as described in the literature have the common characteristic that the active impetus to inflation comes from the side of costs rather than that of demand.

The structuralists do not say that inflation is conducive to growth. They say that it is a necessary evil; that curbing structural inflation by limiting the money supply will also curb investment, the response of supply to new demands, and in general the forces for growth. The only remedial program that will not inhibit growth, they say, is one that will alleviate the "basic factors." This takes time. Meanwhile, if growth is not to be choked off, inflation must be tolerated.

The remedies many of them propose are to have the government (1) act to lessen the country's vulnerability to export fluctuations by promoting import substitution and by pressing for commodity price stabilization agreements; (2) redistribute income to the lower income groups; and (3) bring about increased responsiveness of supply to changes in demand, especially in agriculture, by both direct action and the establishment of incentives for change. The measures would include improvement of the country's infrastructure, irrigation projects, land reform, and tax reform.[12] The discussion of Chapters 5 and 6 suggests that the structuralists have too limited a view of the barriers to economic development, and that these measures would not soon remedy the sluggishness of supply. Only economic development itself will do that.

If among the important causes of the inflation is the exacerbated form of cost-push that I have termed "aggression inflation," measures designed to increase the elasticity of supply will provide only a partial cure. The cure must include actions that will restore the trust in each other of the major socioeconomic groups. The most obvious measure would be the restoration (or establishment) of egalitarianism, honesty, and efficiency in governmental administration. Since proposing this and parallel non-governmental measures with a similar effect is asking the leopard to change its spots, and since the measures might restore a high degree of social trust only when a new generation had grown up, the forecast implied in the "aggression inflation" thesis is not optimistic.

To the writer it seems highly likely that in half a dozen Latin American countries, bringing inflation to a stop by fiscal-monetary restraint would cause severe hardship and would put a curb on growth, even if it were politically possible. However, it does not follow that abandoning attempts to curb inflation by fiscal-monetary policy will maximize the rate of growth. Some monetary braking of the rate of inflation may be salutary. An annual inflation rate of 50% probably causes financial disorder, diversion of energies, and distortion of the pattern of allocation of investment much greater than would a rate of 15%, and it may be possible to slow inflation from the one rate to the other by fiscal-monetary restraint without causing hardship. But perhaps even this degree of retardation is not politically possible in a democracy.

Inflation was checked to some degree in Brazil following the ousting of the elected president and assumption of power by the military in 1964. The method was fiscal and monetary constriction combined with settlement of the cost-push disagreement about the distribution of income

---

[12] See the discussion of structuralist views on this point in Grunwald (1961), pp. 117–21.

through wage decrees which reduced labor's share of the national income. Between 1964 and 1967, the minimum wage rose by 18% less than
did the cost of living index. Real minimum wages, that is, fell by 18%.
Between 1967 and 1970 they fell slightly further. Between 1970 and 1973
they were allowed to rise by 4%, far less than the rise in productivity.
Wages above the minimum level seem not to have been controlled. The
growth of GNP in real terms, which had averaged 7.1% during the 11-
year period 1950–61, had fallen to an average of 3.2% during 1970–73.
The rate of increase in prices (as measured by the cost of living index for
metropolitan Rio de Janeiro) had averaged some 25% per year during
1952–61, but had risen to 55% in 1962, 81% in 1963, and 87% in 1964. It
then fell rapidly, but its lowest level (in 1972 and 1973) was 14%, and in
1974 it rose to 35%. The "indexing" of wages, interest income, principal
payments, and prices in some other transactions had ended or moderated
most of the inequitable effects of inflation.

The very rapid rise in GNP in 1970 and following years is no doubt
due to the new government policies, and is hailed as evidence of the
effects of financial liberalism. No doubt it is, and especially of the effects
on business investment of fear in 1962–64 of extensive governmental
intervention. The moral concerning the effects of inflation is much less
clear, since inflation continued, though at a moderated rate, and since the
respective influence of cost-push and demand-pull on that continued
inflation is not clear.[13]

CONFISCATION

One added topic concerning government policy to finance economic
development belongs in this chapter. This is the question of confiscation
of private property, not to prevent the supposed malign influence of
foreign companies but in an attempt to maximize the pace of development. Bronfenbrenner, writing in the year 1955, noting the lack or slow-
ness of development in many less developed countries in that year, and
probably considering the success of the U.S.S.R. and China in confiscating private property, suggested that other LDCs could maximize development by confiscating all productive private capital. He illustrated this
with a model in which before confiscation 15% of the national income is
property income, of which one third is saved. There are no other savings.
(Funds equal to depreciation allowances are used to maintain existing
capital.) Of this 5% of national income, 2% is invested productively. He
assumed that the rate of population growth is 1.5% per year, and that the
rate of growth of aggregate national income is 1.7% per year, the causal
factors being as follows:

---

[13] Ronald Krieger (1974) discusses this period in Brazil.

Percent Increase
per Year in
National Income

Investment, 2% of national income, with a marginal
   productivity of capital of 0.15 .... 0.3
1.5% increase in labor force, with marginal productivity of labor of 0.6 .... 0.9
Innovation 0.5
     Total 1.7

The rate of increase in income per capita is thus only 0.2% per year.

He assumed that after confiscation of all capital goods, without compensation, one third of the previous return on capital is lost through less efficient management or is dissipated. The remainder is invested productively, thus multiplying the previous rate of investment by five. He assumed also that the marginal productivity of capital falls to 0.125%, the marginal productivity of labor to 0.55%, and the contribution of innovation to 0.4%. Nevertheless, because of the increase in the rate of investment, in 20 years per capita income would have risen by 20%, even if the rate of population growth rose somewhat. He assumed no redistribution of income, and hence termed this model "confiscation, Russian-style." With redistribution (confiscation Chinese-style), and hence development investment of only 5%, the increase in per capita income at the end of 20 years would be only 6%.

Confiscation, he noted, would not be advantageous in (1) areas that have already developed high living standards and social mobility; (2) areas in which there is nothing worth confiscating (e.g., Libya or Nepal); (3) areas, such as the petroleum countries, where the yield of capital is sufficient to satisfy both growth needs and foreign investors; (4) areas close to a Western power that may intervene (interestingly, he suggests Cuba as a case in point); or (5) areas where close racial, religious, or cultural ties with the West make default on obligations to the West repugnant. In some other areas, he saw confiscation as becoming increasingly attractive to the governments concerned. Recent history has contradicted two of his assumptions, concerning Cuba and the oil countries.

Later (1963, p. 367), Bronfenbrenner recognized that he had been inconsistent in assuming that only the marginal productivity of capital, and not the average productivity of existing capital, would decline under government management. On the revised assumption, the advantage of confiscation is less than his original calculation indicated.[14]

---

[14] In his original essay, he argued that Western governments would benefit by curtailing economic aid to a certain minimum, thus inviting confiscation, rather than transferring more capital to be confiscated ultimately in any event. Granick later disputed this conclusion, on social and diplomatic rather than merely economic grounds. See Granick (1963, 1964) and Bronfenbrenner (1963).

BIBLIOGRAPHICAL NOTE

A. R. Prest, *Public Finance in Underdeveloped Countries* (1963) is an excellent introduction to the subject. Three sources of data concerning revenue sources used in the text are J. F. Due (1963), U.N. ECAFE (1961), and A. Martin and W. A. Lewis (1956). H. H. Hinrichs (1966) adds analysis of trends.

Most but not all of the major essays on both sides of the monetarist-structuralist controversy are set forth in H. S. Ellis, ed. (1961), A. O. Hirschman, ed. (1961), and A. O. Hirschman (1963). Among other essays, see especially R. Prebisch (1961). R. Mikesell (1967) is valuable for both facts and analysis.

For summary information concerning country development banks, see P. Perera (1968).

The Allocation of Resources: Criteria and Mechanisms

15

The reason for postponing the discussion of capital inflow as a means of financing domestic investment was noted at the beginning of Chapter 13. It is repeated briefly here. Logically, a discussion of capital inflow should follow the discussion of domestic saving which has been presented in the preceding two chapters. However, the question of capital inflow is so intimately related to the policy question of import-substitution or export expansion, or more broadly, of "outward-looking" versus "inward-looking" policies, that capital inflow should also logically be discussed as a part of the discussion of those policies, which are allocation policies. The latter placement was chosen, and so capital inflow is discussed in Chapter 17.

The allocation that will be discussed in this and the following chapters is the allocation of investment, the prior question of allocation between consumption and investment having been covered in the preceding two chapters.

Allocation should not be thought of as a result primarily of governmental decisions; in large degree it is the outcome of market forces that influence the actions of individuals and firms. In this chapter, the criteria by which an economist would judge whether a country's allocation is optimum for its people's welfare, and then the mechanisms that determine allocation, are summarized. The discussion in this chapter is therefore abstract. The principles discussed apply to any economy. In the following two chapters, substantive questions of allocation that arise in developing countries are discussed: allocation among methods using differing degrees of capital- and labor-intensity, between consumer

387

goods production and capital goods production; among different types of capital goods; and among sectors. This last topic includes the question of "import substitution" versus export expansion. The discussion of these topics involves application of the principles discussed in the present chapter.

MAXIMIZATION AS OPTIMIZATION: PRESENT VERSUS FUTURE

The problem of allocation is a problem of increasing one type of production at the sacrifice of some output of another type. The shift should be made, and relative prices and profit opportunities will usually cause it to be made, though imperfectly, if the increased output is valued more by users than that which is sacrificed. If it is, then the value of aggregate output has been increased by the shift.

The distribution of income determines the relative demand for various types of goods, and therefore affects the basket of goods that will have the greatest aggregate value. If for institutional reasons it is not possible to have the income distribution regarded as most equitable with a given market-determined allocation of resources, then the government may intervene by administrative action to alter allocation. In this case, because the ratio between one person's aggregate consumption of goods and that of other persons affects the satisfaction felt by the people of the society, the basket of goods yielding the greatest satisfaction will not be the one with the greatest aggregate money value. The weights given to goods are not their money prices. An important example is the question of floors under industrial wage rates. For the moment, it is assumed here that there are no such institutional obstacles: that the desired distribution of income is obtained by secondary redistribution or in other ways that do not require administrative interference with the market. The value of aggregate output that is pertinent is then aggregate market value.

The rate of growth of aggregate output over time depends in part on the effectiveness with which innovation is being carried forward in the country. But it also depends on the allocation of inputs, most grossly on the share of inputs that are allocated to capital formation. Up to the present point in this book, we have assumed that growth in per capita income over time is desirable, and that therefore every country will or should sacrifice some present consumption in order to increase the future flow of consumption, but we have not asked how much present consumption it should sacrifice.

Formally, the question is answered by using some method of evaluating the present value of future consumption. We may then state that the objective of allocation is to maximize the present value of the entire stream of present and future production of consumption goods. If we value one unit of consumption at any future period as equal in value to one unit of present consumption, then any unit of investment that yields future flows of output totaling more than one unit—for example, even an infinitesimal flow of output if it is perpetual—will be undertaken. More strictly, all current inputs with a positive yield—that is, inputs that will produce future output whose present value is equal to that of the input plus any added increment—however small, will be devoted to investment. Enough consumption goods must of course be produced to keep workers working efficiently, but in a correct forecast of the future, that effect on future production will be included in the calculation. If we value one unit of future consumption less than one unit of present consumption, then our decision between present consumption and present investment will depend not only on the productivity of that investment but also on how much less we value consumption at any given future period than present consumption. At a 10% per year rate of discount—1 unit now equal in value to 1.1 units one year from now or to $(1.1)^2$ units two years from now, and so on—then we should divert all present inputs from the production of consumption goods to investment whose productivity is 10% or more.

In the abstract analysis of human welfare, it would seem that a zero rate of discount—one unit of future output equal in value to one unit of present output—is the appropriate criterion, since the welfare of future men and women is as precious as that of men and women now alive. Actually, to some degree, individuals take the same view. Most persons would give up one unit of consumption now to have one unit in their old age, up to a certain amount, and many persons, thinking of their children and children's children as extensions of themselves, would give up one unit of consumption now to obtain one unit for *those* future persons, up to a certain amount. But this is presumably not the general human view, and so investment takes place only if it is expected to yield a return considerably above zero. As was noted in Chapter 13, in the past economists often assumed that the prevailing rate of interest in a society is determined by the aggregate of such valuations of present versus future by individuals, but this seems less certain today.

In any event, the decisions of individuals, firms, and the government to save determine the amount of domestic resources that will be allocated to investment in any economy, provided that the capacity and desire to invest all of the intended saving is present.

CRITERIA FOR ALLOCATION: EQUALIZING MARGINAL PRODUCTIVITY

Equalizing Marginal Productivity as a Criterion

It is a standard proposition of the economic theory of allocation that at least in certain simplified conditions the play of market forces will cause the marginal productivity of each factor in production to become equal throughout the economic system, and that this equalization will maximize output (and thereby material welfare) in the system. When no shift of any input from one use to another will increase its marginal value product, then the value of the output of the system is at a maximum. The proposition applies to choice between present consumption and investment as well as to other allocation.

The conditions in which this result will follow are that (1) all factors of production are perfectly mobile, (2) perfect competition including entirely correct forejudgment of the future results of economic choices prevails, (3) every producer has to pay in full for any costs which his productive activity imposes on someone else and, on the other hand, can collect fully for any benefit which his productive activity confers on anyone else, and (4) there are no economies of scale and no "public goods" (defined below).

In an economic system that fulfilled these four conditions, so long as an increased amount of one productive activity is more profitable than some existing activity, some producer will move into it; and so long as the marginal value product of a factor anywhere is greater than the current rate of payment for the factor's use, some producer who sees the opportunity will offer that factor a higher rate of pay to draw some units of it to that use. Competition to obtain that higher income will cause a shift of slight amounts of that factor from all other uses to that use, and a slight increase in its marginal value product and its rate of pay everywhere in the system. In these ways the equalization of marginal products and maximization of the value of output will occur.

Many consumers may feel that while they alone would not wish to make additional provision for the future, still if through collective action all consumers were made to share equitably in the present sacrifice required, then a higher rate of investment would be desirable. Because of that fact, one qualification must be made on the proposition that in the system described above the market would cause the optimum allocation of productive resources to be made. Even in a system with perfect competition, perfect mobility of resources, and no uncompensated costs or benefits or economies of scale, the government should consider the question of public saving (positive or conceivably negative) to be added to private saving.

The Empirical Complexity of Marginal Calculations

The image conveyed in the equalize-productivity model is one of attaining equilibrium by shifting small increments of input from the production of one final product to that of another and comparing the results. Workers in Firm A seek jobs in Firm B because wages are 8%

higher, whereupon the proprietor of Firm B considers that he can reduce wages by 3% in view of the competition among workers for his jobs, and that will then pay him to hire 18 additional workers and thereby expand production by 6%; while the proprietor of Firm A decides that he must raise wages by 5% to keep his workers, but that in that event, raising his prices, he will lose some sales and must therefore reduce production by 5% and let 18 workers go. By such shifts—of all types of inputs—is the marginal productivity of each made equal throughout the system and the aggregate value of output maximized.

Implicitly, the model is one in which final goods are produced from raw materials in each establishment and each producer's production is therefore independent of that of every other producer. In practice, however, because of input-output relationships among firms and industries, and because of joint costs and joint products, the evaluation of the advantage or disadvantage of shifts is enormously complex. It will not pay to make a few more of any intermediate product unless there are going to be a few more final products using the components. The marginal productivity of enlarging a port depends on industrial plans in the entire region served by the port.

It is possible that a country may need to ponder two alternative productive complexes, in each of which the marginal productivity of each input is identical throughout the economy, but in one of which it is higher than in the other, while choices between are inferior to both. This situation violates the assumptions of marginal productivity analysis, which are that there is complete continuity of choices among methods and product choices, and only a single optimum. The situation in a gross form is admittedly uncommon; it arises mainly where large choices among new alternatives are faced, as in oil countries whose revenues have suddenly been greatly increased; but in more subtle degree it faces the producers of any country in which technical change is being considered. Producers must estimate the future situation in which they will be operating.

For such reasons, to consider the preferred among alternative allocations of resources it is often necessary to visualize alternatives for the system as a whole, not merely local marginal changes. It is necessary, that is, to program the entire productive system.

Many innovators program the economy, in the sense that they have at least a hunch about its larger future outlines. Programming more rigorously defined is a complex econometric exercise. Programming techniques are still so rudimentary in spite of the use of high-speed computers, that programming models can do little more than point out the gross requirements and gross implications of rather simple alternative choices. Even this, however, may give planners knowledge that they could not otherwise have. The Chenery-Strout (1966) and Chenery-Eckstein (1970) models provide examples of this. Chapter 19, on planning, presents an elementary description of one programming model, the Eckaus-Parikh model for India.

Yet with these considerable difficulties the principle of equalizing the marginal productivity of all units of each input throughout the system offers an indispensable yardstick for evaluation of policies. With some qualification concerning dynamic considerations, a country should seek to approximate the first three conditions stated above and to take advantage of economies of scale and the existence of "public goods."

Monopoly

One deviation from the conditions presumed to lead to the optimum allocation of resources is the existence of monopoly. If monopoly exists, the price of the good produced will be held too high, and too little will be produced, and in static theory, at least, monopoly not only distorts the distribution of income but reduces aggregate output. An exception exists where concentrating production in a single plant is necessary to attain the maximum economy of scale; in this case, regulated monopoly or government operation is beneficial. Schumpeter argued forcefully for another and more general benefit of monopoly: that it maximizes the rate of technical progress and thus of rise in income; for if a company can for a time have an exclusive gain from its technical advance, the incentive to technical progress will be greatly strengthened. The argument is cogent; permitting monopoly of the fruits of technical progress for a limited period, as for example by a patent system, no doubt raises a country's rate of growth. However, the argument does not apply to other types of monopoly, such as monopoly of a natural resource.

The problem of monopoly is faced in the early stages of industrialization in an acute form. The market for a given manufactured product is often no greater than can be served efficiently by one factory. The first factory is therefore free from competition; any prospective competitor knows that if he enters the field, both will lose money. If there are no close substitutes for an early industrial product, the producer may therefore be able to hold his price considerably higher than would meet the criteria for obtaining allocation, considered statistically. But the successful establishment of an early factory is a difficult and uncertain task, and the entrepreneur often would not attempt it if he anticipated competition, price regulation, or nationalization. In these circumstances, the rate of economic growth may be maximized by permitting private production without price regulation in a wide range of products. It requires far-sightedness to appreciate the advantages and perhaps a high degree of impulse control to adhere to the principle.

Imperfect Mobility

To maximize the marginal productivity or marginal utility of outputs, competition among producers for inputs and among the suppliers of inputs must operate so as to bring the marginal product of each input to equality throughout the system and to equality with its price. So long as the opportunity cost of an input—the production in its present employment that will be lost by shifting it—is less in value than the production that may be gained by shifting it, the economy suffers if the shift is not made. This loss may occur if an input is not perfectly mobile.

If the reason capital stays in the urban centers is that risk is greater in agriculture, and the reason workers stay on the farm is that they feel that the higher money wages in town do not compensate for certain unpleasant features of urban life, then marginal products are actually equal, for risk is a cost and psychic income is income. But if capital stays in town and loses higher returns available in agriculture because its owners are not correctly informed about the opportunities of lending or investing in agriculture, and if workers stay on the farm and lose higher wages available in the city because they are uninformed about urban opportunities or the condition of urban life, then opportunities for increasing the country's production are being missed.

Both forms of imperfect mobility no doubt exist, but their presence may often have been exaggerated. To cite interest rates of 8% in urban lending and 30% in rural lending does not prove misallocation of capital until it is also known how much greater the cost of loan supervision is and how much more frequent defaults are in agriculture. And differences between rural and urban incomes do not demonstrate that factor immobility is at work. Migration from farms to cities, even when the immigrants face unemployment for part of the year, argues that the workers are mobile (see Chapter 9). Their competition for jobs simply fails to bring industrial wages down. The difficulty is institutional interference with factor prices, rather than imperfect mobility.

Insofar as there is imperfect mobility, a recommendation for partial remedy is the improvement of transportation, communication, and information. A further recommendation is the subsidization of industrial employment. For if the productivity of labor is 8¢ per hour in agriculture and 35¢ per hour in industry, but the labor will not be attracted to industry except at a wage of 45¢ per hour, then if the industrial employer is paid a subsidy of 10¢ per each man-hour of newly-recruited workers, the new workers will gain 37¢, whoever bears the burden of the subsidy will lose 10¢, and the two together, and the economy as a whole, will have gained 27¢ worth of output. This argument is stated in expanded form in Chapter 16.

However, to adopt increasing the flow of labor from farm to city too facilely as a goal overlooks certain economic burdens and social disadvantages of increasing that flow. The economic burdens are the use of scarce resources to augment urban infrastructure. This will be a net drain upon the economy, for facilities needed in the villages—if they do not already exist—will be much simpler. The social burden is antisocial behavior that may result. The sons and daughters of migrants from farm to town, like the sons and daughters of migrants from one country to another, are culturally uprooted and tend to be asocial and antisocial. It is reasonable to suppose that if governmental neglect of rural life left a residue of bitterness in the hearts of the migrating parents, that result will be accentuated.

The remedy which maximizes welfare may be to improve amenities in the villages: schools, health facilities, recreation facilities. Paradoxically, increasing the contentment of workers and preventing urban congestion may also maximize the rate of economic growth. In spite of the increase in attractiveness of rural life, the concomitant increased information about the cities is likely to bring as large a flow of men and women to them as industrialization can absorb. Actual conditions and optimum rates of course vary among countries.

Factor Price Rigidities

It was noted above that what appears to be factor immobility may actually be a result of factor price rigidities. In any economy, the market price of a factor in some use may deliberately be held at a level above its opportunity cost. Labor may have a zero marginal product in one sector—for example, agriculture—and a positive marginal product elsewhere, so that a shift of labor would increase aggregate output; yet by law or convention the minimum wage that can be offered elsewhere may be above the marginal product of added labor, and may prevent the shift, so that the surplus labor remains in agriculture and produces nothing. The development of industry in some LDCs is retarded by the requirement of unemployment compensation, sick pay, terminal leave, etc., higher than can be afforded elsewhere in the economy. The labor costs imposed by law reduce the number of workers the industry will hire, and thereby force more workers than otherwise to earn a poorer living elsewhere. If industrialists were allowed to pay only the wages (including fringe benefits) needed to attract workers from their low-productivity pursuits in agriculture or services, the value of aggregate output in the economy (at a constant price level) would be increased.

The conventional recommendation therefore is that the minimum wage or high fringe benefits should be eliminated, so that the marginal productivity of labor might reach equality everywhere apart from the differential needed to induce mobility.

This advice overlooks the problem of income distribution. The price elasticity of demand for labor in industry may be so low that industrial wages would be greatly reduced and agricultural and service incomes only slightly increased before the marginal productivity of labor was equalized across sectors. For production coefficients may be fixed in many industrial processes, so that a reduction in wage rates would induce no increase in the amount of labor employed. The inequality of income distribution, measured by either the Gini ratio or the income share of the lowest-income 20% or 40% of the population, might be greatly worsened.

The ideal solution in an ideal economy would be to maximize aggregate output by eliminating barriers to marginal productivity equalization, then to decrease the inequality of income distribution by "secondary redistribution"—progressive taxation, direct governmental services to the poor, perhaps money subsidization of their incomes. If these measures are not possible, because of public attitudes, administrative incapacity, or the political influence of groups that would be taxed, then a second-best solution may be to set a minimum wage, including fringe benefits, in industry, to improve income distribution there, and then to tax industry to support expenditures enhancing the welfare of the nonindustrial low-income groups. If the government feels unable to assess and tax a company's profits, an excise tax is a third-best measure. But of course the political power of influential groups may bar this solution also. Whether some such measures would serve the public welfare, somehow defined, better than would a policy of maximum encouragement to the equalization throughout the system of labor's marginal productivity is discussed further in Chapter 16. (The problem of fixed coefficients in production, so that changes in relative factor prices do not cause changes in the relative quantities of factors used, is also discussed further in the next chapter.)

It is often asserted that the rigidity of social security requirements greatly discourages the expansion of industry, and especially discourages the use of labor-intensive methods. There is surely some unmeasured amount of truth in this. The major deterrent seems often to be the inability to lay off workers except at very high cost. To impose on employers the retention of unneeded workers is a crude device by which to fight unemployment. Welfare would surely be increased if the government itself faced the problem of providing employment.

Since the results of policy measures depend upon both social considerations and inelasticities that cannot be evaluated a priori, it is impossible without empirical investigation to state what may be the optimum feasible policy for any given country.

Institutional rigidities also often exist in the capital and foreign exchange markets.

Although capital may be scarce enough so that all that is available can yield a marginal product of 18% per year, interest rates in certain uses may be limited by law to 10% per year. The law, if enforced, will prevent those uses from getting capital even though the marginal product there is above 18%, and the capital will be used somewhere else where its marginal product is less than 18%.

The third factor whose market price often differs from its opportunity cost is foreign exchange. The foreign exchange rate may be 10 units of the country's money to the dollar, but foreign exchange may be so scarce that every dollar's worth of goods imported has productivity (or, if it is consumer goods, utility) equal to domestic goods worth 17 units or more. At 10 units to the dollar, bidders for foreign exchange would buy far more than the supply being earned; the available foreign exchange must be rationed, and some uses in which imports priced at $1 are worth 20 domestic units may not get them, while other uses in which they are worth only 12 units do get them. Other inputs, such as some natural resources, may also be over- or undervalued for institutional reasons.

In all of these cases, underneath the market price of the input an economic analyst may estimate its "shadow" price, the price for each factor which is equal to its marginal productivity when every unit is employed optimally, so that no shift would increase its productivity. The shadow price is the opportunity cost. To maximize production, every input should be shifted from any use in which it is earning less than its shadow price to one in which it will earn its shadow price, the only qualification being the one mentioned above about income distribution. Though complete freedom of international trade may not be an optimum condition, because there may be faster routes to future comparative advantage (see Chapter 18), to establish artificially exchange rates favorable to imports, and then of necessity to ration imports, is hardly the optimum policy.

Externalities

The marginal productivity to a private employer of a certain use of an input may not be identical with its marginal productivity to the society as a whole, because of technological external economies and diseconomies. Private marginal productivity plus uncompensated benefits conferred and minus uncompensated burdens imposed on other parties is termed social marginal productivity. Production (that is, welfare) will be maximized if inputs are allocated so that social marginal productivity, not private marginal productivity, is maximized, for these external economies and diseconomies must also be considered in evaluating whether a shift of a factor would increase welfare. The supposed existence of externalities often enters into argument about the advantages of industry compared to agriculture, capital-intensive methods compared to labor-intensive ones, and other allocation choices. The officials of some less developed countries evaluate the external diseconomies of manufacturing industry less weightily than the industrial countries of the world have recently come to do. Japan has concentrated so singlemindedly on industrial growth that she permits pollution of her air and waterways that would be intolerable in even the most negligent European or North American country. "Export your pollution-creating industries to us," Brazilian officials have said; "we will be glad to have their pollution along with them." It may be doubted that these policies truly reflect the desires of publics fully informed about the future effects of present pollution. There is a contrasting case in which the presence of technological external economies warrants government action to bring about technical advance more rapidly then the market would do. This is the case which W. A. Lewis (1966, p. 35) has termed "input industrialization," to distinguish it from the problems of infancy of a single industrial enterprise. If an industrial complex develops, the resulting "specialization, research, and learning" may reduce costs well below those that a single prospective industrialist could anticipate. Both single private investors and private investors as a group may be insufficiently bold to anticipate the effects of development of the entire complex. Hence, industrialization that will be economical may be retarded somewhat. (That it will be prevented for this reason is a limiting case that is less likely.) It may therefore be advantageous for the government to provide support and stimulus to induce an allocation of resources to industry sooner than the market would do so. The point should not be overemphasized. The government should not incur any costs of industrial development that private investors would not find it advantageous to incur themselves if they were sufficiently imaginative and could act in concert. In practice, an impatient government may waste resources trying to accelerate the development of an industrial complex, for the government may overlook the conditions other than merely the absence of complementary firms that set a limit to the pace of industrialization. The attempt of the government of Italy to foster rapid industrialization of the "heel" of Italy's boot, discussed in Chapter 7, provides a convenient example.

Economies of Scale: Public Goods

With the qualifications noted, to optimize material welfare a developing country should endeavor to eliminate the conditions mentioned in the previous sections. But, as noted, policy measures to take advantage of economies of scale and public goods, not to counter their existence, are appropriate.

If a plant is enlarged, the cost per unit of the added units produced may be less than the previous average cost in the plant. If so, then satisfaction in the economy as a whole is increased if the added goods are produced and are sold at their marginal cost, for productive resources will thereby be shifted from some use in which they are producing goods that yield lesser satisfaction per dollar of their price. But if the total output of the larger plant is sold at a price equal to marginal cost, total costs will not be covered. Should the plant be erected if its operations as a whole are run at a loss which someone must bear?

A parallel case is that of indivisible costs or benefits. A lighthouse provides an excellent example. There may be no economies of scale in the ordinary sense; the physical volume of production is not increased; but if the light shines, an added ship may see it at no extra cost. The scale of consumption of the service, rather than of its provision, can be increased with zero added cost. Radio and television broadcasts are other examples. Samuelson has termed such goods, whose provision to one recipient does not decrease the amount available to others, "public goods." There are few other pure examples, but roads, bridges, national defense, education, police and fire protection (within a given geographical area), and certain other services usually provided by government approach the condition. If the price to the specific recipient should be zero, because the marginal cost is zero, what should be the criterion for providing the service? No private producer would provide public goods or would establish a plant in which there are economies of scale unless he expected to have a monopoly or an oligopolistic arrangement, so that competition would not drive the price down to the marginal cost.

The criterion in the case of either economies of scale or public goods is that the benefits to users in excess of the marginal cost ("rents" or "consumer surpluses") should in the aggregate equal the difference between receipts and the aggregate production cost. A government that provides a service of which this is not true is using resources for purposes less productive than other uses to which they might be put. Moreover, the cost should be collected from persons who benefit directly or indirectly (unless for reasons not related to this service it seems equitable to redistribute income from other taxpayers to these recipients and providing this service happens to be a convenient way of redistributing it).

In almost all countries, public goods are provided by the government, since to maximize welfare they ought to be provided free. In the more developed Western countries, large private firms in some industries in which economies of scale prevail are allowed to gain the large profits that result from the inability of new firms (with small sales) to compete. The automobile industry is an example. Other industries, regarded as more essential, or in which competition is especially wasteful, are regulated in some countries, and run by the government in others. This is true of the group of industries usually termed public utilities. In less developed countries, regulation is likely to be excessive, rather than deficient, if the public utility or enterprise embodying economies of scale is foreign-owned. Perhaps a reasonable policy prescription would be parallel to that stated above for early monopolies. The public interest in the increase in productivity created by such enterprises is such that an enlightened government might well welcome them even if a pricing policy that would be optimum in a static economy cannot be enforced. As in other cases, the optimum policy decision in any given case depends on the specific circumstances.

Market Imperfections; Technical Change

A last group of factors that in the opinion of some may cause divergence between the optimum allocation of resources and that which the price system would bring about relates to the nature of the market. Some writers have suggested that the market operates less well in less developed economies than elsewhere in causing knowledge of future benefits to motivate present investment because the local or sectoral markets of these societies are not integrated into one national market, and also because the market forces of relative costs and profits are best adapted to produce marginal changes, whereas larger changes are needed in these economies.

The argument concerning the market is controversial. It was noted in Chapter 5 that the peasants in various countries have demonstrated ready response. There is no organized capital market in the least developed countries, and only a halting one until development is rather far along. But it is doubtful that this is because inadequacy of information about investment opportunities causes savers to fail to bring their funds to a capital market. Rather, their attitudes toward various types of economic activity and toward trusting their savings to strangers cause their action. Government construction of transportation and communication facilities at appropriate times may accelerate development by increasing interpersonal contracts. This may be regarded as improving the market. Otherwise, it is easy to exaggerate the importance of market imperfections that are unique to less developed countries.

One alleged market imperfection relates to the question of the significance of pecuniary external economies. The argument that investment will be too small (and perhaps will not be undertaken at all) because the prospective investor cannot anticipate the increase in demand for his product that would come about if other individuals or firms invested simultaneously was discussed in Chapter 7. It was concluded there that the logic is faulty. It may be that the entire concept of the effects of market imperfections in LDCs is not of great empirical importance.

For a quite different reason, it is impossible for investors to know with certainty whether investment will be advantageous: they cannot anticipate discovery of new natural resources or discovery of new techniques in their own country or elsewhere. This inability is not limited to prospective investors in the less developed countries. The great Lever Brothers built a very large vegetable and fruit canning plant in England, to achieve economies of scale, just before the development of food freezing reduced their market for canned foods much below the capacity of the plant. Some U.S. companies invested heavily in plants to make vacuum tubes for radios and television sets just before the development of the transistor. And so on. It is sometimes suggested (1) that this inability to pierce the veil of the future is true in greater degree of entrepreneurs in the less developed countries than in the more developed ones, and (2) that governments of the less developed countries should therefore intervene.

Both are empirical, not analytical, questions. There is probably some validity in suggestion (1). In part, technical advances cannot be forecast, precisely because they are discoveries (or inventions) of new techniques. However, the trend of scientific and technical advance and of research often (but by no means always) gives some suggestion of likely near-future developments, and companies in countries in which advanced research is going on are somewhat more likely to anticipate near-future technical changes than companies in the less developed countries.

The second assumption, that a remedy is government intervention, is ill-founded. Neither 1 man nor 20 can anticipate future technical change merely because they are government officials. The likelihood is great that private entrepreneurs (or effective managers of government enterprises, in a socialist country) will anticipate technical change more effectively than government planners. The opposite assumption derives from the fallacy of comparing realistic imperfect private action with hypothetical perfect governmental action. The case for governmental intervention on this score is a very weak one.

CRITERIA STATED IN DIFFERENT TERMS

Some writers have argued the appropriateness in a growing economy of allocation criteria which at first glance may seem to have nothing to do with marginal productivity.

One of these is that capital shall be allocated among alternative uses so as to minimize the incremental capital-output ratio. Since capital is scarce, it is recommended that in its investment a less developed country choose among available methods of production those that use least capital per unit of value added, and among alternative products those whose production requires least capital per unit of output. This advice concerning choice of products is most commonly applied specifically to foreign trade; it is stated that a less developed country should specialize in less capital-intensive products, exporting them and importing more capital-intensive ones. However, the advice can be applied also to the choice among alternative products for use within the economy. A country in which capital is scarce may be advised that it will achieve the highest value of output with a given supply of inputs if it specializes in the less capital-intensive products until their increasing relative supply, and hence the fall in the value of output per unit of input, raises the ICOR to equality with the ICORs of alternative products. It is not necessarily implied that the government shall determine this allocation of production by command.

This criterion for allocation would be valid only if capital were the only scarce factor in the system—only if other factors, such as labor, natural resources, and foreign exchange had zero or negligible opportunity costs. In the disequilibrium condition in which there is labor with zero marginal productivity, this is true of labor, but is nowhere true of natural resources and almost nowhere true of foreign exchange—and where it is, capital is as costless as foreign exchange. The thesis of using ICOR-minimization as the sole allocation criterion presumably arose from the fallacious view that scarcity of capital is the basic cause of "underdevelopment."

A related investment criterion is the ratio of capital inputs to labor inputs. It is suggested that as among countries or regions those which have a higher ratio of labor to capital will thereby have a higher ratio of marginal capital cost than of labor cost per unit of output, and should specialize in products and methods that use more labor relative to capital, and trade for goods of the opposite type. This criterion would be valid as among countries with the same production functions and with no inputs except capital and labor. However, if in some industries in the two countries the ratio of the productivity of capital differs from that of labor (because of differences in the state of technology), then the relative amount of capital and labor does not determine the relative average or marginal productivity, and the criterion fails. It also fails if natural resources are inputs for some of the products and if the countries have different endowments and opportunity costs of these resources, and of course these two conditions prevail in virtually every comparison between two countries.

Capital is often much the scarcest input in a less developed country. Where this is true, the capital-output or capital-labor ratio does give a good rough guide for policy. But capital scarcity must not be confused with foreign exchange scarcity. The appropriate rough guide is often, and probably more often, the minimizing of foreign exchange use.

The Galenson–Leibenstein Thesis

Galenson and Leibenstein (1955) have suggested that the capital intensity criterion should be reversed. Projects with the *highest* capital-labor ratio should be favored. They reach this conclusion because they start with unconventional assumptions. There are two aspects to the unconventionality. First, they propose a social welfare function based on the aim of maximizing per capita income at a distant future time. Present and near future per capita income are given no weight. Second, they assume that the governments of less developed countries cannot affect the rates of saving in the economies by fiscal measures, and cannot greatly affect them by any measures. Political considerations prevent levying taxes or compulsory saving on wage earners. On the further assumptions that wage earners will not save voluntarily, that profit-receivers do, and that projects with the highest capital-labor ratios will maximize aggregate profits, they advocate such projects as means of maximizing saving and thereby investment and far-future per capita income. They propose maximizing the "marginal investment quotient" rather than maximizing social marginal productivity as the allocation rule.

Otto Eckstein's Generalization

Eckstein (1957) has pointed out that the Galenson-Leibenstein criterion is not actually in conflict with the marginal productivity criterion; rather, the two are both special cases of a general case. The general criterion of maximizing the present value of the future income stream applies in both cases. If the rate of discount of the future is high, present consumption will be emphasized. If the rate is zero, indefinitely distant future consumption will be absolutely favored so long as present consumption is not reduced so much as to reduce the capacity to work. This is one of the two Galenson-Leibenstein assumptions.

Eckstein also assumes, as the general model, that a different saving (and reinvestment) coefficient is associated with each project. In his model, the rate of saving out of wages and also out of profits may vary from zero upward (or downward). Within these limits, the assumption that the saving behavior of the two groups is the same, or that the government can determine the aggregate saving rate, yields the conventional case; the assumption of differential wage earner-profit receiver behavior, plus the assumption that the government cannot control its own saving rate, yields the Galenson-Leibenstein case.[1]

Choice between the two models depends on judgment concerning which assumptions are closer to reality, or are more useful. Governmental

---

[1] Eckstein suggests that the "marginal growth contribution" of a given project be thought of as consisting of two parts: an "efficiency term" consisting of the present value of the consumption stream, and a "growth term" consisting of the additional consumption to be achieved by reinvesting saving. On the assumption that the society's discount rate and the aggregate saving rate will be the same regardless of the choice of projects, the second term is identical for all projects and allocation depends only on the rate of discount.

action in any country, including the less developed countries, does affect the ratio of saving to the national product. A surplus of government revenues over current expenditures will constitute saving in these economies as elsewhere. Politically, the range of governmental choice concerning saving does seem more limited in many of these countries than in more developed ones. The aggregate rate of saving does often depend in considerable degree on the share of the national income that goes to mercantile and industrial profits. Hence, the choice of projects that maximize those profits may maximize saving. Galenson and Leibenstein argue that the most capital-intensive projects have the highest rate of return on capital. This assumption is shaky, since it ignores relative demand for different projects. The intent of their proposal is that the highest profit projects shall be chosen, to minimize the rise in labor income and thus maximize saving.

It should be noted that wherever this tactic is necessary to maximize the saving rate, it runs counter to the wishes of the great majority of the members of the society, for where the range of governmental choice concerning saving is limited, this fact is associated with a high valuation on current consumption. Would this normative rule, to negate the popular will, be advantageous? Will the peoples of less developed societies be happier, or the societies more stable, if far-future affluence at the cost of minimum or zero rise in per capita income during the near future, and quite possibly a rise in underemployment, is held out as a goal? Or if policy is oriented in this direction without informing the people? Galenson and Leibenstein do not assume increased underemployment as a concomitant of the policy they propose, but if available capital were concentrated on capital-intensive projects it would almost certainly occur.

The judgment is a political and social one. The model is an intriguing bit of theory, but as an empirical recommendation the proposal does not seem soundly based.

That the Galenson-Leibenstein model has parallels is indicated by the suggestion by W. Stolper (1966) that the tax yield to be expected from a project should be a criterion of some importance in weighing its desirability. This case, too, would fit neatly within Eckstein's general framework.

THE ALLOCATIVE MECHANISM

The criterion for optimum allocation of resources is not "culture bound"; in a socialist as well as a capitalist economy, except where there are external economies or indivisible benefits, output is maximized if the social marginal productivity of every unit of each input is equalized. Even a socialist economy completely committed to the principle of "From each according to his ability, to each according to his need" should maintain an accounting and control system aimed at the maximization of accounting profits in its enterprises under pricing and resource allocation that simulates that of market competition. The question of what type of economic system is preferable, so far as it is an economic question, is one concerning how productive energies will best be evoked and how this criterion of allocation can be most efficiently applied.

The possible allocative mechanisms are government commands and the market, if the former term is defined to include governmental regulation of private productivity through the establishment of rules and through subsidies and the imposition of penalties.

The market is a marvelously efficient mechanism. The market-induced search by thousands of individual minds for maximum efficiency creates an optimizing effect of great force. Not all producers work vigorously to this end. Many of those who do not would not under any system. Some have such attitudes that they might do so more effectively if production were socialized. Offsetting them and probably in most cultures much more than offsetting them are the others who would be less efficient under socialism. In most economies the optimizing effect of market inducements is great. True, the quest for maximum income often leads to attempts to avoid competition. Moreover, that quest will normally disregard externalities. But the listing of ways in which the market mechanism leads to less than optimum allocation should not lead one to overemphasize the importance of those considerations relative to the drive for optimization which is inherent (along with certain diversionary tendencies) in the operation of the market. In most industries the disadvantageous effects of market forces can be remedied fairly well by regulation, subsidies, penalties, etc.

Even in the Soviet Union, after publication of a noted article by the economist Liberman, there has been vigorous discussion of introducing the stimulus of market competition to improve the efficiency of the use (i.e., allocation) of resources. Since 1963 Yugoslavia and Czechoslovakia have returned the determination of many prices and profits to the control of the market. Paradoxically, the effect in Yugoslavia is partially perverted by the fact that many locally controlled enterprises are monopolies or quasi-monopolies, and act as private monopolies would. Yugoslavia has a law against collusive price-fixing, but has discovered, like capitalist societies, that when a few producers watch each others' prices, policies contrary to the public interest are possible without collusion.

On the other hand, since the Bolshevik revolution of 1917 the Soviet Union, in which the market has played only a small part in the allocation of productive resources, has maintained an impressive rate of economic growth. It is therefore obvious that very effective stimuli may exist under socialism.

The discussion above of the criteria of optimum allocation has indicated the circumstances in which the market falls short of the optimum.

All of them may be placed under one or another of three heads: absence of perfect factor mobility (including the effect of monopoly and oligopoly), economies of scale, and externalities. Comments were made above concerning possible government actions to move allocation toward the optimum, where these circumstances are present.

BIBLIOGRAPHICAL NOTE

Among a series of articles by H. B. Chenery on allocation criteria, perhaps the most useful single one, one which summarizes allocation theory succinctly, is Chenery (1961). Concerning the effects of interdependencies among productive units, see Chenery (1959). The basic argument, in its modern form, goes back to J. E. Meade, *A Neo-Classical Theory of Economic Growth*, of which the second edition appeared in 1963. Concerning the role of government, see H. G. J. Aitken, ed. (1959), and A. H. Hanson (1959).

Concerning allocation in general, see also the "Bibliographical Notes" to Chapters 16 and 18.

Capital-Intensive versus Labor-Intensive Methods; Allocation by Type of Good

16

One of the simple facts of economic "underdevelopment" which ought to puzzle economists more than it has is that the capital-output ratio is about the same in low-income countries as in high-income ones. The ratio of direct labor employed to output is much higher. This is not surprising. If the total number of units of input per unit of output was not much higher in low-income countries than in high, they would not be low-income countries. But why is the use of their scarce and expensive factor, capital, as great per unit of output as in countries where capital is much cheaper and more plentiful? To an economist, it seems so obvious as to be indisputable that a good manager in a low-income country should be using more labor and less capital per unit of output than his counterpart in an industrial country. Yet he is not. This chapter asks why.

During the past two centuries, through continuing investment, the countries of the West have progressively increased the amount of capital equipment in use per worker, so that at present the amount is far more than that in the lower income countries. As the latter obtain more capital through saving or capital inflow, they have some freedom of choice whether to use it to equip a few workers each year or each decade with the latest Western capital-intensive equipment or to provide more of their workers with more moderate amounts of equipment.

The choice is not whether to follow the historical path of the West. For example, a producer in an LDC will not follow the path from animal power to water power to steam engine to internal combustion engine to diesel generator to electricity from a central source; he will skip several but not necessarily all of the intermediate steps. But even though he passes over some historical development he will face the question of how elaborate the equipment he invests in should be.

THE COSTS OF CAPITAL-INTENSIVITY

Before we ask why the common choices are what they are, let us consider the economic theory which states that output will be maximized if the limited amounts of capital available are allocated to the widespread use of moderate amounts of equipment rather than to limited use of elaborate equipment. The conclusion follows from the theory of the diminishing marginal productivity of any factor as its amount is increased relative to those of other factors. If the first $1,000 of equipment per worker raises his output more than the second $1,000, and that more than the third, then aggregate output will be maximized by giving each of three workers $1,000 worth of equipment, not by buying a $3,000 machine for one worker alone.

Suppose that output in the economic system is homogeneous, so that its production can be pictured on a single production function. Then the argument can be stated simply in the terms of Figure 16–1. Assume that the capital inputs available in the economy are represented by OK_2, and the amount of labor by OL_2. If capital-intensive methods, which use

FIGURE 16–1
Economic Loss through Capital-Intensive Production, One-Sector Economy

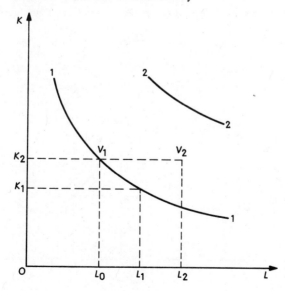

relatively little labor, are used, production will be at V_1, and not all of the
labor will find employment. If methods which use more labor per unit of
capital are adopted, OK_1 of capital combined with OL_1 of labor will
produce the same output, and since K_1K_2 of capital and L_1L_2 of labor
remain, obviously total production can be increased. Aggregate production could be at V_2. If the perfect competition of economic theory
prevails, the play of the market will bring output to the point V_2, for so
long as some workers are unemployed, their competition for jobs will
bring wages down relative to capital costs until all are employed, at
which point the ratio between the two will be equal to the slope of the
isoquant that passes through V_2.

If the economic system produces two commodities, say, manufactured
goods and agricultural products, then the situation is a little more complex. The situation is portrayed in Figure 16–2. The two production
functions are drawn to the same scales. Suppose that the total amount of
capital and labor inputs in the economy are O_MK_1 and O_ML_1 respectively. Capital-intensive methods, employing O_MK_2 of capital inputs and
only O_ML_2 of labor, are used in manufacturing, yielding output of
M_1 on the MM isoquant. Remaining capital and labor inputs, K_1K_2
$(= O_AK_3)$ and $L_2L_1(= O_AL_3)$, are available for use in agriculture, and
are used there.

As the relatively steep negative slope of the isoquant MM at the point
M_1 shows, production methods using a moderately smaller amount of
capital (say K_2K_4 less) would not have to use much more labor to
produce the same volume of output. On the other hand, if the capital

FIGURE 16–2
**Economic Loss through Capital-Intensive Production, Two-Sector
Economy**

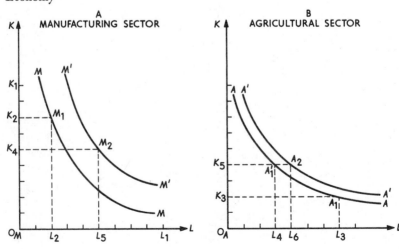

saved were transferred to agriculture, the isoquant AA could be reached (at A'_1) with a much smaller amount of labor. If the net amount of labor thus saved (the difference between the labor freed in agriculture and that added in manufacturing, to maintain the same volume of output in each) were divided between agriculture and industry, output in both could be increased above the original output—to points M_2 and A_2 respectively.

In a geometric representation, no further shift will permit increased output in both sectors when production arrives at points at which the slopes of the two isoquants (drawn to the same scales) are equal. This is approximately true at M_2 and A_2. By the statement that production in one industry is too capital-intensive and in another too labor-intensive, or the statement that concentration of capital in one industry is starving another industry and reducing total output in the economy, is meant that in geometric terms production is at points such as M_1 and A_1, rather than M_2 and A_2.

As in the one-product economy of Figure 16–1, in a perfectly competitive system the play of the market will bring production of the two products of Figure 16–2 to the points M_2 and A_2, at which not merely will the slopes of the two isoquants be equal to each other, but the relative cost of capital and labor will be equal to that same slope.

The analysis of this section, which relates to equalizing marginal productivity, is subject to the same qualifications relating to income distribution and second- or third-best solutions as is the analysis in the preceding chapter. These qualifications do not alter the point being made about the effects of relative labor- and capital-intensivity.

THE SUPPOSED VIRTUES OF CAPITAL-INTENSIVITY

Let us return, then, to the problem of the apparent attractiveness of capital-intensivity to entrepreneurs in low-income countries. Some observers judge that capital-intensivity has advantages to the individual producer (and to the economy) that do not appear in the simple analysis above.

First, the capital-intensive processes are often ones established by foreign investors who would not have entered the country except to establish these operations. There is therefore no sacrifice of capital for other uses; the capital would not have been available for any other use. The point may be granted. A country in which a license must be obtained by a foreign firm may then consider merely whether the proposed operation is advantageous, not whether some alternative use of the same amount of capital would be more advantageous. However, this fact does not explain the phenomenon in question, since capital-intensivity characterizes the production methods of many indigenous entrepreneurs, not merely foreign ones.

Second, it is stated that since workers in low-income countries do not have industrial skills, it pays to use automatic machinery that will reduce the skilled worker requirement, and requires instead only a small number of highly trained technicians (who can be imported if necessary). Less capital-intensive methods would not be as productive as assumed in the diminishing marginal productivity argument, because the skilled labor and therefore the productive process would be inefficient.

Insofar as the facts are as stated, this reason for capital-intensivity is also sound. The basic problem is often the innovational timidity of foreign engineers and managers, the greater ease with which they use methods they are acquainted with, and their assumptions about the inferiority of indigenous workers, rather than the actual qualities of those workers. The scarcity of skilled workers and workers who can handle machinery well is not an enduring situation. Managers, including indigenous ones, may be insufficiently resourceful in training workers. However, there are sometimes, probably often, cultural barriers and adverse motivations, and decisions to avoid the problem have some basis though perhaps often an insufficient one. The U.S. economist F. W. Taussig stated that devotion of energy by U.S. innovators (in the 19th and early 20th centuries) to devising labor-saving machinery was due to the unskilled nature of European immigrants.[1]

Third, as wage costs per man-hour rise, increasingly capital-intensive methods will become the most economic ones. Therefore, it is argued, an entrepreneur or a country should not waste resources in less capital-intensive equipment that will later have to be scrapped. The argument is confused. It overlooks the impermanence of capital equipment and the passage of time. The thesis rests upon the entirely sound proposition, expounded in the following chapter, that a country's comparative advantage depends upon the methods and products that will be advantageous in the future, with technical advance, not those that were most advantageous in the past. But this consideration should relate to a near-future plant, not one that may be optimum a quarter century in the future. Technical advance causes slow, not rapid, rise in labor costs relative to capital costs. By the time a more capital-intensive method is advantageous, the former capital equipment, having been used for, say, 20 years, having paid for itself and contributed advantageously to production, and now being largely worn out or at least obsolescent, can then be replaced by a more capital-intensive piece of equipment. (By this time, the amount of capital equipment in use per worker throughout the system

---

[1] F. W. Taussig, *Some Aspects of the Tariff Question,* quoted by Hla Myint (1954), p. 136.

will have increased. Investment in the more capital-intensive method will not then starve any other industry.)

Fourth, the greatest advantage of the introduction of capital-intensive methods in some uses in less developed countries is none of these three, but simply that in many processes less capital-intensive processes do not exist. In Figure 16–2, a shift from M_1 to M_2 may be impossible because the method represented by M_2 does not exist. Only the capital-intensive method at M_1 has been invented. It was observed as long ago as 1961 that "relatively efficient sectors in Japan (petroleum products, coal products, steel, nonferrous metals) are characterized by high capital-intensivity, large plants, and continuous processing."[2] The reason presumably was that even at the relative labor-capital costs of Japan in the 1950s there were no known processes in these industries in which output per unit of input was as high as in capital-intensive, continuous-process operations. This may even have been true of output per unit of labor taken alone.

It is easy to substitute labor-intensive methods for capital-intensive ones in some processes. This is notably true of in-plant transportation. In introducing Western processes, managers in LDCs have often and probably typically made this substitution. In India, in Latin America, even in the Soviet Union, with its intermediate level of income, one will see workers pushing carts about the factory floor or the mine works to accomplish transportation that in the United States is much more often done by cranes or electrically powered overhead trolleys. But in the central processes, there may be no known method except the capital-intensive one that will produce the wanted product. This will be true where uniformity or precision of dimensions is required for the adequate functioning of the product, where certain chemical transformations are involved in its manufacture, or in various other circumstances. There may be no way in which the capital equipment can be operated to produce a larger volume of output by the use of more labor. Or if a method is known in which lighter capital equipment can be used, by also using a larger quantity of labor, the output per unit of capital, as well as per unit of labor, may be less. That is, it may require more than one half as much capital, as well as more workers, to produce only one half as much output.

These are statements of extreme cases. They should not be taken as applying absolutely in most manufacturing processes. Within certain limits, factor substitution is sometimes possible even in central processes. For example, 1,000 workers operating with hand tools cannot drill a cylinder hole in a motor block to precise tolerances; but a dozen workers operating with general-purpose machine tools may be able to do it to as

---

[2] Arrow, Chenery, Minhas, and Solow (1961), p. 243.

fine tolerances, and to drill as many cylinders as one worker operating a much more elaborate special-purpose machine. And since it may take 20 workers to produce enough output elsewhere to pay for the added annual depreciation and interest costs of the special-purpose machine, output in the country may be increased by using 11 added workers.[3] The nine thus freed can be producing something else. But managers often argue that conditions often approach the situation of a fixed method, with no alternatives, closely enough so that subsitution of labor for capital is impossible.

In terms of a production function, the situation is said to be that portrayed in Figure 16–3A or Figure 16–3B. In Figure 16–3A, a production method with fixed coefficients is shown at the corner of each equal product curve. Neither added capital nor added labor will add to output. In Figure 16–3B, a small account of possible substitutability at each "corner" is indicated. In Figure 16–3A, only one method of production is known. If twice the production of the point V_1 is wanted, the only way to obtain it is to duplicate the plant, thus moving to point V_2.

In Figure 16–3B three isoquants, with relative outputs proportionate to the numbers given them, are shown. A method using about twice as much capital and less labor than the corner point on isoquant 1 will produce four times the output. Even if wages were zero, the cost of production by the more labor-intensive method would be uneconomic, because the capital input per unit of output is also higher. (Visualize the amounts of capital and of labor needed in four plants employing the process of isoquant 1, which together would produce the output obtainable by the method of isoquant 4.)

FIGURE 16–3
Conditions in Which Capital-Intensive Methods Maximize Output

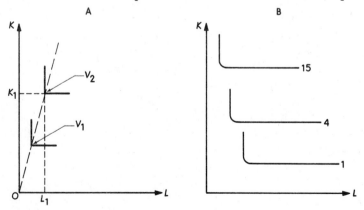

---

[3] In monetary terms, the added capital cost may equal the wages of 20 workers.

Undoubtedly the one situation or the other exists for many industrial processes or part-processes, in the sense that no method is known to engineers at the present time in which less capital can be used per unit of output if more labor is available. There is no reason to assume that this fact is a quality of the physical universe. There are no verities of nature or of physics or chemistry that decree that less capital-intensive methods do not exist. Rather, the situation exists in many processes because of historical trends in the West. As wages rose, in their search for increased productivity, Western innovators have turned increasingly to capital-intensive methods.[4] Only the left ends of more productive equal-product curves, curves pulled in closer to the origin, were invented. The right or labor-intensive ends presumably have a conceptual or "virtual" existence, but they have never been created in the West. Or if they were invented at some time in the past, they have been forgotten.

There is a fifth reason for economically excessive capital-intensivity. It is the existence of government policies and social practices that make it advantageous to the individual entrepreneur. Tariff exemptions on machinery, interest rates to industrial investors made artificially low by governmental regulation, and wage costs greatly increased by minimum wage laws, the imposition of heavy social security costs on industrial producers, and by social attitudes that demand wages in large-scale industry that are extremely high relative to other wages: all of these are common. In the presence of artificially low capital costs and artificially high labor costs, the method of production most advantageous to the firm is one much more capital-intensive than is most advantageous to the economy.

Do the absence of alternative methods that have been invented and the presence of distortions of relative factor costs make the use of capital intensive methods inevitable in most industry in low-income countries? Two facts suggest that they do not, and that there are still other forces at work. One of these facts is that where the presence of competition forces the most careful attention to unit costs, the greatest use of labor relative to capital is found. Much industry in lower income countries is quasi-monopolistic, since the first producer monopolizes the national market and there are few entrepreneurs ready to challenge him rather than to find their own quasi-monopoly in another field. However, where the manufacturer produces for a foreign market, he must meet foreign competition. The government of Mexico has established an industrial zone near the northern border of the country in which producers who make

---

[4] It is not immediately obvious why they should have done so. The logic underlying the assumption that rising wages would necessarily cause this trend becomes fragile on closer examination. The question has been discussed in the technical literature. Whatever the logic underlying the process, the process has occurred.

goods only for export are exempt from all customs duties. It is said that methods of production there are much more labor-intensive than in comparable plants elsewhere in Mexico. The same statement is made about many industrial plants in South Korea that have been given inducements to produce for export. The writer has no firm knowledge that these statements are correct, but accepts the statements of observers of these areas. Certainly it is true that an occasional plant is found in a low-income country successfully exporting in competition with producers in industrial countries by using much more labor-intensive methods.

The other fact is that many industrial producers in low-income countries have not only too capital-intensive plants but too large ones. If a factory is operated for five eight-hour shifts during each week, its machinery is used 40/168, or about 24% of the time. This is the average utilization rate in the United States. A study of West Pakistan showed a utilization rate of 14%, and one of South Korea, 16%.[5] Studies of Indian industry, though less comprehensively quantitative, make it clear that by the standard of a 40-hour week there is widespread under-utilization of industrial capital equipment there as well.[6]

The producers in the Mexican export zone presumably are subject to the same social security laws and hence the same relative costs of labor and capital as other Mexican producers. (I do not have firm facts.) Certainly the exporters in South Korea are. The probable explanation of their use of methods of production that are more labor-intensive than those used on the average by other manufacturers in their countries is that they need to use these methods to compete most effectively, and that rather highly innovative producers chose to venture into production for export. The implication is that many other manufacturers, enough to affect the national averages markedly, ape Western methods too closely, perhaps because they are not highly innovative, perhaps because they are driven by a noneconomic urge to be "modern."

This is also the implication of the prevalent too-large factory size in a number of lower income countries. That all of the manufacturers of a country "misjudge" their market so that they build plants so large that they cannot sell the output of even a 40-hour week is not a random event, but requires explanation. The explanation in some cases is that factory size may be accepted as a criterion for import quotas or for the volume of materials on which tariff exemption is obtained (some of which may then be resold). There are no doubt other such economic explanations. However, they probably do not provide a full general explanation. The remaining one that comes to mind is that desire to have large "modern"

---

[5] Y. C. Kim and Gordon C. Winston (1975), forthcoming.
[6] See George B. Baldwin (1959).

factories biases the judgment of many producers in lower income countries.[7]

Correctives through Ingenuity

The difference in labor-intensivity between producers for export and other manufacturing merits field research. It would be of interest to learn what the innovations have been.

Americans sometimes refer to "Yankee ingenuity." "Yankee ingenuity" has been demonstrated by persons in very non-Yankee lands who were seeking to economize on capital. Japanese engineers developed the three-wheel truck, involving essentially the substitution of a motorcycle for a truck engine. In the process of evolving larger and larger three-wheel trucks, the Japanese developed unprecedentedly powerful motorcycles. Japanese engineers have developed "mini-machines," farm machines so small that their use is economic even on farms of one to three hectares (about 2.5 to 7.5 acres). In Vietnam, insertion of the particular type of outboard motor useful in Vietnam's shallow inland channels into a casing has created an inexpensive type of tube-well pump now widely used.[8] In Colombia, the writer has seen buildings as high as 13 stories constructed with cantilevered floors and "curtain" walls, with no steel rod or shape in the structure thicker than reinforcing rods 1¼ to 1½ inches in diameter.[9] This construction is found in other Latin American countries in which good quality heavier steel structural shapes are not produced.

Somewhat more pedestrian practices which serve a similar purpose are the employment of workers in two or three shifts and on holidays, the use of more labor per machine than would be standard in the west, in order to prevent idle expensive machine time by having an abundance of inexpensive labor, and the employment of large repair crews even though they are idle more of the time than would be economic where labor is more expensive.

Some of the very successful adaptations may not save capital. Others certainly do. Some adaptations, of course, have not been successful. Examples are the "backyard blast furnaces" of China's "great leap forward," and the "ambar charka" of India, a spinning machine designed to

---

[7] A further argument that capital-intensivity benefits an economy, the Galenson-Leibenstein argument, was discussed in the preceding chapter.

[8] The outboard motor in question, used in Vietnam's shallow canals, has a long shaft with a propeller rigidly mounted at the end. The shaft extends rearward from the boat at a very shallow angle, dipping only a few inches into the water.

[9] In the process of construction, a bundle of the rods, imbedded in a concrete pillar, projects above the level of one story. A core of rods at the center is left projecting upward. The rest are bent horizontally in four directions, lying along channels in which a rich mixture of cement is poured to form beams. When the concrete floor of each story has hardened, the process is repeated at the next story.

increase the productivity of labor-intensive work. Cottage industry may seem to the eye to employ little capital, but often it employs both more labor and more capital per unit of output than do factory methods.

OUTPUT OR EMPLOYMENT?
THE FACTOR–PROPORTIONS PROBLEM

Where such capital-saving adaptations are not made on a widespread scale, and where goods that can be produced only by capital-intensive methods are in considerable demand, a country may have to choose between maximum output and full employment. It may be possible to maximize output only by using so much capital in a few industries whose products are desired that there is too little capital left to provide productive employment for the workers remaining in other industries.[10] Suppose that there are two industries in the economy, one producing by highly capital-intensive methods and knowing no other methods. The amount of capital available is limited. The situation shown in Figure 16–4 might then exist.

Sector M produces a product in considerable demand. Production is at M_1, on isoquant 6. $O_M K_1$ of capital is used in Sector M, leaving only $O_A K_3$ for Sector A. So much labor remains available in that sector that its marginal productivity in connection with that small amount of capital is zero, as indicated by the horizontal slope of isoquant 4 at the point A_1. The marginal productivity of labor in Sector M beyond the quantity $O_M L_1$ is also zero, but the marginal productivity of labor up to the quantity $O_M L_1$ is extremely high, and fairly high wages are paid. Some labor—the amount $L^* L_3$ in Sector A—is simply not offered employment anywhere (though if the workers are members of peasant families they may be sustained by those families).

It would require a shift of capital equal to $K_1 K_2$ from Sector M to Sector A to create a positive marginal productivity of labor in Sector A. Production would be at A_2, on isoquant 5 (increased by 25%, if we assume that the isoquant numbers measure cardinally the output on each). But one half the output of Sector M has had to be sacrificed. If in the eyes of the members of the society, the output sacrificed has more value than the increased output obtained in Sector A, then the economy created full employment only by reducing its output.

This, Eckaus suggests, or a situation very much like it, may be a cause of surplus labor in agriculture in the LDCs. If so, the country must choose between maximum output and maximum employment. It is quite possible, though not necessarily the case, that maximum output will be

---

[10] The conditions in which this choice exists were rigorously set forth and their possible empirical significance demonstrated in Eckaus (1955).

FIGURE 16–4
Maximum Output or Maximum Employment

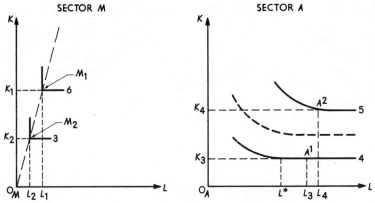

associated with a maximum rate of growth, so that some reduction in the rate of growth as well as in current output must be accepted to maximize employment.

It is possible that production at M_1 and A_1 is not the optimum situation for the economy. The added output of Sector A represented by point A_2 may have little value in the economy. It may for example be rice, of which the people are already eating as much as they want. But, if exported, the extra rice may yield more than enough foreign exchange to import the industrial products lost by reducing output from M_1 to M_2. If so, the country will gain by specializing in rice production and importing the industrial products. But this is not necessarily the case. The problem is discussed at greater length in the following chapter.

POLICY CHOICES

Even if the decision to have the goods rather than employment is socially justifiable, production by these methods is certainly a second-best solution, inferior to their production by less capital-intensive methods if that can be arranged. Governmental actions to equalize the cost of labor and of capital in different sectors of the economy, by providing improved information that will increase the mobility of capital and labor, is a step in the right direction in many economies, but it would not reduce unemployment in the situation shown in Figure 16–4. Governmental subsidies to wage payments in industry and to interest costs in agriculture, even if desirable in principle, will have little effect in the short run or even the long run, since one basic element in the problem is that methods that are less capital-intensive have not been invented.

There is little that a government can do to stimulate the ingenuity illustrated by the more successful examples of capital-saving inventions cited above. Innovational ingenuity cannot be created by formal training, or on demand. However, improved general education will presumably increase labor mobility. Improved technical educational and increased technical knowledge will presumably increase managerial and technical ability. True, improved Western technical education may be counter-productive, in that it causes the individual to become wedded to "modern" Western practices, and lessens his ingenuity. We do not know much about the degree to which such attitudes are increased by one or another type of education, or on the other hand are latent in the individual because of social attitudes inculcated earlier in life.

It is sometimes suggested that a government can induce capital-saving practices by encouraging the importation of used machinery from an industrial country when producers in that country discard it in favor of still more capital-intensive equipment that is appropriate in their high-wage economy. Use of such equipment is sometimes advantageous. To the degree that the machinery has been discarded in favor of more labor-saving equipment, it has precisely the quality of lesser capital intensivity that may make its use in an LDC economic. The shipment of its automobile machinery to Argentina by the Kaiser Motor Company, when it discontinued production in the United States, it is a well-known example of such shipment, but this is a very special case. The cause was failure of the company to capture a share of the U.S. automobile market sufficient to warrant continued U.S. production, and not the labor-intensive character of its equipment. Because the equipment had become of no use in the United States, its capital cost to the Argentinian operation was low, and the operation may have been an economic one on this financial ground rather than on a technical one. In general, used machinery is subject to imperfections or lack of durability resulting from the wear and tear which it has already experienced. The expense of dismantling and shipping it may be considerable, even if its cost at the site of its original use is not great. Hence even apart from the "instinctive" tendency of LDCs to regard the shipment of used machinery as an attempt to foist something out of date onto them, the circumstances in which the practice is advantageous to them are probably limited.

The possibilities of obtaining technical assistance in the devising of methods not highly capital-intensive are also limited. Engineers of the West who are creative enough to appreciate the desirability of such methods and to aid in devising them are likely to find their creativity in such demand in their home countries to serve other purposes that few are available as technical advisers. Technicians from countries whose productive practices do not differ too radically from those of the country being advised may be more helpful than advisers from, say, the United States.

Thus, advisers from Japan may be more helpful than advisers from Germany. Because of Israel's experience with her special problem of increasing productivity rapidly in a small land area with a labor force that includes many members without mechanical experience, in some instances her technical assistance has been very effective.

Labor-Intensive Projects

A country may do well to try to remedy the results of concentration of capital, rather than trying to prevent it. The most ambitious attempt at remedy would be a large-scale program of "rural public works" or labor-intensive works projects. These have been discussed in chapter 13. It was noted there that carrying out such a program itself requires a high degree of administrative and innovational ability, and also interest in village conditions.

ALLOCATION OF INVESTMENT BY TYPE OF GOOD

The allocation of investment among increase in inventories, equipment, and structures, and within this last class among residences, infrastructure facilities, and other structures, does not depend to any great degree on choice between capital-intensive and labor-intensive methods. It is discussed here primarily because it merits discussion but not a separate chapter.

The share of investment to be allocated to housing, the degree of congestion to be permitted in the use of transportation, communication, and other urban facilities, and the risk to be run that the power supply will be inadequate at peak times are all subject to variation if investment is controlled by government decision. To a greater degree, investment in increase in inventories and the allocation between plant and equipment in any given industry are determined by technical considerations and by the rate of interest. All are affected by the composition of output. A country's investment in structures may be high relative to that in equipment because the country's natural resources lead it to specialize in processes using a large amount of electric energy and to produce it in hydroelectric plants. Norway provides the example. One would expect residential construction and therefore total construction to be lower in tropical countries than elsewhere. An agricultural country will have a high ratio of inventories to total capital, because holding agricultural crops for consumption from harvest to harvest requires holding average stocks equal to a normal carry-over plus almost one half of a year's production.[11] But although the distribution of capital among types will

---

[11] Not quite one half, if there is more than one harvest, as there is in tropical agricultural countries.

TABLE 16–1
Distribution of Investment by Type of Good and Income Level,
Modern Times

	Income Level	
	Low	High
Housing	Less than ⅕	More than ⅕
Infrastructure	25–30%	25–30%
Other construction	Less than 10%	Less than 10%
Producers' durables	35% or so	More than 40%
Increase in inventories	12% or so	5%

vary among countries at any given time, there is a fair degree of uniformity in the trend over time, as income rises.

Few estimates are available of the total amounts of different types of capital in existence except for some of the industrialized countries, but a considerable amount of such information exists concerning additions to the capital stock, that is, concerning investment. Table 16–1 presents a summary distilled from various data sources.

Investment in Inventories

Note the decline as income rises in the share of investment that goes into increases in inventories. The most commonly overlooked component of capital formation is the increase in stocks. Perhaps investment needs (for a firm or a country) have been underestimated more often through neglect of the inventory requirement than through any other error. As the volume of production rises, the volume of goods in inventories—raw materials, goods in process, and finished products—must rise also. The fraction inventory increase must constitute of total investment depends on how great an increase in inventories is required to serve the larger volume of production and consumption as income rises, and on the other hand on the amount of fixed capital formation required to increase productive capacity. If the rise in inventories must be one third of the rise in annual output, and if it requires 2.7 units of fixed investment to increase productive capacity by one unit (of output per year), then increase in stocks must constitute one ninth of investment. But if the rise in stocks need be only one fifth of the rise in annual output, and if it requires four units of fixed investment to increase output per year by one unit, then the increase in stocks will constitute less than 5% of investment.

The volume of inventories needed depends on the length of the production cycle. In agriculture, if there is only one crop per year, inventories must constitute, on the average, at least one half of annual output. The production of some custom-made heavy producers' goods requires more than one year; inventories must then be equal to more than six months' output. However, agricultural plus heavy durable goods production together usually constitute a small part of the total output of industrial countries, whereas agricultural production constitutes a fairly large part of the output of a low-income country. The reduction in the share of inventory increase in total investment as income rises is probably accounted for mainly by reduction in the share of agriculture in GDP.

The ratio of inventories to output, and hence the share of increase in inventories in total investment, also depends on the composition of non-agricultural output, the system of production and distribution, and the system of inventory reporting and control. Japan's system of production of components in many small plants and her very poor transportation system have required extremely large inventories. The national income accounts of Japan indicate that inventory increases were 79% of the increase in GNP during 1931–39, 87% during the reconstruction years 1947–52, and 80% during 1953–55. The accounts probably overstate the inventory increase figures, but the true ratio can hardly be as low as 50% in any of these periods.[12]

In recent years, the volume of inventories required to handle a given volume of output has been declining in the United States and probably in many other countries for a number of reasons, among them computerized control of inventories and increasingly fast and dependable transportation. During the period 1935–40, the value of the increase in stocks in the United States was 27% of the increase in GNP, but for the years 1948–53 only 23%,[13] and during the years 1961–64 inclusive a still smaller share, 21%. For this last period, the average ratio of increase in inventories to increase in GDP in Japan was 50% and in Western Europe 24%. It is not clear whether the Japanese figure is comparable to the earlier official ones and therefore represents a marked decrease.[14]

The Distribution of Fixed Investment

Construction apparently takes, very roughly, about one half of investment at all income levels, though not necessarily a constant share, and investment in equipment plus increase in inventories the other half. The share of investment needed for nonresidential structures other than

---

[12] This conclusion is stated in E. E. Hagen, F. W. Herring, and others (1956), p. 154. Its basis is stated more fully in underlying unpublished studies.

[13] U.S. Department of Commerce, *National Income*, 1954 ed. (Washington: U.S. Government Printing Office, 1954); and *U.S. Income and Output* (Washington: U.S. Government Printing Office, 1958).

[14] The data for Western Europe and Japan are from U.N. *World Economic Survey, 1963*, Tables 1–1 and 1–6 (for 1961 and 1962) and *World Economic Survey, 1965*, Table 16 (for 1963 and 1964); and for the United States. *Economic Report of the President*, January 1967 (Washington: U.S. Government Printing Office, 1967), Table B–2. Since the percentages for Western Europe and Japan are calculated from figures for GDP increase for groups of countries rounded to the nearest percent, there is a margin of error.

infrastructure is small—probably less than 10%—at all income levels; less than that needed for increase in inventories at low-income levels and not much more at high-income levels. Other data support this generalization.

Investment in infrastructure requires a fairly constant fraction of total investment, one between 25% and 30%. As was noted in Chapter 7, such other data as are available for low-income countries support the conclusion that no burst of investment in infrastructure at the beginning of economic growth is necessary as a basis for growth.

Both cross-section data and historical data for the United States and the United Kingdom indicate that the share of investment going into dwellings increases as income rises. Data for eight countries for the 19th and 20th centuries do not indicate this; the average percentage in the eight countries is about the same in the 19th century as in the 20th.[15]

APPENDIX

INCREASING CAPITAL-INTENSIVITY AND TECHNICAL ADVANCE IN THE WEST

In technical terms, innovation in the West has been capital-intensive rather than neutral or labor-intensive, on the average. The concepts are illustrated on Figure 16–5. Isoquants VV, V_1, and V_2 represent production of the same volume of output with different technologies. Isoquant V_1 reflects a capital-intensive innovation and isoquant V_2 a labor-intensive one. The test is as follows. The reader should remember that to minimize his costs a producer must produce at the point at which the relative cost of capital and labor (shown by the downward sloping straight lines, the "relative price" lines) is equal to their relative marginal productivity, also termed the marginal rate of substitution (equal to the slope of the isoquant). At a given relative cost of capital and labor, the method that is most economical on isoquant V_1 uses a lower ratio of labor to capital than that most economical on VV. Therefore, by definition, it is more capital-intensive. At a given relative cost, a method on V_2 uses a higher ratio of labor to capital, and is more labor-intensive.[16] The three parallel price lines indicate this at specific points on the three isoquants. As the three isoquants are drawn in Figure 16–5, it is also true at any other points.

On the average, innovation in the present technically advanced countries has been capital-intensive. Methods have moved to the left as well

---

[15] Kuznets (*Q.A.E.G.N.*, 6) Table 13, except for the United States, for which the data are from Kuznets (*Q.A.E.G.N.*, 5), p. 81. The data for the 19th-century period are for varying two-decade periods between 1850 and 1890, except that for Canada they are averages for the years 1870, 1890, and 1900.

[16] This is the Harrod definition of capital-intensive and labor-intensive innovations.

FIGURE 16–5
Capital-Intensive and Labor-Intensive Innovation

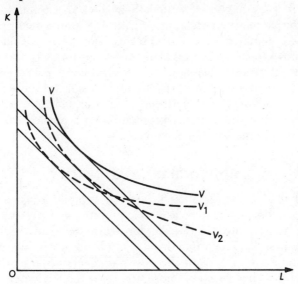

FIGURE 16–6
Economic Growth in the West

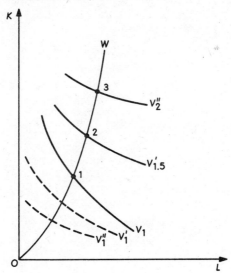

as in toward the origin. But producers as a group have not in fact dismissed workers (except, of course, cyclically) as they economized on labor. Rather, they have augmented their stock of capital so much that even with the increasing capital-labor ratio the employment of labor has also increased secularly. In technical terms, they have introduced capital-intensive innovations and moved along an expansion path simultaneously. Figure 16–6 illustrates. Isoquants with the same prime-marks reflect indentical states of technique, the numerical subscripts indicating the volume of production. As the left end of an isoquant has been drawn in by capital-intensive innovation, production has pushed out to higher isoquants, in a continuing secular process.

BIBLIOGRAPHICAL NOTE

The analytical basis for choice between capital-intensive and labor-intensive methods, on the neoclassical assumptions of perfect mobility of factors, etc., is presented in the standard texts. See the "Bibliographical Note" to Chapter 15. The article by R. S. Eckaus (1955) discussed in the text is the standard analysis of the possible effects of lack of mobility. J. H. Boeke (1953) has received more attention than it deserves, perhaps because of the sensational nature of his "East is East and West is West" thesis. J. P. Lewis (1962), Chap. 3, discusses the problem in the development programs of India.

External Finance 17

At last we come to the foreign sector. We shall view it first as a source of finance for development and then as a source of imports and a market for exports. When those two surveys have been completed, we shall be able to discuss the question: How can the optimum allocation of resources to development and then their optimum allocation among the various sectors and among various uses for development be achieved? We will return to the question of financial liberalism versus comprehensive intervention. That discussion will in a sense be the climax of the analysis presented throughout the book. We shall reach it in the next to last section of Chapter 18.

THE FUNCTION OF CAPITAL INFLOWS

Every country's major source of resources for capital formation is its own saving, but any country may also receive a capital inflow. By a capital inflow is meant a loan or grant from abroad to the government or residents of a country, or direct investment in the country by a foreign firm or individual.

This definition encompasses a variety of flows. The government may obtain a long-term loan from the International Bank for Reconstruction and Development or from another government or a consortium of governments plus the World Bank. The loan may be on quasi-commercial terms, payable in hard currencies, or may be on concessionary terms, or payable in its own currency. The government may sell long-term

425

bonds or short-term securities to private investors, though the opportunity to do so is much less since the disruption of the international financial system caused by the Great Depression and World War II than it was in the 19th century and the first quarter of the 20th. Foreigners, mainly foreign firms with business interests in the country, may place funds on deposit in banks of the country. The International Finance Corporation, a "window" of the World Bank group, may invest in and lend to private enterprises within the country. The World Bank or another government may lend funds to a government development corporation of the country, which in turn may extend loans or purchase stock of private enterprises. Or foreign firms may make either portfolio or direct investments in the country. These are the main but not all possible forms of inflows. They have differing consequences.

The capital inflows will have one or more of three effects. They may simply augment the nation's resources, that is, may supplement the savings of the country; they may provide the country (by which term I include the private entrepreneurs of the country) with foreign exchange needed to purchase goods abroad; or they may carry with them technology or managerial expertise.

Some economists state that except in the short run the first and second of these effects are the same. That question will be discussed later in this chapter. Whether they are the same or quite different, of all the world's countries only the Netherlands and Japan began their modern economic growth without a capital inflow. The economic rise of the Netherlands in the 16th and 17th centuries was financed from their income as seafarers. Japan neither received nor permitted any capital inflow until after 1900. England's early development was also almost entirely self-financed, but wealthy Netherlanders invested some fairly small amounts in England, and the Lombard merchants who settled along the street in London that became known as Lombard Street brought at least their stocks of goods. Beyond these fairly small amounts, which at the time may possibly have exceeded England's investment abroad, England had no net capital inflow during the entire period of her economic growth until she sold off foreign assets to finance the purchase of munitions from the United States in World War I. And has the Netherlands ever had a net capital inflow?

No other country has a comparable record.

France and Germany borrowed abroad in the early stages of their industrialization, mainly to finance railroad building. As Table 17–1 shows, in both Australia and Canada, for a period of four decades, as immigrants and money flowed in to develop "empty lands," the capital inflow exceeded 35% of gross domestic capital formation, which of course means an inflow more than half as large as domestic saving. Probably nowhere else in the world, at least in modern times, has a capital inflow been so large relative to domestic saving. The United States received net

TABLE 17–1
Capital Inflow Ratios, Peak Periods, Selected Countries

Country and Period	Ratio to GDCF	Ratio to Imports	Approximate Ratio of GDCF to Imports
Australia, 1861–1900	.37	.25	0.7
Canada, 1870–1914	.40	.31	0.75
Norway, 1885–1914	.29	.11	0.4
1920–29	.31	.14	0.45
Sweden, 1861–1910	.11	.13	1.2
United States, 1869–98	.02–.03	.07	3.0

Source: Ratios to GDCF: Kuznets (*Q.A.E.G.N.*, 6), app. tables; ratios to imports: Kuznets (*Q.A.E.G.N.*, 10), Table 13, pp. 62–63. The ratio of GDCF for Canada is a simple average of estimates for the single years 1870, 1890, and the periods 1896–1905 and 1906–15. Ratios of GDCF to imports calculated from the other two columns.

capital inflows until about 1900. Her record is discussed below in the paragraphs on the stages of a country's balance of payments.

Even Japan, the exceptional case, who neither received nor wanted any capital inflow at all during her early growth, began to receive an inflow of capital after 1900, when her success in industrialization had made her an attractive candidate for loans. British firms and individuals invested fairly heavily in Latin America, largely in public utilities, for four or five decades beginning late in the 19th century, and United States investors joined after 1900. The saving of each of the present lower income countries, not merely the Latin American countries, has been augmented by a capital inflow, which in their cases has financed typically between 5% and 20% of their gross domestic capital formation.

The capital flow from industrial to developing countries during the 19th and early 20th centuries consisted of both loans and direct investments. In the circumstances, there was little fear of confiscation of the direct investments. They were in colonies, new nations formed by Anglo-Saxon immigrants (the United States, Canada, Australia, New Zealand, South Africa, Rhodesia), or independent countries in Latin America whose rulers, democratic or nondemocratic, were friendly, and where in any event it was expected that the sanctity of international business contract would be enforced by gunboats if necessary. Many of the loans were purchases of bonds of companies that had been established by these direct investments, and were loans not to the less developed countries but to one's fellow countrymen doing business in them. During the 1920s, many less developed countries, mainly but not only those in Latin America, sold governmental bond issues in Britain and the United States. They were attractive to buyers because they bore higher interest rates than domestic issues.

Since 1930, and except for a period after World War II, the international financial exchanges have been disturbed. Political distrust since World War II makes many types of international investment no longer welcome. It is no longer possible for the governments of lenders to enforce payment of debts by "gunboat diplomacy," though they apply what diplomatic pressure they can. In these circumstances, although a private capital inflow to the lower income countries is continuing, one comparable to that of the late 19th and early 20th centuries is impossible. These facts seem to justify the statement that economic aid by governments, directly or through international organizations, is merely a new form of a flow that has "always" been essential for development, a flow that is no longer possible in its old form.

Stages of a Country's Balance of Payments

Samuelson (1973, pp. 659–60) has suggested four stages as typical of the changes in the balance of payments during the growth of an agricultural country into a well-developed industrial one. With slight adaptation, they are as follows. First, there is a period of capital inflow, during which the country goes increasingly into debt. Then, its exports begin to grow relative to its imports. The country has passed into the second stage when its exports become great enough to pay for its imports plus the interest and dividends on the past investments by foreigners; that is, when net capital inflow ends. As its exports continue to increase relative to imports, it uses the proceeds to invest abroad. In due time, its investments abroad come to equal and then exceed past foreign investments in it, and it becomes a creditor nation. In this third stage, so long as it uses its surplus of exports plus the net interest and dividends due it for continued investment abroad, its debtors abroad will have no difficulty in paying the interest and dividends annually. The country's imports rise relative to its exports, with its growing income and the increasing capacity of other countries to produce attractive goods, and—the fourth stage—it uses the interest and dividends due it to pay for an excess of imports over exports. If the country ceases to be a net lender-investor before it becomes a net importer, foreign countries will not be able to obtain enough of its currency to service their debts to it, and some of them will have to default.

The United States was in the first stage—a young and growing debtor nation—from the Revolutionary War until about 1900. She financed an average of about 5% of imports by capital inflow during the four decades 1820–60, 23% during the reconstruction period 1864–68, and about 7% during the three decades 1870–1900. The 1870–1900 inflow financed between 2% and 3% of her domestic capital formation. She then began a net capital outflow, and was a "mature debtor nation"—still with net indebtedness to the rest of the world, but steadily decreasing it—until

1914, and a "new creditor nation" until about 1929. Then, when U.S. investors ceased to lend abroad, but the United States increased its tariffs during the depression to prevent an excess of imports, debtors were forced to default. After World War II, imports of the United States, investment abroad by her citizens and firms, and her expenditures abroad for economic and military aid plus her own military activities together exceeded her exports by more than enough to enable foreign countries to pay the net dividends and interest they owe her and rapidly during the 1960s the "dollar shortage" turned into a dollar glut.

There is no historical or economic law which states that every nation must move smoothly from each of these stages to the next, or that a nation, having entered one of the stages, may not slip back into the one before it, but this is uncommon. As noted above, England became a net borrower (on a large scale) during World War I. She did so again during World War II. Australia exported capital during the decade 1901–10 and again during World War II, but was a net borrower from 1910 to 1940 and has been one again since World War II.

The first stage is of most interest here, for apart from the oil-rich countries the less developed countries are all in this stage. Indeed, a classification of countries as capital importers or capital exporters would provide a division between "less" and "more" developed countries that has a qualitative rather than merely an ordinal quantitative basis. The dividing line would probably be at a higher level of income, on the average, than the usual two-class division based on income, and as between the two classifications a number of countries would shift from the one to the other side of the line.

The Effect on Domestic Saving

It has been charged that a capital inflow lessens domestic saving. The national income accounts of many countries show that this is true. The conclusion is drawn that if there is a capital inflow the people of the country relax and are, so to speak, parasites on the inflowing capital. The conclusion is false, for the decrease in domestic saving is an accounting anomaly, not a result of changed behavior. When capital is invested in a country by means of a loan or by direct investment, the national income accounts show no increase in investment, for the domestic investment is offset by negative foreign investment, namely the increase in foreign claims on the country. If, therefore, so much as a penny of the added income created by capital inflow is spent for consumption, the national income accounts will show net disinvestment in the transaction and thereby a decrease in aggregate saving, even though every person (and organization) in the country who previously was saving is saving as much as before. So no implication of a change in human behavior should be drawn from the fact that capital inflow reduces domestic saving. The accounting result of course does indicate that part of capital inflow is spent for consumption, but econometric tests indicate that where there is a foreign-exchange constraint on growth (see the following section), the productivity of a capital inflow is high. In most cases, Chenery and Carter (1973, p. 468) indicate: "Were we to reduce the capital inflow, savings would rise, but output, investment, and consumption would fall."[1]

Capital inflow is only very loosely if at all associated with growth rates in intercountry comparisons. This presumably means that capital inflow occurs in as large volume into countries that would otherwise have low growth rates as into those that would otherwise have high ones, and also that foreign exchange is as frequently a bottleneck in the one case as in the other.

THE MAGNITUDE OF "NEEDED" CAPITAL FLOWS

The magnitude of the capital inflow that may be "needed" or "useful" or "desirable" depends on the purposes it will serve and the criteria by which one judges how fully those purposes should be served. Some economists, as we shall see in Chapter 18, believe that the optimum level of governmental aid, in the best long-run interest of recipient countries, is zero. Waiving for the time being this argument about the long run, it may be granted that in the short and intermediate run a capital inflow into almost any country can make possible an increased rate of economic growth. Some of the "least developed countries," and countries with such a dismal record as Burma's, may possibly be exceptions. Granted this, one may ask what limit there is to the inflow that a country can use with a reasonable degree of productivity.

Absorptive Capacity

Every economist would agree that in any country there is some limit to the rate of capital formation that can be carried out at any given time with a resulting increase in productivity. There are technical and other limitations. Among the technical ones are the size of the construction industry, the availability of materials for capital construction and of workers for construction and subsequent operation, the capacity of the ports and transportation system to carry capital goods, of the communication system to carry messages, of the country's housing to house expatriate or migrant builders and workers, and of the existing productive

---

[1] Concerning the negative saving effect, see Papanek (1972), who demonstrates the accounting effect noted in the text, and also Chenery and MacEwan (1966), K. Griffin (1973), and Papanek (1973).

complex into which or onto which the new enterprises must be fitted and on which they must depend in part for their productivity. Other limitations would include the number of individuals in the society with adequate managerial and technical capabilities, including in the extreme case the capability of making contracts with foreigners to do the capital formation, and the values and motivations of many groups in the society: of workers, which affect their availability for new enterprises; of government officials, which will determine the degree of waste, corruption, and misdirection of investment; and so on. Some of the human problems can be met by the importation of managers, engineers, and technicians, but even an unlimited supply of them would run into the other limits. In any event, there is a limit to the tolerance of the societies of less developed countries for such an invasion.

Hence there is undoubtedly such a thing as "absorptive capacity." Richard S. Eckaus (in Bhagwati and Eckaus, 1972) has argued that absorptive capacity is largely a learning and adaptation phenomenon, hence that even if "too many" projects are executed at one time, so that execution and management of some are substandard, their efficiency can be expected to increase and in due time to approach that of more effectively executed projects. But not, he agrees, necessarily to equal it, because individuals of permanently lesser capability may be involved. On this argument, which seems unexceptionable, a low level of absorptive capacity should be expected to be temporary. Absorptive capacity should be expected to expand steadily as more and more persons gain experience in new functions. It is also to be expected that the technical limits can be steadily pushed back.

The concept has been much used by some writers.[2] Other economists object to its use on the ground that it can be given no specific quantitative value. It could be given a value for each country with only a small range of ambiguity if the situation were as portrayed by the curve MNP in Figure 17-1—that is, if when a certain rate of investment was reached, the economic system became rather abruptly unable to handle more. The objection is that the situation is as portrayed by the curve MNO, and that furthermore we do not know the location of the curve. The objection is not a valid one, even though the absorptive capacity function certainly is as on the curve MNO. For while the concept of the diminishing marginal productivity of capital relates to the quantity of capital in use, another concept is needed that relates to the quantity of investment per time period. That concept is diminishing absorptive capacity. The reader will find the concept quantified with good effect in the analyses of capital flows in this section.

Max Millikan and Walt W. Rostow (1957) assumed that each low-

---

[2] See, e.g., Millikan and Rostow (1957) and Rosenstein-Rodan (1971a).

FIGURE 17–1
Absorptive Capacity

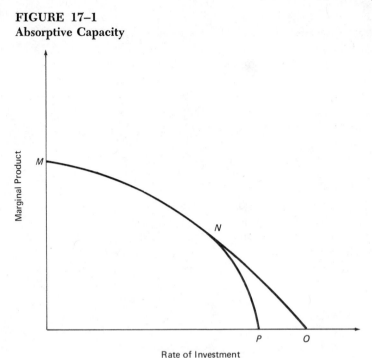

Rate of Investment

income country can within a few years increase its ratio of investment to GNP by one third to one half of the existing rate, and later Rodan (1961) made a similar type of assumption; but the empirical basis for these assumptions was at best informed judgment. Hollis Chenery and Alan Strout (1966) provided an estimate for each of 31 lower income countries that is at least reasonable and objective. They assumed that a country can increase its volume of investment from year to year by the maximum percentage by which it has done so during any five-year period in the near past. The authors implicitly dismiss the group of difficulties setting limits to absorptive capacity that were listed above, or perhaps encompass them all within a simple term; they see no factor limiting investment except "the 'skill limit,' reflecting the skill formation required of managers, skilled labor, and civil servants in order to increase productive investments" (1966, p. 686). But, whatever verbal definition is used, the data show the increases in investment that a country's entrepreneurs were able to make during the period from which the data were taken.

The periods of fastest investment growth vary from 1950–54 to 1960–64. The authors select for comment some of the facts they found. "Sustained rates of increase in investment of 12–15 percent per year are common" (p. 682). "The highest observed value for the skill limit over any recent five-year period is about 20 percent per year, but few countries have sustained a growth of investment of over 10 percent for as long as ten years" (p. 686).[3]

The Two Gaps

Until the 1960s economists assumed that a capital inflow served only one purpose (apart from possible accompanying provision of technical expertise), to augment a country's total investible resources. But in the 1960s the conception was advanced by Hollis Chenery and his associates that there were two "gaps" which may keep a country from using its full capital formation potential, either of which a capital inflow may meet.[4]

Any developing country that is not already industrialized needs some capital goods imports as well as some domestic capital formation for an investment program. Suppose that a country has the entrepreneurial capability and also sufficient saving capacity to carry out a higher level of investment than it is carrying out. It may be prevented from doing so, the proponents of the two-gap thesis argue, by either of two situations. First, at full employment the country may not be saving enough to finance capital formation up to the absorptive capacity limit. If, then, a capital inflow finances the import of consumer goods of the types the country uses, some domestic resources will be freed from their production and will be available to put in place the capital goods imports which the excess of exports could finance.

Or the country may have enough slack at home so that it could put more labor and other resources at work both constructing capital projects and producing the added consumer goods that would be wanted because of the multiplier effect of the investment. However, it cannot carry out the investment because it is not exporting enough to pay for the capital goods that would have to be imported for the projects. There is plenty of saving capacity, that is, but not enough importing capacity. If the country obtains a loan from abroad to cover the cost of capital goods imports, or if someone from abroad makes a direct investment and ships in the capital goods, the country will be able to use its idle labor and other resources to put those imported capital goods in place and carry out the projects. The difficulty thus remedied is the foreign-exchange gap. The former one is the savings gap.

Notice that the foreign exchange gap could not exist in the absence of certain rigidities in the country. If the idle resources can be used to increase exports, then the gap will disappear. Or if the investing entre-

---

[3] The upper and lower quartiles for the highest five years were .19 and .10.

[4] See the "Bibliographical Note" to this chapter for references to literature on the "two gaps."

preneurs modify their project design to use capital goods that can be made in the country, and the idle resources can be put at work to make those capital goods, then the gap will disappear. A government may induce an increase in exports, it is suggested, by devaluing the currency, subsidizing exports, or by other means. Or it can put the idle resources at work at labor-intensive capital formation projects. To remedy a savings gap, any government can increase the taxes it levies and make the funds available for investment. Or it can let interest rates rise to whatever level the market sends them to, thus perhaps increasing saving and certainly eliminating the advantageousness of some investment projects, until there no longer are investment projects desired by capable entrepreneurs that cannot be executed.

Chenery's argument concerning elimination of the foreign-exchange gap is that, whatever may be true in an ideal economy, or might have been true if a government had adopted ideal policies in the past, rigidities do exist, will exist, and cannot be quickly remedied, so that in fact there will be foreign-exchange gaps. If the idle resources could be put at work at investment projects by substituting capital goods that can be made in the country for imported ones, they would be working with reduced productivity. As for filling the savings gap by governmental action, we all recognize the political impossibility for governments in technically advanced countries to adopt policies that may be economically desirable; we should recognize the same in countries with less developed economies. By filling the gap with a capital inflow, we can permit a country to operate more productively.[5] These are sound points and, accepting them, we may recognize the existence of either of two "gaps" that capital inflows may fill. Both gaps may exist at once, in the sense that if one is filled the other may appear. A capital inflow may then fill first the one and then the other (if they are defined as above).

The ratio of a country's exports to its gross product does not give any necessary indication of the foreign exchange the country will have available to pay for capital goods imports, for high exports may imply low production of consumer goods. Proceeds of the exports may be needed to import those goods. The ease of taxing exports, mentioned in Chapter 14, suggests that high exporting countries may also be high savers. Figure 17–2 indicates only a faint and uncertain positive relationship. However, the suggestion of a positive relationship is confirmed by econometric analysis in the Chenery-Eckstein model (1967). If a country is both a high saver and high exporter, it may be guessed that (given a high ability to invest) a savings gap will appear before a foreign exchange gap, but no sure statement can be made.

A few cases suggest themselves of countries in which exports are

---

[5] A clear succinct statement by Chenery is in his "Reply to Bruton" (1969).

FIGURE 17–2
Saving Rates, 1970, Related to Export Rates, 1970
(less developed countries)

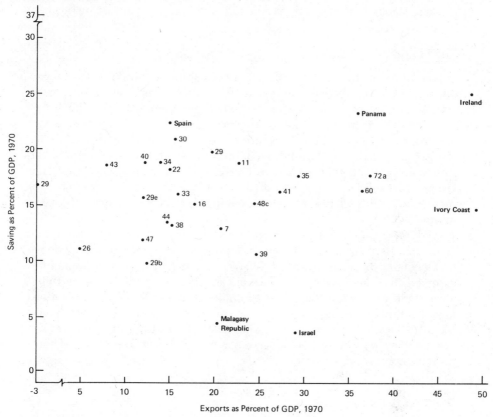

Source: Exports, *International Financial Statistics,* vol. 25, 1972; Savings, Economic Analyses and Projections Department, World Bank.

conspicuously above the demand of the economy for imports. Mainly, these are some of the oil-producing countries and a few small countries each possessing a rich mineral deposit. But these cases are few. On the other hand, whenever the terms of trade turn against a country whose exports are dominated by one or a few primary materials, the crippling effect on the economy of the lack of foreign exchange becomes apparent. The results in Colombia of the fall in coffee prices in the early 1960s provides one example. The effects of sharp declines in tin and rubber prices provide others. The inflation-cum-depression in India in 1966 and 1967, and the stagnation there in 1973 and the following years, are dramatic illustrations (though lack of entrepreneurial vigor, associated with great mutual distrust between government and business, might have caused trouble in any event). Leff (1967) argues that a reduction in industrial production in Brazil in the early 1960s, forced by the curtailment of imports because of a fall in foreign-exchange earnings, was the cause of slack in the economy even while inflation was proceeding.

The Magnitude of the Gaps

A number of studies have estimated the capital inflow "needs" of lower income countries by calculations that, in the terms used above, were estimates of one or the other of the two gaps. A number of estimates of each type were made in the 1950s and early 1960s.[6] From base years varying from 1949 to 1961, they projected capital needs and availability or foreign exchange needs and availability to a year 10 to 15 years in the future. Consistently the former estimates showed a savings gap ranging around $10 million (in prices of about 1960) in the final year of the projection, and the latter a foreign-exchange gap larger by some $5 to $10 million.

Today, the main interest these early estimates may have for many economists is their consistency in estimating some "gap" and the evidence that economists were aware of two gaps, even though they sometimes assumed that these were only different manifestations of the same thing. Two more recent and far more thorough and solidly-based projections have been made of the rates at which the lower income countries would be able to grow if resource limitations did not constrain them, and of the gaps between the required investment and forecast savings or the required imports and forecast exports.

The UNCTAD Study

One of these, published in 1968, was by the secretariat of the United Nations Trade and Development Organization (UNCTAD). It calculated the trend rate of growth from 1950 to 1965 for each of 40 countries, then projected that rate and alternatively a moderately accelerated rate of growth to 1975. Capital requirements were then calculated through estimates of ICORs, savings through their relationship to the national product, and import requirements through their relationships to the level and composition of output. Exports were then estimated by calculations of growth in the higher income countries and projections of world trade in

---

[6] See concerning savings gaps, United Nations (1951b) and (1962), M. F. Millikan and W. W. Rostow (1957), and P. N. Rosenstein-Rodan (1961a), and concerning foreign exchange gaps, GATT (1962), UN World Economic Survey, 1962, part 1, Balassa (1963), and Ohlin (1966). The savings estimates usually estimated average needs over a period of years rather than for a single year. Some of the estimates for the final year, referred to in the text above, were implicit rather than explicit.

each of the main commodities exports by the lower income countries. The two "gaps" were then estimated. In making the projections, 18 of the 40 countries were studied in some detail. Altogether, the study is much the most solidly-based and comprehensive that has been done.

The growth rate derived is of interest in itself. The higher of the two projections yielded a weighted average rate of 6% over the period 1965–75 for the 40 countries as a group. India, growing slowly, had a heavy weight. If India is excluded, the rate of the remaining 39 countries is appreciably higher. This compares with an actual average rate of 5.3% from 1960 to 1971 for all countries with per capita incomes of $1,000 or less.

The conclusion was reached that in 1975, with growth and the other magnitudes having proceeded at the rates calculated, the sum of the gaps between foreign exchange earnings and requirements to meet imports and current services including interest, dividends, and other profits on foreign capital, would be between 19 and 28 billion.[7]

This estimate of the trade gap excludes "negative gaps," that is, foreign exchange accumulation by the oil countries. A total estimate of savings gaps could not be estimated because of lack of savings estimates for some African countries. All trade gaps were included, whether larger or smaller than savings gaps, and while the sum of the dominant gaps would be larger than that of the foreign-exchange gaps above, Marris suggests that it would not be much larger.

This estimate may be compared with the suggestion of persons who are advocates of increased foreign aid that the high-income countries should provide a (private plus public) capital flow to the LDC's equal to 1% of the high-income countries' GNP. That criterion would yield a flow in 1975, in 1968 prices, of about $22 billion.

The Chenery-Strout Estimates

The Chenery-Strout estimates published in 1966 indicate a possible decline in capital inflow requirements. The two authors prepared an econometric model which, using data for 31 less developed countries and partial data filled in by plausible estimates for 19 more, projected trends

---

[7] More specifically, the UNCTAD study estimated that the gap between earnings and requirements for trade, related services, and tourism would be $10 billion, but that $5 billion of this might be eliminated if high-income countries adopted measures to permit a more rapid increase in their imports from the LDCs. It was estimated that if the latter were done, the foreign exchange needed to offset interest, dividends, and other profits would be $14 billion. Robin Marris (1970) estimates that if the LDC exports were not accelerated, and the deficiency were made good by higher capital inflow, by 1975 the sum of interest, dividends, and other profits would be $18 rather than $14 billion.

during 1957–62 to 1975. Their projections are based solely on these data. They did not arrive at an estimate of global foreign-aid needs.

In one respect, their method differed significantly from that of the UNCTAD researchers. Chenery and Strout assumed the rate of growth of the countries to be limited by the rate at which the entrepreneurs of each country could increase investment if given the necessary resources (their "absorptive capacity," termed by Chenery and Strout the "skill limit"— discussed above). The rate of growth was derived by applying an ICOR to the increase in capital.

The question was asked concerning each of the 31 countries whether this rate of increase in investment would yield a 5% per year rate of increase in GNP during the period from about 1957–62 to 1975. The answer for almost all of the countries was Yes. The study then asked whether, projecting to 1975 the 1957–62 rate of growth of exports and the 1957–62 marginal rates of imports and of saving to GNP, each country would need a capital inflow until 1975 to sustain the 5% rate of growth. All or almost all were receiving economic aid during 1957–62. On the basis of this protection, 12 of the 31 would no longer need aid.

For all of the 50 countries, more optimistic estimates of possible trends in output were projected—estimates such as a country might include in a five-year plan, and still higher estimates which in the subjective judgment of the authors each country had only a 25% chance of attaining. Altogether, 18 alternative projections of possible developments from 1962 to 1975 were made for each of the 50 countries. In all of the combinations of these alternatives that were most likely in the authors' view, the amount of foreign aid needed in 1975 was greater than that which was provided in 1962.

In only 3 of the 18 sets of projections of the Chenery-Strout study did the saving gap exceed the foreign-exchange gap in half or more of the 50 countries. In the other 15 sets of projections, the foreign gap was the larger in more than half of the countries. In the UNCTAD study, there was no such predominance of the foreign-exchange gap, at least if only large differences between the two gaps are considered. In the higher of the two alternative sets of projections, the saving gap was larger in almost half of the countries for which the difference between them was equal to 1½% of GNP or more.

In the 1960s, even though capital inflows fell short of those calculated as needed in the Chenery-Strout estimates, growth rates were by and large much as estimated. A significant acceleration of growth was projected for 40 of the 50 countries; in 35 countries some acceleration was achieved. Chenery and Nicholas Carter analyzed developments during the 1960s in 37 of the countries with those projected. The unweighted average of the growth rates of these countries rose from 4.4% in 1957–62 to 5.25% in 1960–70, about as projected. In 25 of the 37, growth was within 1.2% above or below that projected. In five, it was faster than this; in seven, slower. Among the seven is India. Chenery and Carter attribute the very slow rate of growth in India to a 45% shortfall of capital inflow below that calculated as needed to sustain a growth rate of 5.3% (as projected). Other analysts believe that India's growth would have been slow in any event.

"Trade or Aid"

The explanation of the achievement in spite of a shortfall of projected required capital inflow is that exports of the countries increased faster than projected. Chenery and Strout had estimated the annual growth of exports of manufactured goods and services at 6% in the 37 countries; the actual rate of increase was 15%. That trade seems within limits to have been an adequate substitute for aid indicates the importance of the foreign-exchange gap. It reinforces the views of persons who present the slogan which has been used as the title for this subsection.

Present tariff and other barriers to imports erected by the industrial nations of the world are in no cases higher for the products of low-income countries than for other countries, and on the whole are moderate. They do, however, provide special barriers to certain products of especial importance to the low-income countries, such as textiles and leather products. They did not prevent increases in the exports of the less developed countries in the 1960s that are impressive both absolutely and relative to the 1950s. Table 17–2 relates to their exports to the European Economic Community, the United Kingdom, the United States, Japan, and the Soviet Union.

The share of the less developed countries in world trade declined during the two decades. Their exports and imports accounted for 29% of

TABLE 17–2
Exports of Less Developed Countries by Region, 1951–52 through 1968–69

	Value in $ Millions		Annual Percentage Change	
Non-Oil Producers	1951–52	1968–69	1950s	1960s
Latin America	5,512	10,047	0.7	6.2
Africa	3,507	7,506	3.1	6.1
Middle East	1,106	3,172	4.2	8.4
Asia	7,945	11,885	−0.8	5.3
Total above	18,070	32,694	0.8	6.0
Oil Producers*	3,783	12,526	7.2	7.4

* In the four regions, respectively: Venezuela, Netherlands Antilles, Trinidad; Libya; Iran, Iraq, Kuwait, Saudi Arabia; Brunei.
Source: Cohen and Sisler (1971), computed from various issues of *International Financial Statistics*.

world trade in 1951–52, 24% in 1959–60, and 20% in 1968–69.[8] This relative decline, due to the rapid increase in trade among the industrial nations, has no direct significance in relation to the capital and foreign exchange needs of the less developed countries. It is significant that the rapid growth of the industrial nations produced a rapid increase of demand for the products of the lower income countries.

To test whether the increases of the 1960s in exports of the less developed countries were due to their agility in taking advantage of expanding markets, Cohen and Sisler (1971), taking 26 primary products of great trade importance for the low-income countries (excluding mineral fuels), ranked them by the annual rate of growth between 1959–60 and 1967–68 in imports of each from the entire world by the industrial nations, and ranked them also by the change in the share of those imports from the less developed countries. The two authors then did a rank correlation between the two rankings. Their thesis was that if the less developed countries were agile exploiters of increasing opportunities, a positive correlation between the rate of rise in demand and the change in their shares should be expected. If they were passive or rather sluggish beneficiaries, then the correlation should be negative. The correlation coefficient was −0.44, significantly different from zero at the 95% level. For the 21 agricultural commodities alone, the correlation coefficient was −0.60, significant at the 99% level. However, other reasons than sluggishness of response to opportunity enter. The populations of the less developed countries increased much faster during the 1950s and 1960s than did those of the industrial nations. As a result, the margin between their production of agricultural products and their domestic demand also decreased faster. This alone might account for the result Cohen and Sisler noted.

The less developed countries did take increasing advantage of the markets for low-technology manufactures. Table 17–3 provides the evidence. The "primary" and "manufactures" classes include not all commodities of these types but only 21 agricultural, 5 nonagricultural primary, and 6 manufactured commodities or groups that bulk large in trade.

Less developed country exports, especially of manufactures, continued to accelerate during 1970–73, the latest period for which data are available as this is written. Measures for further liberalization of trade barriers that affect their exports were discussed during the 1960s and early 1970s, but without actions of great consequence.

A "Kennedy round" of negotiations for reciprocal tariff reductions, conducted under the General Agreement on Tariffs and Trade, was brought to a highly successful conclusion in 1967. The reductions related

---

[8] Computed by Cohen and Sisler (1971).

TABLE 17–3
Annual Percentage Change in Imports, E.E.C., U.S., U.K., Japan, and
U.S.S.R.—1950–60 to 1967–68

| | Annual Percentage Change in Imports | |
Commodity or Group	From the World	From LDCs
Mineral fuels	9.5	9.0
Other primary		
Agricultural	3.5	1.7
Nonagricultural*	4.5	3.8
Manufactures	12.0	15.0
Clothing	13.3	18.7
Cotton fabrics	3.4	9.3
Footwear	11.7	15.6
Jute fabrics and jute	5.5	6.0
Pearls and precious stones	19.6	28.0
Veneer	7.3	19.8
Other commodities	6.6	6.1
Total imports	8.0	5.5

  * Coffee, fish, iron ore, tin, and wood.
  Source: Cohen and Sisler (1971).

largely to trade among the industrial nations; the trade concerns of the less developed countries received little attention. However, the countries of the European Economic Community had agreed when the Common Market was formed to admit the products of the former African colonies of some of them without duty. Following the GATT agreement, UNCTAD negotiated an agreement with the industrial nations for the establishment of "Generalized System of Preferences" (GSF), that is, preferential tariff rates for the less developed countries by which duties on some imports from those countries would be reduced below the most-favored-nation duties on imports from other countries. In 1971 and 1972 such systems of preferences were adopted by all of the industrial nations of the non-Communist world except the United States and Canada. However, the United States was already relatively more open to manufactured goods imports from the less developed countries than were the European countries or Japan. The GSF systems adopted continued high tariffs on textile and leather products, and in general did not cover a very large share of the exports of the low-income countries.[9]

The accelerating increases in exports indicate that for at least some of the lower income countries their exports may fill their foreign-exchange gaps much sooner than had been anticipated a decade ago. The effect, however, will be somewhat uneven, and a saving gap will still exist even

---

[9] Not surprisingly, in view of the "import-substitution" policies of the less developed countries, the tariffs of the industrial nations average far lower than those of the less developed countries.

for some of the countries that no longer have a foreign-exchange gap. The conclusion one can draw is that net capital inflow is still needed, and will be needed for some time, if all of the lower income countries are to grow as fast as they have the entrepreneurial capability to grow, but that that need is not eternal, even though in the balance of private capital flows in the world there must always be capital inflows somewhere. The conclusion may also be drawn, though the data which provide the basis have not yet been presented, that the private capital flow will not be enough to do the job; that even apart from the serious problem caused by the rise in oil prices governmental aid will continue to be needed for some time if the maximum growth for which the countries have the capability if given the resources is to be achieved.

The 1973 rise in oil prices and that in foodgrain prices create added serious problems, even though the rise in foodgrain prices benefits some low-income countries. A World Bank study released in April, 1974, estimated that before a series of changes in 1972–1975, the capital flows projected for 1974 and 1975 were adequate "to support the development objectives" of 40 developing countries studied, but that because of certain changes an additional $9 billion would be needed for the two years 1974 and 1975 to meet those objectives. The changes were the sharp increase in energy and grain prices, that in fertilizer prices plus the shortage of supply, increased prices for nonfood raw materials, and the prospect of a recession in the industrial countries, which would reduce foreign-exchange receipts of the less developed countries.[10]

The foreign-exchange receipts of the less developed countries increase if the physical volume of their exports at given prices increases. Receipts also increase if the prices of experts rise. The countries of one group, the oil-producing countries, have found a method of improving their terms of trade and remedying any foreign-exchange or saving gap, namely, to form a cartel and quadruple the price of their product. In the cases of some other important minerals, as in oil, a small number of countries produce a large share of the world supply. The tabulation below indicates the most important of these.[11] In addition, a major portion of the world production of phosphate, of coffee, and of bananas is concentrated in a few countries. Can these countries unite in imitation of the oil producers?

The cement that might hold them together is the lure of much higher prices, though any of them would gain still higher revenues if it stayed out of the cartel and maximized its sales at prices a little below the cartel prices. The producers in the cases of mercury, zinc, chromium, and nickel seem unlikely bedfellows, in view of either their political distance from

---

[10] *New York Times,* April 16, 1974.
[11] *U.S. News and World Report,* May 6, 1974.

Mineral	Number of Major Producers	Percentage of World Supply	Names of Major Producers
Bauxite 6		70	Australia, Jamaica, Surinam, Guyana, France, Guinea
Tin 4		62	Malaysia, Bolivia, Indonesia, Thailand
Mercury 5		56	Spain, Italy, Mexico, Yugoslavia, Canada
Zinc 5		48	Canada, Japan, Australia, Peru, Mexico
Chromium 5		75	Soviet Union, South Africa, Turkey, Philippines, Rhodesia
Nickel 3		58	Canada, New Caledonia, Cuba

each other or their political relationships to the rest of the world. Coffee may be in relatively short supply for some years, but when trees probably being planted now begin bearing, there is likely to be "overproduction" again. If Brazil withheld a large share of her production from the market, she might be giving the market to someone else. The last coffee cartel succeeded because the major consumer, the United States, cooperated in enforcing the cartel's limits on sales, but the United States has refused to renew. The price elasticity of demand for bananas is high. A new large deposit of bauxite within the United States is reported, seemingly reliably. If one is developed, the demand of the rest of the world will hardly sustain a cartel. If these considerations are influential, the problem is limited to phosphate and tin. In the case of oil, the major producing nations are united by a bond other than greed or a sense of economic injustice, namely, strong political emotion associated with a religious and for some an ethnic bond, the stronger because the opponent is ethnically related and the need to deny this reality intensifies the complex emotions.

Perhaps because these conditions will not be duplicated, no other minerals cartel will succeed. Perhaps, on the other hand, this assessment is unrealistically optimistic. Of two recent assessments, one (F. J. Bergsten, 1974) argues that others will succeed, the second (R. Mikesell, 1974) that others will not. In any event, only a few lower income countries will benefit even if two or three of these cartels are formed and stick together. The remaining lower income countries will still face the problem of resources for development.

Economic Aid after World War II

Since World War II, government lending to the less developed countries has risen and become important, and there has been a great prolifer-

TABLE 17–4
Net Flow of Financial Resources from DAC Countries, 1962–72 (Million US$)

Net disbursements	1962	1963	1964	1965	1966	1967	1968	1969	1970*	1971*	1972*
I. Official development assistance	5,438	5,772	5,952	5,895	5,984	6,536	6,309	6,621	6,832	7,759	8,654
1. Bilateral grants and grant-like flows	4,020	3,940	3,806	3,714	3,701	3,578	3,344	3,251	3,323	3,634	4,360
2. Bilateral loans at concessional terms	907	1,465	1,740	1,833	1,947	2,222	2,282	2,320	2,384	2,786	2,395
3. Contributions to multinational institutions	511	367	405	348	336	736	683	1,050	1,124	1,339	1,898
II. Private flows	2,453	2,557	3,729	4,121	3,959	4,381	6,462	6,586	6,949	8,215	8,430
1. Direct investment	1,495	1,603	1,572	2,468	2,179	2,105	3,151	2,919	3,563	3,877	4,306
2. Bilateral portfolio	147	327	837	655	480	800	948	1,201	726	757	2,030
3. Multilateral portfolio†	239	-33	461	247	175	469	767	419	474	771	667
4. Export credits‡	572	660	859	751	1,124	1,007	1,596	2,047	2,185	2,810	1,427
III. Grants by private voluntary agencies	—	—	—	—	—	—	—	—	858	913	1,028
Total net flow	7,891	8,329	9,681	10,016	9,496	10,409	12,013	12,606	13,487	15,616	16,571
Memo: Other (i.e., nondevelopment) official flows	546	243	-36	304	447	518	738	571	1,152	1,271	1,541
1. Bilateral	531	246	-28	299	394	499	748	586	879	1,004	1,169
2. Multilateral	15	-3	-7	5	53	19	-10	-15	273	267	372
Percentage to GNP of Official Development Flows											
DAC countries	0.52	0.51	0.48	0.44	0.41	0.42	0.37	0.36	0.34	0.35	0.34
Of which, U.S.	0.56	0.59	0.56	0.49	0.44	0.43	0.37	0.33	0.31	0.32	0.29
Private capital flows											
DAC countries	0.23	0.23	0.30	0.31	0.27	0.28	0.38	0.36	0.39	0.41	0.37
Of which, U.S.	0.14	0.15	0.29	0.27	0.20	0.26	0.28	0.17	0.31	0.32	0.35

* Including grants by private voluntary agencies.

† These funds of private origin are mingled with those under I.3 and Memo.2 and other funds from non-DAC sources, in programs governed by criteria similar to those applied in bilateral official development assistance programs.

‡ Measured by some countries as change in outstanding amounts guaranteed, by others as change in outstanding amounts due on disbursed credits. Interest is included in the sums recorded as outstanding, so that the net flow tends to be over-stated if gross new guarantees are rising and vice versa.

Source: *Development Cooperation: 1973 Review*, a report by Edwin M. Martin. (Paris: OECD, 1973), pp. 42, 189, 190.

ation of international agencies through which the economically advanced countries lend multilaterally.

The Magnitude of Flows

Summary data concerning the net flow of financial resources from the high-income countries of the West to the lower income countries are shown on the somewhat complex Table 17–4. The table refers to flows of "financial resources" rather than of capital because it includes such flows as grants of food to meet famines and the provision of technical assistance, which while useful is not capital. The data are net of capital repayments. They are not net of interest and profit flows. The Development Advisory Committee (or DAC) countries are the countries of Western Europe plus the United States, Canada, Australia, and Japan. Bilateral grants or loans are grants or loans directly from one government to another. In quantity they are predominantly from the United States to low-income countries. Loans at concessional terms are loans with interest rates below market rates, perhaps with an initial period in which no interest is charged, or loans repayable in the local currency. The last are no longer used. Multilateral portfolio private flows are the private purchase of securities of the World Bank. The nondevelopment flows shown in the Memorandum item are largely transfers of munitions.

The table begins with a year, 1962, in which official aid was well established and had reached a large magnitude. The reader will note that it remained on a plateau in absolute amount from 1963 to 1966, then began to rise again. Both official development assistance and that plus private capital flows reached a peak as a percentage of GNP of the contributing countries in 1964. The increase from 1971 to 1972 in bilateral grants and grant-like flows consists largely of grants of non-military goods and funds from the United States to the states of Indo-China. The bilateral portfolio investment consists largely of loans to governments and corporations in middle-income countries. The sharp rise in 1972 consists almost wholly of loans of Euro-dollars, dollar-denominated deposits held in European banks. These in 1971 and 1972 may be much larger than shown in the table, for many of them escape the recording net.

The reader will note the large share of the United States in the total official flow in spite of the low ratio of the United States contribution to U.S. GNP. (See both Table 17–4 and Figure 17–3.) The two sets of figures reflect the huge economic size of the United States. The United States contribution is somewhat overstated because U.S. shipments of foodgrains are valued at U.S. rather than world prices. Correction for this would not alter the totals or percentages greatly. The value of all bilateral aid is somewhat overstated from the early 1960s and especially the mid-1960s on, because by that time the practice had become widespread of

FIGURE 17–3
ODA as Percentage of GNP

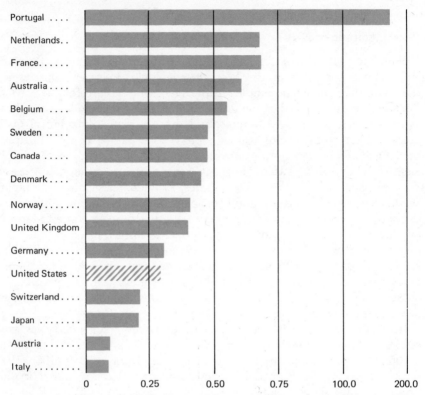

Portugal	
Netherlands..	
France......	
Australia	
Belgium	
Sweden	
Canada	
Denmark	
Norway.......	
United Kingdom	
Germany......	
United States ..	
Switzerland....	
Japan	
Austria	
Italy	

0   0.25   0.50   0.75   100.0   200.0

Source: *Development Cooperation: 1973 Review,* a report by Edwin M. Martin (Paris: OECD, 1973), p. 44.

tying the aid to purchases from the donor country, which often prevented the recipient country from buying goods or equipment as well suited for its purposes at lower prices elsewhere. Ichizo Miyamoto (1974) has estimated that because of tying, the value of bilateral aid to Indonesia during 1967, 1968, and 1969 was 19% less than if it had not been tied. The ratio may be similar for other aid-receiving countries.

From 1971 to 1972 the purchasing power of the official and total flows dropped, and those contributions in relation to GNP dropped even further. That decline in official contributions continued in 1973 and 1974 and will continue in 1975 because of the severe cuts in economic aid enacted by the U.S. Congress, cuts that reflect a sense of U.S. voters that their incomes are inadequate, and also perhaps some sourness at the world after the debacle of intervention in Vietnam. The decline in total official flows would have been greater except for the vigorous expansion of its lending activity by the World Bank. As the data in Table 17–4 show, in 1963 and 1964 bilateral loans and grants constituted more than 93% of all official flows, and in 1965 and 1966 more than 94%. Then the multilateral share rose to around 11% for two years, then to 16%, 16%, and 17% and in 1972 to 22%. It rose further during the three ensuing years, both because of the sharp reductions in United States bilateral aid and because of the expansion of World Bank activity. Except for the loans on concessional terms by the International Development Authority, expansion of World Bank lending is in large degree independent of governmental contributions to the Bank, since its credit is well established and it can borrow in the private capital market.

Although the data of Table 17–4, expressed each year in current prices, are not readily comparable with the estimates of "gaps" presented in the previous section of this chapter, some conclusions may be drawn. The total flows are much under 1% of the aggregate GNP of the contributing countries. Moreover, they include technical assistance expenditures rising from $747 million in 1962 to $1,839 million in 1972, or around 10% of the total in each year. The UNCTAD estimate of the gaps indicated (by Marris's analysis) that a flow above 1% is needed. This comparison must be tempered by the fact that in 1971, 1972, and in later years, there may have been Euro-dollar loans to the lower income countries much in excess of those included in the estimates of Table 17–4. Possibly if there had been no oil price rise and no associated rises in the prices of other products, such as fertilizers, it might have been possible to state that in a few years private plus official financial flows would be filling virtually all of the foreign-exchange gaps and most of the savings gaps, so that a considerable majority of lower income countries would experience no constraint on their growth except their own capabilities. Whether or not this might have been true in other circumstances, in the conditions of 1974 and 1975 the supposition is academic.

Capacity to Repay

The burden of debt service (scheduled repayments of principal plus interest) has been mounting for a number of low-income countries, calculated as a percentage of either their GNP or their foreign-exchange earnings. This does not necessarily mean that their previous loans have burdened their foreign exchange positions; countries with high debt-service ratios may have higher net foreign-exchange earnings after debt service than if they had not made and used the loans.

Whether interest payments and repayments of principal on foreign capital inflow are burdensome is in part a matter of definition. The capital inflow on which a country must now pay interest and principal may have increased its income and perhaps also increased its exports or decreased its need for imports by more than the amount of the payments. Capacity to repay depends on (1) an increase in productive capacity in the recipient country, plus (2) construction of added productive capacity in the production of export goods or the domestic production of goods formerly imported equal to or greater than the amount of the debt service, and (3) an equal increase in saving, so that the increase in exports or diversion of demand from imports to domestic production does not cause shortages in the country. Capital inflow, of course, will not directly provide (3). It may pay for itself even if it does not directly provide (2), for if the capital inflow makes possible an increase in productive capacity, that increase in turn may make possible diversion of resources elsewhere to export expansion or import substitution.

For some countries which have borrowed relatively heavily, these conditions have not been fulfilled. In a 1971 article, Charles Frank and William R. Cline report on a study of the problem for 17 low-income countries, 15 of which were among the top 20 countries in total capital inflow in the 1960s. The authors made plausible alternative assumptions about export, import, and economic aid trends during the 1970s, and by an econometric model analyzed the debt-service problem. They reported the high probability that even if the country's exports grow at the rate of 8% per year, four of these countries would have debt-service difficulties during the 1970s. The four are India, Indonesia, Pakistan, and Tunisia. Since 1971 the problem has been relieved for Indonesia—at least for the time being—by a large inflow of capital, some of it associated with petroleum explorations. Frank and Cline reported a lesser probability that some of eight other countries would have difficulty meeting debt-service obligations, especially if exports did not grow as fast as 8% per year. Of these, Brazil and Korea are doing well because of both rapid increases in exports and large capital inflows. The other six are Chile, Colombia, the Dominican Republic, Israel, Peru, and Turkey. Among the 17 countries, only for Mexico, Argentina, Bolivia, Iran, and Nigeria did the writers see little probability of debt-service problems.

Institutions and Programs

Historical ties, strategic considerations, fear of Communism, and the desire of individual countries to promote trade ties all have played their part in the governmental extension of economic aid and technical assistance. In 1962, for example, France extended 95% of her official bilateral assistance to former and present colonies, the United Kingdom 92%, and the Netherlands and Belgium 90%; and 20% of the U.S. disbursements went to a group of small countries with a combined population of only 60 million that have been termed "military wards" of the United States

(Laos, Cambodia, South Vietnam, Taiwan, South Korea and Jordan). That percentage soared during the Vietnam war. (See Ohlin, 1966, p. 69.) France's total disbursements for assistance have been especially heavy, relative to her GNP, because of her aid to her African ex-colonies. The less developed countries whose independence is of long standing, in Latin America and elsewhere, have obtained bilateral aid primarily from the United States and, in lesser amounts, Germany. If any countries have extended aid from motives almost wholly free of self-interest, it is the Scandinavian countries that have done so. But it is fair to state that in all of the countries giving technical and financial assistance humanitarianism and a sense that "no nation is an island, entire unto itself" have played a considerable part.

If there is any bias to be noted in the allocation of aid among countries when one has totaled up the loans and grants of all aid-giving countries, it does not result so much from these motives of self-interest as from the tendency to give more aid per capita to small countries than to large ones.

Official aid to the lower income countries and intellectual discussions of the development problem have both undergone successive changes in emphasis since the initiation of aid programs just after World War II.

At first, technical assistance was stressed; it was thought that if only the lower income countries were shown the methods of the technically advanced countries, they could quickly adopt them and raise their incomes rapidly. President Truman's call to Congress for his "Point IV" program and the establishment by the United Nations of its Expanded Program of Technical Assistance both occurred in 1949. To show the low-income peoples American "know-how"—one of the least felicitous of popular phrases—was thought by Americans to be the key.

When it became apparent that technical advice is not magic, emphasis on the provision of economic resources increased. In the 1950s, IBRD loans to less developed countries rose rapidly. As United States grants to European countries under the Marshall Plan tapered off in 1951–53, capital aid to the less developed countries was increased to a considerable multiple of the funds available to the World Bank. The United States Export-Import Bank (originally set up late in the 1930s to promote exports) was also given increased funds.

Late in the 1950s, stress by one school of academicians on the importance of "investment in human resources" as the missing ingredient in the aid program increased, as did emphasis in the program on technical assistance in education and training.

Then gradually during the 1960s, with added experience, fuller knowledge on the part of academics, and more mature judgment, the complexity of the growth process became increasingly appreciated, and it became increasingly understood that there is no one uniquely important key, that technical assistance is not merely a matter of telling people something but rather is the complex process described in Chapter 6, and that with the best of rounded programs and effective initiative on the part of the low-income peoples they will not be able to spring with great rapidity to high incomes. By 1970 development aid programs may be said to have become mature.

From the mid-1960s on, programs to curb population increase expanded.

In both bilateral and multilateral official lending, early emphasis had been on loans for large manufacturing projects and for transportation, communication, and power facilities. The emphasis on manufacturing projects was perhaps due partly to the fact that such projects, which were relatively large, could be appraised much more readily than a larger number of other smaller projects, but partly also to the mistaken notion that because economically advanced countries have much manufacturing, the establishment of manufacturing ventures would quickly bring modernity. Leaders of many low-income countries held this view; lending officials may have concurred in it.

Five subsequent changes of emphasis in loan policy merit comment. The first was a diversification of loans to other, including smaller, projects. Secondly, loans were made in increasing amounts for "social infrastructure"—schools, housing, health facilities, and the like. In the 1960s the world "food problem" became appreciated, and contributors of development aid increased their stress on aid to agriculture. Recipient countries, bemused with the desirability of industry, were slower than donors to understand the importance of increasing productivity in agriculture; perhaps the Indian drought of 1966–67 was influential in changing their attitudes. Fourth, as the relationships among the various components of the development process became better understood, and the indirect ways in which investment increases foreign exchange needs also became better understood, there came a certain degree of willingness on the part of some aid-giving countries, as well as the IBRD, to grant loans to support the foreign-exchange needs of a development program as a whole, rather than merely to finance imports for a given project. The United States was a leader in this change. More recently, there has formally been some reversal, but because of increased understanding of the foreign-exchange problem there is increased willingness to grant loans (which provide foreign exchange) to finance the local as well as the foreign-exchange costs of a project.

Lastly, in the aid-giving countries that were not concentrating their aid on colonies and ex-colonies, and especially in the United States, there was initially a tendency to spread aid widely even if it meant spreading it thinly or a little haphazardly. The policy seems to have been rooted in a sense of equity and a sense that the United States aid program ought to be represented everywhere. In the last half of the 1960s, at the insistence of the Congress, the number of countries served by U.S. aid programs has been progressively reduced, in the interest of effectiveness. Unfortunately, by the end of the decade, so much emphasis was given to Vietnam and the few other countries thought of as military wards of the United States that U.S. aid programs everywhere else were fed a very low calorie diet, if not starved.

The International Monetary Fund and the International Bank for Reconstruction and Development had been formed in 1944. Their central purposes visualized then were to promote the reconstruction of the technically advanced countries and financial stability in the relationships among them. The title initially proposed for the latter institution was simply International Bank for Reconstruction. The last two words in its title were added somewhat as an afterthought.

When the United Nations Organization was formed in the following year, it spawned various specialized agencies, including the Food and Agriculture Organization (FAO), the World Health Organization (WHO), the United Nations Economic, Social, and Cultural Organization (UNESCO), and the United Nations International Children's Emergency Fund (UNICEF), and took over an older agency that had been fostered by the League of Nations, the International Labor Office. These agencies offered technical assistance in their special fields, and pretty much went their separate and uncoordinated ways in doing so. The U.N. created a Technical Assistance Administration (TAA) to offer technical advice in other fields. Much of its work has related to cottage industry and industry.

The United Nations sent a "resident representative" to each country to which it was extending technical aid. Since he had no authority over the specialized agencies, for a decade or so the coordination was minimal. During the 1960s, there was a modest degree of improvement. However, coordination between the United Nations advisers and those sent directly by the United States or other governments or by private foundations continues to depend upon the cooperativeness of individuals who happen to be in the field offices.

The IBRD began lending operations in 1946. Its loans were initially "bankers' loans," loans toward large industrial (including transport, communication, and power) projects, and covering only the foreign exchange costs of these projects. They were granted at a rate of interest 1 and a fraction percent above that at which the bank itself borrowed, 1% being to reimburse the Bank for its services, and the added fraction to set up an insurance fund against losses.

As the bank's position as a borrower in the financial markets became secure, its income from interest on its loans increased, the understanding of its staff (like that of other professionals) of development problems grew during the 1950s and 1960s, and the foreign exchange problems of less developed countries (including their repayment obligations on earlier loans) worsened, four changes have occurred in IBRD operations. First, to a limited extent the bank became willing on occasion to grant "balance of payments" loans, that is, loans to cover foreign exchange needs of a country not tied to the capital goods for a specific project, or to finance the local costs of a project as well as the foreign exchange costs, which has the same effect. Second, a subsidiary, the International Development Association, was established to meet other needs. IDA, initially given a capital of $1 billion, makes loans for infrastructure projects, with low interest rates, long maturities, often a grace period before interest payment begins, and often repayable in local currencies. Because loans by IDA are not self-supporting, IDA must depend for its funds on subscriptions by governments plus such a share of IBRD profits as the Bank feels it can donate. Third, another subsidiary, with initial capital of $100 million, the International Finance Corporation, was established to provide funds directly to private business concerns in the less developed countries. These funds sometimes consist partly of purchase of preferred stock, rather than merely of bonds. The three institutions together are self-titled the World Bank Group. A fourth organization, the International Center for Settlement of Investment Disputes, has become attached to the Group but is entirely autonomous.

By the end of 1972, a little more than 25 years after the IBRD began active loan operations, the Bank and IDA had extended loans and credits totalling $20 billion, perhaps one third of U.S. bilateral aid expenditures, but impressively effective. Net commitments of the IFC had exceeded $500 million.

Largely through the offices of the IBRD, in six or eight important instances from the mid-1960s on, aid-giving countries have formed consortia to coordinate large loan programs—to India, Colombia, Turkey and other countries. For example, in a consortium for aid to India following the 1966–67 drought, the IBRD was joined by the governments of Austria, Belgium, Canada, France, Italy, Japan, the Netherlands, the United Kingdom, the United States, and West Germany in a concerted pledge of aid. Other coordination of agencies and governments giving aid also developed during the 1960s. The Organization for European Economic Cooperation had been set up in 1948 by the governments of Western Europe to coordinate their reconstruction programs and to allocate Marshall Plan aid among these countries. In 1961 the OEEC converted itself into the Organization for Economic Cooperation and Development after adding Canada, Australia, Japan, and the United States as members of the new organization. The OECD in turn formed the Development Assistance Committee (first termed the Development Assistance Group). In addition to serving a statistical function, the DAC has somewhat increased communication among aid personnel of the member governments. Because of the work of the DAC and the formation of consortia, economic assistance programs are somewhat more multilateral than is indicated by data relating only to the multilateral organizations.

While its loan activities were evolving, the IBRD realized the need to give technical assistance to countries receiving loans, to make the loans both more effective and more secure. Today it has large resident technical assistance staffs in a number of countries.

Even more recently there has emerged another new emphasis in IRBD policy: its announced intention to consider the income distribution effects when making loans. The emphasis placed by the Bank's president, Robert McNamara, on relieving "absolute poverty" was noted in Chapter 1. In part this intention is reflected in the volume of its loans for agricultural development. In the three years beginning July 1, 1968, loans and credits by the Bank and IDA for agricultural development equalled the total for the preceding 21 years of the Bank's operations. The Bank now provides not far from half of all foreign financial assistance to agriculture. Moreover, the Bank is seeking deliberately to make loans that will help small farmers, though McNamara has acknowledged that major efforts to improve income distribution must be by the initiative of the low-income country governments. In Kenya, as an example of the new emphasis, a Bank project related to tea production provided credit and extension services for smallholders scattered throughout the tea-growing areas of the country, and also financed processing factories and access roads.

Such projects will do their bit to reduce the inequality of income within agriculture. But unless agricultural prices rise steadily relative to other prices, and even if technical advances in agriculture continue steadily and fairly rapidly to increase the labor-intensivity of agricultural production, the labor force of low-income countries must move fairly rapidly from agriculture to industry if a continuing worsening of income distribution is to be avoided. And as noted in Chapter 9, the problem is the more difficult in the lowest income countries, which have the smallest industrial sectors.

BIBLIOGRAPHICAL NOTE

The articles by Chenery and Bruno (1962), Chenery and Strout (1966), Chenery and MacEwan (1966), and Chenery and Eckstein (1967) all present two-gap models. Chenery and Strout imply an intractability in the difference between the two gaps that does not seem entirely realistic. A concise verbal statement is given in Chenery and Strout, pp. 681–82. See also Chenery's "Reply to Bruton" (1969), mentioned in n. 4 of this chapter. For a fuller statement, see McKinnon (1964). J. Vanek

(1967) presents an abstract of the two gaps and applies it to Colombia.

An annual report by the OECD presents the best summary of the magnitude of economic aid from the more to the less developed countries. The 1973 report provides data for the previous decade. See also the annual reports of the IBRD, IDA, and IFC.

Mason and Asher (1973), an authoritative history of the World Bank since its establishment, presents also a judicious analysis of the impact of the Bank's operations and of their present trend.

Outward- or Inward-Looking Orientation

18

The major issue in allocation among sectors is sometimes said to be emphasis on agriculture versus emphasis on manufacturing. But this is not quite the correct way of putting the problem, since analysts on both sides of the controversy agree that any country must move from a base in agriculture to increasing emphasis on industry if it is not to face an awkward and constraining limit on its growth. The issue is not even whether manufacturing shall be for the domestic market or for export, since every analyst agrees that for continuing increase in manufacturing productivity, bringing its contribution to continuing rise in per capita income, much maufacturing must be for the world market to gain economies of scale. The issue is how a country may best attain that goal; whether policies should initially be inward-looking and, if so, when and how the reversal to outward-looking policies shall be made. Associated are a host of policies about the relationship of the government to the economy.

Of course some countries especially favored by nature for agricultural production will advantageously maintain greater emphasis on agriculture than other countries do, forever. New Zealand, the Netherlands, and Denmark provide examples. But even these countries will develop a good deal of manufacturing (perhaps not only in processing their agricultural specialties), and for an international market.

The issue of inward- versus outward-looking policies is closely related to—or some would say a part of—the issue of financial liberalism versus comprehensive intervention discussed in Chapter 13. But before we return directly to that issue, it will be well to sort various strands in the analysis.

THE APPEAL OF INDUSTRY

Spurious Arguments

Rapid industrialization is attractive to many countries for a variety of wholly or partly unsound reasons. Among them are the following:

1. "Industry is modern." This is at times a way of stating some of the other reasons listed here, but often the desire to be modern and to overcome the humiliation of being looked down on by Western countries is so strong that a country's leaders are unable to understand that adopting and subsidizing methods that have a modern look, but for which the country does not yet have the basis, will reduce the country's level of living.

2. "Industrial life is associated with a modern outlook, an innovational spirit." This argument for forced industrialization overlooks two facts. The association cited is due in part to the fact that industrial life is a result of an innovational technical spirit. Trying to establish the external result will not establish the cause. Second, insofar as there is mutual causation and industrial life is a cause, it is industrial life, a far more complex phenomenon not to be evoked by building a factory, that is the cause.

3. "Industry has external economies that agriculture does not have." It spews out trained workers, has linkages which induce other industries to develop, etc. For this reason, and because of the advantages of "growing points," it is argued that the concentration of investment at such points, even at the cost of relative starvation of primary production, will increase the rate of growth of GNP. Perhaps industry does yield greater external economies than agriculture. Certainly up to the point at which congestion outweighs the effect, the enterprises that gather together in growing points yield such economies to each other. But attempts to establish growing points artificially, overlooking the need for the evolutionary development sketched in chapter 6, is very costly and is likely to be futile.

4. "A high rate of investment will cause a high rate of growth. The development of industry leads to the development of a capital goods industry. If a large capital goods industry is established, and turns out a large volume of capital goods, there will be a high rate of investment, by definition. The economic fact is forced by the technical fact."

This argument is drawn from Soviet experience. The Soviet government decreed that there should be much capital goods production, and there was. But there will be no investors ready to buy the capital goods that are produced, unless a market for their products is seen. In the Soviet Union, the government provided that market, to build capacity for producing still further capital goods and armaments. It prevented the income paid out in the process from creating a high demand for consumer goods, by taking a forty percent mark-up on goods bought or produced by the state and sold to consumers. In any other country, a large volume of production of capital goods will assure a large volume of investment only if, by some equivalent of the Soviet policies, the government buoys up the demand for capital goods and holds down that for consumer goods.

5. "High-income countries have industry; therefore, establishing industry will give us high income." Or—a milder version of the same argument: "The value of output per worker is higher in industry than in agriculture. Therefore emphasis on industry will raise per capita income." The fact of higher productivity in industry, and its causes, were discussed in Chapter 4. The argument is sound only insofar as rising productivity has created sufficient demand for industrial goods, or insofar as the evolution of a productive industry permits profitable industrial exports. Neither result is created by creating the symptom.

These arguments imply that the relevant concentration is on productivity, not on industry as such, and that within that concentration the appropriate questions are: What industry? When? (As well as: What primary production? By what method?) The market and the government may join in providing answers.

Factor Price Disequilibrium and Allocation

One argument relating to the allocation of resources between agriculture and industry is that more industry is advantageous than market forces would induce, since the conditions necessary for the equalization of marginal productivity do not exist. The equalization throughout the economic system of the marginal value product of each factor in production is possible only if the unit cost of each factor is equal throughout the system. Economic growth causes wages to differ in different sectors of the economy (See Chapter 4). Action to counteract this factor price distortion is advantageous. So the argument runs. It was stated in one paragraph in Chapter 15, and will be elaborated here.

Suppose that labor costs $1 per day in agriculture and turns out products each day worth $1 (after allowing for the cost of other inputs). Suppose that wages and the marginal product of labor in industry are $1.45, but that if 1,000 added workers transferred to industry, the marginal product would fall to $1.30, while the agricultural output would be lost. Suppose, lastly, that either living costs or the discomforts of living in cities, where industry exists, require an added 10¢ per day above agricultural labor incomes to compensate workers for moving from agriculture to industry. Then if 1,000 workers move from agriculture to industry, the computation of net benefit per worker is as follows: The society will lose output worth $1.00 but will gain output (for convenience, call it one unit of output) worth $1.30. The worker will incur discomfort or added costs costing $0.10. Net, the society will gain $0.20. If the worker receives a wage of $1.30, he will gain the $0.20 benefit. If he receives a wage of between $1.10 and $1.30, he and the employer will share the gain.

Suppose, however, that the worker, overanxious about moving to the city, would not move unless he received $1.45 per day, or that wages were held at that minimum by labor union action. The society would then gain if the government subsidized industrial employers in the amount of 15¢ per day for each worker recruited. The worker would then gain an increase in material welfare of $0.35 per day, while some other member of the society who bore the cost of the subsidy would lose $0.15 per day. On balance, welfare would be increased by $0.20.[1]

The actual facts would be more complicated than in this simple example. Presumably, agricultural output would fall not by $1.00 per day, but by some lesser amount. The social gain would then be greater. If there were competition in industry, the price of the product would fall from $1.45 to $1.30 per each day's output. Every individual who had been consuming the product at $1.45 would then gain a consumer surplus of $0.15, while the producers would lose this amount. On this account there would be no net change in welfare in the society as a whole; hence this transfer was ignored in the preceding paragraphs.

More important, before the government subsidized employment the manufacturing industry may not have existed at all. This would be true if the product could be imported at a price of $1.35, and if free trade prevailed. Domestic industry could not produce at the imported price. The country will export 1.35 units of agricultural products to gain each unit of the industrial product. However, if all industrial wages were subsidized by $0.15 per day, and the domestic industry were established, the country would give up only one unit of agricultural product and suffer 10¢ worth of added discomfort or expense per worker to gain each unit of industrial product.

The competition of imports can of course also be compensated for by imposing a sufficiently high trade barrier. In an earlier essay (Hagen,

---

[1] There is likely to be an opposite industry-agriculture disparity in interest costs, but this is of minor importance relative to the labor cost disparity. Much of the industry-agriculture disparity in interest rates is due to differences in risk and in the cost of administering loans, that is, is not a true difference. However, a subsidy to interest costs in agriculture, where a disparity not justified by differences in costs seems to exist, is also justified.

1958), in which I presented the argument above more rigorously, I also argued that while a prohibitive trade barrier which induced the establishment of industry would not fully remedy conditions, because it would still leave a wage differential and some misallocation of labor, nevertheless it would be an improvement on free trade. Two later papers pointed out that while this may be true it is not necessarily true, and that a lower tariff may be superior to a prohibitive one.[2]

A subsidy is clearly the ideal remedy. However, a subsidy is not likely to be politically feasible. It seems contrary to popular emotions to subsidize industry, whose profitability (mythical or not) is well known or to subsidize industrial workers so as to increase the differential between their wages and the incomes of cultivators. It often does not seem contrary to "common sense" to require the public that consumes an industrial product to pay a penalty, in the form of a higher price, larger than the aggregate amount of subsidy that would be required. Hence, economically perverted though the policy choice is, if industry is to be stimulated in a low-income country, it is likely to be by protectionism. The strongest arguments in favor of this in addition to the welfare argument presented above are that it will tend to make possible the benefits of economies of scale (which apply in industry rather than in agriculture), will protect infant industry and infant industrialization, and, possibly most important of all, that it will induce a shift in allocation in the general direction which consideration of the inexorable future trend in demand indicates that it ought to occur. These are persuasive arguments; protectionism in developing countries is much more likely to increase welfare than is admitted in the conventional economic argument based on static assumptions.[3] However, it involves the danger of creating vested interests that will prevent or delay the later establishment of policies conducive to the export of manufactures. This ideal remedy from the viewpoint of economic theory is to increase the mobility of labor and other factors so that the disparity in wages (or payment per unit of other factors) no longer exists, and the question arises whether policies toward this end are not also the wisest policies in practice. This question is discussed later in this chapter.

---

[2] Bhagwati and Ramaswami (1963) and Bardhan (1964). The most general statement of the relevant economic principles is by Bhagwati (1972).

[3] It is of interest to ask whether world welfare, rather than merely that of the developing country applying protectionism or a subsidy, is increased by these measures. In the case of protectionism, whether applied by one developing country or all developing countries, of high and low income, the result is ambiguous, as it is in the case of the single country. It can be proved rigorously that application of an appropriate subsidy (with tax to finance it) in a single country increases world welfare as well as welfare in that country, and that application of appropriate subsidies by all developing countries, while concomitantly they maintained free trade, would bring the world to an *optimum optimorum* so far as trade policies were concerned.

THE DYNAMICS OF COMPARATIVE ADVANTAGE

Limitations of the Static Principle

The law of comparative advantage (or comparative costs) is simply an application to international trade of the principle of maximizing the value of production by shifting each input to the production in which it has the highest marginal value productivity. The law states that a country or region will maximize its income if it specializes in production of the goods in which it has the greatest comparative advantage in productive efficiency. Consider two countries and two goods. Suppose that Country A can produce 20 units of good 1 or 10 units of good 2 per unit of input, and that Country B can produce 6 of good 1 and 4 of good 2. Country B has a higher ratio of output to input in producing good 2 (4/6 versus 10/20), and Country A a higher ratio in good 1 (20/10 versus 6/4); hence B should specialize in good 2 and A in good 1. When the resources of each country are shifted to the specialization indicated, their products will trade for more of the alternative goods than the inputs can themselves produce directly. Hence their marginal value productivity will be greater.

In the case of two goods and two countries, a rigorous proof of the principle is easy. Intuitively, it is clear that the principle applies equally to any number of countries and any number of goods. Of course a country will not normally specialize completely in one good as the example suggests. It is assumed here that the reader is familiar with the principle of comparative advantage, and beyond this summary reminder the underlying argument will not be spelled out here.

With free international trade, the forces of the market will lead every country to production which utilizes its full comparative advantage and thereby results in maximum welfare in each country and in the world, on the same assumptions on which the market will maximize production by equalizing marginal productivity: perfect competition including perfect foresight and perfect mobility of factors within each country, so that each factor is paid the same income in all uses throughout the economy, no economies of scale, no uncompensated externalities, and unchanging techniques. On these assumptions, comparative advantage exists because of difference in the relative quantity of different inputs in different countries. A country (say Burma or Argentina) rich in agricultural land relative to its supply of labor or of capital should specialize in producing commodities whose production is lowest cost when much land is used; a country with a large number of deft skilled workers (say Switzerland) should specialize in production requiring large amounts of skilled handicraft for lowest cost production; and so on. And each will be led by the relative prices of various products in the world market to do so. Insofar as monopoly, economies of scale, external economies, and other conditions contradicting the assumptions exist, the government may have to intervene to achieve optimum allocation.

But the principle of comparative advantage is backward-looking. It would have a country continue do what it has always done. It ignores both technical and economic changes that will cause the comparative advantage of today to be the disadvantage of tomorrow.[4]

Among other changes, technical advance changes factor endowments. A country's stock of capital increases through capital formation, its supply of labor through immigration, natural increase, and education and training, and its quantity of natural resources through discovery of resources not previously known. (Nothing else can drastically change the comparative advantage of a small country as rapidly as the discovery of a large petroleum or mineral deposit.) As the basket of productive inputs changes, the specialization that is most advantageous changes in ways to which the principle of comparative advantage gives no clue in advance. Above all, techniques change, so that a country's relative cost of producing different products (say agricultural and manufactured products) from the same old natural resources changes drastically.

Then, also, as world income rises, the world's relative demand for primary, secondary, and tertiary products changes. With these changes, comparative advantage changes.

Yet previous comparative advantage is the point of departure from which allocation should be decided. Only if there is a sea change in resource availability and costs, such as the discovery of large new petroleum deposits and then later a quadrupling of petroleum prices, will comparative advantage change abruptly. Moreover, a country does not move today to its comparative advantage 30 years from today. Rather, starting with the mix of products that has been advantageous in the past, a country's producers ask: "Considering the likely changes in our capabilities, in the resources available to us, and in the world economy, what comparative advantage five years from now shall we prepare for today? Ten years from now?" For to try to build the comparative advantage of, say, 25 years from now into structures now is futile. Capital becomes obsolescent and is replaced by a new generation of equipment in shorter periods. And a cost incurred now to gain an advantage foreseen 25 years from now can mount prohibitively through compound interest during the 25-year interval.

Trends in World Demand and Supply

It is of course relative value productivity, not merely physical productivity, that causes one allocation of resources to be more advantageous

---

[4] R. Robinson (1956), parts 1 and 2, makes the standard and compelling presentation of the argument.

than another. Changes in relative value productivity are caused by changes in the relative prices of different types of goods and services, and those changes in turn are caused by increases in demand with rising world income, income and price elasticities of demand, changes in relative production costs with technical progress, and price elasticities of supply.

Let us consider agriculture versus industry. And let us consider the lower income countries as a single group before taking the viewpoint of individual countries.

Within the world as a whole, the lower income countries are the primary sector and the higher income countries are the industrial sector. This broad statement must be accepted with care. Latin America, Asia other than Japan, and Africa together produce manufactures worth some five times the value of their imports of manufactures, and on the other hand the more developed countries produce more food than they import. But the statement is true in two senses: the new flow of primary products is in one direction and that of industrial products in the other, and industrial products exports of the higher to the lower income countries are much larger than their primary exports, whereas the reverse is true in the other direction.

What then are the factors that will determine the trends over time in the relative per capita income yielded by industry and agriculture?

It was noted in chapter 4 that the income elasticity of demand for industrial products as a group is, say, 1.2–1.4, and that for food 0.8 or less. As per capita income rises, the income elasticity of demand for food falls below 0.8. That figure is probably a maximum estimate of the income elasticity of demand for all agricultural products, over a range of income of, say, $100 to $600 per capita, since that for other agricultural products is also below unity.

The price elasticity of demand for agricultural products as a group is also below unity. That is, a given percentage fall in their price will cause a less than corresponding increase in the quantity purchased, so that total expenditures for them will fall. From the producers' viewpoint, a given percentage increase in the quantity marketed will cause a more than corresponding fall in the price, so that total revenues received will be less than they would have been for a smaller crop. This is also true of other primary products as a group, excluding ones for which synthetic products are close competitors. As a result, if the aggregate volume of agricultural products or of all primary products marketed rises, without change in the demand, aggregate revenues received for them by the primary sector will fall; and if the demand for agricultural (or primary) products rises by x percent, but the quantity marketed rises by more than x percent, the price decline will be sufficient so that aggregate agricultural (or primary sector) revenue rises by less than x percent. On the other hand, if a shortage of supply causes the price of agricultural products to rise by 1%, the quantity demanded will fall by less than 1%. Thus short supply will raise, not reduce, the aggregate income of agricultural producers.[5]

Consider the joint effect of the low income and price elasticities.

As productivity and per capita income rise in the world as a whole, aggregate demand for the products of agriculture rises at a slower rate than that for industrial products—not more than two thirds as fast, given the income elasticities of demand cited just above, and perhaps only one half as fast. If the output of agriculture per head of the world population is increasing at a rate more than two thirds as high as that in industry, assuming that the income elasticities of demand are 0.8 and 1.2 respectively—or more than one half as fast, if the income elasticities are 0.7 and 1.4—then the supply of agricultural products will be increasing faster than the relative demand for them, and agricultural prices will be falling relative to industrial prices. Relative per capita incomes of agricultural producers will be falling more rapidly than prices if the agricultural population is increasing more rapidly than the urban population. For world agriculture as a whole, there is no escape except the sufficiently rapid provision of additional jobs outside of agriculture. The faster the rate of increase in the agricultural labor force, and the faster the rate of increase in productivity in agriculture, above the rates that yield the relative increase in output calculated just above, the more rapid the decline in relative real income in agriculture will be. Absolute real income in agriculture may not decline. Agriculture may merely not share in the benefits of the world's increase in productivity. Decline in absolute income is a little farther along the range of adverse effects than decline in relative income.

On the other hand, if because of slow relative increase in productivity, the relative supply of agricultural products is rising no faster than the relative demand, then the ratio of agricultural to industrial prices will remain constant. Aggregate agricultural income would nevertheless be rising less rapidly than in industry, because of the slower rate of increase in output, and per capita income would be increasing still more slowly relative to that in industry if the farm population was rising more rapidly than the urban population.

However, if agricultural productivity rose still less rapidly, relative agricultural prices would rise, and even with a rising relative population in agriculture, real per capita income in the sector might be rising as fast as or faster then in industry. The cultivators of the world, taken as a group, would benefit by precisely the development that persons alarmed

---

[5] Though if a single agricultural commodity for which others are close substitutes is in short supply, an increase in the price will cause a shift of purchasing to the alternative product. The price elasticity of such a single commodity is greater than unity.

about the world's population growth fear: growing food scarcity. Suppose that world agricultural production did not rise at all, while productivity and output in industry were rising. In that case, because both the increase in aggregate demand for agricultural products and the low price elasticity of demand would work in favor of producers, there would be a continuing considerable rate of rise in agricultural prices and agriculturists would fare better than in any alternative case considered above.

It was argued in Chapter 3 that neither this nor any approach to it is likely. It was recognized that the world may be entering a period of climatic conditions inferior to those of the 1960s, but it was argued that though this may cause a downward shift in the level of agricultural production, it will not cause a secularly worsening trend.

Moreover, effective world cartels in major agricultural commodities are highly unlikely, because there are many producing countries, because the major ones are high income industrial countries, and because there are close substitutes for natural fibers and for rubber.

If this forecast of future conditions is correct, it will in general be to the greatest advantage of the low-income countries to shift their productive effort increasingly to manufacturing. But there will be exceptions: countries or regions within a country that because of especially advantageous soil and climate have the greatest comparative advantage in the production of some given crop. The operating principle is not, "Shift to manufacturing," but, "Make whatever changes in methods and products that most increase your value productivity." But the operation of the several factors discussed above is such that following that principle will lead to a continuing shift from agriculture to manufacturing, insofar as the producers of a country have the entrepreneurial capacity to introduce and operate manufacturing enterprises well in the conditions of that country.

Historically, international migration of labor has been important, but it will not be so in the future except into sparsely populated and affluent oil-countries seeking to expand their labor forces. It is prevented by the immigration policies of the MDCs and each LDC alike. Avoiding continually worsening terms of trade for primary and especially agricultural products will therefore require that the LDCs as a group increase industrial production within their own countries rapidly at the expense of increase in their primary and especially agricultural production. Individual LDCs can benefit from continuing concentration on agricultural production only in the degree that other LDCs move out of this field. A few with especially favorable natural resources and climate may prosper by specializing in the production of agricultural products for which the income elasticity of demand is high even at high incomes. New Zealand's success in sheep raising provides an example. Denmark and the Netherlands have gained high incomes in the production and processing of dairy products and meat. Other countries may specialize in production of certain fruits. But the LDCs as a whole could not profit by following their example, even if they had favorable climates and skills. The fallacy of composition must be avoided. Advice to lower income countries as a group that they should continue to specialize in those products for which their natural resource endowment is now favorable is misguided. But the appropriate advice to each individual country is that it should increase its productivity in primary production as rapidly as possible even while a shift to other sectors is occurring, for whatever the world supply-demand and price situation in each primary product is, each individual country (unless its output materially affects the price of total world exports) will benefit by selling more and thus earning more income.

The Terms of Trade: Historical Trends

Trends in the terms of trade indicate the shifts in demand-supply relationships since 1800. Between 1800 and the 1860s or 1870s, new agricultural lands were opened up and the volume of world trade in primary products rose rapidly. But industrial output and the demand for primary products rose even more rapidly, for judging by British data for industrial and primary product prices the relative price of primary products rose steadily and considerably throughout that period.[6] Diminishing returns probably were important throughout the period.

Controversy about whether on balance the terms of trade have turned against agriculture since the 1860s has raged for a long time.[7] The first comprehensive empirical study (League of Nations, 1945), using British data from 1878 to 1938, showed a marked secular trend adverse to primary products. However, the series is an uncertain indicator, for two reasons. It ends during a deep depression, when relative primary products prices were at a cyclical low. Moreover, the prices of manufactures in the LDCs have certainly risen much less than in Britain, and the prices received for primary products in the LDCs have risen much more, because of large reductions in transportation costs in both directions. Just before World War II, transportation costs constituted an average of 10% of the value of total world trade.[8] Morgan (1959) estimates that a century earlier their share was 30% to 70%.[9] For this reason it is entirely possible that the terms of trade between primary and industrial products

---

[6] Schlote (1952), cited by Morgan (1959).

[7] Morgan (1959) summarizes the argument and the data.

[8] United Nations, 1945, *Relative Prices*.

[9] His estimate seems to depend on the assumption that ocean transport costs fell as much during the century as land transport costs in the United States. This may not be correct, but the fall in ocean costs from the day of the sailing vessel to that of the small steamer to that of the large ocean freighter must have been considerable.

changed in favor of industrial products in Britain but in favor of primary products in the countries producing them. From the end of the depression of the 1930s to the "Korea boom" of 1950–52, the terms of trade of primary products rose; subsequently, they have fallen. Altogether, taking some sort of average of relative prices in the industrial and in the primary product countries, the relative price of primary products in the 1960s was probably lower than a hundred years earlier.[10] The physical production per worker in primary production probably also rose less than that in manufacturing during the century. On both counts the relative real income per capita of primary product producers fell. This means that part of the benefit of the increase in physical productivity in the production of primary products was captured by industrial producers, just as from 1800 to the 1860s part of the fruits of technical progress in industry was captured by primary product producers. In 1973 and 1974 foodgrain prices soared, and as this is written in mid-1974 are much above their 1960 level and probably also much above their 1860 level.

C. P. Kindleberger studied the trend from 1913 to 1952 in the prices of all exports of the lower income countries, both primary and manufactured, relative to that in all exports of Western European countries. He concluded that the trend in the overall terms of trade was considerably less favorable to the lower income countries than was that between primary and industrial products alone. Between 1913 and 1952, Europe's export prices rose by 20% relative to those of the recently settled areas, and by 55% relative to those of the lower income countries. Kindleberger concluded that the more developed countries are "quicker on their feet," and shift out of fields of declining advantage sooner than do the lower income countries. The other side of this coin is that the higher income countries create new areas of advantage by technical advance in industry, whereas few less developed countries have yet acquired enough industrial expertise to do so. Many of these advances have the double-edged effect of also displacing or economizing on primary products. Humphrey (1955) estimated that during the preceding 20 years, United States tariff rates had fallen by 75%, because of tariff reductions and because inflation raised product prices while specific tariff rates remained fixed. But he concluded that during this period the displacement of raw materials by synthetics had reduced total United States imports by a greater amount than the tariff reduction increased them. The impact was on agricultural raw materials. As United States reserves of minerals have shrunk, some mineral-producing lower income countries have done well.

---

[10] The terms of trade of Denmark, which specialized in dairy and meat products, for which demand rose much more than for cereals, improved from 1875 to 1930, deteriorated to the mid-1950s and improved again to 1963. Whether they were higher in 1963 than in 1875 depends on the weighting system used in the computation. See Ølgaard (1966) Chap. 12.

EXPORT EXPANSION VERSUS IMPORT SUBSTITUTION: THE PRODUCTION-TRADE SEQUENCE

Industrial expansion may be accomplished by either the expansion of exports or, in a limited way, by the replacement of imports of manufactures by their domestic production, or by first the latter, then the former. The question of foreign exchange needs enters the equation. Here I shall first discuss the almost invariable sequence of changes in production and trade, then how it may be accelerated—or retarded.

Export Expansion: Primary Products

When economic change begins in a traditional economy, the import needs of the country will almost inevitably grow, for except perhaps in the very first rude innovations an increase in investment activity will almost necessarily involve an increase in the demand for imported capital goods. Except perhaps in centrally directed economies, an increase in the demand for imports will not in itself generate an increase in exports to pay for them, and if the country's foreign receipts and payments were previously in balance, one may reasonably ask how the increased imports were paid for. The increased demand for foreign exchange may cause depreciation of the currency, thus discouraging the import of both consumer and capital goods until import-export balance is achieved. Often, however, exports were expanded and balance achieved without it. This is not necessarily coincidence; the same stirring of innovational energy that caused the increased demand for capital goods imports perhaps also caused increased production for the foreign market.

Karl Deutsch and Peter Eckstein (1961) cite data tending to show that early increase in the capacity to import capital goods is mainly through the expansion of exports rather than the substitution of domestic production for other imports. The logic of the situation also suggests this. The imports of a traditional economy are likely to be either industrial products or primary products which it does not have the climate or natural resources to produce. Early innovators are more likely to be able to increase exports than to achieve much displacement of either type of imports. If early economic change in the country includes the exploitation of mineral or forest resources by foreign concerns, or the entry of foreign traders to purchase agricultural staples for the world market, a considerable increase in the country's importing capacity will occur. For even if large profits are retained abroad, the foreign traders must pay for their purchases and foreign producers of minerals or forest products must pay for their domestic expenses, with foreign exchange—or, more precisely, they must sell foreign exchange within the country to pay their domestic expenses.

Apart from the exploitation of mineral or forest resources by foreigners, the export possibilities open to domestic producers are agricultural products or handicrafts. Japan is the limiting case at one end of a continuum, and the United States, Canada, and Australia the limiting cases at the other (or one may regard the oil-producing countries as such). Because of the comparative advantage of the three countries, primary products loomed large in their exports even at a fairly advanced stage in their industrialization—and indeed do so today. Primary and semimanufactured products constituted more than half of United States exports, in value, until almost 1900. Japan had no natural resources out of which to extract primary product exports, except for silk, but its industrious and ingenious producers, who had long been increasing their productivity in the production of handicrafts, could export them in considerable volume. Japan is almost alone in this respect; producers of other countries, who had not been innovational in handicrafts, found it easier to increase agricultural exports. In the early days of British entry into India, Indian exports included finished cotton textiles, but this phenomenon of a time when Western industry was only beginning to develop and India had a handicraft product superior to its close competitors in the West is not likely to be repeated by nonindustrial low-income countries today.

If all of the nonindustrial countries of the world had begun simultaneously to increase their primary products exports to the industrial West, the fall in their terms of trade might have been catastrophic. Because they began this export expansion seriatim, so that some were engaged in import replacement and even the export of some industrial products before the primary product exports of others reached their full flow, the export expansion was possible without a more drastic dislocation than has occurred. Even so, one of the causes of the decline in the terms of trade of the LDCs after the 1870s certainly was the rapid expansion of their search for world markets for primary products.

Import Substitution

The second stage of the production-trade sequence has usually been replacement of some industrial imports by domestic production. This aspect of the economic development of the LDCs during the present century was largely unnoticed until compilation and analysis of the data since World War II drew attention to it. Once observed, it emerges as a rather spectacular feature of the process of development.

Maizels (1963) analyzed the imports of industrial products of the "semi-industrial countries" of the world from 1913 to 1959. The classification "semi-industrial" includes all of the LDCs except those with no significant manufacturing sector. Those excluded are most African countries, some smaller Latin American countries, and a few others. At 1955 prices, in 1913 the industrial imports of the semi-industrial countries totaled $4.1 billion. In 1959, with much larger income and much larger investment programs, the volume of industrial products that they used annually had risen to $15.7 billion. But their imports of industrial products had risen by only $2.7 billion; they were producing an added $8.9 billion of industrial products themselves. Maizels concludes that by 1959 the "semi-industrial countries" had largely eliminated the import of "low technology" consumer manufactures.

The point is made vividly, in more detail, in another tabulation prepared by Maizels. It is presented in Table 18-1. Between 1899 and 1959, the share of textiles and clothing in the manufactured imports of the semi-industrial countries fell from 55% to 9%. These countries are now making these themselves. The share of the products of complex and heavy industry, namely machinery and transport equipment and chemicals, rose from 14% to 64%. Even in the still lower income countries, where manufacturing is quantitatively unimportant, the share of textiles and clothing in manufactured imports fell from 44% to 15%.

The two sets of data suggest an important conclusion. Almost the only added import substitution open to the LDCs is the production of more complex industrial products, as they acquire the technical capability to produce them.[11] Little added import substitution can be done except gradually, as they advance further in technical capability. To refer to import substitution as a choice open to the LDCs in the short run is misleading. There are some exceptions even among the countries classed by Maizels as semi-industrial, but those exceptions cannot be very important. Some import substitution remains undone in the countries that are still almost wholly unindustrialized. These countries do not loom large in the world picture.

The results of a regression analysis done by Chenery are consistent with the facts analyzed by Maizels. In a study referred to earlier in this book, Chenery (1960) classified industrial products into three classes, "investment and related products," "other intermediate goods," and "consumer goods." From a cross-section analysis of production, import, and volume of use (domestic use and export) of the three classes of industrial goods in 38 countries in postwar years, he calculated the changes that will occur as annual per capita income rises from $100 to $600, if each lower income country duplicates the average pattern in higher income

---

[11] McKinnon (1965), in a review article, provides a very useful analysis of major conclusions of Maizels' volume.

TABLE 18–1
Composition of Manufactured Imports, by Country Groups, 1899 and 1959

Year		Metals (1)	Machinery and Transport Equipment (2)	Chemicals (3)	Textiles and Clothing (4)	Other Manufactures (5)	Percentage Total (6)	Total Value ($ Billion) 1955 Prices (7)
				Percentage Share				
Industrial countries	1899	16	10	7	38	29	100	5.1
	1959	16	35	12	11	26	100	22.6
Semi-industrial countries	1899	8	11	3	55	23	100	2.1
	1959	11	50	14	9	16	100	6.8
Rest of the world	1899	11	17	6	44	22	100	2.8
	1959	13	39	15	15	18	100	14.0

Source: Maizels (1963), p. 174.

countries as its income rises.[12] On this assumption, as per capita income rises, the demand for all three classes of industrial products (for domestic use plus export) will increase at a faster percentage rate than income —investment and related goods at 1.6 times the percentage rate, and other intermediate goods and consumer goods at 1.3 times the percentage rate. With respect to all three classes of goods, the ratio of domestic production to imports will rise. But the ratio will rise markedly with respect to investment and intermediate goods, and much less with respect to manufactured consumer goods. That is, a comparison of the lower and higher income countries in the 1950s indicates that from the 1950s on, as income rises there will be little import substitution in consumer goods. In the light of the historical facts presented by Maizels, this conclusion should not be interpreted to mean that little import substitution occurs in the production of these goods. Rather, it has already taken place, even in the present lower income countries.

The process was probably hastened by the experience of these countries during the depression of the 1930s. The unit value of agricultural exports and the importing capacity of these countries both sank so low during the 1930s that they took steps to lessen their need to import.

Export Expansion: Industrial Products

As countries industrialize, they may become capable of competing on the world market in the sale of one and then another industrial product. South Korea and Taiwan in the 1960s and Brazil in the 1970s provide examples of dramatically rapid increase in such capability. The shift to export of manufactures must not be overstated. Figure 18–1 shows the limited association between GDP per capita (which may be taken as a measure of the state of techniques) and the share of manufactured exports in total exports. But in spite of the wide scatter, an association between income and share of manufactures in exports is clear.

There are nonmarket advantages of entry upon manufacturing production for export. First, foreign trade is a vehicle for the transmission of technical knowledge, general knowledge, and managerial skill. It is a vehicle also for the movement of capital. The reference is not to capital goods, but to a flow of resources. The flow into a given LDC of private foreign capital advantageous to the country is likely to be larger if that country's stream of exports and imports are large than if they are small, for the added trade will transmit knowledge from that country to the MDCs as well as in the opposite direction. Lastly, production for an export market permits a volume of production that is not otherwise possible in a small country. Thereby it makes possible not only whatever

---

[12] Of course the lower income countries will not. Among other factors, future technical change will intervene. But this does not invalidate the point made by Chenery.

FIGURE 18–1
Manufactured Exports and GDP Per Capita

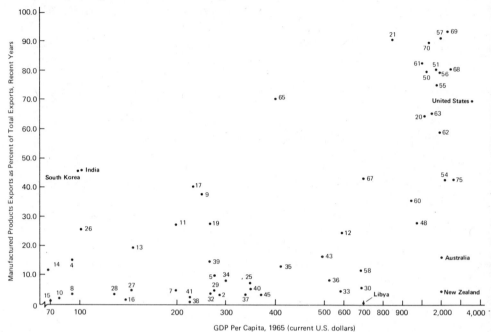

GDP Per Capita, 1965 (current U.S. dollars)

economies of scale there are with prevailing techniques in the country but also the adoption of technical advances that are economic only in production on a larger scale.

THE POLICY CHOICES

And so we come to the question, What policies should a country adopt in order to facilitate and accelerate the rise in value productivity in the country?

Almost all lower income countries, dreaming of the glory of the smoke-stacks of the West, have asked themselves not quite that question. They have asked, "How can we get manufacturing?" And, sure that their infant factories, if established, could not compete with the factories of industrial countries, in answer to their own question many of them have given prospective manufacturers a domestic market by barring the import of almost any manufactured product that an indigenous producer has said that he could produce. Some countries have done the same for any foreign producer who has said that he would establish a factory in the country. The question of the price at which either producer could or would manufacture has often and even usually hardly seemed to enter at all. The average tariff rates of the LDCs are several times as high as those of the industrial nations,[13] and the tariffs are supplemented with quotas, absolute import prohibitions, import licensing, and other devices. Associated with protection will be quotas to permit the import of the materials or components needed for the domestic manufacture, and often also the granting of special foreign exchange rates for the importation of capital goods.

The result is not necessarily an increase in value productivity. That may result, either in the conditions of factor price disequilibrium discussed early in this chapter or because the domestic market is large enough and the state of the country's industrial complex sufficiently advanced so that the factory is efficient, once past its infancy. But the result often is the appearance of modernity, but at the cost of low-productivity, high-cost production that lowers the level of living and contributes little to economic growth.

If imports are sufficiently restricted by a web of such controls, it is possible to set the foreign-exchange rate at a level that gives the country's currency a high value and still export enough to pay for the imports. This is not a necessary part of protectionism, but typically a low-income country will set an official exchange rate that sets a high value on its currency—one, that is, by which one unit of its currency will buy a relatively large amount of foreign currency. The motive often seems to be national vanity: a high currency value seems to dignify the currency. A more prosaic motive is that the imports that are allowed are then cheap in terms of the domestic currency. But if the domestic currency buys much foreign currency, foreign currency buys little domestic currency, and the result is that domestic goods are expensive to foreigners. So it is difficult to produce for export, and exports are low. (And earnings of foreign exchange are low, and on the surface the need to curtail imports by a web of controls seems confirmed.)

Yet protection from foreign competition does stimulate the establishment of domestic factories, and will presumably lead to the establishment of at least the early ones sooner than otherwise. It can be argued that a country cannot export a manufactured product successfully until it has first produced it to meet domestic demand. For only in production for the domestic market, in which it is often protected from foreign competition by tariffs or the equivalent as well as by transportation costs, can it hope to gain the efficiency needed to compete in the world market. The argument is persuasive, with the limited exception that the capability needed for one product may be transferrable to another. This of course is the "infant industry" argument. W. Arthur Lewis extends it. Protection is

---

[13] See United Nations, *Economic Bulletin for Latin America*, 9 (March 1964), Table 5, p. 75.

needed, he states, not only for individual infant factories, but for "infant industrialization." That is, the early stages of development of an industrial complex (sketched in Chap. 6) cannot occur or can occur only very tardily without protection.

The evil of protection of infant industry, as the advocates of financial liberalism see it, is triple. The government, they argue, will protect not merely the "correct" infant industries, ones that will have high value productivity once they gain experience, but also ones that will never be highly productive in the country, ones that the country should never have specialized in. It must be agreed that to foresee the most advantageous specialization for a fairly small country requires a degree of prescience not necessarily possessed by government officials eager for manufacturing, and that the record of governments in this respect is not good. Secondly, though avowedly protection may be temporary, it is politically far more difficult to remove a tariff then to impose it, and, especially on manufacturing that is inefficient in the country, the protection is likely to continue indefinitely. Lastly, the producer given an import quota for supplies, a favored exchange rate, etc., is protected from not only foreign but also domestic competition, may not have any great motivation toward efficiency, and often will indefinitely be less efficient and noninnovative than he would be under the spur of competition.

The advocates of financial liberalism argue, moreover, that protection of infant industry through tariffs, import prohibitions, quotas, etc., is not necessary. If foreign trade is opened wide, the foreign-exchange rate will of course settle at a level at which exports equal imports. This rate, the advocates point out, will make imports more expensive, and exports cheaper to foreigners, than did the artificial rate, and they argue that at that level manufacturing, the manufacturing for which the country has the most favorable conditions, can develop. This is the manufacturing which will be able to export, and so a solidly based industrial complex will develop and will steadily contribute to raising the country's level of living much higher than import substitution will raise it. The question whether initial industry will appear as soon in an almost wholly non-industrial country under such a policy as under protectionism has not been much discussed, but the more fervent advocates of financial liberalism would no doubt argue that it will. They argue also that the whip of competition and potential competition from abroad and at home not only will induce the establishment (and survival) of only the manufacturing ventures in which the country truly has a comparative advantage but will also insure that the survivors are the firms that are efficiently and innovatively managed.

Some of the most fervent advocates point to the great success of South Korea and Taiwan in increasing their exports in the 1960s as proof of the efficacy of the policy. The examples are badly taken. The growth of the two countries from 1960 to 1971 has been very rapid: 7.4% per year in South Korea and 7.1% per year in Taiwan. The association with the growth of increasing productivity in production for export may be granted. The two countries did adopt fairly liberal policies, in the sense in which the word is used here, and their exports and income levels have risen very rapidly. Between 1953 and 1970, the value of Taiwan's exports rose by 1,016% and those of South Korea by 1,418%, just a shade under Japan's increase of 1,429%. Typical increases of other less developed countries are between 50% and 200%.[14] But other factors also worked so forcefully toward this end that it is not possible to say what the relative contribution of each is. First, U.S. military purchasing and U.S. economic aid poured liquidity and a most unusually high and assured demand for exports into both countries, especially into South Korea. Second, each people embodies that Sino-Japanese-East-Asian-Buddhist personality—or culture—whose efficacy is manifested in Japan, in overseas Chinese from Taiwan to Singapore, and presumably also in the Koreans—North as well as South. Lastly, the economic policies involved were not merely liberalization. South Korea illustrates the "artificial" inducements to exporting and virtual guarantees of its success. Larry E. Westphal and Kwang Suk Kim (1973) present the following estimates of the quantitative value of certain export incentives in 1968:

Form of Subsidy	Total Subsidy Payments as a Percent of Total Commodity Exports
Tariff exemptions	14.4
Wastage allowance	2.4
Indirect tax exemptions	7.0
Overhead rate reductions	0.4
Direct tax exemptions	1.1
Interest subsidies	4.5
Total	29.8

The two authors note that exporters also seem to be given a quasi-monopolistic privilege of charging higher prices for their products in the domestic market than for export. In addition, Balassa (1971) notes, exporters received a reduction of 50% on income taxes on profits earned from exports: export credit and loans for the purchase of raw materials and equipment at preferential rates: and through an export-import linkage system were permitted to import goods on the prohibited list (which were scarce and expensive) for their own use or for domestic resale.[15]

---

[14] McKinnon (1973), p. 136.

[15] B. Balassa (1971), p. 63. I am indebted to Youngil Lim for reference to these studies.

Moreover, during the 1960s Korea's ICOR decreased markedly; this fact suggests that in part the rapid growth may have been accomplished through fuller utilization of capacity, and may be a short-run Keynesian phenomenon.

But though the data are too complex for unqualified statements, it is plausible that financial liberalization was among the important influences.[16]

Gustav Ranis (1971) labels the liberalization that is now going on in some low-income countries the "second postwar restructuring," the first one being comprehensive intervention. The term is perhaps an overstatement; not enough countries have yet moved toward more outward-looking and more liberal policies to make the term entirely appropriate.

Whether protection is necessary for the young plants of industry to take root is a moot question today for most lower income countries. The data of Maizels and Chenery indicate that young industry already exists in most of them. Regardless of disagreement about the appropriate policy toward an infant industrial complex, most development economists would probably agree that a shift toward an outward-looking policy now would benefit all or almost all of the so-called "semi-industrial" countries.

An added effect of outward-looking policies, some advocates argue, would be the lessening of inequality in the distribution of income. The argument may be granted in part. Intervention to foster industry logically includes policies to hold down agricultural prices in order to hold down the costs of industrial production. Argentina provides the extreme example of the policy and its ill effects. Whether or not such special policies are adopted, overvaluation of the currency which dampens foreign demand and measures which permit high manufactured goods prices have the same effect. Two dozen or more countries in Latin America, Africa, and Asia provide examples of one or both policies. The devaluation of the currency which is associated with outward-looking policies, by favoring agriculture, redresses the balance.

The remainder of the argument is that the pressure of competition will force producers to use the cheapest rather than the "most modern" methods of production, and thus to use more labor-intensive methods. The result, it is argued, will be to increase labor's share of the national income. This effect, it is asserted, is noticed in the duty-free industrial zone, producing for export, along the northern border of Mexico, and in Korea. The evidence offered thus far has been episodic and unquantified.

Until it and other evidence is quantified, one may be skeptical of the force of the argument. Because technical advance in the industrial coun-

---

[16] B. Balassa (1970), noting the much superior economic performance of Norway and Denmark than that of Argentina, Chile, Czechoslovakia, and Hungary from 1950 to 1965, contrasts the outward-looking policies of the former two with the inward-looking policies of the latter four.

tries during the last two centuries has concentrated on capital-intensive methods, the choice among methods in manufacturing production is limited. In the manufacturing of the great majority of products, the price-elasticity of demand for labor is probably so low that it would require a large fall in wages to induce a fairly small increase in labor-intensivity. If so, while the removal of wage supports might cause the margin between agricultural and manufacturing wages to shrink, this might occur largely through a reduction in real wages in manufacturing, with a fall, not an increase, in labor's share in the national pie. The argument is made that the effect of this particular bit of liberalization would be exerted largely through a change in specialization—that is, a change in the composition of the basket of goods produced. The effect may be granted, but its magnitude is uncertain. It may be conceded, however, that if outward-looking policies speeded up manufacturing production for export and the rise in per capita income, that effect would probably materially hasten the arrival of the period in which continuing economic growth reduces rather than increases the inequality of income distribution. The reader is reminded of the discussion in Chapter 9. Anyone interested in the amelioration of income inequality, however, and not dogmatically committed to complete liberalism, would probably as a minimum insist on major steps of labor-intensive public works, secondary redistribution of income through tax policy, and other measures.

The choice of financial liberalism or, more specifically, outward-looking policies is of course not merely a choice de novo among alternative policies. It requires abandonment in lesser or greater degree of already established interventionist policies. Abandonment even in degree will be resisted, and with some justification, by men with vested interests who feel that they committed their resources on the basis of an implicit commitment by the government. Moreover, devaluation of the currency will raise the cost of the imports that did previously come in, and will also raise the cost of agricultural products if, at the new exchange rate, the world price is higher than the equivalent domestic price. In these and indirect ways devaluation may considerably raise the cost of living. But the importation of goods that were not previously available has at least a mitigating effect. C. P. Kindleberger suggests that three conditions for a successful devaluation and accompanying liberalization of trade are a good harvest, an adequate and price-elastic short-run supply of imported raw materials so that output, especially of export goods, can expand rapidly, and a political consensus that the change of policy is a wise one.[17]

In Ranis (1971), Richard Cooper surveys the effects of 24 devalua-

---

[17] C. P. Kindleberger (1967), cited by Gustav Ranis in Ranis, ed. (1971), p. 446.

tions in 19 different countries during the period 1959–66. He concludes that in general, devaluation:

> improves the balance of payments on current goods and services account.
>
> does not seem to worsen the devaluing country's terms of trade, as might be the case if its exports were sufficient in amount to affect world prices.
>
> causes price increases in imports, in domestically produced goods that compete with imports, and in export goods.
>
> often initially tends to depress economic activity in the country. He suggests that causes may be a shift of income from low to high savers and a large drain on domestic purchasing power created by a rise in the domestic currency price of imports. Another cause may be suggested: an immediate depressing effect on production that cannot stand the competition of imports, while organizing to take advantage of the new export possibilities takes more time, and takes longer, the "less developed" the country.

He concludes also that a decision to devalue does not typically mean the death of the administration making it, but "does seem to be associated with a somewhat higher likelihood of a fall in the government." He advocates an expansive credit policy following devaluation in circumstances in which there is likely to be a deflationary effect.

The case is not conclusively made that outward-looking policies including a general relaxation of intervention and controls are more effective in stimulating exports and increasing the rate of rise in income than are outward-looking interventions such as high export subsidies. Most economists, however, would be willing to make the assertion, outside of their own field of expertise, that the likelihood of administration judicious enough to adopt interventionist policies as effective as a general liberalization is not great.

Economic Isolationism

A school of thought far outside either the financial liberalism or comprehensive intervention schools should be mentioned here. I have termed it economic isolationism. Adopting the Spanish word, Sanjaya Lall (1974) refers to the *dependencia* school, the group whose attitudes arise out of fear of dependence on or, more precisely, control by, foreign corporations. "Economic isolationism" encompasses this but perhaps is somewhat broader.

It arises from fear of a foreign-exchange drain to service foreign debt or equity, fear of the presence of foreign experts, and, especially, fear of control by foreign corporations. This last has three aspects: fear of political control through financial power; fear of economic exploitation of the country through monopolistic pricing, evasion of profits, taxes, etc.;

and fear that the dominance of foreign managers using capital-intensive methods will stifle native ingenuity and prevent that progressive innovation on which continuing rise in income rests. The fear of a foreign-exchange burden is irrational until individual projects or categories of projects have been evaluated. The fear of foreign experts as individuals lacks clarity; a country firm enough in its views to keep them out is presumably also firm enough to prevent the exercise of undue political, social, or economic influence by them. It may be granted that multinational corporations may evade taxes through transfer pricing, and by other methods and, like indigenous corporations, may charge prices as high as the traffic will bear. The thesis of political dominance by foreign capital is probably overdone.

No coherent set of policies flows from the economic isolationist view. If foreign aid and direct investment from abroad are rejected shall the exchange rate be allowed to fall to a level at which exports will pay for imports including capital imports? Or shall state intervention to control trade be exceptionally comprehensive? Shall the country condemn itself to inventing de novo the Western innovations of the last century or two? If not, how shall the inflow of technical knowledge be managed—and maximized? The dependencia school has no clear answers to such questions; its adherents only feel sure that the presence of foreign investment, aid, and managers poses a danger which low-income countries must avoid.

CUSTOMS UNIONS AND FREE TRADE AREAS

We have contrasted "import substitution" and export expansion. Customs unions among low-income countries seem a way of having it both ways: of having export expansion (among the members) through import substitution (with respect to imports from other countries). In that superficial paradox lies a dilemma that goes far to determine whether and how much a customs union contributes to economic growth.

A customs union is an arrangement among countries which, in the ideal version, makes them a single integrated economic area. Such a complete customs union involves elimination of all tariff and trade barriers among the member countries, also of all governmental regulations or aids which provide differential advantages in producing costs; establishment of a common tariff against the outside world; and elimination also of all restrictions on the movement of labor or capital among the members of the union. A free trade area, on the other hand, involves only elimination of tariff and trade barriers with respect to specified products, without harmonization of the tariffs of the member countries and without other types of economic integration. Since a free trade area is usually a weak substitute for a customs union among countries who find it inexpedient to go the whole way, the emphasis here will be on customs unions.

The great model of a customs union is the European Economic Community, which approaches but does not quite reach the ideal defined above. The EEC was composed from its formation in 1958 through 1972 of France, West Germany, Italy, and the Benelux countries, and since January 1, 1973, of these countries plus England and Denmark. In 1968 the EEC completed the elimination of tariffs among the members, subsidies to any industrial production, and almost but not quite all governmental or private measures which directly or indirectly give any advantage to the producers of one member country over those of another in trade within the community. Subsidies on major agricultural products continue. The movement of labor is entirely free. Individual members still maintain barriers against free entry by other members to their capital markets, and during the currency upheavals since 1971 it has not been possible to maintain fixity of exchange rates among the currencies of member countries.

In the western hemisphere the movements for a Central American Common Market (CACM) and a Latin American Free Trade Area (LAFTA) are noteworthy.

In 1958, a series of bilateral agreements and then a multilateral agreement among the five Central American countries were signed announcing general intentions to proceed to internal tariff removal and establishment of a common external tariff on all products except a specified list. Then in 1960, the three countries of El Salvador, Guatemala, and Honduras agreed to free trade by 1965 except on a specified list of items, and by 1962 a similar five-party treaty had been put into effect. Free trade was in effect for almost the entire list by 1966 or 1967. A common external tariff, low on raw materials not produced in Central America and on capital goods, and high on consumer goods, was put into effect simultaneously.

A declaration for the creation of a Latin American free trade area was set forth in the Treaty of Montevideo in 1960. Like CACM, it was stimulated largely by the example of the EEC. Negotiations within LAFTA from 1960 to the present have been largely frustrated by the almost complete inability of the Latin American governments to find any products for which they could agree on the removal of intra-Latin American customs. Because of problems of transportation costs, the larger market has not appeared extremely attractive. A large number of inefficient industrial enterprises have been fostered in various Latin American countries. Contentment with their sheltered markets is more attractive to them than the lure of a larger but competitive market. Nationalism gives support to their resistance to having the barriers that protect them lowered. Fear of the industrially less capable countries that free trade would check their development has been paralyzing. Altogether, the weakness of the economic incentives and the political resistances have prevented much progress.

The automobile industries of Brazil and Chile agreed in 1962 or 1963 that Chile would import partial automobile assemblies from Brazil and in return would ship components to Brazil, both without tariffs. At about the same time, the industries in a number of countries producing electronic tubes, "statistical machines," and glassware agreed to free trade except on listed items. Later, Chile and Argentina reached an agreement for the barter of automobile parts similar to that between Brazil and Chile. In each, Chile largely makes upholstery and receives metallic parts in return. The governments concerned ratified the several agreements, and they are in effect. Beyond these and some recent discussions for very limited similar moves, LAFTA is a concept which has not yet attained much reality.

In September, 1967, the five coastal countries along the Andes—Chile, Peru, Ecuador, Colombia, and Venezuela—formed the Andean Development Corporation. This is not actually a development corporation, but rather an arrangement among the five countries for a trading group within LAFTA. The Andean countries visualize a common market, at least for certain products, and the provision of incentives to investment. This movement has made more progress than has free trade in Latin America as a whole, but is still very far from being a customs union.

Attempts to establish customs unions in Africa have failed. At the time of political breakup of the Federation of Rhodesia and Nyasaland, the customs union also broke apart. Even aside from the political difficulties, it would probably have been doomed to failure by the great disparity in industrial capability. Five countries of equatorial West Africa that had been French colonies formed a pact for a customs union, but the union did not emerge. When the three countries of Kenya, Uganda, and Tanzania (minus Zanzibar) were British colonies, the colonial authorities had instituted a customs union, the East African Community, among them. Some 20% of their foreign trade was among themselves. But at independence 70% of the manufacturing in the Community was in Kenya, and the trade balances of the other two countries with Kenya showed a continuing deficit. Gradually, the belief of Uganda and Tanzania that the benefits of the union were unequal had its effects. Presently, the common currency and common tourist services of the three countries were broken up, and breakup of other common services—notably, the railroads and telecommunications—threatened. Restrictions were imposed on trade. Then, an earnest attempt by the three countries in 1967 to salvage the customs union led to the signing of a treaty which took effect on December 1, 1967. It has three main provisions. (1) Administration of the common services was split. (This was official recognition of an existing fact.) (2) A Community Development Bank was created. Kenya is to contribute one third of the capital, and to receive a maximum of 22% of the bank's loans. (3) Free trade within the Community was re-established, but when any trade deficit country (in practice, Uganda and Tanzania) is offered a factory which would produce a traded industrial product, it might levy a transfer tax of up to 50% of the common external tariff on the product and use the funds to subsidize the infant enterprise. The tax might be continued in effect for a period of not more than eight years. This piece of economic statesmanship offered some uncertain promise, but that promise was not allowed to be tested; the union foundered on political differences.

No customs union (except through political union as in Malaysia) has been proposed in Asia.

The potential advantages of a customs union are two: it permits industries for which national markets are not sufficient to achieve the economies of scale attainable in production for the larger market. And by providing competition in the larger market it increases competition and reduces the opportunity for monopoly. The advantages apply almost exclusively to industrial production; there are few economies of scale in other production. In general, the two advantages do not apply with respect to the same industrial establishments. If a national market is too small for a single plant, then at best there will be oligopolistic competition among two or three firms in a customs union.

Among the requirements for a success of a customs union are: that the physical circumstances of the union are such that transportation costs do not bar economical trade; that the members have something to trade with each other; and that their technical productive capacities are reasonably equal, so that union does not condemn one of them to a prolonged period of production of primary products only while the others develop manufacturing. These requirements have already been discussed in part in the comments above on the difficulties of the East African Community and LAFTA. A fuller comparison of the degree to which the Western European countries, those in Central America, and those in Latin America as a whole meet these requirements will illustrate the significance of the requirements.

The members of the EEC occupy a compact area within which there is excellent and cheap transportation. The Central American countries also occupy a compact area, within which there is reasonably good transportation. On the other hand, the transport costs between the industrial area of Brazil and that of Chile or Colombia are probably greater than between New York and any of these three points. Though an increase in the volume of traffic would reduce the intra-Latin American costs, for many products it would not do so enough to make this trade economic for various points in Latin America relative to trade with the United States or Europe.

International trade is largely among industrial countries, or between them and countries producing primary products. Within modern industry there is a large degree of specialization. Among primary producers, there is, also, but—except for minerals—in products that are substitutes rather than complements for each other. The trade is between such countries and industrial countries, not with each other. Of the foreign trade of the industrial countries of the West, in the period since World War II, about three fourths has been with each other. Of the foreign trade of the LDCs of the world, only about one tenth is with each other.

There is no advantage in the availability of a large market for products which the producers of the area are not yet technically competent to produce. It may nevertheless be true that trade among LDCs in which the less complex types of industrial production have been established or are beginning to be established may be advantageous. That trade in these products forms a small percentage of total trade is not highly relevant. But early industrialization raises in acute form the question of relative industrial capability.

The conception that LDCs of a given continent (say, Latin America), all being low-income countries, have equal industrial capability, is an illusion. Per capita income can be taken as a rough first approximation measure of technical capacity. In 1965, the highest income country of the European Economic Community, West Germany, had a per capita income only about 80% greater than that of the lowest income country, Italy. And the technical capacity of the industrial area of Italy, that country's north, was much more nearly equal to that of the other members than the per capita comparison would suggest. In Central America the per capita GDP of the highest income country, Costa Rica, was also less than twice that of the lowest income country, Honduras, and the industrial capabilities of the five countries were not too unlike. On the other hand, the per capita income of Bolivia was only one fourth, and that of Paraguay only one third, of that of Argentina. (That of Venezuela was still higher, but only because of its oil.) The industrial capacity of these two low-income countries was not remotely comparable to that of São Paulo (Brazil) or even that of Cordoba (Argentina). It would be extremely awkward politically to form a customs union or free trade area that omitted them (or other Latin American countries), yet formation of a Latin American free trade area with fairly comprehensive product coverage would require special measures to prevent dooming Paraguay, Bolivia, and in lesser degree some other countries to being agricultural hinterlands for a long period of years. It is for this reason that some Latin American economists have declared that among the purposes of a customs union of less developed countries must be promotion of industry, not merely facilitation of its expansion. The principle is not readily given effect unless a fair degree of entrepreneurial vigor is present.

When this problem is considered by economists interested in promoting the economic development of the LDCs, one solution sometimes proposed is that the establishment of new industrial enterprises shall be allocated among the member countries, rather than left to private initiative and the inducements of the market. The extreme proposal is that industrial establishments of each given type shall be barred by law except in the country or countries selected as their sites. The more usual proposal is that when an allocation of industrial establishments among the member countries has been decided upon, an establishment in the preferred country shall be given technical aid, financial aid from a development bank, and exemption from profit or other taxes and from internal customs duties for, say, 10 to 15 years, whereas any competitor from another member country would receive none of these benefits.

In the CACM it was recognized that Honduras and to a lesser degree Nicaragua would need special help. The agreements of 1958 provided that a firm given "integration-industry status" should like other firms be exempt from tariffs in its trade within the common market, but that competitors should not. These were not to be barred, but they would have initially to pay the external tariff on their intra-common-market sales, though they would receive a reduction of 10% of the original tariff rate each year. Later it was provided that new industries might be granted higher tariffs if they agreed to produce at least half of the requirements of the common market, with the qualification that the Executive Council might eliminate the excess tariff if it saw fit. Under these provisions, the common market performed just as individual countries following an "import substitution" policy have done. It granted the favor to a number of firms, notably five, which could not achieve high value productivity within the CACM, and whose prices therefore raised prices and somewhat lowered the level of living. The five were producers of galvanized sheets, rayon cloth, tires, cardboard boxes, and electric wire and cable. These and some other cases, then, were "trade-diverting" rather than "trade-creating," in Jacob Viner's use of these terms. The effect, however, did not loom large in the total production of the CACM. Many other firms induced by the common market arrangement to enter were "trade creating," that is, given the larger market, they did achieve economies of production that reduced costs markedly.

But even the entire CACM provided a market that was large enough for only some types of manufacturing production, largely so-called low-technology production—textiles, shoes, clothing, and the like. The total population of the area in 1970 was some 15 million, and the total GDP some $5 billion. During 1962–66, the CACM as a whole boomed, though Nicaragua had its troubles. In 1950, about 3% of the foreign trade of the five republics was among themselves. In 1966, this was true of 20% of their trade, though this figure is somewhat misleading, since much of the intracountry trade is in imports which arrive at the most convenient port and are then transshipped. But by 1968 import substitution seemed to have run its course, and since that time the CACM has faced the problem that many individual low-income countries face—the need to be able to export if it is to continue its industrial expansion.

Price and Income Stabilization

To conclude this chapter, one last problem of foreign trade for the lower income countries should be discussed: the problem of fluctuations in export prices and therefore in foreign-exchange revenues. For many lower income countries it is a serious problem.

In 1953, the following less developed countries obtained more than one half of their export proceeds from their sales of a single primary product:[18]

Materials for Beverages	*Other Foods*
Angola	Mauritius
Ethiopia	Nigeria
French Cameroons	Cuba
Ghana	Ecuador
El Salvador	Formosa
Brazil	Honduras
Colombia	Panama
Guatemala	Thailand
Haiti	

Agricultural Raw Materials	*Minerals*
Egypt	Bahrain-Kuwait-Qatar
Liberia	Belgian Congo
Sudan	Iraq
Uruguay	Northern Rhodesia
Pakistan	Saudi Arabia
	Bolivia
	Chile
	Venezuela

To this fact should be added another: the average year-to-year fluctuation in the world market prices of some 50 primary commodities from 1900 to 1958 averaged 13%.[19] Insofar as the price fluctuations resulted from variations in world supply, price and quantity compensated in some countries and the fluctuations in income were less than those in price. But when sharp changes in world demand occurred, because of two world wars, inflations following them, the Great Depression and lesser depres-

---

[18] Yates (1959), p. 180.
[19] United Nations (1952), and U. N. *World Economic Survey, 1958.*

sions, and the invention in industrial countries of synthetic materials and new techniques, price and quantity sold fell together and the fall in income was exacerbated. The average year-to-year fluctuations in the export receipts of all of the LDCs during the decade 1948–58 varied between 9% and 12%. For some countries for which a single export whose price varied sharply was important, the average for the decade was 18%.[20] No industrial country is subject to comparably large frequent economic fluctuations.

These fluctuations in foreign exchange earnings cause "boom and bust" cycles. If the exporters invest the increased proceeds within their own country when export earnings rise, they may spend part of the foreign exchange for the import of capital goods and sell part to the country's commercial banks to obtain domestic funds with which to pay the domestic costs of the investment. The monetary result is the same as if there were a sudden burst of credit-financed investment, combined with the sudden availability of foreign exchange. By a multiplier effect, consumption will also increase. By depositing some or all of the foreign exchange with the central bank, the commercial banks will also have the reserves to expand credit, thus pushing the boom higher. If the exporters obtain domestic currency but spend it for consumption purposes rather than investment, the immediate effect on income in the country is the same, but when the boom is over no capital goods will have been added to the country's productive system. In either case, when foreign exchange earnings drop, the boom is sharply cut off.

Tax, fiscal, and monetary policies combined can do something to mitigate these violent savings. Assuming perfect knowledge of the course of a fluctuation, action might be as follows. Taxes on exports, graduated with respect to the price of the exports, plus graduated income taxes, should be imposed and collected. The domestic investment or consumption boom will thereby be curbed somewhat, and the government will also become the owner of some of the increased foreign exchange receipts. It should hold them, and sell them to the central bank when a fall in foreign exchange earnings occurs. The government can then counter the domestic deflation by spending the funds obtained, and the central bank can make foreign exchange in excess of current earnings available to importers. Ideally, the upswing and downswing in both domestic income and spending and in importing could be eliminated.

The difficulties with this policy, even assuming that the government can police exporters and capture the foreign exchange in the way indicated, are two. First, the fluctuations are not known in advance. In any year, it must be decided to what extent an increase in foreign exchange earnings reflects a rising secular trend and to what extent it is a tempo-

---

[20] United Nations (1961), pp. 3–5.

rary upsurge. Even a rough approximation to correct forecasts of the fluctuations is extremely unlikely. The error will not be a random one. There will always be agencies eager to spend the funds as they accumulate, and there will always be individuals who claim that the prosperity is not really a boom, but only normal prosperity which the government should not curb by hoarding foreign exchange or domestic funds. And they may be correct in the sense that the boom may be doing no more than causing full utilization of the country's productive resources. It is not certain that governmental adjustments to the situation in response to these pressures will reduce rather than increase the amplitude of the fluctuations.

Second, during the upswing, the primary increase in investment or consumer spending will be by the exporters. During the downswing, the impact of the increased government spending will be experienced elsewhere in the economy. Even though the fluctuations in aggregate national income were completely eliminated, there would be surges forth and back within the economy. Since sufficient mobility of resources to shift fairly rapidly (and repeatedly) from one sector to another will hardly exist, the policy would cause sectoral expansions and contractions within the economy. Perhaps this would be an improvement over economy-wide booms and busts, but combined with the almost inevitable errors in execution it is not likely to be a great improvement.

Remedies: Marketing Boards

A more drastic governmental intervention in private economic activity, designed to remedy the second of these problems, is for the government to take over the exporting function. Ideally, the government would then insulate the domestic economy from world fluctuations. It would (1) pay the producers a fixed price, regardless of the international fluctuations; (2) sell its foreign exchange earnings to the central bank, for resale to importers, at a constant (or secularly rising) annual rate, regardless of the international fluctuations; and (3) similarly spend at an even rate its earnings of domestic funds from the sale of foreign exchange. The administrative difficulties referred to above are then compounded by the need to be an efficient exporter.

A number of state trading boards, to serve these purposes, were set up in LDCs after World War II. The rice marketing board of Burma, the cocoa marketing board of Ghana, a group of marketing boards in Nigeria, and similar boards in other West African countries are examples. An examination of the experience of Burma and Nigeria will illustrate the problems and operations of these trading organizations.

The only one that was in position for a time to affect the world price of the commodity handled was the State Agricultural Marketing Board of

Burma during the period of post–World War II rice shortage. The stabilization operations of boards not in this position must be to interpose themselves between the cultivators and the world market, and hold either the domestic price or aggregate domestic earnings stable by accumulating funds at times of high world prices (if they can judge when this condition exists) and paying them out at times of low world prices or low domestic production. A similar accumulation and disbursement of foreign exchange earnings by the government would stabilize the economy's foreign exchange earnings and income—provided in each case that the marketing board and the government can somehow judge correctly when to act.

The extreme bad example is provided by Burma's State Agricultural Marketing Board. The board did stabilize the incomes of rice cultivators. It held them at a level which in real terms was below that of the prewar days of the foreign traders, while the board accumulated huge profits. The foreign exchange thus earned became income of the government, which not only spent but squandered it without regard to a possible future decline in receipts. The board cost the country enormous potential revenues by holding its rice for still higher prices while production in other countries recovered and prices fell; and by inefficient storage and handling which cost the country the benefit of grade differentials and permitted the rice to deteriorate in quality and in part to disappear.[21]

The experience of the several Nigerian marketing boards presents a happier picture. The commodities handled were cocoa, groundnuts, palm oil, palm kernels, and cotton. Helleiner (1966a) analyzes the effects of the boards' operations during periods from about 1949 to about 1961.

The boards have had a high degree of success in holding prices stable throughout each marketing year. In only one year—when world cocoa prices dropped drastically in the middle of a marketing season—was any of the boards compelled to change its buying price within a marketing year. The result has been orderly marketing, reduction of speculative marketing activity, and improvement in the quality of produce. The judgment of the marketing board managers with respect to year-to-year price changes has also been good enough so that in all cases Nigerian prices have fluctuated less than world prices. But, surprisingly, the price changes were so associated with changes in quantities marketed that in cocoa and palm oil incomes were about as unstable from year to year as if world prices had prevailed, incomes from groundnuts and cotton were more unstable, and only for palm kernel sellers were incomes clearly stabilized. Gerald Helleiner concludes (p. 76): "These results lend weight to the view that Nigerian marketing boards are better defended in their role as [successful] earners of tax revenues than in their role as

---

[21] This account is from the personal experience of the writer. See also Levin (1960).

stabilizing authorities." The comment applies not only to Nigerian marketing boards, but to those in other countries as well.

Remedies: International Stabilization Schemes

Hope for the stabilization of commodity prices or of the incomes of producers must rest with international stabilization operations. In principle, an international stabilization organization could fully prevent wide annual fluctuations in the prices of readily storable commodities, provided only that it had accumulated a sufficient stock before a world shortage appeared. It could do so by holding a buffer stock, a procedure that is useless for a board of a single country. If the organization agreed to permit the price of, say, tin to fall no more than 5% below the moving average of the price of, say, the preceding three years, or to rise no more than 5% above that average, it could limit price changes to a maximum of 10% and an average of much less by its buying and selling operations.[22] A large secular decline in world demand would embarrass the organization only temporarily, for after (as a maximum) the period of the moving average, the organization's selling price would drop by 5% each year until such time as it had caught up with the decline in world demand and the organization was unloading the stock it had accumulated.

This brief account passes over serious difficulties which even such an operation, which made no attempt to influence the long-run trend of prices, might have. But in principle the possibility sketched above exists. For the stabilization of fluctuations in the price of many commodities, the cooperation of the United States would be needed, because it is the buyer of so large a share of world exports. The United States government, which until some time in the 1950s looked with disfavor on almost any international commodity agreement, has since become more favorably inclined to agreements which attempt no more than is sketched above. However, the difficulty with such agreements is that the producing countries are not much interested in merely this prevention of short-run swings. By commodity price stabilization they usually mean stabilization at a higher price than would otherwise obtain in the world.

International commodity agreements have been classed in three types.[23] The first is a buffer stock scheme, like that just sketched, operated by formula or by a manager with discretionary authority. The

---

[22] It might have difficulty initially, if prices had fluctuated wildly during the years immediately preceding the beginning of operations, so that the moving average fluctuated widely. Ad hoc initial rules could take care of almost any probable situation, even if not of all conceivable situations.

[23] Papers by Swerling, Mikesell, and Reynolds, in 1963, with discussions by four other individuals, treat various aspects of the problem. The classification is that of Mikesell.

second is an agreement under which each producing country agrees to an export quota. Unless each country also takes measures to limit production, great pressure to break the agreement will build up as stocks accumulate. The third is a multilateral agreement under which producing countries agree to sell specified minimum amounts each year if desired by buyers at a specified maximum price, and buying countries agree to take specified maximum amounts, at a specified minimum price. This sort of agreement also requires production controls for continued effectiveness.

The first international commodity agreement was the Stevenson rubber scheme of the 1920s. This attempt to form a world monopoly and raise the price sharply broke down as the high price caused rubber production to appear in new areas.

The International Wheat Agreement, first entered into in 1949 and renewed periodically since, is of the third type. The agreement to maintain minimum prices caused record accumulations in the United States and Canada. China's large purchases in 1962, and subsequently disposal of United States surplus stocks by "concessionary" sales (sales which contain a grant element of some sort) to LDCs reduced the accumulations. Then the very large purchases by the Soviet Union in 1972 caused prices to explode through the ceilings.

The International Sugar Agreement, formed in 1953, set export quotas. Cuba was the dominant member. The stocks accumulated were not sufficient to meet the threat of shortage when the first Suez crisis temporarily closed off supplies from Southeast Asia, and prices about doubled in a few months. The stabilization attempt of the International Tin Agreement broke down when the U.S.S.R., not a member, sold large quantities of tin. Through the cooperation of the United States, the major consumer, the International Coffee Agreement of 1963 was executed successfully. The United States agreed to limit its imports from each member producing country. The agreement was threatened by the rapid rise in production of lower grade ("robusta") coffee in low-cost areas in Africa. This grade is satsifactory for making instant coffees. However, the African producers came into the agreement. Brazil has since mounted a program to reduce considerably the number of her coffee trees. Minor evasion has occurred by sale of coffee to third-party countries, whose shipments to the United States were in turn not subject to quotas, since they were not producers. However, the agreement still functioned with marked success. United States participation, contrary to its short-run interest as a consumer, was accounted for by a desire to help to improve and stabilize economic conditions in the producing countries. But by the early 1970s the Brazilian reduction in coffee tree numbers plus a continuing rise in world, and especially U.S., coffee consumption had greatly increased demand relative to supply, and Brazil led producers in pressing for a considerably increased price floor in a new agreement, and the

United States withdrew. Because of the lag between tree planting and increased coffee yield, there will be a sellers' market for some years unless producers in some producing countries planted added trees half a dozen years ago in anticipation of the present situation. Probably they did not; trade journals apparently have carried no reports of such actions.

A 1961 report by a committee of experts appointed by the United Nations proposed the stabilization of the export proceeds of the LDCs by establishment of an insurance fund in which both low-income and high-income producing countries would be members. A country would receive a benefit payment when its export proceeds fell, and would make a repayment when they rose, but the schedules of payments and receipts would be so adjusted that the low-income countries would only partially repay the sums they had received, while high-income countries would be net contributors. In a scheme proposed by a committee appointed by the Secretary-General of the Organization of American States, high- and low-income countries would both contribute premiums, but those of the high-income countries would be purely a form of economic aid; they would receive no compensation payments.[24] To date, neither proposal has been given serious consideration in governmental discussions.

The instability of export proceeds is sometimes mentioned as justification for economic autarky. The argument is rarely if ever justified for the countries to which it is applied, for these are countries without the diversified natural resources needed for autarky, which will have high import needs, must continue the export of their dominant crop, and will find their economies subject to foreign-exchange swings even if they do opt for import substitution. The remedy will be minimal; they need to find relief in one of the types of measures discussed above.

BIBLIOGRAPHICAL NOTE

General statements from the neoclassical viewpoint of the advantages of international specialization and pursuance of the dictates of comparative advantage are made as lucidly and trenchantly in two prewar works as in later statements. These are G. Haberler, *The Theory of International Trade* (1936) and J. Viner, *Studies in the Theory of International Trade* (1937.) In many later essays, both men have restated the argument and applied it to specific points in controversy. See for example Haberler, "Terms of Trade and Economic Development," in H. S. Ellis (1961). Essentially the same viewpoint is applied specifically to the question of economic growth in an elegantly simple statement in G. M. Meier (1963).

The basic sources of terms of trade data and their analysis—by Hil-

---

[24] Mikesell (1963) mentions both.

gerdt, the GATT annual reports, C. P. Kindleberger, and T. Morgan—are discussed in the text. To these should be added the essay by R. Prebisch (1962), which presents the thesis of the inevitably falling terms of trade of the LDCs.

For excellent introductions to the entire range of relevant trade and monetary policies, see H. G. Johnson (1967) or S. B. Linder (1967), or, for a brief survey not including monetary aspects, Chap. 26 of R. E. Caves and R. W. Jones (1973).

Maizels (1963) is a valuable source of the types of data relevant to the discussion of this chapter, as is H. B. Lary (1968).

A. I. MacBean, *Export Instability and Economic Development* (1966), is a recent book on this topic. The symposium in the *American Economic Review* for May, 1963, by Swerling, Mikesell, and Reynolds, with discussions by four other individuals, gives an introduction to the problem of commodity price stabilization.

Concerning Latin American integration, see M. S. Wionczek, ed. (1966), and for a more recent account of the Central American Common Market, D. H. McClelland (1972). See also Inter-American Development Bank, *Multinational Investment Programs and Latin American Integration* (1966).

Development Planning

19

In this book I have tried to balance the theoretical and the "practical": to surround the economic theory with information that would make its relationship to action clear. In this final chapter I shall do the same. The first section summarizes the components of good planning, broadly defined, that have been discussed in preceding chapters; following ones present fairly rigorously the elementary requirements of planning models; and the last discusses the process of formulating and administering a plan.

THE ELEMENTS OF GOOD PLANNING

A joke among development economists a decade ago, told usually in the French because in French the three relevant words have the same rhythm, was that there are three kinds of planning: *imperatif, indicatif,* and *decoratif.* The first was practiced in the Soviet Union, the second in France, and the third in a number of countries which it is not necessary to name here. While decorative planning is only too real, in most countries whose governments avow their intention to accelerate economic development there is significant planning, not merely decorative, which is partially imperative (in government projects) and partially more than indicative in that it endeavors to influence economic parameters and arrange economic inducements so as to influence private choices.

Development planning, most broadly defined, includes whatever the government can do to facilitate and optimally accelerate development. The governmental action will ideally include maintaining favorable insti-

493

tutions, providing appropriate education, opening channels of information, countering the biases of the market, and complementing it by government operation of enterprises. All of these types of actions will have important purposes other than the promotion of economic development. With respect to economic development, the first three will be aimed mainly though not solely at maximizing the rate of innovation, and the last two at achieving the optimum magnitude and allocation of resource use. The term "development planning" is usually used to include not only the planning but also the execution of the relevant measures.

The general body of economic theory is in the main a theory of the conditions and characteristics of equilibria. Often disequilibrium enters the theory only as the state from which equilibrium is approached. On the other hand, development theory must analyze the results of the action of disequilibrating forces that continue indefinitely to counter the tendency of the system toward equilibrium. This assumption of indefinitely continuing disequilibrium is the assumption that opens for consideration most of the theoretical problems discussed in this book.

Moreover, development theory must recognize that continuing technical change is continually causing alteration not merely in economic magnitudes but in the functional relationships among the varying elements. This is the consideration that requires development theory, in considering balance versus concentration or the causes of economic development, to leave the rigor of economic models and turn to economic history, sociology, and personality theory.

Lastly, development theory must recognize that the limits of technical capability or incapability restrict the range of economic choice, and that the pace of change in technical capability sets limits to the speed with which some economic choices can be carried out. This recognition renders allocation theory based on perfect competition and mobility suspect, and permits the formulation of such aspects of development theory as that of the two gaps.

What, then, are the essential elements of good development policy?

1. The government must maintain institutions which will make it as easy and as rewarding as possible for men interested in increasing the productivity of their sector of the economic system to achieve their aim. The relevant policies include maintaining law and order, enforcing or inducing the use of convenient devices such as uniformity and clarity of weights and measures, maintaining an appropriate and consistent balance between personal rights and social responsibilities, sanctioning and protecting an observable and dependable relationship between economic achievement and reward, insofar as prevalent social values will permit, and the like. Within limits the government can intervene to endorse and effectuate the values of one social group rather than another. A pertinent example is the execution of land reform.

Stated in this general way, these measures are as appropriate in a socialist as in a private enterprise society, given that in each case the social values of the groups who make up the society sanction the form of organization. The historical record will not support the proposition that in all countries private enterprise is superior to socialism for the promotion of economic development. This was noted in Chapter 11. However, the historical record will support the proposition that absence of the institutions mentioned above is adverse to development. It has been said that government in Malaysia, Thailand, and the Philippines has been more conducive to economic development since 1950 than that in Burma and Indonesia, not so much in that the three governments have been more favorable to private enterprise as that in the three countries government has at least existed. There is point in the comment.

2. The second basic pro-development policy is to make available to the people of the society the full measure of relevant education to which they are receptive. Educating a person takes time. The government must be continually vigilant that so far as possible it is providing far enough in advance the facilities and opportunities that will yield a sufficient number of workers of various skills and a sufficient number of technically and professionally trained men when they are needed. Insofar as time does not permit it to do this, it should permit and facilitate the in-migration of the needed men, and quite possibly should facilitate in-migration, temporary or permanent, in large numbers even though its goal is the maximum welfare of its own previous citizens.

3. The third policy is to arrange contacts and open channels of information among the groups and regions of the society and with the rest of the world. These channels were discussed in Chapter 3, dealing with difficulties in increase in agricultural productivity and in Chapter 5, dealing with the development of industry.

4. For the sake of both development and current welfare, the government should fear idle productive resources as it would the plague, and should zealously consider whether its fiscal, monetary, and foreign exchange policies are such as to induce the maximum efficient use of resources.

5. It was argued in Chapter 14 that the individuals of a society may prefer a higher rate of saving than otherwise if each knows that all others are being required to contribute their margin. The government must be concerned with its optimum contribution to the nation's rate of saving.

6. As the progress of development permits, the government should foster the evolution of the institutions of a capital market.

7. The government should keep a sharp eye on externalities, immobilities, monopoly, and the possibility of economies of scale, in order that by taxes and subsidies, and also various other policies, it may compensate for the failure of the market to lead to optimum allocation in the presence

of these conditions. It is in this process that the judgment of future terms of trade and "dynamic comparative advantage" is required.

8. Lastly, the government will itself be an investor in the fields of transportation, communication, power, and urban utilities where monopoly is the economic form of organization, and in other fields where the values of the society lead to government proprietorship. In these it must be eternally vigilant to forecast the location and magnitude of likely future demand far enough in the future, and with sufficient allowance for the delays of governmental administrative procedure, so that needed projects can be planned, designed, constructed, and ready for use in time to avoid constricting economic growth.

For this purpose, as well as to provide an estimate of manpower needs at successive future periods, a five-year plan, preferably one that rolls forward every two or three years, is useful. It may usefully be set in the very general framework of a "perspective plan" of, say, 15-year goals. Its formulation, or the planning of projects in the absence of a formal plan, will require some judgment of the flows of materials and components among the industries of the country in the process of producing the basket of final products that is anticipated. That is, it will require preparation of an "input-output" table or of a programming model, formal or informal. Because of the heroic simplifications that are necessary, preparation of a formal model is likely to lead to an utterly spurious and sometimes dangerous sense of precision. Whether or not a formal model is computed, it is important that the analysis be in the nature of a model, so that all assumptions that affect the conclusions importantly are made explicit, and the degree to which the information available is inadequate for full analysis is also made explicit.

Before discussing macroplanning models, it will be useful to discuss briefly the requirements of good planning of projects that are components of the overall plan. It is not implied that projects are planned first and then added to form a macroplan. Planning at the two levels must be interwoven in time.

PROJECT PLANNING

In many of the least developed countries, comprehensive planning is impossible or can be only symbolic or at best highly imperfect, for the elementary facts of population size and rate of growth, gross national product and its composition, and the like are not known. Planning may consist mainly of the consideration of individual projects, not even of comparison among projects, for projects may occur to the planners one at a time. The questions asked are whether a proposed project seems worth its cost in an absolute sense and whether it can be financed. The calculus is like that which may be employed by a banker in deciding whether to make a loan, an investor in buying stock, or a businessman in deciding whether to add a new element to his business. The planning of the International Bank for Reconstruction and Development was almost wholly at this level, with the addition of some regard for the allocation of its funds among countries, during the first decade and more of its existence.

Project planning at a level of sophistication one step higher will include selection among projects by comparison of their expected yields or returns in some broad sense, with less or more careful recognition that the project expenditures must fit into a budget total. Expenditures for roads, schools, dams, and agricultural extension services must be weighed against each other.

However, even in the absence of comprehensive or macroplanning, project planning may and should involve much more than this. If the project has several components, all of which must be completed before operation can begin, their construction must be programmed. If it is not, a factory may stand idle because no power is available or irrigation ditches may blow full of sand because they were dug two years before the deep wells to provide the water were completed, or because the nomads who were expected to become farmers do not choose to do so, or have not been taught how.

Programming must begin by considering the finished project and working backward to see what must be done when to bring it to coordinated completion. Take construction of a textile mill as an example. The questions must be asked: If a building, machinery, a power plant, access roads, a supply of intermediate or long staple cotton, management, and skilled workers will be required, what must be done with respect to each so that all will be ready at the year t? With respect to, say, the power plant, if it will take one year to install the turbines when all else is completed, then what things must be done by the time $t-1$ (where the time unit is one year) in order that installation of the turbines can begin? When must the turbines be ordered if they are to be at the site by $t-1$? When must dam construction begin to be ready at $t-1$? Perhaps at $t-3$, for a small dam. Then when must construction machinery be ordered so that it will be at the site at $t-2\frac{1}{2}$ or $t-3$ as needed? Or when must construction tenders be asked for an order to enter into a contract at a time that will permit construction to begin by $t-3$? So for the access roads, the expansion of cotton production, the arrangement for management, the training of workers, the arrangements for marketing, etc. Some of these segments may depend on others; access roads, for example, may have to be ready before dam construction can begin. If so, their construction time must be subtracted from $t-3$, and the elements in the road construction planned within that prior period. In good project planning, execution of all segments of a project will be programmed so that it is known what things must be done at t-5 so that by t-4 those things are done which will permit execution by t-3 of the operations necessary to complete by t-2 the things that must be done by then in order that the segments may be completed by t-1 on whose execution by that date the completion of the whole by time t depends.

This multi-pronged coordinated House-That-Jack-Built programming is termed critical path analysis or PERT. It is primarily physical or engineering rather than economic planning, though it may become purely economic if a government too inexperienced to program the construction itself contracts with a construction firm to manage the whole. (This is a "turn-key" operation; the contractor undertakes, so to speak, to build the building and hand over the key to the door. In this case the government need only see that it has the funds on hand to make payments at the times called for in the contract—though if it is wise, it will also employ a consulting engineer to keep an eye on the work of the contracting engineer.

Programming, of course, is not sufficient. It is also necessary to see that each segment of the work proceeds at the pace that was programmed or, if it does not and the lag cannot be remedied, to readjust the program. A good reporting system to obtain prompt periodic reports of the rate of physical progress as well as of the rate of expenditure is a necessary part of good project planning.

With the qualification noted above, programming is an engineering rather than economic process. I shall refer to programming again in discussing sectoral planning.

MACROPLANNING

Project planning is of less interest to the economist than macroplanning, the allocation among major uses of the aggregate of resources of the economy. Macroplanning may refer merely to the allocation of resources among private consumption, private investment, and government expenditure. In principle, however, such allocation can be made only with evaluation of the detailed use of resources for each of these sectors.

Macroplanning must begin with a set of national income accounts. Suppose that on the output side these take the simple form for year zero, the present year:

$$Y(O) = C(O) + I(O) \tag{1}$$

where Y, C, and I refer to GNP, consumption, and investment respectively. Investment includes both private and government investment.

The government planner may then estimate GNP for the next time period if he has two additional facts, the estimated ICOR for the economy as a whole and the estimated lag between investment and the initiation of a flow of output from the new investment projects. Assume a lag of one year. The planner may then write:

$$Y(1) = Y(O) + 1/A\,[I(O)] \qquad (2)$$

or, more generally, for a period of years,

$$Y(t+n) = Y(t) + 1/A\left[\sum_{t=1}^{n-1} [I(t)]\right] \qquad (3)$$

where A = the ICOR.

Equation (3) is derived from a set of equations:

$$Y(t+1) = Y(t) + 1/A\,[I(t)] \qquad (4.1)$$

$$Y(t+2) = Y(t+1) + 1/A\,[I(t+1)] \qquad (4.2)$$

$$Y(t+3) = Y(t+1) + 1/A\,[I(t+2)] \qquad (4.3)$$

$$\cdots\cdots\cdots\cdots\cdots\cdots\cdots$$

$$Y(t+n) = Y(t+n-1) + 1/A\,[I(t+n-1)] \qquad (4.n)$$

If the planner can estimate different ICORs for the value added contributed by investment in different sectors, for example, private investment and government investment, he can separate the second term on the right-hand side of each of equations (2) and (3) into two or more terms.

The formulations in equations (2) and (3) are usually said to assume that the increase in Y depends solely on the increase in the capital stock. Capital, in this formulation, is the only scarce input; there is no shortage of labor, unskilled or of any level of skill, training, or education to impede the rise in GNP. However, A is necessarily estimated from the previous experience of the economy or from the experience of other economies, and all that can be said about it assumes implicitly the same combined impact that was experienced previously in this or other economies. Or, some adjustment may have been made in estimating A if it is thought that the impact of these factors will differ from that in the place and period from which the estimate is being derived. In any event, A is estimated independently of the formulation of equation (2) and in that equation is a *datum*.

Planning may consist merely of trying to maximize the selection of projects within I_g (government investment) and the efficiency of their execution. Or, it may consist of this plus the planning of measures intended to maximize the efficiency of private investment. That is, it may aim at minimizing the incremental capital-output ratio A. If, given this effort, we assume that the level of consumption in each year is determined by behavioral relationships outside the equation, and that A is determined by technical relationships outside the equation, then Y and C for each future year are also determined and the planning process is at an end. (These are Harrod-Domar-like assumptions.)

Usually, however, the planner will have magnitudes of Y and C in the future as targets (say a rise in per capita income of 15% during the next five years) and will not accept passively the magnitudes yielded by equation (2) after minimizing A. Suppose for the moment that magnitudes in the year n, the last year of a plan period, are the targets, and that we can ignore intervening years except as steps on the way. That is, $Y(n) - Y(t)$ or some related magnitude is the target variable. More precisely, the target variable will usually be, subject to certain constraints to be discussed below, $Y(n)/P(n) - Y(t)/P(t)$, or, more probably, $C(n)/P(n) - C(t)/P(t)$, where P is the population size. If P is expected to grow at the annual rate r and it is planned to raise per capita income or consumption by the annual rate g, then the target variable will be:

$$Y(n) = Y(t)(1+g)^{n-t}(1+r)^{n-t} \qquad (5)$$

or

$$C(n) = C(t)(1+g)^{n-t}(1+r)^{n-t} \qquad (6)$$

To achieve the indicated level of consumption, it will be necessary to achieve a level of $Y(n)$ which will permit $C(n)$ after allowance for $I(n)$, the investment needed in year n to attain targets beyond the plan period. Equation (5) will still remain a basic planning equation.

To achieve the target of equation (5), it will be necessary to raise I for the period $n-t$ to the level at which

$$\sum_{t=1}^{n-1} I = A \left[Y(t)(1+m)^{n-t}(1+r)^{n-t} - Y(t) \right] \qquad (7)$$

In a closed economy, the remaining question will then be how to raise the rate of saving in each year of the plan period to the level needed to finance the investment targeted for that year. If the economy is operating at less than full employment, the full employment level of government and private saving for each year can be estimated from the national income accounts. If government plus private saving will equal government plus private investment at full employment, then the macroplanning process is complete. However, if a deficiency of saving is indicated, the planner must then propose measures to reduce consumption by a sufficient amount, and if this is not deemed feasible, the targeted investment rates and the income target must be reduced.

Or, if measures can be taken to increase the efficiency of government or private investment, then perhaps the ICOR can be reduced and the income target achieved with less saving and investment than initially planned. However, reductions in the anticipated ICOR in order to make macroplans consistent are usually mainly decorative, and are a way of disguising the fact that the income target will not in fact be achieved.

In practice, of course, the economy will not be closed. In an open economy, the problem of determining whether the level of investment will be high enough and of taking measures to increase it if it is not high enough is more complex.

In such an economy, for each year, from the saving-investment identity:

$$I_d = S + M - X \tag{8}$$

where M = imports, X = exports, and I_d = investment within the economy (that is, excluding investment abroad), the sense in which the term investment is used throughout this discussion of planning.

Also,

$$I_d = S + I_{-f} + R_{-f} \tag{9}$$

where I_{-f} = net capital inflow, that is, the negative of investment abroad, and R_{-f} = net official plus private foreign aid, that is, transfers into the economy. For the excess of imports over exports must be financed by capital inflow and inward transfers.

In a neoclassical economy, in which it is assumed that productive resources are instantaneously shiftable from one use to another, it would be unnecessary to consider the terms on the right-hand of equation (8) separately. Only their sum, the analog of saving within a closed economy, need be considered by the planner. For in a neoclassical open economy, any deficiency of saving to finance intended investment—that is, any excess of demand within the economy—would immediately cause a shift from exports to production of goods for the domestic market. The excess of demand, which implies competition between consumption and investment for available goods, would also cause a rise in interest rates. The decline in net exports or rise in net imports would be lessened by a worsening of the foreign-exchange rate, making exports more and imports less attractive than at the old rate. The decrease in net exports or rise in net imports that did occur would temper the rise in interest rates. At the same time, the rise in interest rates and the worsening of the foreign exchange rate would increase I_{-f} (which in such an economy is only another aspect of the decrease in net exports or rise in net imports).

An equilibrium in equation (8) and simultaneously in equation (9) would be reached at full employment. If that equilibrium involved a rate of investment too low to permit carrying out the plan, the job of the planner would be to alter saving schedules (presumably through fiscal policy) so that the flow of saving increased sufficiently. There would be no other constraint on I_d.

Any excess of saving, that is, deficiency of domestic demand, would cause shifts opposite to those resulting from excess demand, and by permitting I_d above the planned level would permit the planner to raise his sights.

However, in a two-gap world, in which productive resources are not readily shiftable among uses, there would be a second constraint in I_d. Domestic investment would require a technically-determined flow of imports because of inability to produce various types of investment goods within the economy. Let us assume that there is no substitutability whatever between investment goods produced at home and those imported. We must then write:

$$I_d = H_I + M_I \tag{10}$$

where H_I = investment goods produced at home and M_I investment goods imported. Quite separately from his estimate of total resources available for investment, the planner must then estimate whether the volume of imports in each year technically necessary to carry out the plan can be financed. The sources of finance are exports, capital flow, and foreign aid.

$$M = X + I_{-f} + R_{-f} \tag{11}$$

Under the assumptions of the two-gap model, the terms on the right-hand side of equation (11) are determined outside the planning system, that is, are *data*. Exports may be estimated by extrapolation of past trends, by relationship to expected income in customer countries, by judgment of new opportunities, or by these plus other methods. Foreign exchange receipts from capital inflow and official and private foreign aid must also be estimated. The sum of the three indicates the imports that can be financed.

Further, the planner has,

$$M = M_C + M_I \tag{12}$$

If time series are available for government consumption expenditures, government investment, private consumption, and private investment for a past period, and if a classification of imports during the same period into those for these four purposes can be made, then the four types of future imports can be estimated by use of the indicated four relationships,

$$M = M_{CG} + M_{IG} + M_{Cp} + M_{Ip} \tag{12a}$$

If the data needed to estimate the four magnitudes on the right-hand side of equation (12a) are not available, some other (quite possibly cruder) method of estimating future import demand must be used. If the indicated total of imports is greater than the total that can be financed, the alternatives to be considered are restraint on private or government consumer imports, augmentation of foreign exchange receipts, or reduction in planned investment and in the income or consumption target.

At this point, also, interrupting his macroplanning, the planner will do a PERT analysis of the port and transportation facilities to be sure that the country will have the physical facilities to handle the capital goods imports (and other imports) at the time when it is planned to use them.

In these ways the planner will have established investment in years t, $t+1$, $t+2$, etc. (see equation [2]) at levels to serve his purposes within the constraints imposed by the initial conditions and the availability of resources. He will also be constrained by the availability of labor, management and administrative ability, entrepreneurial judgment, skills at all levels, and natural resources, but here we subsume all of those things within the value of A.

Up to this point we have been discussing how the planner arrives at a plan that is internally consistent. However, he wants to choose among alternative consistent plans the optimum one. Let us consider what his targets may be.

He will always balance the magnitudes of two or more variables. That is, he will optimize, rather than maximize. However, he may do so by maximizing some magnitude at some point in time or during a period of time subject to certain constraints about the level or rate of change of other magnitudes. (If he is doing his planning on a computer, he will follow this method because it is technically more feasible.)

If he wished to maximize the rate of output at the end of the plan period, he would adopt measures to reduce consumption during the period to the minimum necessary to permit working efficiency (or the minimum below which there would be successful social revolt). If he wished to maximize the rate of consumption at the end of the plan period, he would minimize consumption similarly until shortly before the end of the period (in order to maximize investment and thereby the growth of output), and then a short time before the end of the plan period would not only end all investment but so far as possible would convert capital goods to consumer goods up to the point at which the conversion was just balanced by the loss of production of consumer goods at that final point in time consequent on the reduction in capital inputs.

But he usually wishes to do neither of these things, though some periods of planning in the Soviet Union came close to the first alternative. Rather, he may wish to maximize output (or some type of output, for example military output or consumption) at the end of the plan period subject to the constraint that consumption per capita during the plan period shall not fall below a certain level, or shall rise at a certain rate. Or, he may plan to maximize the average level of consumption during the plan period, given some weights for the averaging that we have not yet defined. The averaging may give equal weight to each unit of consumption at any time period. It may discount future consumption at some positive rate of discount (thus regarding the material welfare of present consumers as of more importance than that of consumers at any future time). Or it may use weights derived from some other function that takes cognizance of the declining marginal utility of consumption, perhaps with a trend line that recognizes a rise in that marginal utility over time if the average level of consumption rises. Or there may be various other weighting devices, most of which are of more interest to the economic theorist than to a "real life" planner. In any event, his plans in any economy that has existed up to the present will be subject to the constraint that he wishes consumption or some other type of output to continue to rise after the end of the plan period.

Instead of explicit weights for averaging, he may adopt a rule such as: What is the maximum uniform rate of increase in consumption per capita that can be maintained during the plan period while leaving at the end of the period the capacity also to continue that rate indefinitely further in time? Or, some economic theorists have played with the problem: Given certain initial conditions, what are the qualities of various paths of approach to a continuing and equal rate of growth of capital and consumption?

MULTISECTORAL PLANNING

During much of the discussion above, we have implicitly treated the economy as though all consumption was homogeneous and all investment was also homogeneous except for the technically required imports. This assumption evades a central problem of planning. The planner must of course consider not only the allocation of resources between consumption and investment, or between government and private output in each of those categories, but also the allocation of investment and current inputs among the many sectors of the economy. He may conceivably ignore the distribution of income and consumption among sectors, letting the chips fall where they may, but he does so at his peril.

He will need to consider the allocation of resources not only among the major sectors of, say, agriculture, industry, transportation and communication, housing, and other services, but among the many subsectors of some of these fields, so that in discussing multisectoral planning we may have in mind from, say, 25 to 500 sectors. (Conceptually, each set of establishments producing a product different from other products is a separate sector, so that there are far more than 500.)

In practice, the planner will have been doing sector planning in some sectors before he did macroplanning, for he will have faced specific problems long before he had enough information about national income accounts to do macroplanning, and probably also long before he has enough levers of control to do macroplanning. He will plan certain sectors or establishments and, will-nilly, let the market do the macroplanning. He is likely to do some degree of planning concerning government output before he does much concerning private output. However, since the choice among government investment projects or current government outputs affects both the market supply of and demand for inputs and outputs, his planning will alter the outcome of the market forces even in sectors concerning which he is doing no explicit planning.

These comments of course apply to a mixed rather than centrally controlled economy, but they apply to the historical development of planning in present socialist economies as well. Only of primitive communism, in which control of production by decree existed from the dawn of time, would they be untrue.

There are two problems in multisectoral planning. One is a value question, the other a technical matter. The first may be thought of as a question of the competitive claims of sectors for resources; the second, as a matter of coordination among sectors. The first relates to the marginal utility of final products; the second, to supply relationships. One sector may not be able to produce without inputs from another.

Disregarding for the moment the problem of coordination, the planner must decide the optimum volume of output to be produced by each sector and therefore the amount of investment to be allocated to each sector.

In early economic theory, output was treated as though it was by atomistic firms producing a final product each entirely independently of the other firms. In such an economy, there would be no problem of sectoral planning except the relative utility of each type of output. The planner would need merely to allocate resources so as to equate the marginal utility of every type of product, so far as he could estimate marginal utility. There could hardly be said to be sectoral planning at all.

In an economy in which each sector provides inputs to other sectors, the criteria for allocation are more complex. Yet the same principles still apply, even though the utility (productivity) to one producer of the intermediate products produced by another must enter the calculation. What is the marginal utility of food or clothing, relative to that of industrial products? Roads are used for direct consumer enjoyment as well as to transport material products. What is their marginal utility for this final product use, relative to that of television sets or wheat? These questions are one aspect of the problem of balanced growth. The planner must take into account all of the considerations concerning balance or unbalance in growth discussed in Chapter 8: questions of the relative prices of different goods, of income distribution, of employment, and of the stimulus to further growth that will result from alternative allocations. He must also weigh external economies and diseconomies in deciding the true social marginal utility of each type of output, and then must decide whether the producer must bear the cost of the diseconomies, thus increasing the direct marginal utility his product must have to justify its production, or whether on account of external economies the cost of the diseconomies should be borne by some larger sector of the economy or perhaps widely by the economy as a whole.

In one-sector macroplanning, apart from the question of technically required imports, the problem of consistency in planning was primarily that of consistency between the demand for and supply of productive resources in the abstract—that is, generalized productive resources— though the calculation of the ICOR implicitly included consideration of many technical factors. In multisectoral planning, the question of the technical consistency of resource allocations becomes central. The output of every sector requires inputs from other sectors. (There may be minor exceptions.)

There are few intermediate products for which the amount required as an input per unit of some other product is absolutely fixed, regardless of price. As a first approximation, however, in much of his planning the planner will assume that there are fixed coefficients. He will do so not merely to simplify his already complex job but also to avoid putting too much strain on the adaptability of producers. The required volume of an intermediate product used in only one other sector may be estimated by simple regression. Where technical change is not rapid, the estimates derived thus may be satisfactory. If it was assumed that the increase in demand for chemical fertilizer in each type of agricultural production would be proportional to the increase in output, or in acreage seeded, or in the volume of seed used, the estimate would be badly in error. The error involved in ignoring the use of natural fertilizers might not be serious, but that in ignoring the rapid increase in fertilizer use because of technical change would be fatal. However, for the time being let us set aside the problem of technical change.

Disregarding it, the needs of each sector of the economy from every other sector in the production of any feasible final bill of goods can readily be calculated on a high-speed computer if the planner has the information needed for an input-output matrix. (It is assumed that the reader understands input-output analysis.)

A matrix for any one year is of only limited use for planning purposes. A matrix is wanted for some future year, say the last year of a plan period, $t + n$. First, then, a bill of goods for that year must be determined. It must depend on the level of aggregate output that can be attained, but that in turn depends on the inputs that will be available, the sectors in which they will be employed, and the productivity they will have attained in those sectors. The problem is very complex, for we cannot ignore the increases in capacity in the various industries that will be needed to produce the $t + n$ bill of goods, and should not ignore the increases in output per unit of input that will presumably accompany the needed investment, and indeed may occur even in the absence of investment.

The capacity in each industry will depend on the investment projects that have been completed by the year $t + n - 1$. Some of these will not be completed then unless they were in progress in the year $t + n - 2$ and unless other projects had been ready by that year. So on back to the present year, with the further important provision that the capital and consumption goods output that must be produced in the present year t in order to achieve the results in the year $t + 1$ that are needed to achieve the needed output in the year $t + 2$, and so on up to $t + n$, must be consistent with the productive capacity that exists in the year t. Perhaps the problem is not solvable. Perhaps, given the economy's capacity in the year t, there is no sequence by which the desired bill of goods for the year $t + n$ can be produced. To determine by successive approximations whether the problem is solvable and to determine the pattern of production from t to $t + n$ by which it can be solved would be impossibly complex except for the existence of high-speed computers.

Chenery wrote in 1971 that such matters could be handled, using linear relationships, for 200 sectors and a single time period, 10–30 sectors and 5–10 time periods, or 1 or 2 sectors and 100 time periods. Four years later, the statement is obsolete. The computational capacity of computers has doubled or tripled. The increase in complexity of models that can be handled will presumably continue to increase at this very rapid rate.

In an appendix to this chapter, I outline briefly one programming model, that of Richard S. Eckaus and Kirit Parikh for India. It illustrates the problems of modeling mentioned above, and others. Even though now, almost ten years after that model was prepared, far more complex models are possible, three fundamental problems still remain.

It is possible to design a pattern of investment and output, year by year, to construct the necessary set of equations to test whether the pattern is *consistent* with the availability of resources and the final bill of goods, and to solve the set of equations on a high-speed computer. If the plan is not consistent, the planner can then prepare alternative ones and submit them to the computer, one by one. However, the technique by which the computer could be given criteria and then asked to select the *optimum* pattern of investment and output—one that would maximize some one set of magnitudes, for example, a consumption mix varying depending on how large the total might be, subject to constraints about total investment, government expenditures, exports, and imports year by year—involves computational requirements that are very large even for the latest electronic computers.

Second, the algebraic relationships assumed to exist in the economy must be linear, because of the computational complexity if they involve higher powers. The direct incorporation into the model of income or price elasticities, economies of scale, and diminishing returns to investment is thereby ruled out. In some cases, linear approximations may substitute. If changes in input coefficients from year to year resulting from any of these factors, or from investment or technical advance, can be estimated, they can be allowed for by changing the coefficients in the model from year to year. (An input coefficient is the number of units of an input—which may be the output of another sector—required per unit of output.) Other rather awkward substitutes for nonlinear relationships may be devised. Exponential trends or relationships may be handled by means of logarithmic linearity.

The other problem has little to do with computational capacity. Over any time period, because of technical advance, changes in input-output coefficients will occur that are not merely uniform increases in output per unit of each input. Because of these changes, the coefficients used in a matrix for the year $t + n$ will be considerably in error. Moreover, even in the most advanced economy, equipped with elaborate statistics, the computation of an input-output matrix requires several years because of the complexity of the data that must be gathered and analyzed. A set of coefficients available in the year t will be those of a year at least several years earlier, and will therefore be somewhat obsolete. By the year $t + n$ they will be more obsolete because of technical changes that will have emerged in production in the meantime. The computation for the year $t + n$, in short, requires movement from obsolescing coefficients to speculative ones. There will therefore be considerable error.

Even if the planning matrix for a future year in some sense were precisely accurate, only an economy that was already superbly well developed technically and institutionally could respond to inducements, constraints, and administrative directions so as to fine-tune its performance in the ways indicated by an elaborate plan. Witness the shortage of petroleum refining capacity in the United States in 1974 and the prospective shortage in that year of primary processing capacity in a number of U.S. industries. Indeed, only an imaginary economy could comply with the programming involved in the use of an elaborate input-output matrix in development planning.

It is apparent, then, that the conception of guiding development planning in a less developed economy by even an only modestly elaborate input-output matrix and programming based on it is a fantasy. By definition, the problem of economic development is the problem of the absence

of the necessary administrative, managerial, entrepreneurial, and technical ability, and in any event the necessary information for so elaborate a
techno-economic operation. Even in the Soviet Union at the present time
the planning process is much cruder than the process described above. In
economies in which the price system is allowed within modest constraints
to equate demand and supply in the short run and to induce increased
supply in the somewhat longer run, there may be a reasonably good fit in
the interindustry relations, but this carries no implication that the relationships will be what a planner had anticipated. Models involving elaborately quantified input-output and programming analysis are of interest
to economic theorists, not to planning bodies or administrators in LDCs,
though of course there is much variation among LDCs and the degree of
irrelevance of the computations depends on the state of development of
the country.

Yet the *concept* of an input-output matrix is of use in planning in all
but the least developed countries. A picture in the minds of officials
involved with development planning that output in any sector requires
flows from other sectors may remind the officials of questions they ought
to ask. Will we have enough power in that region if these projects are
carried out? Will there be enough water for both the factory and the
power plant? Where will the cement be obtained? Will there be repair
and service facilities for the machinery we intend to make available to
farmers? Will our port facilities and transportation from the ports be
adequate? Etc. A mental schema that will place a nagging question
always in the minds of planners: What have I overlooked? is an invalu-
able adjunct to planning. This, one may judge, is the main value of the
concept of input-output matrices and economy-wide programming in all
or almost all of the LDCs of the world. Implicitly, the planner is filling in
the matrix, and even if the filling in must by the crudest of subjective
judgment, it is important that the necessity to do it be realized.

There are two equilibrating mechanisms that will adjust for some of
the inadequacies of planning as planning has been discussed above:
prices and foreign trade. Input-output analysis assumes that a production
function has fixed coefficients. Almost no production function has; there is
almost always some adjustment that can be made in the use of a given
input, and that will be made if its price rises or falls markedly. The
dependence of any development program on imports of some inputs has
been discussed above. Indeed, in planning more adequately defined,
prices and imports are not correctives but rather integral instruments of
planning.

THE LIMITATIONS OF PLANNING

Planning is not achievement. The formulation of plans may become a
substitute for achievement. A reader who has experience in governmental

administration of economic development in a less developed country, and who has read this chapter, may have said to himself with some dismay, "What does all this have to do with economic development?" and may have answered his own question, "Very little."

There is a sense in which this is true. Colin Leys made the attack piercingly at a conference on development planning: "The underlying concept of planning contradicts the basic concept of politics." "Central planners seemed doomed . . . to progressively lose touch." "Indeed the very choice of economics—which is well known to be a branch of metaphysics—may imply a preference for dealing with concepts rather than people."[1]

The implication of these remarks is that planning ignores the realities of political structure and political processes, the need to get persons to do things. The criticism has substance; if it were possible to rank all development plans with respect to their elegance, and to rank the effectiveness of countries' performance, there might be zero or negative correlation between the two rankings. But it would not follow that the elegance of the formal plans caused the lack of achievement. Officials who are not much interested in economic welfare or who shrink from attempting to bring about the changes necessary for more effective performance may take refuge in contemplating formal plans, but to assume that they would act more effectively if they did not have the plans to contemplate is a non sequitur.

It is rare that the precision of requirements indicated in an input-output matrix of say 40 sectors has much relevance to the development problems of a low-income country. The judgment of a judicious planner concerning where the bottlenecks will be—skilled workers, steel capacity, port congestion, ability to budget—may be as good a guide to needed action as the indications given by the input-output matrix, or by the best linear programming model that the data available make possible. Yet the model may be a powerful aid. The model is not a substitute for his judgment, but a way of quantifying that judgment, of testing his "intuitions." The purpose of planning is to indicate to officials the indirect economic technical requirements and results of their programs.

PERSPECTIVE PLANNING

I have referred at several points above to the need in any plan to lay the basis for continuing development beyond the plan period. In a certain sense, the operational plan period is always a single year, since this is virtually everywhere the budgeting period. A multiyear (say five-year) plan is a necessary frame for the annual budgeting, since an annual horizon is completely inadequate.

---

[1] M. Faber and D. Seers, eds. (1972), vol. 1, pp. 62, 74, and 30, respectively.

By parallel, a "perspective plan" containing a vision of the goal for say 15 years in the future is a necessary frame for the 5-year plan. The parallel is not complete. The perspective plan will usually not contain three elaborated five-year plans. Its presentation of what will be done beyond the first five years will usually be only sketchy. But a picture of the volume and general content of output that can realistically be expected 15 (or 20) years in the future will both constrain the 5-year plan and, especially, determine some of its emphasis.

A new program is less threatening and more interesting to individuals, the greater the degree to which they regard it as their program. For this reason, which may be of especial importance in "traditional" societies, a plan worked out in cooperation with the operating agencies that looks highly imperfect to a development economist may be much superior to a "better" plan worked out solely by more capable individuals in the planning agency. For the first plan may be carried out, while the second one remains on paper. The problem is compounded if the plan was worked out not even by the indigeneous officials of the planning agencies, but by foreign advisers.

A plan must be worked out with the operating agencies, not merely collected from them. A plan cannot be merely a sum of what individual ministries wish to do, precisely because of the intersectoral relationships that have figured prominently in the discussion of this chapter. One duty of the planner is therefore to create an understanding in each agency of those interrelationships and thereby of the need for each ministry to adjust its plans to take account of the needs of development projects and programs in other agencies. That is, the traditional prerogative of each minister to have the little-qualified right to do what he pleases within this area of authority with the resources available to him must be infringed upon. In some cases, this adaptability cannot be achieved except by the replacement of subministerial officials or of the ministers themselves. This may be impossible for entirely valid political reasons. One alternative is to bypass the ministers by creating new positions to accomplish the functions, while leaving the ministers in their positions. This device, far from a perfect substitute for replacement, was much used by President Franklin D. Roosevelt in the United States in the 1930s, even though no traditional prerogatives were involved. To the degree that one or the other device is impossible, or that qualified individuals motivated to perform the necessary functions cannot be found, development may falter. That faltering should not be blamed on the existence of development planning or modeling. It may be due to the inadequate understanding of the chief planning official of the necessary nature of a realistic planning process, but on the other hand it may be due to obstacles that no man, no matter how resourceful, could have overcome. In the process of trying to overcome them, the development economist is only the handmaiden, not the sole architect, of development, but he is a very important handmaiden.

APPENDIX

THE ECKAUS-PARIKH PROGRAMMING MODEL

Illustrative of multisector planning models are S. Chakravarty and Louis Lefeber (1965), Alan Manne and Thomas E. Weisskopf (1969), M. Bruno, M. Fraenkel, and C. Daugherty (1968), and Richard S. Eckaus and Kirit Parikh (1967). That by Eckaus and Parikh is outlined briefly here.

Within the limitations stated in the text and the limitations of available data, the feasibility or consistency of a proposed production program—for example, a five-year plan—can be checked by linear programming.

It is also possible by linear programming to calculate the most efficient allocation of resources to meet given objectives, in a similarly aggregated and simplified model of the economy. The simplifications made necessary by the requirement of linearity are such that the procedure will usually evaluate only rather gross allocational alternatives, but even this evaluation may indicate significant implications of development programs that are not revealed by other analysis. The method, and both its limitations and value, may be illustrated by outlining the Eckaus-Parikh linear programming analysis of India's third Five Year Plan, for this period 1961–62 to 1966–67.[2]

The model has 11 sectors: agriculture and plantations; mining and metals; equipment; chemicals and fertilizers; cement, glass, and wood; food and clothing manufacturers; electrical generation; transportation; construction; housing; and other and margin. The only scarce inputs other than the intersectoral inputs and productive capacity (capital equipment) at the beginning of the plan period are capital and foreign exchange; labor is treated as available in excess supply.

Each sector's input coefficients of capital, imports, and outputs of other sectors were estimated from Indian data. The model takes as one constraint the increase in productive capacity in each sector during the five-year period stated or implicit in the Five Year Plan. The model assumes that to yield productive capacity in any year t, one third of the investment indicated by the capital coefficient (the incremental fixed-capital-output ratio) must be made in year $t-3$, one third in $t-2$, and one third in $t-1$.

---

[2] Eckaus and Parikh (1967). A summary of the model is presented in Eckaus (1967), in which comments by E. S. Mason and Alan S. Manne are included. I am grateful to Professor Eckaus for comments on the first draft of my summary of the nature of the Eckaus-Parikh model. He bears no other responsibility for the final draft.

Other constraints are increase in inventories (estimated as a ratio to increase in output in each sector), exports from various sectors (estimated at a constant 4% rate of annual increase from the initial level), government consumption of the products of each sector (estimated at a 2.5% rate of annual increase from the initial level), and the replacement of capital fully depreciated in that year (estimated exogenously), if the calculations show that the replacement of the capacity for later use is justified. Initial conditions are capacity in each sector, that coming into being during the first years of the plan period from earlier investment, and the initial levels of imports, exports, and government consumption. Terminal conditions are enough capital formation going on at the end of the plan to sustain in the postplan period the programmed rate of growth of output during the plan period. Imports not competitive with Indian production are estimated at ratios to output in the importing sectors; remaining foreign exchange available from exports plus foreign aid (assumed to be $500 million per year) is allocated among other imports in ratios proportional to the previous quantities of these imports, with the qualification that not more than a given share may go to any sector. These are competitive imports; they augment the supply of inputs to the various productive sectors.

Consumption is treated as a single composite good composed of output from the various consumer goods sectors in fixed proportions. (In view of the fairly slow increase in per capita incomes, no annual variation in the weights of the components to reflect differing income elasticities was thought necessary.) The result is that in the initial model, total estimated consumption in each year is limited by the consumer goods output capacity of any sector that is a bottleneck, even though excess capacity exists in other consumer goods sectors.

The model is programmed to maximize the weighted value of consumption during the five-year period subject to these constraints. A rate of discount of 10% per year is used, to weight the consumption of the various years. One difficulty typical of models of this general nature arose: the model tended to concentrate all production of consumer goods in the last years of the period if any rate of discount up to a certain rate was used, then to concentrate it all in the first years at higher rates of discount. At a 10% discount rate, the latter occurred. This "flip-flop" behavior was prevented by a "monotonicity constraint": the model was instructed to increase consumption from each year to the next by not less than a specified percentage. Such a constraint is of course reasonable on social welfare grounds; it was not introduced merely to prevent a "flip-flop."

The solution of such a model yields the optimum allocation price of each primary input (in this case, capital and foreign exchange); the price of imports derived from the world price and the shadow foreign exchange rate; and from the cost of the inputs, the shadow price (what might be termed the shadow cost) of each sector's output. Subject to the capital needs in sectors in which the model is instructed to produce specified amounts of output (for government, exports, etc.), and to the need to maximize over the period a steadily increasing level of output, the model allocates capital to bottleneck sectors until bottlenecks are broken, and thereafter to all sectors in such a way as to maximize the weighted value of total consumption. Where excess capacity is shown in any year, investment is allocated to the sector only if the calculations show that investment to increase capacity for later use is justified relative to investment in other sectors.

The solution showed that no possible allocation of productive re-sources, even with consumption at zero, would yield the 5% per year increase in aggregate productive capacity implicit in the Five Year Plan. The main reasons no doubt are the magnitude of the capacity increase targeted, the existence of capacity bottlenecks in some sectors, and the assumption of lags before investment would remove them. Because of the assumption of fixed-input coefficients, plus the assumption that capital already in place in one industry cannot be shifted to another, neither imports nor excess capacity in other sectors could be applied to remove the bottlenecks, and even massive investment in the first year would not necessarily remove them until the fourth. In the first year a bottleneck in the construction industry prevented full utilization of capacity in any other sector, and until the last year bottlenecks in the construction, equipment, and mining and metals sectors prevented full utilization of capacity in any sector except these three.

A reduction of the planned growth in aggregate productive capacity of 4%, or from 5% to about 4.15% per year, made the plan technically feasible, but with average aggregate annual consumption only a little more than one half that in 1959–60. When the assumption of fixed-input coefficients was abandoned, and the idle capacity in the major consumer goods sectors was allocated among the various sectors, the model showed that with the reduced growth target consumption could be maintained at an average annual rate of a little above the 1959–60 level—too little above to hold per capita consumption constant with a population increase of 2% per year. If 100% of the planned growth rate were to be achieved in the model, consumption would have to be appreciably lower, even if it is assumed that idle productive capacity in one industry could be immedi-ately shifted to increase production of the products of another sector. Thus the model suggests that the plan's targets were inconsistent with a politically feasible level of consumption. Specifically, the model brings the capital-output ratios implicit in the plan into question. The model indicates that to attain output capacity equal to 96% of the Third Plan targets, net investment of more than 160 billion rupees would have been required, whereas the plan estimated a need of only 100 billion rupees to achieve the full targets.

The authors programmed various other alternative "runs." In some of these they increased exports, to finance increased imports. This turned out to make the attainment of a higher growth rate (or higher consumption) possible, even though it simultaneously reduced the amount of domestic resources available for investment and thus left the saving rate unchanged. That is, in this Indian model, as in most of the alternative cases of the simpler Chenery-Strout model, the import gap is greater than the saving gap.

The model is, of course, rather inflexible. The inability of the model to allow for adaptations in consumption and production occasioned by the relative scarcity of some inputs and some goods is very unrealistic. So also is not permitting the use of idle capacity in some consumer goods industries because of the low level of capacity in others—but not as unrealistic as it might seem, for a chief bottleneck industry in the model was food production, and Indian consumers did in fact divert income from other uses to food purchases when food scarcity caused food prices to rise. Moreover, the inflexibilities were allowed for by the authors in a rough way in the supplementary runs after the first runs had shown excess capacity. The aggregative input coefficients have wide margins of error. But this is because of inadequacy of data, not because of the programming technique; if more precise capital-output ratios are not available for use in a programming model, they are not available for any other use. The authors did not allow for changes in input coefficients made possible by investment and by technical advances. Neither did they take into account many policy alternatives.[3] However, in any other planning procedure these changes in coefficients and the possible effects of these policy alternatives can be allowed for only in a rough-and-ready way, and similar allowances can be made in the results shown by the programming model. In spite of its inflexibility, linear programming can improve the basis for planning by showing in precise quantitative form the implications of whatever is known about input coefficients.

BIBLIOGRAPHICAL NOTE

H. B. Chenery, ed. (1971), is much the best one volume as introduction to the construction of planning models. See also the models mentioned above in the first paragraph of the appendix of this chapter.

---

[3] E. S. Mason lists many of these in his "Comments" in Eckaus (1967).

List of References

References are listed alphabetically by author, and under each author by year of publication, with the following exceptions. Annual publications are listed by title, before publications by the same organization listed by date. Since several United Nations publications, other than annual reports, which are listed, may bear the same date, a short form of the title has been used in the text which is easily identifiable by reference to the complete title listed here. The series of publications by Simon Kuznets, *Quantitative Aspects of the Economic Growth of Nations,* referred to in the text as (*Q.A.E.G.N.,* 1), etc., is listed as a group before other publications by Kuznets listed by date.

The following books of reprinted essays are referred to by the abbreviations indicated. Indication that an essay is reprinted in one or more of these volumes is given following the citation of the original source. In all of the volumes except that by Agarwala and Singh, passages are sometimes omitted in reprinting.

A–S AGARWALA, A. N., and S. P. SINGH, (eds.), *The Economics of Underdevelopment* (London: Oxford University Press, 1958).

M MEIER, GERALD M., *Leading Issues in Development Economics* (New York: Oxford University Press, 1964).

M–B–C MORGAN, THEODORE, GEORGE W. BETZ, and N. K. CHOUDHRY, eds., *Readings in Economics Development* (Belmont, Calif.: Wadsworth Publishing Co., Inc., 1963).

O–R OKUN, BERNARD and RICHARD W. RICHARDSON, *Studies in Economic Development* (New York: Holt, Rinehart and Winston, 1961).

Following are abbreviations of the titles of journals and names of organizations used in the text and in the listing below, together with the full title.

517

A.E.R. . . . . .   *American Economic Review*
E.D.C.C. . . .   *Economic Development and Cultural Change*
E.J. . . . .   *Economic Journal*
J.E.S. . . . . . .   *Journal of Economic Studies*
J.P.E. . . . . . .   *Journal of Political Economy*
Q.J.E. . . . . . .   *Quarterly Journal of Economics*
U.N. . . . .   United Nations
R.E. Statistics   *Review of Economics and Statistics*
FAO . . . . . .   Food and Agriculture Organization
IBRD . . . . . .   International Bank for Reconstruction and Development
N.B.E.R. . . .   National Bureau of Economic Research
OECD . . . . .   Organization for Economic Cooperation and Development
U.N.:ECAFE   United Nations Economic Commission for Asia and the Far
                     East
U.N.:ECLA   United Nations Economic Commission for Latin America
W.D. . . . . . .   *World Development*

ABEGGLEN, J. C.   **1958.** *The Japanese Factory.* Glencoe, Ill.: The Free Press.
———   **1973.** *Management and Worker: The Japanese Solution.* Tokyo:
Sophia University.
———, and W. L. WARNER   **1955.** *Occupational Mobility in American Business and Industry, 1928–1952.* Minneapolis, Minn.: University of Minnesota Press.
ABRAMOVITZ, M.   **1956.** *Resource and Output Trends in the United States Since 1870.* N.B.E.R. Occasional Paper 52. New York: N.B.E.R. Reprinted from *A.E.R.,* 46 (May 1956): 5–23.
———, and others.   **1959.** *The Allocation of Economic Resources.* Stanford, Calif.: Stanford University Press.
ADELMAN, I.   **1962.** *Theories of Economic Growth and Development.* Stanford, Calif.: Stanford University Press.
———   **1963.** An Econometric Analysis of Population Growth. *A.E.R.,* 53 (June): 314–39.
———   **1966.** A Linear Programming Model of Educational Planning: A Case Study of Argentina. With comment by S. Bowles. Chap. 14 of Adelman and Thorbecke (1966).
———, and C. T. MORRIS   **1965.** Factor Analysis of the Interrelationship between Social and Political Variables and Per Capita Gross National Product. *Q.J.E.,* 79 (Nov.): 555–607.
———   **1967.** *Society, Politics, and Economic Development: A Quantitative Approach.* Baltimore: Johns Hopkins Press.
———   **1973.** *Economic Growth and Social Equity in Developing Countries.* Stanford, Calif.: Stanford University Press.
———, and E. THORBECKE, eds.   **1966.** *The Theory and Design of Economic Development.* Baltimore: Johns Hopkins Press.
AITKEN, H. G., ed.   **1959.** *The State and Economic Growth.* New York: Social Science Research Council.

ALEXANDER, A. P.   **1960.** Industrial Entrepreneurship in Turkey: Origins and Growth. *E.D.C.C.*, 8 (July): 349–65.

ALLEN, R. G. D.   **1953.** *Mathematical Analysis for Economists.* London: Macmillan and Co., Ltd.

ALMOND, G. A., J. S. COLEMAN, and others   **1960.** *The Politics of the Developing Areas.* Princeton, N.J.: Princeton University Press.

ALTER, G. M.   **1961.** The Servicing of Foreign Capital Inflows by Underdeveloped Countries. In Ellis (1961).

AMERICAN ECONOMIC ASSOCIATION and THE ROYAL ECONOMIC SOCIETY **1966.** *Surveys of Economic Theory: Growth and Development,* vol. 2 New York: St. Martin's Press.

AMES, E., and N. ROSENBERG   **1963.** Changing Technological Leadership and Industrial Growth. *E.J.*, 73 (Mar.): 13–31.

ANDERSON, C. A., and M. J. BOWMAN, eds.   **1965.** *Education and Economic Development.* Chicago: Aldine Publishing Co.

ANDERSON, H. H.   **1959.** *Creativity and Its Cultivation.* New York: Harper & Bros.

ARAK, M.   **1967.** *The Supply of Brazilian Coffee.* Unpublished dissertation, Massachusetts Institute of Technology.

ARROW, K. J.   **1962.** The Economic Implications of Learning by Doing. *R.E. Statistics,* 29 (June): 154–94.

———, H. B. CHENERY, B. S. MINHAS, and R. M. SOLOW   **1961.** Capital Labor Substitution and Economic Efficiency. *R.E. Statistics,* 48 (August): 225–50.

ASHER, R. E., and others.   **1962.** *Development of the Emerging Countries: An Agenda for Research.* Washington: Brookings Institution.

ASHTON, T. S.   **1948.** *The Industrial Revolution, 1760–1830.* London: Oxford University Press.

———   **1955.** *An Economic History of England: The 18th Century.* London: Methuen & Co., Ltd.

AUJAC, H.   **1954.** Inflation as the Monetary Consequence of the Behavior of Social Groups: A Working Hypothesis. *International Economic Papers,* 4: 109–23.

AUKRUST, O., and J. BJERKE   **1959.** Real Capital and Economic Growth in Norway 1900–1956. In I.A.R.I.W., *The Measurement of National Wealth,* Income and Wealth series 8. London: Bowes and Bowes.

AZIZ, SARTAJ   **1973.** The Chinese Approach to Rural Development. *Internal Development Review,* 15, no. 4: pp. 2–7.

BAER, W.   **1973.** The Brazilian Boom 1968–72: An Explanation and Interpretation. *W.D.*, 1 (Aug.).

BAERRESEN, D. W., M. CARNOY, and J. GRUNWALD   **1965.** *Latin American Trade Patterns.* Washington: Brookings Institution.

BAIROCH, B., and J. LIMBOR   **1968.** Evolution de la Population Active dans le Monde par Branches d'Activite et par Regions, 1880–1960. *International Labour Review,* 98 (Oct.).

BALASSA, B.   **1963.** *The Problem of Growth in Less Developed Countries and Its Significance for O.E.C.D. Policy.* Paris. OECD.

———— **1964.** The Capital Needs of the Developing Countries. *Kyklos,* 17, 197–206.

———— **1970.** Growth Strategies in Semi-industrial Countries. *Q.J.E.,* 84 (Feb.).

———— **1971.** Industrial Policies in Taiwan and Korea. *Weltwirtschaftliches Archiv,* band 106, heft 1: 63.

———— **1973.** Just How Misleading Are Official Exchange Rate Conversions? A Comment. *E.J.,* 83 (Dec.): 1258–67.

BALDWIN, G. B.   **1959.** *Industrial Growth in South India.* Glencoe, Ill.: The Free Press.

BALDWIN, R. E., and others.   **1965.** *Trade, Growth, and the Balance of Payments—Essays in Honor of Gottfried Haberler.* Chicago: Rand McNally.

BANFIELD, E. C.   **1958.** *The Moral Basis of a Backward Society.* New York: Free Press.

BARAN, P. A.   **1952.** On the Political Economy of Backwardness. *The Manchester School,* 20 (Jan.): 66–84. Reprinted in A–S.

———— **1957.** *The Political Economy of Backwardness.* New York: Monthly Review Press.

BARDHAN, P. K.   **1964.** Factor Market Disequilibrium and the Theory of Protection. *Oxford Economic Papers,* 16 (Oct.).

———— **1967.** Chinese and Indian Agriculture: A Broad Comparison of Recent Policy Performance. Unpublished draft manuscript, Massachusetts Institute of Technology.

BARNETT, H. J.   **1959.** *Malthusianism and Conservation.* Washington: Resources for the Future, Inc. (In slightly abridged form in N.B.E.R., 1960.)

————, and C. MORSE   **1963.** *Scarcity and Growth—The Economics of Natural Resource Availability.* Baltimore: Johns Hopkins Press for Resources for the Future.

BARRACLOUGH, S. and A. L. DOMIKE   **1966.** La Estructura Agraria en Siete Paises de America Latina. *El Trimestre Economico,* 33 (April–June): 235–301.

BASTER, NANCY, ed.   **1972.** *Measuring Development: The Role and Adequacy of Development Indicators.* London: Frank Cass and Company, Ltd.

BATEMAN, M.   **1965.** Aggregate and Regional Supply Functions for Ghanaian Cocoa, 1946–1962. *Journal of Farm Economics,* 48 (May): 384–401.

BATES, M.   **1952.** *Where Winter Never Comes.* New York: Charles Scribner's Sons.

BAUER, P. T.   **1954.** *West African Trade: A Study of Competition, Oligopoly and Monopoly in a Changing Economy.* Cambridge: Cambridge University Press.

———— **1972.** *Dissent on Development: Studies and Debates in Development Economics.* Cambridge, Mass.: Harvard University Press.

————, and B. S. YAMEY   **1951.** Economic Progress and Occupational Distribution, *E.J.,* 61 (Dec.): 741–55. Reprinted in O–R, M–B–C.

BECKER, G. S.   **1960.** An Economic Analysis of Fertility. In *Demographic and Economic Change in Developed Countries.* Princeton, N.J.: Princeton University Press.

————— 1962. Investment in Human Capital: A Theoretical Analysis. *J.P.E.*, (supplement, Oct.).

BECKER, G. T. **1964.** *Human Capital*, N.B.E.R. New York: Columbia University Press.

BECKERMAN, W. **1966.** International Comparisons of Real Incomes. Paris: OECD.

—————, and associates **1965.** *The British Economy in 1975.* New York: Cambridge University Press.

—————, and R. BACON **1966.** International Comparisons of Income Levels: A Suggested New Measure. *E.J.*, 76 (Sept.): 518–36.

BEHRMAN, J. **1966.** The Price Elasticity of the Marketed Surplus of a Subsistence Corp. *Journal of Farm Economics,* 48 (Nov.): 875–93.

BENOIT, E. **1972a.** A Rejoinder to Professor Dorfman's Comment. *International Development Review,* 14, no. 1.

————— **1972b.** Growth Effects of Defense in Developing Countries. *International Development Review,* 14, no. 1.

BERGSMAN, J. **1970.** *Brazil: Industrialization and Trade Policies.* Oxford: Oxford University Press. (For the OECD Development Center)

BERGSTEN, F. C. **1974.** The New Era in World Commodity Markets. *Challenge* (Sept.-Oct.).

BHAGWATI, J. N. **1966.** *The Economics of Underdeveloped Countries.* New York: McGraw-Hill Book Co.

————— **1969.** *Trade, Tariffs, and Growth.* Cambridge, Mass.: MIT Press.

—————, and P. DESAI **1970.** *India: Planning for Industrialization.* Oxford: Oxford University Press. (For the OECD Development Center)

—————, and R. S. ECKAUS, eds. **1972.** *Development and Planning.* London: George Allen & Unwin.

—————, and others, eds. **1971.** *Trade, Balance of Payments and Growth,* Papers on International Economics in Honor of C. P. Kindleberger. Amsterdam: North Holland Publishing Co.

—————, and V. K. RAMASWAMI **1963.** Domestic Distortions, Tariffs, and the Theory of Optimum Subsidy. *J.P.E.*, 71 (Feb.): 44–50.

BIRD, R., and O. OLDMAN, eds. **1964.** *Readings on Taxation in Developing Countries.* Baltimore: Johns Hopkins Press.

BLITZ, R. C. **1958.** Capital Longevity and Economic Planning. *A.E.R.*, 48 (June): 313–29.

BOEKE, J. H. **1953.** *Economics and Economic Policy of Dual Societies.* New York: Institute of Pacific Relations.

BOGUE, D. J. **1966.** Recent Developments in Family Planning That Promise Hope in Coping with the Population Crisis in Asia and Throughout the World. Paper no. 1 prepared for *Congress Symposium No. 1, Population Problems in the Pacific, 11th Pacific Science Congress,* August 23–26. Tokyo: University of Tokyo.

BOSERUP, E. **1965.** *The Conditions of Agricultural Growth: The Economics of Agrarian Change under Population Pressure.* Chicago: Aldine Publishing Co.

BOWEN, W. G.   1962. *Assessing the Economic Contribution of Education: An Appraisal of Alternative Approaches.* Paris: OECD.

BOWLES, S.   1967. The Efficient Allocation of Resources in Education. *Q.J.E.,* 81 (May): 189–219.

———   1970. Aggregation of Labor Inputs in the Economics of Growth and Planning: Experiments with a Two-Level CES Function. *J.P.E.,* 78 (Jan.–Feb.): 68–81.

BOWMAN, M. J.   See Anderson, C. A.

BRADY, D. S.   1951. Research on the Size Distribution of Income. *Studies in Income and Wealth,* vol. 9. New York: N.B.E.R.

BROADBRIDGE, S.   1966. *Industrial Dualism in Japan.* Chicago: Aldine Publishing Co.

BRONFENBRENNER, M.   1953. The High Cost of Economic Development. *Land Economics,* 29 (May–Aug.): 93–104, 209–18. Reprinted in M–B–C.

———   1955. The Appeal of Confiscation in Economic Development. *E.D.C.C.,* 3 (Apr.): 201–18. Reprinted in A–S.

———   1963. Second Thoughts on Confiscation. *E.D.C.C.,* 11 (July): 367–71.

BROWN, E. H. P.   See Phelps Brown, E. H.

BRUNO, M.   1962. *Interdependence, Resource Use and Structural Change in Israel.* Jerusalem: Bank of Israel Research Dept.

———, M. FRAENKEL and C. DAUGHERTY   1968. *Dynamic Input-Output, Trade, and Development.* Jerusalem: Bank of Israel and Hebrew University. Mimeo.

BRUTON, H. J.   1965.   *Principles of Development Economics.* Englewood Cliffs, N.J.: Prentice-Hall, Inc.

———   1969. The Two-gap Approach to Aid and Development: Comment. *A.E.R.,* 59 (June): 439–46.

———   1974. Economic Development and Labor Use: A Review. In E. O. Edwards (1974).

BUCK, J. L.   1937. *Chinese Farm Economy and Land Utilization in China.* Chicago: University of Chicago Press.

CAIRNCROSS, A. K.   1962. *Factors in Economic Development.* London: George Allen & Unwin, Ltd.

———.   1964. Capital Formation in the Take-Off. In Rostow (1964).

CAMPBELL, R.   1965. Economics: Roads and Inroads. *Problems of Communism,* 14 (Nov.): 23–33.

CAMPOS, R.   1961. Inflation and Balanced Growth. In Ellis and Wallich (1961).

CARLIN, A.   1967. Project versus Programme Aid: From the Donor's Viewpoint. *E.J.,* 77 (Mar.): 48–58.

CARROLL, T. F.   1961. The Land Reform Issue in Latin America. In Hirschman (1961).

CARTER, C. F. and B. R. WILLIAMS   1958. *Investment in Innovation.* London: Oxford University Press.

CARUS-WILSON, E. M.   1941. An Industrial Revolution of the Thirteenth Century. *Economic History Review,* vol. 11, no. 1. 39–60.

CAVES, R. E.   1965. Vent for Surplus' Models of Trade and Growth. In R. E.

Baldwin and others, eds., *Trade, Growth and the Balance of Payments: Essays in Honor of Gottfried Haberler.* Chicago and Amsterdam: Rand McNally and North Holland Publishing Co., pp. 95–115.

————, and R. H. Holton 1959. *The Canadian Economy: Prospect and Retrospect.* Harvard Economic Studies, no. 112. Cambridge, Mass.: Harvard University Press.

————, and R. W. Jones 1973. *World Trade and Payments.* Boston: Little, Brown and Co.

Chakravasty, S. and L. Lefeber 1965. An Optimizing Planning Model. *Economic Weekly* (Bombay), 17 (Feb.): 237–52.

Chaudhury, U. D. R. 1966. Technological Change in the Indian Economy, 1950–60. *Economic and Political Weekly,* 1 (Aug. 20): 37–48.

Chenery, H. B. 1953. The Application of Investment Criteria. *Q.J.E.,* 47 (Feb.): 76–96.

———— 1955. The Role of Industrialization in Development Programs. *A.E.R. Papers and Proceedings,* 45 (May): 40–57. Reprinted in M, A–S.

———— 1958. Development Policies and Programmes. *Economic Bulletin for Latin America,* 3 (Mar.): 55–60. Reprinted in M.

———— 1959. The Interdependence of Investment Decisions. In Abramovitz (1959).

———— 1960. Patterns of Industrial Growth. *A.E.R.,* 50 (Sept.): 624–54.

———— 1961. Comparative Advantage and Development Policy. *A.E.R.,* 51 (Mar.): 18–51.

———— 1960. Paterns of Industrial Growth. *A.E.R.,* 50 (Sept.): 624–54.

———— 1969. The Two-gap Approach to Aid and Development: Reply to Bruton. *A.E.R.,* 59 (June): 446–49.

————, ed. 1971. *Studies in Development Planning.* Cambridge, Mass.: Harvard University Press.

————, M. Ahluwalia, C. L. G. Bell, J. Duloy, and R. Jolly, eds. 1974. *Redistribution with Growth.* London: Oxford University Press.

————, and M. Bruno 1962. Development Alternatives in an Open Economy: The case of Israel. *E.J.,* 72 (Mar.): 79–103.

————, and N. G. Carter 1973. Foreign Assistance and Development Performance, 1960–1970. *A.E.R.,* 63 (May): 459–68.

————, and P. Eckstein 1970. Development Alternatives for Latin America. *J.P.E.,* 78 (July): 966–1006.

————, and K. S. Kretschmer 1956. Resources Allocation for Economic Development, *Econometrica,* 24 (Oct.): 356–99.

————, and A. MacEwan 1966. Optimal Patterns of Growth and Aid: The Case of Pakistan. *Pakistan Development Review,* summer.

————, and A. M. Strout 1966. Foreign Assistance and Economic Development. *A.E.R.,* 56 (Sept.): 680–733.

Choi, K. I. 1967. *The Development of the Japanese Modern Cotton Spinning Industry in the 19th Century.* Unpublished manuscript: Williamsburg, Virginia.

Clark, C. 1957. *Conditions of Economic Progress.* 3d ed. London: Macmillan and Co., Ltd.

———— **1969.** The "Population Explosion" Myth. *Bulletin of the Institute of Development Studies* (May).

COALE, A. J. **1974.** Too Many People? *Challenge* (Sept.–Oct.).

————, and E. M. HOOVER **1958.** *Population Growth and Economic Development in Low-Income Countries: A Case Study of India's Prospects.* Princeton, N.J.: Princeton University Press.

COHEN, B. I. **1971.** *Tariff Preferences for the Third World.* New Haven: Yale Universty Economic Growth Center. Center Paper no. 159.

————, and D. G. SISLER **1971.** Exports of Developing Countries in the 1960s. *R. E. Statistics,* 53 (Nov.): 354–61.

COLE, A. H. **1946.** An Approach to the Study of Entrepreneurship. *Journal of Economic History,* 6: 1–15. Reprinted in Lane, F. C. and J. C. Reierson, eds., *Enterprise and Secular Change, Readings in Economic History.* Homewood, Ill.: Richard D. Irwin, Inc., 1953.

———— **1955.** A New Set of Stages. *Explorations in Entrepreneurial History,* 8 (Dec.): 99–107.

COLE, H. S. D. and others **1973.** *Models of Doom.* New York: Universe Books.

COMITE INTERAMERICANO DE DESAROLLO AGRICOLA **1966.** *Chile: Tenencia de la Tiera y Desarollo Socio-Economico del Sector Agricola.* Santiago: Comita Interamericano de Desarollo Agricola.

COOPER, C., ed. **1973.** *Science, Technology and Development: The Political Economy of Technical Advance in Underdeveloped Countries.* London: Frank Cass.

CORREA, H. **1963.** *The Economics of Human Resources.* Amsterdam: North-Holland Publishing Co.

CORTEZ, A. B., D. R. GADGIL, G. HAKIM, A. LEWIS, and T. W. SCHULTZ **1951.** *Measures for the Economic Development of Underdeveloped Countries.* New York: United Nations.

CRAFTS, N. F. R. **1973.** Trade as a Handmaiden of Growth: An Alternative View. *E.J.,* 83: 873–83.

CUMMINGS, R. W., JR. **1967.** Wheat Production Prospects in India. Minneapolis, mimeographed.

———— **1974.** Comment on Paper by Evenson. *Journal of Economic History,* 34 (Mar.): 84–90.

CURRIE, L. **1966.** *Accelerating Development: The Necessity and the Means.* New York: McGraw-Hill Book Co.

DALY, D. J., ed. **1973.** *International Comparisons of Prices and Output.* Studies in Income and Wealth, no. 37. National Bureau of Economic Research. New York: Columbia University Press.

DAVID, P. A. **1972.** Just How Misleading Are Official Exchange Rate Conversions? *E.J.,* 82 (Sept.): 979–90.

———— **1973.** A Reply to Professor Balassa. *E.J.,* 83 (Dec.): 1267–76.

DAVIS, K. **1963.** Population. *Scientific American,* 209 (Sept.): 62–71.

DEAN, E. R. **1966.** *The Supply Responses of African Farmers.* Amsterdam: North Holland Publishing Co.

DEANE, P. **1955.** The Implications of Early National Income Estimates for the Measurement of Long-Term Economic Growth in the United Kingdom. *E.D.C.C.*, 4 (Nov.): 3–38.

———— **1957.** The Industrial Revolution and Economic Growth: The Evidence of Early British National Income Estimates. *E.D.C.C.*, 5 (Jan.): 159–74.

————, and W. A. COLE **1962.** *British Economic Growth 1688–1959: Trend and Structure.* Cambridge: Cambridge University Press.

DELL, S. **1966.** *A Latin American Common Market?* New York: Oxford University Press.

DENISON, E. F. **1962.** *The Sources of Economic Growth in the United States and the Alternatives Before Us.* New York: Committee for Economic Development.

———— **1966.** Measuring the Contribution of Education to Economic Growth. In Robinson and Vaizey (1966).

———— **1967.** *Why Growth Rates Differ.* Washington: The Brookings Institute.

———— **1969.** Some Major Issues in Productivity Analysis: An Examination of Estimates by Jorgenson and Griliches. *Survey of Current Business,* May, part 2, pp. 1–27.

———— **1972.** Final Comments. In *The Measurement of Productivity* (no author, no ed.). Washington, D.C.: The Brookings Institution.

———— **1974.** *Accounting for United States Economic Growth, 1929–1969.* Washington, D.C.: The Brookings Institution.

DESAI, A. V. **1968.** The Origins of Parsi Enterprise. *The Indian Economic and Social History Review,* 5 (Dec.).

DESAI, E., and D. MAZUMDAR **1970.** A Test of the Hypothesis of Disguised Unemployment. *Economica,* 37 (Feb.).

DEUTSCH, K. and A. ECKSTEIN **1961.** National Industrialization and the Declining Share of the International Economic Sector, 1890–1959. *World Politics,* 13 (Jan.): 267–99.

DIAZ ALEJANDRO, C. F. **1967.** Essays on the Economic History of the Argentine Republic. Mimeo.

———— **1973.** *The Future of Direct Foreign Investment in Latin America.* Center Paper no. 198. New Haven: Yale University Economic Growth Center.

DITELLA, G. and M. ZYMELMAN **1967.** *Las Etapas del Desarollo Economico Argentina.* Buenos Aires: Editorial Universitaria de Buenos Aires.

DORFMAN, R. **1972.** A Comment on Professor Benoit's "Conundrum." *International Development Review,* 14, no. 1.

————, P. A. SAMUELSON, and R. M. SOLOW **1958.** *Linear Programming and Economic Analysis.* New York: McGraw-Hill Book Co.

DORRANCE, G. S. **1963.** The Effect of Inflation on Economic Development. *International Monetary Fund Staff Papers,* 10 (Mar.): 1–47.

DOUGHERTY, C. R. S. **1971.** Optimal Allocation of Investment in Education. In Chenery, ed., *Studies in Development Planning,* 270–92.

DUE, J. F.   1963. *Taxation and Economic Development in Tropical Africa.* Cambridge, Mass.: MIT Press.

DUESENBERRY, J. S.   1949. *Income, Saving and the Theory of Consumer Behavior.* Cambridge, Mass.: Harvard University Press.

EARLE, E. M., ed.   1951. *Modern France.* Princeton, N.J.: Princeton University Press.

EASTERLIN, R. A.   1966. Economic-demographic Interactions and Long Swings in Economic Growth. *A.E.R.*, 56 (Dec.).

ECKAUS, R. S.   1955. The Factor Proportions Problem in Underdeveloped Areas. *A.E.R.*, 45 (Sept.), 539–65. Reprinted in A–S.

———   1962. Technological Change in the Less Developed Areas. In Asher (1962). Reprinted in M.

———   1964. Economic Criteria for Education and Training. *R.E. Statistics,* 46 (May): 181–90.

———   1967. Planning in India. (With comments by Edward S. Mason and Alan S. Manne). In Millikan (1967).

———   1973. *Estimating the Returns to Education: A Disaggregated Approach.* Berkeley, Calif.: Carnegie Commission on Higher Education.

———, and K. PARIKH   1967. *Planning for Growth.* Cambridge, Mass.: MIT Press.

ECKSTEIN, A.   1966. *Communist China's Economic Growth and Foreign Trade: Implications for U.S. Policy.* New York: McGraw-Hill Book Co.

———, and K. W. DEUTSCH   1961. National Industrialization and the Declining Share of the International Economic Sector, 1890–1957. *World Politics,* 13 (Jan.), 267–99.

ECKSTEIN, O.   1957. Investment Criteria for Economic Development and the Theory of Intertemporal Welfare Economics. *Q.J.E.,* 71 (Feb.), 56–85.

ECLA. See U.N.: ECLA

EDDING, F.   1966. Expenditure on Education: Statistics and Comments. In Robinson and Vaizey (1966).

EDEL, M. D.   1965. *The Adequacy of Food Production for Economic Development in Latin America.* Master's Thesis, Columbia University.

———   1967. Food Supply and Structural Inflation in Latin America. Unpublished manuscript, Massachusetts Institute of Technology.

EDWARDS, E. O., ed.   1974. *Employment in Developing Nations.* New York: Columbia University Press.

———, and M. P. TODARO   1974. Education, Society and Development; Some Main Themes and Suggested Strategies for International Assistance. *W.D.,* 2 (Jan.), 25–30.

EICHER, C., and L. WITT, eds.   1964. *Agriculture in Economic Development.* New York: McGraw-Hill Book Co.

ELLIS, H. S., and H. C. WALLICH, eds.   1961. *Economic Development for Latin America.* New York: St. Martin's Press.

EPSTEIN, T. S.   1962. *Economic Development and Social Change in South India.* New York: Humanities Press.

EVENSON, R.   1971. Economic Aspects of the Organization of Agricultural Research. In W. L. Fishel, ed., *Resource Allocation in Agricultural Research.* Minneapolis: University of Minnesota Press.

————. **1974a.** International Diffusion of Agarian Technology. *The Journal of Economic History,* 34 (Mar.), no. 1.

———— **1974b.** The "Green Revolution" in Recent Development. *American Journal of Agricultural Economics,* 56 (May), no. 2.

————, and Y. KISLEV **1973.** Research and Productivity in Wheat and Maize. *J.P.E.,* 81 (Nov.–Dec.), no. 6.

FABER, M. and D. SEERS, eds. **1972.** *The Crisis in Planning.* London: Chatto and Windus.

FALCON, W. **1964.** Farmer Response to Price in a Subsistence Economy: The Case of West Pakistan. *A.E.R.,* 54 (May): 580–91.

———— **1970.** The Green Revolution: Generations of Problems. *American Journal of Agricultural Economics,* 52: 698–712.

FAUNCE, W. A., and W. H. FORM, eds. **1969.** *Comparative Perspectives on Industrial Society.* Boston: Little Brown and Co.

FEI, J. C. H., and G. RANIS **1961.** A Theory of Economic Development, *A.E.R.,* 51 (Sept.), 533–65.

———— **1964.** *Development of the Labor Surplus Economy.* Homewood, Ill.: Richard D. Irwin, Inc.

FELIX, D. **1960.** Structural Imbalances, Social Conflict, and Inflation: An Appraisal of Chile's Recent Anti-Inflationary Effort. *E.D.C.C.,* 8 (Jan.): 113–47.

FERGUSON, C. E. **1965.** Substitution, Technical Progress and Returns to Scale. *American Association Papers* (May).

————, and J. P. GOULD **1975.** *Microeconomic Theory.* 4th ed. Homewood, Ill.: Richard D. Irwin, Inc.

FISCHMAN, L. and H. LANDSBERG. **1972.** In R. Ridker ed., *Population, Resources, and the Environment.* Washington: GPO.

FISHEL, W. L. (Ed.) **1971.** *Resource Allocation in Agricultural Research.* Minneapolis: University of Minnesota Press.

FISHER, A. G. B. **1935.** *The Clash of Progress and Security.* London: Macmillan & Co., Ltd.

———— **1939.** Primary, Secondary, and Tertiary Production. *Economic Record,* 15 (June), 24–38.

———— **1945.** *Economic Progress and Social Security.* London: Macmillan & Co., Ltd.

FLEMING, J. M. **1955.** External Economies and the Doctrine of Balanced Growth. *E.J.,* 65 (June): 241–56. Reprinted in A–S, O–R.

FOOD AND AGRICULTURE ORGANIZATION **1955.** *Uses of Agricultural Surpluses to Finance Economic Development in Underdeveloped Countries.* Rome: FAO.

———— **1962.** *Agricultural Commodities Projections for 1970, FAO Commodity Review 1962, Special Supplement.* Rome: FAO.

———— **1964.** *Production Yearbook.*

FORRESTER, J. W. **1971.** *World Dynamics.* Cambridge, Mass.: Wright-Allen Press.

FRANK, A. G. **1967.** *Capitalism and Underdevelopment in Latin America.* New York: Monthly Review Press.

FRANK, C. R., and W. R. CLINE **1971.** Measurement of Debt Servicing Capacity: An Application of Discriminant Analysis. *Journal of International Economics*, 1: 340–42.

FREDERICK, K. **1965.** Coffee Production in Uganda: An Economic Analysis of Past and Potential Growth. Unpublished dissertation, Massachusetts Institute of Technology.

FREJKA, TOMAS **1973.** Prospects for a Stationary World Population. *Scientific American*, 228 (Mar.): 15–23.

FRIEDMAN, M. **1957.** *A Theory of the Consumption Function.* Princeton, N.J.: Princeton University Press.

FROMM, E. **1947.** *Man for Himself.* New York: Rinehart.

——— **1959.** The Creative Attitude. Chapter 4 of H. H. Anderson, ed. (1959).

FURNIVALL, J. S. **1931.** *Political Economy of Burma.* Rangoon: Burma Book Club, Ltd.

——— **1948.** *Colonial Policy and Practice: A Comparative Study of Burma and Netherlands India.* Cambridge: Cambridge University Press.

GAATHON, A. L. **1961.** *Capital Stock, Employment and Output in Israel, 1950–59.* Jerusalem: Bank of Israel.

GALBRAITH, J. K. **1947.** The Disequilibrium System. *A.E.R.*, 37 (June): 287–302.

GALENSON, W., and H. LEIBENSTEIN **1955.** Investment Criteria, Productivity, and Economic Development. *Q.J.E.*, 69 (Aug.): 343–70.

GEERTZ, C. **1963a.** *Agricultural Involution: The Process of Ecological Change in Indonesia.* Berkeley: University of California Press.

——— **1963b.** *Peddlers and Princes.* Chicago: University of Chicago Press.

GENERAL AGREEMENT ON TARIFFS AND TRADE (GATT) **1962** (Annual report) *International Trade.* Geneva.

GERSCHENKRON, A. **1952.** Economic Backwardness in Historical Perspective. In B. F. Hoselitz, ed. (1952).

——— **1953.** Social Attitudes, Entrepreneurship, and Economic Development. *Explorations in Entrepreneurial History*, 6 (Oct.): 1–19.

——— **1954.** A Rejoinder. *Explorations in Entrepreneurial History*, 6 (May): 287–93.

——— **1954.** Second Rejoinder. *Explorations in Entrepreneurial History*, 6 (May): 297.

——— **1962.** *Economic Development in Historical Perspective.* Cambridge, Mass.: Harvard University Press.

——— **1964.** The Early Phases of Industrialization in Russia: Afterthoughts and Counterthoughts. In Rostow (1964).

GIBB, A., JR. **1972.** Report on Ongoing Research: Some Evidence on the Impact of Agricultural Modernization on Nonagricultural Market Centers. Discussion Paper no. 72–4. University of the Philippines: Institute of Economic Development and Research, School of Economics (April 11, 1972).

GILBERT, M., and associates. **1958.** *Comparative National Products and Price Levels.* Paris: Organization for European Economic Cooperation.

———, and I. B. KRAVIS **1954.** *An International Comparison of National Products and the Purchasing Power of Currencies.* Paris: Organization for European Economic Cooperation.

GILBERT, R. V.   **1964.** The Works Programme in East Pakistan. *International Labour Review,* 89 (Mar.): 213–26.

GLADE, W. P.   **1967.** Approaches to a Theory of Entrepreneurship Formation, *Explorations in Entrepreneurial History,* n.s. 4 (spring–summer): 245–59.

GOLDSMITH, R. W.   **1961.** The Economic Growth of Tsarist Russia, 1860–1913. *E.D.C.C.,* 9 (Apr.): 441–75.

———   **1973.** A Century of Financial Development in Latin America. Center Paper no. 196. New Haven: Yale University Economic Growth Center.

GRANICK, D. H.   **1963.** The Appeal of Confiscation Reconsidered: A Gaming Approach for Foreign Economic Policy. *E.D.C.C.,* 11 (July): 353–66.

———   **1964.** Further Thoughts on Confiscation. *E.D.C.C.,* 12 (July): 425–27.

GREGORY, P.   **1960.** The Labor Market in Puerto Rico. Chap. 9 of Moore and Feldman (1960).

———   **1972.** Economic Growth and Structural Change in Tsarist Russia: A Case of Modern Economic Growth? *Soviet Studies,* 23 (Jan.): 418–34.

GRIFFEN, K.   **1973a.** The Effect of Aid and Other Resource Transfers on Savings and Growth in Less-Developed Countries: A Comment. *E.J.* 83 (Sept.): 863–66.

———   **1973b.** An Assessment of Development in Taiwan, *W.D.* (June).

GRIFFIN, K. B., and J. L. ENOS   **1971.** *Planning Development.* London: Addison-Wesley.

GRILICHES, Z.   **1963a.** Estimates of the Aggregate Agricultural Production Function from Cross-Sectional Data. *Journal of Farm Economics* (May).

———   **1963b.** The Sources of Measured Productivity Growth: United States Agriculture, 1940–60. *J.P.E.,* 51 (Aug.): 331–36.

———   **1964.** Research Expenditures, Education, and the Aggregate Agricultural Production Function. *A.E.R.* (Dec.).

———   **1967.** Production Functions in Manufacturing: Some Preliminary Results. In M. Brown, ed., *The Theory and Empirical Analysis of Production, Studies in Income and Wealth,* N.B.E.R., 31.

———, and D. W. JORGENSON   **1966.** Sources of Measured Productivity Change: Capital Input. *A.E.R. Papers and Proceedings,* 56 (May): 50–61.

GRUNWALD, J.   **1961.** The "Structuralist" School on Price Stabilization and Economic Development–The Chilean Case. In Hirschman (1961). Reprinted in M.

HABAKKUK, H. J.   **1962.** *American and British Technology in the Nineteenth Century.* London: Cambridge University Press.

———   **1963.** Population Problems and European Economic Development in the Late Eighteenth and Nineteenth Centuries. *A.E.R.,* 53 (May): 607–18.

HABERLER, G.   **1936.** *The Theory of International Trade.* London: W. Hodge & Co. Also, New York: Macmillan & Co., 1937.

———   **1959.** International Trade and Economic Development. Cairo: National Bank of Egypt Fiftieth Anniversary Commemoration Lectures. Reprinted in M, M–B–C.

———   **1961.** Terms of Trade and Economic Development. In Ellis (1961).

HAGEN, E. E.　**1958.** An Economic Justification of Protectionism. *Q.J.E.,* 72 (Nov.): 496–514.

———　**1959.** Population and Economic Growth. *A.E.R.,* 39 (June), 310–29.

———　**1962.** *On the Theory of Social Change.* Homewood, Ill.: Dorsey Press.

———　**1972.** An Observation on the Benoit and Dorfman Analyses. *International Development Review,* 14, no. 1.

———, and O. HAWRYLYSHYN　**1968.** World Product, and World Growth, 1955–1965. *E.D.C.C.*

———, and F. W. HERRING and others (the Watkins Mission)　**1956.** *Kobe-Nagoya Expressway Survey for the Ministry of Construction, Government of Japan.* Tokyo.

———, and S. F. T. WHITE　**1966.** *Great Britain: Quiet Revolution in Planning.* Syracuse, N.Y.: Syracuse University Press.

HANSEN, B. **1966.** Marginal Productivity Wage Theory and Subsistence Wage Theory in Egyptian Agriculture. *Journal of Development Studies,* 2 (July): 367–99.

HANSEN, N. M., ed.　**1972.** *Growth Centers in Regional Economic Development.* New York: The Free Press.

HANSON, A. H.　**1965.** *Public Enterprise and Economic Development,* 2d ed. London: Routledge & K. Paul.

———　**1966.** *The Process of Planning: A Study of India's Five Year Plans, 1950–1964.* London: Oxford University Press.

HARBERGER, A.　**1965.** Investment in Men versus Investment in Machines. Chap. 2 of Anderson and Bowman (1965).

HARBISON, F.　**1956.** Entrepreneurial Organization as a Factor in Economic Development. *Q.J.E.,* 70 (Aug.): 364–79. Reprinted in O–R.

———, and C. A. MYERS　**1959.** *Management in the Industrial World.* New York: McGraw-Hill Book Co.

———　**1964.** *Education, Manpower and Economic Growth: Strategies of Human Resource Development.* New York: McGraw-Hill Book Co.

HARRIS, J. R.　**1967.** *The Development of Industrial Entrepreneurship in Nigeria.* Unpublished doctoral dissertation, Northwestern University.

———, and M. P. T. TODARO　**1970.** Migration, Unemployment, and Development: A Two-Sector Analysis. *A.E.R.,* 60 (Mar.): 126–42.

HARROD, R.　**1948.** *Toward a Dynamic Economics.* New York: Macmillan and Company.

HAYAMI, Y., and V. W. RUTTAN　**1971.** *Agricultural Development: An International Perspective.* Baltimore: Johns Hopkins Press.

HAYN, R.　**1962.** Capital Formation and Argentina's Price-Cost Structure 1953–1958. *R.E.Statistics,* 44 (Aug.): 340–43.

HEBREW UNIVERSITY　**1958.** *The Challenge of Development.* A symposium held in Jerusalem, June 26–27, 1957.

HELLEINER, G. K.　**1966a.** Marketing Boards and Domestic Stabilization in Nigeria. *R.E.Statistics,* 48 (Feb.): 69–78.

———　**1966b.** *Peasant Agriculture, Government, and Economic Growth in Nigeria.* Homewood, Ill.: Richard D. Irwin, Inc.

―――― **1966c.** Typology in Development Theory: The Land Surplus Economy (Nigeria). *Food Research Institute Studies,* 6: 181–94.

HICKS, J. D. **1932.** *The Theory of Wages.* New York: Macmillan and Company.

HICKS, J. R. **1959.** *Essays in World Economics.* Oxford: Clarendon Press.

HINRICHS, H. H. **1966.** *A General Theory of Tax Structure Change during Economic Development.* Cambridge, Mass.: Harvard Law School.

HIRSCHMAN, A. O. **1958.** *The Strategy of Economic Development.* New Haven, Conn.: Yale University Press.

―――― **1963.** *Journeys toward Progress: Studies of Economic Policy-Making in Latin America.* New York: Twentieth Century Fund.

――――, ed. **1961.** *Latin American Issues: Essays and Comments.* New York: Twentieth Century Fund.

HIRSCHMEIER, J. **1964.** *The Origins of Entrepreneurship in Meiji Japan.* Cambridge, Mass.: Harvard University Press.

HLA MYINT. See Myint, Hla.

HOFFMAN, W. G. **1958.** *The Growth of Industrial Economies.* Translated from the German by W. O. Henderson and W. H. Chaloner. New York: Oceana Publications, Inc.

HOGAN, W. P. **1958.** Note. *R.E.Statistics,* 40 (Nov.): 407–11.

HOLLAND, S., ed. **1972.** *The State as Entrepreneur. New Dimensions for Public Enterprise: The IRI State Shareholding Formula.* London: Widenfeld & Nicholson.

HOLLISTER, W. W. **1958.** *China's Gross National Product and Social Accounts, 1950–1957.* New York: Free Press.

HOSELITZ, B. F. **1960.** *Sociological Aspects of Economic Growth.* New York: Free Press.

―――― **1960.** *Theories of Economic Growth.* New York: Free Press.

――――, ed. **1952.** *The Progress of Underdeveloped Areas.* Chicago: University of Chicago Press.

HOU CHI-MING **1965.** *Foreign Investment and Economic Development in China, 1840–1937.* Cambridge, Mass.: Harvard University Press.

HOUTHAKKER, H. S. **1957.** An International Comparison of Household Expenditure Patterns, Commemorating the Centenary of Engel's Law. *Econometrica,* 25 (Oct.): 532–51.

HOWE, C. **1971.** *Employment and Economic Growth in Urban China.* New York: Cambridge University Press.

HSING, M-H., J. H. POWER, and G. P. SICAT **1970.** *Taiwan and the Philippines: Industrialization and Trade Policies.* London: Oxford University Press. (For the OECD Development Center.)

HUDDLE, D. L. **1971.** Disequilibrium Foreign Exchange Systems and the Generation of Industrialization and Inflation in Brazil. Paper no. 12. Houston, Tex.: Rice University.

HUMPHREY, D. D. **1955.** *American Imports.* New York: Twentieth Century Fund.

HUNTINGTON, E. **1945.** *Mainsprings of Civilization.* New York: John Wiley & Sons, Inc.

HYMER, S. and S. RESNICK   1967. *The Responsiveness of Agrarian Economies and the Importance of Z Goods.* Center Discussion Paper no. 25 (revised), Economic Growth Center, Yale University. Mimeo.

INTER-AMERICAN DEVELOPMENT BANK   1966. *Multinational Investment Programs and Latin American Integration.* New York.

ISHIKAWA, S. 1965. *National Income and Capital Formation in Mainland China; An Examination of Official Statistics.* Tokyo: Institute of Asian Economic Affairs.

JACKSON, D., and H. A. TURNER   1973. How to Provide More Employment in a Labour Surplus Economy. *International Labor Review* (Apr.).

JAPAN, GOVERNMENT OF: Economic Research Institute, Economic Planning Agency   1963. *Analysis of Price Comparisons in Japan and the United States.* Economic Bulletin no. 13, Sept.

JEWKES, J., D. SAWERS, and R. STILLERMAN   1958. *The Sources of Invention.* London: Macmillan & Co., Ltd. New York: St. Martin's Press.

JOHANSEN, L.   1959. Substitution versus Fixed Production Coefficients in the Theory of Economic Growth: A Synthesis. *Econometrica,* 27 (Apr.): 157–76.

———   1961. A Method for Separating the Effects of Capital Accumulation and Shifts in Production Functions upon Growth in Labour Productivity. *E.J.,* 71 (Dec.): 775–82.

JOHNSON, D. W., and J. S. CHIU   1965. Growth and Investment According to International Comparisons: A Comment. *E.J.,* 75 (Sept.): 626–29.

JOHNSON, H. G. 1958. *International Trade and Economic Growth.* London: George Allen & Unwin, Ltd.

———   1967. *Economic Policies toward Less Developed Countries.* New York: Frederick A. Praeger.

JOHNSTON, B. F., and J. W. MELLOR   1961. The Role of Agriculture in Economic Development. *A.E.R.,* 51 (Sept.): 571–81. Reprinted in M.

JOHNSTON, B. F. and P. KILBY   1975. *Agriculture and Structural Transformation.* New York: Oxford University Press.

JONES, W. O.   1960. Economic Man in Africa. *Food Research Institute Studies,* 1 (May): 107–34.

JORGENSON, D. W.   1961. The Development of a Dual Economy. *E.J.,* 71 (June): 309–34.

———   1966. Testing Alternative Theories of the Development of a Dual Economy. In I. Adelman and E. Thorbecke, eds. (1966), pp. 45–60.

———   1967. Surplus Agricultural Labour and the Development of a Dual Economy. *Oxford Economics Papers,* n.s. 19: 288–312.

———, and Z. GRILICHES   1967. The Explanation of Productivity Change. *Review of Economic Studies,* 34 (July): 249–83.

———   1972. Issues in Growth Accounting: A Reply to Edward F. Denison. In *The Measurement of Productivity* (no author, no ed.), Washington, D.C.: The Brookings Institution.

———   1972. Final Reply. In *The Measurement of Productivity* (no author, no ed.). Washington, D.C.: The Brookings Institution.

JOURNAL OF POLITICAL ECONOMY   1962. Investment in Human Beings. 70, supplement (Oct.).

KAHN, A. E.   1951. Investment Criteria in Development. *Q.J.E.*, 65 (Feb.): 38–61.

KALDOR, N.   1957. A Model of Economic Growth. *E.J.*, 67 (Dec.): 591–624.

—— 1960. *Essays on Economic Stability and Growth*. London: G. Duckworth & Co., Ltd.

——, and J. A. MIRRLEES   1962. A New Model of Economic Growth. *Review of Economic Studies*, 29 (June): 174–92.

KAMARCK, A. M.   1972. Climate and Economic Development. *Economic Development Institute, IBRD* (June 30), EDI Seminar Paper no. 2.

KAO, C. H. C., K. R. ANSCHEL, and C. K. EICHER   1964. Disguised Unemployment in Agriculture: A Survey. In Eicher and Witt (1964).

KELLEY, A. C., J. G. WILLIAMSON, and R. J. CHEETHAM   1973. *Dualistic Economic Development. Theory and History*. Chicago: University of Chicago Press.

KENDRICK, J. W.   1961. *Productivity Trends in the United States*. Bureau of Economic Research, General Series, no. 71. Princeton, N.J.: Princeton University Press.

KENNEDY, C. and A. T. THIRLWALL   1972. Surveys in Applied Economics: Technical Progress, *E.J.*, 82 (Mar.): 11–72.

KENNEDY, K. A.   1971. *Productivity and Industrial Growth: The Irish Experience*. Oxford: Clarendon Press.

KERR, C., J. T. DUNLOP, F. H. HARBISON, and C. A. MYERS   1964. *Industrialism and Industrial Man*. New York: Oxford University Press. Paper. Slightly revised, with bibliography augmented, from 1961 editions.

—— 1971. Postscript to "Industrialism and Industrial Man." *International Labor Review*, 103 (June), no. 6.

KHALAF, S., and E. SHWAYRI   1966. Family Firms and Industrial Development: The Lebanese Case. *E.D.C.C.*, 15 (Oct.): 59–69.

KILBY, P.   1961. African Labour Productivity Reconsidered. *E.J.*, 71 (June): 273–91.

—— 1971. *Entrepreneurship and Economic Development*. New York: The Free Press.

——, and B. F. JOHNSTON   1972. The Choice of Agricultural Strategy and the Development of Manufacturing. *Food Research Institute Studies in Agricultural Economics, Trade and Development*, 11 (no. 2): 156–75.

KIM, Y. C., and G. C. WINSTON   1975. The Optimal Utilization of Capital Stock and the Level of Economic Development. *Economica*, forthcoming.

KINDLEBERGER, C. P.   1956. *The Terms of Trade: A European Case Study*. New York: MIT Press–Wiley.

—— 1961. Foreign Trade and Economic Growth: Lessons from Britain and France, 1850 to 1912. *Economic History Review*, 14 (Dec.): 289–305.

—— 1964. *Economic Growth in France and Britain, 1851–1950*. Cambridge, Mass.: Harvard University Press.

—— 1965. *Economic Development*, 2d ed. New York: McGraw-Hill Book Co.

—— 1967. Liberal Policies vs. Controls in the Foreign Trade of Developing Countries. Agency for International Development. Discussion Paper no. 14 (Apr.).

———— 1973. *International Economics,* 5th ed. Homewood, Ill.: Richard D. Irwin, Inc.

KING, T.   1970. *Mexico: Industrialisation and Trade Policies since 1940.* London: Oxford University Press. (For the OECD Development Centre.)

KRAVIS, I. B.   1970. Trade as a Handmaiden of Growth: Similarities between the Nineteenth and Twentieth Centuries. *E.J.,* 80: 850–72.

———— 1973. A Reply to Mr. Crafts' Note. *E.J.,* 83: 885–88.

KRIEGER, R. A.   1974. Inflation and the "Brazilian Solution." *Challenge* Sept.–Oct.).

KROEBER, A. L.   1944. *Configurations of Culture Growth.* Berkeley and Los Angeles: University of California Press.

KUZNETS, S.   *Quantitative Aspects of the Economic Growth of Nations.* (All published as issues of *E.D.C.C.* Part 1 is the October 1956 issue. Part 2 is a supplement to the July 1957 issue. Each other part is part 2 of the *E.D.C.C.* issue indicated.)

1. Levels and Variability of Rates of Growth. Vol. 5, no. 1 (Oct. 1956).
2. Industrial Distribution of National Product and Labor Force. Vol. 5, no. 4 (July 1957).
3. Industrial Distribution of Income and Labor Force by States, United States, 1919–1921 to 1955. Vol. 6, no. 4 (July 1958).
4. Distribution of National Income by Factor Shares. Vol. 7, no. 3 (April 1959).
5. Capital Formation Proportions: International Comparisons for Recent Years. Vol. 8, no. 4 (July 1960).
6. Long-Term Trends in Capital Formation Proportions. Vol. 9, no. 4 (July 1961).
7. The Share and Structure of Consumption. Vol. 10, no. 2 (Jan., 1962).
8. Distribution of Income by Size. Vol. 11, no. 2 (Jan. 1963).
9. Level and Structure of Foreign Trade: Comparisons for Recent Years. Vol. 13, no. 2 (Oct. 1964).
10. Level and Structure of Foreign Trade: Long-Term Trends. Vol. 15, no. 2 (Jan. 1967).

———— 1947. Measurement of Economic Growth. In *Tasks of Economic History;* supplemental issue, *Journal of Economic History,* 7.

———— 1949. *Problems in the Study of Economic Growth.* New York: N.B.E.R., 137–72.

———— 1953. *Economic Change.* New York: W. W. Norton Co.

———— 1954. Underdeveloped Countries and the Pre-industrial Phase in the Advanced Countries. *Proceedings of the World Population Conference.* Rome: Papers, vol. 5.

———— 1959. *Six Lectures on Economic Growth.* New York: Free Press.

———— 1964. Notes on the Take-Off. In Rostow (1964). Reprinted in M–B–C.

———— 1966. *Modern Economic Growth: Rate, Structure, and Spread.* New Haven, Conn.: Yale University Press.

——— 1967. Population and Economic Growth. *Proceedings of the American Philosophical Society,* 3 (June), 170–93.

LALL, S. 1974. Less Developed Countries and Private Foreign Direct Investment: A Review Article. *World Development,* 2 (April-May): 43–48.

LAMARTINE YATES, P. See Yates, P. L.

LANDAU, L. 1971. Differences in Saving Ratios among Latin American Countries. Unpublished Ph.D. Dissertation, Department of Economics, Harvard University, 1969. A condensed version is reproduced in H. Chenery, ed., *Studies in Development Planning.* Cambridge, Mass.: Harvard University Press.

——— 1971. Saving Functions for Latin America. In H. Chenery, ed., *Studies,* Chap. 3. Cambridge, Mass.: Harvard University Press, 299–321.

LANDES, D. S. 1949. French Entrepreneurship and Industrial Growth in the Nineteenth Century. *Journal of Economic History,* 9 (May): 45–61.

——— 1954. Social Attitudes, Entrepreneurship, and Economic Development. *Explorations in Entrepreneurial History,* 6 (May): 245–72.

LARY, H. B. 1968. *Imports of Manufactures from Less Developed Countries.* New York: N.B.E.R.

LEBERGOTT, S. 1966. Labor Force and Employment, 1800–1960. In *N.B.E.R.* (1966), 117–204.

LEE, D. H. K. 1957. *Climate and Economic Development in the Tropics.* New York: Harper and Row.

LEFF, N. H. 1967. A Note on Brazilian Economic Development before 1939. Unpublished manuscript.

——— 1967. Import Constraints and Development: Causes of the Recent Decline of Brazilian Economic Growth. *R. E. Statistics* (49).

——— 1973. Tropical Trade and Development in the Nineteenth Century: The Brazilian Experience. *J.P.E.,* 81 (May-June), no. 3.

LEIBENSTEIN, H. 1954. *A Theory of Economic-Demographic Development.* Princeton, N.J.: Princeton University Press.

——— 1957. *Economic Backwardness and Economic Growth.* New York: John Wiley & Sons, Inc.

——— 1966. Incremental Capital-Output Ratios and Growth Rates in the Short Run. *R.E. Statistics,* 48 (Feb.), 20–27.

——— 1974. An Interpretation of the Economic Theory of Fertility. *Journal of Economic Literature,* 12: 457–79.

LEONTIEF, W. 1953. Domestic Production and Foreign Trade; the American Capital Position Re-Examined. *Proceedings of the American Philosophical Society,* 97 (September): 332–49.

——— 1956. Factor Proportions and the Structure of American Trade: Further Theoretical and Empirical Analysis. *R.E. Statistics,* 38 (Nov.): 386–407.

LEVIN, J. V. 1960. *The Export Economies: Their Pattern of Development in Historical Perspective.* Cambridge, Mass.: Harvard University Press.

LEVINE, H. S. 1960. A Small Problem in the Analysis of Growth. *R.E. Statistics,* 42 (May): 225–29.

LEWIS, J. P. 1962. *Quiet Crisis in India.* Washington: The Brookings Institute.

LEWIS, O. 1951. *Life in a Mexican Village: Tepoztlan Restudied.* Urbana, Ill.: University of Illinois Press.

LEWIS, W. A. See also Martin, Alison. 1954. Economic Development with Unlimited Supplies of Labour. *The Manchester School,* 22 (May): 139–91. Reprinted in A–S, M–B–C, O–R.

——— 1955. *The Theory of Economic Growth.* London: George Allen & Unwin, Ltd.

——— 1958. Unlimited Supplies of Labour: Further Notes. *The Manchester School,* 26 (Jan.): 1–32.

——— 1966. *Development Planning. The Essentials of Economic Policy.* New York: Harper & Row.

——— 1971. *Tropical Development 1880–1913: Studies in Economic Progress.* Evanston, Ill.: Northwestern University Press.

——— 1972. Reflections on Unlimited Labor. *International Economics and Development, Essays in Honor of Paul Prebisch.* Luis Eugenise di Marco, ed. New York: Academic Press.

LINDER, S. B. 1967. *Trade and Development.* New York: Praeger.

LINDZEY, G., ed. 1954. *Handbook of Social Psychology,* vol. 2. Cambridge, Mass.: Addison-Wesley Publishing Co.

LIPSET, S. M. 1959. Some Social Requisites of Democracy: Economic Development and Political Legitimacy. *American Political Science Review,* 53 (Mar.): 69–105.

LIPTON, M. 1967–68. The Theory of the Optimising Peasant. *Journal of Development Studies,* 4: 327–51.

——— 1970. Interdisciplinary Studies in Less Developed Countries. *Journal of Development Studies* (Oct.): 5–18.

LITTLE, I., T. SCITOVSKY, and M. SCOTT 1970. *Industry and Trade in Some Developing Countries: A Comparative Study.* London: Oxford University Press. (For the OECD Development Centre.)

LUNING, H. A. 1967. Economic Aspects of Low Labour Income Farming. Agricultural Research Reports 699, Department of Agricultural Economics of the Tropics and Subtropics, Agricultural University, Wageningen, Centre for Agricultural Publications and Documentation, Wageningen.

MACBEAN, A. I. 1966. *Export Instability and Economic Development.* Cambridge, Mass.: Harvard University Press.

MCCLELLAND, D. C. 1953. *The Achievement Motive.* New York: Appleton-Century-Crofts, Inc.

——— 1961. *The Achieving Society.* Princeton, N.J.: D. Van Nostrand Co., Inc.

——— 1966. *Does Education Accelerate Economic Growth?* E.D.C.C., 14 (Apr.): 257–78.

MCCLELLAND, D. H. 1972. *The Central American Common Market: Economic Policies, Economic Growth, and Choices for the Future.* New York: Praeger.

MACURA, M. 1967. The Long-range Population Outlook: A Summary of Current Estimates. Unpublished manuscript.

MCDERMOTT, W. 1966. Environmental Factors Bearing on Medical Education in the Developing Countries. A. Modern Medicine and the Demographic-Disease Pattern of Overly Traditional Societies: A Technologic Misfit. *The Journal of Medical Education,* 41 (Sept.).

McDonald, J. S.   **1969.** Migration and the Population of Ciudad Guayana. In Lloyd Rodwin and associates, *Planning Urban Growth and Regional Development: The Experience of the Guayana Program in Venezuela.* Cambridge, Mass.: MIT Press.

McGreevey, W. P.   **1965.** The Economic Development of Colombia. Unpublished dissertation, Massachusetts Institute of Technology.

————   **1974.** The Policy Relevance of Recent Social Research on Fertility. Occasional Monograph Series, no. 2, an ICP Staff Report. Smithsonian Institution: Interdisciplinary Communications Program, Sept.

McKinnon, R. I.   **1964.** Foreign Exchange Constraints in Economic Development and Efficient Aid Allocation. *E.J.,* 74 (June): 388–409. Reprinted in M.

————   **1965.** Maizels on Industrial Growth and World Trade: Implications for Economic Development. *E.D.C.C.,* 14 (Oct.): 94–106.

————   **1974.** *Money and Capital in Economic Development.* Washington, D.C.: The Brookings Institution.

McNamara, R. S.   **1973.** Address to the Board of Governors, World Bank Group (Nairobi, Kenya), September 24. Washington, D.C.: IBRD.

Maizels, A.   **1963.** *Industrial Growth and World Trade: An Empirical Study of Trends in Production, Consumption and Trade in Manufactures from 1899–1959 with a Discussion of Probable Future Trends.* Cambridge: Cambridge University Press.

————, assisted by L. F. Campbell-Boross and F. B. W. Raymond   **1968.** *Exports and Economic Growth of Developing Countries.* New York: Cambridge University Press.

Mandelbaum, K.   **1945.** *The Industrialization of Backward Areas.* Oxford: Blackwell.

Manne, A., and T. E. Weisskopf   **1969.** A Dynamic Multi-Sectoral Model for India: 1967–1975. In A. P. Carter and A Brody, eds., *Applications of Input-Output Analysis.* Amsterdam: North Holland Publishing Co.

Manoilesco, M.   **1931.** *The Theory of Protection and International Trade.* London: P. S. King & Son, Ltd.

Marris, R.   **1970.** Can We Measure the Need for Development Assistance? *E.J.,* 80, 319.

Martin, A., and W. A. Lewis   **1956.** Patterns of Public Revenue and Expenditure. *The Manchester School,* 24 (Sept.): 203–44.

Mason, E. S.   **1958.** *Economic Planning in Underdeveloped Areas.* New York: Fordham University Press.

————   **1966.** *The Diplomacy of Economic Assistance.* Middlebury, Vt.: Middlebury College.

————, and R. E. Asher   **1973.** *The World Bank since Bretton Woods.* Washington, D.C.: The Brookings Institution (Oct.).

Massell, B. F.   **1962.** Another Small Problem in the Analysis of Growth. *R.E.Statistics,* 44 (Aug.): 330–35.

MEADE, J. E.   **1963.** *A Neo-Classical Theory of Economic Growth.* 2d ed. New York: Oxford University Press.

MEADOWS, DONELLA H., DENNIS L. MEADOWS, and others.   **1972.** *The Limits to Growth.* New York: Universe Books.

MEIER, G. M.   **1963.** *International Trade and Development.* New York and Evanston: Harper & Row.

———   **1964.** *Leading Issues in Development Economics.* New York: Oxford University Press.

———, and R. E. BALDWIN.   **1957.** *Economic Development: Theory, History, Policy.* New York: John Wiley & Sons, Inc.

MELLOR, J. W.   **1974.** *The Economics of Agricultural Development.* Rev. ed. Ithaca, N.Y.: Cornell University Press.

MELLOR, J. W., and R. D. STEVENS   **1956.** The Average and Marginal Product of Farm Labor in Underdeveloped Economies. *Journal of Farm Economics,* 38: 780–91.

MEYER, A. J.   **1959.** *Middle Eastern Capitalism, Nine Essays.* Cambridge, Mass.: Harvard University Press.

MICHAELY, M.   **1965.** On Customs Unions and the Gains from Trade. *E.J.,* 75 (Sept.): 577–83.

MIKESELL, R. F.   **1961.** The Movement toward Regional Trading Groups in Latin America. In Hirschman (1961).

———   **1963.** International Commodity Stabilization Schemes and the Export Problems of Developing Countries. *A.E.R.,* 53 (May): 75–92.

———   **1967.** *Survey of the Alliance for Progress: Inflation in Latin America.* 90th Congress, 1st sess., Committee Print, Sept. 25.

MIKESELL, R. F.   **1974.** More Third World Cartels Ahead. *Challenge,* (Nov.–Dec.) 24–31.

———, and J. E. ZINSER   **1973.** The Nature of the Savings Function in Developing Countries: A Survey of the Theoretical and Empirical Literature. *Journal of Economic Literature,* 11 (Mar.): 1–26.

MILLIKAN, M. F., ed. **1967.** *National Economic Planning.* New York: Columbia University Press.

———, and D. HAPGOOD   **1967.** *No Easy Harvest: The Dilemma of Agriculture in Underdeveloped Countries.* Boston: Little, Brown & Co.

———, and W. W. ROSTOW   **1957.** *A Proposal: Key to an Effective Foreign Policy.* New York: Harper & Row.

MIYAMOTO, I. **1974.** The Real Value of Tied Aid: The Case of Indonesia in 1967–1969. *Economic Development and Cultural Change,* 22 (Apr.), no. 3.

MOORE, W. E.   **1951.** *Industrialization and Labor: Social Aspects of Economic Development.* Ithaca, N.Y.: Cornell University Press.

———, and A. S. FELDMAN, eds.   **1960.** *Labor Commitment and Social Change in Developing Areas.* New York: Social Science Research Council.

MORGAN, J., and M. H. DAVID   **1963.** Education and Income. *Q.J.E.* (Aug.), 423–37.

MORGAN, T.   **1959.** The Long-run Terms of Trade between Agriculture and Manufacturing. *E.D.C.C.,* 8 (Oct.): 1–23. Reprinted in M–B–C.

MURRAY, T.   **1973a.** E. E. C. Enlargement and Preface for the Developing Countries. *E.J.,* 83 (Sept.), no. 331.

———— **1973b.** How Helpful Is the Generalised System of Preferences to Developing Countries? *E.J.* (June).

MYINT, HLA **1954.** An Interpretation of Economic Backwardness. Oxford Economic Papers, n.s., 6 (June): 51, 132–63.

———— **1954–55.** The Gains from International Trade and the Backward Countries. *Review of Economic Studies*, 22: 129–42.

———— **1958.** The Classical Theory of International Trade and the Underdeveloped Countries. *E.J.*, 68 (June): 317–37. Reprinted in M–B–C.

———— **1964.** *The Economics of the Developing Countries.* London: Huchinson & Co., Ltd.

———— **1971.** *Economic Theory and the Underdeveloped Countries.* New York: Oxford University Press.

MYRDAL, G. **1956.** *An International Economy.* New York: Harper & Bros.

———— **1957a.** *Economic Theory and the Underdeveloped Regions.* London: G. Duckworth & Co., Ltd.

———— **1957b.** *Rich Land and Poor.* New York: Harper & Bros.

MYREN, D. T. **1969.** The Rockefeller Foundation Program in Corn and Wheat in Mexico. *Subsistence Agriculture and Economic Development,* Vlifton R. Wharton, Chicago: Aldine Publishing Co.

NAFZIGER, E. W. **1969.** The Effect of the Nigerian Extended Family on Entrepreneurial Activity. *E.D.C.C.,* 18 (Oct.): 25–31.

NAKAMURA, J. I. **1966.** *Agricultural Production and the Economic Development of Japan, 1873–1922.* Princeton, N.J.: Princeton University Press.

NASH, M. **1958.** *Machine Age Maya: The Industrialization of a Guatemalan Community.* New York: Free Press.

NATIONAL ACADEMY OF SCIENCES **1973.** *U.S. International Firms and R,D&E in Developing Countries.* Washington, D.C.: National Academy of Sciences.

N.B.E.R. **1958.** *A Critique of the United States Income and Product Accounts.* Vol. 22 of *Studies in Income and Wealth.* Princeton, N.J.: Princeton University Press.

———— **1960.** *Demographic and Economic Change in Developed Countries.* Princeton, N.J.: Princeton University Press.

———— **1966.** *Output, Employment, and Productivity in the United States After 1800.* New York: N.B.E.R.

NELSON, J. **1970.** The Urban Poor: Disruption or Political Integration in Third World Circles. *World Politics,* 22 (Apr.), no. 3.

NELSON, R. R. **1956.** A Theory of the Low-level Equilibrium Trap. *A.E.R.,* 46 (Dec.): 894–908.

———— **1960.** Growth Models and the Escape from the Low-Level Equilibrium Trap: The Case of Japan. *E.D.C.C.,* 8 (July): 378–88.

————, T. P. SCHULTZ and R. L. SLIGHTON **1971.** *Structural Change in a Developing Economy: Colombia's Problems and Prospects.* Princeton, N.J.: Princeton University Press.

NESS, W. L., JR. **1974.** Financial Markets as a Development Strategy: Initial Results from the Brazilian Experience. *Economic Development and Cultural Change,* 22(3) (Apr.): 453–72.

NEWLYN, W. T. **1973.** The Effect of Aid and Other Resource Transfers on

Savings and Growth in Less-Developed Countries: A Comment. *E.J.* (Sept.).

NICHOLLS, W. H.　　1960. *Southern Tradition and Regional Progress.* Chapel Hill, N.C.: University of North Carolina Press.

———　　1961. Industrialization, Factor Markets and Agricultural Development. *J.P.E.,* 69 (Aug.): 319–40.

———　　1971. Agriculture and the Economic Development of Brazil. In Saunders (1971).

NIITAMO, O.　　1958. The Development of Productivity in Finnish Industry 1925–1952. *Productivity Measurement Review* (Nov.).

NORDHAUS, W. D.　　1973. World Dynamics: Measurement without Data. *E.J.,* 83 (Dec.): 1156–83.

NORTH, D. C.　　1961. *The Economic Growth of the United States, 1790–1860.* Englewood Cliffs, N.J.: Prentice-Hall, Inc.

———　　1964. Industrialization in the United States (1815–60). In Rostow (1964).

NURKSE, R.　　1953. *Problems of Capital Formation in Underdeveloped Countries.* New York: Oxford University Press.

———　　1958. The Conflict between Balanced Growth and International Specialization. *Lectures on Economic Development,* Faculty of Economics (Istanbul University) and Faculty of Political Science (Ankara University), Istanbul.

———　　1961. *Equilibrium and Growth in the World Economy.* Cambridge, Mass.: Harvard University Press.

OECD　　(Annual reports) *Development Assistance Effort and Policies.*

———　　1964. *The Residual Factor in Economic Growth.* Paris.

———　　1970. *National Accounts of Less-Developed Countries, 1959–1968.* Paris: OECD.

OHKAWA, K., and H. ROSOVSKY　　1962. Economic Fluctuations in Prewar Japan. *Hitotsubashi Journal of Economics,* 3 (Oct.): 10–33.

OHLIN, G.　　1966. *Foreign Aid Policies Reconsidered.* Paris: OECD.

ØLGAARD, R.　　1966. *Growth, Productivity and Relative Prices.* Copenhagen: G.E.C. Gads Forlag.

OLSON, E. C.　　1948. Factors Affecting International Differences in Production. *A.E.R. Papers and Proceedings,* 27 (May): 502–22.

OSPINA VASQUEZ, L.　　1955. *Industria y Proteccion en Colombia, 1810–1930.* Bogota: Editorial Santafe.

OWENS, E.　　1967. The Local Development Program of East Pakistan. *International Development Review,* 9 (Mar.) 27–30.

PAAUW, D. S.　　1956. The Role of Local Finance in Indonesian Economic Development. *E.D.C.C.,* 4 (Jan.): 171–85.

———, and J. C. H. FEI　　1973. *The Transition in Open Dualistic Societies.* New Haven: Yale University Press.

PACKARD, V.　　1972. *Nation of Strangers.* New York: David McKay Co., Inc.

PAGLIN, M.　　1965. Surplus Agricultural Labor and Development: Facts and Theories. *A.E.R.,* 55 (Sept.): 815–33.

PAPANEK, G. F.   **1967.** *Pakistan's Development: Social Goals and Private Incentives.* Cambridge, Mass.: Harvard University Press.

——   **1972.** The Effect of Aid and Other Resource Transfers on Savings and Growth in Less Developed Countries. *E.J.,* 82 (Sept.): 934–50.

——   **1973.** A Reply to Dr. Griffin and Professor Newlyn. *E.J.,* 83 (Sept.): 870–74.

——, D. M. SCHYDLOWSKY, and J. J. STERN   **1971.** *Decision Making for Economic Development.* Boston: Houghton Mifflin Co.

PARKER, W.   **1954.** Entrepreneurial Opportunities and Response in the German Economy. *Explorations in Entrepreneurial History,* 7 (Oct.): 26–36.

PARKER, W. N.   **1961.** Economic Development in Historical Perspective. *Economic Development and Cultural Change,* 10 (Oct.): 1–7.

PATRICK, H. T.   **1966.** Financial Development and Economic Growth in Underdeveloped Countries. *E.D.C.C.,* 14 (Jan.): 174–89.

PAZOS, F.   **1961.** Private versus Public Foreign Investment in Underdeveloped Areas. In Ellis (1961).

——   **1973.** *Chronic Inflation in Latin America.* New York: Praeger.

PEATTIE, D. C.   **1935.** *Almanac for Moderns.* New York: G. P. Putnam's Sons.

PERERA, P.   **1968.** *Development Finance: Institutions, Problems, and Prospects.* New York: Praeger.

PERROUX, F.   **1955.** Note sur la Notion de "Pole de Croissance." *Economie Applique,* 8: 307–20.

PETERSON, W. W.   **1967.** Returns to Poultry Research in the United States. *Journal of Farm Economics,* 49 (Aug.): 656–69.

PHELPS BROWN, E. H.   **1953.** *Economic Growth and Human Welfare.* New Delhi: Ranjit Printers & Publishers.

PIGOU, A. C.   **1932.** *Economics of Welfare,* 4th ed.; London: Macmillan & Co., Ltd.

——   **1951.** Real Income and Economic Welfare. *Oxford Economic Papers,* N.S., 3 (Feb.), 16–20.

POLEMAN and FREEBAIRN   **1973.** *Food Population, and Employment: The Impact of the Green Revolution.* New York: Praeger.

PORTER, R. C.   **1964.** The Optimal Price Problem in Buffer Fund Stabilization. *Oxford Economic Papers,* 16: 423–30.

PREBISCH, R.   **1961.** Economic Development or Monetary Stability: The False Dilemma. *Economic Bulletin for Latin America,* 6 (Mar.): 1–25.

——   **1962.** The Economic Development of Latin America and Its Principal Problems. *Economic Bulletin for Latin America,* 7 (Feb.): 1–22. Reprinted in M.

PRESIDENT'S SCIENCE ADVISORY COMMITTEE   **1967.** *The World Food Problem.* Washington: Superintendent of Documents.

PREST, A. R.   **1963.** *Public Finance in Underdeveloped Countries.* New York: Frederick A. Praeger, Inc.

PRYOR, F. L.   **1966.** Economic Growth and the Terms of Trade. *Oxford Economic Papers,* 18 (Mar.): 45–57.

RABBANI, A. K. M. G.   1966. Measurement of Underemployment in Rural Households: A Case Study of Rice Cultivation in East Pakistan. East Pakistan Bureau of Statistics, reprinted from *Cento Symposium on Household Surveys,* Dacca.

RANIS, G.   1963. Allocation Criteria and Population Growth. *A.E.R.,* 53 (May): 619–33.

————, ed.   1971. *Government and Economic Development.* New Haven: Yale University Press.

RAUP, P. M.   1963. The Contribution of Land Reforms to Agricultural Development: An Analytical Framework. *E.D.C.C.,* 12 (Oct.): 1–21.

————   1967. Land Reform and Agricultural Output. *Agricultural Development and Economic Growth,* Herman M. Southworth and Bruce F. Johnston, eds. Ithaca: Cornell University Press.

RAVENHOLT, R. T., and J. CHAO   1974. *World Fertility Trends, 1974.* Washington, D.C.: George Washington University Medical Center Population Report, series J, no. 2 (Aug.).

REDDAWAY, W. B., and A. D. SMITH   1960. Progress in British Manufacturing Industries in the Period 1948–1954. *E.J.* (Mar.).

REISCHAUER, E. O., and J. K. FAIRBANK   1958. *East Asia: The Great Tradition.* Boston: Houghton Mifflin Co.

REPORT ON THE SEVENTH SESSION   1971. Committee for Development Planning. Economic and Social Council, Official Records: 51st Sess., supplement 7 (Mar. 22–Apr. 1).

REYNOLDS, C. W.   1963. Domestic Consequences of Export Instability. *A.E.R.,* 53 (May): 93–102.

RIDKER, R. G., ed.   1972. *Population, Resources, and the Environment.* Washington: U.S. Government Printing Office.

ROBBINS, L.   1952. *On the Nature and Significance of Economic Science.* 2d ed. London: MacMillan & Co., Ltd.

ROBINSON, E. A. G. (ed.)   1960. *Economic Consequences of the Size of Nations.* New York: St. Martin's Press.

————, and J. E. VAIZEY, (eds.)   1966. *The Economics of Education.* New York: St. Martin's Press. London: Macmillan & Co., Ltd.

ROBINSON, J.   1954. The Production Function and the Theory of Capital. *Review of Economic Studies,* no. 2.

————   1956. *The Accumulation of Capital.* London: Macmillan & Co., Ltd.

————   1962. *Essays in the Theory of Economic Growth.* London: Macmillan & Co., Ltd.

ROBINSON, R.   1956. Factor Endowments and Comparative Advantage. *Q.J.E.,* 70 (May): 169–92; 70 (Aug.), 346–63.

ROBINSON, S.   1971. Sources of Growth in Less-Developed Countries: A Cross-Section Study. *Q.J.E.,* 85, no. 3.

RODAN, P. N. R.   See Rosenstein-Rodan, P. N.

ROEMER, M.   1970. *Fishing for Growth: Export-Led Development in Peru 1950–1967.* Cambridge, Mass.: MIT Press.

ROSENBERG, N., ed.   1971. *The Economics of Technological Change.* London: Penguin.

————— 1972. Factors Affecting the Diffusion of Technology. *Explorations in Entrepreneurial History,* 10 (Fall).

ROSENSTEIN-RODAN, P. N.   1943. Problems of Industrialization of Eastern and South-Eastern Europe. *E.J.,* 53 (June-Sept.): 202–11. Reprinted in A–S, O–R.

————— 1961*a.* International Aid for Underdeveloped Countries. *R.E. Statistics,* 43 (May): 107–38.

————— 1961*b.* Notes on the Theory of the Big Push. In Ellis and Wallich (1961). Reprinted in M–B–C.

ROSTOW, W. W.   1955. Trends in the Allocation of Resources in Secular Growth. In L. H. Dupriez, ed., *Economic Progress.* Louvain: Institut de Recherches Economiques et Sociales.

————— 1956. The Take-Off into Self-Sustained Growth. *E.J.,* 66 (Mar.): 25–48. Reprinted in A–S, O–R.

————— 1960. *Stages of Economic Growth.* Cambridge: Cambridge University Press.

—————, ed.   1964. *The Economics of Take-Off into Sustained Growth: Proceedings of a Conference Held by the International Economic Association.* London: Macmillan & Co., Ltd.

RUTTAN, V.   1973. Induced Technical and Institutional Change and the Future of Agriculture. (Preprint). In *Papers and Reports,* Fifteenth International Conference of Agricultural Economists, São Paulo, Brazil. Forthcoming.

SAKSENA, R. M.   1972. *Regional Development Banking.* Bombay: Somaiya Publications.

SALTER, W. E. G.   1960. *Productivity and Technical Change.* New York: Cambridge University Press.

————— 1966. *Productivity and Technical Change.* 2d ed. New York: Cambridge University Press.

SAMUELSON, P. A.   1948. International Trade and the Equalisation of Factor Prices. *E.J.,* 58 (June): 163–84.

————— 1949. International Factor-Price Equalisation Once Again. *E.J.,* 59 (June): 181–97.

————— 1950. Evaluation of Real National Income. *Oxford Economic Papers,* n.s. 2 (Jan.), 1–29.

————— 1973. *Economics: An Introductory Analysis.* 9th ed. New York: McGraw-Hill Book Co.

SAMUELSSON, K.   1961. *Religion and Economic Action.* New York: Harper & Row.

SANDBERG, L. G.   1966. World-Wide Famine Just around the Corner? *E.D.C.C.* (15): 94–98.

SAUNDERS, J., ed.   1971. *Modern Brazil: New Patterns and Development.* Gainesville: University of Florida Press.

SAWYER, J. E.   1951*a.* Strains in the Social System of Modern France. In Earle (1951).

—————— **1951b.** Social Structure and Economic Progress. *A.E.R. Papers and Proceedings,* 41 (May): 321–29.

—————— **1954a.** In Defense of an Approach: A Comment on Gerschenkron's "Social Attitudes, Entrepreneurship, and Economic Development." *Explorations in Entrepreneurial History,* 6 (May), 273–86.

—————— **1954b.** A Note on Professor Gerschenkron's Rejoinder. *Explorations in Entrepreneurial History,* 6 (May).

SAYIGH, Y. A. **1962.** *Entrepreneurs of Lebanon.* Cambridge, Mass.: Harvard University Press.

SAXENHOUSE, G. **1974.** A Table of Japanese Technological Diffusion in the Meiji Period. *Journal of Economic History,* 34 (Mar.): 149–65.

SCHLOTE, W. **1952.** *British Overseas Trade, from 1700 to the 1930s.* Oxford: Clarendon Press. (German original, 1938.)

SCHOTT, F. H. **1959.** Inflation and Stabilization Efforts in Chile, 1953–1958. *Inter-American Economic Affairs* (Winter): 4–14. Reprinted in M.

SCHULTZ, T. P. **1967.** *A Family Planning Hypothesis: Some Empirical Evidence from Puerto Rico.* Santa Monica, Calif.: Rand Corporation.

—————— **1973.** Explanation of Birth Rate Changes over Space and Time: A Study of Taiwan. *J.P.E.,* 81, no. 2 (part 2) Chicago: University of Chicago Press.

SCHULTZ, T. W. **1961a.** Economic Prospects of Primary Products. In Ellis (1961).

—————— **1961b.** Investment in Human Capital. *A.E.R.,* 51 (Mar.): 1–17.

—————— **1963.** *The Economic Value of Education.* New York: Columbia University Press.

—————— **1964.** *Transforming Traditional Agriculture.* New Haven and London: Yale University Press.

—————— **1967a.** The Rate of Return in Allocating Investment Resources to Education. *Journal of Human Resources,* 2 (Summer): 293–309.

—————— **1967b.** Significance of India's 1918–19 Losses of Agricultural Labour—A Reply. *E.J.,* 77 (Mar.): 161–63.

——————, ed. **1973.** New Economic Approaches to Fertility. Proceedings of a Conference sponsored by the National Bureau of Economic Research and the Population Council, June 8–9, 1972. *J.P.E.,* 81, no. 2 (part 2). Chicago: University of Chicago Press.

—————— **1974.** Marriage, Family, Human Capital, and Fertility. Proceedings of a Conference sponsored by the National Bureau of Economic Research and the Population Council, June 4–5, 1973. *J.P.E.,* 82, no. 2 (part 2). Chicago: University of Chicago Press.

SCHUMPETER, J. A. **1934.** *The Theory of Economic Development.* Cambridge, Mass.: Harvard University Press. (First German ed., 1912.)

—————— **1939.** *Business Cycles.* New York: McGraw-Hill Book Co.

—————— **1942.** *Capitalism, Socialism, and Democracy.* New York: Harper & Bros.

SCHURR, S. H. **1963.** Energy. *Scientific American,* 209 (Sept.): 110–27. Reprinted in *Technology and Economic Development.*

SCIENTIFIC AMERICAN   1963. *Technology and Economic Development*. New York: Alfred E. Knopf.

SCITOVSKY, T.   1957. Two Concepts of External Economies. *J.P.E.*, 62 (Apr.): 143–51. Reprinted in A–S, M–B–C.

———   1959. Growth—Balanced or Unbalanced? In Abramovitz (1959).

SCRIMSHAW, N. S.   1963. Food. *Scientific American*, 209 (Sept.): 72–88. Reprinted in *Technology and Economic Development*.

SEN, A. K.   1961. On Optimising the Rate of Saving. *E.J.*, 71 (Sept.): 479–95.

———   1966. Peasants and Dualism With or Without Surplus Labour. *J.P.E.*, 74 (Oct.), no. 5.

———   1967a. Surplus Labour in India: A Critique of Schultz's Statistical Test. *E.J.*, 77 (Mar.): 154–61.

———   1967b. Surplus Labour in India: A Rejoinder. *E.J.*, 77 (Mar.): 163–65.

SHANNON, L. W., ed.   1957. *Underdeveloped Areas*. New York: Harper & Row.

SHAW, E. S.   1973. *Financial Deepening in Economic Development*. London: Oxford University Press.

SHONFIELD, A.   1965. *Modern Capitalism: The Changing Balance of Public and Private Power*. London: Oxford University Press.

SIGURDSON, J.   1974. Technology and Employment in China. *W.D.* (Mar.).

SILBERMAN, B. S., and H. D. HAROOTUNIAN, eds.   1966. *Modern Japanese Leadership: Tradition and Change*. Tucson, Ariz.: University of Arizona Press.

SIMEY, T. S.   1946. *Welfare and Planning in the West Indies*. Oxford: Clarendon Press.

SIMMONS, J.   1974. Education, Poverty, and Development. *Staff Working Paper*. Washington: International Bank for Reconstruction and Development.

SINGER, C., E. J. HOLMYARD, A. R. HALL, and others, eds.   1954–58. *A History of Technology*, 5 vols. Oxford: Clarendon Press.

SINGER, H. W.   1949. Economic Progress in Underdeveloped Countries. *Social Research*, 16 (Mar.): 1–11.

———   1953. Obstacles to Economic Development. *Social Research*, 20 (Spring): 19–31.

———   1960. A Balanced View of Balanced Growth. In E. Nelson, ed., *Economic Growth: Rationale, Problems, Cases*. Austin: University of Texas Press. Reprinted in M.

SINGH, S. K.   1972. *Development Economics: Theory and Findings*. Lexington, Mass.: D. C. Heath.

SMITH, T. C.   1955. *Political Change and Industrial Development in Japan: Government Enterprises, 1868–1880*. Stanford, Calif.: Stanford University Press.

———   1959. *The Agrarian Origins of Modern Japan*. Stanford, Calif.: Stanford University Press.

SOLO, R. A., and E. M. ROGERS   1972. *Inducing Technological Change for*

Economic Growth and Development. East Lansing: Michigan State University Press.

SOLOW, R. M.   **1956.** A Contribution to the Theory of Economic Growth. *Q.J.E.,* 70 (Feb.): 65–94.

——— **1957.** Technical Change and the Aggregate Production Function. *R.E. Statistics,* 39 (Aug.): 312–20.

——— **1960.** Investment and Technical Progress. Chap. 7 in Arrow, K. J., S. Karlin, and P. Suppes, eds., *Mathematical Methods in the Social Sciences, 1959: Proceedings of the First Stanford Symposium.* Stanford, Calif.: Stanford University Press.

——— **1962.** Technical Progress, Capital Formation, and Economic Growth. *A.E.R., Papers and Proceedings,* 52.

SOUTHWORTH, H. M., and B. J. JOHNSTON, eds.   **1967.** *Agricultural Development and Economic Growth.* Ithaca, N.Y.: Cornell University Press.

SPENGLER, J. J., ed.   **1954.** Demographic Patterns. In H. F. Williamson and J. A. Buttrick, eds. *Economic Development Principles and Patterns.* New York: Prentice-Hall, Inc. (1954).

——— **1961.** *Natural Resources and Economic Growth.* Washington, D.C.: Resources for the Future.

STALEY, C. E.   **1961.** Response to Agricultural Prices in Costa Rica. *E.J.,* 71: 432–36.

STEVENS, W. J.   **1971.** *Capital Acsorptive Capacity in Developing Countries.* Leiden: A. W. Sijthoff.

STIGLER, G. J.   **1951.** The Division of Labor Is Limited by the Extent of the Market. *J.P.E.,* 59 (June): 188.

STOETZEL, J.   **1955.** *Without the Chrysanthemum and the Sword: A Study of the Attitudes of Youth in Post-War Japan.* New York: Columbia University Press.

STOLPER, W. F.   **1966.** *Planning without Facts: Lessons in Resource Allocations from Nigeria's Development.* Cambridge, Mass.: Harvard University Press.

STONIER, A. W., and D. C. HAGUE   **1957.** *A Textbook of Economic Theory.* 2d ed. New York: Longmans, Green & Co.

STREETEN, P.   **1959.** Unbalanced Growth. *Oxford Economic Papers, n.s.,* 11 (June): 167–90.

——— **1963.** Balanced versus Unbalanced Growth. *The Economic Weekly* (April): 669–71. Reprinted in M.

STROSSMAN, W. P.   **1968.** *Technological Change and Economic Development.* Ithaca, N.Y.: Cornell University Press.

SUNKEL, O.   **1960.** Inflation in Chile: An Unorthodox Approach. *International Economic Papers,* no. 10: 107–31. London: Macmillan & Co., Ltd.

SUTTMEIER, R. P.   **1974.** *Research and Development: Scientific, Political, and Societal Change in China.* Lexington, Mass.: D. C. Heath & Co.

SVENNILSON, I.   **1954.** *Growth and Stagnation in the European Economy.* Geneva: U.N. Economic Commission for Europe.

SWAMY, S.   **1973.** Economic Growth in China and India, 1952–1970: A

Comparative Appraisal. *Economic Development and Cultural Change,* 21 (July), no. 4 (part 2).

SWERLING, B. C.   1963. Problems of International Commodity Stabilization. *A.E.R.,* 53 (May): 65–74.

TANG, A. M.   1958. *Economic Deveolpment in the Southern Piedmont, 1860–1950.* Chapel Hill: University of North Carolina Press.

TAYLOR, C. L., and M. C. HUDSON with collaboration of K. H. DOLAN and others   1972. *World Handbook of Political and Social Indicators,* 2d ed. New Haven: Yale University Press.

———   1973. *Technology and Economic Development,* a Scientific American book, New York: Alfred A. Knopf.

THIRLWALL, A. T.   1972. *Growth and Development.* London: MacMillan & Co., Ltd.

THORN, R. S.   1967. The Evolution of Public Finances during Economic Development. *The Manchester School,* 35 (Jan.): 19–51.

TINBERGEN, J.   1958. *The Design of Development.* Baltimore: Johns Hopkins Press.

———, and H. C. Bos   1962. *Mathematical Models of Economic Growth.* New York: McGraw-Hill Book Co.

———   1964. A Planning Model for the Educational Requirements of Economic Development. In OECD (1964).

TODARO, M. P.   1969. A Model of Labor Migration and Urban Unemployment in Less Developed Countries. *A.E.R.,* 59 (Mar.): 38–48.

TRIANTIS, S. G.   1953. Economic Progress, Occupational Redistribution, and International Terms of Trade. *E.J.,* 63 (Sept.): 627–37.

TUMIN, M. M.   1960. Competing Status Systems. Chap. 15 of Moore and Feldman (1960).

TUN WAI   1956. Interest Rates in the Organized Money Markets of Underdeveloped Countries. *International Monetary Fund Staff Papers,* 7 (Aug.): 249–78. Reprinted in M.

———   1957. Interest Rates Outside the Organized Money Markets of Underdeveloped Countries. *International Monetary Fund Staff Papers,* 6 (Nov.): 80–125. Reprinted in M.

———, and H. T. PATRICK   1973. *Stock and Bond Issues and Capital Markets in Less Developed Countries.* Center Paper no. 200. New Haven: Yale University.

TURNHAM, D., and I. JAEGER   1971. *The Employment Problem in Less Developed Countries: A Review of the Evidence.* Paris: OECD.

UNITED NATIONS   See also Cortez and others.

UNITED NATIONS   (Annual report) *Demographic Yearbook*

———   (Annual report) *Statistical Yearbook*

———   (Annual report) *World Economic Survey*

———   (Annual report) *Yearbook of National Income Accounts*

———   1949. *Relative Price of Exports and Imports of Underdeveloped Countries.* Lake Success, N.Y.

———   1951a. *Land Reform: Defects in Agrarian Structure and Obstacles to Economic Development.* New York. Reprinted in M–B–C, N–L, O–R.

―――― **1951***b*. *Measures for the Economic Development of Underdeveloped Countries: Report by a Group of Experts.* New York.

―――― **1952.** *Instability in Export Markets of Underdeveloped Countries.* New York. Reprinted in M–B–C.

―――― **1961.** *International Compensations for Fluctuations in Commodity Prices.* New York.

―――― **1962.** *The Capital Developing Needs of the Less Developed Countries.* New York.

―――― **1963.** *Compendium of Social Statistics.* New York.

―――― **1966.** *World Population Prospects as Assessed in 1963.* New York.

UNITED NATIONS   **1968.** *Trade Prospects and Capital Needs of Developing Countries.* New York.

―――― **1972.** *Growth of World Industry.* New York.

―――― **1973.** *The Determinants and Consequences of Population Trends.* Population Studies, 1, no. 50, ST/SOA/SER. A/50. New York: United Nations Sales Section.

UN.: ECAFE   (Annual Report) *Economic Survey of Asia and the Far East.* New York.

U.N.: ECLA   (Annual Report) *Economic Survey of Latin America.* New York.

UNITED STATES BUREAU OF LABOR STATISTICS   **1964.** *Consumer Expenditures and Income: Detail of Expenditures and Income, Urban United States, 1960.* Washington, D.C.: U.S. Government Printing Office.

UNITED STATES BUREAU OF MINES   **1970.** *Mineral Facts and Problems.* Bureau of Mines Bulletin 650. Washington, D.C.: U.S. Government Printing Office.

UNIVERSITIES–NATIONAL BUREAU OF ECONOMIC RESEARCH   **1955.** *Capital Formation and Economic Growth; A Conference of the Universities–National Bureau of Economic Research.* Princeton, N.J.: Princeton University Press.

UPHOFF, N. T., and W. F. ILCHMAN, eds.   **1973.** *The Political Economy of Development.* Berkeley: University of California Press.

UPPAL, J. S.   **1969.** Implementation of Land Reform Legislation in India–A Study of Two Villages in Punjab. *Asian Survey,* 9 (May): 362–71.

URQUIDI, V. L.   **1962.** *Free Trade and Economic Integration in Latin America.* Berkeley: University of California Press.

――――, and ROSEMARY THORP, eds.   **1973.** *Latin America in the International Economy.* London: Macmillan & Co., Ltd.

VANEK, J.   **1967.** *Estimating Foreign Resource Needs for Development, Theory, Method, and a Case Study of Colombia.* New York: McGraw-Hill.

VINER, J.   **1937.** *Studies in the Theory of International Trade.* New York: Harper & Bros.

―――― **1952.** *International Trade and Economic Development.* Glencoe, Ill.: Free Press.

―――― VOGEL, E. F.   **1963.** *Japan's New Middle Class: The Salary Man and His Family in a Tokyo Suburb.* Berkeley: University of California Press.

WAI, U TUN. See Tun Wai (U).

WALKER, K. R.   1965. *Planning in Chinese Agriculture.* London: Frank Cass & Co., Ltd.

WALLICH, H. C.   1961. Stabilization of Proceeds from Raw Material Exports. In Ellis (1961).

———   1970. Money and Growth—A Country Cross-Section Analysis. Center Paper no. 141. New Haven: Yale University Economic Growth Center.

WALTERS, A. A.   1966. Incremental Capital-Output Ratios. *E.J.,* 76 (Dec.): 818–22.

WARNER, W. L. and J. C. AGEGGLEN   1955. *Big Business Leaders in America.* New York: Harper and Bros., 1955.

WARRINER, D.   1962. *Land Reform and Development in the Middle East.* N.Y.: Oxford University Press.

———   1969. *Land Reform in Principle and Practice.* Oxford: The Clarendon Press.

WATANABE, T.   1965. Economic Aspects of Dualism in the Industrial Development of Japan. *E.D.C.C.,* 13 (Apr.): 293–312.

———, and R. KOMIYA   1958. Findings from Price Comparisons, Principally Japan vs. the United States. *Weltwirtschaftliches Archiv,* band 81.

WATERSTON, A.   1965. *Development Planning: Lessons of Experience.* Baltimore: Johns Hopkins Press.

WATKINS, M. H.   1963. A Staple Theory of Economic Growth. *Canadian Journal of Economics and Political Science,* 29 (May): 141–58.

WEBER, M.   1930. *The Protestant Ethic and Spirit of Capitalism.* New York: Charles Scribner's Sons (German original, 1904–5.)

WEISBROD, B. A.   1964. *External Benefits of Public Education: An Economic Analysis.* Princeton, N.J.: Princeton University Press.

WELLISZ, S.   1968. Dual Economies, Disguised Unemployment, and the Unlimited Supply of Labour. *Economica,* 35 (Feb.), no. 137.

WESTPHAL, L. E., and K. S. KIM   1973. *Industrial Policy and Development in Korea.* Draft version, mimeo. (July), 1–13.

WHARTON, C., ed.   1969. *Subsistence Agriculture and Economic Development.* Chicago: Aldine Publishing Co.

WHITE, J.   1972. *Regional Development Banks: The Asian, African, and Inter-American Development Banks.* London: Pall Mall Press.

WHYTE, W. F., and L. K. WILLIAMS   1967. "Toward an Integrated Theory of Development: Economic and Non-Economic Variables in Rural Development." Cornell University, mimeo.

WILLIAMS, B. R., ed.   1973. *Science and Technology in Economic Growth.* Proceedings of a Conference held by the International Economic Association at St. Anton, Austria. London: Macmillan & Co., Ltd.

WIONCZEK, M. S., ed.   1966. *Latin American Economic Integration: Experiences and Prospects.* New York: Frederick A. Praeger.

WISE, J., and P. A. YOTOPOULOS   1969. The Empirical Content of Economic Rationality: A Test for a Less Developed Economy. *J.P.E.,* 77 (Nov.-Dec), no. 6.

WOYTINSKY, W. S., and E. S. WOYTINSKY   1953. *World Population and Production.* New York: Twentieth Century Fund.

YAMAMURA, K.   1968. A Re-Examination of Entrepreneurship in Meiji Japan (1868–1912). *Economic History Review,* 21 (Feb.): 148–58.

YANG, M. C.   1948. *A Chinese Village, Taitou, Shantung Province.* London: Kegan Paul, Trench, Trubner & Co., Ltd.

YATES, P. L.   1959. *Forty Years of Foreign Trade.* London: George Allen & Unwin, Ltd.

YOTOPOULOS, P. A.   1968. *On the Efficiency of Resource Utilisation in Subsistence Agricultural.* Food Research Institute Studies in Agricultural Economics, Trade and Development. Stanford, Calif.: Food Research Institute, Stanford University, 8, no. 2.

YOUNGSON, A. J.   1959. *Possibilities of Economic Progress.* New York: Cambridge University Press.

————, ed.   1972. *Economic Development in the Long Run.* London: George Allen and Unwin, Ltd.

Indexes

Name Index

A

Abegglen, J. C., 295, 270, 299
Abramovitz, M., 133 n, 255–58, 266
Adelman, I., 55 n, 192–93, 215, 218, 227, 235 n, 245, 249, 313–14, 322
Agarwala, A., 27
Agency for International Development, 47, 51 n, 61
Ahluwalia, M., 226 n, 227 n, 228, 249
Aitken, H., 405
Allen, R., 267
Almond, G. H., 86 n
Anderson, C. A., 322
Arrow, K. F., 260, 261 n, 411 n
Asher, R. E., 454
Ashton, T. S., 67 n

B

Bairoch, B., 76
Balassa, B., 15 n, 436 n, 475 n, 476 n
Baldwin, G. B., 414 n
Baldwin, R. E., 215
Baran, P. A., 175–76, 215
Bardhan, P. K., 108, 459 n
Barnett, H. J., 32 n, 38
Bates, M., 190 n
Bauer, P., 93 n
Becker, G. S., 54 n, 70
Becker, G. T., 255 n, 260 n, 306, 307 n
Beckerman, W., 15 n, 351 n
Bell, C. L. G., 226 n, 227 n, 249
Benoit, E., 261

Bhagwati, J., 177, 205 n, 431, 459 n
Boeke, J. H., 202, 424
Bos, H. C., 314 n
Boserup, E., 70
Bowles, S., 313 n, 322
Bowman, M. J., 322
Brady, D., 168 n, 170
Broadbridge, S., 202
Bronfenbrenner, M., 384–85
Bruno, M., 257, 453, 512
Bruton, H. J., 215, 242 n, 249
Buck, J. L., 125–26
Bureau of Mines, U.S., 33, 34

C

Cairncross, A. K., 167
Campbell, R., 154
Carter, C., 267
Carter, N., 430, 439
Carus-Wilson, E., 30 n
Caves, R., 177–78, 180, 492
Center for International Studies, 112, 116
Chakravasty, S., 512
Chenery, H. S., 89–92, 95, 160 n, 187 n, 226 n, 227 n, 234, 248 n, 249, 320–22, 343, 391, 405, 411 n, 430, 432–34, 437–39, 453, 469, 476, 507, 515
Chiu, J. S., 255
Choi, K. I., 147 n
Chou, En-lai, 108
Clark, C., 89
Cline, W., 448
Cohen, B., 439–41

Subject Index